BRITISH SECURITY COORDINATION

BRITISH SECURITY COORDINATION

The Secret History of
British Intelligence in the Americas
1940–45

Introduction by
Nigel West

ST ERMIN'S
PRESS

A *St Ermin's Press* Book

First published in this form in Great Britain
in 1998 by St Ermin's Press
in association with Little, Brown and Company

Copyright © 1998 by St Ermin's Press
Introduction copyright © 1998 by Westintel (Research) Ltd

Moral right has been asserted.

All rights reserved.
No part of this publication may be reproduced,
stored in a retrieval system, or transmitted,
in any form or by any means, without the prior
permission in writing of the publisher, nor be
otherwise circulated in any form of binding or cover
other than that in which it is published and without
a similar condition including this condition being
imposed on the subsequent purchaser.

A CIP catalogue record for this book
is available from the British Library.

ISBN: 0 316 64464 1

Typeset by Palimpsest Book Production Limited
Polmont, Stirlingshire
Printed and bound in Great Britain
by Clays Ltd, St Ives plc

St Ermin's Press
Brettenham House
Lancaster Place
London WC2E 7EN

Contents

INTRODUCTION BY NIGEL WEST ... ix

FOREWORD BY WILLIAM STEPHENSON ... xxi

EDITORIAL NOTE ... xxii

GLOSSARY ... xxiii

INTRODUCTION: ORIGIN, DEVELOPMENT AND FUNCTIONS ... xxv

PART I: GROUNDWORK OF LIAISON WITH THE AMERICANS ... 1

CHAPTER 1: Liaison with Hoover ... 3
CHAPTER 2: Liaison with Donovan ... 8
CHAPTER 3: Contacts for Political Warfare ... 16
CHAPTER 4: Donovan's Organization ... 24
CHAPTER 5: Collaboration with the FBI after Pearl Harbor ... 47

PART II: POLITICAL WARFARE FOR SO.1 ... 51

INTRODUCTION ... 53
CHAPTER 1: Political Warfare against the European Enemy ... 55
CHAPTER 2: Campaign against Axis Propaganda in the United States ... 66
CHAPTER 3: Political Warfare against Japan ... 88

Contents

CHAPTER 4: Disguised Channels of Propaganda and
Rumour Spreading 102
CHAPTER 5: After Pearl Harbor 115
POSTSCRIPT: Intelligence and Propaganda 123

PART III: ECONOMIC WARFARE 133

CHAPTER 1: The Campaign against German Business 135
CHAPTER 2: German-American Indebtedness 156
CHAPTER 3: The Prevention of Smuggling 161

PART IV: SECRET INTELLIGENCE 185

INTRODUCTION 187
CHAPTER 1: The Vichy French 188
CHAPTER 2: The Italians, the Spaniards and the Japanese 214
CHAPTER 3: Western Hemisphere Intelligence 219
CHAPTER 4: External Intelligence 231

PART V: SECURITY OF PROPERTY AND PERSONNEL 237

CHAPTER 1: The Security Division before Pearl Harbor 239
CHAPTER 2: Industrial Security Officers 253
CHAPTER 3: The Security of Personnel 264
CHAPTER 4: Security in the Final Phase 269

PART VI: SPECIAL OPERATIONS IN LATIN AMERICA 273

CHAPTER 1: Three Phases 275
CHAPTER 2: Brazil and Argentina 288
CHAPTER 3: Chile 301
CHAPTER 4: Colombia 310
CHAPTER 5: Ecuador 323
CHAPTER 6: Miscellaneous Operations 330

Contents

CHAPTER 7: The Belmonte Letter ... 335
CONCLUSION ... 343

PART VII: COUNTER-ESPIONAGE ... 345

CHAPTER 1: Purposes and Methods ... 347
CHAPTER 2: Sources of Information ... 353
CHAPTER 3: Some Illustrations of Espionage in the
   Western Hemisphere ... 360
CHAPTER 4: Double Agents ... 385
CHAPTER 5: Far Eastern Counter-Espionage ... 399

PART VIII: ORGANIZATION FOR SECRET ACTIVITY
   OUTSIDE THE WESTERN HEMISPHERE ... 405

CHAPTER 1: Foreign Exiles and Minority Groups ... 407
CHAPTER 2: Recruiting Secret Agents ... 416
CHAPTER 3: Training ... 423
CHAPTER 4: Supplying the Underground ... 426
CHAPTER 5: Agents at Work ... 431
CONCLUSION ... 442

PART IX: COMMUNICATIONS NETWORK ... 445

CHAPTER 1: Developing Speed and Security ... 447
CHAPTER 2: Hydra and the South American Scheme ... 460
CHAPTER 3: Illicit Wireless Intelligence ... 466
CHAPTER 4: Complexities of Traffic Exchange ... 478
CHAPTER 5: Purchasing Secret Equipment ... 498
CONCLUSION ... 507

INDEX ... 509

This publication has not been officially endorsed by Her Majesty's Government.

INTRODUCTION

by Nigel West

The origins of this remarkable document, much talked about, often misquoted but never before published in its entirety, lie in the appointment in June 1940 of William Stephenson as the British Passport Control Officer (PCO) in New York. A Canadian who had fought in the Royal Flying Corps in the First World War, Stephenson was a self-made millionaire whose business interests had brought him into contact with the Industrial Intelligence Centre in London, a clearing-house of information about strategic commodities headed by (Sir) Desmond Morton.

The role of the PCO was, of course, a rather transparent cover for the local representative of the Secret Intelligence Service (SIS), and the decision to select Stephenson to replace the elderly Captain Sir James Paget RN Bt, a retired naval officer who had been in the post since July 1937, had been made by the SIS Chief, Colonel (Sir) Stewart Menzies. The precedent for despatching a new SIS station commander, to take on the code symbol 48000, had been set in 1915 when another Canadian, Sir William Wiseman, had taken up the key liaison position.

A small but dynamic character, Stephenson arrived in New York aboard the SS *Britannic* on 21 June 1940 and used much of his own wealth to relocate the PCO from a dingy suite of rooms in the Cunard Building off Wall Street to the thirty-fifth and thirty-sixth floors of the Rockefeller Center on Fifth Avenue. From here Stephenson directed SIS's liaison with the Americans, an undertaking that was to develop into an umbrella organization entitled British Security Coordination (BSC) that eventually represented MI5, SIS, Special Operations Executive (SOE) and the Political Warfare Executive throughout the western hemisphere, establishing offices across the Caribbean, Central and South America, and supervising large censorship bureaux in Bermuda and Trinidad.

However, when Stephenson arrived in New York, he had

inherited only Paget's secretary, his assistant Walter Bell and a small office, together with a brief to work within the limitations of the American Neutrality Act to cultivate closer relations with the Federal Bureau of Investigation. Hitherto, SIS's contacts with the FBI had been minimal, a reflection of the low priority SIS placed on local operations, although on one celebrated occasion in 1938 Paget had delighted J. Edgar Hoover by tipping off the FBI to a large German spy-ring headed by Gunter Rumrich, a US Army deserter. Paget's information had come from MI5's surveillance in Dundee on Mrs Jessie Jordan, who had acted as a postbox for various German agents and had inadvertently drawn attention to herself by her exceptionally large international postbag. Acting on information revealed by MI5's interception of Mrs Jordan's letters in Scotland, the FBI convicted Rumrich and almost all of his spies, and acknowledged the value of its link with MI5 through SIS's tiny office in downtown Manhattan.

Beyond New York, SIS ran only two other stations in the region, at Montevideo (codenamed 75000) and Rio de Janeiro (75200), which reported direct to London. Hitherto, responsibility for security issues had rested with Hamish Mitchell, the senior security officer attached to the British Purchasing Commission, who had concentrated on protecting from Nazi sabotage British *matériel* bought by the Ministry of Supply. It was following Mitchell's initially unpromising attempts to expand his relationship with the FBI and the State Department that Stephenson had flown to Washington DC in April 1940 on a reconnaissance for Menzies, and subsequently had taken up his appointment as PCO two months later. He was to be joined by Mitchell and, in July, by an experienced SIS professional, Colonel C.H. ('Dick') Ellis. In due course, BSC's Secret Intelligence division would be headed by John Pepper, the Security branch by Walter ('Freckles') Wren of MI5, Special Operations by Louis Franck and the propaganda arm by Richard Coit. Incidentally, none of these names appears in the history of BSC, which discreetly avoids identifying individual officers.

Shortly before the end of hostilities in Europe, when BSC had almost outlived its usefulness, Stephenson received a knighthood in the New Year's honours list, but was ambitious to keep his hand in the intelligence world and was anxious to place on record what had been accomplished. Whatever his motives, which would subsequently become a matter of controversy, Stephenson commissioned one of his subordinates, Gilbert Highet, to collate BSC's files and prepare an account of BSC's wartime achievements. Highet, who was married to the spy writer Helen MacInnes, was later to take American citizenship and be appointed Professor of Mathematics at Columbia University. Apparently the arrangements for Highet's project were extraordinary, with all the BSC files escorted under armed guard from New York, across the Canadian border to SOE's Special Training School, a facility that had been set up at Oshawa, some miles outside Toronto, to provide preliminary courses in clandestine work for aspiring agents, under the Canadian Army cover of 'Military Research Centre No. 2'. Officially designated STS 103, the site on the shores of Lake Ontario had become redundant, so Stephenson, who never visited the base while it was operational, used its facilities to provide secure storage for the records and a suitable location for Highet to complete his task.[1] However, Stephenson seems to have rejected Highet's first draft as being too dry and too academic, and instead asked another BSC subordinate, Tom Hill, to start again, using his journalistic skills. Having previously edited trade journals in Canada, Hill had been put to work in BSC compiling the *Western Hemisphere Weekly Bulletin*, a summary of developments in countries where BSC was operational, for the consumption of BSC staff, as well as for SIS headquarters in London and the British Embassy in Washington DC. Devoid of classified operational data, Stephenson had considered the *Bulletin* to be a useful boost for wartime morale and a method of reminding others of what BSC was up to.

Working alongside Hill on the preparation of the history was Roald Dahl, later the highly successful author of stories for children, who had been posted to the Washington Embassy by the RAF in 1942 as an assistant air attaché, having served with his fighter squadron in Greece, Syria and North Africa, where he was injured when his aircraft crashed. Dahl had been recruited by Stephenson soon after his arrival in the States and had acted as a liaison with the US Office of Strategic Services, but he did not last long on Stephenson's history and, after an initial period of collaboration with Hill, left the bulk of the work to him.

Hill seems to have completed his work in the late summer of 1945 and his manuscript was then edited by Giles Playfair, who had joined BSC after his evacuation from Singapore, where he had worked as a radio journalist for the Malaysian Broadcasting Company. Clearly satisfied by his handiwork, Stephenson arranged for a local printer in Oshawa to run off twenty copies, and a bookbinder in Toronto was contracted to cover them in leather and place each individually in a separate locked box. Once these precautions had been taken, Hill and his wife were instructed to gather up the entire BSC archive and destroy it in a huge bonfire, thus ensuring that the twenty copies were all that remained of BSC's historical record.

Stephenson is believed to have distributed up to ten copies to Winston Churchill, SIS and SOE in London, and maybe to the White House, but none of these has ever emerged. He certainly kept two himself, but the others were placed in a bank vault in Montreal until sometime in 1946, when Tom Hill received instructions to have them destroyed. Accordingly, he took the ten books to a farm in Quebec and burned them. Thus, by the end of 1946, it seems that apart from four or five copies in official archives in London, and a copy presented to Norman Robertson, Under-Secretary in Canada's Department of External Affairs, Stephenson controlled the last two, and there is no evidence that he showed them to anyone until he invited Harford Montgomery Hyde to write his biography.

Like *British Security Coordination* itself, the background to this part of the story is complicated. Hyde had served in British Security Coordination between May 1941 and 1944, having been posted to New York from the Imperial Censorship and Contraband Control office in Bermuda. He had previously worked for SIS's sabotage unit, known as Section D, and for a while had been based in Gibraltar.[2] After the war, Hyde had been elected the Unionist Member of Parliament for North Belfast and had written a number of biographies, including that of Oscar Wilde. In 1961, having kept in contact with Stephenson, he agreed to give up his academic post teaching history at the University of the Punjab in Lahore, Pakistan, and devote himself for a few months to a book he was to call *The Quiet Canadian*, a reference to a flattering description given to Stephenson coined in 1948 by the author Robert Sherwood in *Roosevelt and Hopkins: An Intimate History*. One condition of Hyde's acceptance of the commission was that Stephenson, who had by then retired with what remained of his fortune to Bermuda, should pay his expenses. According to Hyde's papers, his advance amounted to £600, a considerable sum in those days.

Although Hyde was working as a legal adviser to the British Control Commission in Austria when Giles Playfair was editing Tom Hill's manuscript, he was not unfamiliar with the content, for back in March 1943 he had completed a 200-page document entitled *Report on British Security Coordination in the United States*

Introduction by Nigel West

of America, a copy of which is now lodged with Hyde's papers at Churchill College, Cambridge.

A comparison between *British Security Coordination* and *The Quiet Canadian* shows that the latter relied very heavily on the former, and that Hyde lifted many very long passages directly from the text, without attribution, although some passages were placed in quotation marks and presented as Stephenson's own words. On the issue of sources, the author said only that he had used 'Sir William Stephenson's official and private papers, supplemented by my own correspondence and personal recollections'.[3] In the estimate of Tim Naftali, a Canadian academic at the University of Hawaii who has made a detailed study of the two, eighty-five per cent of Hyde's narrative is either 'direct reproductions or faithful executive summaries' of the history.[4] The remainder was either more biographical data about Stephenson, or Hyde's own material, recalling his experiences first as a Contraband Control officer in Bermuda and then as a case officer for the SIS agent Elizabeth Thorpe, referred to in both texts simply as 'Cynthia'.[5] As for Hyde's personal contribution, much of it was mischievous. He had been particularly irritated by the behaviour of his first wife during the war and, in a departure from the history's text, made a sly reference to the BSC double agent codenamed SPRINGBOK, 'a man of powerful attraction to women, judging by the fact that he successfully seduced the wife of the BSC officer in whose charge he was for a time'.[6]

Clearly Hyde's methodology must have received Stephenson's full support, for he lent the author his copy of *British Security Coordination*. He also encouraged Hyde to discuss another similar project that he had attempted to sponsor recently with Dick Ellis, his old wartime deputy. Ellis had accepted Stephenson's proposal and had discussed it with another BSC veteran, John Pepper, but the scheme had floundered after Ellis had produced an initial 200-page draft, *Anglo-American Collaboration in Security and Intelligence*, which Stephenson had renamed *The Two Bills: Mission Accomplished* and then rejected. His choice of Ellis was particularly interesting, for at the time Ellis had just taken unexpectedly early retirement from the Australian Secret Intelligence Service, having spent much of his adult life in the British SIS. He had joined the Berlin Station in October 1923 and since then had served as an SIS professional, until his switch to the sister service in his native Australia in 1953, by which time he had reached the senior position of SIS's Chief of

Production/Europe. When approached by Stephenson, Ellis was working on an account of his participation in the ill-fated Allied intervention in the Russian Civil War, released initially as articles, 'Operations in Transcaspia 1918–19', and in 1963 published as a book, *Transcaspian Episode*.[7] Unknown to Stephenson, who thought that Ellis had been retained part-time by SIS and the Foreign Office's anti-Soviet propaganda branch, the Information Research Department, Ellis had actually come under suspicion as a traitor who had certainly fallen victim to Nazi bribery before the war, and possibly Soviet blackmail afterwards. Under interrogation Ellis admitted the first offence, so forfeiting his SIS pension, but denied any Soviet connection.[8]

With help from Ellis and Pepper, Hyde completed his manuscript by June 1961. When it was published the following year, it caused a minor sensation, principally because it identified for the first time Sir Stewart Menzies as having been the wartime Chief of the Secret Intelligence Service. Hyde argued that others had named him, but his indiscretion was sufficient to prompt angry questions in Parliament in November 1962, not least because no action had been taken to prevent publication, whereas the Government had not treated other authors so leniently.[9] Significantly, Hyde acknowledged the assistance he had received from Colonel Ellis, who 'read the book in manuscript and has made suggestions which have improved it in many ways';[10] he also mentioned that he had received help from John Pepper, Ingram Fraser, David Ogilvy and Tommy Drew-Brook, all BSC insiders. Clearly, for Whitehall to have taken any action against Hyde, a former MP, would have involved much embarrassment, particularly as the text contained nothing that was likely to compromise the security of current operations. Indeed, although Hyde referred to Stephenson's deputy as having been an SIS professional, he did not specifically identify Ellis in the role, and he also took steps to conceal some of the names which appeared in the original history.[11]

Nevertheless, despite Hyde's best efforts, he soon found himself facing legal actions from Gaston Henry-Haye, formerly the Vichy Ambassador in Washington DC, and the family of the late Admiral Alberto Lais, previously the Italian Naval Attaché. The first litigation centred on Hyde's assertion that Henry-Haye had exploited French resentment towards the attack on the French fleet at Mers-el-Kebir and Oran, and 'at the same time he organised a kind of Gestapo in the Embassy to report upon the activities of supporters of the former French Government and

Introduction by Nigel West

in particular those who had responded to General de Gaulle's patriotic call'.[12] However, the relevant passage in the BSC history asserted that 'It had been ascertained that even before Henry-Haye's arrival, the Vichy Government had organised a so-called French "Gestapo" in the United States, a secret police body whose duty it was to report upon the activities of the supporters of the former French Government and in particular upon the adherents of General de Gaulle' (p. 148). Naturally Henry-Haye, who had no knowledge of the existence of the BSC history, was infuriated by Hyde's libel, and when he started proceedings the author of *The Quiet Canadian* was at a severe disadvantage. The very existence of the original text was a closely guarded secret, if not an officially classified document, and furthermore it provided little comfort because it served only to demonstrate that Hyde had incorrectly paraphrased a passage that did not credit Henry-Haye with organizing a kind of Gestapo in the Embassy. On the contrary, the Gestapo was only said to have operated in the United States and to have been established well before the new Ambassador had taken up his appointment. Accordingly, Hyde was obliged to reach an expensive settlement with Henry-Haye.

Hyde also experienced difficulties with his description of how 'Cynthia' had seduced the Italian Naval Attaché, Admiral Lais. On this occasion he was on slightly firmer ground, partly because his version did not depart too extravagantly from the original text in the BSC history, but mainly because Lais himself was dead. However, in Italian law the families of the deceased can sue for defamation to defend the honour of the dead, and Hyde found himself facing a libel suit over his exaggerated account of Lais's sale of the Italian naval cipher. Unfortunately, Hyde had embroidered the tale by adding the unjustifiable claim that the decisive naval action fought off Cape Matapan in March 1941, in which the British had sunk three Italian cruisers and two destroyers, had been a direct consequence of Lais's duplicity. The movement of the Italian fleet had been 'correctly anticipated with the aid of the ciphers', wrote Hyde,[13] whereas the BSC history had made no mention whatever of the Matapan engagement and had confined itself to the comment that by virtue of his access to the Italian codes, the Commander-in-Chief Mediterranean had been able 'to dispose his meagre forces to such effective purpose that the Italians were constantly deceived concerning the numbers and strength of British units'. The best the BSC history could say was that this 'may have been largely due to the fact that the British had knowledge of the Italian Naval cypher' (p. 166), which, of course, was not quite the same as Hyde's sensationally extravagant assertion. Being able to dodge a superior naval force is certainly useful, but to blame Admiral Lais for the defeat off Cape Matapan was wholly insupportable.

In reality, although cryptography had indeed played a significant part in the Battle of Matapan, it had nothing to do with the codebook provided by Lais. According to the official history of British Intelligence, released in 1979, 'Italy's main naval book cyphers, which were the cyphers used by her fleet for most of her important communications, were never read again after July 1941 except for a few brief intervals as a result of captures after the middle of 1941'.[14] Actually Admiral Somerville's 'vital clue to Italian movements before the Battle of Matapan' had come from the decryption of the Italian naval Enigma traffic, which had been read by the British since it had first been introduced during the Spanish Civil War. A later, improved model of the Italian Enigma machine had been broken at Bletchley Park in September 1940 and information gleaned from this source, together with data from the Luftwaffe's Enigma traffic, had allowed the Royal Navy to spring a skilful trap that had virtually eliminated the Italian fleet from the rest of the war. It was certainly a great triumph for the codebreakers, but an event quite unconnected with any undercover BSC operation in Washington DC.

Whether Hyde realized that his hyperbole had dropped him in hot water again is unknown, but he decided not to defend the case. Consequently, he was convicted of criminal libel and paid £4,000 in damages to the Lais family.

Financially, *The Quiet Canadian* was not a success for Hyde, but it did accomplish Stephenson's objective, to gain recognition as having played a pivotal role in the clandestine war. Hitherto British Security Coordination had been virtually unknown, its name never having emerged in print in public. Stephenson himself had been almost as shy, having been the subject of a rather sensational article entitled 'The Biggest Private Eye of All', published in *Maclean's Magazine* in December 1952, but now he emerged as an impressive figure, his mission to the United States on behalf of Winston Churchill having been revealed in a foreword written by David Bruce, then the widely respected American Ambassador in London, and formerly a senior OSS officer.

It was this political dimension to Stephenson's assignment that raised some eyebrows, for the BSC history makes clear

Introduction by Nigel West

that Stephenson went on his first mission for SIS to New York 'in the early spring of 1940 . . . at the request of CSS' (p. xi) and then returned as the PCO in June for CSS, making no mention of any intervention by Winston Churchill, or any dramatic interview as described by Hyde, in which the new Prime Minister told Stephenson that his duty lay in America. Hyde's enhancement of Stephenson's status extended to the Canadian's alleged involvement in March 1940 in an attempt by SIS to sabotage the Baltic port of Oxelösund in order to prevent Swedish iron from reaching Germany. According to Hyde, Stephenson had travelled to Stockholm with another saboteur, only to have their mission cancelled after a personal plea from King Gustav of Sweden to King George VI. Disappointed not to be planting his consignment of plastic explosives, Stephenson apparently moved on to Helsinki early in March before returning to London.[15]

Hyde's account went unchallenged at the time it was published, but much more is now known about Section D's plan to sabotage the loading facilities at Oxelösund, and it is clear that Stephenson played almost no part in it. The operation had been arranged by the head of Section D's Scandinavian Section, Alexander Rickman, who had completed a thorough reconnaissance in 1938 under journalistic cover, and had been assisted by two members of the local British expatriate business community, Ernest Biggs, a one-legged tea importer, and Harry Gill, the British Petroleum representative. Another Section D adventurer, Gerald Holdsworth, flew in to participate, but Rickman was arrested in April 1940 as he moved the explosives to the target. He was sentenced to eight years' hard labour, and Biggs, who was caught with two suitcases packed with dynamite, received five years. Also convicted were their two Swedish co-conspirators, Elsa Johansson and Arno Behrisch. However, Holdsworth managed to evade the police and took refuge in the British Embassy until he could flee to Finland. Thus, far from being a scheme invented by Stephenson, to whom 'one of 'D's officers was specially attached . . . as an assistant',[16] the entire project proved an embarrassing fiasco which happened long after Stephenson had left Stockholm. As well as changing the dates, Hyde's account omitted the crucial fact that all the plotters except for Holdsworth ended up in prison. Indeed, Hyde's version was also contradicted by what is known of Stephenson's true movements in March 1940. According to US Immigration records, Stephenson was in London on 6 March to apply for a visa to visit America on behalf of the Ministry of Supply, and was in Washington DC on 14 April to meet J. Edgar Hoover of the FBI, before moving on to California. Quite obviously, Hyde's tale of Stephenson's exploits in Scandinavia was nothing more than an invention.

This is but one example of Hyde embroidering Stephenson's story, but worse was to occur when a Canadian author, William Stevenson, wrote another biography, this time entitled *A Man Called Intrepid*.[17] According to Stevenson, he had been invited to consider such a project by Ian Fleming in 1956,[18] and had discussed Dick Ellis's draft with the author in 1972, having been contracted to start work in 1968. Simultaneously, he embarked on a separate venture which was to culminate in the publication in 1973 of *The Bormann Brotherhood*,[19] a curious quest for Hitler's deputy in South America allegedly conducted by secret agents long after the war and directed by Sir William Stephenson, codenamed INTREPID.

In researching *A Man Called Intrepid*, and possibly a television documentary, Stevenson drew on *British Security Coordination*, which Sir William referred to in his foreword as 'the BSC Papers' that 'consisted of many thick volumes and exhibits, covering five years of intense activity and thousands of operations across the world'.[20] In addition, Dick Ellis contributed 'a historical note' in which he recalled Hyde's book, *The Quiet Canadian*, and made the astonishing assertions that publication had been an officially approved 'partial leak' and that 'the reason for the break in the silence about BSC in 1962 was the escape to the Soviet Union of Kim Philby'.[21]

In reality, of course, Hyde's book had been published in November 1962, whereas Philby did not defect for a further two months, on the night of 23 January 1963, so Ellis's account of a leak to mitigate the damage caused by Philby cannot be correct. Indeed, closer examination of *A Man Called Intrepid* showed that it was largely a work of fiction, and was so categorized by the American publishers following overwhelming criticism, thereby ensuring that Sir William's reputation was irretrievably damaged, although he was in such poor physical and mental condition until his death on the last day of January 1989 that he never realized the extent of what had happened.[22] The unpalatable reality was that both his biographies had been hopelessly inaccurate, leaving the authentic version of BSC's operations unavailable, at least until now.

Whatever the different interpretations put by other authors on *British Security Coordination* since it was completed, the document itself, in its complete and unexpurgated form, has

Introduction by Nigel West

been deliberately kept from the public. Some photocopied versions of Sir William's personal edition have circulated among a small circle of intelligence *cognoscenti*, but this present edition is the first time the whole document has been published without editorial comment.* Overall, the history falls into two distinct parts, pre- and post-Pearl Harbor, and reveals the lengths taken to influence US public opinion and isolationist politicians. In particular, the willingness of American radio commentators, then a very influential medium, to peddle what amounted to foreign propaganda, will shock. However, the ingenuity with which the Nazis were outmanoeuvred in North and South America is an extraordinary achievement, both for the organization itself and for Sir William, and one that deserves, at long last, to be told in full, in the form originally intended.

Source Notes

1. For a comprehensive history of STS 103, see David Stafford's *Camp X* (Lester & Orpen Dennys, Toronto, 1986).
2. For Hyde's own account of his wartime activities, see *Secret Intelligence Agent* (Constable, London, 1982).
3. *The Quiet Canadian* (Hamish Hamilton, London, 1962), p. 243.
4. Timothy J. Naftali, *Intrepid's Last Deception* (Intelligence & National Security, Vol. 8, July 1993), p. 72.
5. Hyde subsequently wrote her biography, *Cynthia* (Farrar, Straus, New York, 1963); see also Mary Lovell, *Cast No Shadow* (Pantheon, New York 1992).
6. *The Quiet Canadian*, p. 222.
7. C.H. Ellis, *Transcaspian Episode* (Hutchinson, London, 1963).
8. For details of the suspicions against Ellis, see Peter Wright, *Spycatcher* (Viking, New York, 1987), p. 326.
9. *Hansard*, 8 November 1962, col. 1153.
10. *The Quiet Canadian*, p. x.
11. The double agent TRICYCLE, for example, became 'BICYCLE' (p. 220), the Comte de la Grandville is referred to as 'the Count de la L—' (p. 115) and Charles Brousee became 'Captain Bestrand' (p. 108).
12. *The Quiet Canadian*, p. 95.
13. *Ibid.*, p. 107.
14. F. H. Hinsley, *British Intelligence in the Second World War*, Vol. I (HMSO, London, 1979), p. 210.
15. *The Quiet Canadian*, p. 21.
16. *Ibid.*
17. *A Man Called Intrepid* (Harcourt Brace, New York, 1976).

---

* Typographical errors in the original have been corrected and, due to poor quality, some of the illustrations which appeared in the original have been omitted.

18. See Stevenson's letter to *Saturday Night*, October 1990, in which he wrote that 'Ian Fleming proposed that I write the biography of Sir William in 1956, but we encountered official opposition.'
19. *The Bormann Brotherhood* (Harcourt Brace, New York, 1973).
20. *A Man Called Intrepid*, p. xiv.
21. *Ibid.*, p. xix.
22. For details of Sir William's alleged infirmity, see Thomas Troy's *Wild Bill and Intrepid* (Yale University Press, 1996).

FOREWORD

This account has been prepared, at my instruction, by BSC officers, who have used the organization's files as sources of information. The original purpose was to provide a record which would be available for reference should future need arise for secret activities and security measures of the kind it describes.

That purpose has already been advanced to the point of immediacy by the march of events; for, with the advent of atomic weapons, what is written in the pages following may be considered relevant to the present rather than to a hypothetical future. Against possible atomic attack, the only hope of survival is to be forewarned; and – having regard, in particular, to the various surprise forms of atomic attack which an aggressor nation might employ – to be forewarned clearly necessitates a worldwide Intelligence Service of maximum effectiveness.

This record of lessons learned and of methods evolved under the impetus of war is, therefore, submitted as contribution to the maintenance of such a service. It demonstrates, above all, that, during the period under review, an organization in the Western Hemisphere restricted in its authority to collecting intelligence by established means would have been altogether inadequate and that the success of secret activities was primarily dependent upon the coordination of a number of functions falling within the jurisdiction of separate government departments in London. It was only as a result of such coordination that BSC had the necessary elasticity to meet the urgent demands of the situation and to adapt itself readily to swiftly changing needs. In referring to it, one feels impelled to make specific mention of the close cooperation afforded BSC by HM Embassy in Washington – without which much that was achieved could not have been. Lord Lothian's intimate concern in the early days proved invaluable; and so, too, did the unfailing support subsequently given by Lord Halifax.

The conception of coordinated operations in the field of secret activities, which BSC originally exemplified, was the basis upon which the Americans built, with astonishing speed, their own highly successful wartime Intelligence Service. It is, perhaps, not going too far to suggest that this conception may properly be regarded as essential to the maintenance of worldwide vigilance and national security in the critical years ahead.

WILLIAM STEPHENSON

New York,
31 December 1945

EDITORIAL NOTE

While this history is the work of more than one hand, it has been subjected to a final editing, chiefly with the object of making each separate part an intelligible account in itself – provided always that the Introduction and Part I (Groundwork of Liaison with the Americans) are read beforehand.

British Security Coordination is referred to throughout as BSC and the Director of British Security Coordination as WS. A glossary of other abbreviations used appears on the facing page.

GLOSSARY

AFL	American Federation of Labor
BEW	US Board of Economic Warfare
BIS	British Information Services
CBB	Central Bureau of Brisbane
CD	Head of SOE
CISO	Chief Industrial Security Officer
CIO	Congress of Industrial Organizations
COI	Coordinator of Information
CSO	Consular Security Officer
CSS	Head of SIS
DNI	Director of Naval Intelligence
FEA	US Foreign Economic Administration
FBI	US Federal Bureau of Investigation
FCC	US Federal Communications Commission
FIS	Foreign Information Service of the Office of the Coordinator of Information
GCCS	HM Government Code and Cypher School
G-2	Military Intelligence Division, US War Department General Staff
ISO	Industrial Security Officer
JIC	Joint Intelligence Committee
JSC	Joint Security Control
MEW	HM Ministry of Economic Warfare
MOI	HM Ministry of Information
ONA	Overseas News Agency
ONI	US Office of Naval Intelligence
OPG or OP-20-G	Communication Intelligence Branch of the US Office of Naval Communications
OSS	US Office of Strategic Services
OWI	US Office of War Information
PWE	Political Warfare Executive
RCMP	Royal Canadian Mounted Police
RSS	Radio Security Service

Glossary

SFE	US Survey of Foreign Experts
SI	Secret Intelligence
SIS	Secret Intelligence Service
SO	Special Operations
SOE	Special Operations Executive
SO.1	Political Warfare division of the early SO organization
SO.2	Division of the early SO organization concerned with Special Operations other than those of a Political Warfare nature
SSA	Signals Security Agency, US War Department
WEC	Wireless Experimental Centre
WPB	US War Production Board

INTRODUCTION

Origin, Development and Functions

In the early spring of 1940, WS paid a visit to the United States. Ostensibly private business was the purpose of his journey. In fact, he travelled at the request of CSS.

He had received instructions which were explicit but limited in purpose to furthering Anglo-American cooperation in one specific field. He was required to re-establish on behalf of CSS a high-level liaison with the Federal Bureau of Investigation – a liaison which had been cut off as a result of British belligerency and American neutrality but without which SIS could not function effectively in the United States.

WS saw J. Edgar Hoover, Director of the FBI, and explained the purpose of his mission. Hoover said frankly that, while he himself was not opposed to working with SIS, he was under strict injunction from the State Department to refrain from collaboration with the British in any way which could be interpreted as an infringement of United States neutrality, and he made it clear that he would not be prepared to contravene this policy without direct Presidential sanction. Further, he stipulated that even if the President could be persuaded to agree to the principle of collaboration between the FBI and SIS, such collaboration should be effected initially by a personal liaison between WS and himself and that no other US government department, including the Department of State, should be informed of it.

Accordingly, WS arranged for a mutual friend to put the matter before the President, and Mr Roosevelt, upon hearing the arguments in favour of the proposed liaison, endorsed them enthusiastically. 'There should be the closest possible marriage', the President said, 'between the FBI and British Intelligence.' Later, by way of confirmation, he repeated these words to HM Ambassador in Washington.

Thus an agreement was reached, some six months after the

start of the European war, for Anglo-American cooperation in the intelligence field. The fact that it was reached at all is indication of Mr Roosevelt's remarkable clarity of vision. The fact that it had to be kept secret even from the State Department provides striking illustration of the strength of American neutrality at the time. Moreover, though it was a first essential step by SIS towards combating enemy activities in the United States, it was in itself insufficient to meet the demands of the situation. The enemy was already well organized and well entrenched, and, realizing the extent of Britain's ultimate dependence on American material aid, was directing his subversive propaganda towards buttressing the wall of traditional isolationism by which the President was encompassed. In that task he was experiencing little difficulty and enjoying considerable success, for he was faced by no organized opposition. There were still comparatively few Americans – in or out of Congress – who understood that the safety of their own country would be endangered by Britain's collapse; and many among those who were instinctively pro-British had nonetheless been disheartened by Munich and by what they called the 'phony' war. The American authorities, including the FBI, had no power to suppress enemy subversive propaganda, since this did not menace directly the security of the United States. And meanwhile Britain herself was doing nothing to expose or counteract it.

Furthermore, it seemed likely that the enemy would make a wide-scale attempt to halt or slow down by physical means such supplies as were coming to Britain from the United States, and that if he did so he might well succeed. He could attack at several vulnerable points, and he could presumably recruit sabotage agents without difficulty – particularly among the dock labourers and stevedores who were largely drawn from resident communities of German and Italian extraction. The American authorities were not concerned to take any special measures for the protection of British property, and while the British Purchasing Commission was technically responsible for prevention of sabotage, it was equipped to do little more than minimize the risk in factories turning out war material for Britain. It had no means of instituting adequate safeguards at the various ports where the material was loaded on to British ships and where the threat of enemy interference was most serious.

Upon his return to London, WS reported these findings to CSS, and he advocated that a British secret organization in the

Introduction: Origin, Development and Functions

United States, though founded upon the basis of liaison with Hoover, should not confine itself to purely SIS functions but should undertake to do all that was not being done and could not be done by overt means to assure sufficient aid for Britain and eventually to bring America into the war. On the understanding that he would be empowered to establish such an organization he accepted the appointment of Passport Control Officer* in New York, and in this capacity went back to the United States in June of 1940 – at the time of the catastrophe on the Western Front.

There proved to be no adequate existing foundation, for the Passport Control Office which WS took over had neither sufficient personnel nor physical resources to engage in secret activities on the scale envisaged, and indeed, apart from its overt functions, was concerned only with low-grade counter-espionage work. In effect, therefore, the task of building a secret organization had to be begun from scratch. WS embarked upon it with four definite advantages. The first was his liaison with Hoover which had been previously arranged. The second was his acquaintanceship with a number of convinced interventionists, notably William Donovan, who were in a position to influence both public opinion and Government policy. The third was the goodwill of the Canadian authorities who could give him much assistance which he required. And the fourth was the support which he enlisted, immediately upon his arrival in the United States, of HM Ambassador (the late Lord Lothian), who, in the urgent circumstances of the moment, when Britain was critically dependent on American aid but could make no move to solicit it openly without playing straight into the hands of the isolationists, fully endorsed the need for an organization which, though independent of the Embassy, would in effect act as a covert counterpart of it.

WS had no settled or restrictive terms of reference, and his functions grew out of the broad objective already mentioned. Before he left London, CSS had handed him a list of certain essential supplies of which His Majesty's Government had immediate need. In addition to obtaining these by entering into secret negotiations with the White House, his three primary concerns were to investigate enemy activities, to institute adequate security measures against the threat of sabotage to British property and to organize American public opinion in favour of aid to

---

* The time-honoured cover for SIS representatives abroad.

Britain. It was to fulfil these purposes that his headquarters organization* in New York was originally established and the immediate steps taken in pursuance of each of them were as follows:

1. The Investigation of Enemy Activities

Agents were recruited to penetrate enemy or enemy-controlled businesses, propaganda groups and diplomatic and consular missions, and representatives were posted to such key points as Washington DC, Los Angeles, San Francisco and Seattle. At the same time it was realized that the scope of investigations could not logically be confined to the United States, for in his general purpose of isolating Britain from American material assistance, the enemy could both attack and be attacked at other points in the Western Hemisphere. Accordingly the closest liaison was established with Imperial Censorship, which proved a prolific source of information concerning enemy activities throughout the Western Hemisphere and also with the Canadian Security authorities. Direct communication was established, too, with SIS stations in Latin America. A number of these stations proved to be hardly better equipped for engagement in secret intelligence than the Passport Control Office in New York had been, and WS's organization, therefore, undertook the task of rehabilitating them, despatching representatives, for that purpose, to Mexico City, Havana, Guatemala City, San José, Haiti, Bogotá, Barranquilla, Caracas and Panama. Furthermore WS was entrusted with responsibility for directing the activities of MI5 officers in Bermuda, Jamaica and Trinidad, who were often in a position to interrogate and, if necessary, apprehend suspects *en route* to and from the United States and Latin America. A sketch map showing the various points in the Western Hemisphere with which the headquarters organization maintained direct contact for the purpose of investigating enemy activities is reproduced opposite.

---

* At its outset it operated under cover of the Passport Control Office, and was inevitably small, though it grew rapidly as necessity required and opportunity permitted. Apart from a senior SIS officer who was sent out from London and whose assistance proved of great value, it was staffed exclusively by officers whom WS recruited after taking up his appointment. With one or two exceptions none of them had had any previous experience in secret work, but were chosen by virtue either of having held responsible professional positions in private life or of special knowledge which suited them to undertake the various tasks involved. A number of officers and virtually all the secretarial staff were recruited in Canada.

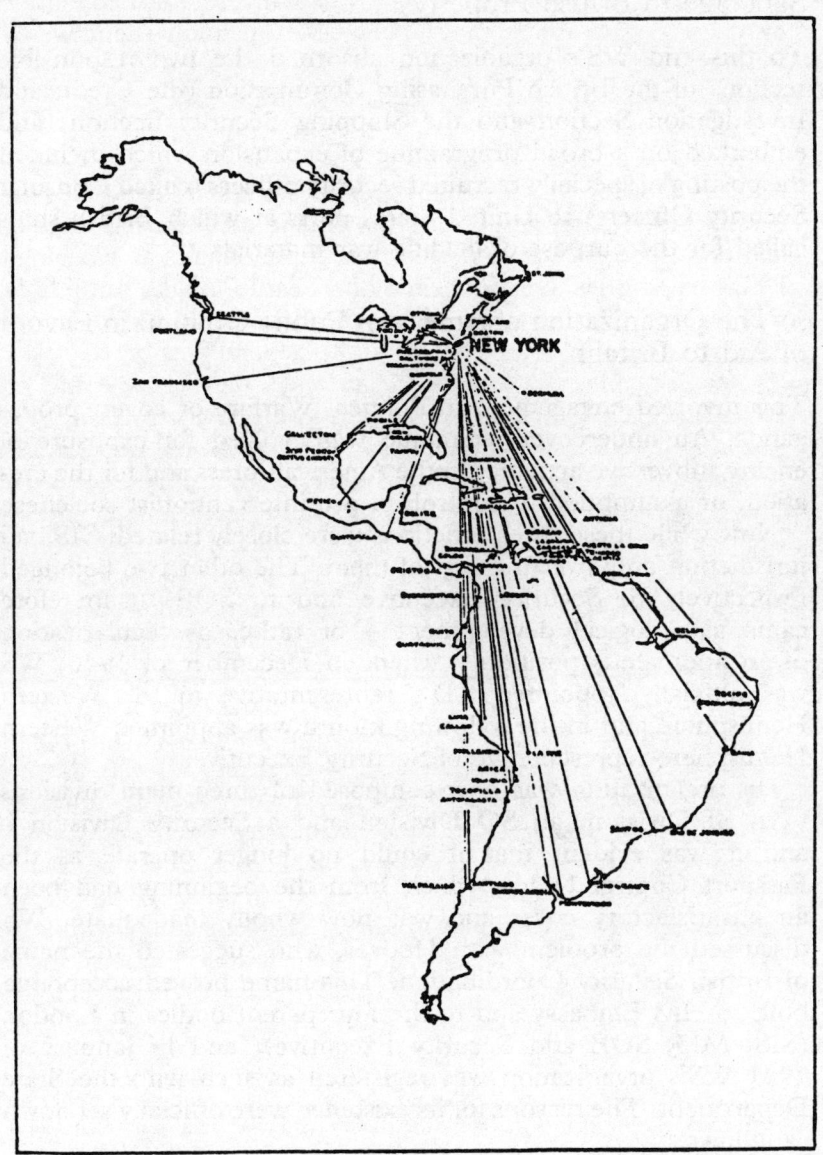

Map showing principal cities in which BSC had direct representation.

2. Institution of Security Measures against the Threat of Sabotage to British Property

To this end WS's organization absorbed the two responsible sections of the British Purchasing Commission (the Credit and Investigation Section and the Shipping Security Section) and embarked on a broad programme of expansion which included the posting of specially recruited security officers (called Consular Security Officers) to United States ports at which British ships called for the purpose of loading war materials.

3. The Organization of American Public Opinion in Favour of Aid to Britain

This involved engagement in Political Warfare or covert propaganda. An undercover technique was evolved for exposure of enemy subversive activities in the American press and for the creation, or assumption of control, of pro-interventionist societies.

Now while these three functions were closely related, SIS had jurisdiction only over the first of them. The other two belonged respectively to Security Executive and to SOE. It therefore came as a logical development – or rather as regularization of an anomalous position – when, in December of 1940, WS was officially appointed CD's representative in the Western Hemisphere and in the following month was appointed Western Hemisphere representative of Security Executive.

His organization was now composed of three main divisions – an SI Division, an SO Division and a Security Division – and it was evident that it could no longer operate as the Passport Control Office, which from the beginning had been an unsatisfactory cover and was now wholly inadequate. WS discussed the problem with Hoover, who suggested the name of British Security Coordination. This name proved acceptable both to HM Embassy and to the four parent bodies in London (SIS, MI5, SOE and Security Executive); and in January of 1941 WS's organization was registered as such with the State Department. The reasons for its existence were officially set down as follows:

> Consequent on the large scale and vital interests of the British Government in connection with the purchasing and shipment of munitions and war material from the United States, coupled with the presence in this country

Introduction: Origin, Development and Functions

of a number of British official missions, a variety of security problems have been created, and these, affecting closely as they do the interests of the British Government, call for very close and friendly collaboration between the authorities of the two countries.

Thus, for example, the presence in large numbers of British and Allied ships engaged in loading explosives and other war materials, and the existence of large quantities of similar materials in plants, on railways and in dock areas throughout the country, presenting as they do a tempting target to saboteurs and enemy agents, constitute in themselves a security problem of considerable magnitude.

With a view to coordinating the liaison between the various British missions and the United States authorities in all security matters arising from the present abnormal circumstances, an organization bearing the title *Security Coordination* has been formed under the control of a Director of Security Coordination, assisted by a headquarters staff.

For a brief period in 1941, Political Warfare was conducted under special journalistic cover, and the Passport Control Office continued as such to discharge its overt functions throughout. Otherwise BSC, though Security was its only declared purpose, became cover for all the varied activities with which WS was concerned, and the work it undertook before Pearl Harbor, in addition to that mentioned above, may be briefly summarized as follows:

> 1. The collection of intelligence concerning United States and Latin American affairs – both foreign and domestic – affecting British interests.
> 2. The collection of external intelligence – intelligence, that is to say, derived from sources within the Western Hemisphere but relating to areas outside the Western Hemisphere.
> 3. The penetration of unfriendly, as well as enemy, diplomatic and consular missions.
> 4. The establishment in Latin America of an SOE organization, with the primary purpose of preparing for underground activities in the various republics against the possibility (which at the time seemed far from remote) of Axis invasion or Axis-inspired revolution.

5. The organization of 'free' movements among foreign exiles and minorities in the Western Hemisphere for the purpose of encouraging and strengthening resistance in the occupied countries.
6. The direction of subversive propaganda from American sources both to Europe and the Far East.
7. The institution of measures to prevent the enemy from smuggling supplies both to and from the Western Hemisphere.
8. The institution of security measures in Latin America through the posting of security officers to Latin American ports where British ships called.
9. The recruitment of agents in the Western Hemisphere to undertake either SI or SO work in enemy-occupied countries.
10. The training of agents for SI or SO work. To this end arrangements were made for the establishment in Canada of a special training camp which was opened coincidentally with Pearl Harbor.
11. The procurement in the Western Hemisphere of special supplies for the underground in occupied countries.

Although it is true that a number of these functions had no obvious connection with WS's initial purposes, yet in fact they developed logically from them, for all BSC's work before Pearl Harbor had one thing in common: it proved as useful to the United States as it did to Britain. Had there been no BSC, it is likely that when the Americans entered the war they would have possessed little knowledge concerning enemy activities in the Western Hemisphere; would have been embarrassed by many more agents, subversive businesses and organizations than in fact they were under compunction to suppress; and in Latin America, where United States security was particularly vulnerable, would have had to contend with an enemy holding virtually unchallenged sway. Furthermore, it is certain that without BSC they would have been far less well equipped than they were for engagement in their own secret work abroad.

In contradistinction to the task of investigating and exposing enemy subversive activities, which served the objective of fostering American intervention, such functions as the organization of 'free' movements, inasmuch as they helped to prepare the United States as a base for operations against the enemy outside the Western Hemisphere, were undertaken on the supposition of America's eventual entry into the war and represented essentially a move from the defensive to the offensive. The climax of that offensive was reached some six months before Pearl Harbor when BSC secured, through the establishment of the organization which eventually came to be known as the Office of Strategic Services, an assurance of full American participation and collaboration with the British in secret activities directed against the enemy throughout the world.

Thus, though its first objective was fulfilled when Pearl Harbor came, BSC was already in a position to take advantage of the changed situation and to act thenceforward as the organization responsible for ensuring that the Americans undertook secret work, both within and without the Western Hemisphere, not divergently but in the closest possible alliance with the British. As such its functions, though subjected to considerable adjustment, were hardly less manifold than they had been before Pearl Harbor, and may be briefly summarized as follows:

1. Activities in the United States

(a) There was no longer any need to carry out direct investigations of enemy activities, for this work was now fully within the competence of the American authorities. Nor, as it happened, was there freedom to do so, for according to the terms of a Bill (known as the McKellar Bill) which was enacted in the early summer of 1942, all foreign intelligence agencies were prohibited, *inter alia*, from employing their own agents within the United States. On the other hand, there was increased opportunity for engagement in liaison with the FBI in counter-espionage work – work which hitherto had been subordinated to the more urgent need of suppressing subversive propaganda – and in order to take full advantage of it a special counter-espionage section was established at the beginning of 1942. Furthermore, the task of penetrating certain foreign missions, which had been begun before Pearl Harbor, was completed, and the results were shared with the American authorities.

(b) Security work was continued, though in far closer liaison with the Americans than had hitherto been possible.

(c) The collection of intelligence about American affairs was continued, for this was clearly of no less importance than it had been previously.

(d) Political Warfare designed to influence American public opinion was, for obvious reasons, largely abandoned. However on occasion covert arrangements were made, at London's request, for placing special material in the American press.

2. Activities in Latin America

One of the results of the Rio Conference of January 1942 was to enable the Americans to undertake large-scale secret work of their own in Latin America. While this represented a great step forward, BSC's responsibilities increased rather than diminished thereafter, because, at the outset at least, the Americans were far from adequately equipped to undertake sole responsibility for Latin America, which, inasmuch as it was the only remaining neutral source of strategic supplies, had become the chief target of enemy activities in the Western Hemisphere and was still extremely vulnerable. Moreover, it would in any case have been impolitic to allow the Americans monopoly in an area where British interests were heavily involved, and thus BSC was concerned to ensure first that British Intelligence, Security and Special Operations should be as effective as possible and secondly that American parallel activities should be conducted in harmony with them. To these ends BSC (a) continued to maintain close contact with SIS stations and for a period was entrusted with administrative control of them, (b) retained its SOE organization until 1944 by which time the need for Special Operations had clearly passed and (c) retained its Security Organization until the war ended, increasing the scope of its activities in the summer of 1942 through the execution of an Industrial Security Plan. In these undertakings collaboration with the Americans was effected both locally and at a headquarters level.

3. Activities Directed against the Enemy outside the Western Hemisphere

All BSC's functions directed against the enemy abroad – which have been previously listed – were conducted in close collaboration with the Americans after Pearl Harbor. While responsibility for Political Warfare was assumed by a PWE mission in the summer of 1942, the recruitment and training of agents continued until the beginning of 1944.* The collection of external intelligence and work with minority groups remained BSC's concern until the war ended.

4. Communications Division

Late in 1941, BSC added to its three existing Divisions a Communications Division whose work largely developed after Pearl Harbor. It was originally founded for the triple purpose, first of devising a secure means of rapid communication between BSC and its Washington office; secondly of purchasing special wireless equipment for Britain which was available in the United States and nowhere else; and thirdly of devising a secret communication network in Latin America in case underground activities were rendered necessary there by Axis invasion or Axis-inspired coups d'état. BSC was in direct contact with US Service Intelligence Departments, and it became the transmitting channel for the exchange of intercepted enemy messages between American and British terminals. This traffic steadily increased, and when the war ended had reached formidable proportions. By that time BSC's Communications Division was the largest unit of its kind in the world, having handled, at its peak, a regular average of a million groups a day.

Such then were the chief functions of British Security Coordination, and in the account which follows they are described under the broad headings of Political Warfare for SO.1, Economic Warfare, Secret Intelligence, Security of Property and Personnel, Special Operations in Latin America, Counter-Espionage, Organization for Secret Activity outside the Western Hemisphere and Communications Network. They were, however, closely related and inevitably have defied any attempt at rigid separation: inevitably because coordination was the very premise of BSC's work, and without it little could have been achieved.

To sum up, it may be said that in the final analysis all BSC's functions were the logical consequence of four initial purposes – three essentially defensive in character and one offensive. They were:

1. The establishment of a secret organization to investigate

---

* For Europe only. Recruitment of Canadian Chinese continued until 1945.

enemy activities and to institute adequate security measures in the Western Hemisphere.
2. The procurement of certain essential supplies for Britain.
3. The fostering of American intervention.
4. The assurance of American participation in secret activities throughout the world in the closest possible collaboration with the British.

It is obvious that none of these purposes could have been fulfilled without American assistance – both official and unofficial. For, while it is true that before Pearl Harbor BSC was largely under compunction to take independent action in the United States, it could not have come into being at all without American approval on the highest level. Furthermore, apart from the Consular Security Officers, the majority of those who, knowingly or unknowingly, served BSC – as intelligence agents, intermediaries, propagandists and political organizers – were not British but American. WS's first task, therefore, was to lay the groundwork of liaison with the Americans – and it is appropriate that this should be discussed in the opening Part which follows.

PART I

GROUNDWORK OF LIAISON WITH THE AMERICANS

CHAPTER 1

Liaison with Hoover

J. Edgar Hoover is a man of great singleness of purpose, and his purpose is the welfare of the Federal Bureau of Investigation. The FBI had already been in existence some years when, as a young man, Hoover was appointed its director nearly a quarter of a century ago. But he became its personification. He transformed it from a little known federal agency into a national institution, with a fabulous reputation for efficiency and achievement, an institution which is now regarded as the surest possible guarantee that crime in the United States cannot pay. Although Hoover is occasionally criticized in the liberal press on account of his suspected right-wing bias and anti-Communist phobia, the FBI has to endure none of that newspaper sniping against its usefulness to which other federal agencies, almost without exception, are periodically subjected. Its record has placed it above criticism.

Hoover has little time for leisure and few interests outside the FBI. His acquaintances are, therefore, predominantly made up of those with whom his work brings him into contact. To them he can be extremely affable, provided he is satisfied that they threaten neither directly nor indirectly the prestige and influence of the agency which he directs with such devotion. Hoover is in no way anti-British, but in every way pro-FBI. His job is at once his pride and his vanity. These facts are emphasized because they are fundamental to an understanding of the course of BSC's relationship with the FBI, which did not run smoothly throughout.

At the outset – and indeed until a few weeks before Pearl Harbor, when events, to be described in a subsequent chapter, caused a radical change in his attitude – Hoover could hardly have been more cooperative. Clearly WS's organization employing, as it did, not only its own intelligence agents but what amounted to its own police force (see Part V) represented an obvious threat to United States neutrality and could not have existed at all without the FBI's sanction. But Hoover was more than its licensor. He was, in a very real sense, its patron. He suggested its cover name. He placed at WS's disposal an FBI wireless channel which for a long while provided BSC with its only means of telegraphic communication with SIS headquarters (see Part IX). On a personal basis he worked very closely with WS to further the wholly unneutral purpose of protecting British interests, and he instructed his officers to assist BSC in every way open to them. In short, he led his Bureau into a full-fledged alliance with British Intelligence, as the President had urged.

The results of that alliance form a not inconsiderable part of the material in this book and are described in detail elsewhere (see, in particular, Parts V and VII).

WS helped him to escape from that dilemma by making available to him the resources of British Intelligence developed under the impetus of war. He afforded him opportunity for studying the organizational prerequisites of secret intelligence work. To that end he made arrangements in the autumn of 1940 for two of Hoover's senior officers to visit SIS headquarters and subsequently for one of Hoover's assistant directors to discuss the planning of an FBI field organization in Latin America with the heads of all SIS stations there. He accepted as a major responsibility of BSC the instruction of the FBI in SI methods and practice. The results of this work are described in some detail in Part VII, but, as one example, it may be remarked here that early in 1941, FBI laboratory technicians were taught by a BSC expert how to open and reseal – without leaving a trace of tampering – certain high-grade types of intercepted correspondence.

Further, WS pooled with Hoover information derived not only from BSC's agents in the field but from such prolific sources as SIS stations in Latin America and Imperial Censorship. The total volume was considerable and, while it contained much material of assistance to the FBI in its immediate purpose of counter-espionage (see Part VII) and its potential purpose of combating all enemy subversive activities in the Western Hemisphere, included besides a quantity of operational intelligence which was not of direct interest to Hoover but which he could (and did) pass on to the US Service Intelligence Departments (ONI and G2). It should be said here, for it is germane to what follows, that the opportunity thus provided him of furnishing ONI and G2 with information which they required but could not otherwise obtain, pleased Hoover, for it gave his Bureau a commanding position in the overall US Intelligence picture.

Liaison with Hoover

Before Pearl Harbor, although WS was personally friendly and in frequent touch with the heads of the US Service Departments, he had no liaison with ONI and G2. They were, in fact, opposed at that time to collaboration with the British, but the arrangement whereby he furnished them with material through Hoover proved well worthwhile. In the sense that it increased Hoover's desire to assist BSC, it resulted on some occasions in a measure of what amounted to direct US intervention at a time when the State Department was adhering to a policy of strict neutrality. An example is provided by the following case:

In the autumn of 1940, WS's representative in Mexico City reported grounds for believing that sixteen Axis vessels, tied up in the ports of Tampico and Vera Cruz, were planning to run the blockade. Four of these ships were German and the remainder Italian. There was a likelihood that, if they made their attempt, they might succeed in it, for the Royal Navy was, of course, forbidden to maintain a patrol in Mexican territorial waters. WS passed the information to Hoover for transmittal to ONI. Meanwhile he advised SIS/London of the position, and was authorized by them to take whatever action he considered appropriate, provided he kept HM Embassy informed.

As a first step he arranged for a quantity of 'limpets' – small explosive charges fixed to a magnetized frame which would cling to the steel plates of a ship's hull – to be despatched to agents in Mexico. However, while this provided a possible means of causing sufficient damage to the ships to delay their departure, it was evident that no really effective counter-measure could be taken without the assistance of the US authorities. Accordingly, after discussions with HM Ambassador, WS suggested strongly to Hoover that a US Navy patrol should be despatched to Mexican territorial waters.

This suggestion obviously entailed an infringement of US neutrality, and to persuade the State Department to countenance it and the Navy Department to act upon it was, therefore, no easy matter. But Hoover – anxious to secure reciprocal action for the information he had supplied to ONI – eventually succeeded. With the State Department's approval, four US destroyers were despatched to Mexican territorial waters, where they were stationed off Tampico under orders to watch and report by radio *en clair* any movements which the Axis ships might make.

On the night of 15 November, the four German vessels steamed out of port into the Gulf of Mexico. The US destroyers approached and trained the full battery of their searchlights upon them. This was not in itself a bellicose act but it had the effect of an all-out attack. In the ensuing panic one of the German ships – the *Phrygia* – either caught fire or was deliberately scuttled. Her crew took to the boats and she was abandoned as a total wreck. The others turned tail and fled back to port at full speed. Intelligence reports subsequently revealed that the German captains evidently believed they had encountered some of the over-age American destroyers which had recently been transferred to the Royal Navy. They informed acquaintances in Tampico next day that they 'had been ordered to surrender by British battleships'.

A fortnight later, two of the three remaining German ships steamed out to sea in broad daylight. The American destroyers shadowed them and, by transmitting position signals, enabled British warships to intercept them before they could get very far. The one German and the twelve Italian vessels left behind were apparently too intimidated to make any further attempt to run the blockade. They remained impotently in port until, in April 1941, they were expropriated by the Mexican Government.

This particular case, inasmuch as it did not concern even indirectly enemy subversive activities in the Western Hemisphere, provides evidence that Hoover was willing to carry his assistance well beyond what he might justifiably have regarded as the limits of his common interest with WS, and indeed it may be said without exaggeration that for all practical purposes he was in the war from the moment he began collaboration. As further illustration of this, it is, perhaps, worth recording that he agreed early on to 'plant' SIS strategic deception material on the German Embassy. SIS/London would send such telegrams as the following to WS:

> Give consideration to Hoover passing to German Embassy following report: 'From highly reliable source it is learned USSR intend further military aggression instant Germany is embroiled in major operations' . . . For your information underlying motive is to try cause Germany delay any major operations . . .

and:

> It would be valuable if you could place through Hoover following reports in German Embassy . . . that in event Germany using poison gas Britain will use their secret weapon consisting of some kind of glass balls containing chemical

producing such terrific heat that they cannot be extinguished by any known means . . . also that British Government circles have quite recently been greatly elated at news from Moscow.

WS would then pass the relevant material to Hoover, who would, in turn, transmit it to the German Embassy through one of his agents, acting under cover of an Axis sympathizer.

Such, in very broad terms, was the nature and scope of Hoover's collaboration. And while there has been no attempt in this chapter to record details of it, for these are related in subsequent Parts, it is hoped that enough has been said to show that in the critical period before Pearl Harbor, Hoover was persuaded to render very valuable service to Britain's cause. The price of his cooperation, however, was always conditioned by his overwhelming ambition for the FBI, and this led him, after the United States entered the war, to the untenable position of insisting in effect upon retaining for the FBI, among US Intelligence agencies, monopoly of liaison with BSC. It was an untenable position, because the FBI was not recognized as a coordinating centre of American wartime intelligence and its sphere of operations was limited to the Western Hemisphere. But it was the rock upon which WS's good relationship with Hoover for a while foundered.

CHAPTER 2

Liaison with Donovan

The liaison with Hoover provided WS with a foundation upon which to build a secret organization in the United States. To achieve his immediate parallel purpose of obtaining certain essential supplies for Britain, he needed an intermediary *par excellence* for negotiations with the White House. In that respect it was fortunate that he was already well acquainted with William Joseph Donovan.

Donovan may be described as in every way a big man. He has great generosity of spirit, many enthusiasms and considerable breadth of interests. He is a former American football star and holder of the Congressional Medal of Honor which he won in the First World War, when he commanded the famous 'Fighting 69th' and earned for himself the title 'Wild Bill' Donovan – somewhat inappropriately, for though he is energetic and has a commanding personality, he is by nature modest and unassuming. In private life, he is a highly successful New York lawyer. He is self-made and has risen to his present eminence in what Americans like to call 'the hard way'.

Though a member of the Republican Party, he exercised considerable influence in the inner councils of the Roosevelt Administration, for the Secretary of State, Cordell Hull, the Secretary of War, Henry Stimson, and the Secretary of the Navy, Frank Knox, were all his friends of long standing. Further, he was one of the President's most trusted personal advisers.

Donovan, by virtue of his very independence of thought and action, inevitably has his critics, but there are few among them who would deny the credit due to him for having reached a correct appraisal of the international situation in the summer of 1940. At that time the United States Government was debating two alternative courses of action. One was to endeavour to keep Britain in the war by supplying her with the material assistance of which she was desperately in need. The other was to give

Britain up for lost and concentrate exclusively on American rearmament to offset the German threat. That the former course was eventually pursued is due in large measure to Donovan's tireless advocacy of it.

Immediately after the fall of France, not even the President himself could feel assured that aid to Britain would not be wasted in the circumstances. His ambassadors in London and Paris had advised him that Britain's cause was hopeless, and the majority of his cabinet ministers were inclined to the same conclusion. In its negative sense only, their attitude found vigorous expression in organized isolationism (see Part II), which, with men like Colonel Lindbergh and Senator Wheeler as its sponsors, was exerting a powerful hold on the American people.

Donovan, on the other hand, was emotionally convinced that, granted sufficient aid from the United States, Britain could and would survive. It was WS's task, first to inform him of Britain's foremost requirements so that he could make these known in the appropriate quarters and secondly to furnish him with concrete evidence in support of his contention that American material assistance would be, not improvident charity, but a sound investment.

In June of 1940 – very shortly after WS had taken up his appointment in the United States – Donovan arranged for him to attend a meeting with War Secretary Henry Stimson and Navy Secretary Frank Knox. At this meeting WS stressed the fact that Britain lacked sufficient destroyers with which to protect her Atlantic lifeline from U-boat attack, and the way was explored towards finding a formula for the transfer, without legal breach of United States neutrality and without affront to American public opinion, of fifty over-age American destroyers to the Royal Navy.

In the following month, WS suggested to Donovan that he should pay a visit to Britain with the object of investigating conditions at first hand and of assessing for himself the British war effort – its most urgent requirements and its potential chances of success. Donovan referred the proposal to the President. On 15 July, WS sent the following telegram to CSS:

> Colonel William J. Donovan personally representing President, left yesterday by Clipper . . . US Embassy not being informed of visit . . .

On the next day he cabled:

Groundwork of Liaison with the Americans

Donovan may be regarded as key man . . .

This last statement was no hyperbole, as events soon proved. In London CSS arranged, in accordance with WS's suggestion, for the President's special envoy to be afforded every opportunity to conduct his enquiries. Donovan was received in audience by His Majesty the King. He interviewed the Prime Minister and prominent members of the Government. He visited war factories and military training centres. He spoke with industrial leaders, union leaders and with representatives of all classes in the community. He learned what was true – that Mr Churchill, in defying the Nazis, was no mere bold façade but the very heart of Britain, which was still beating strongly. Donovan flew back to Washington at the beginning of August. On 8 August, WS telegraphed to CSS:

Donovan greatly impressed by visit and reception . . . has strongly urged our case re destroyers . . . is doing much to combat defeatist attitude Washington by stating positively and convincingly that we shall win . . .

The destroyers for bases agreement was now under consideration by the US Government. Donovan persuaded Frank Knox of the urgent necessity of implementing it without delay, and stood powerfully behind him in his efforts to press for a conclusion against what WS subsequently described as 'strong opposition from below and procrastination from above'.

On 21 August, WS informed CSS:

Donovan has urged upon President to see promised matters through himself with definite results . . . Donovan believes you will have within a few days very favourable news . . . thinks he has restored confidence as to Britain's determination and ability to resist . . .

Two days later he sent CSS a telegram prefixed 'Most Immediate':

Informed that fifty destroyers agreed last night . . . forty-four are in commission for delivery . . .

It is certain that the destroyers for bases agreement, which now belongs to History, could not have eventuated when it did without

Donovan's intercession, and in recognition of this fact WS was instructed to thank him in behalf of His Majesty's Government.

There were other essential supplies which Donovan was largely instrumental in obtaining for Britain during the same period and by the same means – among them a hundred Flying Fortresses for the RAF Coastal Command and a million rifles for the Home Guard. Moreover, while in London, Lord Beaverbrook had informed him of the British Government's particular desire for knowledge of the secret American bombsight, and upon his return he urged both Knox and the President that they should make this available. At first they objected – and with logic on their side – that to do so would be detrimental to American interests inasmuch as the bombsight, if fitted to aircraft operating over Europe, would sooner or later be bound to fall into enemy hands. Fortunately, WS was able to overcome this objection by advising Donovan that upon the basis of recent SIS information it seemed likely that the Germans already possessed details of the invention; and on 24 September 1940 he telegraphed CSS:

> President has sanctioned release to us of bombsight, to be fitted henceforth to bombers supplied to us . . .

WS's work with Donovan can be described, for want of a better title, as covert diplomacy inasmuch as it was preparatory and supplementary to negotiations conducted directly by HM Ambassador. At first consideration it may seem that this work was far removed from his responsibilities as director of BSC and indeed that it necessitated, since it was strictly a personal undertaking, no organizational machinery of any kind. But the truth is that whatever he was able to accomplish in the way of obtaining certain essential supplies from the United States Government during the summer of 1940 was largely assisted by his connection both with Secret Intelligence and Political Warfare work. As may be judged from the preceding paragraph, it would in all probability have been impossible for him to overcome the objections raised to releasing details of the bombsight to Britain, had he not had ready access to SIS sources of information. Furthermore, Donovan would certainly have found it harder to achieve success in his negotiations if WS had had no means at his disposal for influencing American public opinion in favour of aid to Britain. In fact, covert propaganda, one of the most potent weapons which BSC employed against the enemy (see Part II), was harnessed directly to this task. For example,

General Pershing was persuaded through an intermediary to make a speech in support of the destroyers deal, and, since General Pershing is a national hero, without suspected political ambitions or partisan affiliations, his voice carried much weight. Again, Donovan, upon his return from London, wrote five articles dealing with 'German Fifth Column Tactics'. These were based on SIS material supplied to him by WS and they were published in the influential *Chicago Daily News*, owned by Frank Knox. They were reproduced in many other papers throughout the country, including the *New York Herald Tribune*, and were also the occasion for a broadcast talk by Donovan over a nationwide 'hook-up' – the first ever afforded to a speaker other than the President. Knox himself wrote a follow-up article to the series.

On 14 September 1940, WS telegraphed to CSS:

> Our American friends desire guidance as to what requirements in addition to Flying Fortresses they may assist to fulfil . . .

That meant, in effect, that the United States Government was by now convinced in principle of the wisdom of providing material aid to Britain. WS's immediate task of obtaining certain essential supplies was, therefore, accomplished, or rather became inextricably a part of the broader purpose of fostering American intervention to which, in turn, all the Intelligence and Political Warfare activities of his organization were initially directed. In pursuing that purpose Donovan's cooperation continued to be of inestimable value, and though some of the more important services he rendered Britain were, in fact, removed from BSC's sphere of operations, it seems appropriate to relate them here – not only because they flowed, as it were, from WS's liaison with him, but because they have not been recorded elsewhere.

During the early winter of 1940, His Majesty's Government was especially concerned to obtain assistance from the American Navy in convoying British merchant shipping across the Atlantic. This was a measure of intervention which the US Government was reluctant to take for fear that the Germans would regard it as a *casus belli*. WS discussed the problem at length with Donovan, who was persuaded, first, that it seemed unlikely on the basis of the evidence available that Germany, until she had defeated Britain, would be provoked into a war with the United States by anything short of direct aggression and, secondly, that for the American Navy to participate in convoy duty should be regarded as an essential step in the United States policy of playing for time, that is to say in the policy of enabling Britain to keep the enemy at bay until American preparedness was sufficiently advanced to meet the German challenge. These arguments Donovan advanced at a conference, in December of 1940, with Knox, Stimson and Cordell Hull, who were impressed by them but needed more concrete evidence before they could take action, in particular evidence supporting the contention that the necessity of agreeing to the British proposal outweighed the risk inherent in so doing.

To obtain such evidence, Donovan decided on the advisability of another exploratory trip – to London and thence to the Mediterranean area, where Britain's position was at the time in considerable peril. On this occasion arrangements for his visit were formally made by HM Embassy, and he travelled officially as Knox's representative. At his request WS accompanied him as far as London, and before leaving cabled CSS as follows:

> Impossible over-emphasize importance of Donovan's visit . . . He can play a great role perhaps a vital one . . . but it may not be consistent with orthodox diplomacy nor confined to its channels . . . You should personally convey to Prime Minister that Donovan is presently the strongest friend we have . . .

At the same time the Director of Naval Intelligence sent a telegram to the Commander-in-Chief, Mediterranean Fleet, describing in some detail Donovan's position, from which it is, perhaps, pertinent to quote the following extract:

> Donovan exercises controlling influence over Knox, strong influence over Stimson, friendly advisory influence over President and Hull . . . Being a Republican, a Catholic and of Irish descent he has following of the strongest opposition to the Administration . . . It was Donovan who was responsible for getting us the destroyers, the bombsight and other urgent requirements . . . There is no doubt that we can achieve infinitely more through Donovan than through any other individual . . . He is very receptive and should be made fully aware of our requirements and deficiencies and can be trusted to represent our needs in the right quarters and in the right way in the USA . . .

While he was in London, Mr Churchill requested Donovan to

visit the Balkans in Britain's behalf. The general pattern of future German aggression was already apparent, and what Mr Churchill wanted was some upset in Hitler's timetable for the subjugation of the Balkan countries which would delay, even if only slightly, the date of his contemplated attack on Russia.

Donovan went first to Sofia. He did not dissuade the Bulgarian leaders from their pro-German policy, but he did implant in their minds a measure of doubt as to the wisdom of that policy. In result, they hesitated before implementing their proposed intervention on Germany's side by allowing German troops unrestricted passage through their country for the eventual invasion of Greece. Mr Churchill had intimated that he would be content with a delay of twenty-four hours. Donovan secured a delay of eight days.

In Yugoslavia, Donovan paved the way for the *coup d'état* which resulted at the eleventh hour in Yugoslav resistance to, instead of acquiescence in, German aggression. He interviewed General Simovic, who asked him whether Britain could hold out against the Nazis and whether the United States would enter the war. After warning Simovic that he could do no more than express his own personal views, he answered both questions in the affirmative; and at his persuasion Simovic agreed to organize the revolution which a few months later overthrew the pro-German Government of Prince Paul.

During an extensive tour of the Middle East, Donovan had talks with General Wavell and Admiral Cunningham, among others, and was convinced that Britain's military position in an area of great strategical importance was extremely precarious and that to secure it American supplies would have to be made available in abundance.

Donovan returned to Washington on 18 March 1941. Next morning he had breakfast with the President, to whom he reported his findings. He urged, in particular, the importance of sending war materials directly to the Middle East. The President instructed him to consult with the government departments concerned 'to see what could be worked out'.

On 5 April 1941, WS informed CSS:

> ... Donovan expects ships will be loading within two weeks
> ... The Embassy has been asked to list our requirements ...

Having been persuaded to invest so heavily in Britain's defence, it was now a logical step for the United States Government to protect that investment by participating in the guardianship of the Atlantic life line. About this time BSC learned, as a result of its penetration of the Italian Embassy in Washington (see Part IV), that the Axis intended to attack any American warships that might be employed in convoy duty, and WS arranged for the information to be passed to the President. But there was no longer any question of withdrawal. It is common knowledge that the United States Navy began to assist in convoy duty in the summer of 1941 and that, following an attack on the USS *Greer* by a German submarine in September of that year, the President ordered American warships 'to shoot first'.

At Mr Roosevelt's request, Donovan had broadcast to the nation shortly after his return from the Middle East. His speech, which was widely publicized, was designed to create a favourable public atmosphere for the pending announcement of new measures of American intervention. It was essentially a plea for the US Government's policy of 'enlightened self-interest' – delivered by a man who had had a considerable share in shaping that policy.

CHAPTER 3

Contacts for Political Warfare

Through Hoover, WS was enabled to establish an organization which was adequately equipped both to investigate enemy activities and to put into effect requisite security measures for the protection of British property. Through Donovan, he was enabled to engage in covert negotiations with the United States Government, and thus to achieve his immediate objective of obtaining urgently needed supplies. For the purpose of fostering the cause of intervention – or in other words of conducting Political Warfare – he enlisted assistance from other Americans who were in a position, directly or indirectly, to influence American public opinion. Those who helped can be roughly classified under three headings – high-level contacts, private individuals who served as intermediaries, and newspaper and radio contacts. It is appropriate to deal briefly in this chapter with each in turn.

1. High-Level Contacts

Inasmuch as the cause of American intervention was symbolized in the foresight and determination of the President himself, the ultimate purpose of all BSC's Political Warfare was to assist Mr Roosevelt's own campaign for preparedness. This was not merely an abstract conception, for WS kept in close touch with the White House and as time went on the President gave clear indication of his personal concern both to encourage and take advantage of BSC's activities. In October of 1941, a sensational piece of information relating to enemy plans for the eventual domination of South America, which BSC agents unearthed, provided Mr Roosevelt with an opportunity to attack the Axis in more forthright language than he had yet been able to employ (see Part VI). In this particular instance, the information was handed to the President by Donovan, but Donovan, though without doubt the most important, was not WS's only intermediary with the White House. Two others merit brief mention.

The first was Robert Sherwood, who, as his plays reveal, is an anglophile and a passionate anti-Fascist. It is now an open secret that Sherwood had a considerable hand in writing the President's more important speeches on international affairs, and he made a practice of showing each of these to WS while it was still in draft form, thus affording WS opportunity to suggest modifications, additions or deletions from the British point of view. He did this with the President's knowledge and approval.

The second was the well-known Vincent Astor, a close friend of the President. On 4 February 1941, WS telegraphed CSS:

> President has appointed Vincent Astor as his personal liaison with me ... This arrangement is a great step forward and should considerably facilitate our efforts ...

In WS's behalf, Astor kept the President regularly informed of any specific desires of His Majesty's Government which could not properly be communicated through diplomatic channels, and also passed to him the more important results of BSC's investigations into enemy activities – for example, a comprehensive report on Vichy intrigue in the United States (see Part IV). He brought back from the President comment, information and advice, thus enabling BSC to plan its Political Warfare in correlation with the White House.

Similarly, WS maintained close contact either directly or through intermediaries with Cabinet Ministers and other influential members of the Administration. Some of them, like Frank Knox and Henry Stimson and Cordell Hull, were already well disposed to Britain and it was necessary only to suggest to them ways in which they could be of assistance. But others were not, and their goodwill had to be assiduously canvassed.

Moreover WS was concerned to enlist the sympathy of anti-Administration leaders, for it was clearly of the utmost importance that the cause of American intervention, although it had become symbolized in President Roosevelt, should be preserved, as far as possible, as a non-party issue. For example, he had a lengthy discussion with Wendell L. Willkie before the latter left for London on a special mission for Mr Roosevelt shortly after the Presidential election of November 1940. He found that Mr Willkie had little of that liberal internationalism which later became his trademark, but on the contrary was both reactionary and sectarian in his outlook, believing, among other things, that, since Britain was likely to go 'red' after the war, it would probably serve American interests better in the long run to allow Britain to be defeated. At the same time, WS realized what was not then obvious in London, that Mr Willkie was a considerable political force in the United States, far more influential, actually and potentially, than Mr Roosevelt's two previous victims; for while he had been severely defeated on paper, he had in fact polled a larger number of votes than any other Republican candidate in history. Accordingly, WS sent a long telegram to CSS, setting out in detail Mr Willkie's views and position, and suggesting strongly that special arrangements should be made to ensure the success of his visit. CSS took appropriate action on this telegram, and in result Mr Willkie, like Donovan before him, returned from London immensely impressed both by his reception and by what he had seen and heard. It is common knowledge that throughout 1941 he lent powerful and ungrudging support to the President's foreign policy, though at the time many of the Republican Old Guard – including Willkie's successor, Thomas E. Dewey – were still voicing isolationism.

2. Private Individuals who Served as Intermediaries

It is not appropriate in this context to list all – or even a few – of the many intermediaries who assisted BSC in its task of disseminating British propaganda through American channels. One of them, however, deserves especial mention because he rendered very valuable service during the critical period when the question of United States aid to Britain was in the balance.

Reference has been made in the previous chapter to the speech which General Pershing delivered in support of the destroyers deal. General Pershing was contacted in WS's behalf by a wealthy American businessman, named Albert Younglove Gowen.

He was pro-interventionist by persuasion of his own experiences. He had been in Denmark* at the time of the German occupation and had spoken with German officers who had boasted to him that, after conquering Great Britain, Hitler would attack the United States. The propaganda value of his story was evident. At WS's suggestion he recounted it in an article, and arrangements

---

* At WS's behest on a job for SOE.

were made for this to be published in *Life* magazine. The sting of the article was in the tail, which read:

> ... It is my hope that this will be of some influence in convincing the United States of the reality of Germany's threat to our existence. The British Fleet is still our first line of defence. In my opinion we must do all we can to help England maintain it because if it fails, there is no salvation ...

Gowen's article, appearing as it did in one of the most powerful organs of the Republican opposition (*Life* has a registered circulation of 3,934,484 and is published by Henry Luce, who was a bitter opponent of President Roosevelt), provided a strong impartial rebuttal of the argument that Germany did not menace the United States – an argument which was the mainstay of the nationwide campaign led by Lindbergh to block the destroyers deal. General Pershing's speech provided a still stronger one, and for that too, Gowen was responsible. Further, he did much to win over public opinion in the traditionally isolationist Mid-West (where he had his business and was well known) by platform speeches, by the organization of independent committees and round-table discussions and by personal canvass of prominent industrialists. When WS informed CSS, in a telegram dated 4 September 1940, of the tribute due to Donovan for his part in bringing about the destroyers agreement, he added:

> ... Suggest you make a note to acknowledge Gowen's efforts too ... He kept the issue alive throughout the country, checkmated Lindbergh with Pershing, and made numerous other tactical moves which in themselves have created a powerful truth-telling entity which can now be used for the next job ...

3. Press and Radio Contacts

The cooperation of newspaper and radio men was of the utmost importance. Without it, as will become apparent later on, many of BSC's operations against the enemy would have been impossible. Yet, in enlisting it, whether directly or through intermediaries, the greatest care had always to be exercised, for clearly if BSC had ever been uncovered or had the sources of its information been exposed, it would at once have been in the position of an overt British propaganda organization and as such considerably worse than useless. The conduct of its Political Warfare was entirely dependent on secrecy. For that reason the press and radio men with whom BSC maintained contact were comparable with sub-agents and the intermediaries with agents. They were thus regarded.

Several of BSC's more important press contacts were established directly by WS before he had the advantage of a working organization. The number was subsequently increased – and radio contacts were added – through intermediaries. There is no need to list them all, but among those who rendered service of particular value were George Backer, publisher of the *New York Post*, Ralph Ingersoll, editor of *PM*, Helen Ogden Reid, who controls the *New York Herald Tribune*, Paul Patterson, publisher of the *Baltimore Sun*, A. H. Sulzberger, President of the *New York Times*, Walter Lippman and several other columnists, William L. Shirer, the commentator, and Walter Lemmon, owner of Station WRUL.

While such a team was clearly in a position to exercise considerable influence on public opinion, it remained true that the American press was in a large measure controlled by men of anti-British and isolationist persuasion. To overcome this handicap WS employed three methods. First, he made use of pro-Administration columnists, who, though their columns appeared in the hostile press, were free to write what they pleased because of their mass appeal – for example, Walter Winchell (see Part II). Secondly, he enlisted the cooperation of individual employees of isolationist newspaper owners who were prepared in the cause of anti-Fascism to work surreptitiously against the interests of their masters – for example, the head of International News Service (a Hearst-controlled news agency) was persuaded to render great assistance to one of BSC's major campaigns (see Part III). Thirdly, in a few instances, he made contact, initially through intermediaries and latterly directly, with hostile publishers in an endeavour not so much to win them over as to neutralize them. As example, he undertook a prolonged wooing of Roy Howard, President of the large chain of Scripps-Howard newspapers, though it should be said here in parenthesis that Howard's immediate assistant was persuaded to work actively in BSC's behalf. WS learned that Roy Howard was anti-British largely by reason of a well-developed inferiority complex; he was a little man – vain, ambitious and overdressed; a clever reporter with a thirst for political power. The first definite move to tame him was made in August 1940, when he visited Australia and at WS's suggestion was paid special attention. Apparently he remained unimpressed, for upon his return he pursued his anti-British and isolationist policy with more vigour than ever before, and though invited – in December of 1940 – to visit England, ignored the invitation. It was not until June of 1943 – by which time, of course, the isolationist issue was dead, although the question of Anglo-American relations was still very much alive – that WS's efforts at conciliation reached, as it were, a climacteric. In that month it was arranged that Lord Beaverbrook should invite Howard to visit England and on this occasion he accepted. He flew to London with Lord Beaverbrook, WS, Donovan and Harriman in Lord Beaverbrook's private plane. Either on the way over or during his stay he experienced a slight but quite perceptible change of heart. Shortly after his return to the United States he remarked to a BSC source:

> American feeling toward Britain has improved considerably in the past year or so . . . Americans do not like Britishers better, but they have a fuller appreciation of what Britain has done and is doing . . . Most Americans, including myself, are now out of patience with criticism of British internal management . . .

Other newspaper owners – more warped and deeply embedded in the isolationist doctrine than Roy Howard – were beyond hope of conversion and the possible advantage to be gained from contacting them would clearly not have discounted the danger of so doing. Yet during the critical period before Pearl Harbor they represented such a grave menace to the British cause that serious consideration was given to the possibility of putting them out of business; and an opportunity for silencing in this way the elderly but extremely powerful William Randolph Hearst did in fact occur.

In June 1941, WS learned that the Hearst syndicate owed $10,500,000 to Canadian paper manufacturers – all in the form of demand notes which were renewable every six months. Upon further investigation, it was found that any one of the creditor companies, by demanding payment, could have quickly brought about the liquidation of the entire Hearst syndicate; and its collapse would have been rendered all the more certain by the fact that if one company had taken action, the others would inevitably have followed suit. Up to that time they had not pressed for payment, because their only hope of recovering the sums due to them was to keep the syndicate alive. On the other hand, if the Canadian paper supply had ceased or been interrupted, publication of all the Hearst newspapers would have become impossible within thirty days, since paper could not be obtained elsewhere.

Through friends in Canada WS ascertained that it would be possible to buy one or more of the demand notes, since these were negotiable. Had this been done, the buyer would have been able either to force the Hearst syndicate to suspend publication altogether or to bring about a radical change in its policy. The matter was referred to the Treasury but, after due consideration, the Treasury stated that it was unwilling to provide the necessary funds.

As a footnote to this chapter, it should be observed that just as BSC's various functions, though divided by name and performed under the jurisdiction of separate organizations in London, were closely related, so, too, the American assistance described above served needs additional to those of Political Warfare. It is clear that WS could not have used the Administration as a medium of propaganda if he had had no means of passing information to the White House. It is equally clear that he would have been severely handicapped in planning any Political Warfare operations if he had had no means of receiving information from the White House. But by the very fact of securing such means he became equipped also to engage in covert diplomacy and to collect secret intelligence about American affairs. As already stated, WS undertook secret negotiation with the White House through men like Donovan, Astor and Sherwood, and through them, too, he was given advance information of the President's intentions and engagements in foreign policy.

These and other high-level contacts were a prolific source of intelligence and for that reason were maintained after Pearl Harbor, when to influence American public opinion was no longer a matter of major concern. In result, WS was able to keep CSS constantly advised concerning trends and likely developments in United States affairs – both foreign and domestic. (See Part IV.)

Newspaper contacts also yielded a certain amount of intelligence. This may seem a surprising statement at first sight, but the truth is that the majority of American politicians, not excluding Cabinet Ministers, are willing to supply influential members of the press with 'inside' information in return for favourable publicity. Such information is, of course, usually handed out under pledge of secrecy – to be used as 'background material'

Contacts for Political Warfare

and not for publication. But it is given out nonetheless, and during the war, as BSC discovered, contained much material of political interest as well as several operational secrets of vital importance.

CHAPTER 4

Donovan's Organization

(a) Coordinator of Information
(b) Office of Strategic Services

(a) Coordinator of Information

To go over from the defensive to the offensive, that is to say to secure full American participation in secret activities directed against the enemy outside the Western Hemisphere, WS needed something which did not exist at the time he founded BSC. He needed an agency responsible for conducting, in behalf of the United States Government, secret activities throughout the world; an agency with which he could collaborate fully by virtue of its being patterned, in the matter of coordinated functions, exactly after his own organization.

As early as June of 1940, in his discussions with Donovan, WS had pleaded the necessity of establishing such an agency. Donovan agreed in principle, and during his subsequent visits to London had several exploratory talks with CSS and CD. Indeed, on the occasion of his second visit, CD showed him around some of the SO stations; and upon his return to Washington the need for expanding the scope of American secret activities was one of the subjects which he discussed with the President.

In April of 1941, Mr Roosevelt began to give serious consideration to the question, for by then his policy of intervention had won a sufficient measure of Congressional acceptance to make some positive move towards establishing the kind of agency which Donovan had urged a practicable as well as a desirable proposition. On 5 May 1941, WS telegraphed to CSS:

> I have been attempting to manoeuvre Donovan into accepting job of coordinating all US Intelligence . . .

The idea that he himself should direct the new agency did not at first appeal to Donovan nor was it by any means a foregone conclusion that he would be offered the appointment. Yet from WS's point of view he was obviously the man for the job. In the first place, he had the confidence of the President, of the Secretary of State and of the civilian heads of the Service departments. Secondly, he had made some study of, and had given considerable thought to, the conduct of secret activities. Thirdly, he had all the requisite vision, energy and drive to build swiftly an organization of sufficient size and competence to play an effective part in the war. Lastly – and most important – he had already shown himself willing to cooperate fully with BSC – and the worth of his cooperation had been abundantly proved.

It seemed, therefore, a matter of the first importance to assure his appointment as head of the new agency, and to that end WS worked not only by personal persuasion of Donovan but by exerting outside pressure through various high-level contacts. His efforts were at length rewarded. On 18 June, he was able to advise CSS:

> . . . Donovan saw President today and after long discussion wherein all points were agreed, he accepted appointment . . . He will be Coordinator of all forms intelligence including offensive operations equivalent SO.2 . . . He will hold rank of Major General and will be responsible only repeat only to the President . . . Donovan accuses me of having 'intrigued and driven' him into appointment . . . You can imagine how relieved I am after three months of battle and jockeying for position in Washington that our man is in a position of such importance to our efforts . . .

Donovan was appointed head of the Office of the Coordinator of Information (COI) by Presidential Executive Order of 11 July, which defined his responsibilities as follows:

> To collect and analyse all information and data which may bear upon national security, to correlate such information and data, and make the same available to the President and to such departments and officials of the Government as the President may determine, and to carry out when requested by the President such supplementary activities as may facilitate the securing of information important for national security not now available to the Government.

This directive was necessarily vague in terminology, for clearly the President could not be specific about the functions of an agency created to undertake work which was both secret and potentially offensive in character. But, in fact, Donovan had been entrusted with responsibility not only for collecting intelligence but for coordinating this work with preparations to conduct Special Operations and subversive propaganda; and thus COI was in effect, if not in name, the American counterpart of BSC which WS had desired.

Collaboration began at once. Indeed Donovan drew up the initial plans for his agency, both as regards establishment and methods of operation, in consultation with WS. On 9 August 1941, WS telegraphed CSS as follows:

> Donovan's organization rapidly taking shape . . . Central offices in Washington now working with nucleus of staff and liaison is established and functioning . . . Understanding with Chiefs of Staff seems satisfactory and Donovan feels confident their cooperation . . . He has several competent assistants who seem to know their job and to have practical outlook . . . He now has working apparatus here and in Washington and should be able to safeguard secret documents . . .

For the purpose of ensuring the closest possible day-to-day working liaison between BSC and COI, WS set up a branch office in Washington, to which officers both of the SI and SO Divisions were attached, while Donovan in turn established a branch office in New York. The results are described in some detail later on, but it should be said here that, though they included immediate advantages to BSC, the establishment of Donovan's organization five months before Pearl Harbor represented more the promise – in itself a considerable step forward, of course – than the fact of American participation in secret activities abroad. From the British point of view, COI was essentially a long-term investment, and for some time it required far more help than it could give in return.

This was inevitably so for four main reasons. First, there was the obvious one that COI was a pioneer body lacking previous experience of its own upon which to draw. Secondly, so long as the United States remained at peace, Donovan's position was equivalent to Hoover's in the intelligence field – that is to say he had responsibilities without power. For example, to conduct propaganda operations he needed, among other things, control of short-wave radio facilities. But broadcasting in the United States is a private industry, and before Pearl Harbor the owners of short-wave stations could not be ousted or even coerced. In many instances they refused to follow the COI directives or to use COI material (see Part II). Again, the State Department was fundamentally reluctant to risk identification with an agency whose covert functions clearly endangered United States neutrality, and, despite initial promises to the contrary, largely withheld its cooperation which Donovan needed to provide 'cover' for his operations abroad.

Thirdly, the older agencies, whose collaboration he required in order to carry out his task of correlating intelligence, were at the outset somewhat hostile – partly through scepticism regarding the worth of an organization which, of necessity, was staffed by amateurs and partly through fear that COI would infringe on their own prerogatives. This was particularly true of the FBI – of which more is said in the next chapter. To a lesser extent it was true also of the Service Intelligence departments.

Lastly, when war came, Donovan was expected by the Chiefs of Staff, as justification for the continuance of his organization, to produce immediate results, despite the fact that he had had insufficient time and authority to make adequate preparations.

It is likely that if Donovan had been unable to rely upon BSC's assistance, his organization could not have survived, and indeed before he had his own operational machinery in working order, which was not until several months after Pearl Harbor, he was entirely dependent upon it. The provision of such assistance was reinsurance of COI's full collaboration and, while it is described in detail in the appropriate Parts, to illustrate its comprehensive character it may be well to enumerate briefly hereunder the following points:

1. The bulk of COI's secret intelligence, before Pearl Harbor and for several months thereafter, was supplied by BSC from its various sources.
2. BSC controlled through intermediaries two short-wave radio services – the one for broadcasts to Europe and Africa, the other for broadcasts to the Far East. These it made available to COI immediately after Pearl Harbor and they were the foundation of all American short-wave radio propaganda. (See Part II.)
3. COI officers, both of the SI and SO Division, as well as COI

agents were, in the beginning, trained at the BSC school in Canada which was set up in December 1941 under SOE auspices. The school served as a model for COI's own training schools which were later established under the guidance of BSC instructors. (See Part VIII.)
4. BSC supplied COI with all the equipment which it needed for Special Operations for a period after Pearl Harbor when such equipment was not yet in production in the United States. (See Part VIII.)
5. Early in September 1941 (before Donovan could undertake any active preparations of his own for Special Operations work), WS made arrangements with CD for a senior COI officer to visit England. The officer spent some three months in England, where he was given facilities for studying the entire SOE organization at first hand.
6. In January of 1942, the head of SOE's American Department was sent on a special mission to the United States in order to advise and assist Donovan regarding his Special Operations Division which was by then in process of formation.
7. In October of 1941, the director of SIS Communications visited the United States for the purpose of assisting COI to set up a worldwide system of clandestine communications. The head of BSC's own Communications Division acted as an adviser to COI. (See Part IX.)

These are but a few instances of assistance rendered to the nascent COI. In short, BSC, either directly or through its principals, had a considerable hand in the upbringing of the agency of which it was, in a sense, the parent. The effort thus expended would have been wasted only if COI – to carry the metaphor a little further – had never grown to man's estate. In fact, as may be judged from the section following, it proved extremely rewarding. For not only was Donovan's organization eventually equipped to discharge its responsibilities effectively but, since it owed much to British influence, was inevitably prepared to work in fullest accord with both SIS and SOE.

(b) Office of Strategic Services

The period during which Donovan's organization was largely dependent on BSC may be said to have lasted until June 1942. In that month a Presidential Executive Order abolished COI and established two new agencies in its place – the Office of War

Information (OWI) and the Office of Strategic Services (OSS). The former, under Elmer Davis, was entrusted with responsibility, *inter alia*, for all overseas propaganda other than 'black' (i.e. covert) propaganda. The latter, under Donovan, was entrusted with COI's remaining functions. OSS's sphere of operations was restricted to exclude the Western Hemisphere, and Donovan was placed directly under the Chiefs of Staff.

This order, while it limited the scope of Donovan's activities, yet considerably strengthened his position. It removed the causes of friction which had hitherto existed between his organization and other US intelligence agencies, notably the FBI. At the same time, by establishing OSS as an arm of the US Services, it put Donovan above suspicion of being an instrument of Presidential policies and made his organization an essential part of the war effort.

At the time the order was issued both WS and Donovan were in London, and it was, therefore, the occasion for discussions concerning future collaboration between OSS and its British equivalents. Out of these discussions there emerged agreements between OSS and SIS, and between OSS and SOE as follows:

1. Between OSS and SIS

It was decided that there should be as free an interchange of intelligence as possible – and on as high a plane as possible – but no integration of OSS with SIS inasmuch as each organization would remain free to adopt its own methods for the collection of intelligence and would operate independently wherever it pleased. This agreement, which was formalized in a short exchange of letters, remained valid for the duration of the war.

2. Between OSS and SOE

For the purpose of Special Operations, the world was divided into various zones designated as British zones, American zones and British-American zones. It was decided that in British zones, SOE should have command and in American zones OSS; while in British-American zones, such as Germany, both organizations would be free to operate independently, although, wherever possible, their activities should be closely coordinated. This agreement, known as the London Agreement, was, with certain minor alterations, subsequently approved on the American side by the

US Joint Chiefs of Staff and on the British side by the Foreign Office and the British Chiefs of Staff.

Thus provision was made for pooling results of activities, independently undertaken, in the field of Secret Intelligence and for a working partnership in the field of Special Operations. Furthermore, OSS decided to follow the example of SIS by establishing a separate division to undertake counter-espionage, and, so far as Europe was concerned, it was agreed that this work should be administered jointly by SIS and OSS from London. (See Part VII.)

Thenceforward Anglo-American collaboration in all forms of secret activity outside the Western Hemisphere steadily increased in scope and value, and, while its emphasis inevitably shifted from the United States to the various operational theatres, BSC, maintaining liaison with OSS headquarters as representative both of SIS and SOE, had the responsibility of coordination. Its work in this regard, though described in more detail later on, may be briefly summarized as follows:

Secret Intelligence

Immediately following the agreement referred to above, a special liaison officer was appointed to OSS headquarters. It was his responsibility to channel information of American origin back to London, and to advise OSS on such matters as the management of agents, methods of operation and evaluation of intelligence reports. In result, BSC received, and passed on to London, reports – numbering several scores daily – gathered by OSS agents throughout the world. Latterly, an OSS office was established in London, and it was arranged that this office should pass intelligence reports direct to SIS headquarters. But thereafter BSC kept open its liaison channel with the SI Division of OSS, and was thus enabled to draw London's attention to intelligence of exceptional interest.

There were several OSS headquarters establishments, separated from the SI Division, which produced useful intelligence and with which BSC maintained regular contact. Among them were the Survey of Foreign Experts (SFE) and the Research and Analysis Branch. The task of the first named was to interrogate residents of the US who had lived recently in Europe or the Far East and possessed first-hand knowledge of economic or operational interest. BSC passed to SFE regular questionnaires drawn up by various government departments in London, and SFE furnished, *inter alia,* a quantity of information concerning potential bombing objectives throughout Europe.

The work of the Research and Analysis Branch, in producing strategic surveys and maps, was generally regarded as second to none. Although its duties were largely overt, it had access to secret reports from a number of US government departments, and, over a period, it made these available to BSC in addition to its own compilations.

Special Operations

Shortly after the London Agreement, SOE, at General Donovan's request, sent four experts to Washington, each with experience in the different theatres where OSS was operating. Under BSC's auspices, they maintained liaison with OSS on a planning level in regard both to organization and methods.

At the same time, SOE supply experts joined BSC to advise OSS upon the production of special devices and weapons. They made available British specifications and details of new developments and assisted OSS to establish its own production schedules. Subsequently it was their task to assure coordination between OSS and SOE in regard both to the production of devices already in use and to the development of new devices. As a result of their work, special devices, totalling in value six million dollars, were made available to SOE under Lend-Lease. Furthermore, numerous SOE devices were adopted by OSS for standard use, and many new devices were introduced.

OSS, of course, provided the facilities for manufacture, research and testing, but in the majority of cases BSC/SOE furnished the ideas, and indeed it is true to say that the research and development procedure adopted by OSS was largely based on SOE practice.

The material which BSC/SOE acquired from OSS, either by cash payment or under Lend-Lease, included much that could not otherwise have been obtained. In May 1943, for example, SOE London informed BSC that it required three or more ships with a minimum range of 3,000 miles, a maximum speed of at least 16 knots and four tons of cargo space, for irregular operations in the North Sea. WS approached Donovan, who persuaded the US Navy to release three 100-foot sub-chasers in the belief that they were to be used in OSS's own operations. They were fitted with A/A guns, K guns, depth charges and radar. In great secrecy they were transferred to the United Kingdom in September 1943.

Throughout the following winter they ran the German blockade to and from Sweden, carrying not only valuable material but a number of important passengers.

By similar means, landing craft, W/T equipment, cameras, radio valves and kayaks – ostensibly for OSS's use but in fact made available to SOE – were obtained from the US War Department. Against this it should be remembered, of course, that, as previously stated, BSC secured supplies for Donovan during the period when these were not yet in production in the United States. It provided him, for example, with all the equipment which he used in the Torch operation preceding the invasion of North Africa.

To make a detailed assessment of the work of OSS in the field is outside the scope of this book. Yet it can be said for certain that well before the war ended it was comparable quantitatively with the combined efforts of SIS and SOE – in itself a considerable accomplishment when it is remembered how little time Donovan was afforded to build his organization and how many serious obstacles he faced at the outset. Qualitatively, too, much of OSS's work was without doubt of first-class importance by any standard. As just one example, it is, perhaps, pertinent to recall that the head of OSS's office in Berne persuaded an official of the German Foreign Office to provide him with copies of all telegrams which passed through his hands. This material, on the assumption that it was genuine, was clearly intelligence of the greatest value, and for a long while SIS, despite OSS's assurances to the contrary, could not believe that it was other than a 'plant'. However when GCCS were eventually enabled to check it against their own findings, its reliability was established beyond question.

Under Presidential Executive Order of 20 September 1945, OSS has been abolished as a separate agency and its functions divided, for the time being, between the Departments of War and State. This does not mean, however, that its establishment before Pearl Harbor has proved of only evanescent worth. Whatever new arrangements may eventually be made, it is clear that the United States Government is now fully convinced of the need for preserving a coordinated Foreign Intelligence Service which must be built on the foundations laid by OSS. As President Truman wrote to Donovan on the day he issued his Executive Order of 20 September:

> ... Timely steps should also be taken to conserve those resources and skills developed within your organization

which are vital to our peacetime purposes . . . I want to take this occasion to thank you for the capable leadership you have brought to a vital war time activity in your capacity as Director of Strategic Services. You may well find satisfaction in the achievements of the office and take pride in your own contribution to them. These are in themselves large rewards. Great additional reward for your efforts should lie in the knowledge that the peacetime intelligence services of the Government are being erected on the foundation of the facilities and resources mobilized through the Office of Strategic Services during the war.

Many of the more important OSS officials, who collaborated with their British colleagues during the war, will continue to serve the United States Intelligence Service in peace, and, provided proper advantage is taken of the opportunities, there seems no reason why the tradition of Anglo-American cooperation in intelligence work throughout the world, which Donovan helped so largely to establish, should not survive. In this context it is, perhaps, appropriate to quote the letter which CD wrote to Donovan on the day of victory over Japan:

. . . I send to you and to all the Office of Strategic Services the congratulations of SOE upon the splendid contribution you have made to the defeat of our common enemy, and grateful thanks for your cooperation with us all over the world.

It has been a pleasure to work with you and all the men and women under your command. The close association of our two organizations is a forerunner of what can be achieved by the Anglo-American unity which we all feel is so important for the future peace and happiness of mankind.

At the time of writing (November 1945) something concerning OSS's undertakings, which were, of course, kept strictly secret during the war, is being released officially to the press. To illustrate the significance of OSS in American eyes, there is reproduced, immediately following this chapter, a recent account which appeared in *Life* magazine of OSS's contribution to the war effort. The account, written by a journalist who was a severe critic of President Roosevelt, may be regarded as an accurate and impartial assessment of the facts so far as they are within the public domain.

OSS

The cloak-and-dagger boys of 'Wild Bill' Donovan's
Office of Strategic Services waged a successful secret war
behind enemy lines and have demonstrated the need for a
coordinated intelligence office for the U.S.
by JOHN CHAMBERLAIN

In 1941, long months before Eisenhower's and Mark Clark's men started piling ashore on the Moroccan and Algerian beaches, the quality of the U.S. commercial agents in North Africa underwent a sea change that might have perplexed even such a connoisseur of pixies as Barnaby's fairy godfather. If you had gone to one of the new agents on a business matter about the distribution of food from the U.S., you might have got satisfaction. But if you had probed hard on any special business angle you might have discovered that the agent knew considerably less about commercial matters than about the customs of Saudi Arabia or the significance of the brachycephalic head. If, by chance, you happened to have been well-acquainted in U.S. academic circles, you might have been startled to see peering from behind the pepper-and-salt habiliments of the businessman the visage of Carleton Coon, a well-known Harvard anthropologist. And the man who limped, the tall, thin, determined fellow who spoke Arabic – was it possible that he was Marine Colonel 'Bill' Eddy, the missionary's son and World War I veteran who had become president of little Hobart College back home in upstate New York?

In Washington, where the intelligence-gathering Office of Strategic Services was even then a-borning under the deft obstetrical touches of Major General William J. ('Wild Bill') Donovan, a few people who were in on the secret of Colonel Eddy's commercial agents spoke cryptically of our '12 apostles' in North Africa. And, indeed, the 12 apostles were the missionaries of a savior. When the savior, in the collective person of Eisenhower's armies, eventually landed in North Africa in November of 1942, signal lights guided him ashore, guns of Vichy shore installations were spiked, the state of harbor facilities and German troop dispositions was well known and the French officers were in many instances quite ready and willing to 'sell the pass' to the invaders. Colonel Eddy and his agents, working for Donovan on a loose rein that permitted full cooperation with Robert Murphy and the U.S. State Department, had done the job.

It was a job for which little public credit could be given or taken at the time. Unable to remove its light from beneath the bushel, the Office of Strategic Services suffered throughout the war from the jibes of columnists who chattered about OSS standing for 'Oh So Social, . . . Oh Shush Shush' and 'Oh So Secret.' But now that the war is over, it is possible to look into OSS's activities and assess its worth. On the whole the record is impressive. OSS contributed measurably toward victory and in some instances – as in the wangling of German surrender in North Italy – it was a decisive factor. The very fact of OSS successes raises important questions. Why did we have to call on amateurs from scratch to do OSS's job? And what kind of security policy should we now adopt to keep from being caught next time?

Before 1941 the U.S. had no intelligence service worthy of the name, nothing comparable to the 400-year-old British service that currently operates on a free mandate and with unvouchered funds under the Foreign Office, and nothing the equal of the German ABWEHR, whose mysterious Greek head, Admiral Canaris, reported directly to the German General Staff. Nor, on the secret operations side, did we have anything remotely resembling that natural complement to the ABWEHR, the Nazi fifth column, which softened up the European democracies as scurvy softens up the teeth of an arctic explorer. If you wanted a Michelin road map of the Vosges or Haute Savoie in the Washington of early 1941, it was a hundred to one that you could not find one. Nor could you successfully apply to any government agency for the gauge of an Algerian railroad track, the kilowatt-hour supply of the Japanese power grid, the number of wharfside cranes in Casablanca, the quality of drinking water in Tunis, the tilt of the beaches off Kyushu or the texture of the Iwo Jima soil. Our friends in Germany and Japan and adjacent territory were either dead or in jail or unknown to us. The barbed wire was up everywhere, and the few listening posts that we did have –

Groundwork of Liaison with the Americans

at Vichy, at General Weygand's North African Headquarters – were in perpetual danger of sabotage by the well-meaning but essentially stupid remonstrances of the more emotional Left press. Even the facts of prime importance that we did possess remained uncoordinated, unevaluated, uninterpreted and generally in the wrong hands. There was no one in Washington charged with putting the jigsaw pieces together to see what pictures would develop or what pieces of the puzzle were missing. The reason was simply that the government – and country – was not security-minded, perhaps a corollary of life in a free-wheeling, ocean-girded, peace-loving democracy. At any rate, while there were intelligence organizations in Army, Navy, State Department and FBI, there was no broadly organized intelligence.

That was in early 1941. By 1945, during the span of time it ordinarily takes a young man to go through college, OSS had beaten Hushofer's Nazi geopolitikers and Admiral Canaris' secret operatives at their own game, and the work done by OSS in foreign lands to counter the fifth column had helped prepare the liberation of a world. Although OSS's freshman exploits were frequently in a highly romantic vein that came to little or nothing, by senior year the processes of learning had begun to pay off in quantity: in 1945, for example, in the China theater 9,000 Japanese died as a direct result of OSS spy work and behind-the-lines killing.

Lieut. Colonel Ilya Tolstoy's visit to 'Shangri-La' in 1942 and 1943 is the type study of OSS freshman exploit. When the great German pincers, with one arm clamped on the Volga and the other pressing at El Alamein, threatened to snap shut somewhere east of Suez, the joint high command in Washington began worrying about a last-ditch defense of middle Asia. With the Japanese and the Germans threatening to meet in India, even the Dalai Lama, the high priest of Tibet, had become an important pawn in the game of conquest. In Ilya Tolstoy, the grandson of the Russian novelist, OSS had an adventurous character who was willing to dare the fastnesses of Tibet and the portals of the Forbidden City of Lhasa. With Lieut. Brooke Dolan, Tolstoy set out from India, carrying with him presents to the Dalai Lama from Franklin D. Roosevelt. The two men crossed the mountains, traveled through places that had never before echoed to the foot of a white man, bluffed their way past surly and uncomprehending tribesmen and finally reached the Forbidden City. Tactfully the two explained themselves; they had come seeking goodwill, they wished to convey the personal greetings of the head of a country far across the mountains and the sea – a country, parenthetically, that had no designs on anything that was sacred to the Dalai Lama. But just in case the Japanese hoped to knock China out of the war by cutting the line from eastern India to Chungking, they wished to judge the feasibility of a new supply road to China through Tibet. From Lhasa, Tolstoy and his companion went on toward Chungking, climbing the goat-track passes, plodding on through the deserts. Whenever they noticed a good site for an airfield, they jotted it down. Eventually they reached Chungking, where they learned that the threat to Suez and India had already been turned back at Stalingrad and El Alamein. Their expedition had been militarily superfluous.

In the Burmese jungle

The final OSS work in behalf of China was far from superfluous. In the autumn of 1942, when Tolstoy was setting out for Tibet, 20 OSS men, led by Colonel Carl Eifler, jumped from a plane into the north Burmese jungle, seeking contact with the naked, monkey-eating tribe of the Kachins. Eifler had it on the word of a missionary, Father James Stuart, that 250,000 Kachins were ready to fight the Japanese, whom they hated far more than they had ever hated the British. Eifler's work in organizing the Kachins was OSS's bow in the China-Burma-India theater; it paid off in the successful consummation of the campaign that brought General Merrill and his Marauders to the key airport of Myitkyina in 1944. The OSS-led Kachins accounted for 5,447 Japanese in the guerrilla warfare that took the pressure off the Assam-Chungking supply route. And while the Kachins were sniping and spying and tipping off the air force to easy Jap targets, OSS men were busy organizing the intelligence and special operations groups that Wedemeyer was to depend upon so heavily in China itself.

In Europe OSS teams played a ponderable part in preparing ambushes for the Germans. But in China a handful of OSS men did the work of a small army. In July of 1944, OSS Private X was ranging the contested country to the west of Changsha where Japanese units were maneuvering to expel the Chinese from the rice bowl and to cut the north-south railroad to Canton. Near the town of Yiyang, Private X peered out from his hiding place to see the advance units of a Japanese cavalry patrol moving toward a river. For minutes the Japanese rode on; Private X estimated there must be 10,000 of them. Since batteries are practically useless in the damp heat of central China, Private X pumped at his 20-pound portable hand generator to get up the current to flash a message to Chennault's airmen. Frantic with worry because his code signals did not seem to be getting through, Private X repeated his information again and again in 'clear.' For eight hours he ground away at the hand generator, powering the trim 31-pound waterproofed special OSS sending and receiving set. Suddenly he was rewarded by the roar of Chennault's planes; a 14th Air Force mission had come from Kweilin. The planes caught the Japanese cavalry just as it was entering the river and 9,000 of the Japanese were killed.

Between the exploits of its freshman and senior years, OSS men covered the world to fill the gaps left by the specialized intelligence officers of the Army's G2, the Navy's ONI (Office of Naval Intelligence) and the Army Air Force's A2. In Washington, in 1942, OSS men Edward Mason and Walt Rostow assembled the figures to prove that Russia would hold, thus providing a statistical underpinning for the hunch of Harry Hopkins and the on-the-spot minority report from Moscow of the Army's Colonel Faymonville. In Washington, in 1942, Sherman Kent, a Yale academician with the forward slouch of a ready prizefighter, drove through a study of North Africa which the Army found quite useful in planning the operation then known as Torch. It was OSS that finally convinced the Army and State Department that the French resistance forces constituted a valuable D-day and pre-D-day fighting army as well as a source of mere annoyance to the Nazis. In the field OSS men jumped at midnight from planes, landed on hostile coasts from rubber boats, swam underwater to attach explosive 'limpets' to enemy ships, infiltrated past sentries to carry radio sets to Maquis and guerrillas, set up high-powered telescopes on mountainous Mediterranean islands and slipped into German Paris with a pistol in one hand and cyanide pills in the other.

Professors, stockbrokers, screwballs

Critics of OSS in the other services claim a high percentage of Donovan fumbles. Certainly OSS had its failures. It botched a behind-the-lines expedition into Hungary, it put men ashore to almost instant death on the Italian coast, and some of the $100,000,000 it spent during the war may have gone down the drain. Since the 22,000 people who worked for OSS at one time or another ranged from professors to screwballs, movie producers to Communist fellow travelers, missionaries' sons to stockbrokers and millionaires, college presidents to ex-governors of states, and charwomen to the left-at-home wives of servicemen, there was plenty of room for a wide variety of personal performance. But as a team OSS batted at least 260 in General Donovan's estimation, which is a good team figure in any league.

OSS grew out of the character of ruddy-cheeked, soft-spoken Wild Bill Donovan, whose whole life prior to 1941 was an unconscious preparation for the job of World War II U.S. spymaster. Donovan proved his strategic brains when he quarterbacked a good Columbia football team; he proved his fantastic courage in the course of a volunteer career in World War I that won him the DSM, the DSC and the Congressional Medal of Honor. In France he became a close friend of Colonel Ned Buxton, a newspaperman from Providence, R. I. who was Sergeant York's commanding officer. Buxton had a passion for studying the wiles of Hannibal, the Carthaginian general whose G2 produced the intelligence that lured the Romans to destruction in the 'perfect' battle of Cannae, and he lost no time in communicating his ardor to Donovan. After World War I, Donovan, with Buxton to whisper in his ear, kept a geopolitician's idea of the globe suspended in the back of his mind, rising superior to the traditional rebel Irish view that world strategy is a racket practiced by and for the benefit of the British Empire. When the Reds and Whites were tangling in Russia, Donovan went all the way to Siberia to watch Admiral Kolchak's rear-guard action against the Soviets; then he came home to become an antitrust prosecutor for the Department of Justice and to make an unsuccessful bid for the New York governorship. His legal work taught him how to employ academic experts and gumshoe artists, stool pigeons and idealists. Meanwhile he indulged a personal hobby of reading about colonial guerrilla warfare and the use of Pawnee spies by whites in the wars against the Sioux.

The minute the Japanese attacked in Manchuria in 1931, Donovan knew that his job was to scout the globe as an unofficial spy for his country. With Buxton at his elbow he cooked up a way to bait Mussolini into sending him to Badoglio's headquarters in Ethiopia. 'Your excellency,' said Donovan to Mussolini in Rome, 'if your troops are no better than they were in the last war, then this Ethiopian war is only a small colonial affair. But if you've created a new sixth or tenth legion, then the balance of the world may be changed.' Mussolini, falling for the ruse, bridled and said, 'You'll see; I'll send you there.' From Ethiopia, Donovan went on to watch the 'laboratory' war in Spain; after

Dunkirk he made an on-the-spot investigation of the staying power of Britain before moving on to Belgrade and the menaced Balkans.

During his English mission he made a detailed study of British secret intelligence and the 'special services' that had to be developed to keep the flame of resistance alive in German Europe. When he brought the story of British intelligence and secret operative work home to Washington, President Roosevelt made Donovan Coordinator of Information and told him to go to work on the job of pulling together and supplementing the facts turned up by the routine government intelligence agencies. A year or so later, in June of 1942, the office of the COI became OSS, an organization that was responsible not to any single governmental department but to the all-embracing body of the Joint Chiefs of Staff.

OSS a catchall

Functionally speaking, OSS was a catchall organization which, like John L. Lewis' famous District 50 of the United Mine Workers, grew in unforeseen directions to meet unpredictable emergencies. Before it finished it was doing sabotage, organizing undergrounds and doing hazardous spying from Brittany to Korea. But when it began its work in 1941 it consisted largely of the so-called '100 professors' – a group of middle-aged specialists in anthropology, economics and a dozen other fields, plus a few young instructors who had had Ph.D. training in applying the seat of the pants to the seat of the chair in libraries. The 100 professors became the backbone of a fact-grubbing research and analysis department which proved that libraries and microfilmed German magazines could reveal more relevant facts than a whole platoon of Mata Haris.

Donovan picked his administrators for OSS from among his own personal acquaintances in civil life: Buxton naturally became his chief assistant, with able support coming from 'Oley' Doering and Ned Putzell, who left the Donovan law firm in New York to follow their chief to Washington. Although the old-line Washington bureaucrats resented the administrative presence in OSS of Financiers Charles Cheston and Russell Forgan, International Lawyer Allen Dulles, ex-Governor Bill Vanderbilt of Rhode Island, Louis Ream of U.S. Steel, Atherton Richards of the Hawaiian Pineapple Co., Cotton Textileman John Hughes and David Bruce, an in-law of the Mellon clan, the fact that Donovan had his own personal machine made for tight loyalties and smooth operating efficiency.

As the war progressed and as the Army and Navy started flying hundreds of reconnoitering flights over enemy territory from advanced bases, the OSS research and analysis branch continued to do the dray-horse work that was the main contribution of OSS; government policy makers depended on its thousands of background studies. The OSS map division, making topographical maps for General Marshall a specialty, turned out 8,000 map titles from 1942 to the war's end in 1945. Churchill preferred OSS maps to all others; at the Quebec Conference he called Roosevelt to his room, pointed to his wall and said, 'See, I've got them, too.' But since the executive order creating OSS had made provision for a secret intelligence service working behind enemy lines and for special strategic service operations in sabotage, morale subversion, guerrilla organization and aid to partisan resistance, there was plenty of room for OSS to grow in new directions as the character of the war changed. Even the research and analysis functions became more venturesome: an economic objectives unit in London helped the air forces work out the 'optimum maturity' schedule for strategic bombing of ball-bearing, fighter-plane and oil-production targets, and in the field OSS agents pieced together enough information from captured enemy units to arrive at a remarkably accurate estimate of German armament production.

Once in a war theater, an OSS operator was sometimes hard put to it to determine whether he was doing research and analysis work, secret intelligence or any one of a number of strategic service operations. Take the OSS career of Peter Karlow, for instance. Karlow began his OSS life as a field staff man in New York City, later, in the Mediterranean, he examined German armor, a dangerous job when the Nazis were using burned-out tanks for booby traps. In Corsica, Karlow found himself helping OSS guerrillas to improvise a maritime spying operation. Through Leghorn on the Italian coast the Germans were shipping supplies to their armies below Rome. Twenty-one miles southwest of Leghorn the 837-foot island peak of Gorgona rises out of the Mediterranean, and from a high-powered telescope set up on the peak OSS watchers could peer into Leghorn harbor. Another telescope was put ashore on the island of Capraia, farther to the south. From Gorgona and Capraia and Elba, advanced spy units tipped the Allied air forces off to German ship movements and directed the bombing of oil installations on the Italian mainland.

Karlow was badly wounded when his Italian PT boat struck a mine; he returned to the U.S. to do less arduous OSS work.

Radiomen in France

From the 'great empty lot' of French North Africa, OSS discovered it was comparatively easy to infiltrate secret intelligence agents into France. And so it was in France that secret intelligence really began to pick up where common research lagged. When the French gave the order to scuttle their fleet at Toulon, one of the escaping submarines, the *Casabianca*, joined the Allies. Although he was suffering from a leg malady that grew progressively worse as the war went on, Commander L'Herminier of the *Casabianca* ran OSS radiomen into southern France to help organize the 28 active radio chains that were working for us below the Loire prior to D-day. One secret intelligence agent, a French Jew who posed as a fur merchant, mapped three fourths of the French Mediterranean coast for Patch's invasion army. His astounding reports insisted that many of the German coastal 'defenses' were protected by wooden guns which air reconnaissance could not distinguish from the real thing. Another OSS agent, posing as a recruiting official for the Vichy militia, learned the range, trajectory and location of 20 batteries on each side of Marseilles; he also learned the whereabouts of German observation posts and electric controls. Such information, reaching North Africa by radio, by carrier pigeon, by pick-up plane and by couriers slipping across the Pyrenees and through Spain, helped make the invasion of southern France a comparatively painless operation.

To provide a central nervous system for secret intelligence, OSS built up an elaborate radio network that kept secret information flowing from the field to theater headquarters and Washington: operatives received their instructions and sent back data over 1,126 radio circuits established in enemy-occupied areas. At peak operations during the Battle of France, some 90 OSS agents, aided by 500 French accomplices, were busy radioing out information on troop movements, the location of munitions dumps, the condition of factory production and transportation, the movement of German secret-service personnel.

The job of penetrating Central Europe with secret intelligence agents was far more difficult than working with the French resistance forces, but OSS found that it could be done. In Switzerland, where John Foster Dulles' brother Allen sat with ready ears, there was a vast coming and going of agents from Germany and Central Europe. Allen Dulles caught echoes in Bern of the Nazi V-weapon developmental program that was being carried out at Peenemünde on the Baltic coast. With his information added to items that had been gleaned from refugees and British aerial photography, the Allied air command was enabled to blow Peenemünde off the map. The bombing of Peenemünde set the German V-weapon program back from six to nine months and probably saved England as an invasion base for D-day. Later on Dulles used his Switzerland post as a focal point from which to wangle the surrender of the Nazi armies in North Italy.

Since a spy needs a 'friendly house' – *i.e.*, a place to sleep, eat and set up a radio – the job of keeping an agent going inside Germany required considerable craft when the Gestapo was riding high. But when German internal security began to break down amid the chaos of the bombing and the influx of the six to eight million Poles, Russians, Czechs, French and Belgians who were conscripted for labor, the job of keeping cover and manufacturing a convincing background was made relatively easy. OSS had some 250 agents in Germany and Austria from September 1944 until the end of the war, and one man even managed to penetrate the Gestapo. This 'double agent' fed misinformation to the German General Staff that brought about the deployment of 30,000 German paratroopers in the Low Countries at a time when it was important to keep Nazi divisions from reaching the Normandy invasion coast. Other OSS men kept themselves alive in Germany by pretending to be traitors; the cream of the double agent jest came when three OSS agents were actually awarded the Iron Cross.

Rescuing downed airmen

The kindlier manifestations of secret operations resulted in the rescue of more than 5,000 downed Allied airmen from behind enemy lines. Some 3,000 of these were spirited out of the Balkans by various underground channels. OSS's Major Lynn Farish, the originator of the Balkan escape network, parachuted into the Balkans three times and journeyed thousands of miles on foot in search of downed fliers before meeting his death in a plane crash.

The job of recruiting and training an OSS secret agent was something to daunt a republic that had never in its history gone in for large-scale organized secret intelligence and sabotage operations. In the early days of OSS, recruitment was done on a personal basis; the fact that it was well done is proof either of our luck, the bracing circumstances of American life or the quality of Wild Bill Donovan's connections. OSS's 'eager beaver,' Lieut. Colonel 'Jerry' Sage, who became famous as 'Jerry Dagger' and 'the Big X' because of his harum-scarum escapes from German prison camps was picked to join OSS as a behind-the-lines demolition artist on the suggestion of an FBI acquaintance. Jerry, a Procter and Gamble soap salesman, had been a football star and Phi Beta Kappa man at Washington State College; as a boy he had shot ground squirrels and as an early inductee from the ROTC he had learned something about demolition and silent killing, or judo. Jerry went into OSS with no psychiatric screening, and he proved an accession in every way.

The professional recruitment touch, however, was soon applied by psychiatrists working under James McConaugh, former president of Connecticut's Wesleyan University. Whether the prospective OSS overseas candidate was a Norwegian sailor, a Greek refugee, the daughter of a missionary to China, an Italian schoolteacher or simply a halfback from an American college campus, he (or she) was put through an elaborate screening operation to test emotional stability and qualities of leadership under stress. On a property in Fairfax County, Va., Major Henry Murray, a Harvard psychologist, and his screening board put groups of 20 through a three-day grilling that often had the candidates goggle-eyed with incomprehension. One of the group assignments was to move a cannon across a brook, a job designed to winnow natural bosses from natural followers. On one of the evenings at Fairfax a group would be allowed plenty of alcohol, the aim being to test the men on their power of discretion when drunk. After the screening, operatives were trained intensively in such edifying things as gutter fighting, radio operation and repair, coding and decoding, foreign languages, mapping, jugular slashing, the use of explosive 'pencils' and other easily concealed demolition devices, and the keeping of cover under the most impossible circumstances. The art of keeping cover was perhaps the most difficult thing OSS had to teach; men might have gone to their deaths if they had been caught in Germany or France with English tobacco grains in their pockets, or shoes that weren't cobbled according to local standards, or laundry marks that were demonstrably Anglican or American, or hair oil with an Oshkosh smell.

The present plans for conserving the assets of OSS are somewhat nebulous. One plan is to bestow the research and analysis functions and membership upon the State Department and to hand over to the Army the clandestine operations files and personnel. Another plan is to set up secret intelligence under the State Department. But this is going back to the very fragmentation and compartmentalization of intelligence that so bedeviled us in 1941.

An intelligence service should derive from the nature of the country it is intended to serve. The Germans could entrust their intelligence to their army's general staff and its ABWEHR, for Germany was a military nation in the heart of a militarized continent. The British can put their intelligence under their Foreign Office, for the immemorial British instinct for keeping tabs on the balance of power renders British Foreign Office employes peculiarly immune to the blandishments of ideology. But the U.S. Army, unlike an army in continental Europe, is not the nation's first line of defense, and the U.S. State Department, which is enmeshed in protocol and officially devoted to the promulgation of justice and good works, lacks the operating coolness and objectivity needed in the gathering of strategic intelligence.

Our future intelligence

If we had a unified Department of Defense, then there would be a good case for putting any successor organization to OSS under the jurisdiction of a Secretary for Defense. As a service department working for a unified command, the reports and evaluations of such an intelligence-gathering and intelligence-pooling agency would be impartially available to Navy, Army, Air Forces and President. But as long as our military arms are compartmentalized, intelligence under any one of them will remain compartmentalized, too. It is the nature of the compartmentalized beast to be jealous of its own files and to fall into the habit of thinking facts are something to be kept out of circulating use.

General Donovan, who bowed out of the picture when OSS was deprived of its autonomous existence on Oct. 1, would like to see a permanent fact-gathering and fact-pooling organization set up under the control of the U.S. President, who is the sole administrative officer capable of coordinating the work of Army, Navy, Air Forces and State Department. And, since you cannot run a spy service with its financial books open to inspection, he would trust the President to see to it that an intelligence agency's funds were well spent. If Congress, however, objects to putting intelligence under the President, a permanent OSS could

Groundwork of Liaison with the Americans

be made responsible to an Army-Navy-State interdepartmental committee.

Certainly the republic needs its sentinels. Pearl Harbor resulted from bungled intelligence pooling. The blunder wasn't fatal, but if our next Pearl Harbor comes in the guise of atomic explosions set off by time fuses in the New York, Pittsburgh, Detroit and Chicago consulates of a conspiratorial foreign power, there will be no recovery from it. The *next* time our intelligence service must do its big job *before* the war. We need our new OSS, our new General Donovan, now.

CHAPTER 5

Collaboration with the FBI after Pearl Harbor

As already stated, Hoover keenly resented Donovan's organization when it was first established, because he feared that its interests would clash with the authority of the FBI, particularly in Latin America. His resentment extended to BSC. Indeed, realizing that he could attack Donovan's organization most effectively by attacking what was then its mainstay, he began shortly before Pearl Harbor to treat BSC with ill-concealed hostility, and his purpose was quite evidently to suppress its activities if he could. In that purpose he had the backing, among others in the Administration who were latently anti-British, of Adolf Berle, Assistant Secretary of State.

Immediately after the Rio Conference of January 1942, which resulted in greatly increased opportunities for US participation in secret activities in Latin America, a joint committee was set up for the purpose of coordinating all Anglo-American intelligence activities in the Western Hemisphere. At its first meeting, which was attended by Hoover, Berle and WS, among others, Berle proposed that BSC should maintain liaison with no agency other than the FBI. WS resisted this proposal and went on to refer to the McKellar Bill (see Introduction), pointing out that in its present form it would mean the end of his organization inasmuch as it stipulated, *inter alia*, that 'all records, accounts and propaganda material used by foreign agencies (whether allied or neutral, secret or open) would be liable to inspection by US Government authorities at any time'. Berle replied, with a smile, that this was regrettable but that it was too late to effect any modification since the Bill was already on the President's desk awaiting signature.

WS left the meeting before it was over and went straight to Donovan's office. He explained the position to Donovan, who, realizing well enough that the end of BSC would at the present juncture render virtually impossible the continuance of his own organization, telephoned the White House and asked for an immediate interview with the President, which was granted. At Donovan's persuasion Mr Roosevelt agreed not to sign the Bill unless and until it was modified to allow adequate safeguard of BSC's legitimate interests, and a few days later he vetoed it. In the following month an amended version of the Bill, which excluded the crippling clause concerning compulsory disclosure of records, was introduced in Congress, and, as already stated (see Introduction), it became law on 1 May 1942.

This did not end Hoover's efforts to embarrass BSC, but to relate more of them would be merely tedious and probably misleading. Basic to them all was his resentment that the FBI no longer had a monopoly of collaboration with British Intelligence. The fact that it had lost this monopoly was inevitable not only on account of the emergence of Donovan's organization but because, when the bar of neutrality was lifted, the Service Intelligence departments also insisted on maintaining direct liaison with BSC (see Part IX). But Hoover is the kind of a man who does not bow easily to the inevitable – that is at once his strength and his weakness – and it took a long while to convince him that he could not succeed in his determination to exclude BSC from contact with other US Intelligence agencies. Until then he remained obdurate.

Berle, on the other hand, proved more amenable. WS had many discussions with him during 1942 in an effort to temper his hostility, and he was eventually persuaded that – to use his own words – 'as a realist he owed it to his country to find the best method of cooperation with Great Britain'. Towards the end of the year, HM Ambassador reported to the Foreign Office: 'For the past two or three months he (Berle) has been noticeably sweeter.'

Berle's changed attitude eventually provided the means of convincing Hoover that his efforts to control BSC's activities were futile. In June 1943, a memorandum from the Department of Justice, which had clearly been written at Hoover's instigation, instructed BSC to desist from direct contact with the US Armed Services and maintain liaison only through 'approved British Military channels'. Since this proposal was known to be diametrically opposed to the wishes of the US Service Intelligence departments, BSC referred it to General Strong, Head of G-2, who stated unreservedly that 'he was not prepared to submit to an FBI censorship'. At a subsequent meeting with Adolf Berle, attended by all interested parties, Berle endorsed General Strong's decision, and ruled that BSC should be allowed to decide for itself to which agencies and in what manner it would transmit its information. Hoover had no choice but to accept this ruling, and thereafter he abided by it without apparent demur.

Thus what may be described as the period of embitterment in the relationship between the FBI and BSC, which began immediately before Pearl Harbor, continued for approximately eighteen months thereafter. It did not, however, interfere with collaboration on matters of mutual concern, and indeed, as will become apparent later on (see Part VII), some of the best results in counter-espionage work were achieved while it lasted. Nor did it interrupt WS's personal liaison with Hoover, for Hoover's hostility was expressed not openly but in backstage manoeuvres. And while it was regrettable, it was not without value, for it was extremely revealing of Hoover's attitude of mind and served to emphasize the prerequisites of effective dealings with the FBI. One of these is, perhaps, worthy of brief mention.

It was always of the utmost importance never to allow the impression that information to which the FBI could lay just claim by right of common interest was being withheld. On some occasions Hoover made purely reckless charges in this regard. For example, there was a time when he accused BSC of not passing to him intelligence from its sources in Latin America, although the fact of the case was that during the period in question BSC had furnished the FBI with considerably more material than it had received from the FBI in return. Yet on other occasions, it must be admitted, Hoover had reason for complaint. This was not because BSC deliberately withheld information (although that was the interpretation Hoover inevitably put upon it) but rather because BSC did not invariably receive information, for which the FBI had asked and which existed only in London, with sufficient speed and in sufficient quantity to satisfy the FBI's legitimate requirements. For instance, on 9 November 1942, WS telegraphed CSS:

> ... I have arranged with Hoover personally to appoint trusted representative as liaison with us on Communist activities exclusively ... If I am not to be accused once again of withholding relevant material from London, it will be essential that you personally instruct that I should be promptly supplied with all available material so I may implement our promises and so that it will not be necessary for Hoover to turn elsewhere ...

Despite several reminders, seven weeks elapsed before a reply was received to this telegram. It read:

> Every attention is being paid to your repeated requests . . . My officers are already engaged in careful and exhaustive survey of Communist material . . .

The delay in this case, as in other similar cases, may have been unavoidable. But it was the kind of incident upon which Hoover's suspicions and susceptibilities found sustenance, and it is mentioned here only as indication of the difficulties which were experienced in dealing with the FBI and which were inseparable from Hoover's own psychology.

Despite those difficulties, it is possible to report that BSC's relationship with the FBI has left behind it no traces of bitterness and at the end is as cordial as it was at the outset. During a recent discussion with WS, Hoover stated that their liaison had been one of mutual understanding and mutual advantage, and that for his part he would wish it maintained, in the form of regular meetings, during the post-war period. He made clear his conviction on this occasion that since, in his view, Intelligence is the only defence against the atom bomb, there should be the closest cooperation between SIS and the FBI, not necessarily in British or American interests, but – to use his own rather forcible expression – 'in the interests of civilization'.

PART II

POLITICAL WARFARE FOR SO.1

INTRODUCTION

(a) Terms of Reference
(b) Guiding Principles

(a) Terms of Reference

In the early years of its existence SO was divided into SO.1 and SO.2, the former being responsible for subversive propaganda (that is, Political Warfare), the latter for special operations. The SO mission within BSC could, in practice, observe no such division of its responsibilities for the great majority of its special operations were of a non-violent nature and Political Warfare was often an indispensable aid to them. (See Part VI.)

It has been said before – but cannot be overemphasized – that BSC was, unlike any other secret organization, in a position to coordinate all secret activities and, as representative in the Western Hemisphere of various London headquarters, never kept its separate functions in watertight compartments. Thus it used Political Warfare on occasion to further objectives which did not come within the competence of the SO mission, for example the collection of intelligence (see Part IV) and Economic Warfare (see Part III). Further, it used Political Warfare to exploit the advantages gained from the collection of intelligence (see Part IV, hereunder). For example, if it obtained positive evidence as a result of planned investigation that a particular man was working against the interests of Great Britain, it did not have to rest content with forwarding the information to London or filing it away for future reference, but by means of covert propaganda could take positive action to discredit the man in question and thus to undo his capacity for harm.

In the sense, then, that Political Warfare was interwoven with certain other activities it remained one of BSC's principal weapons throughout, though admittedly it was used more sparingly after Pearl Harbor than before. On the other hand, it ceased to be a distinct function of BSC when, as a consequence of SO.1's responsibilities being assumed by the Political Warfare Executive, a separate PWE mission was sent out to Washington, in August of 1942, under the direction of the Hon. David Bowes-Lyon.

Insofar as actual operations are concerned, this part is concerned only with those which BSC undertook strictly in its capacity as representative of SO.1. But the details set down regarding methods and media of subversive propaganda are intended to clarify the manner in which all BSC's Political Warfare was conducted.

(b) Guiding Principles

There were two SO.1 sections within BSC. The first, whose function, very broadly, was to conduct Political Warfare against the European enemy, was established in March of 1941. The second, whose function was to conduct Political Warfare against Japan, was established in the following May. Their lines did not cross. Each had its own distinct objectives. Each employed its own intermediaries, and each utilized its own chosen outlets for material it was concerned to publicize. But both were guided by rules which were fundamental to BSC's conduct of subversive propaganda. The first required all Political Warfare operations to be based, insofar as was possible, on accurate intelligence derived from secret sources and demanded the rejection – save in exceptional circumstances to be mentioned later – of unreliable or fabricated information. BSC accepted the principle that the best propaganda is the truth but recognized in turn that the facts likely to attract the widest attention and exercise the most powerful influence are those which have the greatest news value. Hence there was continual search for material which could and should be publicized for propaganda purposes yet was not available to ordinary news-gathering agencies or overt propaganda organizations. In this, needless to say, the SIS Division cooperated fully.

The second basic rule governing BSC's Political Warfare demanded that the officers responsible should work in strictly covert fashion and should guard against the least risk of their output (or other results of their activity) being traced back to them or identified as British propaganda. The reason for this rule and the technique evolved for observing it will become apparent in the succeeding pages. It should be said here, however, that a major objective of the battle within the United States which the Axis and their isolationist confederates waged against preparedness was to expose British Political Warfare. They did not succeed in a single instance.

CHAPTER 1

Political Warfare against the European Enemy

(a) Objectives and Methods
(b) Use of News Agencies
(c) Station WRUL

(a) Objectives and Methods

Political Warfare against Japan is described in Chapter 3.

In its Political Warfare against the European enemy, BSC had two broad objectives. First, it was concerned to bring the United States into the 'shooting' war by attacking isolationism and fostering interventionism. Secondly, it was concerned to prepare the United States as a base for operations against the Axis by developing American channels of propaganda and assisting the newly established COI. Thus before Pearl Harbor its Political Warfare activities were directed against the enemy within and without the United States, and were both offensive and defensive in character.

BSC used mainly ordinary, overt propaganda channels such as press and radio. It had occasional resort to disguised channels, but since these were controlled directly rather than through intermediaries and since the principle of trafficking only in accurate information did not apply to their use, they fall outside any general survey of BSC's Political Warfare technique. For that reason they are separately described in Chapter 4, which deals also with rumours, based on fiction rather than fact, which BSC put about to achieve certain specialized and short-term purposes.

BSC was able to initiate internal propaganda through its undercover contacts with selected newspapers, such as the *New York Times*, the *New York Herald Tribune*, the *New York Post* and the

Political Warfare for SO.1

Baltimore Sun; with newspaper columnists and radio commentators; and with various political pressure organizations. The method of working through columnists and commentators is described in a postscript to this Part. Operations under cover of organizations are related in the next chapter.

The number of newspapers with which BSC maintained regular contact through intermediaries was extremely limited, but it was sufficient. Because of BSC's insistence, as a matter of policy from which only occasional divergence was allowed, on restricting its output to accurate information which had genuine news value, publicity for a campaign, once it had been launched, was largely self-generating.

An illustration of this point is provided by the case of Doctor Gerhard Westrick, who was a high-level agent of the Third Reich.

Westrick arrived in New York from Japan in the spring of 1940. He posed as a private citizen. He got in touch with a number of important American businessmen and leased an expensive house outside the city.

In the following June, WS began to investigate his activities. He discovered the following facts about him:

1. Westrick was actually accredited as a diplomat and registered with the State Department as Commercial Counsellor to the German Embassy.
2. He was a partner of Heinrich Albert, who had been a German propagandist in America during the first war; and he was assisted by Baroness von Wagenheim, a relative of Ribbentrop.
3. Surveillance of his house showed that he was visited both by many well-known American industrialists (particularly in the oil business) and by comparatively obscure young men of German descent who were employed in strategic factories.
4. One of his chief contacts was a Norwegian-American called Captain Thorkild Rieber, president of the Texas Oil Company. Rieber was suspected of supplying the Axis with oil through the British blockade. He had attended a banquet (at which Westrick was guest of honour) celebrating the fall of France. Westrick described himself as an 'employee' of this company, and in applying for a driving licence gave its office as his business address.
5. His purpose was evidently to convince American businessmen that the war had already been won by Germany, and to enlist their support on a high level for the isolationist

campaign. Their reward was to be business privileges in Axis-dominated Europe.

These facts provided sufficient basis for a first-class news story. The story was written by BSC and placed, through an intermediary, in the *New York Herald Tribune*, where it was published as a series of articles.

The repercussions were spontaneous. The articles in the *Herald Tribune* were reproduced throughout the country and were the cause of numerous editorials on Fifth Columnism in the United States, with particular reference to the fall of France which was attributed to German corruption of her businessmen and politicians. This nationwide publicity resulted in an outburst of public indignation.

Westrick was deluged with threatening letters and abusive telephone calls.

A hostile crowd gathered outside his house. He met this threat, with true German subtlety, by playing 'God Bless America' and 'The Star Spangled Banner', interminably, on his gramophone. But the FBI had to provide him with a twenty-four-hour guard. Eventually his landlord asked him to leave the house. His driving licence was revoked because he had described himself as 'not crippled', whereas the *Herald Tribune* articles revealed that he had in fact lost a leg. His American contacts, unwilling to be labelled Fifth Columnists, all deserted him. When reporters tried to interview them, they were inaccessible or 'away on vacation'. And then the State Department, at the instigation of the FBI (prompted by WS), requested the German Government to remove Westrick from the country for pursuing activities unfriendly to the United States. By 20 August 1940, he was *en route* to Germany on a Japanese liner.

The *Herald Tribune* received literally hundreds of letters congratulating it on smoking out a dangerous emissary of Adolf Hitler, and was praised by the Attorney-General at a meeting of forty-two State Governors. There was even a proposal that the paper should receive the Pulitzer Prize for its good work.

The shares of Texas Oil also dropped. Captain Rieber was considerably alarmed for his own future – and with reason. He told the press he was thoroughly pro-British, but he was forced to resign from the chairmanship of the company at a stormy stockholders' meeting. Although he remained active in the oil business, he was watched most carefully thereafter and lost much of his capacity for doing harm.

The Westrick case is an example of BSC's internal propaganda – of the campaign against German influence within the United States, which is related in full in the next chapter. It has been described here merely to illustrate one of the principal methods which BSC employed in disseminating subversive propaganda. All that was necessary was contact through a reliable intermediary with one influential newspaper.

It should not be thought, however, that the method was simple to apply. The utmost discretion had to be exercised at all times. There was constant danger that an intermediary might be exposed or give himself away or that British influence might in some other way be revealed. Had anything of the sort happened, BSC's Political Warfare would have boomeranged and the whole British cause been put in direct jeopardy. The enemy continually wielded his spotlight to pierce the shadows where BSC lurked. The dividing line between safety and disaster was perilously thin.

(b) Use of News Agencies

Virtually all BSC's Political Warfare against Japan consisted of propaganda which had the appearance of news originating from strictly American sources but which was directed to targets outside the United States. Operations of the same kind were conducted against the European enemy. Their launching was dependent upon the acquisition and control not only of an appropriate American source, as in the case of internal propaganda, but of a channel for external dissemination.

In April 1941, contact was established with the Overseas News Agency, which was a branch of the Jewish Telegraph Agency, owned in part by the rich New York Jew who controlled the liberal and vehemently anti-Nazi *New York Post*. After a series of secret negotiations, BSC agreed to give the ONA a monthly subsidy in return for promise of cooperation in certain specific ways. One of the things the ONA did at once was to increase its representation abroad by sending fifteen newly recruited correspondents to various cities throughout the world. But its value, as is revealed in subsequent chapters, lay in its ability not only to channel propaganda outwards but to assure wide dissemination of material originated by BSC and intended for internal consumption. In April 1941, the ONA clients within the United States already numbered more than forty-five English-language papers which included such giants as the *New York Times*, the *New York Herald Tribune*, the *New York Post*, the *New York Daily News*, the *Washington Times*

Herald and the *Washington Post*, the *San Francisco Chronicle*, the *Philadelphia Inquirer* and the *Kansas City Star*. BSC arranged to expand this clientele. Czech, Italian, Polish and Spanish foreign-language bureaux were opened to supply news to the myriad of foreign-language newspapers, one or more of which are printed in every town of any account in the United States. Practically the entire Polish press in the US became subscribers, and it included eight daily newspapers and no less than fifty-four weeklies. Twelve large Italian daily newspapers and over thirty other foreign publications, such as the *Greek National Herald*, the *Ukrainian Daily News* and the *New Yorksky Dennik*, were likewise persuaded to subscribe as also were twenty-four newspapers in South America, including the greatest of them all, *La Nación* of Buenos Aires.

ONA provided useful cover on occasion for SOE agents. Another agency which BSC controlled was the original cover for the whole SOE mission. It was called British and Overseas Features, and was registered in June 1941 for the overt purpose of transmitting suitable articles, culled from the US press, to Latin American and Far Eastern papers. As cover, it had considerable verisimilitude, for the majority of SOE officers were, in fact, trained journalists and the main outer office in New York was plentifully furnished with the paraphernalia of their trade – ticker tapes and the like. Further, it afforded a useful instrument for rapid dissemination abroad of subversive propaganda originated by BSC in the United States. Regrettably its overt purpose became redundant when a few months later the British Overseas Press Service – a branch of the Ministry of Information – began to expand. Two official British propaganda agencies could not exist side by side when even one was frowned upon. And so British and Overseas Features was dissolved, and the SOE officers assumed the cover of British Security Coordination.

Finally, BSC made occasional use of Britanova, the news agency which was clandestinely controlled by SOE in London. Great care had to be taken to avoid revealing any official contact with Britanova, but messages and funds were passed to its New York director and, as is revealed in subsequent chapters, the agency assisted in disseminating abroad stories planted by BSC in American newspapers.

(c) Station WRUL

Perhaps the most powerful instrument which BSC found for conducting Political Warfare against the European enemy abroad was the short-wave wireless station WRUL. From this station BSC was able to direct its American-made subversive propaganda to listeners through the greater part of the world. But first a whole organization of contacts and intermediaries had to be built up. Running a radio programme was a far more complicated business than placing an occasional article in a newspaper.

WRUL was the only short-wave wireless station in the United States which was not run for profit. It had been founded by Walter Lemmon of International Business Machines and was supported by several great charitable institutions. Its avowed purpose was to spread international goodwill.

Its power, 50,000 watts, was unsurpassed by any other station in either the Americas or Germany. Already, when BSC first encountered it, it had a large international audience, held together by an Association of Listeners in more than thirty countries abroad. These listeners were its regular correspondents, so that its influence could be accurately gauged. During a single week in January 1941, for example, the station received letters from listeners in countries ranging all the way from New Zealand to Great Britain, from Australia to Yugoslavia, and from Algeria to Guatemala. It received letters in that week from listeners in such distant places as the Virgin Islands and from listeners at sea. It received, on an average, 1,000 letters every week. The CBS correspondent in Vichy estimated that it had a daily listening public in France alone of 400,000 strong.

The station was, however, poorly equipped in personnel for multi-lingual broadcasts, and, before BSC's intervention in its affairs, devoted the greater part of its transmitting time to English programmes, which were, of course, entirely unsupervised by propaganda experts. To fulfil adequately its avowed purpose of spreading international goodwill it needed professional assistance. The opportunity to provide this was too good to be missed.

Through cut-outs, BSC began to supply it with everything it needed to run a first-class international programme worthy of its transmitting power and declared policy. BSC subsidized it financially. It recruited foreign news editors, translators and announcers to serve on its staff. It furnished it with material for news bulletins, with specially prepared scripts for talks and commentaries and with transcribed programmes. Rapidly, its foreign-language broadcasts increased in number, variety and influence. By the middle of 1941, station WRUL was virtually, though quite unconsciously, a subsidiary of BSC, sending out covert British propaganda all over the world. It was controlled

Political Warfare against the European Enemy

through a network of intermediaries drawn mainly from the various minority groups with whom BSC maintained contact (see Part VIII).

Daily broadcasts went out in no less than twenty-two different languages and dialects: English, Iraqui, Egyptian, Moroccan, Albanian, Senegalese, Armenian, Czech, Finnish, French, German, Greek, Italian, Persian, Polish, Portuguese, Roumanian, Serbo-Croat, Slovak, Spanish, Swedish and Turkish. Material was prepared in the BSC offices and then passed to the various intermediaries for transmittal to the station, which regarded itself, of course, as completely independent, and was so nominally.

The conduct of the station as a propaganda agency provides a good example of the type of coordinated work which BSC undertook. It was as follows:

1. SOE/London provided BSC with regular directives on policy and requests for instituting specific campaigns. (For example, in May 1941, Sir Samuel Hoare asked for an immediate propaganda campaign designed to convince Spain that she would be the loser if she entered the war on Germany's side. WRUL broadcasts written by BSC agents launched this campaign in June.)
2. The directives contained information for implementing particular campaigns and this was supplemented by material from BSC's own sources, e.g. SIS, Censorship, monitoring of enemy broadcasts. WRUL had a rule against broadcasting material which had not appeared in the American press, but BSC got around this by inserting its own material in friendly newspapers, and then quoting it.
3. Information in directives was further amplified as a result of discussions with the minority groups with whom BSC was in contact.
4. Members of these groups, and reliable American agents of BSC, assisted in preparing broadcasts based on the raw material of the directives. Often contacts or agents of BSC actually broadcast the final version. Their cover was one or other of the pro-British committees secretly supported or influenced by BSC, such as *Free World* (see Chapter 2). When a committee with which BSC was unconnected sponsored the broadcasts, BSC was able to introduce its own material by paying additional subsidies to the writers and speakers.
5. Subsequently material was also furnished by Donovan's

organization, and this was coordinated with BSC's propaganda line.

6. Finally, the broadcasts were coordinated with internal propaganda campaigns currently being carried out, and reference to other channels of covert propaganda controlled by SOE and BSC were introduced objectively. For example, all the prophecies of the propagandist-astrologer, Louis de Wohl (see Chapter 4), were broadcast to the Near East, and a new French broadcasting station 'believed to be controlled by the Vatican', but really directed by SOE, was similarly publicized. Articles in the various 'free' periodicals controlled by BSC – *Austrian Action*, the *Jugoslav Bulletin*, the Hungarian *Igazmondo*, the Arabic *Al Hoda* – were broadcast to the appropriate countries as soon as written. The foundation of *Free World* was made the occasion for a series of important broadcasts to Europe and Latin America by its directors.

Thus it happened that an American wireless station with an unsullied reputation for impartiality was, for many months during the most critical period of the war, unknowingly harnessed to the task of broadcasting British propaganda on a scale almost comparable in quantity of output with the BBC's Overseas Service. But to maintain control over it through intermediaries was no easy matter. None of the instructions which BSC issued covertly had the backing of any legally constituted authority, for even Donovan, when he had entered the picture, in practice had no power to dictate the policy of what was after all a privately owned and administered American concern. The station management, docile enough at first, became more difficult to handle as WRUL's importance and influence increased. The directors sometimes rebelled against the tendentious tone of the broadcasts. And Lemmon himself, enjoying his new-found power, was often given to displays of self-assertiveness. Any attempted interference on his part which ran contrary to BSC's interest could not be arbitrarily or directly brushed aside. It could be overcome only as a result of tactful negotiation through go-betweens.

The enemy, too, was aware of WRUL's value so that strict precautions had to be taken to safeguard the security of the station as a propaganda channel. Close and constant watch had to be kept on personnel and every broadcast had to be carefully monitored.

There were several instances of attempted sabotage. At the time of one of the Syrian crises, for example, when Free French broadcasts were exerting considerable influence on the situation, an Arab named Fuad Mufarrij persuaded an official attached to the station to allow him to organize all programmes to the Near East. Very soon BSC's monitoring service was perplexed by several unauthorized policy changes. These were explained when Mufarrij admitted to a BSC intermediary, Raoul Aglion of the Near East Information Centre, that he had on several occasions deliberately cut out the transcribed Free French programmes on the grounds that they were 'indistinct' and in their stead had substituted his own material without warning.

Another attempt to interfere with Free French output was made by the Germans when they tried to silence an Egyptian broadcaster, a certain Dr Dorra. In July 1941, the Egyptian Consul (acting probably on orders from Berlin relayed through the French Minister in Cairo) summoned Dorra and pointed out to him that his material had a distinctly pro-British and anti-Vichy tone. Since Egypt maintained diplomatic relations with Vichy, the Consul explained, Dorra would have to abstain from critical comment and in future submit his broadcasts to the Egyptian Consulate for approval. The attempt was frustrated. Through BSC's intermediary, Raoul Aglion, Dorra was told to ignore the Consul's instructions and was assured that the Free French would do their best to guard his relatives in Egypt against possible reprisals. At the same time BSC arranged for the State Department to be informed of the Egyptian Consul's unwarranted intervention in the affairs of a free American broadcasting station.

The organization of WRUL to serve the short-term needs of British propaganda represented a considerable step towards fulfilment of the long-term objective of preparing the United States as a base for Political Warfare operations against the Axis. BSC knew from the beginning that its covert control of the station would last only so long as the United States Government was unable to assume official control, and the American authorities were no less aware of this. Although the State Department was at first apprehensive that the tone of the broadcasts might be regarded as an infraction of US neutrality, it was before the end of 1941 contributing heavily to WRUL funds and had its own officials attached to the station, thereby exerting indirect influence on WRUL's policy.

As the war clouds loomed nearer, the Americans realized that preparedness for wide-scale propaganda operations must be regarded as an integral part of military preparedness and the establishment of Donovan's COI in the summer of 1941 provided proof of this. Yet they found it virtually impossible to do the job for themselves, for short-wave broadcasting facilities – indispensable to an adequate propaganda machine – could not arbitrarily be taken over for official use so long as the country remained nominally at peace. In the United States, it should be remembered, radio comes strictly within the domain of competitive private enterprise and not of state monopoly. It is an industry, and before Pearl Harbor the owners of short-wave broadcasting stations resented and resisted anything that smacked of government interference.

Thus it happened that while Donovan had the responsibility of developing broadcasting services for official US propaganda, he lacked sufficient authority to discharge it on his own initiative. In September 1941, after long discussions with BSC, he began his attempt to commandeer the facilities of American short-wave stations, and sent Robert Sherwood, head of his Foreign Information Service, to London to plan coordination of propaganda programmes with the BBC. But he made little headway. NBC rejected an offer of COI translators. CBS, broadcasting an identical news bulletin to France several times daily, could not be dissuaded from this labour-saving but futile practice. And when approached directly all the stations including, ironically enough, WRUL refused to accept COI's directives.

In practice, Donovan could do little more than supply the stations with material. He could not force them to broadcast it, and he had largely to rely on them to translate it into the appropriate foreign language, for he had only sufficient resources to provide Czech, Swedish and Finnish scripts in final form.

This was still the situation but a fortnight before Pearl Harbor, and in such circumstances the value of WRUL can readily be imagined. Here was a station which had been innocently obeying BSC's directives for months past. It was a fully equipped radio propaganda service of exactly the kind Donovan needed but was unable to build for himself. Even though he had been balked in his bid to control it directly, he was already using it jointly with BSC under cover.

The significance of WRUL, then, lay not so much in its value to BSC as an instrument for directing British propaganda abroad (although that was important) as in the fact that it represented a ready-made broadcasting service for American propaganda, which was available to Donovan and was in fact turned over to him as soon as the United States entered the war. Had BSC not undertaken this work, Donovan's Political Warfare activities after

Pearl Harbor would have been considerably retarded, for while WRUL as such would have been at his disposal, he would have found in it little more than a powerful transmitter to serve his immediate needs. All the necessary preparations in the way of recruiting and training news editors, translators, commentators and announcers would still have been ahead of him. Nor was WRUL the only short-wave station which BSC converted into a propaganda broadcasting service for eventual American use. When Pearl Harbor came, a radio organization for Far Eastern propaganda was also available to Donovan – but that story belongs to a subsequent chapter.

CHAPTER 2

Campaign against Axis Propaganda in the United States

(a) Stimulating Pro-British Groups
(b) America First
(c) The Congressional Franking Case
(d) Working with American Labour
(e) Organizing the Irish

The Battle of Words between BSC and the Germans was largely waged in the United States under cover of opposing societies – interventionist on the one side and isolationist on the other. Whereas the enemy never succeeded in unmasking British Political Warfare, BSC was able in several instances to rip off the disguise of German-inspired subversive propaganda.

In planning its campaign, it was necessary for BSC to remember (as the Germans remembered) the simple truth that the United States, a sovereign entity of comparatively recent birth, is inhabited by people of many conflicting races, interests and creeds. These people, though fully conscious of their wealth and power in the aggregate, are still unsure of themselves individually, still basically on the defensive and still striving, as yet unavailingly but very defiantly, after national unity, and indeed after some logical grounds for considering themselves a nation in the racial sense. It is their frustrated passion to achieve a genuine nationalism which leads them to such extravagances – more wishfully assertive than fervently patriotic – as the annual 'I am an American Day' and to such absurdities of expression – often heard – as 'Wishing you a real *American* Christmas'. But protest as they will, they remain essentially a concourse of immigrants and are unable, in the main, to cut the atavistic bonds which bind them to the lands of their origin. While it is true that the memory of the War of Independence is enshrined in the hearts of all Americans –

particularly, perhaps, in the hearts of those whose ancestors had no part in it – there is little evidence of a common emotional rebellion against the European mainland. Indeed, among the ancestral nations, Great Britain alone is unrepresented by a solid bloc of voters with which to influence American policy, both foreign and domestic. There is no recognized British vote in the United States. But the Italian vote, the Polish vote, the Irish vote, the German vote, the Lithuanian vote – all these and more besides have to be carefully considered and wooed by candidates at election time.

For while there is no real national unity, there is considerable group unity, and the fact that the United States abounds with clubs, societies, associations and the like is doubtless expressive both of the desire which Americans have to speak with one voice and of their inability to do so. All the various political pressure groups, however conflicting their views and interests, alike wrap themselves in the *Stars and Stripes*. The ungainly word Americanism enjoys universal popularity, but it is excessively overworked and defies definition. So, too does its opposite, the still more ungainly un-Americanism. Bilbo, the Jew-baiting, Negro-baiting Senator, is considered guilty of un-Americanism by his liberal opponents and he accuses them of the same offence in turn. It is un-American to favour racial discrimination, it is un-American not to favour racial discrimination. It is un-American to be pro-Soviet, it is un-American to be anti-Soviet. Before the United States entered the war it was un-American to help Britain, and it was un-American not to help Britain. By the same token true Americanism meant isolationism. It also meant interventionism.

The attack on Pearl Harbor admittedly harnessed the peoples of the United States to a common purpose, and deep-rooted divergent prejudices were largely put aside, though not forgotten. But before then the country was a playground for spreading discord. No political cause, good or bad, sensible or extravagant, practical or absurd, needed to go begging for a society to sponsor it in the name of Americanism.

(a) Stimulating Pro-British Groups

It was in the critical days of 1940–41, when Britain was on the ropes and needed every kind of assistance from the United States which was still neutral, that the enemy redoubled his efforts to swing American public opinion against Britain.

'He conducted a widespread and efficiently run campaign,

which resulted in isolationist anti-British propaganda splashed over the front pages of the newspapers, shouted at mass meetings, disseminated through special societies and proclaimed in the Senate and in the House of Representatives. The majority of Americans believed that a considerable number of their fellow countrymen were giving vent to their natural feelings and inbred desires. They did not know that the German propaganda machine was at work in their midst.

Paralleling the tactics used by the NSDAP in Germany, the pro-Nazi forces within the United States formed 'patriotic societies' devoted ostensibly to serving the interests of 'Americanism'. There were a great many such organizations ranging all the way from ridiculous little imitations of Fascism like William Dudley Pelley's 'Silver Shirts' to wealthy and powerful organizations such as the America First Committee. The dozens of interlocking isolationist organizations held mass meetings, issued pamphlets and periodical news-sheets, trained street-corner speakers and organized 'educational' meetings under the auspices of existing clubs. Quickly their effectiveness grew, so that by early 1941 the temper of the people all over the country became difficult to assess. It gave the impression of being unstable and dangerous.

In Detroit, Lord Halifax was hit with eggs and ripe tomatoes which were thrown with unusual accuracy by some isolationist women. The Ambassador said: 'We do not have any such surplus in England.' A Senator told 3,000 people in Brooklyn that 'It is not freedom of the seas that England wants, but domination . . .' A Congressman shouted at a large audience: 'the present war was brought upon the Third Reich by England and France'. Many other remarks of the same irresponsible kind were being made by prominent people. The Germans were doing well in the United States.

The situation was becoming serious, for, in contrast to the success of enemy propaganda, British efforts were feeble and ineffective. In April 1941, BSC began to investigate. It was noticed that during and immediately after the Battle of Britain, and even after the sinking of the *Graf Spee*, there had been a sudden growth of sentiment in favour of Britain. However, adequate measures had not been taken to exploit the propaganda advantages of such victories, whereas the German propaganda forces invariably put every opportunity that came their way to fullest use, rallying to the attack whenever a new occasion offered. The news agencies, Transocean and DNB, were always first with the headlines and they would counteract whatever German reverses there were to report in other spheres. Accordingly, WS obtained reports on the situation from Donovan, who was in close touch with the President, discussed the matter with American public opinion experts and, towards the end of April 1941, sent the following two telegrams to CSS in the hope that influence might be brought to bear in the appropriate quarter to remedy the situation:

> Close examination of US press during past fortnight indicates almost complete failure prevent Axis monopoly of war news coverage . . . most journals . . . carry preponderance of Axis news . . . photographs . . . few if any British photographs appear . . .
>
> . . . Axis news reports reach here more quickly than ours . . . rapidly followed by copious flow of descriptive material photographs and films . . . Transocean and DNB keep up flow and build up stories even in quiet periods . . . invariably beat our news to headlines . . . We fail counteract major stories such as Greek withdrawal by good presentation of other stories such as Ethiopian success . . . US newsmen here say Germans show far better sense of news and timing . . . infinitely better understanding US psychology . . .

These warnings went unheeded, and accordingly WS decided to take action on his own initiative. He instructed the recently created SOE Division to declare a covert war against the mass of American groups which were organized throughout the country to spread isolationism and anti-British feeling. In the BSC office plans were drawn up and agents were instructed to put them into effect. It was agreed to seek out all existing pro-British interventionist organizations, to subsidize them where necessary and to assist them in every way possible. It was counter-propaganda in the strictest sense of the word. After many rapid conferences the agents went out into the field and began their work. Soon they were taking part in the activities of a great number of interventionist organizations, and were giving to many of them which had begun to flag and to lose interest in their purpose, new vitality and a new lease of life. The following is a list of some of the larger ones:

1. *The Non-Sectarian Anti-Nazi League to Champion Human Rights*. This society organized boycotts of all firms dealing in German goods, published exposures of Germans and

pro-German Americans in the USA, picketed isolationist meetings and issued a periodical bulletin on Nazi activities in America. As an example of its work, at an America First rally featuring Lindbergh as speaker, the Non-Sectarian Anti-Nazi League distributed leaflets showing Lindbergh in amicable conversation with the be-medalled Erhard Milch of the Luftwaffe.

2. *The League of Human Rights, Freedom and Democracy*. This was a committee aimed at winning the support of organized labour. It had branches in over 200 cities. Its honorary president was William Green, head of the American Federation of Labor; its president, Matthew Woll, vice-president of the American Federation of Labor; and its vice-president, David Dubinsky of the International Ladies' Garment Workers Union. Its theme was that American labour owed it to itself to assist British labour in the fight against Hitler. One of its best achievements was the distribution of a pamphlet contrasting Nazi statements of principle with those of distinguished Americans, under the title of 'Their Aims – Our Aims'. Sample copies of this were sent to 4,800 branch offices of AFL unions, with such success that over 8,000,000 were eventually distributed in the United States alone and 2,000,000 more in Latin America. In addition, it sent selected news items to 400 labour papers and magazines every week.

3. *The American Labor Committee to Aid British Labor* was another affiliate of the American Federation of Labor, also under the chairmanship of Matthew Woll. It held mass meetings, sponsored radio broadcasts and distributed 'Aid British Labor' buttons, 'Help Smash Dictators' circulars, posters, etc. These two committees were particularly useful in the period when much of organized labour was still anti-British because it followed, or was attracted to, pro-Soviet isolationists. It was impossible to do anything with large segments of the Congress of Industrial Organizations before June 1941, but its powerful rival, the American Federation of Labor, was thus induced to side with the British.

4. *The Ring of Freedom*, an association led by the publicist Dorothy Thompson, the *Council for Democracy;* the *American Defenders of Freedom*, and other such societies were formed and supported to hold anti-isolationist meetings which branded all isolationists as Nazi-lovers.

5. *The Free World Association*, which had on its committee the

Spanish Republican politician Julio Alvarez del Vayo, the Uruguayan anti-Nazi propagandist Hugo Fernandez Artucío, the Socialist Louis Dolivet, and other distinguished liberals with whom BSC was closely in touch. Founded in June–July 1941, it functioned in the United States mainly through liberal meetings and articles in liberal weeklies, but had more influence in Latin America, which will be described in the proper place. It also sponsored broadcasts to Europe. In conjunction with the 'Committee to Defend America by Aiding the Allies' and the societies described under (1) and (2) above, it held over a hundred 'Stop Mass Murders' meetings throughout the USA in November 1941 against the shooting of French hostages by the Germans. There were 750 speakers, the estimated attendance was 350,000, and 20,000 newspapers carried announcements or reports of the proceedings.
6. *The Civilian Defence and Information Bureau*, which sent 85,000 copies of an article on the British Empire by Sir Norman Angell, reprinted in pamphlet form, to the American Legion, the Veterans of Foreign Wars, local chairmen of the 'Committee to Defend America', doctors, lawyers, and educators through the USA.
7. Many anti-Nazi groups were organized among the foreign-language minorities in the United States. These communities had been penetrated by German or Italian propagandists.

Obviously the part BSC played in stimulating and encouraging these and many other similar societies throughout the United States had to be carefully concealed. All financing and all contacts were managed through reliable cut-outs so that the fact that Britain was greatly responsible for what appeared to be a new surge of honest American opinion was never revealed.

(b) America First

There was one isolationist society which was so large and so powerful that BSC decided to give it special attention. The America First Committee embraced peoples of all creeds in all places in the United States. Among its members there was Charles Lindbergh, who was then still a national hero. There were Colonel Robert McCormick and his powerful *Chicago Tribune*, Father Coughlin and Father Curran who brought with them the Catholics and the Irishmen, and such men as Henry Ford, General

Robert E. Wood of the huge Sears-Roebuck merchandising firm and many other anti-Roosevelt industrialists who provided sound financial support. Some of the greatest publicity experts in the US, such as Bruce Barton and Chester Bowles, were also members.

America First did not start as a pro-German association. It was founded in Chicago in October 1940 and was designed to compete with the pro-British societies such as William Allen White's Committee to Defend America by Aiding the Allies. Full-page advertisements appeared in newspapers throughout the country. Large-scale propaganda was conducted and the aims and ideals of America First were made known in every town in every state. The propaganda was clever and was calculated to obtain the support of the greatest possible number of groups and cliques. It appealed to pacifists, haters of Roosevelt, haters of Great Britain, anti-Communists, anti-Semites, admirers of Germany, American imperialists, devotees of big business, and to those who hated Europe, who regarded that continent as a corrupt and backward region which stood for all the things from which the Pilgrim Fathers and their successors had fled.

Through the winter of 1940 America First grew monstrously. By the spring of 1941, it was extending itself into a nation-wide movement, founding 'chapters' in all the principal cities and in many universities, building up a huge mailing list for its propaganda, bringing in sympathizers from other isolationist and anti-British societies, holding mass meetings, training street-corner speakers; 'lobbying' in Washington, spreading directions for exercising pressure on Congress, passing out handbills, postcards and pamphlets libelling Britain and the President, funnelling its ideas into foreign-language groups and from time to time picketing the British Embassy, Consulates and other British Missions. By the late spring of 1941, it had 700 'chapters' and nearly 1,000,000 members (with Charles Lindbergh emerging as its leader). The principal call on its energies was a campaign directed against the passing of the Lend-Lease Act and against the proposal for convoying ships across the Atlantic.

In the summer of 1941, the Russo-German treaty was broken, which meant that America First lost nearly all its left-wing support. But the society was so vast that this had no effect upon its continued existence. The Germans had been quick to realize its worth. Many of them had infiltrated into its ranks. As a result, it became more and more openly anti-British and pro-German, while at the same time it lost its original wholly American appearance. Many of its more skilful speakers coupled together the

Campaign against Axis Propaganda

names of Hitler and Churchill or Hitler and Stalin as competitors for European domination. Audiences booed the names of Churchill and Stalin, but remained silent when Hitler was mentioned. Day by day, week by week, the abuse which speech-makers poured upon the British Empire grew more violent and vitriolic. Only a few months before Pearl Harbor Lindbergh publicly intimated that there were only three groups which wanted America to enter the war: the British, the Jews and the Roosevelt Administration. The hysterical blend of hatred and exaltation with which this message was greeted was frighteningly reminiscent of a *Parteitag* in Nuremberg.

From its very beginning WS perceived the potential menace of the America First Committee. As the speed of its growth was observed, agents were despatched to each part of the country to attend its meetings, to keep track of its new members and to ponder upon new and effective ways of instigating counter-propaganda. One agent befriended the woman who was the head of the society's lecture bureau in New York and procured from her a mass of information about its propaganda themes, its financing and its backers, particularly about its German backers, the official ones such as Ulrich von Gienanth of the German Embassy, and the private ones such as Gunther Hansen-Sturm. Another agent, an expert on Japan, investigated the society's dangerous Far Eastern Committee, and in the offices of BSC these findings and many more were collected and pieced together. The disposition of the enemy's forces was thus obtained so that plans could be made for the forthcoming battle.

The counter-offensive was developed along three different lines. First, arrangements were made for a press exposure of the society's close ties with German activities. Secondly, various pro-British American groups were approached and counter-attacks were planned through them. Thirdly, efforts were made to prove that the society was concerned with illegal, treasonous activities. All three of these lines of counter-offensive were successfully pressed home, the while BSC remained in the background, drawing up new plans of battle and giving directions for carrying them out.

For the press exposure, BSC agents collected quantities of material, which was a straightforward intelligence job. Copies were obtained of cheques made out to Congressmen – as, for example, a cheque to Hamilton Fish from G. Hansen-Sturm, the Nazi propagandist. Many stories were written up regarding the evil pro-German habits and sympathies of particular personalities.

The pro-German attitude of the whole society was analysed in carefully prepared essays. All this and much more was handed out by devious means to the great impartial newspapers of the country, and throughout the summer and autumn of 1941 the press featured newsworthy and damaging information about the pro-German society which was a cancer within the nation. Personalities were discredited, their unsavoury pasts were dug up, their utterances were printed and reprinted. Those who read what was written (and they were many) could not but realize that something was wrong. Little by little a sense of guilt crept through the cities and out across the states. The campaign took hold.

The second line of counter-offensive, that of assisting and subsidizing pro-British societies, has been mentioned in the previous section. Nevertheless, because America First was a particularly serious menace, BSC decided to take more direct action. Its agents persuaded one or more of these pro-British societies to cover each important America First meeting and do all that they could to disrupt it and discredit the speakers. When Senator Nye spoke in Boston in September 1941, Fight for Freedom passed out 25,000 handbills attacking him as an appeaser and as a Nazi-lover, inserted a large advertisement in the local newspapers to the same purpose and procured counter-statements answering his speech. Its representatives also called up every radio station in the area asking for time to answer any broadcast that he might make, with the result that the stations in question decided not to give him any facilities.

When Representative Hamilton Fish made a speech at an America First rally in Milwaukee, Fight for Freedom was there too, and just before Fish concluded his inspiring oration, someone handed him a card on which was written 'Der Fuehrer thanks you for your loyalty'. Photographers took a picture of the scene, and the picture, with the contents of Hitler's note upon the caption, made good copy for the newspapers. At the same meeting members of the American Legion acted as pickets outside the hall and numbers of girls inside the auditorium distributed Fight for Freedom literature.

Those are just two examples. Such activities by BSC agents and cooperating pro-British committees were frequent, and on many occasions America First was harassed and heckled and embarrassed. Only once did a plan miscarry, and that was at the Madison Square Garden on 30 October 1941, when Lindbergh was to address a huge rally. It happened then that BSC agents caused duplicate tickets for the meeting to be printed. These were passed out free to members of the friendly societies. The plan was for some of the holders of these illicit tickets to go early and be seated before the legitimate ticket holders arrived, and for others to arrive late and start trouble by demanding loudly the accommodation to which their tickets ostensibly entitled them. It seemed that there was a good possibility of disrupting the whole meeting. But unluckily – for some unexplained reason – there was a very small audience that night. The duplication of tickets was soon noticed and the ushers merely showed all the would-be protestors to many of the hundreds of vacant seats available. There was no trouble. America First merely had a bigger audience than would have been the case without BSC's benevolent intervention.

The third line of counter-offensive, the attempt to prove that America First was concerned with illegal, treasonous activities, is best illustrated by the campaign that developed into what has since come to be known as 'The Congressional Franking Case'. It will be treated separately in the next sub-section because it is a story in itself.

BSC's campaign against America First throughout 1941 did not bring about the complete disintegration of the society, but success was had in reducing considerably its usefulness to the Germans at a very critical time, and the way was paved for the great disrepute into which it eventually fell. It happened that Senator Nye was delivering an address to one of the society's larger meetings when the chairman suddenly announced that the Japanese had attacked the American fleet at Pearl Harbor. Without hesitating Nye remarked: 'It is just what the British planned for us.' But a few days after the United States entered the war, America First was virtually no more than an evil memory.

(c) The Congressional Franking Case

For this campaign, the cooperation of an American friend was enlisted. He worked on his own, in his own time and with his own money, while BSC provided him with information, guidance and extra funds. By profession he was a 'direct mail advertising specialist'. His clients consisted of those commercial companies who wished to be told about new and better methods of advertising by mail.

In the early days of the war, he noticed that German propaganda was being distributed throughout the United States with a degree of skill and economy unequalled by advertising experts such as himself. He began to investigate, and what he found intrigued him greatly. He found that privileges were being abused, if indeed the law was not being broken, as seemed probable. Because he was in the business himself it was to his own advantage to oppose such abuses, but when he discovered further that he was on the trail of a carefully planned system for subjecting the American people to a powerful and skilful campaign of German mass progaganda, the purpose of his investigation transcended his self interest and took on the quality of a one-man crusade.

He traced the most obvious distributors of enemy propaganda such as the German Railroad Bureau. From there he went on to investigate a more subtle method of dissemination, which appeared to involve the dignity of the United States legislature. It is a long-standing privilege of Senators and Representatives to send letters without paying postage, using envelopes which are 'franked' with the signature of the sender. This privilege is constantly and legally used by the Senators and Representatives to distribute to their constituents copies of their own speeches, of articles, poems or anything else which they think should be read. It is, however, illegal to employ the 'frank' for the benefit of clubs or societies, and this is where BSC's friend found a weakness. He noticed that certain Congressmen were using the 'frank' for distributing free through the mails not only their own isolationist speeches but others which had often been specially written by Nazi hacks. Moreover, this material was being sent not only to the Congressmen's own constituents but to people throughout the United States. It almost seemed as if Congress was being converted into a distributing house for German propaganda.

More thorough investigation by BSC revealed that isolationist speeches were going to all persons on the mailing list of the German Library of Information in New York. BSC agents checked this fact by arranging that certain names and addresses should be inserted into the Library's list. Very soon the same names began to appear on 'franked' isolationist mail from United States Congressmen, posted not only in New York but in Washington and elsewhere.

Next the envelopes were compared, and it was found that anyone on the German Library's list would receive 'franked' envelopes – (all were addressed in the same handwriting) – from numerous different Senators or Representatives. In one month an American of German descent in New York received 'franked' mail from the anti-British Representative Holt and from the isolationist Senators Nye, Tinkham, Thorkelson and Wheeler.

All were addressed in identical handwriting and all were posted in New York, although the Representative and the Senators concerned came from such widely separated states as Montana, Massachusetts and West Virginia. It seemed certain there was one single centre of distribution.

Upon investigation of a number of other New York envelopes 'franked' by the notorious Senator Wheeler, it was found that the addresses were stencilled in a peculiar blue ink by a distinctive type of addressing machine. Further investigation proved that the machine was an out-of-date Elliott, of which there were only three in New York. BSC's agents ascertained that one of these three machines was the property of the Steuben Society, a German 'cultural' organization. The next step was to obtain samples of confidential bulletins distributed by this Society. The samples were examined and found to have been stencilled on a similar machine, in the same peculiar blue ink and in the same distinctive style. The address plate bore the same code-number as the one that had been used for Wheeler's envelopes. The bulletins themselves urged members to attend certain meetings of the Steuben Society, at which reprints of speeches by Wheeler would be available in 'franked' envelopes to be mailed to their friends.

In May 1941, the campaign was begun. BSC's friend – the direct mail specialist – published an open letter to Senator Wheeler accusing him of misusing the privilege of the Congressional 'frank', with citations of all this evidence and more. It appeared throughout the United States in newspapers and magazines, while 100,000 reprints were distributed through firms and organizations. Wheeler protested in the Senate, but his reply was evasive and utterly inconclusive, and in the course of it he admitted incidentally that America First had purchased a million of his 'franked' postcards. The immediate result was that the Steuben Society was fined for violation of the postal regulations. Wheeler himself lost considerable prestige.

Although in June 1941 all German consulates and agencies in the USA were closed by Presidential Executive Order, the abuse of the Congressional 'frank' still continued. The volume of direct mail pro-Nazi advertising appeared to increase. BSC agents now concentrated on Washington, where the distribution was evidently centred. The investigation led them to an insignificant bureaucrat called George Hill. His method was as follows:

First, he compiled lists of persons interested in isolationist propaganda. He did this by befriending the secretaries of various isolationist Congressmen and persuading them to hand him all the letters expressing isolationist sentiment which were sent to their employers. From these letters he had lists and card-indexes typed out by a considerable staff of stenographers. He sold these lists to isolationist and crypto-German societies.

George Hill was secretary to the arch-isolationist Representative Hamilton Fish. He also happened to be the Washington Commander of the Order of the Purple Heart, the American wounded ex-servicemen's organization. Both these positions enabled him to arrange for the insertion of isolationist propaganda in the Congressional Record. Such stuff need not be read out in Congress. It is necessary only for the Congressman to rise, obtain the formal permission of the House to insert his own introductory remarks and a document of any length in the Record, and then hand the whole to the Government Printer. Hill had no difficulty in getting his material inserted. If straightforward methods failed, which they seldom did because he was careful to approach only isolationist Senators and Representatives, then he fell back upon the Order of the Purple Heart. He would tell the secretaries of Congressmen that the Order of the Purple Heart wished their employer to have such and such a speech printed in the Congressional Record. The desires of such a respected veterans' organization were naturally never questioned.

Hill's purpose in getting this material in the Record was in order to obtain reprints of it from the Government Printer for distribution. Through Congressmen's secretaries, he got certain Congressmen to sign an order to the Government Printer for the required number of reprints, stating usually that the request came from the Order of the Purple Heart. He paid the secretaries the government price for the printing, which was about a third of the retail price. He sold the reprints to America First or to other organizations at the regular retail price and kept the difference himself.

This much was revealed to BSC agents. Then by the exertion of pressure in certain quarters, a Federal Grand Jury investigation of German propaganda was arranged. During the investigation, an anti-British propagandist called Prescott Dennett was subpoenaed for misusing 'franked' envelopes put out by his anti-British Islands for War Debts Committee. Dennett was working with Hill. The threat of investigation frightened him into telephoning Hill and asking him to remove to a place of safety some bags of 'franked' mail which he, Dennett, had in his possession. Hill ordered a government lorry to pick up the bags and deliver them to a storeroom in Congress used by Hamilton Fish. The lorry picked them up, but by mistake it delivered them to Fish's office. Fish's girl secretary became flustered. She kept some of them and sent twelve others over to the office of America First. All these moves were being watched by BSC agents, and at this point it was suggested that the Federal authorities should raid the America First office.

The raid was made, and the bags were found. The girl secretary was subpoenaed and all the evidence was turned over to the Federal Prosecutor. Further evidence was provided by a reporter who stole two dustbins full of ashes from the headquarters of several isolationist committees, searched the ashes and found legible fragments of 'franked' envelopes of the same type. Hill was brought to give evidence before the Federal Grand Jury investigating German propaganda. During his evidence, he stated on oath that he had not given orders to hide these mail bags. He was prosecuted for perjury and sentenced to a term of two to six years' imprisonment.

Congressman Hamilton Fish himself came under fire. He was invited to testify before the Grand Jury, and, when he did not respond, was subpoenaed. He tried to get the House of Representatives to grant him immunity from questioning, but failed. He was saved by the peculiar laxity of the American legal system. He rejoined the army in great haste and entered the decent obscurity of a training camp, from which he did not emerge until the affair had subsided.

However, in these troubled waters a bigger fish had been caught: George Sylvester Viereck, who had been Hill's paymaster. Viereck was a naturalized American citizen. He was a poet and writer. He had done propaganda work for Germany in the last war. He was a passionate admirer of the Hohenzollerns, claiming incidentally that he himself was a Hohenzollern bastard. BSC agents watched him carefully from the beginning. One of them knew him personally and spent much time with him and his friends. The Bermuda censors regularly picked up copies of his weekly reports to the propagandist Wirsing in Munich. All findings were passed by WS to the FBI and also to General Donovan for the Attorney-General.

The result was that in October 1941 Viereck was arrested for failing to give sufficient information when he registered as a foreign agent. In January 1942, he was tried. Hill, who had already been convicted, was brought out of gaol to give evidence and received a remission of sentence therefor. Hill said he had been introduced to Viereck by Hamilton Fish in July 1940 and had received money from him. A censor from Bermuda testified that she had intercepted an envelope from Viereck containing the manuscript of a book by Congressman Rush Holt, addressed to the German Ambassador in Lisbon. Much other evidence was forthcoming and Viereck was convicted. He appealed and was re-tried with the same result. He appealed again but without success, and was sentenced to one to five years with heavy fines. The Special Assistant to the United States Attorney-General wrote to BSC saying: '. . . I want to express the thanks of the Department to British Security Coordination for the assistance which you have rendered in the Viereck case . . . We have found our association with you personally most pleasant and hope that we shall continue to keep in touch . . .'

In December 1942, when Viereck was already in gaol, he was charged, together with twenty-seven other defendants, including many of the most violent anti-British isolationists, such as Ralph Townsend and Elizabeth Dilling, with seditious conspiracy. The trial which resulted was the biggest sedition case in the history of the United States. After careful consideration, the Assistant Director of Censorship determined that evidence obtained by British Censorship must not be introduced at the trial, because it would be likely to implicate a number of distinguished Congressmen and national figures.

Senator Wheeler and others succeeded in effecting the removal from the case of Federal Prosecutor Maloney, with whom BSC had worked in closest cooperation since the beginning of the investigation of Nazi propaganda; and due largely to the obstructive tactics of the defence the trial dragged on and on, and was apparently far from approaching its end when it was halted by the death of the presiding judge. However, at present writing a new trial is scheduled. Meanwhile Viereck remains in gaol.

The investigations and the events leading up to the exposure of Viereck and Fish and Hill have been set down in a book. Three thousand copies of it were bought and distributed by Fish's opponents in his Congressional District before the elections of November 1944. Fish was not re-elected. He attributed his defeat to Reds and Communists. He might – with more accuracy – have blamed BSC.

(d) Working with American Labour

Working through organizations like the American Labor Committee to Aid British Labor and the Fight for Freedom Committee (both briefly described in a previous section), BSC campaigned to enlist the sympathy of the mass of American workers in favour of intervention. Through the former, contact was established with William Green, head of the American Federation of Labor, and with his chief lieutenant, Matthew Woll.

In March 1941, the American Labor Committee to Aid British Labor held a mass meeting at which Governor Herbert H. Lehman of New York was the principal speaker. President Roosevelt and Mayor LaGuardia were among those who sent messages urging support for the movement. Before mid-summer, other mass meetings had been held, talks over the air had been broadcast by officers of the Committee, and a series of 'Reports to the Unions' had been mailed to union members throughout the nation.

It is worth emphasizing once more that British connection with the societies controlled by BSC was never suspected. British subjects did not belong to them, and British subjects were never employed as intermediaries. Even the American authorities had no reason to believe that the societies were anything but 100 per cent American, and the fact that President Roosevelt himself sponsored a drive for the American Labor Committee to Aid British Labor, which aimed at raising $5,000,000 for the United Nations war relief, offers eloquent proof of this.

The American working class, compared with its counterpart in Great Britain, was found to be uninformed and politically disorganized. Many of the workers came from the uneducated foreign-born population, which, having no political tradition (and often a good deal of language difficulty), was confused and easily swayed by mass emotional appeals of the crudest character. Of the two great unions (the American Federation of Labor, or AFL, and the Congress of Industrial Organizations, or CIO), the AFL, generally representing the right wing, supported Roosevelt and all-out aid to Britain. The CIO, on the other hand, included some locals which were Communist-dominated, and therefore isolationist, in the days before Germany invaded Russia.

CIO's official attitude was even less friendly than the individual views of its members may have warranted, for it was under the dictatorial control of John L. Lewis, of the United Mine Workers, who was violently isolationist and nursed a personal hatred of President Roosevelt and a hardly less virulent loathing of the British. His daughter – also prominent in CIO affairs – was very active on the America First Committee. As the majority of the unions in the vital defence industries were affiliated with the CIO, Lewis's prejudices were a menace to Britain.

In 1941, after Germany invaded Russia, BSC decided to attack John L. Lewis from two angles – through the Communists and through his rivals in the CIO. The Communists were in a delicate position, for they could not afford to sever their connection with Lewis while he controlled the union's funds. Also, they had not yet adopted an official 'line' to cover the new international situation. One of BSC's contacts suggested to the Soviet Embassy that Moscow should bring pressure to bear on the American Communists. Needless to say, Constantine Oumansky, who was the Soviet Ambassador to the USA at that time, rebuked his visitor for suggesting that the Soviet Union would interfere in the domestic affairs of the United States. It seems not unlikely, however, that he reported the suggestion to Moscow.

BSC then requested London to arrange for official enquiries to be made in Moscow regarding the extent of Russia's control over the CIO and her policy towards Lewis. The Russians declared bluntly that they had no influence over the American Communist Party and that they considered the whole US labour movement 'a racket run by racketeers'.

But despite protestations to the contrary, the Russians not only could but apparently did intervene. Shortly afterwards one of BSC's informants reported:

> The isolationist faction of the Communist Party has been bludgeoned into line by the Party Executive, like a circus trainer rapping lions on the nose until they climb down one by one. This belated flip-flop was the most painful for those leaders who . . . had always denied publicly that they were Party members . . .

BSC discovered that there were a great many people in the CIO who would oppose Lewis's policies if given adequate moral support. Among these were the Amalgamated Clothing Workers, under Sidney Hillman, and individuals like R. J. Thomas, head of the United Automobile Workers. Philip Murray, who became national president of the CIO after Lewis and his United Mine Workers had seceded from the large, heterogeneous union, was also an interventionist at heart, although he was not forceful enough to oppose Lewis so long as the latter remained 'boss' of the CIO.

In November 1941, the CIO National Convention in Detroit offered BSC a dramatic opportunity to attack the union's isolationist façade. Lewis had arranged that the convention should coincide with a miners' strike, which was essentially a gesture of defiance directed against the President. There was grave danger that the Union's anti-Roosevelt bias, fostered by the pressure which isolationist organizations were exerting on it, might stampede the convention into adopting isolationist resolutions which would have long-lasting and possibly disastrous results.

BSC attacked under cover of the Fight for Freedom Committee. Agents were despatched to Detroit, where they contacted Philip Murray, Sidney Hillman and others who had long opposed Lewis and were sympathetic to Britain and intervention. The campaign conducted by BSC's agents successfully countered the rise of isolationist sentiment among delegates and brought about a positive trend in the other direction. The following tactics were used:

1. Fight for Freedom conducted a public opinion poll of the delegates on questions relating to intervention in the war. Great care was taken beforehand to make certain that the poll results would turn out as desired and that they would be given the fullest possible publicity. The questions asked were designed to be 'educational', a euphemism in this case for tendentious; they were worded in such a way as to steer the delegate's opinion towards support of Britain and the war. One precaution was to try out the questionnaire in advance on a dozen of the most influential delegates, asking them for suggestions as to how it might be improved. The fact that they had been consulted gave the CIO leaders a vested interest in the poll, and in consequence they took it upon themselves to see that it was given full publicity in the local and labour papers.

   The announcement of the results, which was made immediately, was of course intended to impress the delegates when they were being interviewed. The published results showed that:

   96% thought that defeating Hitler was more important than keeping the USA out of war.

   95% said they would advocate defending the Philippines and keeping the Japanese out of British and Dutch possessions in the Far East.

   90% said they would fight at once, if it seemed certain that Hitler would defeat Britain.

   87% supported Fight for Freedom as against America First.

Lindbergh was voted US Fascist Number One, and Wheeler Number Two.
2. A resolution was then presented to the convention, and passed almost unanimously, expressing full support of the President's foreign policy.
3. BSC agents met most of the union leaders and explained to them the purpose of Fight for Freedom and of the poll. They contacted nearly all the reporters in order to secure maximum publicity in local and labour newspapers.
4. Quantities of literature were disseminated to the delegates, to 'alternates' and to spectators in the gallery. The material included:

25,000 copies of *Hitler – Wanted for Murder*; 2,000 copies of *Fight for Freedom: Labor News*; 2,000 copies of *Labor Union* advertisements, showing a Nazi soldier driving workers with a whip; 2,000 *Smash Hitler* buttons; numerous copies of a pamphlet showing Lindbergh receiving a Nazi decoration, postcards – expressing interventionist sentiment – to mail home, ribbons, posters and pledge cards. The hall and the staircase were covered with posters especially designed for the Convention.

The campaign was particularly appreciated by some representatives of the Roosevelt Administration, who attended the convention as observers. It resulted in a definite advance which pointed the way to further action of the same kind. Plans were made which, had time allowed, would have resulted in the formation of a body similar to the CIO Political Action Committee, which came into being some years later and played a conspicuous part in the 1944 Presidential election. BSC would have used such a body to urge intervention through lecture tours, distribution of literature, public debates, broadcasts and closer communication with British unions. Before the plan matured it was rendered unnecessary by the outbreak of the Pacific War.

(e) Organizing the Irish

Despite the policy of the Eire Government, the Irish in America were anything but neutral. Some, in fact, were militantly anti-British, instinctively hating 'the oppressors who had driven their fathers from home'. Fear of Communism, and to some extent opposition to Protestantism, also affected adversely the attitude of many Irish-Americans towards a war in which America was a potential ally of Communist Russia and Protestant England. And further, those who considered themselves more American than Irish were hostile to the former rulers of the American colonies.

The isolationists were quick to recognize the Irish-Americans as a potential source of recruits, money and moral support. 1939 and 1940 saw a revival of interest in and new financial prosperity for the numerous Irish-American societies, many of which had become severely impoverished. For example, after the old 'rebel' newspaper, the *Gaelic American*, had announced its own impending death, it was provided with help from outside of such a kind that it became violently anti-Roosevelt, isolationist and quasi-Fascist.

Organizations like the American-Irish Historical Society and the Ancient Order of Hibernians were anti-British, anti-Russian and anti-interventionist, and became increasingly so. In 1940, a man named Michael McGlynn formed a new organization – the American Friends of Irish Neutrality – to unify the efforts of the Irish-American isolationists. It was allied with America First; and it had to be fought, as America First was fought.

After the usual preliminary steps had been taken in the way of collecting intelligence, BSC sponsored an Irish interventionist society in the autumn of 1941. Contact with it was maintained by a good cut-out, a man who followed directives from the BSC office and kept BSC posted on every move made. In return, BSC financed the society (after a few months it was self-supporting) and supplied it with propaganda material, much of which was culled from intercepted letters from Eire.

The society was named the American Irish Defence Association. It was run – so far as the public was concerned – by prominent Irish-Americans, few of whom had previously been identified with aid to Britain. They kept themselves clear of Eire-British political differences and emphasized that these were less important than beating Hitler. They concerned themselves with the question of Irish defence bases for America and publicized the disastrous effects 'neutrality' would have on the economy of Eire. They set up committees in New York, Washington, Boston and Chicago, and they began to cooperate with such other 'American' organizations as the Committee to Defend America by Aiding the Allies and the Fight for Freedom Committee. A lecture bureau and a literature committee were set up, and booklets on Irish-American affairs were prepared.

The American Irish Defence Association was launched by a six weeks' publicity drive, which included broadcasts, news releases, dinners, mass meetings, street corner meetings and personal appearances of film stars and other Irish celebrities. 'National roll call' leaflets were issued, pledging the signatories to support of the President's foreign policy. The association organized a revival of memories of the 'Fighting 69th', an Armistice Day ceremony at the monument of the famous Irish chaplain, Father Duffy, and the presentation of a shillelagh to Mayor LaGuardia.

Extensive public opinion polls were conducted among members of the American Legion, the Veterans of Foreign Wars, the Freedom for Ireland organizations of the First World War and among Catholic organizations of all kinds. In Boston, trade union leaders were approached personally, and many who were far from pro-British were nonetheless impressed by the Committee's list of sponsors, were convinced that unity was necessary between the United States and Ireland, and were thus persuaded to cooperate.

In September 1941, Senator Francis MacDermot of Eire visited the USA, and the Association organized wide publicity for him. He made pro-British and interventionist speeches, attended a great many social gatherings and broadcast over a nationwide radio network. Shortly afterwards, the Association made a public appeal to President Roosevelt to negotiate for the establishment of bases in Ireland. In October, it issued, through the American Council on Public Affairs, a pamphlet called *The Case for American-Irish Unity*, which was distributed to local libraries, chapters of the Daughters of the American Revolution, American Legion posts – and to Catholic leaders and Senators, Congressmen and Government officials in Washington. When Edward J. Flynn, one of the most powerful of the Democratic Party leaders in the whole of the USA, joined the Association, it was able not only to ask but to demand the active support of many politicians and office holders who counted on his patronage.

The Association drew fire from the most powerful opposition groups. It was attacked by the United Irish Societies – with results in publicity which won for it many new members.

On 10 November 1941, Burton K. Wheeler spoke in the Senate.

'Where', he demanded, 'did this committee originate?', and, answering his own question, 'It originated in the office of Colonel Donovan, in the office of the Coordinator of Information of the United States Government. Perhaps I should say it originated in New York, in the minds of gentlemen closely associated with the British Government, and was brought down here to

Washington and hatched out in the office of the Coordinator of Information of the United States Government . . . Of course, they (the committee members) do not have to assume financial responsibility, because the expenses are to be paid either by England or probably from funds provided by the Lend-Lease Act, or from money appropriated for the Coordinator, Colonel Donovan.'

It was true that Donovan, as a prominent Irish-American, had supported the movement from the first in a private capacity, but Wheeler's reference to the 'gentlemen closely associated with the British Government' was obviously a shot in the dark. Had he been in a position to name them – or the agency for which they worked – he would certainly not have refrained from so doing.

The American Irish Defence Association, already influential, was rapidly expanding at the time of Pearl Harbor. It issued a public statement then appealing to the fighting spirit of the Irish-Americans to finish the war victoriously, and this did not go unheeded. BSC's connection with it was no longer necessary and was severed.

CHAPTER 3

Political Warfare against Japan

    (a) Primary Objective
    (b) Use of Anti-German Material
    (c) Organization of Publicity in the US
    (d) Channels to Japan
    (e) The Kasai Operation
    (f) Station KGEI
    (g) Secondary Objective
    (h) Assessment of Results

On 22 October 1941, HM Embassy in Tokyo reported to the Foreign Office as follows:

> Mr T. Suzuki, head of the European and American section of the Metropolitan Police, told a reliable informant on October 15th that the police are in disgrace with the Home Office for not having stopped the foreigner or foreigners responsible for the material on the German Fifth Column, which is pouring into Japan from all over the world. The Police are trying to find out who is responsible for this and have come to the conclusion that there must be a foreigner or foreigners collecting information systematically. Mr Suzuki pointed out a room in police headquarters where 10 men were working on this Fifth Column material, investigating post marks, etc., and endeavouring to work out the ramifications of the organization that was 'trying to break German-Japanese friendship.'

So far as is known, the investigators referred to in the above report never arrived at the correct answer to their problem. It is doubtful whether HM Ambassador could have enlightened them at the time, although he was convinced that the cause of their concern had 'proved to be one of the best pieces of propaganda work affecting Japan ever done'. The Foreign Office in London was equally mystified.

In fact, the organization responsible for the material on the German Fifth Column 'pouring into Japan from all over the world' was BSC and to 'break German-Japanese friendship' was the prime, though not the only, objective of its Far Eastern Political Warfare.

(a) Primary Objective

The story begins in August of 1940. At that time HM Ambassador in Tokyo telegraphed a 2,300-word summary of German subversive activities in Japan to HM Embassy in Washington, with a request that HM Embassy in Washington should covertly arrange for it to be published in the United States as a series of articles written by an American author and quoting American sources.

The summary had been drafted by H. V. Redman, MOI representative in Tokyo, and by an SIS agent operating in Japan under propaganda cover. The information it contained was not imaginary but authentic and capable of proof. For there was, indeed, a well-organized German Fifth Column plotting to drag Japan into the war to suit Germany's ends, and to make Japan as surely a German puppet as Italy. Further, its activities were evidently countenanced by the native Fascists – (the Militarists) – not, perhaps, because these men really intended, in the long run, to play the German game, but because the alliance with Germany was the keystone of their expansionist policy.

To this expansionist policy – involving, as it did, war against both Great Britain and the United States – the so-called moderates of the governing class were still showing semblance of opposition, being motivated by prudence if not by ideological conviction. But their position in the State was getting progressively weaker. Certainly they drew no strength from public opinion, for the Japanese people, living under a tyrannic rule of censorship, knew nothing of the realities of the situation – knew nothing of the true causes and dangers of the war towards which they were being guided, of the will and the power of the United States to resist aggression or of German machinations to betray them. So long as they remained politically unaware, their military masters could rely on their instinctive xenelasia, patriotic fervour and Emperor worship as guarantee that they would enter a struggle with the West cheerfully and even jubilantly.

Obviously, then, for the British to thwart the expansionist policy

Political Warfare for SO.1

– and thus to neutralize Japan – it was essential to strengthen the hand of the moderates through the political awakening of the Japanese people. That, it seemed certain, could best be achieved by a successful propaganda designed to turn the full force of Japanese xenelasia against the Germans and thus to smash the German alliance. For Germany, if not the dominating cause of the Militarist policy, was nonetheless indispensable to its execution.

For such a campaign the summary of German subversive activities provided potentially very damaging ammunition, for it indicated clearly enough a German conspiracy, which the Militarists were preparing to implement, to mislead the Emperor into a war that would be catastrophic for Japan, whatever its outcome.

However, in the hands of the British, it could not be effectively used in an overt way, since Britain was already at war with Germany and any attack on the Germans, apparently originating from a British source, would obviously be dismissed in Japan as mere propaganda and would thus largely defeat its own purpose. Therefore the suggestion had been made that it should be disguised as independent American reportage. The United States was still neutral, and American commentators still enjoyed a reputation for objectivity. Further, and very importantly, there could be no doubt that, in the final analysis, the attitude of the United States towards aggression generally would carry far more weight inside Japan, as a deterrent to the execution of the expansionist policy, than the attitude of Great Britain.

It happened that HM Embassy in Washington took no action, doubtless because it lacked the necessary machinery for so doing. But in May of the following year, BSC's Far Eastern Political Warfare Section was formed under the direction of the same SIS agent who had helped to draft the original summary and was now transferred to BSC's SO Division. He, of course, knew that the summary was in Washington and was well aware of its potential value. At his suggestion, therefore, it was obtained from HM Embassy's archives and put to use.

(b) Use of Anti-German Material

In fact, it formed the substance of BSC's attempt to break the German-Japanese alliance. The Japanese police were wrong in their assumption that the German Fifth Column material pouring into Japan could be traced to the activities of some foreigner (or foreigners) collecting information systematically. BSC had no

Political Warfare against Japan

agents inside Japan. It had, indeed, no direct communication with Tokyo – a disadvantage which, without doubt, made its task considerably harder. It worked closely with SO/Singapore, with which it was in regular communication, but was not furnished thereby with relevant, up-to-date material for its anti-German campaign. In the United States it had its own sources of intelligence, including direct contacts with the Japanese Embassy in Washington and with the Japanese Consulates in New York and San Francisco, but while these proved useful (in various ways to be mentioned later) they produced little if any new information on German subversive activities. In short, BSC's anti-German propaganda was largely based on material, which, by the time it had got back to Japan and had begun seriously to alarm the Japanese authorities, was more than a year old.

To maintain its disguise effectively and to eliminate the possibility of its being traced back to British sources, it had to be handled very sparingly and with extreme care. In other words, BSC could use it only when there was some genuine 'news peg' upon which to hang it and no danger of its real origin being disclosed. This put a severe limitation on operations, but if it had not been observed the whole campaign would have been rendered worthless.

(c) Organization of Publicity in the US

The material for anti-German propaganda, then, existed. It was neither as voluminous nor as recent as BSC would have liked; but it would serve. The next step was to find the means and the excuse for securing its publication as independent American reportage.

An opportunity occurred when Dr C.N. Spinks returned to the United States from Japan in May of 1941. He was an American citizen and a considerable Japanese expert, with ability both to read and speak the language and with exceptional inside knowledge of the country's political and economic conditions. Further, he was a trained journalist, having served as editor of the American-owned *Japan News Week* (the last independent English-language newspaper to be published in Japan). What he could report, therefore, at a time when the American public – or at least the American press – was becoming increasingly aware of the Japanese menace, was obviously and essentially news.

In the assurance that he was pro-British and that complete confidence could be placed in his reliability and discretion, he was contacted by a BSC agent and subsequently engaged to work under cover in behalf of BSC's Far Eastern Political Warfare, specifically as a freelance writer on Japanese affairs.

Early in July a 3,000 word article, exposing the German Fifth Column in Japan, was prominently featured under his name in the influential *New York Herald Tribune*. The article had been accepted strictly on its own merit. It comprised information which had all the appearance of being at once authentic and uncoloured by organized propaganda. It was regarded, therefore, as 'hard' news and created something of a sensation. It was syndicated in forty leading newspapers throughout the United States and Canada, and was widely quoted by American radio commentators. A few weeks later, the *New York Post*, under the heading of HITLER'S AGENTS RUNNING TOKYO, published the first of five special articles for the express purpose of showing how closely the Nazi betrayal of Japan paralleled 'the Nazi double-crossing of Italy', which the paper had recently exposed. 'A full dress Nazi Fifth Column,' wrote BSC in the guise of Dr Spinks, 'conducting under cover campaigns to promote a Rightist Revolution in Tokyo and to drive Japan into war with the US, has gained a powerful hold on the Japanese government.'

The story of the German Fifth Column in Japan had 'broken', and it was now up to BSC to keep it alive. Other articles along the same lines as Spinks's were placed in the press, through intermediaries, whenever a suitable opportunity occurred. News commentators were supplied with 'inside information', again through intermediaries. The original Spinks article was republished in pamphlet form by the New York Committee to Defend America (see Chapter 2) – an interventionist body with which BSC had close connections – and was thus widely distributed. This pamphlet was, in turn, translated into Spanish and Portuguese and circulated throughout Latin America, where press and radio took up the cry. A British propaganda campaign had taken on, as intended, the quality of an independently American-led crusade.

(d) Channels to Japan

But enough had not been accomplished to endanger the German-Japanese Alliance, so long as the main target remained untouched. The main target was Japan. There was an incidental purpose to be served in convincing American public opinion of the Nazi menace, but the chief concern was to awaken the Japanese people to it. Accordingly BSC had now to ensure that its German Fifth

Column material, released in the United States as news, and so accepted throughout the Western Hemisphere, should get back to Japan in the same form.

In that task, Japanese representatives abroad were of some considerable help, for while Japan's Militarist clique was cognizant of German machinations, Japan's civilian authorities – at least below the top level – apparently were not. Reference has already been made to BSC's direct contacts with the Japanese Embassy in Washington and with the Japanese Consulates in New York and San Francisco. Through these contacts BSC was able both to gauge official Japanese reaction to specific operations and to use official Japanese communications as 'rumour' channels. One of them reported that the Spinks article had caused a furore in the New York Consulate, and that its contents had been cabled back to Tokyo in full.

It was anticipated that Japanese missions in other countries would react in similar fashion. For that reason BSC, utilizing intermediaries, organized publicity of the Spinks article on a worldwide scale. Republication rights were secured for the Overseas News Agency which telegraphed the article verbatim to London, where SO, having been previously warned, arranged, *inter alia*, for it to be published, together with editorial comment, in the London press; for it to be cabled in full to HM Embassy Tokyo; cabled in full to Melbourne, together with a cypher message recommending that summaries should be broadcast on the Australian radio transmission to Indo-China and throughout the Far East; for it to be summarized in Empax telegrams to Stockholm, Helsinki, Berne, Madrid, Tangier, Lisbon; summarized in a special Britanova cable to the Arab News Agency; and summarized in the Britanova transmission to West Africa and Istanbul. In result, these arrangements contributed to the impression of spontaneous publication all over the world of German Fifth Column material which eventually streamed, multidirectionally, back to Japan.

Japanese residents and visitors abroad were also regarded as providing a potential means of communication. To that end the Spinks article was translated into Japanese and published in pamphlet form by the Anti-Militarist Society of Patriotic Japanese Residing Abroad, which was, in fact, a BSC front invented for the occasion. The pamphlet was printed by a Japanese printer in San Francisco who was a BSC sub-agent. 160,000 copies were distributed in the United States, preponderantly in California where there were large Japanese settlements. 30,000 were mailed to Japanese firms and ships, and one bookshop in Los Angeles was persuaded to enclose a copy in every package wrapped. Many thousands more were mailed to Japanese in Canada, Hawaii and the Philippines. Without doubt, a fair proportion of these eventually reached Japan. Some were enclosed in private correspondence to friends and relations at home; others were taken back by returning travellers. Tokyo evidently became aware that anti-German material was being introduced into Japan in this fashion, for the Japanese Consul in San Francisco was ordered by his Embassy to find out who was behind the distribution of the pamphlets, and subsequently all Japanese passengers on a homebound ship were warned that they would be court-martialled by the Admiralty if any 'dangerous thought' publications were found in their possession. BSC circumvented this last measure by having 1,000 copies hidden in various places throughout the ship before she sailed.

(e) The Kasai Operation

One particular way in which Japanese communications, official and private, were harnessed to the task of directing BSC's anti-German propaganda to its target constituted an operation in itself and is, perhaps, worthy of description in some detail.

Early in September of 1941, Juiji Kasai, a prominent member of the Japanese Diet, known for his moderate views, arrived in the United States on a semi-official visit. He had influential friends in Japan – high Palace dignitaries and statesmen who were basically anti-Militarist and not as yet committed to the expansionist policy. It occurred to BSC that Kasai might be persuaded to write personal letters to some of these men drawing their attention to the anti-German material which was receiving such wide publicity in the United States. They would doubtless be influenced by it and could if they wished make political capital out of it by having it privately printed and circulated.

It happened that if Kasai could be so persuaded, a means of getting his letters safely back to Japan was at hand. For BSC learned that the *Heiyo Maru* – the ship in which Kasai had travelled from Japan – was now in Manzanillo whence she was due to sail shortly on the return voyage. No doubt Kasai could arrange to entrust any letters he might write to the captain of the *Heiyo Maru*, who, in turn, could post them on arrival, after affixing Japanese stamps.

Kasai was contacted at the Mayflower Hotel in Washington by a BSC agent, ostensibly representing the New York Committee to Defend America, which, it will be remembered, had sponsored republication in pamphlet form of the original Spinks article. He agreed to the general proposal that he should write a number of personal letters, enclosing copies of the pamphlet, and should send them to the captain of the *Heiyo Maru* for subsequent mailing in Japan. After some discussion, he accepted a list of thirty addresses, which included the names of Prince Chichibu, Prince Konoye and Baron Matsudaira.*

Kasai wrote the letters, addressed envelopes for them in Japanese, and – as agreed – placed them in an outer cover addressed to the captain of the *Heiyo Maru*. However he could not be allowed to send the packet off himself. For one thing, BSC wished to photostat the contents before they left the country. For another, it was necessary to arrange a rather special method of despatch to Manzanillo, a method which was quite beyond Kasai's competence and, indeed, would have alarmed him considerably had he known of it. Accordingly the agent took the packet from him on the pretext that he would post it for him by registered air mail, special delivery.

To have the letters removed, photostatted and then replaced without leaving telltale signs of tampering was easy enough. But despatch to Manzanillo actually proved the most complicated part of the whole operation, inasmuch as it had to be guided by two apparently conflicting considerations. On the one hand, it was obviously important to avoid subjecting the letters to the hazards of censorship *en route*. On the other hand, it was essential to ensure that the captain of the *Heiyo Maru* should have no cause for suspecting that the packet had not reached him through such postal channels as were available to Kasai.

The problem was solved by enlisting the aid of Captain (now Colonel) James Roosevelt – always a good friend to BSC. Through him, certain special arrangements were made with the Washington Post Office and the State Department, which

---

* The complete list is as follows: – Prince Chichibu, Prime Minister Konoye, Tsuneo Matsudaira, Count Aisuke Kabayama, Marquis Tokugawa, Marquis Nobutsune Okuma, Yosaburo Takekoshi, Dr Kiroku Hayashi, Prince Iyemasa Tokugawa, Shingoro Takaishi, Viscount Tadashiro Inouye, Admiral Yonai, Mr Mukai, Captain Tanaka, Baron Hiranuma, Count Soejima, Foreign Minister Toyoda, Mr Umekichi Yoneyama, Baron Dan, Seihin Ikeda, Matsuzo Nagai, Tokichi Tanaka, Count Kentaro Kaneko, Matsutaro Shoriki, Nobuya Uchida, Mr Ishida, Masatsune Ogura, Shigemichi Miyoshi, Seiichi Takashima, Yoshiharu Nagashima and Chokuro Kadono.

enabled a sort of concealed safe-hand method of delivery to be effected.

The packet was stamped and cancelled 'air mail, special delivery' at the Washington Post Office, but it was not mailed. Instead, on orders from the White House, a special courier flew it to the United States Consulate in Manzanillo, with instructions that it should be delivered by a Mexican messenger boy to the captain of the *Heiyo Maru* on board. In this way censorship was avoided, and the captain accepted his mission from BSC quite unsuspectingly.

Some time later, Kasai received a telegram from the captain stating that the *Heiyo Maru* was approaching Yokohama. No mention was made of the letters, but Kasai interpreted the message as an assurance that his wishes would shortly be carried out. Meanwhile the New York Committee to Defend America wrote a letter of thanks to Kasai, and in this fashion BSC expressed formal obligation to a member of the Japanese Diet for valuable assistance to the cause of British propaganda!

(f) Station KGEI

Potentially, a more direct means of reaching Japan than those outlined above was by short-wave radio from the United States. However the facilities for this were far from abundant. There was, when BSC began its Far Eastern Political Warfare operations, only one American organization engaged in broadcasting to the Far East – and that was station KGEI in San Francisco. Owned and operated by General Electric, its policy was distinctly anti-British. Its news, broadcast in English and Chinese only, was drawn exclusively from Hearst sources. Its Chinese programmes were entirely unsupervised by any responsible authority and – so BSC had reason to suspect – were being used by the enemy to transmit code messages.

Nevertheless it was a powerful, well-equipped station and its transmissions could be well received in Japan. Seeing no alternative in view, BSC cast covetous eyes upon it – and fortunately not in vain.

In July, listeners to station KSFO in San Francisco heard William Winter, well-known American commentator, report on the German Fifth Column in Japan as follows:

'... The chances are that Japan would remain neutral, and would support a peaceful policy towards the United States, if Japan were entirely directed by Japanese. The facts, however, are that there are more than three thousand Nazis in Japan. They are not Japanese; they are Germans. They are reported – and incidentally this is not to be construed as any "inside information" – it is material that has been widely published – the report is that there are more than three thousand well-trained agents, listed as businessmen, technicians, advisers, and just plain tourists, all over the country. The former editor of the *Japan News Week*, an American weekly published in Tokyo, and a member of the faculty of the Tokyo University of Commerce, Dr C. N. Spinks, returned to the United States recently from Tokyo, and reported in print that the ramified network of Nazi agents in Japan centres on the person of General Eugen Ott, the German Ambassador to Tokyo. As a result of what Dr Spinks describes as the Nazi Fifth Column effort in Japan, all non-Nazi Japanese have been driven from positions in Japanese business concerns and schools. And the information tells us that, by this time, German Nazi agents, or at least axis-sympathizers, are in control of the agencies which direct and formulate popular opinion and, indirectly, government policy . . . Whether Japanese intelligence will overcome Nazi persuasion only the future can reveal.'

Mr William Winter, an independently minded newsman, would have been surprised – to say the least – had he been informed that the real source of his Nazi Fifth Column information was British propaganda. He would have been still more surprised a few months later, after he had been engaged as regular news commentator for the short-wave station KGEI, to learn that his real employer was BSC. But it was so. Working through an agent, representing himself as manager of the Malaya Broadcasting Corporation and interested in securing rebroadcasting rights for the Singapore Radio, BSC began negotiations to win control of KGEI's facilities, and by the time the Pacific War broke out had largely succeeded. The former anti-British station was then receiving news from AP and UP; from special US government teletype services in Washington and New York; and from a special SO news service in Singapore. In addition to Mr Winter's English commentary, it was broadcasting daily commentaries in Dutch, French, Chinese, Japanese, Tagalog, Thai and Malay.

These commentaries, directed of course to the Far East were, by arrangement with the relevant SOE missions, picked up and rediffused on short-wave transmission both by the Malaya Broadcasting Corporation and by the Australian Broadcasting Commission. The material for them was supplied through the recently formed COI office (Donovan's organization). Some of it was directly relevant to the anti-German campaign. All of it was angled to suit the general purpose of exposing the aggressive plans of Japan's Militarists.

(g) Secondary Objective

It has already been said that to destroy the German-Japanese Alliance was the prime but not the only objective of BSC's Far Eastern Political Warfare. A secondary objective was to stiffen resistance, both in the United States and throughout the Far East, to the threat of Japanese aggression. This was essentially a matter of gathering relevant material through intelligence sources, and of publicising it, whenever an appropriate opportunity occurred, by the same means as those already described, that is to say by inspired articles and news stories in the US press, inspired commentaries over the American radio (both domestic and short-wave), sponsored publication and distribution of pamphlets, and the planting of rumours in enemy and neutral missions.

Thus the KGEI broadcasts served this secondary objective of BSC's Far Eastern Political Warfare. So, too, did various special operations, whose method and scope can be illustrated by one outstanding example.

In the late autumn of 1941, SO/Singapore sent BSC a summary of a secret agreement between the French and Japanese, which gave the Japanese economic control of Indo-China. This was, of course, political dynamite, and precisely the type of material needed to awaken public opinion in the United States and throughout the Far East to Japan's aggressive intentions. The information was conveyed to the President and the State Department, who requested that it should not be made public property until Mr Hull had had the opportunity to utilize it as ammunition in his negotiations with that Japanese envoy of ill repute, Kurusu.

Thereafter, as BSC urged, it was clearly to the advantage of the United States Government that the information should be released. That, however, could not be done in any way officially inasmuch as the original agreement was not available, and SO's source was a delicate one which had to be protected. Only clandestine methods could be used, therefore, and it was left to BSC to organize them in its own fashion. This it did by having the information released as a straight news story in the *New York Herald Tribune* under the name of a reputable American journalist.

Worldwide publicity for it was then organized in conformity with the course charted when the Spinks article appeared.

(h) Assessment of Results

The actual effects of BSC's Far Eastern Political Warfare operations are still hard to calculate. Historically speaking, the anti-German campaign was obviously begun too late to attain its objective, although there can be no doubt that it gave the Japanese authorities serious cause for alarm. During the months after Pearl Harbor, when Japan's armed might went on a triumphant parade through South-East Asia, it may well have seemed as if nothing had been achieved in the way of undermining Japanese morale. But doubts and fears had been implanted nonetheless, and it may yet become apparent that they contributed to Japan's ultimate downfall.

That, however, is in the field of conjecture. It is obvious enough now that there was never any chance of frustrating the execution of Japan's expansionist policy in the few months which destiny allowed. The attempt was made, and all that can be said for certain is that it produced definite disturbance inside Japan which might, had time allowed sufficient opportunity for its fostering, have grown to the stature of a major political upset.

But BSC's excursion into the Far Eastern Political Warfare field had one result which, though unconnected with its actual objectives, was potentially of major importance. That was the opportunity to exercise a wide measure of influence over American propaganda in the Far East.

Before Pearl Harbor, there was no official American Far Eastern propaganda machine, although Donovan had the responsibility of making preparations for it in the event of war, and meanwhile of coordinating the outward flow from the United States of news and comment. BSC's objective of neutralizing Japan was obviously in harmony with United States policy, and inevitably Donovan was interested in furthering it.

His interest was shared by the White House, from which high source BSC was able, on various occasions, to draw succour not only for its own operations but for the implementation of British Far Eastern propaganda in general. At BSC's request, for example, the President granted a special dispensation under Lend-Lease for the despatch of two high-powered transmitters to Singapore where they were urgently needed by the Malaya Broadcasting Corporation, which was still speaking in somewhat piping tones owing to lack of essential equipment, though intended as the voice of Britain in the Far East.

While the United States had to keep official silence, it was clearly to American advantage that British propaganda should be enabled to speak as loudly as possible. More than that, however, it was to American advantage that propaganda channels in the United States should be prepared for official use – a job which in fact was being done through BSC.

There emerged, then, from BSC's dealings with Donovan's COI office on Far Eastern Political Warfare matters a sort of interdependent relationship based on community of interests. It was only with the help of the COI office that BSC succeeded in securing propaganda facilities over station KGEI and subsequently in arranging for the erection of a new 100 KW short-wave station (KWID) in San Francisco. But the COI office certainly had as much – if not more – to gain as BSC from these operations, even though it could not have undertaken them on its own initiative. The fact is that if there had been no British organization in the United States engaged in the job of exploring and expanding means of directing American propaganda to the Far East, the COI office would probably have felt the need to invent one.

Thus BSC's activities considerably advanced American plans for Far Eastern Political Warfare. And these plans, including official assumption of control of the KGEI and KWID short-wave broadcasting services (both staffed incidentally by BSC recruits), were put into effect as soon as United States neutrality came to an end. There was then no longer any purpose in BSC conducting operations of its own – and indeed no opportunity for so doing. But there was opportunity to maintain the very close relationship which had already been established with the COI office and had proved mutually advantageous. The Americans wanted BSC's continued cooperation. They wanted it because, by accomplishments in their behalf, BSC had proved its worth to them. They wanted it because Far Eastern Political Warfare was a highly specialized business of which BSC had practical experience and they had none; and because BSC could put at their disposal a small but highly trained group of Japanese experts whose knowledge they respected and upon which they could draw.

And so it happened that when the Americans took over responsibility for the active direction of their Far Eastern propaganda, thus stepping into a field explored and cultivated by BSC, the latter retreated no farther than the sidelines, as it were. Through its liaison with the COI office it was still equipped to exert powerful influence in a consultative capacity, and was encouraged to offer suggestions, technical assistance and advice.

The story of that liaison, of its productiveness and of its eventual termination belongs to a later chapter. It should be said here, however, that, as a direct result of its pre-Pearl Harbor operations, BSC was in an admirable position thereafter to guard against the possibility of American propaganda in the Far East ever conflicting with the interest of His Majesty's Government.

CHAPTER 4

Disguised Channels of Propaganda and Rumour Spreading

(a) Propaganda by the Stars
(b) Station M
(c) Rumour Factory

(a) Propaganda by the Stars

A country that is extremely heterogeneous in character offers a wide variety of choice in propaganda methods. While it is possibly true to say that all Americans are intensely suspicious of propaganda, it is certain that a great many of them are unusually susceptible to it even in its most patent form. And while, for reasons previously discussed, there is a general striving after standardization among Americans, yet the United States is still a fertile field for *outré* practices. It is unlikely that any propagandist would seriously attempt to influence politically the people of England, say, or France through the medium of astrological predictions. Yet in the United States this was done with effective if limited results.

In the summer of 1941, Louis de Wohl, a bogus Hungarian astrologer, was sent over to the United States by London. He was to be controlled by BSC, but his instructions were that he must never mention Britain or show in any way that he was especially interested in her welfare. His mission was to shake public confidence in the invincibility of Adolf Hitler.

It was planned that the first prophecies which de Wohl would make upon his arrival in the US should harmonize with pre-arranged astrological and magical predictions of Hitler's fall which would be made in other remote parts of the world. In this way it was hoped not only to convince the public but to alarm that great believer in astrology, Hitler himself. When de Wohl arrived in New York, BSC arranged a press conference for him at which he told newspapermen that Hitler's horoscope showed that his fall was now certain. The planet Neptune, he said, was in the house of death, making for a mysterious fate, and soon the progressed ascendant would be in a place where Neptune was at the moment of Hitler's birth. That very summer, de Wohl added, Uranus would bring the birth constellation into effect with grave consequences for Hitler.

A day or two after these statements had appeared in the newspapers, other stories began to emanate from elsewhere. The arrangements which had been made were working smoothly. In Cairo, an Arabic paper carried a statement by the eminent Egyptian astrologer Sheikh Youssef Afifi, who said: 'Four months hence a red planet will appear on the eastern horizon and will indicate that a dangerous evil-doer, who has drenched the world in blood, will pass away . . . this means that an uncrowned Emperor will be killed, and that man is Hitler.' Steps were taken to ensure that this story was duly picked up by American correspondents in Egypt.

At the same time correspondents in Nigeria filed a story which told of a report by a local District Officer in a far up country district. It appeared that a Nigerian priest called Ulokoigbe had seen a vision. In the priest's own words: 'In the light . . . I saw a group of five men on a rock. One was short with long hair; the second was fat and shaped like the breadfruit; the third monkey-faced and crippled; the fourth had glass in his eyes like the District Officer; the fifth was leopard-faced. After a quarrel the fifth vanished. The cripple stabbed the breadfruit man in the back. The long-haired one cursed the glass-eyed one and pushed him from the rock. Then the cripple jumped from the rock in a panic, leaving Long Hair alone. Long Hair seized the crown from the rock but it did not fit his head and fell off. In a wild rage Long Hair slipped from the rock and fell shrieking like a madman. The crown was left in its proper place in the middle of the rock . . .'

This, too, was carried in the American papers. People began to sit up and take notice. BSC carried the matter further and in order to enhance de Wohl's reputation still more, it was arranged that he should make a prophecy which would be fulfilled in ten days' time. After consulting the stars (and BSC), he told the press that one of Hitler's allies would, within ten days, be found to be mad. BSC arranged that a story confirming this should be published. A French naval officer who had escaped from Martinique was quoted as asserting in Puerto Rico that Admiral Robert had gone violently insane and could be heard shouting and screaming all the night long. De Wohl's public was delighted, and impressed. He really seemed to know what he was talking about. After all here was a prophet who had made a prediction in New York which was immediately confirmed, first by an Egyptian astrologer in Cairo, and secondly by a Nigerian priest in the jungles of Africa. Furthermore, he had definitely said that within ten days one of Hitler's allies would be found to be mad, and, sure enough, it appeared from reports that the Vichy Admiral Robert was mad. For the moment anyway, his reputation shone as brightly as the stars of which he spoke.

From this triumphant beginning de Wohl went out on tour, and all the time, at public meetings, over the air, in private assemblies, in interviews, in widely syndicated articles and at an important convention of American astrologers, he declared that Hitler's doom was sealed. Later, he delivered similar attacks upon the French Ambassador, Henry-Haye, upon Pétain and upon the isolationist Colonel Lindbergh. At the American Astrologers' Convention de Wohl said of Lindbergh that he was part of the plague of technology which makes the weak-minded believe that a man who can handle machines well must be an authority on things of the spirit. He went further than that. He said that the kidnapped Lindbergh baby was still alive and was one of a number of future Fuehrers being trained in the NSDAP school at Vogelsang in East Prussia.

De Wohl delivered many other attacks like these upon anti-British personalities, and there is little doubt that his work had a considerable effect upon certain sections of the people. After Pearl Harbor he returned to England, having completed a fantastic but effective mission.

(b) Station M

BSC controlled directly an organization for fabricating letters and other documents. It had a laboratory in Canada which was set up, with the aid of the RCMP, under cover of the Canadian Broadcasting Corporation, and was run by a small group of technicians. It was called Station M.

It was essentially a disguised propaganda channel, though many of its products were intended to further Special Operations as opposed to Political Warfare campaigns. For example, a notorious Czech traitor was (from the German point of view) wrongly convicted by a military court in occupied Czechoslovakia and put to death as a result of the efforts of Station M. Three letters signed 'Anna' and posted in Santiago provided the evidence which condemned him. These were a blending of truth and fiction. They mentioned facts about the man's personal life which he could not truthfully deny, such as references to 'the strange death of his brother, Jan' and to his former wife who was half Jewish. They contained statements which were incomprehensible to him such as 'I looked after the marks but could do nothing with the zlotys.' 'Father caught 75 fish on Wednesday the 17th. Brother was not well but he caught 82,' and 'I was knitting Karl a sweater in which I had to use 14 skeins of wool, each 60 feet long although two were only 28 feet'.

To the German censors it seemed obvious enough that Anna was attempting to communicate with the man in plain-language code and that he was probably an Allied agent. He was in a very poor position to answer the charge. He had no idea who Anna was, but he could not argue away the clear indications that he was in regular communication with her, for how else could she be familiar with the details of his personal life? And he could not explain the frequent references to numbers. The Germans were unimpressed by unsupported protestations of innocence – even in the torture chamber. They lost a good collaborator.

For the fabrication of letters BSC needed, first, technical facilities in the way of special inks and paper, secondly, a certain amount of accurate information about individuals derived from censorship and other sources, and, lastly, planned inventiveness which had to be based on sound appraisal of political conditions in the various target areas.

Little could have been achieved without the cooperation of Imperial Censorship authorities who facilitated the operations of Station M in every way possible. They agreed to unseal and reseal bags in order to insert suitable material in transit mail. They forwarded all relevant raw material like inks and personal documents impounded by Travellers' Censorship. They furnished specimens of the epistolary paraphernalia used by government departments, banks and other official and quasi-official bodies in various countries, such as notepaper and rubber stamps, and also specimens of private stationery which might be useful for reproduction purposes. And they reported fully on individuals whom they considered possible victims of incrimination or propaganda.

Station M worked on the principle that its output must be good enough to confound microscopic examination. And it produced no document which was not an exact imitation in every detail of what it purported to be. The necessary technical processes were handled by a panel of experts, whose services were for the most part given free. Among them were Canada's leading authorities on the manufacture of special inks and paper.

As already explained, Station M was chiefly concerned with special operations. Besides producing incriminating letters for despatch from fictitious addresses in the Western Hemisphere to quislings in Europe and North Africa, it was the instrument of a number of special operations in Latin America which are described in Part VI.

Its Political Warfare work was represented by the organization of a letter-writing campaign designed to cause alarm and despondency in the enemy camp. The letters were genuine. The writers were recruited individually from among enemy or neutral nationals opposed to the Axis and they did not know they were contributing to a general scheme. They were asked to correspond regularly with personal friends and business acquaintances in occupied Europe and to include in their letters subversive material, prepared by Station M, which revealed lack of faith in the Axis cause but was not so obviously defeatist in tone as to seem like deliberate propaganda. Risk of endangering addressees was kept to the minimum. Frequently letters were purposely sent to deceased persons or to businesses which had been closed down. So long as the subversive material was seen and noted by enemy censors and officials it served its purpose.

On the assumption that the Nazis could (and probably would) undertake letter-writing propaganda of their own – indeed there was some evidence that they were already doing so – BSC planned a campaign to discredit information in letters coming from Germany. It would have been easy to apprise friendly newspapermen of the available evidence, but Station M considered this inadequate, and decided that something more substantial should be fabricated. In due course, Walter Winchell (see below) received a letter mailed in Lisbon by an American merchant seaman, who wrote that (while *en route* from Hamburg to Brazil) he had been told by a Jewish refugee that correspondents in Germany were sent a monthly bulletin of news to be included in their letters abroad.

To substantiate his story, Winchell's informant enclosed:

1. A printed slip inserted by German Censorship in a letter which had been returned to the sender because he had not included the stock sentences;

2. A copy of a bulletin in which these sentences were issued in Hamburg to writers abroad.

It was a fine story for Winchell and his 25,000,000 readers. Neither he nor they had ever heard of Station M.

A by-product of Station M was the game of 'Vik'. Its purpose was to use ridicule as a weapon against the Nazis, and, although the march of events did not allow much time or scope for its practice, it is, perhaps, worthy of brief mention as an idea which might be put to use should the need for it ever occur again.

'Vik' was launched by means of cheaply and anonymously printed booklets in English, French, Spanish and Portuguese, which were the product of Station M and were distributed with the very greatest secrecy by BSC agents throughout South America. Allied sympathizers were urged to organize themselves into teams and to compete with one another by scoring points for every annoyance or embarrassment caused to the Nazis and their confederates. Called 'a fascinating new pastime for all lovers of democracy' the rules of the game were set out in detail, and to make distinction between the dangerous and relatively safe ways of playing it the methods whose application would be punishable by law were marked with an asterisk.

Station M's officers, in a preliminary memorandum, described the kind of petty persecutions they had in mind. A Nazi, they said, 'can be telephoned at all hours of the night and when awakened can be apologetically assured that it is the wrong number; the air can disappear mysteriously out of his motor tyres; shops can be telephoned on his behalf and asked to deliver large quantities of useless and cumbersome goods – payment on delivery; masses of useless correspondence can reach him without stamps so that he is constantly having to pay out petty sums of money; his lady friend can receive anonymous letters stating that he is suffering from mysterious diseases or that he is keeping a woman and six children in Detroit; he can be cabled apparently genuine instructions to make long, difficult expensive journeys; a rat might die in his watertank; street musicians might play "God Save the King" outside his house all night; his favourite dog might get lost. With a little thought it should be possible to invent at least 500 ways of persecuting a victim without the persecutor compromising himself.'

'Remember always', said a note at the end, 'that in playing Vik you are in your own small way acting as a fighting member of the forces of Democracy. Therefore be silent, secret and discreet.'

"PEPINO"

La Tragedia del Superhombre.

¿Quién—gracias a la eficacia fenomenal de Joselito Goebbels—no ha oido hablar del famoso "Herrenvolk", esa noble raza del caballeros teutones? ¡Tan grandes son! ¡Tan potentes! Desgraciadamente la verdad de las cosas, de vez en cuando, no coincide con la apariencia. ¿Quién no se acuerda de ese conocidisimo refrán que dice "Los mayores pepinos nunca tienen buen sabor"? Y de veras que es así con el distinguido caballero,

VON LEVETZOW,

quien era (hasta hace poco) Canciller en la Embajada de la raza aria en Rio de Janeiro. Este hombre erguido (madre danesa—¡Quién más nórdica!) tiene el pelo de lo más rubio yo ojos azules que, por anticipo, han excitado a miles de inocentes doncellas....¡ hasta el momento en que sus lindas manos agarran el pepino famoso! Frau von Levetzow, heredera de los millones Krupp, ella si que descubrió una noche (esa noche nupcial cuando se entregó al superhombre) encontró—¡ pobre de ella!— que su esposo era otro Adolfito—tan

IMPOTENTE

como el gran Fuehrer. Cinco meses aguanto. Cinco meses de hambre—¡y ella vegetariana!—luego huyo para Alemania. ¿Sabes por qué, querido lector? Para pedir a esa enorme fábrica de acero, la Casa Krupp, si no pudieran fabricar un pepiniro, uno solo, para su querido superhombre.

¡Conciudadanos!

Este hombre, este Levetzow, puede robar vuestro dinero, vuestras casas y patria, pero JAMAS *vuestras mujeres* . . . . . NO PUEDE.

Station M's attack on Von Levetzow.

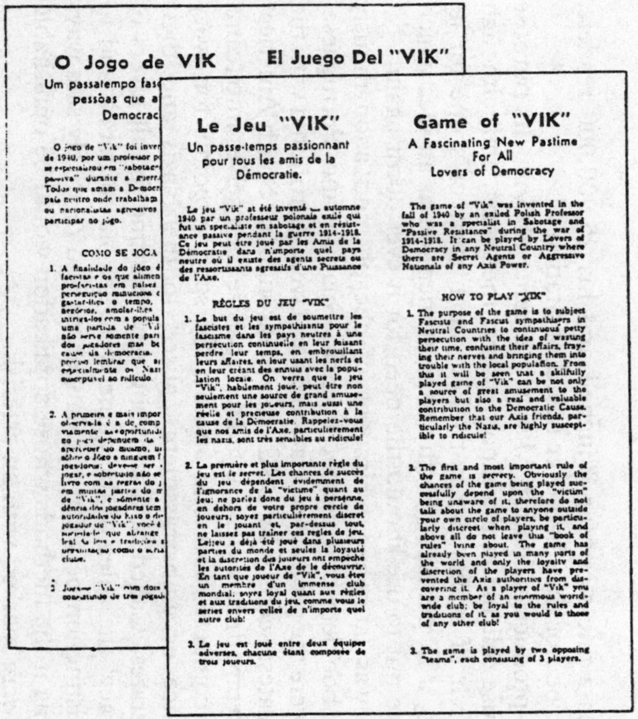

O Jogo de VIK

El Juego Del "VIK"

COMO SE JOGA

Le Jeu "VIK"

Un passe-temps passionnant pour tous les amis de la Démocratie.

Le jeu "Vik" at été inventé — automne 1940 par un professeur polonais exilé qui fut un specialiste en sabotage et en résistance passive pendant la guerre 1914-1918. Ce jeu peut être joué par les Amis de la Démocratie dans n'importe quel pays neutre où il existe des agents secrets ou des ressortissants agressifs d'une Puissance de l'Axe.

RÈGLES DU JEU "VIK"

1. Le but du jeu est de soumettre les fascistes et les sympathisants pour le fascisme dans les pays neutres à une persecution continuelle en leur faisant perdre leur temps, en embrouillant leurs affaires, en leur usant les nerfs et en leur créant des ennuis avec la population locale. On verra que le jeu "Vik", habilement joué, peut être non seulement une source de grand amusement pour les joueurs, mais aussi une réelle et precieuse contribution à la cause de la Démocratie. Rappelez-vous que nos amis de l'Axe, particulierement les nazis, sont très sensibles au ridicule!

2. La première et plus importante règle du jeu est *le secret*. Les chances de succès du jeu dépendent évidemment de l'ignorance de la "victime" quant au jeu; ne parlez donc du jeu à personne, en dehors de votre propre cercle de joueurs, soyez particulièrement discret en le jouant et, par-dessus tout, ne laissez pas trainer ces regles de jeu. Lejeu a déjà été joué dans plusieurs parties du monde et seules la loyauté et la discrétion des joueurs ont empêche les autorités de l'Axe de le découvrir. En tant que joueur de "Vik", vous êtes un membre d'un immense club mondial; soyez loyal quant aux règles et aux traditions du jeu, comme vous le seriez envers celles de n'importe quel autre club!

3. Le jeu est joué entre deux équipes adverses, chacune étant composée de trois joueurs.

Game of "VIK"

A Fascinating New Pastime For All Lovers of Democracy

The game of "Vik" was invented in the fall of 1940 by an exiled Polish Professor who was a specialist in Sabotage and "Passive Resistance" during the war of 1914-1918. It can be played by Lovers of Democracy in any Neutral Country where there are Secret Agents or Aggressive Nationals of any Axis Power.

HOW TO PLAY "VIK"

1. The purpose of the game is to subject Fascists and Fascist sympathisers in Neutral Countries to continuous petty persecution with the idea of wasting their time, confusing their affairs, fraying their nerves and bringing them into trouble with the local population. From this it will be seen that a skilfully played game of "Vik" can be not only a source of great amusement to the players but also a real and valuable contribution to the Democratic Cause. Remember that our Axis friends, particularly the Nazis, are highly susceptible to ridicule!

2. The first and most important rule of the game is *secrecy*. Obviously the chances of the game being played successfully depend upon the "victim" being unaware of it, therefore do not talk about the game to anyone outside your own circle of players, be particularly discreet when playing it, and above all do not leave this "book of rules" lying about. The game has already been played in many parts of the world and only the loyalty and discretion of the players have prevented the Axis authorities from discovering it. As a player of "Vik" you are a member of an enormous world-wide club; be loyal to the rules and traditions of it, as you would to those of any other club!

3. The game is played by two opposing "teams", each consisting of 3 players.

The Game of 'VIK'.

Disguised Channels of Propaganda and Rumour Spreading

As an aid to the campaign of ridicule which BSC was anxious to launch against the Nazis in South America, Station M produced a number of abusive pamphlets which were secretly distributed. An example is the one dealing with Werner Von Levetzow (see illustration). He was the Chancellor of the German Embassy in Rio and was being mentioned as the next German Ambassador to Buenos Aires. He was a fine-looking superman of six feet two, but shortly after the war he had married a Krupp heiress, and she had left him in Rio and had returned to Germany alleging that he was impotent. Naturally he was the butt of many jests in Rio society, and upon these BSC built.

Station M's technical facilities enabled BSC to provide London with a regular supply of documents which were invaluable for agents in the field (see Part VIII). After Pearl Harbor there was no longer opportunity for Station M's collaboration either in Special Operations or Political Warfare, which were themselves largely curtailed. But the laboratory in Canada, working with a reduced staff, was kept open and continued to produce fabricated documents for use elsewhere – for example, atrocity pictures.

(c) Rumour Factory

In 1941, BSC created an organization for spreading rumours, and although this largely ceased to function in the United States after Pearl Harbor, it was maintained in South America until 1944.

Rumour-spreading campaigns were directed from New York. Their objectives ranged all the way from publicizing misleading information about Allied strategy to undermining the prestige of an individual Nazi by encouraging salacious gossip about his private life. Material for particular campaigns was usually supplied by SO/London, but was sometimes originated in New York.

There was never an insufficiency of material. Rumours might be pure inventions or they might be based on half truths derived from such sources as intercepted letters, interrogations of travellers, secretly opened diplomatic mail, German and neutral newspapers. Letters from France proved particularly useful. For example, there was one which stated that after each British air raid German aircraft stationed nearby went up to bomb hospitals and schools.

The rumour organization was made up of the various channels of propaganda at BSC's disposal which have been described in previous chapters – newspapers, magazines, radio commentators, news agencies, short-wave wireless stations and so on. In addition, there were certain special channels – diplomatic and commercial.

Political Warfare for SO.1

The Press Attaché of the Czechoslovak Embassy rewrote material supplied to him in the form of 'underground reports from Europe' for circulation to eighty Czech and Slovak newspapers in the United States. Rumours were planted in the Japanese Consulate (see Chapter 3) and during the early part of 1941, the Yugoslav Embassy regularly cabled BSC's planted material to Belgrade. Rumours were planted in various factories – for example, a story about I.G. Farben circulated rapidly among the 400 employees of a large firm, returning to its originator on the same day that he instigated it. Finally, ships' observers were used to pass rumours by word of mouth on the ships of ten lines plying between Spain, the United States and Latin America (see Part III).

Rumour material was regularly cabled or sent by bag to BSC representatives throughout Latin America, and not only SOE men but BSC Consular Security Officers and Industrial Security Officers made use of it by instituting whispering campaigns among dock workers, seamen and employees of plants and factories.

Much of the rumour spreading in Latin America was done by word of mouth, and whispering campaigns were carried out on many different social levels through the contacts which agents maintained with governmental, diplomatic, professional, social, commercial and working-class circles as well as with various minority groups such as Poles, Czechs, Free French, Basques and Spanish Republicans.

To a limited extent, SOE representatives were able to use the Latin American press and radio as channels of propaganda in the same way as BSC used press and radio in the United States. Their work in this regard is fully described in Part VI. Retransmittal abroad of rumours which allegedly had their origin in South America was accomplished in the following ways.

1. By letters and newspapers sent across the Atlantic. Thus, a representative in Venezuela arranged for letters to be written to the officials of defunct clubs in Spain by ex-members, giving accounts of pro-Allied feeling in Venezuela. Contacts in Spain were tipped off to collect the letters and disseminate the contents. Similarly, letters embodying rumours were sent to the Uruguayan Consuls in Portugal, Spain, Sweden and Switzerland, and there can be little doubt that private correspondents passed on rumours to their friends in Europe.
2. By word of mouth. Trinidad was particularly useful in this respect, for Spanish ships constantly touched at Port of Spain *en*

route between Europe and South America. BSC agents planted high-level rumours ('indiscretions' from inside England) with travelling diplomats, and simpler rumours with crews and third-class passengers. Several rumours initiated in this way were repeated to their originators as gospel truth before the ship had sailed.

3. By South American short-wave wireless stations.

It may be worth recording the more important rules which BSC observed in running its rumour organization. They were as follows:

1. A good rumour should never be traceable to its source.
2. A rumour should be of the kind which is likely to gain in the telling. (On occasion BSC released a rumour in two parts. For example, a story about a ship finding dead German sailors off Kerguelen Island was supplemented a few days later with the name and some details of the raider in which the sailors were supposed to have served.)
3. Particular rumours should be designed to appeal to particular groups. Catholics in South America, for example, were always deeply influenced by stories of Nazi desecration of churches and monasteries. When the Vatican Radio, in December 1942, deplored sexual immorality in Germany, BSC was presented with an opportunity to invent material with which to feed the flames of Catholic resentment.
4. A particular rumour should have a specific purpose. The objectives of rumour spreading may be many, but a single rumour cannot be expected to serve more than one of them.
5. Rumours are most effective if they can be originated in several different places simultaneously and in such a way that they shuttle back and forth, with each new report apparently confirming previous ones.

The last point deserves elaboration, for with the cooperation of the New York correspondent of a leading London newspaper, BSC and SOE/London learned how to spread rumours over a very wide area. SOE would start a rumour in London by planting it in the office of the London newspaper in question. If the subject of the rumour were of sufficient importance, the paper would cable its New York correspondent for further information, because at that time British newspapers were obtaining much of

Political Warfare for SO.1

their news of occupied Europe via the USA. BSC, having been warned by SOE, would then be prepared to 'feed' the New York correspondent with additional information. At the same time, the London newspaper would make inquiries of an American news agency, which in turn would cable its Berlin correspondent. The rumour would thus be planted in Berlin – with the German censors, the Gestapo and the Berlin correspondent of the US news agency, who would in all likelihood discuss it with other newspaper correspondents.

A case history in point is provided by the following extract from a report sent to London by BSC in August 1941:

> This rumour, after publication in the *New York Post* on August 15th, was cabled to Moscow by the *Tass* correspondent in Washington. It was broadcast from Moscow the following day in the form of a report from Switzerland. Presumably it was also published in the Moscow press and was sent thence to London by the British correspondents in Moscow. It was then cabled from London back to the United States by the United Press and was published in a completely new form on August 19th in the *N.Y. Daily News*, *N.Y. Herald Tribune*, and the *N.Y. Daily Mirror*.

A few examples are given below to illustrate the types of rumour which BSC circulated.

1. In November 1941, London requested that BSC disseminate or circulate rumours aimed at shattering the morale of U-boat crews. At once the ONA put out a story under an Ankara dateline which had every appearance of being authentic and which stated that a new super-explosive had been discovered by the British for filling depth charges. The story appeared on the front page of all the leading American newspapers. It reappeared in South America, bounced backwards and forwards across the Atlantic and finally reached Germany and the families of the U-boat crews.
2. On the basis of an intercepted letter, BSC invented a story that General Wilhelm Von Faupel was in North Africa plotting to bring the territory under Spanish–German domination. This was published in the *Christian Science Monitor* and quoted by the influential William L. Shirer in a news commentary over WABC.
3. In the Spanish diplomatic bag a letter was found explaining

the official propaganda line to the Falange in Venezuela. It quoted the Russian paper *Red Star* for details of damage done in Bremen and Hamburg by RAF raids. A story was written by BSC (under a Caracas dateline) to the effect that Spanish propagandists were now quoting Soviet newspapers against Germany. It was sent out through the Overseas News Agency to the New York press and broadcast in German over WRUL. Two days later it was republished by anti-British sections of the American press.

4. In June 1942, the Ministry of Information asked SOE to spread a rumour about a German submarine torpedoing a Brazilian ship. BSC originated the story in Argentina. It was cabled back to London as genuine news and denied with indignation over the German wireless.

Perhaps the most spectacular activity of BSC's rumour organization resulted from a request by the Admiralty that a story should be broadcast from South America just before the Rio Conference (15 January 1942) to the effect that the Axis powers intended to make a display of naval strength off the South American coast, and that British naval forces in the South Atlantic had therefore been reinforced.

On 9 January, the story was released simultaneously in the New York press with a Buenos Aires dateline, and in the Buenos Aires *Critica* with a Dakar dateline. Both the New York and Argentine news agencies cabled it to one another for confirmation, and thus gave it added weight. The Associated Press and United Press were asked for confirmation and they began to make independent inquiries.

On the 10th, it was broadcast to South America from all short-wave stations in the USA and from Montevideo.

Meanwhile, a BSC officer, who was a journalist with wide experience of South America, was spreading it assiduously. On his way by train from Rio to Santos, where he was to meet and interview the delegates to the Conference, he repeated it to the Chilean Military Attaché and the Brazilian diplomat, Afranio Mello Franco – elaborating it with the ingenious suggestion that the Argentine delegates were coming by air because they had forewarning of the demonstration and were afraid their ship might be sunk. In São Paulo he spread it, through a trustworthy intermediary, at the races and in the Cotton Exchange. In Santos he put it about through the coffee trade, shipping circles and officers of the Brazilian Navy. He told it to reporters and customs officials on the docks and finally he told it to the delegates themselves while interviewing them.

By 11 January, the story was widespread in Rio. It had grown alarmingly. The British Press Attaché had heard it from many quarters and had attributed it to German terror propaganda.

On 12 January (three days before the Conference), BSC/Montevideo reported that the American Ambassador had called a meeting of his staff to discuss the matter. His Service Attachés had been warned that the Axis might attempt raids and even landings on the South American coast. He himself had informed the President of Uruguay, urging him to take all possible precautions. Even the BSC officer, who knew nothing of the purpose of the campaign, was disturbed.

The final proof of the story's credibility reached BSC in an unexpected way. A section of the Admiralty which had not been informed of the intended rumour campaign heard the story and asked SIS/London to check it. London, in turn, telegraphed BSC. The rumour had completed a full circle.

Its objective was achieved. Well conceived and widely distributed, it did much towards swinging the Latin American powers against the Axis at the historic Rio Conference.

CHAPTER 5

After Pearl Harbor

(a) Anglo-American Collaboration
(b) The PWE Mission
(c) Training of American Propagandists

(a) Anglo-American Collaboration

Enough has already been written in the preceding chapters to indicate the very close collaboration in Political Warfare matters which BSC established with Donovan's organization before the United States entered the war. This collaboration was maintained for several months thereafter. BSC ceased activities in its own behalf, but continued to assist COI in every way possible. The Americans assumed official responsibility for their own propaganda, but many of the themes they used and the methods they employed were suggested by BSC.

The Political Warfare branch of COI was headed by a group of highly intelligent, war-conscious and pro-British writers like Robert Sherwood, Edmond Taylor and Joseph Barnes. Having assured and distinguished positions in private life, they were not afraid to admit that the conduct of subversive propaganda was a business with which they were still comparatively unfamiliar. They welcomed BSC's advice based on practical experience. And they could hardly be other than grateful for the ready-made radio services at their disposal which were entirely the result of BSC's earlier endeavours.

The European Political Warfare Section undertook in COI's behalf an investigation into Fifth Column propaganda in the United States, the results of which are described elsewhere (see Part IV). It provided COI with all manner of material which was essential to their operations but which they could not readily obtain from any United States agency – for example, BBC monitoring reports of enemy and neutral broadcasts, analyses of Axis propaganda, news digests of the European press, copies of propaganda directives received through SOE, relevant information derived from censorship and SIS sources. In November 1941, COI asked urgently for a complete series of the SO.1 pamphlets which had been dropped by the RAF and clandestinely distributed in occupied Europe, for they wished to implement a similar campaign for themselves. BSC complied. At the beginning of 1942, the RAF dropped the first American-made pamphlets over Europe.

In the following spring, COI were planning – without the knowledge of the State Department – a campaign for sending propaganda-laden correspondence into France and French Africa. With the assurance that this project had the President's approval, BSC passed COI a large file of intercepted letters from the relevant territories. This revealed many addresses of persons sympathetic or hostile to the Allied cause and also provided evidence upon which to decide what particular propaganda points would be likely to prove the most effective.

The Far Eastern Section likewise rendered COI much assistance. For example, it prepared the Japanese text of the first leaflet which COI produced to be dropped by aircraft over Japan. It obtained illustrations of the Paulownia leaf as formalized in Japanese art and persuaded COI to reproduce this in a leaflet symbolizing decay and death falling on Japan. It procured photostats of *Gogai* (Japanese newspaper extras) to serve as models for forgeries. And it was largely responsible for the famous leaflet used by the Americans at Guadalcanal – famous because it induced numbers of Japanese troops, including officers, to surrender despite the gloomy forecasts that such a thing would be impossible. Further, the section was able to persuade COI to abandon several unwise projects. One of their proposed themes was that Japan ought to accept guidance from the United States 'as a younger brother from an elder'. The section pointed out that this would invite ridicule, because most Japanese are convinced that their country is the most ancient in the world and all are quite certain that it is considerably older than the republic of 1776.

It can be said – without exaggeration – that the working relations between COI and BSC in Political Warfare were an example of Anglo-American collaboration at its best. This was so for three basic reasons. First, COI had access through BSC to essential material which they could not obtain elsewhere. Secondly, COI regarded BSC's knowledge and experience, rightly or wrongly, as one of their most valuable assets. Lastly, the individual officers concerned liked and trusted one another personally. They worked together not resentfully as representatives of rival organizations, but as friends in a common endeavour. They were devoted to a practical association which had already accomplished much and might well accomplish more.

Had this association lasted there can be little doubt that Allied propaganda as a whole would have been enriched, for two partners who work well together and stimulate each other in the invention of new ideas and new methods are individually the poorer when they are apart. Had this association lasted there would have been no cause for serious division between British and American propaganda lines. The danger of such division in Europe was, of course, slight. But in the Far East, where the Americans might feel encouraged by public pressure to preach a 'new order' which would be directly opposed to British policy and would prepare for an economic and strategic post-war resettlement of Asia and Oceania on a plan that might suit the United States but would damage the interests of Britain, it was, as WS repeatedly informed London, considerable. So long as the association lasted, American Far Eastern propaganda could be kept in line politically as well as operationally; and one example may serve to illustrate this point.

In May 1942, when Japanese pride and self-assurance were at their height, Rear-Admiral Toshio Matsunaga broadcast a talk from Tokyo to Japanese-speaking audiences abroad, describing a tour of inspection which he had made through the newly acquired empire. He described how American sailors from the *USS Houston* were employed on forced labour, apparently in the Celebes. He said:

> They are engaged in the work of filling the holes in the airfields. They are engaged in comparatively easy jobs. There are many who are suffering from hunger because they are not used to the Japanese type of food, and there are some who get very lazy because of the extreme heat. Those who do not do their part are beaten by the Japanese guards . . . Those who are hard to handle are severely beaten with a rope which is similar to the rope used by sailors. Because of the pain the lazy American prisoners continue the work with painful expressions on their faces. Indonesian natives who have lived on this island for a long time watch these prisoners, and they say: 'Previously these white people treated us like animals, and now the Japanese soldiers, who have faces similar to

ours, are beating them' . . . The natives are very thankful for what the Japanese soldiers have done for them.

This broadcast was withheld from publication by American authorities under the terms of the Japan Plan, which was the US Army's official plan for psychological warfare against Japan, drawn up by Colonel Solbert and his assistants in the Psychological Warfare Branch, and approved by the Chiefs of Staff, Secretary of War Stimson and Secretary of State Cordell Hull. The Army's reasons for opposing the publication of Japanese atrocity stories were that: (a) such stories would provoke savage reprisals against Japanese and Japanese-Americans in the United States; (b) the stories themselves were not substantiated (!); (c) publicity might encourage the Japanese to engage in further brutalities; (d) the Army wished to fight the war according to civilized rules. There was a hint that racial questions, which might induce negroes to side against the white nations, were to be played down.

BSC's Japanese experts pointed out that this policy was based on a misconception of Japanese psychology. It failed to realize that Japanese atrocities were intended to destroy the prestige of the white races – as indeed Matsunaga acknowledged in his reference to the Indonesian spectators, and as was shown by the fact that British prisoners were being worked as coolies in Malaya, where there was no lack of coolie labour. BSC pointed out that by publicizing these facts, in conjunction with strong protests, the United States might help both to alleviate the conditions described and to attack Japanese morale. The Japanese are sensitive to 'loss of national honour'. These atrocities could easily be interpreted as a proof that the Japanese Army was a gang of savage barbarians. Protests against them would, therefore, impel the liberal elements in Japan to curb the excesses of the military and ultimately to accept the Allied propaganda theme that Japan was being betrayed by her militarists. It was recalled that after detailed reports on the looting of Nanking were published in America, the officers responsible for that orgy were severely disciplined; and that conditions in Hongkong improved noticeably after Mr Eden's statement in the House of Commons.

These arguments were passed to Donovan, whose propaganda department unofficially opened a newspaper campaign against the suppression of such stories. The US Navy was also determined to publish such stories wherever possible. As a result of BSC's protests, the Office of Facts and Figures was directed to release the story.

(b) The PWE Mission

Unfortunately the BSC/COI association did not last. In America, interdepartmental rivalries culminated in a Presidential order of June 1942 setting up the Office of War Information under Elmer Davis to control all foreign propaganda. This did not in itself destroy Anglo-American cooperation in Political Warfare, for, as it happened, BSC was able for a while to continue liaison with Robert Sherwood and his officers, who were transferred to OWI, as well as with Donovan's organization, which became OSS.

But several months before the establishment of OWI in Washington SO.1 in London had been absorbed by PWE. For a lengthy period, therefore, SOE officers within BSC were representing, in fact though not in name, the interests of PWE. This was an arrangement of which PWE were either unaware or disinclined to encourage. As early as November 1941, WS had to complain that much material which he had promised Donovan was late or incomplete on arrival. The weekly directives came in two or three days late, the BBC monitoring reports were sometimes nearly a month out of date, and several requests for information were ignored.

In March of 1942, PWE decided that it would be well for them to establish their own separate representation in the United States, and they sent out two officers to investigate the situation at first hand. The officers reported their surprise at discovering that BSC had a section which they described as 'definitely allocated to PWE and functioning as such', and they went on to say:

> We are satisfied that they (BSC) have been wholly engaged on our behalf, and have been sending – whatever may have happened in transit – a wealth of material for our use. They have a large amount of valuable material which will be available for any future organization in America. They have access to many secret reports not only from British sources but from American sources as well. They are therefore in an admirable position to service our intelligence departments, wherever they may be now or in the future. We consider it unfortunate that the existence of (such) a clearing-house had not been fully realized by PWE . . . In considering our future relationship to (WS's) organization, it is important to remember the close relations at present obtaining and material which would certainly not be forthcoming in the event of surgical separation.

But a surgical separation in fact took place. In the summer of 1942, it was learned that PWE proposed to establish a separate mission in the United States under the Hon. David Bowes-Lyon. The proposal was at first resisted by WS on the ground that it represented a threat, not only to the continued operation of arrangements which were working smoothly, but to the whole conception of coordinated activity which his organization had set out to achieve.

It was frowned on, too, by OWI. Robert Sherwood sent a telegram to the US Ambassador in London requesting him to inform Mr Eden that 'his (Sherwood's) liaison with representatives of SOE/New York had been of the greatest value' and that he hoped it could be continued.

He was assured that it could be. But inevitably it was not. For once the new PWE mission was separately established and BSC divested of all official responsibility for Political Warfare, it was obviously impossible for BSC officers to continue day-to-day liaison with OWI. Such liaison would have led merely to duplication and confusion.

BSC handed over all its relevant files to Mr Bowes-Lyon, provided him with full information on current activities and made suggestions for their development. It also did what it could to assist him in the recruitment of expert staff, which he needed urgently, for while his purpose was to influence American operations on a planning level he was in the position of having to build up an organization from scratch at a time when American Political Warfare was no longer in its infancy, but well advanced.

BSC could not pass on to the PWE mission the full benefits of its working collaboration with OWI. That was an intangible asset – the result of common experience and achievements and of friendships forged in circumstances which no longer obtained. It could be exploited by BSC and by no other body, for it was essentially personal. Thus it happened that PWE had to set about building up their own liaison with OWI. Whatever else their accomplishments, they did not succeed in making cooperation as close and productive as it once had been.

(c) Training of American Propagandists

Even after its concern with Political Warfare was over, BSC continued to influence the conduct of American propaganda indirectly. Certain of its officers were seconded temporarily to OWI and were actively concerned with the OWI training programme and with the selection of recruits. In result, arrangements were made for eighty-five OWI men, who had been selected for overseas duty, to undergo courses at the BSC training school for SOE agents, which had been set up in Canada in December of 1941. (See Part VIII.)

By the time these OWI men reached the school they usually knew to what stations they would be sent and what duties they would be expected to fulfil. The instructors at the school were intent on teaching them – *inter alia* – to understand British imperial policy – a subject of which many of them were amazingly ignorant as a result not so much of intellectual indolence as emotional anti-British prejudice. The instructors corrected their misconceptions of the administrative machinery which runs the British Empire, of the conditions in which that machinery has to work and of Empire relations with other Powers. For instance, when an OWI student, who had been assigned to Cairo, bluntly described the late Lord Moyne as Governor of Egypt, he was gently apprised of the real nature of the link between Great Britain and the Kingdom of Egypt. Again, by intelligent and liberal discussion of pertinent problems, the instructors impressed their OWI pupils with the essential sincerity and altruism which dictate imperial policy, and they, in return, were given an invaluable insight into the principles and methods of American Political Warfare as these were understood by the men who intended to apply them in vital British spheres of influence.

In May 1943, it was learned that four out of a team of six OWI students, who had already attended a month's course at the OWI school on Long Island, were, before arrival at the BSC school, extremely sceptical of the worth of undergoing further instruction, and had a predominantly anti-British background. When they were visited by their briefing officer a week later, they had all become unconsciously but enthusiastically pro-British. They compared their own school very unfavourably with BSC's, and even proposed to write a letter to Elmer Davis, urging that every overseas representative of OWI and every executive officer at headquarters should be sent to the BSC school for a month's course.

These men were students in the sense only that they were being specially trained for unfamiliar duties. They were mature in age and experience, had held responsible positions in private life to which they would return after the war, and were shortly to undertake work which would form part of the pattern of United States foreign policy. For that reason BSC considered that their presence at the training school provided excellent opportunity to contribute to the harmony of British and American viewpoints in world affairs; and this work was continued until the training school was closed down at the beginning of 1944 (see Part VIII).

POSTSCRIPT

Intelligence and Propaganda

(a) Walter Winchell
(b) Drew Pearson

As a logical postscript to this Part, it should be said that BSC maintained contact with a number of key American newspapermen until the end of the war. It did so for two reasons: first, because there were occasional items of special concern which London requested BSC to 'plant' in the US press; secondly – and more importantly – because, as already indicated (see Part I), newspapermen often possessed secret intelligence about American affairs which they could be persuaded to divulge provided they were kept supplied with exclusive information from BSC's sources. This was essentially the pre-Pearl Harbor technique of Political Warfare in reverse, and to illustrate how it worked it is pertinent to recount something of BSC's dealings with two newspapermen who were (and still are) very much part of the American scene – Walter Winchell and Drew Pearson.

Both of them, when they embarked upon their careers as columnists, set about obtaining 'hot' news by the infallible method of unearthing all that was discreditable in the past of prominent public figures and threatening to publish it unless their prospective victims would undertake to supply the columnists with other information they might require. This would have been no more than blackmail but for the fact that their victims also benefited. So huge was the audience which the two of them commanded daily that they could make, as well as break, a man. Hence the deference with which they were treated by all alike, from the President himself downwards. They were feared universally, because of their enormous power.

As a result of their profession, Winchell and Pearson were exceptionally well informed of what was going on in America.

They were, therefore, obvious though delicate sources for BSC to tap.

(a) Walter Winchell

Winchell's column, which was printed in more than 800 newspapers, was read by well over 25,000,000 persons daily, or one in every five or six of the entire population of the United States. There was no Senator or Representative whose constituents were not reached by his writings, and since Congressmen like votes, they were obliging to Winchell.

A Winchell column consisted of between twenty and fifty separate references to individuals or events. He wrote seven of these columns each week. Striking an arbitrary average of twenty-five items per column, this makes a total of more than 9,000 items a year – intimate, important, airy or disconcerting notes about people and things. Thus a typical wartime column might contain as its principal feature a forthright, and possibly courageous, denunciation of some native-born Fascist enterprise. But it would also include some score of minor items, ranging from a stroll of Marlene Dietrich along Fifth Avenue to a notice that Mr Fishbein, the gooseberry king, was about to be divorced by Mrs Fishbein.

J. Edgar Hoover was Winchell's friend, frolicked with him, on occasion, at the Stork Club, and was even indebted to him for the capture of the notorious gunman, Louis (Lepke) Buchalter. Buchalter surrendered through Winchell, because he knew that the agents of the law would not shoot him at sight, if he were in the company of so celebrated (and influential) a personage. A telegram which WS sent to London on 3 March 1944, the contents of which were obtained from Winchell through an intermediary, said: 'Lepke reprieved 48 hours . . . Dewey is faced with complex situation for personal decision. He is progressing towards practically certain Republican nomination . . . Lepke's statement (which is being retained by Dewey in extreme secrecy) implicates important New Dealers . . . If . . . worthwhile, Dewey again reprieving Lepke for the purpose of . . . deferring the final great exposé until just before election time, so that he may produce a knockout blow for the President at the crucial moment.'

When Franklin D. Roosevelt entertained Winchell at the White House, he opened the conversation, according to Winchell, by saying: 'Walter, here's an item for you.' Bundists, America-Firsters, Coughlinites and all the lunatic fringe of American isolationism probably concentrated more sheer hatred on Winchell's sleek grey head than upon that of any other one man. It is notable that many of them went to jail or were indicted on charges of traitorous or treasonable conduct as a result of his disclosures.

It is hardly necessary to add that his income was enormous – he himself boasted that he had 'salted away a couple of million' – or that he went in constant fear for his personal safety. The country estate to which he retired by day to sleep, bristled with sirens, electric eyes and other up-to-date forms of alarm.

In the middle of 1943, WS found an excellent intermediary for dealing with Winchell. He was an American lawyer – and one of his duties was to provide Winchell with material. He was considerably prominent in the political world and had direct access to President Roosevelt. Since he was a sincere admirer of Great Britain and was convinced of the necessity of Anglo-American cooperation, his acquaintance with WS and certain members of the staff of BSC soon became a close working partnership. He would provide information which he had obtained either from Winchell or from his other sources. In return he would be given material to pass on to Winchell; and, as the alliance grew closer, BSC found itself able not only to place items in Winchell's column but, on occasion, to write a part or even the whole of the column itself. For example, in October 1943, London cabled WS: 'Between 30 and 40 ex-*Graf Spee* internees released on parole . . . Have you any discreet means of having Argentine public attention drawn to this breach of agreement? . . .'

WS replied: 'Your telegram . . . being dealt with this weekend.'

A column of over a thousand words was written, beginning: 'The following is an exclusive exposure of the attempt of the Argentine Government to send reinforcements to the Nazi submarine fleet . . . The people of the Argentine are not informed of this fact . . . This is the second time that the Ramirez Government has broken its word of honour . . . We cannot shake the hands of men who are helping to send our flag to the bottom of the sea, while our fellow Americans are dying to keep it flying in the sky . . .' It was handed to Winchell through WS's intermediary, subsequently published in its entirety and thus circulated to more than 25,000,000 people. Furthermore, Winchell drew attention to it in his regular Sunday evening broadcast; and after the Argentine Ambassador in Washington had been prompted by this to issue a public denial, BSC wrote another column for Winchell from which the following is an extract: '"Impossible and barbaric" is the quote of the Argentine Embassy about my broadcast and column

... The phrase is too valuable to drop, because "impossible and barbaric" exactly describes the President of the Argentine. Here are the facts . . .' South American radio stations picked up Winchell's broadcast and re-broadcast the story throughout the continent. The result was that President Ramirez decreed that the crew of the battleship *Graf Spee* were to be 'concentrated in small groups, which will be under the supervision of the Army and Navy . . .'.

Winchell was so pleased with the quality of the Argentine material that he said to WS's intermediary: 'This is terrific. For God's sake don't make me a flash in the pan. Keep going.' Thenceforward it was not difficult for WS to place with Winchell any item which London wished to be ventilated.

For example, in December 1944, public opinion in America was beginning to favour a lenient peace for Germany. WS handed the intermediary a column written for Winchell with the title: 'Humanity vs. the German people'. It was a cogent argument against leniency, based on facts. Winchell published it as it stood. Three more articles on the same subject were then prepared by BSC officers. Winchell published these as 'Humanity vs. the German People, Parts 2, 3 and 4'. The evidence suggested that many Americans were profoundly influenced by these indictments, for little was heard thereafter about the desirability of mild peace terms for Germany.

On another occasion, WS's intermediary received a personal request from President Roosevelt to assist him in preparing public opinion for the drafting of army nurses. The intermediary turned to WS for help. It seemed an excellent opportunity to publicize the British war effort (not infrequently underestimated in the United States) and a column entitled 'British Women – Orchids to Some Gallant Ladies' was prepared by BSC. It was published by Winchell as it stood, and WS arranged through his contacts that, on the day of its publication, Representative Celler of New York should request in the House permission to read it in full into the Congressional Record. The Speaker granted Celler's request.

In January 1945, President Roosevelt asked WS's intermediary to assist him in preparing public opinion for the passing of a National Service Act. Once again the latter requested BSC's cooperation, and another column was written for Winchell, entitled 'Things I Never Knew'. It contained a full account of the National Service Act in Great Britain.

WS arranged that all important conversations between himself and the intermediary should be recorded, and a brief extract from one of these may serve to show the double advantage derived from BSC's dealings with newspapermen on an intelligence exchange basis. The extract is from a conversation which took place on 21 October 1944 – a few days before the Presidential election of that year:

Intermediary: 'Hello, Bill.'
WS: 'Hello. So you've just come back from Washington?'
Intermediary: 'Yes. I saw the President. I found him extraordinarily alert, as usual.'
WS: 'Did he have anything of interest to say?'
Intermediary: 'A great deal . . .'
WS: 'He is confident, I suppose, isn't he?'
Intermediary: 'Not as confident as I am . . . but he's in. And I can tell you from his own lips what his strategy is. He said: 'If we can get the vote out we're all right. If we do that, we will have no trouble in fixing Dewey. I certainly got him mad by my last speech, and I'm going to make him madder . . .'

The conversation continued to turn upon the coming elections for a while, and then:

Intermediary: 'Got any more stuff on Argentina? Walter is still after me for more stuff about this. He was crazy about that first batch that you gave him.'
WS: 'I think we should leave that alone for the time being. The public has had about as much as it can stand of that at the moment.'
Intermediary: 'I'm inclined to agree with you.'
WS: 'But there's something here which might interest you. Some details about the V-2's and how tough they make it for the British people. Don't you think it's time they realized over here that London is still being bombed quite heavily?'
(Pause)
Intermediary: 'Goddam it, Bill, I never realized that it was as bad as this. I'll take this along with me if I may . . .'

(b) Drew Pearson

Andrew Russel Pearson is a tall, tight-lipped individual, who looks uncomfortably like a horse, a likeness which is increased by his habit of snorting as he speaks. He has little sense of humour. He is a Quaker, who still occasionally addresses members of his family as 'Thou' or 'Thee'. The garden-pool of his Washington house is stocked with goldfish bearing such names as Harry Hopkins and Harold Ickes. The cows on his Maryland farm are similarly christened: Henry Morgenthau, Ed Stettinius, Eleanor Roosevelt. Cordell Hull was slaughtered in the spring of 1945 and eaten by Pearson and his family with relish.

Washington was Pearson's beat. Cabinet Ministers, Senators, and Congressmen were his servants. His methods of extracting information and rewarding his informants were similar to those employed by Winchell, although Pearson regarded himself as a more serious reporter than his colleague, because he dabbled to a smaller extent in pregnancies, divorces and infidelities. Actually, he was less intelligent, and certainly far less trustworthy, than Winchell. He had a goatish indifference to the feelings of others, and was quite unperturbed if one of his disclosures cost a friend or acquaintance his job.

Pearson kept extensive records, both in his head and on his files, of the misdemeanours of important public men, mainly of politicians in Washington. He knew which Senators and Representatives had taken bribes from business 'lobbyists', and which had been unfaithful to their wives. Moreover, he was adroit at hinting that he would not use the information if they made a point of telling him now and again what was going on in their departments. The results were highly satisfactory to Pearson.

He was said to have in his possession an affidavit, signed by someone in a position to vouch for Sumner Welles's alleged homosexual activities. Whether or not this was true, it seemed strangely inappropriate to observe the suave and snobbish Welles making frequent visits to Pearson's house, in order to keep him *au fait* with events; and strangely inappropriate, too, to hear Pearson say: 'So you say that the Brazilians are doing that? Well, I will ring up Welles and see if he knows anything about it.'

He obviously had a considerable hold on Senator Langer of North Dakota, among others. On one occasion, a BSC officer said to him: 'Drew, if you publish that, you must conceal the fact that it came from the British side.'

'Easy,' Pearson snorted. 'I'll put in my column that Senator Langer of North Dakota said today . . . That will clear you.'

'But won't he object?'

'You bet he won't,' said Pearson. 'He'd better not, anyway.'

Evidently Senator Langer paid a heavy price for his past errors.

Before the war Pearson had a collaborator, Robert S. Allen. But after Allen joined the army, Pearson continued alone. The column itself was started in 1932, just after Pearson and Allen had published a book, entitled *Washington Merry-Go-Round*. Ninety thousand copies of the book were sold, and Washington society was badly jarred by what it had to say of the private lives of leading citizens. Its success led Pearson and Allen to publish a daily column of similar character and with the same title. This column was even more popular and, before long, appeared in 616 newspapers with a readership of over 20,000,000 persons. It was second only to Winchell's in its influence on the public mind. During the war years, when it was written by Pearson alone, it lost none of its popularity, and Pearson's Sunday evening broadcasts, which were made just two hours before Winchell's, had an estimated audience of 15,000,000.

Pearson contrived, despite Cabinet changes, to remain in direct touch with at least three Cabinet Ministers at any given time. He was always able, for example, to ring up or visit Ickes, Morgenthau or Biddle. From these, and other sources, he obtained first-hand reports of all Cabinet meetings and, on occasion, quoted in his column the actual words used by the President or a passage of dialogue between Ministers during a session.

In England, of course, he would have been prosecuted at once for violating the Official Secrets Act. In the United States he was immune, provided that he did not publish information which might have caused the loss of American lives. Like Winchell, he was careful to foster the friendship of J. Edgar Hoover, and at suitable intervals went out of his way to praise him. His foresight paid him well. Once, Hull was so angry with Pearson that he swore to expose both him and his sources. Hoover was, accordingly, instructed by the White House to penetrate Pearson's intelligence system. 'Of course,' said Pearson casually, as he told the story to a BSC officer, 'Hoover came along and told me about it. So I was able to take the necessary precautions.'

Although Pearson was a staunch New Dealer and an admirer of President Roosevelt, the President never liked his column. The trivialities which it contained apparently nettled him as much as disconcerting anecdotes about members of his Administration. Once, when the President made a journey to Warm Springs, the column announced that a standing order for Danish pastry, of which the President was allegedly fond, had not been cancelled before his departure and that consequently Danish pastry was piling up high at the White House. Twenty-four hours later, three high officials paid separate visits to Pearson. 'For God's sake,' they said, 'lay off the boss. Why are you always attacking him?' And they went on to explain that Danish pastry was not, in any case, the President's favourite confectionery. On another occasion, Pearson spread the story that Roosevelt enjoyed the tune 'Home on the Range'. For months afterwards the President could not escape 'Home on the Range', whenever he was within earshot of a band. Unfortunately, it was not Roosevelt, but his secretary, Marvin McIntyre, who liked it. Roosevelt detested it.

More serious was a charge of mendacity which the President brought against Pearson after a broadcast in which the latter said that Hull wanted to see Russia 'bled white'. Both the President and Hull protested that Pearson was entirely wrong, and warned him that such statements might be construed as a dangerous affront to an ally. Pearson replied that the Russians had long been aware of Hull's 'consistently anti-Russian attitude', and added: 'It didn't take me to tell them about it. However, if the President needed a scapegoat, I am glad if anything I have said now assists the Administration to make clear in words what certainly was not clear before in deeds.'

After the President's protest Pearson had large placards made, displaying his own profile and under it the words: 'The Man the President Called a Liar'. For him it was good publicity.

But even Roosevelt acknowledged Pearson's value at election time in 1944, and he sent both Harry Hopkins and Hannegan to speak to him. Each of them told Pearson how much the President admired him for his courage, adding that, although they had had differences in the past, the time was too critical for anyone to allow small personal bickerings to hinder the cause. Pearson was delighted and thereafter campaigned ardently for Roosevelt.

WS gave instructions that Pearson should be cultivated as a potential source of important intelligence, and the necessary contact with him was made. A BSC officer in Washington spent many months gaining Pearson's confidence, and by the middle of 1943 the acquaintance had begun to produce solid results in the form of reports on, *inter alia*, political changes, the President's intentions and the views of high naval and military officials. The friendship grew closer until, early in 1944, the BSC officer was 'regarded as one of the family'.

But Pearson had to have information in return for that which he gave. Accordingly, carefully chosen matter was fed to him. This practice, however, did not produce results comparable with those in Winchell's case; for not only did Pearson refuse to allow anyone to write his column for him but frequently insisted upon putting his own interpretation upon information which he received. Nor was it possible to prevent him from publishing at the same time a considerable amount of anti-British material. This material, some of it very violent, was fed to him assiduously by such highly placed officials as Admiral Leahy, Assistant-Secretary of War McCloy and others. Pearson did not publish it because he was anti-British. He was not. He published it because it was 'hot' news. It was, for example, 'hot' news that Assistant-Secretary of War McCloy told Pearson that he believed Britain to be delaying the second front, and no one could stop Pearson from printing it. On the other hand, his BSC contact dissuaded him from publishing much that would have been damaging to Britain, and at one point Pearson undertook to show him all such material before he used it. A great deal of it was proved to be untrue or inaccurate and was discarded by Pearson. Much of it also he was argued out of using, on the ground that it would be harmful to Anglo-American relations, and therefore to the general war effort. The only time that BSC actually wrote part of a Pearson column was when Pearson described the role which British women were playing in the war. It will be recalled that BSC placed this hitherto meagrely publicized material in Winchell's column also.

Pearson, who had no scruples himself in publishing unauthorized information, was nevertheless enraged when BSC succeeded in penetrating his own intelligence organization, although he never discovered how or by whom this was done.

There appeared in his column one day in July 1944 the text of a letter to the President from his special envoy, William Phillips, containing severe strictures on British policy in India. The stir which this caused is well known. Lord Halifax protested to Mr Hull, and Phillips was recalled. Subsequently on the Foreign Office's instructions Sir Ronald Campbell called upon Eugene Meyer, publisher of the *Washington Post*, and lodged a formal complaint. This, as it happened, was to little avail, since the *Washington Post* was but one among 616 newspapers in which the offending column had appeared and it exercised no direct control over Pearson. However, Sir Ronald reported his conversation with Meyer to the Foreign Office in a secret telegram, and the gist of this was faithfully reproduced in Pearson's column a few days later. Pearson had somehow obtained a copy of the original telegram from the Embassy.

It was an intolerable situation. Cordell Hull swore that he would find out who had given Pearson a copy of Phillips's letter to the President, and the British Embassy began to search for chinks in its own security. Meanwhile BSC's contact with Pearson in

Washington set to work, and, on 3 August, he was able to report to WS that Pearson had told him in the strictest confidence that he had received a copy of the Phillips letter from an Indian. On 25 August, WS cabled London: 'Man who gave Pearson Phillips memorandum was Chaman Lal, Indian nationalist.'

There still remained the matter of the Embassy telegram. On 28 August, WS was asked by London to offer all possible assistance to the Embassy in its investigation, and this was by now a matter of extreme urgency since other serious leakages had come to light. Senator Chandler, for instance, had been able to quote in the Senate the exact text of a cable from Sir Olaf Caroe in India to the Secretary of State for India in London, terming Phillips *persona non grata*.

Six days later, on 3 September, WS sent Sir Ronald Campbell a full report on the case, showing that the leakages were occurring in the Washington office of the Indian Agency General and naming those implicated. As a result, Major Altaf Quadir, a Third Secretary of the Agency and an ardent nationalist, was removed from the country. He had been borrowing telegrams from the Agency's files and passing them to Pearson and Senator Chandler as anti-British, Indian nationalist propaganda.

Thus, much to his discomfiture, Pearson lost one of his best sources. But he still had many others, and as a final example of his usefulness it is worth quoting an extract from a report dated 14 April 1945, which the BSC officer in touch with him compiled:

> Pearson has direct report from Cabinet member regarding Truman's first Cabinet meeting held just before swearing in . . . he said he wanted them all to continue serving. Stettinius said he would be glad to . . . Stimson said he was a soldier and would serve so long as the war lasted . . . Mrs Perkins started weeping . . . Truman lunched with Senators on the Hill yesterday; they all endeavoured persuade him make following changes in staff . . . Byrnes Secretary of State . . . remove Madame Perkins as Secretary of Labor . . . decision already taken make Spruille Braden Ambassador to Argentine . . . You should know that conversations are going on at present between Army, Navy, State Department and Department of Interior re Roosevelt's proposal make conquered Jap islands in Pacific trusteeships. This . . . one of first problems confronting Truman . . .

PART III

ECONOMIC WARFARE

CHAPTER 1

The Campaign against German Business

(a) Schering A.G. and its Associates
(b) I.G. Farbenindustrie
(c) Standard Oil of New Jersey
(d) Pioneer Import Corporation
(e) Economic Agents of Germany

For many years before the war the large German industrial organizations such as I.G. Farbenindustrie and Schering A.G. had been methodically consolidating their interests in the United States. The men in control of these companies worked according to a carefully calculated plan for German infiltration in the Americas. This was carried out in two ways: first, through the branches and subsidiaries in the USA of German-owned companies which were nearly always camouflaged by neutral ownership in Sweden or in Switzerland; and secondly, by the secret cartel agreements of German parent companies with their American subsidiary companies.

When Germany went to war, this vast and intricately organized network of companies became the backbone of the German intelligence and propaganda systems in the Western Hemisphere, and its existence seriously endangered the security and the economy of both Britain and the United States. To devise a way in which to combat and if possible to liquidate it was one of the most important problems which confronted BSC in late 1940.

The United States was neutral. Most of the German subsidiaries were registered as US companies, operating to a great extent with American employees and camouflaged by dummy neutral ownership. BSC had, therefore, to achieve its objective without offending sensitive US public opinion, particularly as represented in Congress. A false step might have created a revulsion against

Britain which would have seriously prejudiced such criticial negotiations as Lend-Lease.

With this in mind, a plan was formulated in BSC's offices. It was decided that the SI Division must obtain absolute proof of the existence of direct connections between Germany and German firms operating under cover in the United States. The SO Division would then expose these connections by means of a powerful newspaper campaign designed to persuade public opinion that American/German firms menaced the security of the United States and to bring pressure upon the US Government to control German and collaborationist business. Further, it was decided that the SI Division must provide the Treasury, the FBI and the Anti-Trust Division of the Department of Justice – agencies which, although anxious to cooperate, had never commanded enough public support to risk bucking Big Business – with evidence for taking action against German-controlled businesses on technical grounds, such as the infraction of the anti-trust laws. This meant that the SI Division would have to find proof of the existence of cartel agreements between the German parent companies and their subsidiaries in the United States.

The plan was put into operation, and the story of how it affected the larger companies concerned is told briefly in the following pages.

(a) Schering A.G. and its Associates

In the summer of 1940, after the fall of France, the large German chemical firm, Schering A.G., was the subject of serious study in three places: London, New York, and Bloomfield (NJ), USA. In London, the Ministry of Economic Warfare, then compiling its Statutory List to help enforce the economic blockade of Germany, realized that the list was full of gaps, because firms like Schering A.G. had built up complicated systems of neutral holding companies in Switzerland and dummy concerns throughout Europe and South America for the express purpose of evading Allied control. In New York, the men who formed the nucleus of what was later to become British Security Coordination had initiated their investigation. About a dozen miles from New York, in Bloomfield, New Jersey, a senior official of Schering/Bloomfield learned with grave concern that the firm for which he worked was in reality a subsidiary of the German firm Schering A.G. and that the professed Swiss ownership was merely camouflage.

This official of Schering, who was a German citizen awaiting

The Campaign against German Business

American naturalization, became so troubled by the state of affairs which he knew to exist that he obtained an interview with the Assistant Secretary of State, Adolf Berle, and told him that Schering A.G./Berlin was evading the British blockade through the use of dummies in South America and through the so-called Swiss-owned Schering/Bloomfield, that it was providing funds and cover for German espionage in the United States and was indulging in large-scale Nazi propaganda. Berle listened to the story, commented politely 'Very interesting', and subsequently wrote a confused report on the subject, which began: 'From a source – the reliability of which is not confirmed – I have learned the following . . .' In effect, the State Department were not interested. The Schering official then told his story to the Department of Justice, but they informed him that there were no legal means available to them for taking action. He decided to get in touch with the British.

Through an acquaintance, formerly the Berlin manager of an American bank, a meeting was arranged with an officer of BSC. (WS's organization during 1940 was not yet known as BSC, but, to avoid confusion, it is called by that name in this narrative.) The BSC officer listened to the Schering man's story, then he told him to go back to Bloomfield, NJ, and to continue with his job for the time being. He urged him to try to obtain documentary proof of his charges.

During the succeeding months, the evidence began to accumulate. BSC's new agent had access to the files of Schering/Bloomfield and these he was able to remove from the office for short periods. Almost daily, he and the BSC officer who was guiding him met in a small hotel in midtown Manhattan. The files and documents taken from the office were picked up in Bloomfield by taxi in the evening; photostatic copies were made and the originals were returned to the office early the next morning. Certain of the records were not ordinarily available to the agent, but Sunday visits to the Bloomfield office enabled him to purloin what he could not pick up during the week.

The management of Schering/Bloomfield were aware, of course, that British censorship could intercept their correspondence with Switzerland. Their most carefully guarded secret was their connection with Germany (through dummies in Switzerland) so they were particularly careful to word their correspondence in such a way that this connection would not be revealed. It was decided, therefore, to manufacture evidence of the facts which had been learned but could not otherwise be proved. BSC instructed the agent to obtain Schering letterheads. Under these letterheads incriminating letters were written in the BSC office for signature by the agent who was still working as a senior Schering official. On each occasion that such letters were despatched, BSC would advise censorship stations and the censors would intercept them and send them back to BSC as submissions.

After several months of work an imposing array of evidence had been amassed. Briefly the story was this. During the period between the wars, Schering A.G. had become one of Germany's largest exporters of pharmaceutical and medicinal products and of fine laboratory chemicals. Its export system, which was extremely bold and competent, had been devised by Julius Weltzien, a Jew who served as president of the company until 1938, and was then transferred to the United States because the Nazis were 'purifying' the German firm from a racial point of view. The Nazis apparently considered him too valuable a man to liquidate.

The American subsidiary, the Schering Corporation, was established in Bloomfield, New Jersey, during 1939, and was developed into a small facsimile of the Berlin firm so that it could act alone in case of necessity. Weltzien was its president in 1940; its vice-president was an American physician called Gregory Stragnell, and its secretary was a US-naturalized German, Ernst Hammer. Here it should be noted that the Swiss dummy companies, through which Berlin controlled its foreign subsidiaries, were financed by the Swiss Bank Corporation of Basle, London and New York. The connection of the Swiss-American firm in Bloomfield with the German parent company was very close, as the following facts go to show:

1. Although itself using a different trademark, Schering/Bloomfield owned all the Schering/Berlin patents and trademarks in the USA.
2. Schering/Bloomfield paid licence fees to Schering/Berlin, although after the beginning of the war the money was diverted through the Swiss Bank Corporation.
3. Until the outbreak of war there was a constant interflow of experience and knowledge between the two companies through visits exchanged between Berlin and Bloomfield.
4. When the Jews were expelled from Schering/Berlin, the most important of them came straight over to Schering/Bloomfield; not only the president Weltzien, but the chief chemist, the chief legal adviser and one of the physicians.
5. After the outbreak of war, and with the advent of the British

The Campaign against German Business

blockade, Schering/Bloomfield, by agreement with Berlin, took over the task of supplying the Schering subsidiaries in Latin America, formerly supplied by Schering/Berlin. This was a complex task, for which Bloomfield had already been supplied with full instructions, sets of German type packages, labels, prescriptions, and so forth, varying from country to country.

When the war broke out, Schering/Berlin took certain carefully calculated steps to retain its world markets in spite of the British blacklist and blockade. Instead of exporting directly from Germany, it did so through its agents in Belgium and Holland, and its subsidiaries in Milan. It cancelled its cartel agreements with Schering/Bloomfield and agreed that Bloomfield should take over the task of supplying its Western Hemisphere markets. A dummy holding company in Switzerland called *Forinvent* had already been formed in order to take over ownership of all Schering interests in the British Empire, except in England and in Latin America, so that they should not be blacklisted. In the same way, Schering firms in England and the USA had been 'sold' to a Swiss holding company called *Chepha*. *Chepha* was, of course, at once placed on the British blacklist. Both *Forinvent* and *Chepha* were controlled by the Swiss Bank Corporation.

Another attempt was then made by the Germans to keep control and escape the blacklist by setting up a trading company in Panama to manage the Schering interests. Dummies were established for all blacklisted Schering firms in Latin America, save only in Mexico, where the manager, with typical German arrogance, refused to admit a disguise. The export business to Latin America was formally distinguished from the export business in the British Empire: the two were ostensibly carried on by different companies, which nevertheless had the same officers; and packages for the British Empire were so constructed as to appear American, while packages for Latin America still looked German. Some of their labels even bore the words *Industria Alemana* – Made in Germany – in order to create the impression that Germany, and not the USA, delivered the goods.

In January 1941, BSC sent to London a report of nearly 400 pages, dealing in detail with the whole of Schering's vast industrial set-up. The report revealed that the Berlin company retained its hold on many important world markets; that a constant flow of contraband passed to Germany through the British blockade and further that half the large cash turnover of the American Schering concern found its way to Berlin through Switzerland. For 1940, the total foreign currency transferred in this way was estimated at over two million dollars a month.

BSC's report contained proposals designed to prevent Germany from benefiting in these ways. For the British Empire, it was suggested that all the former Schering subsidiaries should be liquidated, and that Schering/Bloomfield and any future agent of this company should be prevented from re-establishing sales of its products or re-registering its trademarks within the Empire. Similar steps were suggested for the Dutch agencies. A list of Swiss, American and Latin American dummy firms was proposed for blacklisting.

Obviously it was of the utmost importance to persuade the United States Government at the same time to take independent action. The US Proclaimed List, the parallel of the British Statutory List, had not then come into being, and the only method which appeared likely to influence the government departments was that of arousing public opinion by a widespread publicity campaign, even though this might mean that the Schering agent whom BSC was employing would be exposed and consequently 'expended' in the process.

The plans were made. It was decided that the only direct legal accusation which could be made against Schering/Bloomfield was that of having been involved in cartel agreements and of thus having violated the Sherman Anti-Trust Act, a decree under which monopolistic combines could be prosecuted on charges of 'restraining trade'.

This was the line BSC decided to follow. A friend in the International News Service was contacted. He was shown four photostatic copies of Schering documents, all of which proved in one way or another Schering's anti-trust violations. He realized at once that here was a story of major importance, and in return for exclusive rights to it, he agreed to follow a course of action which BSC suggested to him and promised at the same time not to divulge his source. As instructed, he paid a call on the Department of Justice before publishing any of the facts. There he saw Joseph Borkin and told him that he had some documents that he thought would be of interest to the Department's Anti-Trust Division. As he handed the documents to Borkin, he said, 'What I want to know is whether or not the Department of Justice knows that this sort of thing is going on. And if so, what is the Department going to do about it?'

Borkin glanced at the documents and asked from where they

came. The newspaperman replied that they came from the Schering Corporation, as the name on the letterhead indicated. He added that in three weeks' time they would be reproduced in every one of the INS subscriber newspapers from coast to coast, accompanied by the complete story of the manner in which the German cartels were violating American law. He told Borkin that he was going to allow him the chance to prosecute before publication, provided Borkin would give him exclusive rights to the story thereafter. 'If you do not prosecute,' the newspaperman said, 'the headlines will read 'Why is the Department of Justice sleeping at such a critical time?"' The newspaperman was obeying his instructions.

In fact, Borkin was one of several American officials who had long felt that some action should be taken against the German chemical trusts, so the visit from the INS official strengthened his hand in subsequent arguments with those who advocated a policy of *laissez-faire*. An investigation into the affairs of the Schering Corporation was started by the Department of Justice. Nevertheless, the wheels of the Justice Department turn slowly, and BSC realized that, although it had succeeded in making some initial headway, the press campaign would probably have to proceed in order to ensure decisive action.

At that time, BSC learned that Armand Dreyfus, the managing director of the Swiss Bank Corporation (which through its control of the holding companies professed to control Schering USA), was visiting New York. A BSC officer approached Dreyfus, who, after being told that the Schering properties in the US were in danger of imminent seizure by the authorities, was ultimately persuaded to provide against this contingency. A tentative agreement was placed before him, under which a Canadian holding company would be formed to take over the assets of the Swiss dummy holding companies, *Chepha* and *Forinvent*. A nominee of the Canadian Custodian of Enemy Property would sit on the board of the new Canadian company and Schering/Bloomfield; share certificates of the latter would be lodged in Canada; the Canadian Foreign Exchange Control Board would have the power to decide on all movements of cash pertaining to the companies; and royalty payments owed by Schering/Bloomfield to Germany would be accumulated on the books of the Bloomfield concern. The use of dummy companies would be discontinued; goods would be sold in Latin America under US trademarks instead of German; and certain specific precautions would be taken to prevent Schering profits being used to pay for enemy propaganda. It is obvious that these arrangements would have solved the Schering problem in a very satisfactory manner. By switching control of the company to British territory, the maximum degree of supervision would be possible and valuable enemy assets would become British owned. In return for all this, the Swiss Bank demanded the removal of *Chepha* and *Forinvent* from the Statutory List, and in addition asked for certain guarantees against seizure of the properties.

After Dreyfus had agreed to these proposals, and Canadian officials had approved the plan, BSC despatched a telegram to London, outlining the position and stating that the newspaper campaign would be called off if this alternative suggestion were approved. An urgent reply was requested because steps had already been taken to put the press campaign into effect and it was scheduled to begin in six days' time. The six days passed and no reply was received. At the last moment, the newspaper campaign and Federal investigation instigated by BSC were too far advanced to be called off. But even after the campaign started, BSC had hoped it would still be possible to carry out the proposed agreement with the Swiss Bank Corporation, and London were again asked by telegram to approve the proposal to remove *Chepha* and *Forinvent* from the Statutory List in exchange for the formation of the proposed Canadian holding company. Twelve days after the despatch of the first telegram a reply came. It stated that the Ministry of Economic Warfare could not 'commit themselves in advance to supporting removal of companies from the Statutory List, and on the facts are not repeat not very disposed to do so'. The Canadian Custodian, who had cooperated whole-heartedly with BSC, was disappointed. By this time, however, there were Federal investigators in the offices of the Swiss Bank Corporation, Schering Corporation and many other concerns, and their real German ownership had become apparent to the Americans.

On 10 April 1941, after all arrangements had been made, the story 'broke' in the press. It soon took on the quality of a powerful campaign in which more than a thousand papers as well as many magazines and radio commentators had part. For several months it held the attention of the public, and so far as Schering was concerned, its immediate results were as follows:

1. The board was hastily purged of all members of German origin, except the president, Weltzien.
2. The practice of mis-labelling goods for Latin America was stopped.

3. Schering/Bloomfield endeavoured at different times to hand over its stock to new holding companies, to a small American corporation, and to the employees of the firm. All of these manoeuvres were unsuccessful.
4. The company was fined $15,000 and its president and vice-president $2,000 and $1,000 for conspiracy to restrict trade.
5. The Swiss Bank Corporation was ordered to divest itself of stock held in Schering/Bloomfield within three months.
6. Under this pressure and adverse publicity, Schering/Bloomfield was threatened with bankruptcy. To add to its worries, it found itself without sufficient credit to pay for a new factory it had started to build.

Meanwhile, BSC advised the Canadian Custodian of Enemy Property to sell the Canadian subsidiary of Schering to Dr Stragnell, who was trying to obtain control of Schering/Canada on behalf of Bloomfield. Twenty-four hours after selling for $150,000, the Custodian was supplied by BSC with evidence which enabled him to seize the whole Canadian property, thereby taking a net profit of $150,000, while Stragnell and Schering/Bloomfield suffered a corresponding loss which undoubtedly served to discourage them from making future deals of this nature.

That was the situation when the American entry into the war accelerated the firm's disintegration. After Pearl Harbor, the US Treasury took over the entire control of Schering/Bloomfield. All the common stock of the company was acquired by the United States Government. Weltzien, Hammer and other officials of German origin were suspended and the business was run under the supervision of Federal officials.

(b) I.G. Farbenindustrie

The successful campaign against the Schering concern and its associates was notable because it was the first in a series. Yet even while BSC was collecting data and planning operations against Schering, it became obvious that a much more formidable target would soon have to be attacked, namely the *Interessen Gemeinschaft Farbenindustrie Aktiengesellschaft*, more commonly known as I.G. Farben. This concern, with a nominal issued capital of RM 900,000,000, was by all standards of measurement the largest corporation in Europe and one of the largest in the world. Joseph Borkin, US Department of Justice official, has said that the terms 'monopoly' and 'cartel' were inadequate when applied to I.G. Farben; rather it was an 'agglomeration of monopolies and an aggregation of cartels'.

The task of collecting information on the worldwide operations of I.G. Farben and its subsidiaries was begun in earnest by the SI Section of BSC in the winter of 1940, and by May 1941 enough data had been collected for the start of a subversive propaganda campaign aimed at ending I.G. Farben business infiltration in the Western Hemisphere. It became apparent by June 1941 that the operation would be much bigger than any of its kind previously attempted. The export manager of Schering, who was now BSC's special agent concerned with German business, established a separate office as a base of operations.

It was at this time that the Ministry of Economic Warfare completed a plan to attack Germany's sources of foreign exchange, her ability to import and her power to employ and control agents abroad. The keystone of the plan was to expose I.G. Farben as a German espionage and sabotage system, and the plan had been passed to SOE/London, who communicated it to the SO Division of BSC/New York. Consequently, although the SI Division of BSC had done most of the early work on I.G. Farben, the SO Division as such began in the summer of 1941 to take an active part in the campaign against the Farben octopus. Throughout the summer and during the following autumn the two divisions, working in collaboration, concentrated on the task. Questionnaires were sent out to Latin American stations, who returned them with very full and revealing details. London provided much important evidence, in particular evidence revealing the connection between I.G. Farben and the synthetic oil and rubber programmes.

At the same time, arrangements were made by BSC to keep in close touch with what was going on inside the offices of the General Aniline and Film Corporation, a principal US subsidiary of I.G. Farben. Contact was made with the female secretary of the President of the company, and from her much valuable information was obtained.

When sufficient intelligence on I.G. Farben had been collected, a propaganda campaign was opened throughout the Western Hemisphere. Rumours were spread. Articles were placed in newspapers and in magazines. Radio talks and protest meetings were organized, and arrangements were made for picketing certain Farben properties. The attack was begun simultaneously with the one on Schering, and it spread rapidly of its own accord. The firm was pictured as a German power-house greater than the Nazi Party, its branches were depicted as instruments of the German Army and Foreign Office, and its products were characterized as dangerous. One of many rumours maintained that the archives of I.G. Farben in Germany had been hit by the RAF and the formulae destroyed, with the result that there had been many deaths from wrong prescriptions; another that I.G. Farben had been giving German civilians sedatives in ordinary articles of food, such as salt and ersatz coffee, and were feeding their army with stimulants.

A particularly effective propaganda weapon was a booklet which was written under the supervision of BSC officers and called *Sequel to the Apocalypse*. This booklet, which sold for 25 cents, had a wide circulation. Among those whose wartime contacts with I.G. Farben it exposed was Standard Oil of New Jersey, whose officials were greatly disturbed when the publication reached the news-stands. At first they bought up every copy that could be found. The managing director of Standard Oil told an American contact of BSC that he would pay $50,000 to know who was behind its publication, and a principal topic of conversation in business circles in the first weeks after the *Sequel to the Apocalypse* appeared was whether Standard Oil would or would not file suit against the publishers. Wisely, they decided against this. The booklet was distributed by the US State Department to all their embassies in Latin America with instructions that they should pass it to the Foreign Ministers of the countries to which they were accredited, calling their attention to this exposure of German business methods. The Congressional Patents Committee, and a Senate Committee which was then investigating the war effort, were reported in April 1942 to be using the *Sequel to the Apocalpyse* as a handbook.

It would take many pages to describe in detail the campaign against I.G. Farben and only the most significant facts have been mentioned here. Attacks were also launched against a number of I.G.'s associated companies in the United States. Among these were Sterling Products, the largest drug company in America, and its subsidiaries, such as Bayer/New York, Bayer/California and Bayer/Canada; also the Winthrop Chemical Company and the Alba Pharmaceutical Company.

Both Bayer and Winthrop Chemical were doing an extensive 'replacement' business in Latin America for I.G. Farben firms cut off from Germany. A letter written on 30 November 1939 by I.G. Farben directors of Sterling Products had asked the latter to take over the task of supplying all types of pharmaceutical preparations to South America, and by the beginning of 1940 Sterling had taken over the aspirin business in South America and was committed to supplying ethical products needed by the Farben subsidiaries. In supplying Latin American markets, it had been decided that Mexico should be the centre of distribution for Central and northern South America. Drugs and packaging materials were shipped separately from the United States to Mexico, where the packages were assembled and shipped out with the Mexico Bayer Company listed as manufacturer. Mexico was regarded as a particularly good centre of operations since its currency was not controlled, and any payments to Mexico from other Latin American countries could easily be transferred to the United States. Only one 'dummy', situated in Mexico, would be necessary. Other Farben companies in Latin America could import from this sister company under their own names. A number of them immediately sent up samples of their packings from Latin America so that United States supplies would be identical with those formerly received from Germany.

Another aspect of Sterling's operations was an agreement it made with Germany to cut off supplies to the British Empire. In June 1940, I.G. Farben in Germany suddenly demanded a commitment that Sterling would not file, in countries outside the United States, any new patent applications received from I.G. In a telegram dated 25 June, Sterling 'agreed indefinitely' to the condition and sent 'kindest personal regards' to the I.G. Farben head. For some reason the Germans decided that a still more definite commitment was necessary and on 4 July a cable was despatched making it still plainer that British Empire countries were the target of the restrictions. The message said in part, 'We require from you by cable an undertaking to the effect that all manufacturing processes and/or information equivalent to this and/or explanations furnished to Albany since September 1st last year or to be furnished in the future, will under present conditions not be used for manufacturing goods to be sold by you in Canada, England, Australia, South Africa . . .' Sterling hesitated for two days but gave the required commitment on 9 July 1940.

An inspired press attack upon Sterling Products was conducted throughout 1941, and simultaneously the US Department of Justice were kept supplied with new evidence as and when it emerged. Finally in September 1941, the Justice Department filed complaints against Sterling Products and three subsidiary companies, as a result of which each was fined $5,000.

(c) Standard Oil of New Jersey

The Standard Oil Company of New Jersey, although entirely an American concern, maintained close contact with Germany during the period of America's neutrality. Early in 1941, BSC began to investigate, and in April a telegram was sent to CSS which said in part:

> The Standard Oil Company of New Jersey is playing this war at both ends and in the middle . . . their tankers operating under a Panamanian flag ply between Gulf ports and Tenerife ostensibly to supply the Spanish refinery of *Cepsa*. In fact they also supply enemy shipping in the Port of Tenerife with bunker fuel and large cargoes of petroleum products.

This information, together with other data on Standard Oil operations, which was sent to London in a series of telegrams on the same day, was obtained from reliable American sources. London, however, took the view that BSC's American informants were trying to create trouble for Standard Oil, and the Ministry of Economic Warfare frankly did not believe the report. London's reply said *inter alia:*

> MEW suspect behind this some attempt to create bad blood between them and New Jersey, and comment as follows (on the report re supplying enemy shipping at Tenerife): 'this story entirely without foundation'.

BSC rejoined:

> The facts may be disputed by MEW but nevertheless they are unquestionably accurate . . . The 'story' about Tenerife supply is not a story; it is fact known to State Department and derived from official US sources. Also refer to . . .

The reference given at the end of the message was to a censorship intercept of correspondence from the American Consul at Tenerife, who wrote to the US Secretary of State on 24 February 1941:

> Since the outbreak of hostilities in Europe and the arrivals of crude and fuel oil cargoes from American, Venezuelan and Colombian ports, only one oil transfer has taken place in this port . . . However, fuel and/or Diesel oil has been supplied

on several occasions by the local refinery since the outbreak of war in Europe to both German and Italian vessels lying in this port, three of which, two tankers and one cargo vessel, clandestinely cleared for unknown destinations . . .

The relationship between Standard Oil and I.G. Farben began with a series of agreements dating from 1927. Their basic understanding, as described in Standard's own words, was that 'The I.G. are going to stay out of the oil business and we (Standard) are going to stay out of the chemical business insofar as that has no bearing on the oil business.' In 1929, they consummated what has been described by both Standard and I.G. as a 'full marriage'. The parties to these nuptials endowed each other with exclusive monopolies in their respective holdings, vowing 'loyal adherence to each other's welfare' for such time as the union should endure. Standard received *carte blanche* in the oil industry of the world with the exception of the domestic German market. I.G. Farben in turn was assured a free hand in the entire chemical industry of the world, including the United States. This arrangement was to prove embarrassing to Standard at a later date.

The marriage of these two organizations worked directly against the interests of the United States when, after Pearl Harbor, Americans found that their wealthy country was far from self-sufficient. The fall of Malaya and the Netherlands East Indies suddenly created a rubber shortage in America, and there was no alternative source of supply of natural rubber large enough to fill more than a fraction of the US war machine's needs. Standard Oil had been interested in the development of synthetic rubber for several years, but the product fell within the exclusive province of I.G. Farben because of the agreements made in 1929. The two companies nevertheless had an agreement whereby all knowledge should be pooled, and because of this the terms of the agreement had been stretched and Standard had been allowed to carry out certain experiments in the synthetic rubber field. The fact remains that although I.G. Farben did not give the results of its experiments to Standard Oil, yet the latter told I.G. all that it knew and had discovered. Between 1930 and 1938, Standard Oil had developed a form of synthetic rubber known as Butyl, which has a petroleum base. This was given to the Germans and was for them a substantial gain, because Standard's Butyl rubber could be made more easily, using less critical materials than Buna, the I.G. product, and its quality at that time was almost the equal of Buna.

The Campaign against German Business

At the same time Standard could not give American companies the right to manufacture Butyl rubber. Four rubber manufacturers and one chemical company in the years 1932–4 applied to Standard for licences under the Standard-I.G. synthetic rubber patents. In one case (that of the Goodrich Rubber Company) Standard drew up an agreement which would have allowed American manufacture of Butyl, but I.G. refused to ratify it. In this unfortunate respect, therefore, Standard Oil honoured its agreement with I.G. Farben to the letter, and it was not until late in 1939, some time after the outbreak of war in Europe, that the strictures were relaxed and Standard was allowed to license the rubber companies under the I.G. patents to make Buna. Even then, however, Standard was reluctant to license potential competitors because of its instinctive desire to protect and perpetuate its monopoly in the United States. And when Goodrich started to fabricate Buna without Standard's permission, three months before Pearl Harbor, Standard filed suit for infringement of I.G. Farben patents.

Such was Standard Oil's relationship with I.G. Farben. But many more interesting details were uncovered by the investigations which BSC conducted throughout 1941. A report was received from a French oil technician who declared that he was part owner of certain interests in Germany on which he had refused to pay taxes. Standard Oil, also part owner, paid his taxes as well as their own, and told him he 'could square up with them later'. He named one of the officials of the company as being in business communication with the Germans, and apparently on the best of terms with them.

It was known that in October 1939, a month after the outbreak of war, a vice-president of Standard Oil had gone to Europe and had written back to Standard's president a report that is now considered a classic example of the 'business as usual' attitude. The letter included the following words:

> Pursuant to these arrangements I was able to keep my appointment in Holland, where I had three days of discussion with the representatives of the I.G. They delivered to me assignments of some 2,000 foreign patents and we did our best to work out complete plans for a *modus vivendi* which would operate through the term of the war, whether or not the US came in.

Through many channels BSC learned that Standard Oil was

fuelling Vichy ships in the Caribbean and at Dakar. And BSC's informants within the company reported that as late as October 1941, its officials were discussing methods of evading the British blockade in order to continue supplying the Spanish refinery, *Cepsa*, in the Canary Islands. *Cepsa* was known to be bunkering German and Italian ships. It was also a fact that Standard was providing oil for the Italian airline *Lati*, enabling *Lati* to keep its Europe to Brazil route in operation. From Venezuela BSC received information that Germans were being given preference in supervising the development of Standard Oil fields in that territory; and from Wall Street, on good authority, it was learned that a great deal of the anti-British talk about Malaya emanated from Standard Oil executives. The company, therefore, could scarcely be regarded as merely an American business machine. It was a hostile and dangerous agency.

In May 1941, a selection of information about these Standard Oil activities was passed to friendly Americans. Then, working with and through its American contacts, BSC:

1. Instituted a press and radio campaign to expose the connections of Standard Oil with Germany.
2. Arranged that Standard should receive its share of dishonourable mention in the special booklet, *Sequel to the Apocalypse* (the reaction to this phase of the campaign has already been described).
3. Primed stockholders to ask embarrassing questions at the annual meeting of the company.
4. Thus directed the attention of publicists and legislators to its activities.
5. Encouraged law suits by stockholders who desired to recover more than $100,000,000 lost by Standard as a result of its agreements with I.G. Farben.

The results were soon apparent in a new attitude of suspicion which surrounded and embarrassed Standard Oil. In August 1941, the US Economic Defence Board put a stop to the deal under which Standard was to have sold Germany the Hungarian oil company, *Magyar Amerikai Olajipari Resveny Tarsasag*, or MAORT for short. In February 1942, the company was examined by the formidable Senatorial investigating committee headed by Harry Truman. The 'trust-busting' Assistant Attorney-General, Thurman Arnold, gave highly damaging testimony, which included many of the facts unearthed by BSC. Adolf Berle testified that the company had refused two requests by the State Department to stop supplying *Lati*, and had yielded only when its Brazilian subsidiary was placed on the US blacklist. Another witness declared that *Lati*, using Standard's fuel, had carried more than two tons of Axis propaganda books, nearly a ton of Axis films and a quantity of chemical and pharmaceutical products to South America between January and May 1941, and had taken back more than three tons of mica and large amounts of platinum and diamonds.

Thus Standard was forced to sever a number of its Nazi ties before America entered the war.

(d) Pioneer Import Corporation

A brief description of the measures taken by BSC against this American company will serve as a final illustration of the various methods which were employed to combat pro-German business in the US. The Pioneer Import Corporation, which was headed by a naturalized German, Werner Conrad Clemm von Hohenberg, had been engaged in a large number of varied transactions with European intermediaries and connections since the outbreak of war. It dealt in hops, tulips, glue, synthetic stones and diamonds, and it carried on an elaborate correspondence with Germany in an intricate code. Bermuda Censorship compiled many valuable reports on the commercial labyrinth of which Pioneer was part. They summed up the character of its trade in November 1940 by saying that it was 'essentially to develop and wherever possible monopolize German imports to the USA, and to exploit every disaster to the Allied cause for personal profit, e.g. by entering the diamond and tulip business on the breakdown of Dutch resistance'.

Von Clemm and his firm were obviously targets of major importance, and BSC instigated the usual investigation of their activities. By March 1941, the SI Division was in a position to compile a full report, from which the following facts emerged:

Von Clemm was an ex-officer of the German Army, married to the daughter of a rich Anglo-American banker. He had acquired American citizenship in 1922. Two of his sisters were married to German officers of high rank, and his cousin was Ribbentrop's wife. In November 1938, when war between Britain and Germany was imminent, he had founded the Pioneer Import Corporation. But this firm was merely a subsidiary of the International Mortgage Investment Corporation (IMICO), which von Clemm tried to disguise as 'a Maryland corporation' but which was in reality controlled by Germans in Germany. Most of its cash assets were in Reichsmarks not negotiable outside Germany. His brother Karl was his opposite number in Germany, on the board of the controlling company.

The evident purpose of the Pioneer Import Corporation was to promote the German export and import trade without allowing Reichsmarks to leave the country, and incidentally to beat the British blockade. It was obvious that the corporation was doing big business. The Bermuda Censors found reference to 'very large credits' in its correspondence. A good informant who was closely in touch with von Clemm reported that he was importing looted diamonds from Europe under a falsified German certificate of origin. BSC's report contained much additional information which revealed von Clemm's methods of exchanging jewels from Axis Europe for US dollars, his relationship to Ribbentrop and the German control of his firm. This, with the cooperation of the SO Division, was published as a series of articles in a New York newspaper. At the same time, the evidence was handed to the FBI for the Department of Justice, which placed an investigator in the firm's offices, and in January 1942 indicted von Clemm together with his brother Karl, the Pioneer Import Corporation, the International Mortgage Investment Corporation and the High Command of the German Army for violating the Treasury blocking order.

Von Clemm and his partners were accused of conspiring to bring to the USA Belgian and Dutch diamonds, on which the proceeds should have been frozen, as German diamonds (it was permissible before Pearl Harbor to sell the latter openly). One of the crucial points in the trial was that, when von Clemm had opened his files to customs agents, he had destroyed correspondence showing the jewels to be Dutch in origin. He was fined $10,000 and sentenced to two years' imprisonment; his personal funds and $400,000 worth of semi-precious jewels belonging to the corporation were seized. When he appealed, his conviction was upheld and his plea described as 'effrontery'. During the trial, the Treasury thanked its 'newspaper friends' for their assistance in the investigation.

The campaigns against I.G. Farben, Schering and Pioneer Import Corporation, which have been described in the foregoing pages, were part of a general attack on all the subsidiaries and instruments of German cartels in the United States which comprised more than a hundred companies. As has been shown, both the SI Division and the SO Division took part in this attack. The SI Division, through its investigations, obtained proof of German ownership of subsidiary companies in the United States and thus was able to furnish evidence which enabled the Alien Property Custodian to seize companies whose assets totalled $260,000,000. Before that, while the United States was still neutral, the SO Division had helped to create an atmosphere in which the President's freezing orders could be issued. For the American people, having been persuaded by disclosures in the press that German commerical machinations were a menace to their own security, accepted these orders as essential, and American Big Business, conscious of public sentiment, did not dare to oppose them.

(e) Economic Agents of Germany

Among the various German agents who were sent to the Western Hemisphere on commercial missions, two required particular attention because it was part of their purpose to ensure that German business should be organized in such a way that it could continue to flourish in spite of the war.

Kurt Heinrich Rieth was an economic envoy with long experience in undercover activity. He came from a wealthy Hamburg family. His father had made a fortune representing Standard Oil in Antwerp, and he himself had equally productive business contacts. He avoided military service and entered the German diplomatic corps, spending several years in Paris. In 1930, he was appointed German Minister to Vienna and was in the thick of the 1934 conspiracy that had its climax in the assassination of Dollfuss.

There were ugly if unsubstantiated rumours about Rieth's private life, and his behaviour in Vienna had called for official whitewashing. But he was valuable to the Nazis, for he had many excellent business contacts in all parts of the world. In February 1941, Rieth flew to Brazil and there BSC began to follow his movements. It was observed that he travelled much and met a great many people. When he was in Santiago, he attended a gathering of the four German Ministers from Argentina, Chile, Peru and Bolivia, and discussed with them the question of collaboration between the South American countries and Axis satellite nations in Europe. In Buenos Aires, he conferred with Mitsubishi officials, and BSC learned that he was trying to induce German merchants, deprived of their usual stocks, to sell Japanese merchandise.

At the end of March 1941, Rieth entered the United States at Brownsville, Texas, on a visitor's visa. He went to New York and settled in a $600-a-month apartment in the Waldorf-Astoria, where he was shadowed by BSC agents. He saw much of the German officials in New York and he made free and frequent use of Walter Teagle, chairman of the board of Standard Oil of NJ, as a business reference. Soon his objective became apparent. He was in New York to foster post-war cooperation of German and US oil interests in Europe. He discussed patent agreements between I.G. Farben and Standard I.G. with Standard Oil representatives. His main purpose was to negotiate the sale to the Germans of Standard Oil's Hungarian subsidiary company, MAORT (*Magyar Amerikai Olajipari Resveny Tarsasag*). The cash price mentioned was $25,000,000.

After several weeks, BSC had obtained sufficient information to initiate action. A full account of Rieth's 'secret mission' appeared on the front page of the *New York Herald Tribune* on 24 May 1941, and the story was republished in the usual way by newspapers throughout the country. Standard Oil, who were fully implicated, rushed into print with elaborate denials of any connection between their officials and Rieth. They claimed they had never heard of him. Rieth was equally embarrassed and shut himself up in his hotel suite. At first he refused to be interviewed. Finally, he told press reporters over the telephone that he was in the country on 'purely personal business'.

Five days after the start of BSC's campaign, Rieth was arrested for giving a false explanation of his entry into the United States. Subsequently he was deported.

In 1941, while Kurt Rieth was still in the United States, Dr Fritz Fenthol arrived in Rio as an official representative of the German Potash Syndicate.

He was a Roman Catholic married to a Jewess. But he was nevertheless working for the Fatherland. Contact was established with his secretary from whom many details of his plans were obtained, including sight of much of his correspondence. His orders were to enter the US and there to endeavour to negotiate the freeing of German assets before the US entered the war. Like Rieth, he was in touch with Standard Oil; he was also concerned with the MAORT deal. He had a letter from a German finance company to Underwood-Elliott-Fisher, authorizing him to negotiate the sale of 5,000,000 marks' worth of shares which Underwood held in a German office machinery concern. Fenthol told an informant of BSC's in Rio that he was under the orders of the German General Staff, which probably meant he was working for its economic branch.

In Rio, Fenthol set about trying to get an American visa. BSC, however, had kept the FBI informed, with the result that the State Department refused him entry. In due course, Fenthol settled in Brazil and started building a reputation as an anti-Nazi. He cultivated dignitaries of the Catholic Church. He endeavoured to convince his episcopal friends that the German Army was the best bulwark of Christianity against Communism. At one time he went so far as to say that he was a Jew. He offered the US Embassy in Rio information regarding internal conditions in Germany, and he said that he belonged to an anti-Nazi organization known as 'The Friends of Fritsch'. He made friends with the Chief of the Brazilian General Staff.

All this provided Fenthol with cover for what were his most important activities. It transpired that he was a high official of I.G. Farben and was in touch with their directors in Brazil. He had conversations with Mauricio Hochschild, German-Bolivian tin magnate, who was at that time considering the promotion of exports to Japan. Fenthol offered an intermediary a large commission to procure 5,000 tons of Chilean copper to export to Germany. It is believed that, amongst other things, he succeeded in transferring a million Swiss francs to Brazil, paying a commission to Foreign Minister Aranha.

In January 1942, Fenthol was arrested by the Brazilian police as an enemy agent and interrogated at length. He was released, through the intervention of a powerful friend in Standard Oil, but soon he was rearrested and interned. He tried to get himself repatriated, but without success. The Argentine Foreign Minister, Ruiz Guiñazú, assured him he would be welcome in Argentina if he could get there, and the Spanish Embassy in Rio wrote to their Foreign Office urging that he be allowed to go to Argentina in default of being allowed to return to Europe. His Benedictine friend, Dom Odo, Duke of Württemburg, wrote personally to Aranha in October 1943 requesting his freedom. But BSC managed to convince the Brazilian Government that Fenthol was a dangerous individual, and, as a result, he was kept in custody.

CHAPTER 2

German–American Indebtedness

During 1940 and 1941, while efforts were being made to harass the large German-owned and German-influenced corporations in the United States, BSC was also occupied with investigating another German operation. Unlike those already discussed, it was purely financial.

In the summer of 1940, it was observed that Germany was beginning to pursue a rather unusual policy. Having borrowed in the United States and defaulted for many years, the German Government began to pay off its debts. Upon investigation, it was found that the Nazis were buying up outstanding commercial bills representing debts owed by private German companies to banks in America. In these transactions an American bank holding bills against debts owed by a private German firm would be persuaded by the *Reichsbank* to accept settlement of the bill at a large discount on condition that the payment should be made in dollars in the USA. The *Reichsbank* then made payment in New York from German balances held by the Chase National Bank, being at the same time reimbursed by the German firm (the original debtor) in Reichsmarks.

Similarly, bonds issued between 1924 and 1930 in the United States on behalf of German industries and municipalities, which had remained in default since 1931, were being bought up at large discounts. In August and September 1940, transactions involving defaulted German bonds ran as high as $250,000 a day and forced the price up by about 10%. The *Golddiskontbank*, a subsidiary of the *Reichsbank*, had a monopoly on repurchases of all foreign claims against Germany. By buying up dollar bonds in this manner the *Golddiskontbank* made huge profits for the German Treasury.

A simplified description of the procedure will show how the German Treasury profited. The *Golddiskontbank* might pay, in a specific case, $250 for a $1,000 bond. It would obtain the 250

156

American dollars by paying a premium of 100% in Reichsmarks to a holder of dollar exchange. Thus, at 100% premium (5 Reichsmarks per dollar) the American dollars would cost RM 1250. The *Golddiskontbank* would then sell the bond to the German obligor for RM 2500. The obligor would be glad to have the bond at this price since the obligation was outstanding on his books at RM 4200, the old dollar parity for $1,000. The obligor would then use the bond to meet his next sinking fund payment.

It transpired also that Germany was buying up American shareholdings in German companies, again at a heavy discount. For example, International General Electric Company's investment of $22,500,000 in Siemens & Halske was purchased by a German semi-official institution for some $10,000,000. Censorship information showed that Germany had redeemed DuPont's German assets for eight cents per Reichsmark; apparently DuPont's holding in I.G. Farben had been acquired by the German Government.

The International Telephone and Telegraph Corporation, whose financial position was not good, was anxious to sell its entire holdings in its German company and had been offered $23,000,000 by the German Government. The offer was referred to the State Department, who refused to allow the deal to go through unless the German Government could prove that the money was German-owned and not confiscated funds. Although the deal was abandoned, it produced an interesting variation on the same theme.

BSC learnt in the strictest confidence that the President of I.T. & T., Sosthenes Behn, was negotiating the sale of its Spanish subsidiary to the Spanish Government for $50,000,000. The requisite amount of dollars was to be lent to Spain by Germany, on a number of conditions, one of which was that only the Germans should supply telephone material to Spain. In July 1941, it was learnt that a high executive of International Telephone and Telegraph intended to visit Switzerland to negotiate the purchase of the General Aniline and Film Corporation (the US subsidiary of I.G. Farben) by his own company. This was evidently another variation, by which I.T. & T. would barter its Spanish company for General Aniline. BSC informed the Department of Justice, who told the company that no change in the status of the General Aniline and Film Corporation would be acceptable to them.

A change in the method of German dividend payments was also noted at this time. Dividends paid by German firms (or German branches of American firms) had previously been payable only in blocked Reichsmarks. Suddenly the Germans switched their policy, and the first indication of this was in December 1940, when the Rhine-Westphalia Electric Power Corporation, the German branch of the International General Electric, stated its willingness to pay its dividends at a big discount in dollars in the US.

On all sides, the Germans were taking advantage of the desire of Americans to exchange German currency for American dollars. In the pre-war years, the Nazis had developed several different kinds of marks covering various types of financial and commercial transactions, and the selective blocking of this currency enabled the Reich to maintain a tight control over foreign exchange. There were, among others, Registered Marks, Conversion Office Marks, Security Marks, Commercial Marks and Emigration Marks. In 1940, all these were blocked. Obviously any American business house which owned a quantity of blocked commercial marks, which it had received as payment for merchandise delivered, would welcome a chance to exchange them for dollars, and with Europe at war would be glad to sell at a substantial discount.

Thus the Germans began to buy up, through intermediaries, blocked Reichsmarks. Although the *Golddiskontbank* was the principal purchaser, Swiss and Swedish banks also played an important part in many of these transactions. In some instances, Swiss banks with claims against Germany (holdings of securities of Reichsbank balances with German banks) would employ these claims under favourable conditions to pay for purchases of German goods or goods from German-occupied territories, thereby realising Swiss francs which could be changed into dollars, which in turn would be used to purchase American claims against Germany. Thus the Swiss banks, as a result of the lower cost of the American claims, would recover their Reichsmark holdings and make a considerable profit on the deal.

These financial manipulations gave cause for considerable concern. Proof that they were successful was manifest in the rapid rise in price of German dollar bonds, which had been a drag on the New York market for years. The price levels increased by more than 60 per cent. Registered Marks went up from 8 cents to $12\frac{1}{2}$; Conversion Marks from 6 to $9\frac{1}{2}$; Security Reichsmarks from 5 to 9; and Commercial Marks from 3 to 9.

Soon it became obvious that there was more than one reason why Germany was sacrificing her dollar holdings in this way. First, the Nazis wanted to make a good impression on American Big Business. They wanted to prove the desirability of doing business with Germany, thereby strengthening the belief, already strong in certain American financial circles, that it might have been more profitable to allow Britain to be defeated and Europe to be unified under Germany than to assist in the defeat of the Reich.

Secondly, the German Government could well afford to reduce its dollar balance, since it possessed more than enough dollar credits to finance its propaganda and intelligence services in the US, whilst it could not make any large purchases in the country because of the British blockade.

Thirdly, the Germans confidently expected at that time to win the war. Thus, by buying up German indebtedness at a considerable discount, they were getting rid cheaply of obligations which they would have been expected to pay in full after their victory.

Fourthly, in making these transactions, Germany was pursuing the policy of National Socialism, which was, of course, to eliminate foreign investments in Germany and to put German private business under the control of the German Government.

Finally, there was a net profit for the German Government. It seemed probable that, when the *Reichsbank* paid off a German company's debt at a discount of 70% (using otherwise useless dollars for the purpose), it forced the firm to pay the debt at a discount of 25% within Germany. At the same time, German business was expanding over conquered Europe so that the companies themselves could scarcely complain.

A number of individuals who were connected with these financial transactions were carefully watched. There was Ernst Gottlieb, a German Jew and director of the AEB American Corporation, and his colleague, Alfred Romney (alias Rosenfeld), both of whom were particularly active in buying up German indebtedness. In March 1941, it was learnt that they had already purchased 10 million dollars worth, which had been sent to Germany via South America. Gottlieb was in direct touch with the *Reichsbank*'s foreign subsidiary and in one way and another he appeared to be one of the chief paymasters of German finance.

BSC sent full details of Gottlieb's transactions to London, who then made their own investigations, which showed a tie-up between Gottlieb's firm and a London concern called the Transfer Trust Company. The latter was at once dissolved.

Then there was the Swedish banker, Marcus Wallenberg, who arrived in the United States in November 1940, where he engaged in various economic activities, both for the Swedish Government and for his own firm. He spent six weeks in New York buying up German indebtedness – not only German dollar bonds but International General Electric claims against German subsidiaries. In January 1941, Wallenberg sailed for home. Bermuda were advised of his departure, and on his arrival there, they photographed his diary and all his documents, which gave most valuable information on Swedish trade, Swedish interests in the Americas and negotiations on Swedish purchases of war material in the United States.

The SI Division of BSC compiled full reports upon the whole German indebtedness picture, and the information was passed on both to SIS in London and to the Ministry of Economic Warfare. In March 1941, MEW instructed BSC to 'take any action open to it to impede these operations'.

The SI Division, therefore, enlisted the aid of the SO Division and arrangements were made to feed a large quantity of selected material to the press. In preparing the articles, care was taken to link the German financial transactions directly with other better known and much hated Nazi practices and to show that Americans, in dealing with Germany on a financial basis, were assisting her to pursue these. Banking firms engaged in the mark-selling business were described in such a way as to undermine the public's confidence in them. For example, it was related that one such firm, the *Deutscher Handels-u. Wirtschaftdienst*, had a director named von Wimmersberg who was 'a Nazi-speculator-businessman-spy . . . who had a close tie-up with the Gestapo . . .'.

The main task, however, was to collect as much information as possible for the interested departments of His Majesty's Government; and that was done.

CHAPTER 3

The Prevention of Smuggling

(a) Ships Observers' Scheme
(b) Coordinated Counter-Measures
(c) Examples of Contraband
(d) Diamonds
(e) Platinum
(f) Smuggling and Counter-Espionage

(a) Ships Observers' Scheme

The prevention of smuggling was another aspect of economic warfare with which BSC was concerned.

It became apparent early on that the enemy, utilizing channels which were difficult to control, was conducting considerable traffic with the Western Hemisphere in contraband of small bulk and high value.

The professional smuggler often displayed great ingenuity in attempting to get his cargo through the blockade. Preventative measures consequently had little hope of success unless they were equally ingenious and well organized. With the smugglers, sea-chests and lockers with false bottoms were commonplace. A special wireless transmitter was smuggled into Buenos Aires, after three trips across the Atlantic, disguised as a piano. The Spaniards in Venezuela placed diamonds inside their tubes of toothpaste. One report stated that platinum was smuggled in the drinking cups of canary-cages; another that it was smuggled in the form of thin wires placed behind the stamps of ordinary letters. Carlos Valero Alcaraz was caught by the Argentine Customs carrying twenty pounds of the metal in powder form inside a belt next to his skin. Diego Beltram, arrested at Gibraltar for carrying shipping intelligence, had a loaded camera concealed inside the ship's wireless and documents in the airshaft. Platinum was smuggled out of the Argentine concealed in tins of peaches, and once a quantity of it was found in the cook's stock-pot down in the galley. Smugglers melted down gold coins and, having fashioned them into the likeness of brass buckles, fitted them to their trunks. In short, smuggling was an art.

Investigations, started perhaps by an anonymous letter to a British Consul or a tip from a ship's observer, might culminate in the diversion of a British cruiser to intercept and escort some Spanish ship to a British harbour where she would be boarded and examined, hold by hold, parcel by parcel, man by man, paper by paper, down to the seams on the crew's clothing, the coal in the bunkers, the boilers and pipeshafts in the stokehold, the floors in the cabins, the interior of the ballast-tanks, the mattresses in the bunks, the tins in the store-room, the foodstuffs in the galley, the wash-basins in the beauty-shop and the cigarette-papers in the forecastle. There were many searches which produced rich rewards. There were far more which produced nothing whatever. In Bahia, for example, the Consular Security Officer (see Part V), acting on a tip, searched 119 bales of tobacco without finding an atom of smuggled quartz. Ninety-nine pedestal ashtrays were taken to pieces on the *Cabo de Hornos* without revealing the 'documents and money for Nazi agents in Chile' which the American Office of Naval Intelligence believed to be hidden in them.

Neutral shipping was the main channel which the smugglers used and before Pearl Harbor this included of course not only Spanish, Portuguese and Vichy French ships but the vessels of the American merchant fleet. Since it was nearly always the small but valuable items in which the smugglers were interested, many members of ships' crews became regular couriers who regarded the business as a normal method of increasing their incomes. A substantial number of seamen evolved their own minor but lucrative rackets, and during 1941 the classified advertisement columns in North and South American newspapers were studded with notices such as these:

> Discreet American seaman would serve as contractor, commissions or personal N.Y.C. Back every six weeks. References. Reply 'Elm' this office.

or

> Responsible employee, aboard American vessel, will undertake

The Prevention of Smuggling

important confidential commissions, etc., N.Y.C., returning every six weeks. Credentials. Reply 'Pan' this office.

To assist in combating this growing threat, WS and his Economic Section conceived the Ships Observers' Scheme. The essence of it was this. One or more observers would be appointed among the crew of every neutral ship sailing from the United States and Latin America. The observer on each ship would be met by an agent in the principal ports at which the ship touched. He would report any suspicious events he had observed on the voyage: Nazi or Communist talk among the crew, evidence of smuggling, possible Axis agents among passengers or crew, radio messages sent out after a British ship was met, possible German supply vessels or raiders sighted and similar matters. The reports would be sent at once to New York for action.

Recruiting of Ships Observers was begun early in 1941. Reliable persons in the offices of each shipping company were approached, and they chose the observers. The observers were introduced to agents who maintained contact with BSC. In some cases, the shipowners themselves, being genuinely anti-Axis, offered their assistance. Many were induced to assist in the scheme because it increased the security of their vessels if a watch were kept for activities which might compromise them. They knew also that their cooperation with BSC would accelerate the passage of their ships through British control points. By May 1941, BSC had informers stationed upon 145 ships and among these were ships which sailed the Caribbean to Central America, ships which sailed the North and South Atlantic to Spain and other parts of Europe and ships which crossed the Pacific bound for China, Australia and the Netherlands East Indies.

In some respects the scheme fell short of expectation; in others surpassed it. On several occasions Ships Observers produced intelligence which, though unrelated to the primary objective of preventing smuggling, was extremely valuable. For example, the captain of the Portuguese ship *Nyassa*, during one voyage, obtained and photostatted the letters of the agent J.L. Musa, and their contents later became a valuable part of BSC's evidence against the Vichy French (see Part IV). The captain was a resourceful man and he repeatedly used the same trick for extracting mail from unsuspecting passengers. 'We may soon be intercepted by a British ship,' he would announce over the vessel's public address system, 'so anyone with mail for safe-keeping should give it to the captain to evade seizure.' On one trip alone he obtained eighteen important letters in this way, and handed them over to BSC in due course for examination. Another alert Ships Observer, sailing on a Spanish vessel, succeeded in purloining a copy of the sealed sailing orders which had been given to the captains of all Spanish ships by the Chief of Naval General Staff in Madrid – orders which were to be obeyed in the event of Spain going to war. These orders, elaborately sealed and secured by various devices, were secretly opened, photostatted, re-sealed and replaced, apparently intact.

In time, Ships Observers were entrusted with other duties besides those originally planned for them. They kept track of and reported upon events in the neutral countries they visited, and they provided intelligence about enemy ports. They were used to spread rumours and disseminate propaganda literature (see Part II). They provided information on suspect seamen, engaged in carrying letters or contraband or verbal messages from one port of call to another for Axis agents. Their reports provided material for a complete list of suspect seamen which BSC compiled and which was responsible for securing the dismissal or preventing the re-engagement of many undesirables, since British and American shipping agencies made constant reference to it.

The Ships Observers' Scheme, since it involved the use of agents by the British in US ports and on US ships, was inevitably a potential cause of difficulty with the Americans. Consequently when the American agencies themselves began to take an interest in the question of shipping security, BSC decided to relinquish control of the operation so far as the United States was concerned and to hand it over to the Office of Naval Intelligence. That was in the autumn of 1941.

In February 1942, the Office of the Chief of US Naval Operations stated in a letter:

> In cooperation with the British Intelligence unit in the Third Naval District, New York, New York, a plan for placing ship observers on American merchant vessels has been in effect for several months with excellent results. The plan involved cooperation between the British Intelligence and Naval Intelligence whereby certain ship observers placed on American vessels by British Intelligence were put under control of Naval Intelligence and certain additional observers were placed on other American vessels by Naval Intelligence. Provision was made for the mutual exchange of information

obtained from ship observers between British Intelligence and Naval Intelligence.

It has been decided to extend the 'Ships Observers Scheme' to all US Naval Districts and a Directive dated February 14th, 1942, has been issued for this purpose.

It will be appreciated if you will inform the British Intelligence units in the various US Naval Districts of this plan and request their cooperation with Naval Intelligence in placing it in effect.

After Pearl Harbor, ONI repeatedly pressed for resumption of the formerly close cooperation with BSC, on the grounds that they were unable to operate the scheme properly without contact with someone in the BSC office. The final plan left American vessels and ports to the Americans, and neutral vessels and South American ports to BSC. With the responsibilities divided in this way, and with all parties utilizing fully the experience already gained, the scheme worked well. The reports gathered from observers in Latin American ports were of great assistance to BSC in its campaign against Axis smugglers during 1942 and 1943.

A useful by-product of the Ships Observers' Scheme was the close liaison which developed between BSC agents and the shipowners, for this resulted in the latter making available much information in regard to their cargoes and passengers. It was arranged that they should make up the baggage manifests of their vessels, particularly of those sailing to South America and Lisbon, before the ships reached Bermuda *en route* in order to facilitate control at that port. Further, they provided information revealing the age, nationality, occupation and destination of all passengers entering or leaving the USA, by incoming and outgoing vessels on the East Coast, a procedure which simplified the business of controlling passengers. This latter arrangement synchronized well with BSC's general endeavour to keep track of all travellers of enemy or potential enemy nationality entering and leaving ports in the Western Hemisphere. One section of the Observers' organization arranged through contacts within the New York and Mexico City offices of the Japanese *Nippon Yusen Kaisha* and *Osaka Yusen Kaisha* lines to get regular information about all passengers on Japanese ships. The consulates at Seattle, San Francisco and Los Angeles were likewise asked to cooperate. They did what they could, although they were somewhat hampered by the laxity of the US immigration laws, which permitted the passenger lists to be handed in as much as two months after the ships had sailed. By July 1941, BSC was receiving and examining the names and destinations of 20,000 travellers per month. The Ministry of Economic Warfare confirmed the value of this work which became especially important when Russia's entry into the war stopped travel from Axis Europe through the Far East.

During 1941, both the British and the US Governments began to tighten their control of travellers on neutral ships. The FBI, for example, determined in April 1941 to obtain the passenger lists of all Japanese ships entering or leaving Pacific ports. In the same month, BSC asked SIS/London to arrange that all Spanish and Portuguese ships should be diverted to British control points for examination. While the Foreign Office were at first reluctant to provoke diplomatic objections by accepting this suggestion, they eventually agreed that all neutral ships should be compelled to visit British control points. The result was a rich harvest of Axis agents, correspondence and contraband.

(b) Coordinated Counter-Measures

After Pearl Harbor, enemy smuggling activities were concentrated in South America, which was the last neutral source of strategic raw materials in the Western Hemisphere. Accordingly, when WS was instructed by London to take control of all SIS stations in Latin America, he became responsible, *inter alia*, for directing counter-measures.

By January 1942, the *Lati* airline, flying between South America and Europe, had been put out of business as a result of BSC action (see Part VI), and the only remaining channel for smuggling available to the enemy was neutral shipping. Unfortunately the majority of the neutral ships plying the South Atlantic were Spanish and indirectly controlled by Germany.

The three main shipping lines involved were:

(1) The *Ybarra Line*, with which Generalissimo Franco himself had some connection. The line was apparently owned by the Conde de Ybarra and the Conde Mayalde, the ex-Ambassador to Berlin. Though reported to be nearly bankrupt at the beginning of the war, Ybarra bought the American liners *President Lincoln* and *President Wilson* in 1940, rechristened them *Cabo de Buena Esperanza* and *Cabo de Hornos*, and made phenomenal profits out of them. He also owned a few small freighters. All his ships called at South American ports.

(2) The *Naviera Aznar* had a big fleet of Basque freighters. It

The Prevention of Smuggling

had once been owned by two Basque families, De La Sota and Aznar. In 1934, the former bought out the latter's interest but after the Spanish Civil War, in which the De La Sotas sided against Franco, the fleet was confiscated and handed back to the Aznars. The vessels had once been named after Basque mountains. Now they were renamed after obscure Spanish mountains such as *Monte Gurugu* and *Monte Amboto*. Falangist agents travelled on most of the ships.

(3) The *Lloyd Brasileiro* liners *Bage* and *Siqueira Campos*.

There were a number of smaller companies which were of less concern, and a large Swiss fleet, which was carefully watched and which gave little trouble. Practically all the ships on the Spanish and Brazilian lines carried officers, seamen and passengers who were interested, occasionally or constantly, in evading the blockade.

In these circumstances shipping provided a channel for enemy smuggling which it was extremely difficult to control. For that reason BSC was chiefly concerned to prevent contraband from reaching the ships in the first place and its counter-measures were concentrated in and around the ports. These counter-measures, which entailed the closest cooperation between the SI, the SO and the Security Divisions, were, broadly speaking, as follows:

1. In Rio, Buenos Aires and other Latin American ports, very close contact was established with the police, with the port authorities and with the customs. In each of these three departments there were nearly always senior officials who, if expertly handled, were prepared to cooperate fully. To quote but one example among many, the Port Captain in Rosario (Argentina) was persuaded to place a good policeman on all Spanish ships, and in result several smugglers, including Benceny, the port chandler at Rosario, were apprehended. One night a policeman who was standing watch on the deck of a Spanish ship saw Benceny approaching with his launch full of provisions. Benceny, when he looked up and observed that there was a policeman on the ship, immediately dumped a number of cases into the river. They were duly recovered and proved to be corrugated iron sheets, whose export was illegal. Benceny lost his licence and was forbidden to enter the port. Others like him were thereafter forbidden to provision ships from launches; they were compelled to load on the quayside under police control. The Port Captain at Rosario also stationed on each Spanish ship a 24-hour guard to examine

doubtful cargo as it was being loaded, and at the same time he had another guard out of sight on the dock watching the ship.

2. *Consular Security Officers* (see Part V), with their numerous contacts on the waterfront, often obtained valuable information and were thus able to initiate official action more easily than SIS representatives. Indeed the quantity of information which CSOs obtained was so great, and the quality of it was on the average so high, that on WS's instructions several methods were devised for improving and making closer the cooperation between the CSOs and other British Missions. SIS themselves always kept in close touch with the CSOs and with useful results. For example, in June 1943, SIS received information that the *Monte Gurugu* was carrying three bags whose contents had not been declared. The CSO was informed. When the captain had been given his navicert and signed the requisite undertaking, he was asked about the bags by the CSO. There was much procrastination and many denials, but a search revealed eight tons of undeclared stores and four bales of unmanifested cargo.

3. The *Ships Observers' Scheme*, which has already been described, was operating effectively according to the arrangements whereby BSC controlled observers on all neutral ships in Latin American ports. In August 1942, however, London ruled that observers should thenceforward be controlled by European stations. The changeover did not prove altogether advantageous, for Spanish seamen were often reluctant to make contact with British agents in Iberia for fear of being detected by Franco's police.

4. *Crew Control*. By enlisting the cooperation of the ship-owners suspect seamen were transferred to vessels which plied between ports offering no opportunity for smuggling on behalf of the Axis.

5. *Harassing*. A technique for harassing suspects was successfully employed by agents operating in and around the port areas. The suspect was constantly shadowed, not secretly but openly, wherever he went, and this simple routine often unnerved him. For example, a man who was carrying contraband from Europe to South America was harassed to such effect that he went back on board ship and returned to Spain with part of his contraband, having been afraid to land it. In special cases BSC agents allowed themselves the luxury of violence.

The purser of the Spanish *Cabo de Buena Esperanza*, whose name was Guillermo Robertson Guantes, received attention of this kind. While his ship was in Trinidad a Spanish-speaking NCO of the Field Security Police, following instructions, warned him that he was under suspicion and faced severe penalties. Guillermo burst into tears and said that this would be his last voyage, that his career was wrecked, that he would lodge a complaint with his uncle who was none other than 'Franco's right-hand man', and that in this way might even induce Franco to make a major issue of his case. As he spoke of Franco, he began to recover his confidence and to boast that he had indulged in smuggling upon a large scale. He said he was very clever and could always evade British control if he set his mind to it. He threatened violence to any agent who might try to trail him in Buenos Aires. When he reached Buenos Aires, he was picked up outside a bar and given a very thorough and expert 'beating-up', which served effectively to discourage him from further smuggling attempts.

6. *Interrogation*. Interrogation of suspects at British Control points often proved an effective deterrent.

7. *Informants*. Agents recruited informants from inside the smuggling rings. Some of these men were actually Axis agents, so that it was a delicate and sometimes an expensive business to suborn them. Others were merely avaricious natives and they could be bribed with ease.

All operations were controlled from New York, and thus each contributed to the workings of a unified anti-smuggling organization. One example will serve to illustrate this point.

In November 1941, a German agent in Rio sent a message to Germany which was duly intercepted. The agent advised his principals to contact the captain of the *Cabo de Hornos* and to say: 'I come from Señor Mella Alfageme of Buenos Aires. Have you any photos?' At first the name Mella was thought to be merely a password; but in the light of further evidence its owner was identified in May 1942 as one José Alfaro Mella Alfageme, a Spaniard by birth, who worked with the firm of Siemens-Schuckert B.A. and was foolish enough to cash cheques for 4,000 pesos, though his salary at Siemens amounted to no more than 450 pesos a month. Mella, it transpired, was working for the Germans as liaison man between Germany and Spain in anti-Allied activity. In September 1942, SIS agents followed him to the port of Rosario. There he was overheard bribing the master of the *SS Monte Gurugu* to accept contraband. The master protested at first but eventually agreed to load the material, because, as he himself said, his livelihood depended upon trade between Spain and Argentina, and both countries were pro-Axis.

Agents continued to watch the ship. They reported their findings to headquarters, and British naval officials, upon checking, ascertained that the vessel was officially loaded with 200 pounds less than her normal freight. The news was signalled to BSC, New York; and BSC passed it to London with the request that the *Monte Gurugu* should be intercepted and examined. She was met by a British warship before reaching the Canaries, taken to Gibraltar and searched. It was found that Mella had forced the master to load twenty-four cases labelled 'soap', had told him that they were for the Spanish Ministry of Marine and had instructed him to pass them to the captain of the first port of call who would send them on to Madrid. These cases were found to contain 450 pounds of meat extract, 300 pounds of cholesterol and 140 pounds of caffeine.

Having thus discovered that Mella was a dangerous key man in the German organization in Argentina, BSC telegraphed Buenos Aires to suggest either the penetration of his group by a double agent or his elimination by SOE. But before any decision could be taken, the problem was solved in quite a different way. The US Ambassador in Buenos Aires passed to the Argentinians a memorandum on the activities of German espionage organizations in Argentina, based largely upon BSC information which had been passed to the FBI from time to time. The memorandum contained strong evidence against enemy agents and a firm request that their work should be stopped. Mella was included in the list and in November 1942 he was arrested. He was released on bail and for some time was careful to lead a life of model innocence. But gradually he returned to his old habits, and after the revolution of June 1943 was considerably active. Early in 1944 renewed diplomatic pressure was brought to bear upon the Argentinians, and Mella was again arrested on a charge of espionage. When last heard of he was still in gaol.

(c) Examples of Contraband

It would require a volume in itself to relate all the smuggling cases with which BSC was concerned. Of the many materials which the enemy wished to move into or out of Europe, diamonds and platinum were of the greatest value to him and around them his activity was chiefly centred. They are, therefore, treated in some detail in the next two sections. However to indicate the scope of the problem a few sample items are given below of

The Prevention of Smuggling

other contraband whose clandestine import or export BSC took measures to prevent:

1. ESSENTIAL OILS. Only from France could the perfumers of America obtain the essential constituents of good perfume, so that efforts to smuggle essentials oils into the US began at the moment when France fell. BSC, in investigating the activities of the merchants of New York such as Schiaparelli and Fritzsche Brothers, found itself concerned with such exotic sounding contraband as jonquille, oakmoss, rose oil, lavender, mimosa, jasmine, geranium, orange flower, betyver, neroli, bergamot, wormseed, terpineol and ylang ylang. All were valuable and all were urgently required by the manufacturers. In June 1941, Pierre Ernest Massin, passenger on *SS Excalibur* sailing from Lisbon to New York, was detained in Bermuda. From intercepted correspondence and documents, BSC learned that he was in touch with dealers in essential oils and that he was likely to try to smuggle a quantity of these oils through the blockade from France. It was known that Massin was friendly with the Vichy French in New York so that the considerable profit which he would make by selling the contraband would almost certainly find its way back to Occupied France.

When the *Excalibur* docked at Bermuda, Massin was interrogated. It was known at the time that he carried 750 grams of essentials oils, although this fact was not mentioned upon his Customs declaration. After much talk in which he eloquently stressed his hatred of the Germans and told a fanciful story of having been tempted in Marseilles by a beautiful Gestapo agent, he finally had to admit that he was carrying 750 grams of oil. When asked if he had any more, he dramatically pointed to his Legion of Honour ribbon and declared: 'I give you my word as a French officer that this is all I have with me.'

Unfortunately for him, as he said this his cabin was being searched. Hidden in a golf bag were found three canisters each containing 750 grams of essential oils. Six more were found in a box which he had concealed behind his trunk.

The documents which he was carrying were carefully studied and these revealed that he was running a lucrative currency racket with one Georges Dumont, president of the Canadian Club of New York, whereby arrangements were made for French expatriates in the US to transmit money to relatives in France. He was interned in Bermuda for several months. Later, he tried to clear his reputation in New York by joining the Free French, but BSC advised that his application should be rejected, which it was. His business in New York was boycotted and his career as a smuggler and a racketeer came to an end.

His case is but one among many. The careful watch which was kept on the correspondence of the larger merchants and that of their friends in Europe made interception reasonably certain, for all were usually foolish enough to reveal their plans in letters.

2. OPIUM. BSC became involved in tracking down the opium smugglers not so much as a war measure as to assist HM Government in combating the traffic between the US and Britain. On one occasion, BSC informed London that opium was being smuggled back and forth by Chinese crews on ships leaving the Mersey area, and that these men carried the narcotic ashore in the batteries of the torches which they used in the blackout.

Some opium found its way from London to Cuba and from there it was carried to the coasts of Florida and Louisiana in small fishing sloops. This particular business was directed from Miami by two gentlemen who had held respectively the posts of Commander in Chief of the Cuban Army and Chief of the Cuban Navy!

3. INSULIN. Whilst Italy was in the war, the Spanish Embassy in Buenos Aires sent quantities of insulin to the Italian Insulin Society in Milan by diplomatic bag. BSC was unable to prevent this.

4. LIGHTER FLINTS. In 1941, BSC learnt from an observer on the *SS Commandante Pessoa* that a very considerable and lucrative smuggling business in lighter flints was being carried out by the Germans in order to increase their foreign exchange abroad. The method which they used was to despatch the flints to Lisbon from Germany by air, and to load them on to *Lloyd Brasileiro* vessels at Lisbon, concealed in the ships' stores, in baskets containing vegetables and in cases of wine. There was apparently a great demand for lighter flints in Brazil, particularly in the interior where matches were scarce, and a subsequent report received by BSC stated that each *Lloyd Brasileiro* ship was transporting regularly between two and three tons of them. They were sold in Brazil for about $53.00 US per kilo. After an exchange of telegrams between New York and Lisbon, it was decided in December 1941 to inform the shipping company of what was going on and to warn them that if they themselves did not take immediate steps to halt the traffic, their ships

The Prevention of Smuggling

would be stopped on the high seas by British men-of-war and subjected to thorough search. The Brazilian customs officials were also advised and the results generally were satisfactory. Not only were considerable consignments of flints confiscated by the Customs in Rio but *Lloyd Brasileiro* were persuaded to cooperate fully.

5. RADIUM. In 1941, a report was received from London that the Germans were planning to smuggle 70 grams of radium out of America. In view of the fact that the world total of radium is only 180 grams, this was a large undertaking and it was vital that it should be frustrated. BSC investigated immediately, traced all the possible private owners of radium in the US and took steps to ensure that no transfer would take place. Thenceforward the possibility of smuggling radium from the US to Germany by one way or another, including the use of the Spanish diplomatic bag from Havana, was kept constantly in mind. As a result of precautions taken by BSC in conjunction with MEW and the US Foreign Economic Administration, it is doubtful whether any useful quantity ever reached Germany.

6. STAMPS. Late in 1941 BSC obtained evidence that a considerable traffic was being carried out between Lisbon and the USA in foreign stamps, particularly in unused German stamps and stamps of the Principality of Liechtenstein, all of which, when sold in New York, yielded a profit of about 500%. In this way Germany increased her cash resources in the US.

On 16 January 1942, after America had entered the war, the US Government prohibited the import of stamps from Axis or Axis-occupied countries. Germany had probably obtained some twenty million dollars in US currency by this traffic alone.

7. BUTTERFLY TRAYS. Butterfly trays are made in Brazil. The wings of brightly coloured butterflies are arranged in a flamboyant pattern under the glass top of a tray. The Germans bought them in vast quantities, but it was never determined whether their interest in them was aesthetic or material. On several occasions suspects were reported to be handling these trays, and a reliable agent stated that he had seen some women workers in the German Embassy in Rio taking butterfly trays to pieces and putting them together again. Consequently it was suggested that the trays were possibly being used as a means for communicating secret messages. After much difficulty, and after many had been smashed in transit, some specimens reached London intact where they were examined with great care. Nothing

was discovered and the mystery of the butterfly trays still remains unsolved.

(d) Diamonds

There were a number of cases of diamond smuggling which BSC handled before Pearl Harbor. At that time many fine stones cut in Europe travelled into the United States or South America, to be sold for the benefit of the Germans. Diamonds were sometimes moved directly from Europe into the United States. Often they were carried by refugees who said they had escaped with them from the Low Countries. Before permission could be obtained for the export of such diamonds from Britain, the carrier had to prove he owned them, to undertake that they would not reach the enemy or to promise to send their dollar equivalent back to Britain.

There were several violations, including the case of the *SS Serpa Pinto* in April 1941. On this voyage ten lots of diamonds carried by passengers were held at Bermuda because the carriers could not produce any proof of their origin, or evidence that they had been declared to any British authority until just before the ship sailed. Two lots, containing nineteen parcels each marked with different initials, were carried by a certain Maurice Fischer, who admitted that they were not his property and that he did not leave Brussels until some days after the German occupation. The total value of these diamonds was great: one lot alone was worth $61,000.

The smuggling of diamonds in the other direction, from South America to Europe, increased greatly after Pearl Harbor, and BSC agents were required to keep pace with this development. Some diamonds came from Bolivia, but Venezuela and Brazil were the most important sources of supply.

In 1942, Brazil became an active belligerent and plans were made to despatch Brazilian troops overseas. Any diamonds which were smuggled out of the country to Germany might be used indirectly to kill Brazilians, for most of the diamonds were boarts which could be made into tools which in turn could be used to fashion weapons. Further, the Brazilians themselves had a diamond-cutting industry for which boarts were urgently required. For these reasons they should have been both able and willing to cooperate actively in the prevention of smuggling.

Regrettably, however, there was found to be widespread corruption among the police and high government officials in Brazil

The Prevention of Smuggling

with the result that, although many smugglers were successfully tracked down and arrested, a great number of them succeeded by bribery in securing their release.

An example is provided by the case of Mauricy Minoga. In 1943, BSC agents handed the police of the Federal District of Rio a dossier on a large smuggling ring headed by Minoga. The compilation of this dossier, which was complete, entailed much work and time. All members of the ring, including Minoga, were arrested, and the price of diamonds throughout Brazil dropped immediately. A little while later, Minoga and his friends were out of prison and again at large, having been released without official penalty. The unofficial penalty, of course, was represented by the considerable amount of money which they found it necessary to pay to various persons in order to obtain their freedom.

Incidents such as this were frequent and so undermined the worth of precautions which would otherwise have proved effective that it was found impossible to put a stop to smuggling. There is no doubt that until the end of the war considerable quantities of diamonds and boarts continued to find their way out of Brazil into the Argentine and thence to Germany.

Venezuela had less material reason than Brazil to cooperate in suppressing the activities of Axis smugglers, but paradoxically the Venezuelan police and government officials proved far more helpful than their opposite numbers in Brazil.

Early in 1942, a BSC sub-agent was sent up country to the rich diamond mining districts of Gran Sabana near the Brazilian border. To the south the Gran Sabana, which is a vast, isolated plateau, looks down upon Brazil along hundreds of miles of jungle border. The entire responsibility for patrolling that border, so the sub-agent reported, was in the hands of two Venezuelan National Guardsmen and two customs officials.

The sub-agent's report, supplemented by information from a freelance journalist who had made investigations on the spot, confirmed the suspicion shared by BSC and MEW that the diamond market was booming. It seemed almost certain that figures of diamond production which had been obtained from the Venezuelan Ministry of Development were inaccurate, for these did not include stones which had been mined and smuggled out of the country. Yet even so, they indicated a market boom. They showed that 10,457 carats had been mined during the first three months of 1942 as compared with 4,724 carats for the whole of 1940. Upon the basis of information available, BSC estimated that in fact 20,000 carats had been mined during the first three months of 1942, and there could be little doubt that the balance of nearly 10,000 carats was going to Germany. Venezuela, particularly the Gran Sabana area, was inhabited by numerous Germans and German sympathizers, including a number who were reported to be offering high and uneconomic prices to the miners for their stones.

There were several ways in which the diamonds could reach Germany. They could be:

(1) Smuggled across the Brazilian border for disposal to enemy agents and subsequent forwarding to Germany via the Argentine.

(2) Brought to Caracas and sold to agents who would forward them by Spanish or Argentine ships to Germany via Spain and Portugal.

(3) Smuggled aboard a German submarine somewhere along the coast of Venezuela.

(4) Smuggled to Trinidad by river steamer and there disposed of.

BSC agents in Venezuela, after weighing all the possibilities, came to the conclusion that the main channel of smuggling was via Caracas and that the carriers were for the most part Spanish sailors on ships of the *Ybarra* line. The Venezuelan authorities were approached with a view to persuading them that passengers on these ships should be searched before every sailing. But the Spanish Minister, José Antonio Sangroniz de Castro, stood obstinately in the way of completing any agreement of this kind. He protested vigorously against the projected searching of Spanish nationals, and to such effect that BSC agents decided that they would have to investigate him. It might be that he himself was involved in smuggling. If so, he could be denounced to the Venezuelan authorities.

Fortunately, BSC already had a good source inside the Spanish Legation, and he reported that Sangroniz had spent much time recently in close and earnest discussion with a diamond dealer. The dealer, Angel Arpon Gandara, was one of the leading Falangists in Venezuela.

Following up this lead, BSC agents learnt that since Pearl Harbor Arpon had been acting as agent for Sangroniz in many elaborate transactions. These included the releasing of German and Italian funds from Venezuelan banks and the purchasing of diamonds with the money so obtained. The Minister also increased his diamond purchasing power by taking the spare cash of Germans and Italians leaving Venezuela and arranging for them to receive the equivalent when they reached Spain.

But he was not working solely in the cause of Fascism. He had been heard to declare that the *peseta* would be worthless if Franco fell, and that he was amassing as large a fortune as possible in more reliable assets. It was found that he had two contacts, both of them diamond dealers, who could probably be persuaded to talk. One was Dr Pablo Emilio Fernandez and the other Juan Guillermo Aldrey. Through friends in the Venezuelan Government, BSC arranged for both men to be interviewed by Dr Cesar Bonzales, Minister of the Interior, who was himself already suspicious of the Spanish Minister's activities.

Dr Bonzales accused Fernandez outright of dealing in diamonds. Fernandez immediately denied the charge, but when he was confronted with two definite transactions (the details of which had been supplied by BSC), and was told that these could be regarded as clandestine and so subject to heavy fines, he decided to be helpful. He said that the Spanish Minister had requested him to act as an intermediary and had offered him Bs. 100,000 as an advance. He stated further that the Spanish Minister was sending diamonds to Europe by three routes: (1) by diplomatic bag from Caracas to Washington, where they were forwarded by a secretary of the Spanish Embassy; (2) by passengers travelling from Venezuela to Spain on Spanish ships; and (3) by diplomatic bag to Buenos Aires where they were handed to passengers and crews of Spanish vessels.

The Spanish Minister's other contact – Juan Guillermo Aldrey – was by a curious chance a friend of Dr Bonzales. He told his story rather bashfully. He said: 'I am one of the few dealers in Caracas in direct contact with the Spanish Minister on diamond dealing . . . the Spanish Minister has insisted on my keeping his name out of any deals which I transact for his account . . . I am dealing with Angel Arpon who is also buying diamonds with funds supplied to him by the Spanish Minister and by the Spanish Chamber of Commerce . . . The last diamond I sold direct to the Spanish Minister was valued at Bs. 25,000 . . . I have sold many diamonds to Arpon . . . They are in his office . . . and will soon be carried to Europe . . . They will not go in the Spanish diplomatic pouches but will be carried by passengers from Venezuela through Trinidad . . . Arpon will travel on the ship and before the vessel reaches Spain all carriers will hand their diamonds over to Arpon who will carry them through the Spanish customs . . . The Spanish Minister has arrangements with the Administrators of Customs in Spanish ports for his diamond couriers to get through . . . Apart from myself, I can state that only Arpon, Fernandez, Torrente and Walewick are in direct contact with the Spanish Minister in these transactions . . .'

Upon the basis of this information, it was ascertained that Arpon and his friends were due to embark on the *Cabo de Hornos* at Puerto Cabello on 14 February 1943. BSC agents were instructed by telegram from New York to approach the Minister of the Interior again and to arrange with him for orders to be issued that when the ship docked at Puerto Cabello, no members of the crew or transit passengers should be allowed to come ashore; that no visitors should be allowed on board; that no passengers joining the ship should be allowed to come ashore after going on board; that all baggage and passengers joining the ship there should be thoroughly searched; and that all valuables carried by passengers should be declared and signed for by the carriers. This was done, and it was hoped that thereby the diamonds would be discovered and confiscated when the ship reached Trinidad.

Meanwhile the diamond dealer Arpon applied for exit and re-entry permits. The Venezuelans consulted BSC, and it was agreed that the permits should be granted so that Arpon could be caught with the goods.

On 13 February, the *Cabo de Hornos* arrived at Puerto Cabello. The Spanish Minister himself drove down to the port and blustered his way on board in the face of some rather frightened Venezuelan officials. BSC knew from information previously received that he was carrying about Bs. 130,000 worth of diamonds and an observer on the ship reported that he handed these to the Captain. Since there had been no forewarning of the projected search, it did not seem likely that these were the stones which Arpon had been asked to carry, and in fact they were not.

As soon as the Spanish Minister had left the ship, the German and Italian passengers were called into the Customs House for a thorough search. Arpon worked quickly. He disappeared, together with five other Spanish passengers, into a small hotel near the Customs House. When the party returned to submit themselves to examination, it was obvious that Arpon had distributed the diamonds amongst his five friends, for each was found to be carrying stones worth many thousand dollars. Arpon himself had two large diamonds with him and also a letter signed by the Spanish Minister asking the Director of Customs in Spain to give him every facility. During the search the Spaniards showed

The Prevention of Smuggling

themselves surprisingly indifferent to the fate of the jewels. Most of them, upon being questioned, said that they did not remember where they had purchased them. Some said that if the fact that they were carrying diamonds would make it difficult to leave the country, they would readily disown them and leave them behind. However they were all allowed to proceed on board after they had signed declarations to the effect that they were carrying jewels of specified value. Thus evidence was obtained which would prevent any attempted concealment at Trinidad.

The BSC officer who had been in charge of the investigation flew to Port of Spain ahead of the ship. He arrived in time to assist in the interrogation of Arpon and his assistants, and having brought with him a copy of the signed declarations, he was able to ensure that all the stones were produced. In result, approximately $30,000 worth of diamonds were seized. Arpon was persuaded to talk and made a statement which completely incriminated the Spanish Minister, Sangroniz. He and his friends were then allowed to proceed to Spain empty-handed.

That was in mid-February. On 25 February, the Spanish Minister in Venezuela received the following telegram from Madrid:

No. 30 Private and Confidential. To be decyphered by Your Excellency, personally.

Difficulties connected with your representation in the country to which you are accredited, related to us in confidence by the Colombian Government, oblige me to transfer you to San José, and it is regretted that the circumstances referred to (which I hope will not recur in other posts, and which are all the more felt because Your Excellency knows the singular affection in which you have always been held) should make this decision necessary. I hope that in your new sphere you will be enabled to develop your excellent professional qualities.

And so in April, His Excellency sailed for Spain. Immediately there was a slump in the Venezuelan diamond market. Doubtless Sangroniz himself carried with him on his journey a last considerable packet of stones, but BSC after consultation with MEW decided that it would be unwise to search him for fear of provoking the Spaniards to reprisals. When he first arrived in Venezuela, the Minister had deposited $5,000 in his personal account with the Venezuelan Central Bank. When he left that sum had grown to $103,000. He was not allowed to take it away with him, for arrangements were made with the US Government to block his account.

They were not idle words which the Spanish Foreign Minister used in his telegram to his Venezuelan envoy when he spoke of 'the singular affection in which you have always been held'. Sangroniz was soon given another good post. He was sent to Algiers as observer with the French Committee of National Liberation, and there he found new scope for his old tricks. He opened a large account in Swiss francs with a Lisbon bank. A French diplomat denounced him for allowing German agents to use the Spanish diplomatic bag from Algiers. He was still in touch with members of the Spanish mission in Caracas and in all probability he succeeded from time to time in getting a few diamonds out of Venezuela. But he was now far away from the Western Hemisphere, and BSC's concern with him was over.

(e) Platinum

Platinum comes from Colombia and Ecuador. Colombia is the more important source, and the Choco area is the main centre of production. The Choco is a vast jungle area inaccessible except by river boat up the San Juan River or by occasional plane or very poorly constructed road. Several large companies operate in this area, but much of the platinum which was smuggled was that panned by peons from the river bed during the dry season. The peons bartered the panned metal in trade with the Choco merchants, most of whom were, during the war at any rate, representatives of individuals engaged in smuggling.

In order to get the platinum to Europe, it had to be brought first to the Argentine or to Brazil, where it could be given to a carrier travelling east on a neutral vessel. During the first part of the journey overland to the ports the platinum could be carried by several ways and routes: by Panagra plane to the Argentine within specially constructed luggage; by train to the port of Buena Ventura and thence by ship to the Argentine; overland to Ecuador and from there sent to the Argentine by plane or ship; on occasion it was taken by highway and by plane to Venezuela or to Brazil, for both at Caracas and Rio neutral ships called.

BSC found it almost impossible to take any useful preventative action up-country in the mining areas. Sub-agents were sent up there on several occasions, and they came back with reports that little or nothing could be done because of the remoteness of the country and because of the impossibility of tracking down the

The Prevention of Smuggling

hundreds of small-scale smugglers who were scattered through those vast and impenetrable regions. Their reports, however, contained much information which assisted in the tracking down of the receivers and the shippers at the ports of embarkation – at Rio and Buenos Aires.

The methods employed against platinum smugglers were much the same as those used against the diamond smugglers – and indeed it often happened that the same men were engaged in smuggling both diamonds and platinum. These methods have already been described, but a glance at a few messages which have been chosen from the files serves to show how many-sided and how curious the problem was:

From Rio to New York: 'Joaquim Cabral de Queroz carrier for platinum contraband gang . . . on previous trip of *SS Serpa Pinto*. He hid platinum in cook's stock pot during search . . .'

Report received by BSC: 'Piano in Lisbon selling platinum to Germans obtained through Brazil . . . Sousa operating jewelry shop in Rio transporting platinum to Argentina . . . Joao Alberto, Brazilian Minister of Finance, reported buying platinum and selling to German intermediary . . . Alberto may receive platinum through diplomatic pouch from US . . .'

From BSC Informer: 'That platinum goes out on every Spanish ship leaving Buenos Aires is almost certain because of increase in local price when Spanish ship enters port . . .'

From Buenos Aires to New York: '*SS Monte Naranco* carries six kilograms platinum concealed in tins of peaches in case stamped "Bagly" . . .'

From Buenos Aires to New York: 'Our observer on *SS Cabo de Buena Esperanza* reports Mauricio Abaroa Aldecoa carries considerable quantity of platinum in his cabin . . . leaving Buenos Aires 16th March . . . Metal in tins of biscuits hidden inside panelling at head of Aldecoa's bunk . . .'

Later Report: 'Platinum removed from this place by Aldecoa and is now in barrels of manzanilla wine in Captain's cabin . . . This platinum was originally collected from apartment of mistress of ship chandler Carraredo in Calle Pueyrredon 933 . . .'

Report to BSC: 'Platinum is being smuggled to Brazil from US in Panair transport planes . . . handed over by pilots in Rio to Gómez, Customs claims agent for Panair . . .'

From Rio to New York: 'Gómez will probably be arrested in a few days' time . . .'

From Rio to New York: 'Silvestre de Carvalho spent his last

night in Rio with one of chiefs of platinum smuggling ring . . . Carvalho trades in cheap jewelry as cover for smuggling . . . is due to sail . . .'

Reports to BSC: 'Platinum is smuggled ex Rio by José Marinho de Lima, purser of *SS Cuiaba* . . .'

There were many messages and reports like these, and action was taken on each of them. Sometimes it was successful, sometimes it was not. An example of successful action is provided by Dr Teutonio Lança, who was ship's doctor on board the Brazilian *SS Bage*. In October 1942, Rio informed New York that information had been obtained from an informant to the effect that platinum was being smuggled to Europe by Dr Lança. Rio added that they had informed the Brazilian Ministry of Marine and that the Ministry had undertaken to telegraph the captain of the ship, which was then *en route* to Lisbon, ordering an investigation.

When the ship arrived at Lisbon a British representative immediately went on board and interviewed the captain, who said that on receipt of the message from the Ministry of Marine, he had himself searched Lança's cabin while the latter was having a bath. There he had found 800 grams of platinum and 50 grams of commercial diamonds hidden in a false bottom which had been constructed in the Doctor's instrument box. The captain replaced everything in position and a little later asked the Doctor if he was carrying with him any platinum or stones. When the Doctor assured him that he was not, the captain proceeded to search the cabin in the presence of other ship's officers and naturally enough found the platinum and diamonds.

The captain informed the British representative that the contraband would be handed over to the Brazilian authorities when the ship returned to Rio. Accordingly BSC agents in Rio interviewed Dr Lança upon his return and by appropriate measures obtained from him a list of his contacts who were engaged in smuggling platinum and diamonds to Europe. Lança himself was fined 800 contos in the Rio courts and he never again attempted to engage in smuggling. His confederates were tried and sentenced, though unfortunately most of them were subsequently released. Nevertheless their names were now known to BSC agents, who were able thenceforward to keep track of them.

In February 1943, evidence was obtained that the Spanish Legation in Lima was using its diplomatic bag for smuggling platinum and cocaine to Germany. The motive was not solely to assist the enemy; it was partly to facilitate the transfer of funds contrary to the Peruvian fund-freezing regulations. German nationals leaving Peru would liquidate their property, deposit the proceeds in Peruvian money with the Spanish Legation, and get receipts which were negotiable in Europe at fixed rates of exchange. Large sums were involved, and the money was sent over by diplomatic bag in the form of platinum or cocaine which was purchased by the Spanish Legation. BSC arranged that the Peruvian Government should be informed, and the outcome was that the Spanish Minister was warned that, if the practice continued, Peru would cancel her agreement with Spain covering the exchange of diplomatic bags. The warning proved to be effective.

Another method of smuggling which the Spanish diplomats used was to send the platinum overland from Bogotá to Caracas, where it was delivered to the Spanish Legation and placed on board Spanish ships. The overland route was long and tortuous, and doubtless because of this the Spanish Minister in Bogotá approached the Government of Colombia with a view to obtaining permission for Spanish vessels to make a stop at Barranquilla, the port of Colombia.* BSC took steps to ensure that the request would be refused. The Caracas route was rendered altogether useless after the withdrawal of Sangroniz, the Spanish Minister to Venezuela, in February 1942 (see above).

The smuggling of platinum – never carried out on so large a scale as the smuggling of diamonds – decreased considerably after the *SS Monte Albertia* was searched in Gibraltar at the instigation of BSC agents working in Buenos Aires. Two navicerted consignments of 'compressed foods' were found to conceal not only liver extract for the Wehrmacht, and I.G. Farben documents, but also heavy platinum discs fitted into the bottom of the food containers.

Thereafter the smugglers appeared discouraged. By April 1944, London was informed that in the Buenos Aires black market there were no buyers for platinum, and in Lisbon the price had fallen by more than 50%.

(f) Smuggling and Counter-Espionage

WS's responsibility for directing anti-smuggling measures came to an end when control of the SIS stations in Latin America

---

* This information was obtained from a letter written by the Chancellor of the Spanish Consulate at Bogotá to the Spanish Chargé d'Affaires in Panama.

reverted to London in March of 1943. However BSC continued to contribute to the effectiveness of these measures as a result of the information it was able to make available from CSOs and from its SOE representation.

Ultimately the problem of smuggling merged into the problem of counter-espionage and in certain aspects had to be solved by similar methods. The Germans were as anxious to obtain and report shipping information as they were to procure and ship strategical materials, and it was found that in their endeavour to achieve these aims they used parallel organizations which were sometimes controlled by the same men. In view of this, a joint directive was issued in December 1943 by CSS and the Ministry of Economic Warfare providing that the counter-espionage division of SIS should be entrusted with the duty of curbing traffic in contraband of small bulk and high-value passing between the Western Hemisphere and the Iberian Peninsula in Spanish and Portuguese ships. The counter-espionage section of BSC (see Part VII) then took the initiative in coordinating all information on this subject from British and American sources in North and South America, through a system of shipping summaries. Under this plan, the counter-espionage officer in Buenos Aires cabled both London and New York all available information on Iberian ships leaving Argentinian ports. BSC then passed this information to British and US Naval Intelligence in Washington, giving further details from BSC records and asking for additions or corrections. The final result was cabled by BSC to London, Buenos Aires and other stations concerned, so that before such ships had reached Trinidad, a decision could be formed regarding their interception, search of their structure and holds, and interrogation or detention of crew members or passengers. This system functioned satisfactorily until the end of the war.

PART IV

SECRET INTELLIGENCE

Introduction

While this Part deals primarily with activities in which BSC engaged as representative of SIS, it describes several undertakings resulting therefrom which were of purely SOE concern. In that sense its title has been somewhat arbitrarily chosen; but, for the very reason that BSC's various functions were closely coordinated, it has not been possible to treat secret intelligence entirely distinctly from other related activities.

The intelligence which BSC set itself to collect may be broadly classified under three headings, as follows:

1. Western Hemisphere Intelligence, that is to say intelligence concerning United States and Latin American affairs.
2. External Intelligence, that is to say intelligence derived from sources within the Western Hemisphere but relating to areas outside BSC's sphere of operations.
3. Intelligence concerning enemy activities in the Western Hemisphere. Much of this is relevant to other Parts of the book, for it includes the information which BSC used for its Political Warfare for SO.1 (see Part II), for its Economic Warfare (see Part III), for its Special Operations in Latin America (see Part VI) and for its Counter-Espionage (see Part VII). In addition, BSC undertook the penetration of all enemy and unfriendly missions in the United States and, through its representatives, of a number of such missions in Latin America. It secured thereby twenty-eight foreign cyphers, ranging from the highest grade. Since this work was largely carried out before Pearl Harbor, when the maximum secrecy in regard to it had obviously to be observed, its details were in the majority of instances not committed to record. However as much of it as it has been possible to reconstruct from the files is briefly related in the first two chapters following.

CHAPTER 1

The Vichy French

(a) The French Gestapo and J. L. Musa
(b) Penetration of the Embassy
(c) The Press Campaign
(d) Obtaining the Cyphers
(e) Martinique
(f) St Pierre and Miquelon

(a) The French Gestapo and J. L. Musa

BSC's investigation of the Vichy French in the United States involved more than the penetration of the Embassy. Its ultimate purpose was to discredit the whole Vichy organization in America, an organization which was at that time represented by one of the most formidable Fifth Columns in the country.

The new French Ambassador, Gaston Henry-Haye, arrived in Washington in September 1940. A BSC agent in the Vichy Embassy provided a report on the Ambassador's first meeting with his staff. 'Our prime objective', the Ambassador told them, 'is to establish the fact that Britain betrayed France and is therefore her real enemy. Every means at our disposal must be used to convince American officialdom and the American public that this is true.'

In that task Henry-Haye began with certain very definite advantages. Many influential Americans, with investments and/or social connections in France, were inclined to support Marshal Pétain. Further, there was a strong bond of traditional friendship between France and the United States, and Henry-Haye, though an out-and-out collaborationist with a long record of pro-Fascist activity which BSC unearthed, was astute enough to exploit this fact. When presenting his credentials to President Roosevelt, he said: 'France has been terribly wounded and must now submit to the implacable law of the victor. But, Mr President, I can say to you even if my country cannot free itself from the hard obligations

The Vichy French

which are the result of its defeat, the ideal for the defence of which my countrymen courageously took up arms again 20 years after the most bloody of victories still remains alive in the hearts of Frenchmen.'

It had been ascertained that even before Henry-Haye's arrival, the Vichy Government had organized a so-called French 'Gestapo' in the United States, a secret police body whose duty it was to report upon the activities of the supporters of the former French Government and in particular upon the adherents of General de Gaulle. These Vichy agents made numerous attempts to obtain a list of the Frenchmen who were secretly helping de Gaulle, and their endeavours culminated in a number of significant attempts to burgle the offices of the British-American Ambulance Corps at 420 Lexington Avenue, New York, where they pried open and ransacked desks and cabinets, suspecting they would find a copy of the list. Later, they penetrated the Free French Delegation in New York and obtained lists from Captain Roger Brunschwig, assistant to Count Jacques de Sièyes, who was General de Gaulle's chief personal representative in the USA. It was the Vichy 'Gestapo' which supplied the names and records of the French men and women who were deprived of their citizenship by the Decree of 28 February 1941.

Among those who were subject to especial scrutiny by Vichy were Jules Romains, the novelist; the journalists Pertinax and Mme Tabouis; Pierre Cot, former Air Minister, and Henri Kérillis, former right-wing member of the Chamber of Deputies and editor of the newspaper *L'Epoque*. Others were Henri Bernstein, Eve Curie, Jacques Maritain, Charles Boyer, Roussy de Sales, and Pierre Lazareff. But the two most hated of all were Eugene J. Houdry, who was President of the Free French organization 'France Forever', and Maurice Garreau-Dombasle, who was once Commercial Attaché to the French Embassy in Washington and had resigned his post to transfer his allegiance to General de Gaulle.

The Vichy agents adopted every means in their power to prevent their countrymen from joining or supporting the Free French. In true Nazi fashion, they threatened reprisals against the men's families in France. They shanghaied French sailors who were known to have been contemplating joining the Free French. They met all French arrivals in the US and employed with them the means best suited to the particular individual.

When Henry-Haye arrived, the Gestapo organization came under his control. The head of the organization was Count

René de Chambrun, who reported directly to the Ambassador. De Chambrun was ably and energetically assisted by his wife José, Pierre Laval's daughter.

Late in 1940, José de Chambrun made a trip to France by Clipper. In Bermuda the British authorities seized from her a quantity of documents amongst which was a letter from a certain J.L. Musa to Otto Abetz in Paris and letters from other Vichy agents in the United States, including one from André Maurois, who had by now forgotten about Colonel Bramble and had earned the restoration of his French nationality for his contemptible services to the Vichy hierarchy.

In January 1941, de Chambrun returned to France, and so passed out of the American picture, although now and again he attempted from a distance to feed Vichy propaganda to the United States press. After his departure, the responsibility of supervising the activities of the Vichy Gestapo was taken over by Jean Louis Musa, who had been de Chambrun's assistant.

Musa was a close personal friend of the Ambassador. He lived a complicated life, for he not only worked for the Vichy secret police but handled all the unofficial business of the French Embassy and all covert propaganda on behalf of Vichy. Simultaneously, he was involved in numerous shady commercial enterprises. Although born and brought up in Europe, he was a citizen of the United States, whither he had come in 1940 carrying with him orders on behalf of France for armaments and machinery amounting, he claimed, to $4,000,000. On this deal he had expected to make a 10% commission, but before anything could come of it, the armistice had been signed and he had been left high and dry and extremely short of ready cash.

In result, he had got in touch with his old friend and business associate, Henry-Haye, and had acquired the unofficial position of personal secretary to the Ambassador. 'I intend to guard the contact with the Ambassador', Musa told a BSC source, 'because it pleases me. It is extremely agreeable. Henry-Haye is a man I adore and who reciprocates this feeling. He is the type of man that I put on a pedestal as high as the Eiffel Tower.' The Ambassador himself frequently spoke of Musa as his *alter ego* in New York. Indeed Musa was, as he was fond of saying, exactly right for the job. A tall, swarthy man in his early fifties with a dark fluid eye and a fondness for bow ties, he made himself personally very useful to Henry-Haye and to Colonel Bertrand-Vigne, the Military Attaché.

At the outset, he was paid only $300 a month with an additional

$200 per month for expenses, a sum which was quite inadequate for a man of his extravagant tastes, especially when his wife and children joined him. This seemed an appropriate moment for action. For some time he had been under surveillance by BSC and now contact was established with him through the medium of another Frenchman. The latter pretended a hatred of the Free French and had no difficulty in cultivating Musa, who confided in him that the Ambassador paid him 'a perfectly ridiculous sum'.

As cover, BSC's agent had taken an office in New York from where he ran a trading company. Soon he suggested to Musa that the two of them should go into business together and he offered to put an office and a secretary at Musa's disposal. Musa accepted readily and at once settled down in the office which was provided for him. BSC had installed microphones in the office, and recordings were made of all his conversations, both telephonic and otherwise. Moreover, his papers were examined every night and those of interest were photostatted. He used the office for interviews, talked freely over the telephone and left papers, many of them marked *à ne pas laisser passer*, in his desk drawers and in the safe for which BSC had learned the combination. Thus there was little that went on either in Musa's private or business life about which BSC did not know. It knew, for example, all the details of his plan to buy the controlling interest in a company which had the exclusive rights to manufacture the Bren gun in the USA. During a series of protracted negotiations, Musa interested Emil Mathis, the French car manufacturer, in the project, but, when at last it seemed likely that the scheme would mature, BSC informed the British Purchasing Commission, who took the necessary steps to quash it.

A remarkable project with which Musa was associated during early 1941 would have given Vichy France control of some of the most important radio and cable communications in the world, had it materialized. Its idea was to erect, in conjunction with the Western Union Cable Company, a powerful wireless station on the French island of St Pierre, situated off the south coast of Newfoundland. Maurice Cartoux, the European general manager of the Western Union Company, brought the details with him when he arrived in the United States towards the end of 1940. He discussed these with Musa, and the latter put him in touch with the Ambassador, while himself working vigorously in his own way to further the project.

Preliminary negotiations had actually taken place a year before the war broke out. Briefly, the details were as follows. The

Western Union Telegraph Company of New York was to receive from the French Government a long-term concession and sufficient ground was to be placed at its disposal in the French colony of St Pierre for the erection of a wireless station. In return, Western Union was to construct and maintain a station sufficiently powerful to be capable of communicating with the whole world. For this the company agreed to pay a fixed maximum royalty of two gold centimes per word to the colony.

The Western Union Company possessed five cables running into St Pierre. These cables, connected as they were with 34,000 offices in the US, would feed the wireless station, the latter acting as the final transmitting agency for the messages which would be despatched from St Pierre by radio-telegraph. Thus, all countries in the world, particularly those which Western Union did not serve directly by cable, could be reached with ease, and Western Union would no longer have to call upon the assistance of competitive foreign companies in certain spheres.

Cartoux wrote a long memorandum outlining the scheme, sent the original to Henry-Haye and a copy to Musa. The copy was found in Musa's office by BSC officers during their routine nightly search, as were hundreds of other documents relating to it. Musa himself wrote to the Ambassador: 'I hope that you will give the necessary instructions so that this project of the greatest interest takes shape and progresses as fast as possible.'

The plan was dangerous to Britain not only from a commercial point of view, but also because, had it matured, it would have provided Vichy agents with a means of communicating rapidly and on a large scale with Europe without submitting their messages to censorship. Further, it appeared to represent an effort on the part of the Germans to dominate, through Vichy, the wireless communications of the world, for it was definitely known at the time that the Germans were fully cognizant of the plan.

Accordingly, BSC took action. WS's good friend Vincent Astor (see Part I) was a director of Western Union. Astor was informed of the situation and he brought the matter up at a board meeting that same day. Because his colleagues on the board knew that he was President Roosevelt's confidential adviser, they assumed that his statements had the President's backing. They voted at once to drop the proposal. In April 1941, the President of Western Union wrote to Cartoux, 'In view of certain circumstances which have arisen concerning our proposed arrangements at St Pierre, please discontinue all your activities in this connection and do nothing further until you are advised.'

The watch which was kept upon Musa's office revealed the details of many other of his activities. He conducted a regular business in remitting money for food parcels to Occupied France through Antonio Ribeiro Lópes in Lisbon. He helped the Embassy Military Attaché, Colonel Bertrand-Vigne, evade the British blockade and the American freezing regulations by paying dollars on the Colonel's behalf to Louis Arpels, the New York jeweller, while Arpels's company paid the equivalent in francs to the Colonel in France. He dabbled in the passport racket and some of the visas he obtained were for known German agents. He sold exit permits for considerable sums, and on one occasion he endeavoured to work out a scheme whereby French vessels would carry Spanish refugees to Mexico and would return to Marseilles fully laden with cargo, for he calculated that he himself would make $150,000 out of each voyage. He collected information from French girls who had formerly been employed by the French Purchasing Commission, and whom he had arranged to place with French and American business firms. He fostered the pro-Nazi French News service *Havas*. He kept in touch with a news-sheet called *Freedom*, which spread the gospel according to Vichy through the mouth of a discharged member of the British Purchasing Commission, one Paul Seguin. He succeeded in preventing a Montreal French-language newspaper from hiring Paul Lazareff, a French refugee journalist who, so he suspected, might have written articles unfavourable to Vichy.

While his capacity for harm lasted, Musa served the Vichy French and the Germans with almost as much energy and ingenuity as he served his own interests. But the end was not long delayed. It came when he, together with his other Vichy friends, was exposed by BSC. That operation is described in a subsequent section.

(b) Penetration of the Embassy

Musa, although influential, was merely the instrument of Henry-Haye and his Embassy in Washington. BSC's investigations were not, therefore, concerned only with him. Plans were made for effecting a complete penetration of the Embassy itself and for obtaining access to all telegraphic communications passing between the Embassy and Vichy. Credit for their accomplishment belongs in large measure to a woman agent, recruited early on by

BSC, who worked under the direction of the SI Division in New York. It would be difficult to over-emphasize the importance of her work. Not only did she secure *en clair* copies of nearly all the telegrams despatched from and received by the Vichy Embassy, but she was also instrumental in obtaining both the French and Italian naval cyphers.

As her story unfolds, it will become apparent that her feminine charms were the ultimate cause of her success. And yet, remarkably, she had no very obvious sexual allure. She was neither beautiful nor even pretty in the conventional sense, although she had attractive blonde hair. She was tall, with rather prominent features. Certainly there was nothing about her which smacked of easy virtue. She was a pleasant companion, for she was intelligent and talked well – or rather listened well. She had a soft, soothing voice which doubtless in itself inspired confidences. It may be that her appeal to her victims was in the first place intellectual, and that the discovery of her physical attraction came later as an intoxicating realization. That she was physically very attractive cannot be doubted, for the powerful hold she exercised over the worldly wise men whose secrets she sought to obtain was clearly based on sex. But she had many other qualities. She was widely travelled and understood well the psychology of Europeans. She had a keen, incisive brain and was an accurate reporter. She was extremely courageous, often being willing and anxious to run risks which her mentors could not allow. Her security was irreproachable and her loyalty to her employers complete. She was not greedy for money but greedy only to serve a cause in which she believed. In fact she was paid a small salary which represented little more than her living expenses, although the value of her work to Britain could be assessed, if at all, in millions. For convenience sake she will be given a name – Cynthia.

In May 1941, Cynthia was ordered to concentrate her attention upon the Vichy Embassy in Washington. Posing as a newspaperwoman and accompanied by a female assistant, she called at the Embassy to keep an appointment which she had made for a press interview with the Ambassador. The two ladies sat first for a while with Charles Brousse, the Press Attaché, who talked with them while they awaited Henry-Haye. Brousse had been an important newspaper proprietor in France, and now in Washington he was doing an effective propaganda job for the German-Vichy regime.

For nearly an hour he talked with the two girls, and by the end of the interview, Cynthia had achieved her first objective. As Brousse escorted them up to the Ambassador's office, he expressed a desire to see her again.

The two newspaperwomen had a long off-the-record discussion with the Ambassador. He was an excitable man in the best of circumstances, but seemed especially overwrought on this day, for he had previously had a rather unpleasant interview with Secretary of State Cordell Hull. To his discreet and appreciative audience he told of the very difficult mission with which he had been entrusted. He spoke frankly on the subject of relations between France and Germany. 'France's future', he maintained, 'requires cooperation with Germany. If your car is in the ditch, you turn to the person who can help you put it on the road again. That is why we will work with Germany.'

There were many frank replies to a number of penetrating questions. The Ambassador was neither reticent nor particularly cautious. An interview with two newspaperwomen seemed to him to be an opportunity to impress upon the American public the anti-British line he had charted earlier at his first staff meeting. Moreover, he seemed in no hurry to finish the conference – doubtless as a result of Cynthia's soothing influence. When at last he showed her to the door, he told her that he would be glad to see her again at any time she cared to visit the Embassy.

Both the Ambassador and his Press Attaché saw her again. The Ambassador saw less of her than he would have liked. The Press Attaché saw more of her than was good for him. Very soon Charles Brousse was completely infatuated and under her control.

Brousse was married, but was at an age, perhaps, when the chance of a new conquest seemed particularly alluring. He was an emotional man in every respect. He felt strongly and bitterly about both the British and the Americans. He enjoyed the confidence of the Ambassador, perhaps more than any other member of the Embassy staff. He nevertheless despised Henry-Haye as a *parvenu* and a *bourgeois*, and thought that he himself, with his superior culture, would have made a better and more suitable Ambassador.

Like most Frenchmen, Brousse expressed a hatred of Laval, and in so doing gave Cynthia an opportunity of which she made good use. Gradually, under BSC's guidance, she stimulated his dislike of Laval, and as her personal influence upon him grew, persuaded him to talk more and more of Vichy affairs. Soon he was answering prepared questions and giving valuable information about Vichy underground activities in the United States.

In July 1941, the Vichy Government decided to abolish the

post of Press Attaché, but Henry-Haye retained Brousse despite this decision, paying him a salary from secret funds. It meant, however, a substantial cut in his income, and it was at this psychological moment that Cynthia made a partial revelation to him. She 'confessed' that she was an agent of the US Government and suggested that, in return for cash, Brousse should pass her information about Embassy affairs. She pointed out that this was the only possible thing for a patriotic Frenchman to do, the only way to defeat Laval and the Germans.

Brousse agreed and from then on intelligence began to flow into the offices of BSC. As the days went by, Brousse produced more and more material so that eventually there were very few happenings inside the Vichy Embassy of which BSC was not informed. Brousse had a good memory for conversations. Moreover, at some personal risk, he took stenographic notes when the Ambassador read out telegrams each day to his staff.

Then, in November 1941, Cynthia persuaded Brousse to pass her *en clair* copies of all cypher telegrams which were being despatched and received by the chancery of the Vichy Embassy. These did not include the Financial Attaché's telegrams which were obtained in another way. On BSC's instructions, Cynthia also asked Brousse to write a daily report upon what went on in the Embassy, and this report, written as it was in great detail, filled in many gaps, and as a result of it particular telegrams were often more easily interpreted. It told of all the Ambassador's appointments and of the results of his interviews. It told of the plans and the activities of everyone of any importance who worked in the Embassy.

While Cynthia was working successfully with Brousse, BSC agents were penetrating the Embassy in other ways. First, contact was established with a woman called Mme Cadet, who was attached to the French Consulate in New York, working for the Financial Attaché. Mme Cadet was married, but soon she fell in love with the BSC agent who was in touch with her. He gave her money and in return she provided him with all the information and documents he required. She had a woman friend with whom contact was also established, and when the Financial Attaché moved to the Embassy in Washington, Mme Cadet and her friend went with him; Mme Cadet to continue her work as secretary to the Attaché, and her friend to become the Ambassador's secretary.

Mme Cadet was able to provide copies of all telegrams and

Washington, le 15 juin 1941.

DIPLOMATIE - VICHY

No. 1334 - 1337.

De l'attaché naval à l'Attaché Naval Français.

pp. 232-233

1). "J'ai appris de bonne source présence:
2). A Norfolk de l'Illustrious';
3). A Philadelphia du 'Repulse';
déjà signalé.
A New York de un ou deux croiseurs de type 'Kaiser'.

Tous ces bâtiments subissent des réparations de longue durée, le premier prêt sera sans doute le "Kaiser" qui est immobilisé encore au moins pour un mois.

Ceci répond à votre télégramme No. 4075/."

HENRY-HAYE

Vichy telegram showing that Henry-Haye was actively interested in intelligence matters

---

Washington, le 1er mai 1941.

DIPLOMATIE - VICHY

No. 872.

Je me réfère à votre télégramme No. 625.
L'activité de M. Jules Romains aux Etats-Unis est très ralentie. On n'en perçoit plus l'écho depuis quelque temps.

Quant à celle de M. André Maurois, elle mérite l'appréciation favorable formulée par M. Paul Hazard. M. Maurois, par de nombreux écrits et conférences, a contribué à informer l'opinion américaine sur notre véritable situation. Son action loyale à l'égard du Gouvernement français lui a valu d'être violemment pris à parti par M. Henry Bernstein./.

HENRY-HAYE

A reproduction of one of the thousands of telegrams taken from the Vichy French Embassy. This particular one clearly implicates André Maurois.

correspondence which came within the Financial Attaché's competence. Her friend, the Ambassador's secretary, provided telegrams and information from the Ambassador's office, which included *en clair* copies of all the Naval Attaché's cables to Vichy. Meanwhile Charles Brousse was feeding his series of telegrams to Cynthia, so that not only was coverage complete but facts could be checked and counter-checked.

From three separate sources, therefore, BSC was kept informed of the activities of Vichy French officialdom. The quantity of material received daily was considerable and officers of the SI Division spent much time each day sorting it, cabling the more important parts to London and summarizing the remainder for despatch by bag.

Nor was the Consulate in New York neglected. After Madame Cadet had been transferred to Washington, three new contacts were established and through them BSC obtained all the material it required, including copies of cables and other documents, rubber stamps, blank passports and details regarding the secret marks made upon visas which the Consulate issued. These marks were intended to indicate to examiners the degree of reliability, from the Vichy point of view, which should be placed on individual passport holders. Knowledge of their meaning, therefore, was very useful in assessing the danger to which an agent would be exposed if he entered France (see Part VIII).

(c) The Press Campaign

In the summer of 1941, the SI Division of BSC compiled a comprehensive report on the whole Vichy French situation in the United States, together with an appendix of photostatted documents and transcripts of recorded telephone conversations. WS took it to London in July 1941, and meanwhile arranged for a copy to be given to President Roosevelt.

The President read it 'as a bedtime story' and described it as 'the most fascinating reading I have had for a long time . . . the best piece of comprehensive intelligence work I have come across since the last war'. At WS's suggestion, he was asked for permission to publish the details in the USA as part of a projected press campaign, and he agreed. His Secretary of State, Cordell Hull, and Under Secretary, Sumner Welles, were also in favour of such a campaign, Cordell Hull himself having suggested that BSC should 'blow Vichy sky-high'.

This was an SO job, and the cooperation of the SO Division was enlisted in the usual way (see Part II). Plans were made at once. The SI report was rewritten and suitably edited in the form of an article which was passed to a safe contact on the *New York Herald Tribune* staff. The article appeared on the front page of that paper on 31 August, 1941, which was a Sunday. It was illustrated with photographs of Henry-Haye and Georges Bertrand-Vigne, the Military Attaché, and of Count René de Chambrun and his wife, José, and with photostatic copies of some of Bertrand-Vigne's letters to Musa. It contained an attack on Charles Brousse, and this was included purposely so as to deflect suspicion from him.

The article was in the nature of an introduction to a complete exposure of Vichy intrigue. It accused the French Embassy of running a secret agency for collecting intelligence from and for exerting political pressure upon the United States on behalf of Germany, and it alleged that since this work was being undertaken with funds blocked by the US Government it provided proof that the Embassy's purpose was to assist the Nazis in making France a vassal nation of Germany. It stated further that such intrigue ran counter to the interests of the United States and that, incidentally, several men connected with the Embassy were engaged in dubious or illegal financial transactions.

Three days later, another article appeared on the front page of the *Herald Tribune*, and a day after that, on 4 September, yet another. The headline of one of these read 'VICHY AGENTS SOUGHT PLANS OF BREN GUN', with sub-headings: 'Tried to get blue-prints of weapon defending Britain from invasion – Balked mass-scale production in US.' More facsimile letters and photographs were reproduced, and the *Herald Tribune* carried leading editorials supporting the allegations.

In the newspaper world, the exposure was regarded as a colossal scoop for the *Tribune*. It was a first-class 'news' story and undeniably authentic. During the first fortnight of September, it was reproduced in over one hundred newspapers in the United States and Canada, including the *Washington Post*, the *Baltimore Sun* and the New York *Daily Mirror*. Henry Morgenthau, Jr, voiced the general acclaim when he expressed a desire to meet the *Herald Tribune* reporter who had produced the series of articles. He wished to compliment him personally on his outstanding journalistic feat.

The Vichy Embassy was considerably embarrassed. Henry-Haye announced that he intended to make an official protest to Secretary of State Cordell Hull. He denounced the articles as a 'campaign aimed at realizing the ambition of certain Americans

NEW YORK Herald Tribune

Vichy in America

Within recent weeks Americans have been increasingly appalled by the spectacle of the Vichy puppets acting as hangmen for Adolf Hitler. If anything more were needed to round out the sorry picture it would be evidence that the same system of repression and espionage, directed against true Frenchmen, that prevails in France, had been extended to the United States. Last October it was asserted categorically by supporters of General de Gaulle and of the Free French movement in this country that they...

M. Henry-Haye and Jean Musa

M. Henry-Haye, the ambassador of the Vichy government, has denied, with much emotion, that his government operates a secret service in this country, that it has a ...aganda service here or...

Ambiguous Vichy

In his reply to the Herald Tribune's articles on Vichy activities in this country Mr. Henry-Haye, the Vichy ambassador, exclaimed that "the aim is to try to realize the ambition of certain Americans and certain Frenchmen to break up or deteriorate diplomatic relations between the French government and the United States."

Musa Explains Work Here for Vichy's Envoy

Says He Received $300 a Month for Arranging for Ambassador's N.Y. Visits

Jean L. Musa, the...

PRO-NAZI REPORTS STIR HENRY-HAYE

French Ambassador Says Series of Articles Charging Vichy Propaganda Are Untrue

PLANS PROTEST TO HULL

He Asserts Campaign Aims at Break in Relations Between America and France

Henry-Haye Will Protest to Hull

WASHINGTON, Sept. 2 (UP).—French Ambassador Gaston Henry-Haye said today he would protest to Secretary...

Reactions to BSC's campaign against
the Vichy agents.

The Vichy French

and Frenchmen to break up and deteriorate diplomatic relations between the French Government and the United States'. He made no mention of the British, for he did not realize that they were concerned.

He held a press conference. BSC arranged that a friendly reporter should be present, primed with embarrassing questions, and the conference therefore resulted only in further unfavourable publicity. The *Herald Tribune* wrote in an editorial: '. . . The Ambassador speaks as a representative of the French people, a friendly power; yet the government he represents has repeatedly done everything it could to promote the German victory which the United States has declared to be profoundly inimical to its vital interest, and to embarrass the British resistance to which the United States is pledged to render every aid in its power.'

Thereafter Henry-Haye made no further public efforts to explain away the attacks upon himself and his colleagues, but sources in the Embassy reported that he was not a little annoyed. In one of his less restrained outbursts he described the whole affair as 'De Gaullist-Jewish-British-FBI intrigue'. But he never really suspected the British. Nor for that matter did SIS/London. Some weeks after the start of the campaign, London drew the series of articles to BSC's attention, and said: 'We expect you will have seen reference in the *New York Herald Tribune* . . . Please comment.'

The Fighting French in the United States were jubilant. The Vichy Gestapo had to curtail its activities at once, and Musa himself was forced to cut himself off from them, although he was incidentally retained by Henry-Haye at a small salary. His business activities were blocked. He received hundreds of threatening letters and telephone calls. The whole Vichy French organization was completely discredited. Prior to the press revelations, Americans had tended to regard the Vichy Frenchmen with sympathy and some admiration. Now they realized that Henry-Haye and his henchmen deserved neither pity nor praise. They were not proud men trying to put a bold face on defeat, but Nazi hirelings and potential enemies of the United States.

Other Vichyites, besides the Embassy staff, suffered as a result of the press campaign. Camille Chautemps was one. Although a left-winger and a Freemason, Chautemps had, at the time of the armistice, led the support for Pétain, who rewarded him with a South American mission. Laval jockeyed him out of this, but with the assistance of the American Ambassador, William Bullitt, Chautemps managed to get himself sent to the USA in October 1940. In Washington, Chautemps installed his wife and four children in an apartment near the Embassy, but the family kept to themselves. BSC learned from reports inside the Embassy that the Vichy Government was supporting Chautemps to the tune of $2,000 a month. It was believed that he was working on the unfreezing of French funds in the USA, but later BSC agents learned that he was in touch with those politically confused Frenchmen who were pro-Pétain but opposed to collaboration, while beginning to flirt with the de Gaullists. Then, in December 1940, he lunched with Summer Welles and Admiral Leahy and told them that Pétain was first and foremost pro-French, and that he himself and Pétain hated Laval. He also made a show of rebuking the USA for not helping Britain and in this way rendering it difficult for Vichy to oppose Hitler.

When an article on Chautemps was included in the *Herald Tribune* exposure, it caught him at an unlucky moment, for his allowance from France had just been cut off, apparently because he was a Freemason. He tried to get more money through the French Consulate, while at the same time offering his services to the Free French. Throughout the autumn, winter and spring of 1941–2, BSC kept track of his efforts to form a new group of French fence-sitters, with which he hoped to capitalize on the State Department's dislike of de Gaulle, the prestige of Marshal Pétain and the apprehensions of some Frenchmen who wished to reinsure against a German defeat.

In May 1942, BSC learned from a reliable source that Chautemps was being supported by the US State Department. London were informed and, on their instructions, a new campaign was started to break down what was left of his reputation. New and virulent attacks were made upon him through the press – with the desired result. His last public statement was a ridiculous manifesto in which he offered to join the Fighting French under Giraud 'as a soldier of France', although he was then fifty-seven years of age.

It is worth mentioning here two other prominent people who worked unofficially for Vichy. BSC found that André Maurois* spent a great deal of his time with members of the Vichy Gestapo.

---

* BSC recently received the following report from a reliable informant:

For twenty years André Maurois based his literary record in France on his devotion to Britain and the furthering of Anglo-French relations. A virtually unknown figure in French letters before the last war, he burst into instant prominence with his admirable studies of Col. Bramble, which were followed by political studies of Disraeli and King Edward VII and by literary biographies of Shelley and Byron.

He had come to New York in the autumn of 1940 where he lived lavishly at the Ritz Towers. He constantly received violently anti-British letters from his wife's parents in unoccupied France, and later, in 1941, it was ascertained that Vichy had cabled Henry-Haye to restore Maurois's French citizenship and to renew his passport for two years. Irrefutable evidence showed that Maurois was engaged in spreading Vichy propaganda in the United States.

After the invasion of North Africa, Maurois joined General Giraud's forces. His return to army life was, however, brief and

---

Maurois became the leading figure in the Anglo-French literary world, lecturing in the United States on English literature and accepting with pleasure and gratification the role of Britain's friend. He was awarded honorary degrees by the Universities of Oxford and Edinburgh, and in 1938, after considerable 'lobbying' in his own interests, was created a KBE on the occasion of the Paris Exhibition.

This same year saw the realization of another of his personal ambitions; he was elected a member of the Academy of France; to achieve this honour he had abjured his native Jewish faith for that of Roman Catholicism and forsaken his earlier liberal views to write a biography of Chateaubriand.

The outbreak of the Second World War found Maurois as Official Eyewitness at British GHQ, where he remained until the collapse of France in the summer of 1940. With other pro-British journalists he was evacuated to England by the Press Counsellor of the British Embassy in Paris, with whom Maurois made considerable fuss about reserving 'his usual suite at the Dorchester'.

Arrived in London, Maurois pursued a double-faced course of action. To the Queen – who presented him with a pair of jewelled cuff-links on his departure for America – and to his English friends (e.g. Harold Nicolson) he protested his undying devotion to Britain, but to his American friends in London he took the line, which he was later to develop in both the printed and spoken word in the United States, that Britain had no hope of survival against Germany and that the downfall of France was due in great measure to the failure of Britain to honour her pledges to France for adequate military support and assistance.

Maurois's sojourn in the United States was distinguished for his systematic and subtle attempts to sabotage American goodwill toward Britain. His previous record as author and lecturer gave him a ready-made and receptive public, and in his books, articles and platform appearances he consistently pursued the same line.

Nor was his hostility to Britain without its pusillanimity. When a French refugee published, under the pseudonym of André Simon, an attack upon the men of Vichy, calling it 'J'accuse', Maurois – fearing that, as his first name was André and his wife's Simone, the book might be attributed to him – was at great pains to explain that not only was he not the author but that he in no way shared the views expressed.

There are few more outstanding examples of the 'fairweather friends of Britain' among the French than André Maurois and it is to be hoped that his record will not be forgotten in the years to come.

unsuccessful, and soon he was back in New York, officially on leave, although under French law an officer on leave has no right to leave the Metropole, which for him was then North Africa. De Gaulle accused Maurois of being a deserter and declared his intention of treating him as such. Maurois wisely decided to remain in the United States, but he was no longer of any use to Vichy as a propagandist.

Else Schiaparelli, the dress-designer, also worked against Allied interests. BSC sent a full report on her to the Trading with the Enemy Branch of the Treasury, and this revealed clearly that her pro-Vichy sentiments were inspired by avarice and a determination to prosper in the world irrespective of whether or not it was Nazi-ruled.

Both Schiaparelli and Maurois emerged from their collaborationist activities comparatively unscathed. Jean Louis Musa, on the other hand, received the full measure of his deserts. He was eventually arrested by the FBI for failing to register as a foreign agent, and although the prosecution handled the indictment so ineptly that it was set aside, his career was finished nevertheless. When BSC last heard of him, he was destitute.

(d) Obtaining the Cyphers

In March 1942, CSS informed BSC that the Admiralty wished to get hold of the French naval cypher, a copy of which was used by the Naval Attaché in the French Embassy in Washington. At the time, there was doubt about the intentions of the French fleet in the Mediterranean. The possession of the cypher would enable those concerned to keep informed of the fleet's intended movements.

Cynthia was instructed to approach her friend Charles Brousse on the subject. Brousse was flabbergasted. He said that it was an impossible task; that the only people who had access to the code-room were the Chief of Codes, a man named Benoit, and his assistant; that the room itself was always locked and that the telegrams were carried personally to the head of the code-room by the Embassy Counsellor.

'Do you mean that even you haven't access to that room?' Cynthia asked.

'Nobody has,' Brousse said. 'Once the Naval Attaché used to go to the code-room more frequently than seemed necessary because of a curiosity that is second nature to him. The Ambassador

The Vichy French

himself – how do you say it – ticked him off. He sent him a note forbidding further trips to the code-room.'

'What about night-time? Do they work all night?'

'No, but the room is carefully guarded at all times. The Foreign Office sent instructions recently that a permanent watchman should be on duty at nights and on holidays to guard Embassy premises.'

'How big are these code-books?'

'So big that even if anybody could smuggle them out, their absence would be noted at once.'

Cynthia questioned Brousse about the old code-clerk, Benoit.

'He is a bear', Brousse said, 'who has lived 20 years with his work. He has no needs, no ambition and no imagination. He arrives at the Chancery, says good morning to no one and goes directly to the cypher-room.' No arrangement could be made with Benoit, he maintained.

Benoit, it appeared, was confused and unhappy about his country's behaviour. Like many other officials, he did not wish to join de Gaulle. To his prosaic mind the safest way was the best way, and after all was not Marshal Pétain Chief of the French State and therefore entitled to the loyalty of all Frenchmen?

Nevertheless Laval's collaborationist policy, as evidenced in his speeches, finally became too repulsive for Benoit to stomach, and he resigned. At this point Cynthia approached him and told him that she would give him an opportunity to help France. She reported to BSC that she had had the following conversation with him:

'Our desires', she had said, 'and aims are the same as yours. We want to help France because we know that by doing so we are also helping the Allied war effort.'

Old Benoit's eyes filled with tears. 'I am very confused,' he said. 'I have had no time to think. Everything has happened so quickly.'

'The cyphers could provide the key to prove how much the traitors in the French Government are helping the Germans. To turn them over to us would be the greatest service you could perform for your unhappy country.'

'But I cannot do that,' Benoit said. 'Everything is so confusing. Everything has happened so quickly.'

'Your loyalty should be to the French people. Not to the government of traitors.'

'I cannot,' he said with finality. 'I have built up a long record of loyalty to my chiefs. All of them have written me letters. The cyphers have been my responsibility – my own responsibility. To guard them carefully has been my duty.'

Cynthia's attempt was to no avail and she had to abandon it. Yet it was reassuring to find someone amongst the Vichy crowd who remained loyal to his principles. In the traitorous ranks of the Vichy supporters, old Benoit stands out as a man worthy of having served a better cause than the one which he refused to betray.

After Benoit's resignation, his assistant, Comte de la Grandville, was given charge of the code-room. He was a young man with a wife and growing family, and BSC believed, with good reason, that he was short of money. Cynthia, whose energy and persistence were boundless, at once began to cultivate him, though she did not tell Brousse what she was doing.

De la Grandville's wife was then having her second child, and he himself was a little bored and glad to have found a companion as sympathetic as Cynthia. Soon she was telling him of her views about Laval and expressing astonishment that any loyal Frenchman should associate himself with Laval's policies. Gradually, she worked around to the question of the French naval cypher, and she stressed the immense assistance that its possession would render to the enemies of Germany. As further inducement, she offered him a lump sum of money should he procure it for her, and a monthly retainer thereafter if he would keep her advised of any possible changes in it. De la Grandville refused. He professed to be torn by doubt, but his attitude was in fact very definite, for he went to the Ambassador and reported all or nearly all of his conversation with Cynthia, ending with the dramatic announcement that she was in the employ of the United States Secret Service. He exaggerated a little in telling of the sum she had offered him for the cypher.

There was a sensation in the Embassy. Brousse, of course, heard about the affair, but he did not believe de la Grandville's story. He went to Henry-Haye and told him that it was untrue. He told him that de la Grandville was unreliable. Had he not been spreading false rumours about the Ambassador's liaison with the Baroness de Zuylen? Obviously the man was a liar, and having spread such a malicious and damaging story about the Ambassador himself was doubtless addicted to spreading equally untrue and insidious tales about other people. The Ambassador heartily agreed. He summoned de la Grandville and soundly reprimanded him. He informed him at the end of the interview that he was to be withdrawn from the code-room.

Cynthia had been lucky. She had also been astute in concealing

The Vichy French

her friendship with de la Grandville from Brousse. A new plan was devised for procuring the naval cypher. It entailed Brousse's assistance, but his part was to be an easy and congenial one. Eventually he agreed to cooperate.

He supplied a floor-plan of the Embassy, and with the aid of this the final dispositions were made. One evening Brousse arrived at the Embassy door with Cynthia. He told the night watchman that he had nowhere else to go. Washington was crowded, and anyway it would not do for a member of the Embassy staff to be seen at a hotel with his mistress.

The watchman offered no objection, especially after he had received a tip, and he allowed Brousse and Cynthia to spend the night on a divan on the first floor. For several nights after that, they repeated the practice, and the watchman became accustomed to their visits.

One night in June 1942, a cab driven by an expert locksmith deposited Brousse and Cynthia at the Embassy. They were well provisioned with champagne and, in festive mood, invited the watchman to join them in a glass. They handed him a doctored drink, and soon he was sound asleep. They admitted the locksmith, who was awaiting their signal in the taxi outside, and he set about his task at once. First he got the lock off the door leading to the Naval Attaché's office. Then he worked out the combination of the safe in the coding room. He had to labour in complete silence and with the utmost care, for clearly it was essential that he should leave no trace of his presence.

It took him three hours before he was done, and there was by then too little of the night left to allow time for photostatting the cyphers. But the way was now clear, the most difficult part of the undertaking was accomplished. Two nights later, Brousse and Cynthia paid another nocturnal visit to the Embassy. It was considered inadvisable to drug the watchman again lest he should realize that the fact of his falling asleep on a second occasion was something more than coincidence and should report the matter to his superiors in the morning. On the other hand, Cynthia sensed that he was already a little suspicious and was probably intent on finding out the true nature of the business in which she and Brousse were engaged. It was, therefore, essential that some effective method should be used for keeping him well out of the way. The expedient to which she resorted was very simple. When the watchman attempted a surprise entrance (as she had surmised he would) he found her undressed. Very naturally he withdrew in great haste, embarrassed but by now fully reassured that his visitors had no other reason for spending the night in the Embassy than the one which they had intimated.

The watchman was put to flight not long after Cynthia and Brousse had arrived, and they could be reasonably certain he would not come near their room again. They admitted the locksmith who, forearmed with the knowledge he had already gained so laboriously, was able to reach the safe and open it within a matter of minutes. The cypher books were handed through an opened window to another BSC agent who had been waiting in a taxi outside. He rushed them to a vacant house nearby where they were photostatted. By four o'clock next morning – well within the time limit – they were back in the safe, and there was no sign that they had ever been removed. On the following day the photostatic copies were sent by courier to London.

In passing, it may be noted that in Mexico and Colombia also, the Vichy French organizations were penetrated by BSC/SI. In June 1942, a source in the Legation in Mexico City was persuaded to supply verbatim copies of despatches sent to the French Foreign Ministry by the Chargé d'Affaires, Ghislain Clauzel. This information was supplemented by copies of the Legation's coded cables which the secret police of the Mexican Ministry of the Interior furnished to BSC.

In Colombia, contact was established with the French Ambassador's valet, who became a valuable source of intelligence. He passed on drafts of telegrams from the Ambassador to Vichy, copies of letters from the Commercial Attaché to the Minister of Finance and other material, amongst which were copies of the cypher instructions for six different French cypher systems.

(e) Martinique

The strategic importance of Martinique and its challenge as an Axis-controlled stronghold in the Western Hemisphere was apparent early in the war. The island, it will be remembered, was under the iron rule of Admiral Robert who was fanatically loyal to Marshal Pétain and was an astute politician. He had charge of Vichy's gold reserve, valued at $2,883,000,000, which had been sent over to Martinique on the *Emile Bertin* and was now closely guarded in an old stronghold, Fort Desaix, near Fort de France, the capital. He had at his disposal a somewhat over-age but still valuable squadron of the French fleet which included the aircraft carrier *Béarn* (25,000 tons), the cruiser *Emile Bertin* and

The front and another page of one of the French diplomatic cyphers taken from the Vichy French Consulate in New York.

the converted cruiser *Barfleur*. Further, he had almost a hundred aircraft, some of them of American manufacture.

Within three months of the fall of France, plans were made by BSC to liberate the island in collaboration with the Free French in the USA. On 24 August 1940, the first telegram on the subject was sent to London. It said:

> There is possibility of organizing scheme to be carried out by reliable Frenchman for *coup* in Martinique which would release to ourselves gold, ships and aircraft. Before we investigate further should be glad to know if there are any objections.

On 4 September, after an enquiry about the 'reliable Frenchman', came the reply:

> Provided you are not implicated and scheme is entirely organized by French it is viewed favourably.

More details were immediately sent to London. Working with BSC were Jacques de Sièyes of the Free French Delegation in New York, and Eugene Houdry, a rich French industrialist. Houdry considered that the moment was propitious because the psychological effect on the French colonies of a successful *coup* in Martinique would be likely to prove profitable, quite apart from the military advantages of dislodging the Vichyites.

The 'reliable Frenchman' mentioned in BSC's telegram was a gigantic, swashbuckling Martiniquais named Jacques Vauzanges, a one-time member of the *2me Bureau*. He had two sons on the island and many contacts among the naval officers and government officials. The commanders of the two warships were personal friends of his.

On Houdry's advice, Vauzanges had kept up relations with the Vichy Embassy in the USA, and he was thus able to proceed to Martinique without difficulty and without arousing suspicion. He planned to organize the anti-Pétain elements in the colony and to endeavour to alter the outlook of the remainder by propaganda. It was intended that after the *coup d'état* which would result in the islands recognizing de Gaulle, the warships should be sent to Halifax, where they would join the British fleet (under an agreement between de Gaulle and the Admiralty), and the gold reserve should be placed at the disposal of the Free French.

The scheme received the approval of HMG and General de

The Vichy French

Gaulle, and the latter conferred the fullest authority on Houdry and Vauzanges. By 20 September, Vauzanges was in Martinique. He had planned his programme in conjunction with BSC and had been given facilities for communication, although he had no traceable connection with his allies in New York. On his arrival, Vauzanges found the situation more complicated than he had supposed. The local population were indifferent and more concerned with material conditions than with politics. If anything, they were pro-de Gaulle, but their sympathies were excessively passive. Nevertheless, the naval officers appeared to dislike and to mistrust their chief, Admiral Robert. Vauzanges formed the impression that they would welcome a *fait accompli* from outside which would release them from their allegiance to Vichy without endangering their relations at home.

Economically, the colony was in a bad state. Because of the blockade there was a shortage of petrol and important products. There was a glut of sugar and bananas. Unemployment was serious and money scarce. Vauzanges decided that the odds were slightly in his favour and began laying the groundwork for his operation.

Unfortunately, on 23 September, the very day on which he had planned to take action, the Free French suffered their unhappy defeat at Dakar and the prestige of de Gaulle in Martinique slumped sharply. The officers, the backbone of the projected *coup*, were loud in their condemnation of Admiral Muselier's action at Dakar and declared they would make no move which might put them under his command. Vauzanges's plan was hamstrung and he abandoned it.

He spent some time on the island, spreading as much anti-Vichy propaganda as he could, and then he returned to New York. There he made a very full and valuable report to BSC on conditions in Martinique, and expressed his opinion that the problem could be solved by imposing a strict blockade on the island. He said that this would bring the economic crisis to a head and cause a complete collapse within two months. Ultimately it was proved that he was right.

During 1941 and 1942, BSC submitted several alternative plans for wresting Martinique from Vichy control, but these were all rejected on account of American reluctance to interfere with the *status quo*. Meanwhile a careful watch was kept on the situation which, so long as it lasted, represented a grave menace to Allied security. From its various sources of information which included copies of the diplomatic despatches sent to Vichy by

Admiral Robert (these were obtained from the French Embassy in Washington), interrogations of anti-Pétain Martiniquais who had escaped via Santa Lucia, and reports from its own agents who were sent to investigate conditions at first hand, BSC was able to keep London fully advised of political, military and economic developments inside the island.

In 1943, the United States Government was at last persuaded to impose an economic blockade and thus acted on Vauzanges's original suggestion. Within a short time Admiral Robert, despite his obstinacy and fanaticism, was forced to capitulate.

(f) St Pierre and Miquelon

In August 1941, the quesiton of the Vichy-controlled islands of St Pierre and Miquelon was raised in discussions between the Foreign Office and the Canadian Department of External Affairs. The problem was whether or not to occupy the islands. The Chiefs of Staff urged that the removal of Vichy influence, 'preferably by Free French naval forces', was very desirable on the grounds of naval security, for there was reason to believe that Vichy was tapping the Western Union transatlantic cables through St Pierre and also passing convoy information to the enemy. Fishing boats from the islands made convenient cover for espionage.

The Canadians were somewhat fearful of any incident which might tend to strengthen anti-British feeling in other parts of the French Empire and also in Canada, but they suggested that the Free French should be allowed to occupy the islands 'under Canadian supervision'.

However, before any course of action could safely be charted, it seemed essential to ascertain what were the political opinions and aspirations of the inhabitants of St Pierre and Miquelon, for only thereby could it be determined whether or not there was risk of an invasion resulting in a replica of the Dakar fiasco. Accordingly, BSC sent agents into the islands and their investigation revealed that 97% of the inhabitants were pro-de Gaulle. This information was embodied in a comprehensive report which BSC sent to London in the autumn of 1941.

The report was shown to de Gaulle himself, and he was persuaded by it to undertake an invasion of the islands. There followed an exchange of messages between the Foreign Office and the State Department which showed that the latter were strongly opposed to any interference with the *status quo* at that time. Nevertheless de Gaulle, acting on his own initiative, sent

The Vichy French

Free French warships to St Pierre and Miquelon, and there was no resistance encountered. Subsequently a plebiscite was held, and this resulted in a 98% majority in favour of de Gaulle, which showed that BSC's agents had erred in their estimate by only one per cent – on the conservative side.

CHAPTER 2

The Italians, the Spaniards and the Japanese

(a) The Italian Naval Cypher
(b) The Spanish Diplomatic Cyphers
(c) The Japanese

(a) The Italian Naval Cypher

Before Cynthia undertook the operations against the Vichy Embassy, which have been described in the preceding pages, she had already carried out a less spectacular, but, in result, possibly a more important task for BSC.

In the late winter of 1940, WS was advised by SIS/London that the Admiralty urgently required the Italian naval cypher, a copy of which was known to be in the possession of the Italian Naval Attaché in Washington. Accordingly Cynthia's services were enlisted. She had been recruited only recently and this was her first major assignment.

She secured an introduction to Admiral Lais, the Italian Naval Attaché, and began to cultivate him systematically. He reacted to her charms violently and soon, for within a few weeks of their first meeting he supposed himself deeply in love with her and she was able to do with him virtually as she pleased. In retrospect, it seems almost incredible that a man of his experience and seniority, who was, by instinct, training and conviction, a patriotic officer, should have been so enfeebled by passion as to have been willing to work against the interests of his own country to win a lady's favour. But that is what happened.

As soon as she was sure of her ground, Cynthia came directly to the point. She informed the Admiral of her desire to obtain copies of the naval cypher, and he, without any apparent demur, agreed to assist her. He put her in touch with his own cypher clerk,

The Italians, the Spaniards and the Japanese

who produced the cyphers after a suitable financial agreement had been reached. They were photostatted in Washington, and the photostats were sent to London immediately.

At that time Britain was still alone, and the Royal Navy was spread thinly over the seven seas. In the Mediterranean the forces available might well have proved insufficient to meet the demands of the situation had they been challenged by the Italian Navy in strength. Yet it is a matter of history that they never were so challenged, and that the Italian Navy was virtually neutralized and failed to win a single battle. This may have been largely due to the fact that the British had knowledge of the Italian naval cypher, which provided means of learning the enemy's intentions in advance and thus enabled the Commander in Chief, Mediterranean, to dispose his meagre forces to such effective purpose that the Italians were constantly deceived concerning the numbers and strength of British units and did not dare to risk a major engagement.

After she had secured the naval cyphers, Cynthia continued to maintain contact with Admiral Lais and obtained from him a quantity of valuable information concerning Axis plans in the Mediterranean. She was responsible, incidentally, for his eventual downfall, which happened a few months later – in the following way.

In the spring of 1941, there were a number of Italian ships marooned in American ports, ships whose masters did not feel that it was either prudent or possible to run the British blockade to Europe. Lais realized that sooner or later the United States would enter the war and that these vessels would then be taken over by the Allies. Accordingly, he devised a plan to sabotage them. Fortunately he revealed the details of his plan to Cynthia a few hours before they were due to be put into effect. BSC immediately informed the US Office of Naval Intelligence, and thus largely prevented the intended sabotage from taking place. The Italian ships were promptly seized by the US Government, when it was found that wilful damage had already been done to a number of them.

As a result of this incident, the US Government informed the Italian Embassy that Admiral Lais was *persona non grata* and requested his withdrawal. He never suspected Cynthia. As he was about to board the vessel which was to take him back to Italy, two parties were on the quayside to bid him farewell. One consisted of his wife and children; the other merely of Cynthia, who stood alone, some distance away. The lovesick Admiral spent his final minutes with her and ignored his tearful family entirely.

(b) The Spanish Diplomatic Cyphers

The Spanish Embassy in Washington was penetrated in early 1942. In this instance Cynthia's services were not required. The job was done by Spanish Republicans and Basques working with other agents employed by the SI Division.

Original penetration was effected by General José Asensio, who had been Military Attaché in Washington during the Spanish Civil War and headed a small group of Spanish Republicans. His people suborned the butler and the chief messenger at the Embassy, both of whom were able to produce a certain amount of material, which included copies of papers from the Ambassador's desk and specimens of the Embassy seals and rubber stamps.

When SIS/London informed BSC that copies of the Spanish diplomatic cyphers were urgently required, Asensio's people gave further assistance. A typist who was in touch with them worked in the cypher-room of the Embassy, and she was able without much difficulty to procure knowledge of the combination of the safe in which the cyphers were kept. The Secretary who was in charge of the safe had a bad memory and was wont to shout across the room to his assistant asking him for the combination. The typist could always overhear the reply which was shouted back. All she had to do was to make a note of it and pass it on to her friends.

Meanwhile, through independent enquiries, BSC learned that one of the janitors at the Embassy was a Basque. Most Basques had remained loyal to President Aguirre, who had been forced to flee after Franco's victory. Aguirre was then in the United States and already in touch with BSC. Accordingly, it was suggested to him that he should ask the janitor to cooperate with BSC agents in obtaining the Spanish cyphers. This he did, and the janitor readily agreed.

One night shortly afterwards, the janitor, who had by then been informed of the combination, opened the safe and carried the box in which the cyphers were kept to the washroom of a nearby hotel. A BSC agent was awaiting his arrival in one of the lavatories. However, the mechanism of the box proved so complicated that when the time arrived for it to be returned to the Embassy it was still unopened. The next night the janitor brought it out again and this time, the agent, having made previous arrangements, took it to the BSC offices in Washington where the secrets of its

The Italians, the Spaniards and the Japanese

mechanism were unravelled by technical staff. The contents were removed, photostatted and replaced. The box was then returned to the janitor. A description of the special method which was employed for opening the box was sent to Trinidad, where it proved useful because similar boxes were frequently intercepted in the Spanish diplomatic bags.

The photostats of the cypher were sent to London, and thus His Majesty's Government was provided with the means for reading all diplomatic messages passing between Madrid and the Spanish Embassy in Washington.

By way of footnote, it is worth recording that the Spanish Embassy in Venezuela was also penetrated with Aguirre's help. The BSC/SOE representative had recruited the Basque chauffeur and houseman of the Spanish Ambassador as an informant, and in August 1942 arranged for him to be presented to Aguirre, who was then on a tour of Latin America.* At Aguirre's persuasion the houseman agreed to cooperate fully with the British, and two months later managed to purloin the Ambassador's cypher books.

(c) The Japanese

As mentioned previously (see Part II) BSC had contacts inside the Japanese Embassy in Washington and the Japanese Consulates in New York and San Francisco. Some success was also had in direct penetration of the Kurusu mission. (It will be remembered that Saburo Kurusu, Japan's special 'peace' envoy, arrived in the United States a few weeks before Pearl Harbor.) The agent employed in this instance was a British subject who had spent fifty years in Japan and spoke the language fluently.

He contacted Mr Yuki, Kurusu's secretary, and held with him a series of conversations in a Washington flat which had been previously wired for recording. He spoke to Yuki of his love for the Japanese and told him that he felt that he could use his influence to persuade Lord Halifax and the British Government to prevail upon the United States to appease the Japanese war lords. Yuki was convinced of his sincerity and spoke freely, telling him in so many words that Japan's attitude was an unalterable one and that the United States must either give way or face the consequences.

---

* The tour had been arranged by Donovan at BSC's request.

Secret Intelligence

The information obtained from the transcripts of the recordings which were made of these conversations was conveyed each day to President Roosevelt. For the President it provided confirmation of Japan's attitude and of her future intentions which were becoming clearer and more alarming as each day went by. While the White House was still being supplied with information from these transcripts, the President sent his son, James Roosevelt, with a special message for WS.

The message contained information which was not yet known either to the British Embassy in Washington or to the Foreign Office. It was indisputably accurate. WS telegraphed it to CSS on 27 November 1941. His telegram read:

> Japanese negotiations off. Services expect action within two weeks.

CHAPTER 3

Western Hemisphere Intelligence

(a) The United States
(b) Latin America

(a) The United States

It is unlikely, even if space permitted, that a detailed analysis of BSC's intelligence concerning United States affairs would be worthwhile, for in the nature of things what is secret information of urgent importance today is often of no more than academic interest tomorrow. As previously mentioned, the intelligence was derived chiefly from high level contacts (see Part I), and was based on statements of fact privately made, or views and intentions privately expressed, by the President himself,[1] by his advisers and members of his Administration,[2] by the Service Chiefs[3] and by others in a position to determine or influence the shape of policy and strategy. Thus WS was enabled from the beginning to keep CSS constantly supplied with information of secret developments and with advance notice of predetermined developments in United States affairs, both foreign and domestic.

---

1. As one example, a telegram dated 8 December 1941:
   President will give facts to Congress today including loss of four battleships and two battleships and cruiser damaged . . . also over three thousand armed services lost . . . He remarked last night 'at any rate this will be salutary lesson to Navy not to be too free with their criticism of British' . . .
2. As one example, a telegram dated 30 November, 1943:
   Ickes says: No repeat no commitments on oil were made during recent visit of Saudi Arabia potentates to Washington . . .
3. As one example, a telegram dated 4 April 1944:
   . . . Navy and particularly King violently opposed to Russians' active lobbying for quote Lend-Lease for three years after war and assistance to establish large navy unquote . . . King asks: 'Who are they going to use this goddamned fleet against?' . . .

Furthermore, through analysis of the intelligence available to him from his various sources, he was enabled to provide CSS with reliable forecasts of coming events; and as illustration of this it is pertinent to record that he prognosticated the results of the Presidential elections held in 1940 and 1944 with what proved to be complete accuracy. His first message regarding the 1944 election was despatched to CSS on 16 November 1943, and this was followed during the ensuing year by regular cabled reports upon every aspect of the campaign. A few extracts from these may be of interest:

21.11.43 'In spite of all his protestations, Dewey will repeat will accept the draft . . .'

9.12.43 'Disregard claims that Roosevelt does not intend to stand again . . . Republican Presidential stakes: Dewey far ahead . . .'

20.1.44 '. . . Anything we may say publicly which bears on British-American relations will be "used as evidence against us" for election purposes by the opposition . . .'

26.1.44 'Example of what is meant by my telegram of January 20th appears in newspapers here this week quote Yorkshire Post, political mouthpiece of Britain's Foreign Secretary, Eden, jumps on Roosevelt band-wagon, hails Roosevelt as "irreplaceable national leader" . . . unquote . . . This is effective anti-Roosevelt material . . .'

14.2.44 '. . . Roosevelt has undertaken to Party that he will jettison Wallace as Vice-Presidential candidate . . .'

(A BSC officer in Washington, who was in frequent consultation with Wallace, reported that Wallace himself was unaware of this almost up to the day of his rejection by the Democratic Convention five months later.)

10.3.44 'Presidential stakes: according secret White House poll figures, somewhat of a shock, Roosevelt 68% vs. Willkie 32%, Roosevelt 55% vs. Dewey 45% . . .'

5.4.44 'Roosevelt is confident of victory . . .'

20.10.44 'Secret survey completed for FDR within past week indicated Dewey will carry only 10 to 16 states . . . which agrees my estimate giving FDR approximately 200 electoral vote majority . . . Ten days ago White House was worried . . . but heavy registration . . . generated optimism . . . new confidence about New York with its 47 electoral votes . . . Presidential stakes Roosevelt 65–35 . . .'

27.10.44 '. . . FDR said privately this week quote now if we get vote out we're all right . . . I've already got him mad and I'll get him madder . . . the people will only come out for a championship fight unquote . . . We will bait Dewey to achieve this end . . .'

31.10.44 'My estimates have consistently conflicted markedly with those of Gallup and other pollsters and political pundits . . . and now show even greater divergence from largely accepted view than previously . . . *My current analyses indicate victory for FDR in minimum repeat minimum of 32 states with 370 electoral votes and maximum of 40 with 487 electoral votes* . . . Dewey minimum comprises North Dakota, South Dakota, Nebraska, Colorado, Kansas, Wyoming, Vermont and Iowa . . . maximum includes foregoing plus Maine, Idaho, Wisconsin, Indiana, Michigan, Ohio, Minnesota and Illinois . . . Last four are Dewey's most doubtful ones and not improbable result anticipates his losing two, three or all four . . .'

This last telegram is particularly noteworthy, for the results of the election were exactly as it predicted. Dewey won all the eight states listed as his minimum, together with four of the eight listed as further possibilities. Roosevelt won thirty-six states, with 432 electoral votes.

Now inasmuch as BSC employed no agents of its own to carry out investigations, it is obvious that prognostications of this kind* would have been impossible had not sources close to the President upon whom WS largely relied for intelligence about US affairs (see Part II) been themselves well informed concerning public

---

* As one other example, WS predicted on 24 February 1944 that William O'Dwyer would be the next Mayor of New York and that La Guardia would not run. At that time, more than eighteen months before the elections, it was widely accepted – and in the press virtually assumed – that La Guardia would be a candidate to succeed himself. At the time of writing (November 1945) O'Dwyer has just been elected by the largest majority in the history of New York Mayoralty campaigns.

opinion and political trends throughout the country. In contrast, the result of the British election of 1945 was apparently the cause of general amazement in the highest quarters and confounded the most optimistic and pessimistic prophets of both major parties. Yet it is suggested that if scientific methods, similar to those in use in the United States, had been employed for measuring public opinion it would have been possible to arrive at a reasonably reliable forecast. This suggestion may be worth consideration in the future, for while, on the one hand, members of the Cabinet and HM Ambassador in Washington were kept advised of the developments in the Presidential election, as WS reported them, and afterwards expressed their appreciation that they had been so accurately forewarned regarding the outcome, it was found impossible, on the other hand, despite frequent requests, to supply interested American officials with any reliable prediction concerning the British election.

As indicated in the telegram of 31 October, quoted above, the Gallup Poll† did not prove a reliable guide to the Presidential election of 1944. This was so, largely because Gallup is himself a Republican and was a staunch supporter of Dewey. As WS learned, there was little doubt that Gallup deliberately adjusted his figures in Dewey's favour in the hope of stampeding the electorate thereby, and the reliance which Dewey placed upon him is well illustrated by the transcript of a conversation between WS and his intermediary with Walter Winchell (see Part II). The conversation was recorded on 23 October, 1944, and the following is an extract from the transcript:

> Intermediary: 'Jesus Christ, it's unbelievable . . . There are going to be some whitefaced boys in this country . . . Dewey is calling up Gallup so often they have to have a clerk to answer him . . . Imagine a guy shaking so much . . .'
> WS: 'And Gallup is trying to give Dewey service, I suppose?'
> Intermediary: 'Sure, he's one of Gallup's principal clients . . .'

Nevertheless, the Gallup Poll is the best-known, and by far the largest, organization for testing public opinion in the United States, and its findings are more often than not extremely accurate. The Roosevelt Administration made covert use of it. It preferred to employ, not Gallup himself, but one of his colleagues, Hadley Cantril, Director of the Office of Public Opinion

† As the American Institute of Public Opinion is commonly known.

Research at Princeton University. Cantril used Gallup's organization to secure answers to specific questions. He handed these to Judge Rosenman who passed them on to the President, and they had a considerable influence on the political strategy of the Administration.

Clearly, therefore, the Gallup Poll could be regarded as a useful source, even though tainted in particular instances, and reliance could be placed on the intelligence which it produced provided that this was assessed in the light of information from other sources. Since the results of many of the polls were kept secret, access to them could be had only by penetrating the organization. This was effected towards the end of 1941, when one of Gallup's assistant directors – a British subject – was approached and readily agreed to cooperate.

Thenceforward, BSC was kept continually advised of Gallup Poll secret findings, including a number of Cantril's confidential reports to the President, and, at the beginning of 1942, arranged through its contact in the Gallup organization for a series of polls to be conducted with the object of analysing the exact state of American public opinion toward Great Britain. These continued for several months and they revealed, *inter alia*, that the defeats which Britain suffered at the time, as presented by malignant or misinformed American publicists, were having a most damaging effect on the American attitude both to Britain and to the Roosevelt Administration. They showed that, in the middle of February, 63% of the American public believed that the British were doing all they could to win the war. Three weeks later this figure had fallen to 49%, the lowest point to which British prestige had sunk since the beginning of the war. Furthermore, the reports showed that there was a loss of confidence in the US Government: one American out of three now believed that the United States, and therefore the Roosevelt Administration, was not doing its utmost to win.

The results of these secret polls, together with supporting evidence independently collected, enabled BSC to draw up a series of memoranda, entitled 'Fifth Column Propaganda of the Axis in the United States'. As these memoranda had a far-reaching effect, it is worth digressing for a moment in order to observe the circumstances in which they were compiled.

Before Pearl Harbor, BSC had successfully spread covert propaganda, designed to discredit the isolationist and strengthen the interventionist groups throughout the country (see Part II). As soon as the United States was formally at war, the second task became superfluous. But BSC continued to analyse the publications and broadcasts of former isolationists, and it found that as the bellicose spirit brought about by Pearl Harbor subsided and the Allies continued to suffer crushing defeats, so the isolationist press was encouraged to print anti-Roosevelt, anti-British, anti-Russian and anti-Semitic propaganda of increasing vehemence and in increasing quantity. There seemed to be a pattern in these attacks. An anti-British theme would appear in one organ and be taken up by others, until it had spread throughout the country. Or, more commonly, some incident, such as Mr Churchill's remark that he had hoped and prayed for America's entry in the war, would be seized on by commentators of various types – from the highly paid hirelings of William Randolph Hearst to renegade Englishmen like Boake Carter – who would distort it in the same fashion, thus producing an apparently unanimous cry of hatred. The New York *Daily News*, for example, was urging in February 1942 that the bases in the Western Hemisphere which the British had leased to the US should be 'confiscated', in case, some day, they should play the same part as the Japanese mandated islands in the Pacific had played in the Pearl Harbor attack. Thus the *Daily News* at once appealed to American acquisitiveness, stigmatized Britain as a potential enemy of the US and opened up a vista of future wars.

BSC's findings were confirmed by the records of an interventionist society called *The Friends of Democracy*, to which BSC had free access and which, together with the results of the secret Gallup polls, were embodied in the series of memoranda already mentioned. The first of these covered the period between 7 December 1941 and 24 January 1942; the remainder ran in unbroken sequence down to June 1942.

The reports analysed all the tricks which the isolationists were using and showed that, while much of their propaganda was devised by native Americans, much was also dictated by the Germans, either through propagandists of the Viereck type or through short-wave broadcasts. They showed how the same themes were used throughout the country in a way which implied a consistent policy guided by a single group.

The first volume of BSC's 'Fifth Column Propaganda of the Axis in the US' was handed to General Donovan. It was studied by him and by leading members of his staff. It was then passed to President Roosevelt, on whom it made a considerable impression. He had not hitherto realized how widespread and how purposeful this propaganda was, for at the time no US agency had been engaged in studying it. On 23 February 1942, the President delivered a speech to the nation, in which, for the first time, he denounced 'rumour-mongers and poison-peddlers in our midst'. Robert Sherwood and Archibald MacLeish, who had collaborated in the preparation of this address, had asked BSC for permission to keep the borrowed copy of its report until the speech had been delivered. The President made use of a number of the ideas it contained, and one long paragraph in his address was directly inspired by it.*

Thereafter, the President's advisers, particularly those attached to the Donovan organization, requested BSC to pass them each memorandum as it was completed. On the President's instructions, a vigorous counter-attack was started, and Edmond Taylor of COI used the BSC reports consistently during the campaign. Joseph Barnes, Sherwood's chief assistant, passed numerous extracts from them to the *New York Herald Tribune*, which embodied them in a series of articles. Every night for a week the Columbia Broadcasting System, drawing its information almost exclusively from the reports, devoted its principal news period to talks on enemy propaganda, and did the same with

---

* The relevant passage from BSC's report, and the paragraph from the President's speech (with echoes italicised), read as follows:
BSC: 'The objective of the Axis propagandists now is (1) weaken American unity and war morale; (2) meantime, separate the US from the Allies; (3) thus, achieve the Axis plan – 'Divide and Conquer' . . . They cannot now demand that the US sever ties with Britain and Russia and China as Allies; instead, they demand that the US pick out its own theatre of war and fight there, and withhold supplies from all Allies' . . . 'Britain is finished as a great power' . . . 'Russia will quit, and turn against us' . . . 'Whispering and rumour-mongering are the chief weapons of . . . the Axis propagandists following Axis radio lines, and of the Axis radio quoting misstatements by American people such as Hearst . . .'
The President: '*The object* of the Nazis and the Japanese *is to separate the US, Britain, China, and Russia*, and to isolate them from one another, so that each will be surrounded and cut off from sources of supplies and reinforcements. It is the old familiar Axis policy of "Divide and Conquer" . . . There are those who . . . advise us to *pull our warships into our own home waters, and concentrate solely on last-ditch defence* . . . The consequences of Pearl Harbor have been wildly exaggerated . . . originally by Axis propagandists, but repeated by Americans in and out of public life . . . *Almost every Axis broadcast directly quotes Americans who* by speech or in the press *make damnable misstatements* . . . *The Axis propagandists have tried* in various evil ways *to destroy our determination and our morale*. Failing in that they are now trying to destroy our confidence in our own Allies. They say that the *British are finished*, that *the Russians and Chinese are about to quit* . . .'

its coast-to-coast programme, *Report to the Nation*. Dozens of articles, editorials and cartoons along similar lines followed. Finally, Archibald MacLeish's Office of Facts and Figures* issued a booklet, which the author had obviously written with the BSC reports on his desk, analysing Axis propaganda themes and showing the public how to detect them.

Having thus prepared public opinion for more direct action, the President was enabled to make a series of frontal attacks. A large number of the propaganda organs used by Axis sympathizers and isolationists were banned from the mails: Coughlin's *Social Justice*, William Dudley Pelley's *The Galilean, X-Ray* and *Publicity*, to name only a few. Their publishers, with the exception of Coughlin, whose indictment might have offended Catholic voters, were all arrested, and thirty-three of them were indicted at the largest sedition trial in American history (see Part II).

As the campaign against Fifth Columnists in the US continued, BSC was able, through the Gallup Poll, to see how its progress was affecting American public opinion. The results, as polled by Gallup, were most gratifying. On 11 March, only 49% of the American people thought that Britain was doing her utmost to win the war. On 23 April, this proportion had jumped to 65%, although no important naval or military victory had occurred during this period to influence the public in Britain's favour.

Gallup's assistant, who eventually joined the staff of BSC, was able to ensure a constant flow of intelligence on public opinion in the United States, since he had access not only to the questionnaires sent out by Gallup and Cantril and to the recommendations offered by the latter to the White House, but also to the findings of the Survey Division of the Office of War Information and of the Opinion Research Division of the US Army. The mass of information which BSC collected in this way was obviously of interest to London. But it was most immediately useful in helping the British Information Services, the Embassy and the Consulates throughout the country to plan effective counter-measures against anti-British propaganda in the United States. The BSC reports were described by one Department of the Embassy as 'the most reliable index of Anglo-American relations available'.

---

* Established in October 1941 to facilitate dissemination of factual information within the United States. Transferred and consolidated into the Office of War Information, June 1942.

Gallup himself was by no means unreservedly pro-British, but BSC's contact was able to dissuade him from publishing the results of certain polls which would have had a damaging effect on British prestige. It would have been unfortunate, for instance, if Gallup had released to the hundred or more newspapers which published his findings the fact that only 50% of the British people believed that Britain was doing her utmost to win the war and only 54% believed that America was doing hers. Yet these were the results of a poll conducted by Gallup's representative in England in 1942. Nor, again, could it have proved other than harmful had it become generally known that a large number of Americans were in favour of immediate self-government for India and of the formation of a Palestinian army.

His knowledge of Gallup's methods led this same officer to the conclusion that a poll, if secretly organized in other countries, could assist in settling many political or ethnological problems without the confusion and possible corruption of a plebiscite. The results of such a poll, conducted in Spain at any time during the war, might have been used not only to guide British policy regarding Franco, but also to determine what types of Allied propaganda would be most effective. By the same means it would have been possible to assess the true strength of such political movements as the Integralist in Brazil or the Fascist in Great Britain.

These ideas were set out in a report, entitled *A Plan for Pre-determining the Results of Plebiscites, Predicting the Reactions of People to the Impact of Projected Events, and Applying the Gallup Technique to Other Fields of Secret Intelligence*, which was forwarded by WS in August 1943 to London.

Though it was received without enthusiasm at the time, the fact remains that a year later the Psychological Warfare Board of SHAEF successfully conducted polls in Europe in the manner it had advocated. For that reason it is suggested that it may be worthy of further consideration.

(b) Latin America

Inasmuch as both were collected, broadly speaking, by the same organizational means, it is not practical to deal separately with BSC's intelligence concerning Latin American affairs and BSC's intelligence concerning enemy activities in Latin America. For that reason the subject is largely treated in other Parts of the book to which it is relevant.

Much of the intelligence which BSC received from Latin America was a by-product of its Special Operations work (see Part VI) and some of it was supplied by Consular and Industrial Security officers (see Part V). While SIS stations, whose task it was to report on economic and political conditions in the various republics as well as upon enemy activities (see Parts III and VII), worked independently of BSC – except during the comparatively brief period when they were under WS's administrative control – BSC remained in close touch with them throughout, for it was responsible for coordinating their undertakings with those of the relevant US Intelligence agencies.

BSC was always concerned to increase the productivity of its intelligence sources in Latin America, and to that end instituted the *Western Hemisphere Weekly Intelligence Bulletin* which was edited in New York and was a composite report of current information. The first issue appeared in August 1942, and thereafter the *Bulletin* was produced weekly for just over two years. Each issue summarized events in the Americas of interest to British Services, and the material was drawn from all pertinent sources to which BSC had access with the exception of Top Secret sources, for the distribution of the *Bulletin* was fairly wide. It went to:

- London, for SIS, SOE and Security Services, and through them to the Foreign Office, Colonial Office and Ministry of Economic Warfare.
- Washington, for various departments of the Embassy.
- Ottawa, for the Department of External Affairs and the RCMP.
- British Imperial Censorship Stations in the Western Hemisphere.
- All SIS Stations and SOE representatives in the Americas.
- Consular Security Officers (see Part V).
- Chief Industrial Security Officers (see Part V).

It was of practical use to interrogators at British Control Points who found in it much material of assistance to them in carrying out their duties. And it was of particular value, too, to field representatives in Latin America, who needed something of its kind to keep them *au courant* with the problems of Western Hemisphere Intelligence as a whole, to inform them of new methods which were being successfully carried out elsewhere and which they might themselves employ to advantage, to forewarn them of likely developments with which they might have to contend and to reassure them that their activities were not isolated or remote but part of a general design.

Experience taught BSC that intelligence agents (and agencies) thrive on reaction to their efforts, and are correspondingly discouraged by silence from their principals which may lead them to the depressing conclusion that they are serving a void. The *Bulletin* in itself provided Latin American stations with proof that their reports were being read and put to use. Thus it stimulated production, which was its prime purpose.

By the same token comments sent to representatives in Latin America from London or New York also stimulated production. When BSC assumed control of SIS Stations in Latin America in June of 1942, it inaugurated a system of commenting which proved advantageous. Officers were required to comment on every report of interest to them, and comments were also supplied by such official bodies as the FBI, OSS, HM Embassy in Washington, the Canadian Department of External Affairs and the Royal Canadian Mounted Police to whom reports from Latin America were circulated. At their own request, BSC continued to supply the stations with comments, after they had reverted to London's administrative control.

As already stated (see Introduction), in the early days before Pearl Harbor, when there was little information forthcoming from any Allied source in Latin America, BSC undertook the rehabilitation of a number of SIS stations. Two types of organizational machinery which eventually developed for collecting secret intelligence in Latin American countries may be briefly described by reference to the charts reproduced opposite.*

It will be seen from the first chart that the Chief Representative, while under compunction not to risk being uncovered, had to secure access to all the sources of information listed on the outside circle. He achieved this through the establishment of what might be termed a *cordon sanitaire*. Inside that circle were the official agencies to whom he was known as the Chief Representative of SIS. In this case they were HM Embassy, the Consuls, the Canadian Embassy, the FBI, ONI and G-2. Apart from them, there were only four people in the country with whom he was in direct contact. They were the four head agents shown on the inside circle. Each of them knew him, but they did not know each

---

* [These charts did not appear in the copies of *British Security Coordination* which still exist and therefore cannot be reproduced here.]

other. It was their responsibility to set up organizations to cover the various fields allotted to them and to maintain their own security to the fullest extent possible.

Security was protected principally through the system of cut-outs shown on the chart. In case of trouble, the agent removed the cut-out, replacing him if possible, and thus the channel remained secure. An example of this is the line running from 510 to USSR activities. The head agent identified as 510 was in direct touch with 511, who was aware that he was working for British interests but, of course, did not know the Chief Representative or the rest of the organization; 511 contacted 549, but through a cut-out who could be removed in case of necessity; 549 himself only knew the cut-out and did not know for whom he was working; 549 had the direct line into USSR activities.

Another example, on the same chart, is that of the Secret Police of the Interior. This was a useful organization into which to run lines, because it possessed a considerable amount of required material. In this case three of the head agents had independent lines to the Secret Police. 516 had direct contact; 529 had two lines through two separate cut-outs; while 536 also had a line through another cut-out.

The second chart is illustrative of a station which, owing to exceptional circumstances, did not require a large field organization. The National Secret Service was of unusual calibre and enjoyed a number of unusual advantages. It had its own police organization, as seen on the right-hand side of the chart, and was also served by the whole organization run by the Ministry of the Interior. The President of the Republic made personal use of the Secret Service, and consequently there was complete secrecy regarding all its investigations. It was, therefore, possible, through cooperation at a high level, to make enquiries through the Secret Service without the lower grades being able to identify the source of such enquiries.

In this way the entire country was covered by utilizing an organization which had at its disposal all the normal facilities of censorship, telephone tapping, surveillance and so on, and it was unnecessary for the station to maintain more than a 'shadow organization' of its own. The shadow organization was necessary for an occasional check on the products of the National Secret Service and as a skeleton alternative establishment on which to build in case the existing arrangement was at any time placed in jeopardy.

CHAPTER 4

External Intelligence

(a) Minorities
(b) Individual Informants

BSC received the bulk of its external intelligence – and this represented a high percentage of the total volume of material made available to SIS from all quarters – as a result of its liaison with US Intelligence agencies. Among these OSS was, of course, by far the most prolific source, and indeed it may be said that the assurance of a regular supply of high-grade external intelligence from official American sources – one of BSC's principal objectives – was eventually brought about through the establishment of Donovan's organization (see Part I).

There were, however, certain unofficial sources of external intelligence available in the Western Hemisphere and these BSC was already tapping before it was enabled to maintain direct liaison with any US agency other than the FBI and before Donovan's organization came into being. They may be classified under two headings: Minorities and Individual Informants.

(a) Minorities

Reference has already been made to President Aguirre and to the cooperation which BSC received in various intelligence activities from the Basques. With BSC's assistance the Basques were eventually enabled to establish or rather re-establish their own intelligence service in the Western Hemisphere and so, too, were a number of other exiled groups, notably the Free French, who ran 'lines' into Europe. Indeed the organization, both in the United States and Latin America, of 'Free' movements composed of refugees and certain members of the resident minorities, was one of BSC's major undertakings. While this work had as its main objective the strengthening of resistance movements in occupied countries and was closely related to the task of recruiting agents for despatch into enemy territory, it inevitably resulted in the acquisition of external intelligence. For that reason attention has been drawn to it here, although it is described in detail in Part VIII, which is the more appropriate context.

(b) Individual Informants

For a period of two years, beginning in 1940, BSC sent London a weekly cable detailing the production figures of the Hungarian and Roumanian oil fields, and at regular intervals kept London supplied with information concerning the current overall oil position of the Axis. During 1941, it furnished reports on recent trends in Japanese heavy industry, which revealed, *inter alia*, that the Japanese had been able to deceive the world by a peculiar method of bookkeeping, and that their production figures were, in fact, rising and not falling as had generally been supposed.

These are but two examples among many others which could be quoted of external intelligence – of operational and political as well as economic interest – largely derived from individual informants. A list of all the various individuals who assisted BSC either by supplying relevant information already in their possession or by obtaining information through their own contacts would clearly be of little interest. But one in particular merits some mention, because his position is of concern to Allied authorities at the time of writing.

It will be remembered that in 1940 Captain Fritz Wiedemann was the German Consul-General in San Francisco.

Wiedemann had been Hitler's commanding officer in the First World War, and, according to general belief, had been one of his right-hand men at least until the outbreak of war. His apparent banishment to San Francisco was, therefore, something of a mystery. He himself explained it by the fact that Hitler had become aware of his increasing disillusionment with the Nazi regime, and, having told him he could not employ anyone as his adjutant who did not fully accept his policies, had given him the choice of leaving the service of the German Government entirely or of going to San Francisco. In substantiation of his story, Wiedemann professed to be a 'German rather than a Nazi', and put it about that he favoured a Hohenzollern restoration.

On the other hand, it was clear that, from the Nazi point of view, he had been placed in an important strategic area and in a post he was well qualified to fill. He had travelled in the United States in

1937 and had reported to Hitler on the undeveloped potentialities of the West Coast as a field for political and economic exploitation. Furthermore, San Francisco was a logical coordination centre for German and Japanese espionage in the United States and a logical headquarters, too, from which to direct Nazi activities in Mexico and South America.

In April 1940, the British Consul-General in San Francisco informed the Embassy that he had been approached by an acquaintance of Wiedemann who apparently wished to establish relations with the British. The acquaintance – a British subject of doubtful reliability named Wooten – said that Wiedemann expected to be ordered back to Germany, that he was afraid to return because of a quarrel with Ribbentrop and that he desired to renew his acquaintance with Lord Halifax in order to secure entry into Great Britain.

Meanwhile, the FBI had been keeping Wiedemann under surveillance, and had intercepted a telephone conversation between him and the German Embassy which indicated that the Embassy had adopted a 'domineering attitude' towards him. Accordingly there seemed grounds for believing that Wiedemann's story might not be without foundation in fact – and certainly there seemed good reason for listening to it.

BSC discussed the matter with the FBI, who agreed on the advisability of making contact with Wiedemann. In October 1940, WS arranged for Sir William Wiseman, who already had some slight acquaintance with Wiedemann, to go to San Francisco and interview him. During the next two months Sir William had several long conversations with Wiedemann and, while he held out no promises, encouraged him to talk freely.

Wiedemann furnished a great deal of information about Germany, much of which was proved to be both accurate and valuable. He said that he himself had been opposed to the Nazi regime ever since the murder of von Fritsch. He claimed to be in communication with a number of high officers who felt that the only hope for Germany was a restoration of one of the Hohenzollerns, because the monarchists did not share Hitler's ideal of world conquest and wanted only security for Germany. The Crown Prince, so he suggested, would be the right man to organize a revolution against the Nazis, although he would not become Kaiser. Wiedemann gave the names of six high officers (including Halder), saying that they had conferred with the Crown Prince and that the Prince or one of his right-hand men would be glad to meet a British representative in Switzerland to discuss their plans.

There was, he said, another opposition group in Germany called the *Tatkreis*, which had been responsible for the beerhall bombing in Munich. It was headed by a Berliner named Eustace Koch and was sympathetic to the Crown Prince.

He made some accurate prognostications concerning German strategy. Although he did not mention Hitler's intentions to invade Russia, he did say that the visit of Soviet Foreign Commissar Molotov to Berlin had proved a failure. In his estimation, Molotov had been given instructions to discuss everything and agree to nothing. Furthermore, he emphasized that Hitler had never liked or trusted the Russians and that this fact should not be forgotten.

He revealed that Hitler, who had expected Britain to be defeated by the beginning of October 1940, was now off balance for the first time, and that the persons chiefly responsible for misleading him about the British will to resist were Lord Rothermere and Unity Freeman-Mitford, who had both reported that England was on the verge of a Fascist revolution. He said that there had been a sound and detailed plan for invading England, drawn up by Beck, but that it had been superseded by an impractical and amateurish plan which no one favoured except Hitler and Goering. When Hitler had been told that on this basis an invasion of Britain would be suicidal he had retired into cavernous gloom for three days. However, Wiedemann continued, the Army leaders now intended to subjugate Britain by heavy and persistent air raids. Hitler was himself convinced that Britain could not withstand prolonged bombing. But, Wiedemann added, while Hitler hinted at secret plans, it seemed probable that he was marking time and was uncertain what to do next.

It was in connection with forthcoming Mediterranean operations that Wiedemann supplied his most valuable piece of intelligence concerning German strategy, for in November 1940 he told Sir William Wiseman that the German High Command intended to close the Mediterranean at both ends by persuading Spain to collaborate and by inducing the Balkans to join the Axis. 'From a transportation point of view,' he said 'a movement through the Balkans would not be so difficult as some people think. The problem has been very carefully studied.' Five months later, on 6 April 1941, the Balkans were invaded.

These are but a few examples of the intelligence which Wiedemann supplied, much of which, as already stated, proved valuable. However, the State Department suspected that Wiedemann was attempting to engineer a negotiated peace, and, in December of 1940, informed HM Embassy of an intention to deport Sir William Wiseman because of his association with him. While WS was able to provide assurance that Sir William's meetings with Wiedemann (which had, of course, been held with the FBI's full knowledge and approval) were of an entirely unofficial nature and implied no threat to the interest of either the British or the United States Governments, it was nevertheless decided to terminate the contact largely because it was impossible to offer Wiedemann any encouragement in the course of action which he professed himself anxious to follow.

London commented as follows on BSC's first report of Sir William Wiseman's conversations with him:

> Information of considerable interest. Policy in dealing with Wiedemann should be not to discourage him from talking if he wishes to do so, but not to encourage him from our side.

After the enforced closure of the German Consulate in July 1941, Wiedemann went first to South America and thence to China. Whatever the colour of his actions during the ensuing years, in retrospect it seems logical to suggest that his offer to assist in organizing a rightist anti-Nazi revolution may have been sincere and might indeed, had he been able to implement it, have hastened the march of events which culminated in the attempted assassination of Hitler in 1944.

PART V

SECURITY OF PROPERTY AND PERSONNEL

CHAPTER 1

The Security Division before Pearl Harbor

(a) BSC Takes Over
(b) The Factories
(c) Consular Security Officers

(a) BSC Takes Over

During the year and a half of the European war which elapsed before the passage of the Lend-Lease Act, Britain was in the position of having a vast amount of her resources of production, supply, shipping and foreign investment situated in a country which was under no obligation to protect them. Yet it was vital that they should be protected.

In the United States there are 6,000,000 German-speaking Americans and 4,000,000 Italian-speaking Americans. Many of these American citizens were employed as workers in the factories producing British war material. Some of them were labourers in the freight yards or employees of the railways which transported British property, and others were stevedores loading British ships. It was a dangerous situation; for a wide-scale sabotage campaign in the private factories producing arms for British account or against the large proportion of Britain's 20,000,000 tons of shipping which used American ports could have proved disastrous.

Moreover, it was known that the organization and resources of the enemy in the United States, in combination with the potentially subversive elements which already existed there, were ample for this task. Enemy agents were scattered throughout the forty-eight states, and each one knew well that he could rely upon the assistance, active or passive, of the many thousands of members of militant German Bunds. And there were others who would help. There were the isolationists; there were the businessmen with European interests; there were the nationalist Indians, the anti-British Irish and, in increasing volume, the Communist-influenced left-wingers, preaching against 'the imperialist war' while Soviet Russia was still apparently on friendly terms with Germany. The Communist-dominated National Maritime Union of America was bitterly attacking the despatch of American ships into the war zones and any form of US intervention. Its lawyers had developed various ingenious techniques of delaying Allied vessels by suborning members of Chinese and other crews to refuse to sail at the last moment without new and extravagent equipment. All these groups and organizations were giving either direct or indirect help to the Nazis.

In the summer of 1940, before BSC came into being, some tentative steps had been taken to combat the danger. A Credit and Investigation Section and a Shipping Security Section had been formed under cover of the British Purchasing Commission. These two sections were doing what they could with the meagre resources and facilities available to them. The former endeavoured to establish the reliability of firms working for British account. The latter took measures designed to ensure the safe loading of supplies from wharf to ship. But their work, in comparison with the magnitude of the danger, fell far short of necessity.

What was required was a security organization that would maintain specialized departments to devise measures for the physical protection and security of British property; to advise on security steps and anti-sabotage precautions for factories, railroads, shipyards and docks; to investigate and report upon sabotage, subversive activities, Communist influence amongst labour unions and the suborning and desertion of crews; to vet the reliability of manufacturing companies and also of individuals applying for jobs in British missions in the USA; finally, to establish the closest possible liaison with the American and Canadian departments concerned with these activities – with the FBI, the RCMP, the US and Canadian Service Intelligence organizations, the Customs and Immigration and the local police and port authorities.

Shortly after his arrival in the United States, WS suggested that a security organization should be formed to undertake these duties, and as a result BSC came into being in January of 1941. While it provided cover for SIS and SOE activities, its sole overt purpose was the safeguarding of British interests in the United States.

A programme of expansion was at once launched. The Security Division within BSC absorbed the old Shipping Security Section and the Credit and Investigation Section. It was responsible for the security of (i) British war material in production and in transport to ships, (ii) shipping, and (iii) personnel and premises of British Missions in the USA. In time, it was entrusted with other important duties (to be described hereunder) and shortly before Pearl Harbor assumed responsibility, too, for the safeguarding of British interests in South America.

(b) The Factories

British orders for war materials in the United States prior to Pearl Harbor amounted to some $4,000,000,000. Of this, $300,000,000 was invested in British government-owned plants and extensions of existing plants. It was the duty of the Security Division to safeguard these assets in every way possible. The first step was obviously to vet the firms producing the war materials. In order to do this, the British Purchasing Commission, whenever any contract was in negotiation, approached the Security Division of BSC and asked for a check of the contractor from two points of view. Was he financially reliable, and was he completely free from any connection with the enemy? The first check was made through credit agencies, banks and financial houses; the second through direct investigation and by obtaining all possible information from the FBI and other relevant US Government agencies.

After the firm had been vetted and the contract signed, it was necessary to make sure that the factory producing the war material was secure. Here advantage was taken of an existing clause in all British contracts with American firms, which provided for technical inspection of the product at various stages of manufacture and upon its completion. These inspections were carried out by the Inspection Board of the United Kingdom and Canada, with headquarters in Ottawa, an office in New York and a large technical staff in the field. BSC established liaison with this field staff and secured the assistance of one of the administrative officers of the Board. The latter's particular duty was to visit all factories working for Britain, to safeguard the welfare of the resident inspection staff and to settle a large variety of other personnel problems. In collaboration with him, BSC prepared a standard form, covering the security status of each factory, to be completed by the administrative officers in the course of their inspection. At the same time the officer recruited assistants of his own to report back to him on the maintenance of protective measures. With the resultant information, the Security Division was able to draw up a complete survey of all British contracts placed with US factories and to examine the security conditions prevailing in each plant.

Essential as it was to adopt rigid security measures, BSC had no legal authority to enforce such measures in American factories on American soil, and before the passing of the Lend-Lease Act there was little assistance forthcoming from the US military authorities. BSC, therefore, approached the manufacturers themselves, and, though great care and tact had to be exercised, was eventually able to persuade nearly all of them to cooperate in taking every possible precaution against sabotage in their own plants. At the same time the British Purchasing Commission was prevailed upon to adopt a sabotage clause in its standard form of contract. In this clause the manufacturer undertook to maintain all reasonable precautions against sabotage, and to advise the Purchasing Commission of any actual or attempted sabotage in his factory. Obviously the fact that the manufacturer would himself have to sustain any losses made him all the more willing to take care that official security measures were enforced. In this he was assisted by a set of recommendations which was issued by BSC to all American plants working for British account. Therein advice was given upon how to prevent the infiltration of saboteurs or enemy sympathizers.

After the passage of the Lend-Lease Act, American defence production began to increase, and American authorities took a much more active interest in the prevention of sabotage in factories. The liaison with the FBI and with the War Department, which the Security Division had already established, became closer. The FBI, however, were on the point of relinquishing their responsibility, although they retained the right to investigate all cases of possible sabotage after they had occurred. The War Department, and specifically the Office of the Under-Secretary of War, became the main point of contact, and in September 1941, the Under-Secretary circularized all departments of the US armed forces, inviting them to cooperate with the British in:

physical protection of factories;
vetting of employees;
enforcing regulations applying to visitors;
controlling guard personnel;
investigating suspected sabotage;
investigating slow-ups;

investigating subversive activities;
investigating labour conditions generally.

It was specified that the cooperation should be with the Administrative Officer of the Inspection Board who was now formally transferred to the staff of BSC. This move put the Security Division in direct touch with about one thousand inspectors employed by the British Government in factories throughout the United States.

At the same time BSC set about the task of instructing the Americans in what good factory security meant. It was found that the most effective method was to take them on inspection tours of protected British factories, pointing out the dangers and the safeguards and allowing them to draw their own conclusions. In November 1941, the US Government issued a directive which stated, *inter alia*, '. . . the plant protection project of the US Government will be extended to include . . . inspection of plants in which British orders only are undertaken . . .' This, it should be remembered, was at a time when America was still neutral.

After the material had been produced in the factory, the next step was to get it safely to the ship. Officers of BSC's Security Division undertook a twenty-four-hour inspection of all railwayyards, railway termini and deep-sea piers which handled goods for Britain. They contacted the local police and fire departments, the port control officers, the Coast Guard, the shipping boards and the Army and Navy agencies. They talked with them all at length and eventually each was persuaded to cooperate fully in instituting proper systems of protection to ensure that goods and munitions found their way safely from the factory to the wharf. Whenever goods were not delivered, whenever they were damaged in transit or appeared to have been inadequately protected, BSC investigated the causes and took steps to have them removed. A series of reports were compiled dealing in detail with the innumerable issues involved, and the recommendations made in the reports were adopted as basic rules by the Americans when they entered the war.

(c) Consular Security Officers

Having done all that was possible to ensure that the war material was not sabotaged either during manufacture or on its journey to the coast, the next step was to see that it was loaded safely from the wharf to the ship; to see also that those British ships which

Security of Property and Personnel

came to American ports to collect the cargo were not damaged whilst in harbour.

The problem of handling and loading presented a number of difficulties, of which labour trouble was the chief. Not only were the dock workers potential trouble makers but also the seamen from the ships. In the ports, Nazi-inspired anti-British groups and organizations spread their propaganda. The Communist-influenced National Maritime Union and the Scandinavian Seamen's Club did much to foster desertions amongst Greek, Chinese and Scandinavian seamen. Other organizations instigated strikes amongst the dock workers and in one way or another did everything they could to prevent or slow down aid to Britain.

To meet this situation, WS decided that an organization must be set up under the Security Division which would cover all the major ports in the United States; that men should be selected who had a wide experience of merchant shipping and a profound knowledge of the district in which they were to serve. Plans were made and discussed with HM Embassy in Washington, with DNI Ottawa and with various authorities in London.

They were approved. Men who would henceforth be known as Consular Security Officers (CSOs) were appointed to serve at:

Baltimore	Mobile	San Francisco
Boston	New Orleans	San Pedro
Galveston	New York	Savannah
Houston	Philadelphia	Seattle
Los Angeles	Port Arthur	Tampa
Miami		

These ports served 95% of all the British shipping which touched the United States, and the duties of the new CSOs included the maintenance of constant vigilance against the entry aboard of saboteurs in the guise of visitors, repairmen, stevedores, ship-chandlers; the checking of physical anti-sabotage equipment, such as screens and nets; the protection of seamen from the attentions of those anxious to learn their secrets; the suppression of news of ships' cargoes, movements and convoys.

Despite the exposed situation of many port areas in the United States, particularly New York, where one of the more successful German informants (later arrested) needed only to ride back and forth on the Staten Island Ferry to secure his information, the system proved effective. In fact, by midsummer of 1941, the experience gained, combined with the ever-increasing spread of war activity, demonstrated beyond doubt that a similar system was essential in the ports of South America, where British vessels called for foodstuffs and strategic minerals. In August, just a year after the German High Command had sent to Rio de Janeiro a coordinator and administrator for their embryonic sabotage organization, the head of the Security Division of BSC left New York with the mission of establishing CSOs in the south. In this task, the intimate knowledge which he possessed of South America, and particularly of British shipping problems there, proved invaluable. As a result of six crowded weeks of travelling, CSOs selected mainly from among the personnel of the great British shipping houses were appointed and instructed in their duties in twenty-six ports of nine countries, covering over 90% of British-controlled shipping in South America. They were stationed at:

Antofagasta (Chile)
Bahia Blanca (Argentina)
Bahia do Sao Salvador (Brazil)
Barranquilla (Colombia)
Belem do Pará (Brazil)
Buenos Aires (Argentina)
Callao (Peru)
Caripito (Venezuela)
Cartagena (Colombia)
Cumarebo (Venezuela)
Güiria (Venezuela)
Iquique (Chile)
La Guayra (Venezuela)
La Libertad (Ecuador)
Las Piedras (Venezuela)
Mamonal (Colombia)
Maracaibo (Venezuela)
Montevideo (Uruguay)
Panama (Panama)
Puerto La Cruz (Venezuela)
Recife (Brazil)
Rio de Janeiro (Brazil)
Rio Grande do Sul (Brazil)
Santos (Brazil)
Tocopilla (Chile)
Valparaiso (Chile)

BSC was thus ready for the intensive submarine campaign which opened with such ferocity in the Caribbean and upon the western shores of South America six months later.

It is perhaps worth while to review the situation existing in October 1941, when the head of the Security Division returned from South America. Though the German attack on Russia had won over the Communists and their large labour following to support of aid to Britain, a month-long strike at the Federal Shipyards at Kearney was holding up two American cruisers under construction, while John L. Lewis was about to order a serious coal stoppage. The isolationist America First organization (see Part II), though showing signs of strain, boasted a membership of 900,000 and was working feverishly to blacken the Allied cause and avert

Standard Anti-Sabotage Precautions for Merchant Shipping

(APPROVED BY THE ADMIRALTY, MINISTRY OF WAR TRANSPORT AND FOREIGN OFFICE. JUNE, 1942)

Consular Seal

1. **MOORING** — Vessel to be so moored as to limit means of access as much as possible. Pontoons to be placed between ship and quayside wherever practical.

2. **GUARDS and WATCHMEN** — A 24-HOUR WATCH to be set. Guards (armed, if possible) to be posted FORE, AFT and at GANGWAY and NOT to leave their posts unless relieved. An Officer to be on duty day AND NIGHT and to check frequently that all watchmen are at their posts. A responsible crew-member to be stationed at the gangway throughout the vessel's stay in port. Watchmen to be provided with WHISTLES and TORCHES. Arrangements to be made, wherever possible, for the provision of quayside guards and barriers.
   IMPORTANT: Exact scope of Guards' and Watchmen's authority must be clearly defined to them.

3. **CREW PASSES** — Officers and crew to be in possession of a ship's pass before leaving the vessel. Crew-member at gangway to verify that persons holding crew-passes are actually members of crew. Any crew-member returning without his pass to be closely questioned as to its loss, and immediate steps taken to prevent the lost pass being used by an unauthorized person to get aboard.

4. **VISITORS** — NOBODY to be allowed aboard without an approved pass plus adequate identification plus legitimate ship's business. Books or sheets to be kept at the gangway and EVERY visitor to sign when boarding and leaving vessel, giving time and business affiliations. All visitors to be kept under continuous surveillance while aboard.

5. **LIGHTING** — Vessels to have STRONG LIGHTING during darkness. Light-clusters to be hung over the bow, off-shore side, stern, gangway and any open hatch. A movable-floodlight or powerful portable electric-torch to be available for examining approaching harbour craft, etc.

6. **HARBOUR CRAFT and LIGHTERS** — To be challenged on approaching the vessel and not allowed to remain alongside without legitimate reason. Lighters required for working cargo or stores not to remain alongside at night-time unless absolutely necessary, in which case they are to be inspected by a ship's Officer and thereafter KEPT UNDER CLOSE WATCH.

7. **STEVEDORES and SHORE WORKMEN** — To be carefully checked and, if possible, searched at gangway and NOT allowed to carry unexamined packages aboard.

8. **PACKAGES** — ALL Packages brought aboard to be examined at gangway. This includes passengers' luggage.

9. **HOSES** — To be RIGGED, ready for immediate use. Extinguishers and sand always to be available throughout the vessel.

10. **GUNS and AMMUNITION** — Gunners to maintain 24-hour watch and not to allow unauthorised persons in guns' vicinity. Ammunition to be under lock and key and examined daily.

11. **BRIDGE COMPANIONWAYS, ETC.** — To be roped-off to protect compass and other navigating instruments against tampering. Chartroom, Wheelhouse, Wireless-room, etc., to be securely locked when not occupied.

12. **CABINS** — To be locked when not in use.

13. **ENGINE and BOILER ROOM ENTRANCES** — One entrance only to be in use, this to be kept under close watch.

14. **VENTILATORS and SKYLIGHTS** — To be covered by stout wire-netting (mesh half inch max.). Covers (canvas or wood) to be kept handily accessible for closing ventilator-shafts in case of fire.

15. **PORTHOLES** — To be closed or barred, especially if easily accessible from outside.

16. **HOLDS and HATCH-COVERS** — A crew-member to be in each hold while working cargo. HOLDS TO BE CAREFULLY INSPECTED BY AN OFFICER BEFORE BEING CLOSED. Hatch-covers to be replaced immediately work ceases. Bunker hatches especially to be kept closed whenever possible.

17. **GOOSE NECKS to TANKS** — To be protected by stout gauze or other effective covering.

18. **SOUNDING PIPES ETC.** — Caps of sounding pipes to fresh-water tanks to be tightly SCREWED DOWN AND SEALED in order to prevent poison, etc. being injected into the water. The same care is to be taken with sounding pipes leading to bilges and tanks, especially to tanks containing water intended for use in boilers. ALL water to be tested before using.

19. **REPAIRS** — Especially welding and burning to be done under CLOSE SUPERVISION. Fire extinguishers, hoses (rigged) and sand always to be within reach.

20. **OIL FILTERS and DRAINS** — To be CHECKED FREQUENTLY against abrasives.

21. **TURNING MACHINERY** — The main engines to be carefully turned over with the turning-gear once before starting.

22. **DEGAUSSING EQUIPMENT** — To be frequently tested, especially before sailing. Particulars of tests to be entered in ship's Log.

23. **LIFEBOATS** — To be frequently examined, especially before sailing. Particulars of examinations to be entered in ship's Log.

24. **STORES** — To be examined (not merely checked) before being brought aboard.

25. **OIL and COAL** — Bunker and/or lubricating oil, if taken, to be sampled before use. Careful scrutiny to be given to bunker-coal as taken aboard.

26. **GAS-CYLINDERS for REFRIGERATION** — Any gas-cylinders bought locally to be examined and tested before use.

27. **SEARCH of SHIP and EXAMINATION of SHIP'S HULL** — EFFICIENT SEARCH of ship and examination of SHIP'S HULL to be made by Master or responsible Officer immediately prior to leaving port. Note of search to be duly entered in ship's Log. Any (apparently forgotten) object found which is not the property of a crew-member, to be thrown overboard without examination, unless a Police explosives-expert is available.

INCIDENTS of SABOTAGE — A full report to be made immediately to CONSULAR SECURITY OFFICER.

S.A.S.P. 1.

Anti-sabotage precautions for merchant shipping, prepared by the Security Division of BSC and translated into Dutch, Greek, Serbo-Croat, Spanish and Norwegian. Their use became standard practice in the Western Hemisphere.

BRITISH SECURITY CO-ORDINATION
SHIP INSPECTION REPORT

PORT: .... DATE: ....

SS/MV .... Port of Registry .... Gross Reg. Tons ....

Master .... Agents ....

Arrived .... Berth .... From ....

Sailed .... For .... Days delayed ....

Is vessel: Loading ☐   Discharging ☐   Repairing ☐

Nature of cargo loaded .... Hatches Nos. ....

Crew: Nationality .... Attitude ..../............

Number of Watchmen on duty: Crew { Day .... Night .... } Shore { Day .... Night .... }

Rank and name(s) of Officer(s) interviewed ....

Ship inspection. Mark X against any deficiencies noted:

☐ Poor lighting (night-time)   ☐ Forward   ☐ Midship   ☐ Aft   ☐ Off shore side
☐ No crew-member at gangway   ☐ Door to Radio Room open
☐ No guard on armaments   ☐ Door(s) to unoccupied Cabin(s) open
☐ No Officer on duty (night-time)   ☐ Magazine not locked
☐ Sounding pipes unsealed   ☐ No lighting over open hatches (night-time)
☐ Goose necks not protected   ☐ Open hatches unattended
☐ Ventilators not protected   ☐ Unattended lighters alongside (night-time)
☐ Skylights not protected   ☐ Fire hoses not rigged and connected
☐ Open portholes not protected   ☐ No extinguishers or sand available
☐ Bridge companionway not roped off ☐ Inadequate supervision during repairs
☐ Both doors to Engine room open   ☐ Unauthorized persons boarding vessel
☐ Door to Wheelhouse open   ☐ Packages brought aboard without search
☐ Door to Chartroom open

To whom were they reported? (Name and rank) ....

Were they rectified? ....

REMARKS (on deficiencies, crew troubles, etc.)

Ship Inspection Report form used in South American ports.

US aid. At Camp Nordland, New Jersey, the German Bunds met Sunday by Sunday, while in the streets of Hoboken, where a German Seamen's Mission overlooked the waterfront, Allied seamen were openly suborned to desert their ships. The US vessel *Panuco*, lying in dock in Brooklyn and loaded with drums of oil for the great US naval base at Guantanamo, Cuba, caught fire and was completely destroyed with pier and barges and the loss of twenty lives.

It was in such an atmosphere that the machinery of the Security Division began to work at full pressure. As regards shipping security, CSOs in the United States had long since established liaison with local naval, coast guard, FBI, customs and police officials, though relations were unofficial and in many cases extremely delicate. CSOs now supplied and vetted shore-watchmen for British vessels and inspected the latter's anti-sabotage measures. They guarded crews against suborners and combated the mass desertions of Chinese seamen. They watched the security of cargoes of material lying on the docks for shipment. And they participated whole-heartedly in welfare work which was a major contribution to security.

In all the posts in the United States where CSOs were stationed and in many of those in South America, clubs and hostels were established for seamen. These clubs did excellent work. They served the triple purpose of keeping Allied seamen in good heart, of protecting them from Axis-inspired attempts to provoke discontent and strikes, and of steering them away from resorts where drink or other inducements might loosen their tongues.

Further, it was the task of the CSOs to persuade their American colleagues to become security-minded. Before Pearl Harbor the latter had begun to provide information about enemy agents, labour agitators and such unusual arrivals as the Swiss *SS St Cergue* which sailed into New York on 31 July 1941, from German-occupied Rotterdam, with one of the most suspect crews ever assembled.

At the same time, the head of the Security Division established contact with the British National Union of Seamen in America. The liaison, which was made with the Union delegates, produced the most salutary results, for the delegates assisted in solving labour disputes and in seeking out undesirables. They reported upon every genuine difficulty which was encountered. Men would complain that they were unfit for work, that their ship was dirty or unseaworthy, that their officers were harsh and so forth. The Union delegate would investigate. If the seamen were malingering or exaggerating, he had the authority, as the representative of their own Union, to quash their complaint. If he found it justifiable, the matter was reported to the CSOs who in turn informed BSC headquarters, and action was taken to meet it.

A system of communication was set up between the Security Division and the CSOs in the various ports, and between one CSO and another. Cable communications were sent in code, whilst a weekly safe-hand service was established for less urgent reports. The CSOs were encouraged to send full reports on their activities to the Security Division. Whenever a ship arrived in port, the CSO filled in a standard Ship Inspection Report, noting the essential facts about the ship's arrival and departure, cargo, crew and watchmen. This contained a chart showing deficiencies in security found by the CSO during an inspection, and space for remarks. One copy of this report was sent to the Security Division; a second was placed in a sealed envelope and handed to the master for transmission to the CSO at the next port of call; and the third was kept by the CSO himself for the record. Any grave or repeated violation of security regulations was reported to BSC, which in turn passed the report to London for action.

The CSOs in South America not only carried out similar duties but had to adapt themselves to the varying political conditions and sympathies of local port officials and police. Only later was it confirmed that even as they were being appointed to their posts, clandestine German radios were already transmitting to Berlin the names, departures and cargoes of the vessels which the CSOs were bound to protect. A Nazi sabotage network had been standing by for word from Berlin to strike at British shipping in South American harbours.

When the United States entered the war in December 1941, American officials expressed the desire that the CSO organization should continue to concern itself with British and Allied shipping. Some time later, the US Coast Guard agreed to accept CSO – in lieu of their own – inspection of an Allied ship. In US ports, the Americans supplied military guards for British transports, but the responsibility for their safety was shared by the CSOs. In New York harbour, the CSO had ten assistants. He divided the harbour into three zones. A round-the-clock watch was kept on each of these by members of his staff who reported hourly by telephone to a central number. Continuous eight-hour watches were kept upon the two most important British vessels, the *Queen Mary* and the *Queen Elizabeth*. In their case, as in all others, the closest attention was paid to preventing smoking and to keeping out unauthorized visitors and anyone under the influence of alcohol. A pass system was rigorously enforced. Workmen and crew were searched both upon embarking and debarking. All packages and tool-kits were inspected.

In result not a single British ship was lost or seriously held up by accident or sabotage in a United States port throughout the war. When the *Normandie* caught fire, sank and capsized in February 1942 – because sparks let fly by a welder fell upon a heap of Kapok lifebelts – later enquiry showed that of the eight British recommendations regarding welding practice, copies of which had already been supplied to the Captain of the Port of New York, no less than five were being violated.

Meanwhile, in Latin America the CSO organization was expanded and consolidated, and with the increasing establishment of US naval security officers, Anglo-American liaison there became likewise of primary importance. Many CSOs had desks in the US Naval Intelligence officers' rooms, or vice versa. Hundreds of ONI reports were passed to BSC. In the spring of 1942, a British-US Naval Routing Agreement provided for the transfer of the protection of merchant shipping 'within strategic waters of the Western Hemisphere' from the British to the US Navy, and except for a skeleton liaison service, British Naval Control withdrew from South American ports. However the CSOs were specifically exempted from this order by the Combined Chiefs of Staff, and the incoming US naval officers were directed to collaborate with them unreservedly. Thus the money, drive, diplomatic and economic pressure available to the Americans were reinforced by the knowledge and experience of the CSOs, many of whom, as remarked above, were professional shipping men.

These arrangements were completed just in time. The intensive German submarine campaign upon the Atlantic shores of South America began in the spring of 1942. Tankers were sunk carrying crude oil from Maracaibo to the Netherlands West Indies. Vessels were torpedoed by the dozen from the Carolines to Curaçao, and between February and September 1942 no less than twenty-three ships carrying bauxite from the sole British source in the Guianas to Canada were sent to the bottom.

These campaigns involved the CSOs in concentrated effort to suppress leakage of shipping information and to track down suspicious longshoremen, port officials, newspaper reporters and others who might be serving as German informants. In the United States, countless bars where seamen were reputed to have been pumped for information were investigated with the help of the

FBI and Army G-2, who in some cases undertook day and night surveillance of the suspects. In South America, much of this work had to be done by the CSOs themselves, in default of local aid. They drew up lists of undesirable resorts in every port to warn crews of incoming vessels. Further, they were concerned to stop the publication of information about shipping movements in the press and to prevent communication of such information by radio, letter or telegram. As a result of joint British-US diplomatic pressure, legislation to this effect was secured in most South American countries in the first half of 1942, but in many cases there remained the problem of securing its enforcement. CSOs had to plead with, cajole and threaten local port officials. They had to go over their heads to higher authorities, and they had laboriously to gather proof of the offences committed and the dangers involved.

Gradually the situation was improved. Newspapers dropped their shipping columns, photography in port areas was forbidden, docks were cleared, cables censored and pass-systems instituted. There was in some cases a natural wave of local resentment as citizens found their seashore promenades curtailed, their communications made more difficult and their right to dispose of bad liquor to ships in the bay denied.

By the summer of 1943, the Security Division was employing 31 CSOs with their staffs in the United States and 45 in Latin America. In a single period of three months, CSOs in North America carried out over 5,000 inspections on nearly 800 ships, and in South America over 2,500 inspections on 859 vessels. This gives an annual total of approximately 30,000 anti-sabotage inspections aboard British-controlled merchant ships.

In this way the CSOs helped to preserve the ships. But second only to the preservation of the ships themselves was the saving of tonnage time by providing for their quickest possible turn-around in the various ports of call. Here CSOs were able to help by arranging with local police to return drunken seamen to the gangplank rather than hold them in gaol, and by establishing launch services to vessels lying in the stream. In some ports, and particularly at Buenos Aires, they assisted in the prevention or the terminating of strikes by stevedores and shipyard workers.

The CSOs in Latin America cooperated with other BSC agents in preventing the smuggling of small bulk strategic commodities such as platinum and industrial diamonds. With their multiple waterfront contacts and with their countless 'shady' sources, they were able to contribute a continual flow of dependable information on the traffic and the elements responsible.

CSOs were required by Consuls-General to assist in the control of neutral vessels. In particular, they were able to help in preventing the abuse of ships' stores facilities. The CSO at Buenos Aires, for instance, drew up a scale of stores allowable to Spanish ships, which was later adopted by MEW for general use. Soon after, in January 1944, the CSO at Montevideo noted that Spanish ships calling at Brazilian ports were in the habit of loading excess stores there, on the plea of ignorance. Necessary action was taken and the traffic satisfactorily curbed.

Then just before the invasion of France, to prevent accidental leakage of information concerning it, a system was introduced whereby US Censorship intercepts of indiscreet letters from seamen on British-controlled ships could be passed to the appropriate CSOs, who in turn would arrange for masters to reprimand the writers. Admiralty cable channels were made available to reach ships which had already sailed, in no matter what part of the world they might be. As a result, seamen who had posted indiscreet letters in the United States or South America were surprised to find themselves being severely reprimanded in Karachi or Cape Town. The deterrent effect of such cases resulted in a sudden decrease of violations to a negligible level.

These are but a few examples of the tasks performed by CSOs. There were many more, and not all of them were undertaken as a result of directives from headquarters. CSOs had, above all, to be men of initiative with ability to improvise according to necessity.

CHAPTER 2

Industrial Security Officers

(a) The Vital Industries of Latin America
(b) The Beginning of the Organization
(c) ISOs in Operation

(a) The Vital Industries of Latin America

From the oil wells of Venezuela and from the refineries of the Dutch West Indies came 80% of the fuel oil used by the Royal Navy, and a great quantity of the aviation petrol used by the RAF. From the bauxite mines of the British and Dutch Guianas came 76% of the aluminium available to the Allies. While it was the job of the Consular Security Officers organization to protect the tankers carrying the crude oil from Venezuela to the Dutch West Indies and to protect the ships carrying aluminium ore from the Guianas to North America, it became obvious that another branch of security was essential: an industrial security organization which would undertake the protection of vital sources of strategic materials in South America, the factories where they were processed and the transportation channels along which they moved to the sea.

In July 1941, the BSC representative in Trinidad had visited the bauxite mines of British Guiana. These mines, which produce over a million tons of bauxite annually, became, after the Germans overran the European countries, the only important source from which Great Britain and Canada could obtain the ore. The mines lie at Mackenzie, sixty-five miles up the Demerara River from Georgetown. Destruction of the power plant would, it was estimated, have stopped production for nine months. And since ore is carried down river by shallow-draught ships and two of the bars could not be passed by a loaded vessel except at high tide, the scuttling of a single vessel at the right point would have choked the channel for weeks.

Unrest among the negro labourers and among the British 'East'

Security of Property and Personnel

Indians in the colony had, early in 1941, led to a strike and something approaching a riot. Guards for the Mackenzie plant were twenty negro police, who could hardly be expected to ward off a really determined attack. Previous recommendations by the officer commanding troops in Trinidad had not been carried out, and the Governor, agreeing that the danger was great, added that he would welcome the presence of white British troops. In his report the BSC representative recommended an increase in guards on ships and in the factory, the erection of an unclimbable fence around the factory area, and full examination of the bauxite ships by naval boarding personnel. The first two recommendations were met, after a fashion; the third was neglected. The Governor was supplied with fifty sub-machine guns and instructed to mobilize the local militia.

But as the war spread and Japan conquered most of the Far East, it was plain that these precautions were inadequate. In February 1942, the Security Executive suggested a thorough survey of the entire bauxite position in British Guiana, covering every stage between the mining of the ore and the final shipment to Canada. The head of the Security Division set out immediately, visiting British Guiana, Dutch Guiana, and the new dump at Chaguaramas in Trinidad and the trans-shipment port of St Thomas in the Virgin Islands.

Briefly, it was found that in British Guiana there was some security and no defence. In Dutch Guiana there was defence and no security, while in St Thomas there was crew trouble, which grew more serious every week after the Caribbean submarine campaign had started, and there was no defence whatever. In Dutch Guiana the Americans had already landed some troops, but the officers did not regard factory protection as part of their duties, and neither the Governor nor the Alcoa officials were interested in security. The BSC officer impressed upon the management both necessity and method of this, and persuaded a colonel of US Army Intelligence to explain them to the officers and to the Governor. For St Thomas he made suggestions for starting a canteen and for advancing US currency to Canadian crews, and held a meeting of the American and Canadian aluminium company heads with their shipping managers, at which he obtained a promise that all his recommendations would be carried out. For British Guiana he recommended once more that white troops should be provided. And after some negotiation between the Colonial Office and the War Office and the Government of Canada, a detachment of hand-picked Canadian officers and men was seconded to British Guiana, where it arrived in May 1942.

This instance has been described in some detail because it is illustrative of the general problems of industrial security in Latin America, which the Japanese conquest of the Far East had now made vital to the Allied war effort. The continent was rich. Eventually it could supply everything the Allies needed except rubber. But it was under-populated, its communications were poor, its societies weak and unstable. Most of its areas producing strategic material were not integral parts of a state like the Black Country or the Ruhr, but rather colonial developments, sometimes standing by themselves far in the jungle or isolated in the desert, so that it was difficult to provide them with effective military or police protection. Finally, the inhabitants who did not own these resources had little interest in safeguarding them.

The risk of direct military attack receded as the United States despatched troops, aircraft, coastal guns and light patrol boats to the Galapagos, Natal, Tocopilla and elsewhere. But there remained the probability that the Axis would attempt to disrupt the sources of strategic supplies in Latin America by sabotage or by fomenting strikes and revolutions; and this fear was proved well grounded by the subsequent unmasking of a widespread German sabotage ring (see Part VII).

Before appropriate action could be taken, it was necessary to convince both London and Washington of the danger inherent in the situation and of the need to combat it. At WS's instruction, the SOE Division compiled a report on Axis strength in Latin America which was based on information supplied by agents in the field. It drew attention to the large German colonies; to the active and well-organized Nazi organizations; to the widespread influence of Germany upon governments, officials and army officers; to the vulnerable and unguarded coastal areas; and to like factors which jeopardized the security of strategic industries. The report was sent to HM Embassy, to the headquarters of SOE and SIS, to the FBI, to General Donovan and to the RCMP.

At the same time, full lists of essential commodities, arranged in order of priority, were obtained from the Ministry of Economic Warfare in Washington and from American sources. In May 1942, an experienced British chemical engineer was recruited in Trinidad and requested to survey the possibilities of sabotage in all the industries which were essential to the war effort. He worked with the assistance of the SOE staff, and had access to all relevant information from expert sources. In result, a report entitled 'The

Physical Security of Strategic Raw Material Supplies from Latin America' was produced, and this estimated that the following were the most important materials supplied by Latin America. They are set out in order of the percentage of total Allied needs:

Metals	Antimony	43% from Mexico
		35% from Bolivia
	Bauxite	40% from Dutch Guiana
		36% from British Guiana
	Tin	54% from Bolivia
	Mica	28% from Brazil
		10% from Argentina
	Vanadium	37% from Peru
	Tungsten	19% from Bolivia
		7% from Argentina
	Chromium	26% from Cuba
	Mercury	26% from Mexico
	Petroleum	12.4% from Venezuela
		2.3% from Mexico
		1.3% from Colombia
		1.2% from Argentina
		1.15% from Trinidad
	Copper	17% from Chile
Other Products	Balsa Wood	99.55% from Ecuador
	Quinine	45% from Bolivia, Colombia, Ecuador and Peru
	Sisal	28% from Mexico
	Rubber	12% from Brazil

The report pointed out that enemy sabotage could attack these materials at seven distinct points:

1. Source of the material – oil wells, mines, growing crops.
2. Processing plants – ore dressing mills, refineries, sawmills.
3. Stocks of materials – oil, timber, cotton.
4. Means of transport – railways, river channels, airlines.
5. Services – water supplies, electric power installations and hydro-electric plants.
6. Staff – skilled technicians.
7. Labour.

In the light of these conclusions, the report examined every material separately, indicating the danger point which would have to be safeguarded. Antimony, for example, is sorted and crushed mostly by primitive methods, so the only two danger points are labour and transportation. Labour troubles can be avoided only by cultivating good labour relations. As regards transportation, Bolivian antimony has to pass over more than 500 miles of lofty mountain and deep valley by the Antofagasta railway. Sabotage can be avoided only by protecting the railway.

(b) The Beginning of the Organization

The report was sent to the Chiefs of Staff in London, who, after studying it, telegraphed to the Joint Staff Mission in Washington on 9 June 1942:

> We are anxious to see an end of Axis machinations in Latin America which constitute serious potential threat to Allied supplies . . . Our policy in regard to secret anti-Axis activity has been one of *laissez faire* to avoid risk of upsetting Latin American states . . . Although overt security measures to prevent sabotage to ships and cargoes have been organized in all major ports by British Security Coordination . . . except for this Axis have virtually had a free run . . . It is therefore highly important that secret work should start quickly . . . We have recommended to Ministers concerned that resources of both SIS and SOE should be made available . . . We have also recommended that British Security Coordination should extend their overt security measures . . .

Two weeks later the head of Security Executive in London wrote to WS as follows:

> . . . It has been agreed by the Departments concerned here that British Security Coordination in New York and Washington should take immediate steps, either in conjunction with the appropriate US authorities or otherwise, to carry into effect the recommendations contained in . . . the Chiefs of Staff telegram . . .

On 5 August 1942, the Chiefs of Staff again cabled the Joint Staff Mission saying:

> The recommendations . . . have been approved by the Foreign Secretary and the Ministry of Economic Warfare . . . should now discuss this matter with the US authorities . . .

South American sources of strategic materials required by the Allies, and (opposite) principal threats to the security of these materials prior to the formation of BSC's Industrial Security Organization.

LATIN AMERICAN RAW MATERIALS
VULNERABILITY TO SABOTAGE

	Source	Processing Plant	Storage	Transport	Services	Personnel & Labour
ANTIMONY: Mexico, Bolivia				Antofagasta Rly.		Labour trouble
BAUXITE: B.Guiana, D.Guiana		Drying Plants		River Channels	Power Plants	Labour trouble
TIN: Bolivia		Ore-dressing Plants		Antofagasta Rly, Arica-LaPaz Rly	Power Plants	Labour trouble
MICA: Brazil, Arg.			Damage by fire & water			Few skilled overseers
VANADIUM: Peru		Concentrating Plants		Central Rly.	Power Plants	Labour trouble
TUNGSTEN: Bolivia, Arg., Peru				Antofagasta Rly.		Labour trouble
CHROMIUM: Cuba				Rly.		
MERCURY: Mexico	Flooding workings				Power Plants	
PETROLEUM: Ven., Mexico, Col.		Refinery Distillation units	Tanks	Maracaibo tanker service	Power Plants	
COPPER: Chile		Concentrating Plants		Antofagasta Rly	Power lines: Power plants: Pipelines	Labour trouble
BALSA WOOD: Ecuador			Damage by fire			Skilled overseers; Labour trouble
CINCHONA BARK: Bolivia, Colombia, Ecuador, Peru						(Labour (trouble
SISAL: Mexico			Damage by fire			
RUBBER: Brazil, Cent.Am.				Adulteration; fire		Overseers

Serious dangers shown thus: ▒

Less serious dangers shown thus: ▨

Now SOE's report 'Axis Strength in Latin America' had laid down certain basic rules applicable to all the strategic industries of Latin America which, it suggested, should be enforced by locally recruited men who had full knowledge of the particular industry involved and the dangers to which such industry was exposed. WS had then drawn up plans for a new organization formed along these lines. He envisaged a scheme whereby reliable men from the factories, mines and refineries could be recruited by BSC, trained in security work and then returned to act as Security Officers at their places of employment.

An Industrial Security Plan was therefore ready to be put into effect. But first, in conformity with the instructions of the Chiefs of Staff, discussions were held with the US authorities. It was found impossible to obtain their effective collaboration despite much endeavour and despite the fact that American interests owned many of the companies involved. This was partly because of the rivalry between competing US agencies and partly because of the ever-present desire to exclude Britain from South American affairs.

In July 1942, when its scheme was in process of development, BSC asked the US Chiefs of Staff to determine which American agency was responsible for industrial protection in Latin America, and to lay down the basis on which BSC should collaborate with it. The US Army nominated G-2, but J. Edgar Hoover had already put some FBI agents to work on the security of Royal Dutch Shell and Gulf Oil in Venezuela and of Standard Oil in Aruba, whilst US Naval Intelligence had set up its own organization for factory security in Argentina. It was a straightforward case of one agency competing with another, and it was clear that no satisfactory cooperation would be obtained in this way. BSC could not afford to wait. It went ahead with its own arrangements.

Lists of British or British-controlled companies in Latin America were compiled. A chart of danger areas was built up. In London, the Chairman of the Security Executive held a meeting with the Board Chairman of over thirty British South American companies. He explained to them the principle upon which BSC's scheme was based and the vital necessity of putting it into operation. The companies at his request willingly agreed to release officials for training as Industrial Security Officers.

It was only when arrangements were near completion – in December 1942 – that an agreement was reached whereby the FBI was designated the responsible American agency. This tardy decision proved more embarrassing than helpful; for the FBI produced their own plan which they had drawn up without consulting BSC, and it was found to provide for the protection of many British companies to which BSC had already appointed Security Officers. Much negotiation was necessary before the FBI could be persuaded to modify it.

(c) ISOs in Operation

One or more representatives were chosen from each of the companies in Latin America which had been designated by BSC as being the producers of vital material. These men were flown up to the BSC school in Canada, where they were given an intensive two weeks' course of training in the basic principles of anti-sabotage. At the end of that period, each wrote a thesis on the special security problems of his own firm. The problems raised therein were discussed with the head of the school, then again with BSC in New York, and the man was returned quickly to his post in the south, a fully-fledged Industrial Security Officer, ready and qualified to take up his new duties. ISOs served without pay; but in order to concert measures of protection over wider areas and to keep the ISOs informed and enthusiastic, a small number of full-time paid supervisors were appointed as Chief Industrial Security Officers (CISOs), each one covering a certain zone. For this purpose Latin America was divided into six Security Zones:

Zone A: Peru, Bolivia, and Northern Chile
Zone B: Brazil
Zone C: Colombia, Venezuela, and Ecuador
Zone D: British Guiana (supervised by the Defence Security Officer)
Zone E: Southern Chile
Zone F: Argentina, Uruguay and Paraguay.

In each of these zones, the CISO travelled from point to point throughout the strategic areas, urging local governments and officials to improve security, making recommendations which the companies themselves could adopt after due discussion, and maintaining liaison with American security officers where such existed. CISOs also reported on other companies whose security was a matter of British interest but which were not important enough to warrant the expense of training an official.

The first recruits entered the school in August 1942. A year later the work was complete. Six supervisory officers and sixty-one ISOs had been recruited, appointed and trained, of whom seventeen were railway managers, ten oilfield technicians, two from oil storage plants, seven officials of the *frigoríficos* supplying Britain with frozen meat, six representatives of merchant houses, and five from power companies. Though it cost a thousand dollars (three-quarters of which was air passage to Miami) to bring a recruit up for training and to return him to the field, the loss of even a week's operation of any one of the enterprises concerned would have made this figure dwindle into insignificance.

Under WS's direction the SOE Division had been primarily responsible for developing the scheme, for it was originally believed that the scheme would provide excellent means for large-scale SOE penetration of South America. But the Chiefs of Staff laid down the principle that it should be kept entirely separate from both SOE and SIS in order to reassure local governments and to avoid possible denunciations by the Americans. Its control was therefore transferred in October 1942 to the Security Division of BSC. The head of the Security Division controlled the CSO organization, and now that he also had under him the ISOs he was able to ensure that both organizations worked along parallel lines and in full cooperation so that between them they could ensure the safety of all valuable materials, at the source of production and at the docks and upon the high seas.

In November 1942, the ISO organization was officially recognized in a circular telegram from the Foreign Office to Chanceries in South America, which stated that its functions were:

> to cover the security of war materials from the place of production until safely shipped, and to bring within its scope the railway over which these materials are carried to the port of embarkation, and such power and other utility services as are essential to their transport or production.

That, indeed, was what the ISOs did. As they returned to their posts and began to apply the lessons they had learned, reports and recommendations started to reach New York. As early as August 1942, an ISO visited the oilfields at Talara and suggested – *inter alia* – the installation of night lighting, the employment of more Anglo-Saxon watchmen and the creation of an informant service. Progress reports and detailed examinations of vulnerable areas increased from sixteen in November 1942 to eighty-nine in June 1943, and all of them helped to build up the detailed security plan of each company and each area kept by the CISO for each zone. As a by-product, a considerable amount of political and general intelligence was passed to SIS and SOE in New York. Many reports also went to the FBI and US Army Intelligence, and in return the FBI provided copies of certain South American surveys made by their own agents, although, it should be added, there were no reports on American-owned enterprises. In several spheres of common interest, such as the balsa mills in Ecuador, however, security surveys were carried out by the CISO and the FBI agent jointly.

The success of the scheme from the British point of view was complete. No major act of sabotage was successfully perpetrated by the enemy to hinder the flow of essential materials at any time during the war, despite the proved existence of a widespread and well-organized enemy sabotage ring. And though there were numerous accidents – particularly as the rolling stock of the strategic railways began to wear out – the vigilance of the ISOs made them far less frequent and serious than they might have been.

In fact, a large part of the work of the ISO organization lay in preventing or remedying small stoppages and inefficiencies, all of which would have held up material in its urgent passage to the sea. A typical example occurred in January 1944, when the Duperial ammonia factory in Buenos Aires broke down. Without ammonia the *frigoríficos* could not freeze the beef waiting for transport to Britain. Through quick cooperation between the CISO in Buenos Aires, the Security Division in New York and the Security Executive in London, tubes of the chemical were sent out from Britain with the highest priority, and thus a disastrous reduction of British rations was averted.

Indeed much of the ISOs' work may prove of more than transient worth. Latin America is likely to suffer from wars and revolutions for decades to come and during such civil commotions there are always and inevitably attacks on foreign companies. The safeguards which the ISOs instituted have already become routine, and most of the ISOs are themselves still employed by the companies they were called upon to protect during the war.

CHAPTER 3

The Security of Personnel

The Security Division of BSC safeguarded the material resources of Great Britain on the American continent. That work has been described. But there was another more subtle problem of security with which the Division had to deal, the problem of preventing enemies and undesirables from infiltrating into positions where they might gain special knowledge of the British war effort. The undesirables included employees who, being weak, garrulous, of divided loyalty or in financial difficulty, would become easy prey for an enemy agent remaining in the background.

Sound security in these matters involved the checking of countless individuals. Prior to Pearl Harbor it involved the checking of British and Canadian citizens applying for work in British missions as accountants, clerks, secretaries and guards; American employees for these missions; Allied personnel volunteering for service in the armed forces; American citizens volunteering for the Eagle Squadrons and other sections of the RAF; American citizens for the armed medical services or for the technical corps; American defence workers going to British territory, and employees of US commercial airlines who would be going abroad.

A few months after Pearl Harbor, recruiting for the RAF, which had been done through the Canadian Aviation Bureau, ceased. But Pan-American Airways began to enlist many more recruits, pilots, air-crew and ground staff for overseas, all of whom had to be carefully vetted. Then there were freelance British lecturers or writers catering to the American public; American employees of British-controlled war plants; American patent attorneys entrusted with secret British information; deserting seamen and suspect seamen.

In all cases, the person's record was examined and judged in the light of his access to information or his opportunity to commit sabotage. For example, the Security Division during the second six months of 1942 made 1,560 detailed personnel examinations for Washington, 928 for the British Ministry of Supply Mission in New York, and 1,348 for other enquirers. In the same period they vetted 1,405 Allied service personnel, mostly Norwegian and Dutch, 537 British volunteer civilians, 237 technicians, 723 recruits for three American airlines and 194 for British Overseas Airways.

In practice, these different types of investigation were allocated among different sections of Security Division. Cases of applicants for jobs in British missions in the US were handled by a section which enjoyed close contact with the FBI and the police. Examinations were conducted in different ways according to the nature of the case; sometimes through a special investigator, sometimes through a credit bureau, or, in cases of distant or foreign background, the CSO or SIS representative was called upon. References were then taken up and those who had given them were asked for further information. The applicant's name was checked through the various New York registries, the FBI subversive files and in some cases through the local police at the place of residence. The field reports, together with information from those giving references, were then closely compared with the claims made on the application form; discrepancies and contradictions were re-checked. Finally, an assessment was made and the mission concerned was notified.

Over 20,000 such investigations were carried out, and though most of them concerned American citizens, not one complaint was received. The work had to be undertaken with considerable discretion, and it was greatly assisted by the devotion of the American employees engaged in it.

An extension of personnel security was the general security of the British missions in the United States.

Sooner or later, tired from long hours, the man busy on secret plans leaves a document lying on his desk, which catches the eye of an inquisitive cleaner. A messenger puts down his bag in a public place to buy a packet of cigarettes and, turning, finds it has vanished. Under strain, a man begins to drink to heavily, and, under the influence of alcohol, talks. All such problems refer to the security of missions.

In principle, of course, this phase of security is an unpopular one, since heads of missions naturally wish to retain full powers over their own departments. At first there was neither agreement that a single authority responsible for the security of missions was necessary nor, if it were, that such authority should properly be vested in BSC. The first step was taken in March 1942, however, when representatives of the Embassy, the Joint Staff Mission, the Admiralty Delegation, the Air Commission, the Treasury, the Supply Council and the Purchasing Commission, as well as the Coordinator of Empire Requirements, met to discuss a basic set of security regulations with a BSC representative. The resulting British Security Manual was accepted by all departments concerned.

The next stage was to have these basic rules enforced. In June 1942, the head of the British Army Staff Mission in Washington expressed his alarm at the laxity which still persisted, suggesting that all security arrangements should be coordinated under one officer directly responsible to the Embassy. The head of the Security Division saw representatives of the various British delegations and missions once more in July 1942, and they agreed that guards and safe-hand messengers should be controlled by BSC. A Chief Security Officer was appointed, and he made a tour of British-occupied buildings in Washington and submitted a report on them. This showed that elementary rules were being neglected; important papers were being left unattended in unguarded rooms and mere boys were being employed to carry sacks of safe-hand mail containing highly confidential documents. BSC's investigators found a similar situation in several New York offices and contrasted it with the strong security prevailing in American buildings occupied by the FBI, the Navy and the Joint Staff. A number of urgent recommendations were eventually accepted by representatives of the various missions in Washington, and BSC took over control of their guards and physical security from 1 September, 1942.

During the ensuing months, similar reforms were instituted in the British missions in New York. BSC employed a corps of 74 guards in New York, 26 in Detroit and 220 in Washington, as well as receptionists and messengers. Each month approximately 56,000 pounds of confidential waste were burned under the supervision of these guards. All the while the situation was watched and a regular monthly survey of security errors was compiled and circulated amongst the missions in order to remind their staffs of the need for constant vigilance.

BSC did not, however, have jurisdiction over the distribution of secret telegrams, minutes and reports within British missions, and it was felt that this created a certain risk of leakage. Civil servants are not all security minded. Also, Washington presented a peculiar problem in that the personnel of many missions had become largely Americanized. American advisers had been appointed,

The Security of Personnel

American girls were taken on as secretaries and staff members married American citizens.

One serious example of the result of this situation may be worth noting in detail. On 25 July 1944, the columnist Drew Pearson published part of a confidential report to President Roosevelt on India by the former US Ambassador to New Delhi, William Phillips (see Part II). By 10 August, BSC's own informants in Washington had learned that Pearson had obtained the report from an anti-British Indian agitator connected with the India League of America. Pearson already had contacts with the League. So far, although grave, this affair did not concern the security of British missions. But on 28 August Pearson printed a report that the Foreign Office had asked for Phillips's recall from London, and he quoted, almost verbatim, several telegrams from Whitehall to the Embassy. This was taken up by Senator Chandler in the Senate and with even more energy by Representative Calvin Johnson in the Lower House. Chandler also made public the text of a cable from the Department of External Affairs in New Delhi to the India Office.

After the Embassy's own Security Officer had attempted without success to trace the leakage, BSC was called upon for assistance. An investigation was carried out and within two days a full report was submitted by WS to Sir Ronald Campbell in Lord Halifax's absence. The report told that the leakages were emanating from the Indian Agency General in Washington, where at least one Indian Nationalist sympathizer was being employed in an important position. Names were given and recommendations were made. It was emphasized that both civilian and military security were in jeopardy and that action should be taken immediately.

Enquiries were then instituted regarding the security of telegrams and documents in the Washington missions and in the Embassy itself, and in result WS submitted a short report to the Ambassador which indicated considerable inefficiency and danger of leakage. Lord Halifax at once requested WS to report fully upon the situation and to submit specific recommendations for safeguarding confidential communications both within the Chancery and Embassy, and in each separate mission.

This was done, and the final report revealed a most unsatisfactory state of affairs. American citizens were being employed as assistants and secretaries in positions where they could read cables on post-war subjects, which were specifically prefixed 'GUARD' (Not to be shown to the Americans). One of these American employees, a secretary, was the wife of an FBI official; another had a husband in the War Department. Foreign Office telegrams which should have been circulated only to thirty people were available to sixty persons or more. The keys of safe-hand boxes were being carelessly handled, and in one instance they were in the custody of an American secretary.

After the Ambassador had received the report, he summoned the heads of all the British missions in Washington to a meeting and discussed the situation with them. Thereafter he requested WS to appoint a BSC officer to assist the mission heads in putting into effect the recommendations contained in it. The chief representative of the Security Division in Washington undertook this duty, and under his guidance adequate measures were enforced against security breaches.

The Security Division had also to deal with deserters from British and Allied merchant vessels. The intensity of the campaign and the long ordeal of the Merchant Navy inevitably resulted in desertions on a considerable scale. There was the additional temptation of high wages in American war factories ashore, for the owners of these were only too glad to get labour with few questions asked. Through 1944, nearly 100 British seamen a week continued to desert their vessels in United States ports. Desertion of Chinese seamen, with their closely organized communities ashore, provided a particularly difficult problem.

Although the US Immigration authorities were at one period of the war reluctant to take appropriate action against deserters because of the acute labour shortage in the port areas, they were eventually persuaded to do so by the argument that one of the easiest ways for a saboteur or agent to secure entry into the United Kingdom or the British Merchant Fleet was by getting himself picked up as a deserting British seaman. Accordingly, they agreed to enable BSC to vet all deserters before they were returned to their ships or deported home. Further, under the American ruling which permitted deportation of deserters to countries adjacent to their own (if their own countries were enemy occupied), the US authorities facilitated a scheme which resulted in the deportation of Greeks and Yugoslavs to the Middle East and of Chinese to India, where in many instances they were drafted into the Allied Armed Forces.

CHAPTER 4

Security in the Final Phase

As the Allied position improved, the threat of sudden emergencies with which the Security Division might have to deal receded. For example, the North African campaign of 1942 removed the danger of direct German assault on Brazil and the growth of US naval power in the Pacific eliminated the possibility of Japanese raids on the Panama Canal or on oil installations in Peru.

By 1943, the responsibility of the Security Division was largely a matter of applying measures previously devised and tested. But it was by no means simple to discharge. Provision of security in the United States, with the exception of the work of the CSOs, had, after much change and experiment, been placed in American hands. It would be perhaps more accurate to say in many American hands, for the agencies responsible included the FBI, the Office of Naval Intelligence, the Coast Guard, the US Army G-2, the Provost-Marshall General's Office and the Immigration authorities. These various agencies divided the duties among themselves in a manner which was so confused that there was constant likelihood of inter-organizational disputes. Thus BSC's liaison with the Americans on security matters, which had once amounted to no more than unofficial contacts with a handful of friendly individuals, now resembled the conduct of a highly intricate telephone exchange in which the operator has to know the exact interest and mutual relations of all subscribers and must never make a wrong connection. In addition to the many official liaisons with the headquarters of US and Canadian agencies in Washington, New York and Ottawa, there existed innumerable local liaisons between CSOs and the officials of the interested American services in their respective ports. Consequently the work, though unspectacular, was considerably intricate.

As 1943 passed into 1944, the work of the Security Division was concentrated on assisting the extraordinary precautions which had to be taken to safeguard the forthcoming invasion. The smallest

Security of Property and Personnel

risk of the enemy securing forewarning of any detail of the Allied plan could not be afforded, nor could so little as a day's delay in the sailing of a ship carrying men and supplies to the United Kingdom.

In nearly every British Mission there was a senior Administrative Officer who had in his possession a fragment of vital information which would have contributed valuably to the mosaic which the enemy was endeavouring to piece together. To meet the special circumstances, the War Office made security recommendations of exceptional severity to British Civil Missions, and BSC's Chief Security Officer in Washington helped to implement these. Regulations governing the carriage of secret documents by British officials within the US were once again reviewed, safety plug-in telephones were installed in the offices of senior executives, a committee was formed to coordinate practice in handling classified documents and the various British courier systems were thoroughly checked and consequently improved.

Towards the end of March, security services in the UK began to note an increasing number of alien seamen on American-controlled ships. These were seamen who had recently emerged from Axis-occupied territory in the Mediterranean, but had nevertheless been allowed to pass through a US port without any effective security vetting. Investigation by BSC revealed many loopholes in the American system whereby enemy agents might well make their way on to United States ships in Mediterranean ports, and without difficulty obtain seamen's documents in the US. They could then sail freely to the UK. Urgent pleas to the Americans for remedial action brought no improvement, for no less than eight separate US agencies, each endowed with conflicting and overlapping authority, were involved.

Four flagrant and different cases were submitted to ONI who replied that these were not under naval jurisdiction and suggested an appeal to a higher authority. The situation was then brought to the notice of the British Joint Staff Mission, who in turn laid it before the Combined Chiefs of Staff.

As a result, the US Chiefs of Staff clarified the functions of the eight agencies involved. They instructed the Coast Guard to cease issuing to alien seamen documents which would enable them to sail without interrogation. Those already in possession of documents were to be interrogated forthwith. These measures were regarded as adequate on both sides of the Atlantic, and it is gratifying to record that subsequently the US Coast Guard, at the Security Division's suggestion, invited an experienced UK

Security in the Final Phase

Security Control Officer to visit the United States for the purpose of instructing them in British methods of seamen's interrogation and port control.

The pre-invasion travel ban on the movement of Allied service personnel from the Western Hemisphere to the UK was imposed barely a month before D-Day. The application of the ban was carried out by the appropriate section of Security Division with much expedition. All Allied military missions in the US and Canada were informed at once. Special visits were paid to Washington, Montreal and Ottawa to check arrangements, and a satisfactory test case was conveniently provided by a certain French officer who approached both British and American authorities in the United States to obtain passage to the UK. Being unsuccessful, he endeavoured to obtain first sea and then air transport from Canada, only to find himself in each case referred back to the Security Division.

D-Day came and went, and with it the work of the Security Division began to decrease. But so long as the war in Europe lasted, and there was the smallest chance of a sudden reversal in Allied fortune, it was essential and could not be abandoned. Indeed one new security plan, which had worldwide implication, was put into effect after the invasion.

The Security Division had always maintained close working relations with relevant British agencies in the United States. It worked, for example, with the Ministry of War Transport in regard to shipping, with the War Trade Department of the Embassy on contraband and with NID18 on naval intelligence affairs. It had maintained liaison, too, with the RCMP, DNI, Canadian Military Intelligence and the Department of External Affairs in Ottawa. Now it began to develop liaison with security authorities in other British countries, and in June 1944, direct communication was established with the Australian Commonwealth Security Service at Canberra, with the Director of Security Intelligence in New Zealand and with the South African Security authorities. In each case the object was to coordinate the protection of British, Australian and New Zealand ships plying between the Americas and the Antipodes, at both ends of their voyage, and to narrow the watch on suspect seamen and troublesome crews, who formerly disappeared from view in faraway waters.

This expanding field of inter-communication began to give a new significance to the system of Security Coordination Ship Inspection Reports, by which each vessel visited carried on it a sealed copy of the CSO's report to the Security Officer at the next

British-controlled port of call. A brief explanation of the scheme was circulated to British Security Officers all over the world. Security Service links throughout Africa and the Mediterranean became familiar with the system, and in Australia and New Zealand it was arranged that receiving officers should reseal and return such reports after adding their own comments. The system thus provided the nucleus of a progressive security check on individual ships and seamen from port to port throughout British-controlled territory.

The Security Division was finally disbanded after V-J Day, when its work was done. It had been given the wartime task of guarding from sabotage all British interests of strategic importance in the Western Hemisphere. Among these, there was British-controlled shipping in American ports and there were the vast stores of war materials in manufacture in the US factories; there were the oilfields in Venezuela and Peru supplying the bulk of the needs of the Navy and the RAF and there were the bauxite mines of the Guianas; there were the wheat and the meat from the Argentine, the tin from Bolivia, the balsa wood for Mosquito bombers from Ecuador, the copper from Chile, the platinum and iron ore from Brazil.

There can be no doubt that the Security Division succeeded in its purpose. The record shows that the total enemy sabotage score against British property throughout the whole American Continent, apart from a number of insignificant interferences with industrial undertakings which may or may not have been inspired by Berlin, amounted to no more than six vessels damaged. None was sunk.

PART VI

SPECIAL OPERATIONS IN LATIN AMERICA

CHAPTER 1

Three Phases

(a) Before Pearl Harbor
(b) After the Rio Conference
(c) After the Invasion of North Africa

This is a brief outline of the work which was performed by agents in the field of Special Operations throughout South and Central America during the war years. The territory covered was large, the opportunities for embarrassing the enemy were numerous, and several operations – as for example the incident of the Belmonte letter in Bolivia and of the Lati letter in Brazil which are described later – were spectacular in themselves and had spectacular repercussions. On the other hand there were many small, unspectacular operations which produced useful results.

Agents and sub-agents, and their paid and unpaid informers and assistants, were active in all the South American and Central American countries. Their objective varied according to the country in which they worked. In Chile it was to force the Government to break relations with the Axis. In Brazil it was to fulfil another equally specific but quite different purpose. But in every country the agents themselves and the policies they adopted were controlled and coordinated by BSC headquarters. New York was the Operations Room. There the plotters sat and to them the facts and the findings came and from them the orders went out. By them new methods and plans were devised. The work occupied much of WS's own time and required his personal attention.

Originally the Special Operations organization in South America was formed to oppose a campaign of disorder and revolution which might be inspired by the Germans or the Japanese or both, and at the same time to prepare an underground organization which would carry on resistance in the event of the invasion and subjugation of South America by the Axis.

Later, after the danger of direct invasion was eliminated, it had to be adapted to do a different job; a many-sided one involving such duties as those of countering the danger of sabotage to strategic supplies, of countering Axis-inspired revolutions and subversive activity of all forms. This necessitated the employment of methods unlike those used by SOE elsewhere in the world.

The history of the Special Operations organization in Latin America falls into three distinct phases, corresponding to three main developments in the war situation.

(a) Before Pearl Harbor

The BSC/SOE organization in Latin America was set up in 1941. At that time every American republic was neutral. There was no immediate prospect that the USA would enter the war, and it was perfectly possible that the South American republics would swing increasingly to the side of the Axis. Many had governments which were directly or indirectly under Axis influence. The colonies of German, Italian and Japanese immigrants were large, powerful and well organized. The Germans were in North and West Africa. The danger of a German invasion of South America, coordinated with Axis-inspired revolutions in the most important states, was too near to be ignored. Early in 1940, the Fuhrmann plot had been uncovered by the Uruguayan Government. Arnulf Fuhrmann and his German accomplices, as they subsequently confessed, had planned to occupy Uruguay in five days and to mobilize all German residents in Argentina. Then in October 1941, a German courier whom BSC agents had been following met with an accident. The courier's despatch case was taken and opened, and among the contents there was found a document of the greatest importance. It was a map of South America. The map showed the subcontinent radically redistributed into four areas and one colony, all under German domination. The four areas and the colony were:

Brazil
Argentina, including Uruguay, Paraguay and lowland Bolivia, with a corridor to the Pacific at Antofagasta
Chile, including upland Bolivia and Peru
New Spain, composed of the three Bolivarian republics *and* Panama *and* the Panama Canal
Guiana, the three Guianas united as a French colony.

Reproduction of the original 'map of South America' which BSC purloined from a German courier. Translation of the handwriting is:

On the left—'(1) Is a fuel monopoly planned? (2) Can private capital participate in expansion? Under what conditions? (3) To what extent will Mexico F participate in installation and expansion F as furnisher of fuel?'

On the right—'Fuel reserves for transatlantic traffic (a) with what capacity, (b) whom to interest for installation, (c) estimate.'

The entire area was covered by a comprehensive airline network leading to Panama and to transatlantic terminals at Natal. Handwritten notes in German referred to 'fuel reserves for transatlantic traffic' and to 'Mexican fuel'. All names were in German.

The map was sent to New York. Obviously it was a plan for redistributing the territory of Latin America after the war and for covering it with a network of German airlines which would link up with Axis Europe. WS passed the map to General Donovan, who handed it to President Roosevelt. On 27 October 1941, the President made a forthright speech in which he referred to the map as a proof of German plans for aggression against the Western Hemisphere.

> ... Hitler has often protested that his plans for conquest do not extend across the Atlantic Ocean ... I have in my possession a secret map, made in Germany by Hitler's Government, by planners of the New World Order ... It is a map of South America as Hitler proposes to reorganize it ... Today in this area there are 14 separate countries ... The geographical experts of Berlin, however, have ruthlessly obliterated all the existing boundary lines and have divided South America into five vassal states, bringing the whole continent under their domination ... and they have also so arranged it that the territory of one of these new puppet states includes the Republic of Panama and our great life-line, the Panama Canal ... This map makes clear the Nazi design, not only against South America but against the United States as well ...

Three weeks later a BSC agent in Argentina, who was in touch with the German Embassy, reported that after President Roosevelt's speech Hitler had at once asked the German Ambassador in Buenos Aires, von Thermann, for an explanation of the leakage. Apparently there were only two copies of the map. One was in Hitler's safe; the other was with von Thermann. Hectic discussion took place in the German Embassy and the blame was eventually fastened upon Gottfried Sandstede, a former civil attaché and NSDAP leader. He was accused of allowing the map to be copied.

The discovery of the map was convincing proof of Germany's intentions in Latin America and came as a tremendous shock to all good citizens of the United States. Throughout 1941, the magnitude of the danger was alarming. In addition to denying

Britain and America many priceless strategic materials, it was entirely possible that Axis strategy would plunge the subcontinent into civil war, break one of the few remaining reservoirs of British economic strength, and offer the United States a military challenge which might well keep her out of the European war altogether. For Germany, the gamble was less risky than the attack on Russia, and for a long time there was no knowing for certain that she would not make it.

BSC/SOE was at first organized in Latin America, then, against a campaign of disorder and revolution inspired by the Germans – a campaign which might possibly culminate in invasion. The lesson of the Balkans was still in mind. There the enemy had gained an enormous advantage by completing his attack before any underground organization had been created to aid the Allies and before the economic strength of the region could be denied to him. As a result, months of careful planning and recruiting and many dangerous aerial operations were necessary before agents could re-enter the occupied areas to organize resistance and cut some of the enemy's sources of supply.

Therefore in 1941 and early 1942 (when the Japanese danger still threatened), BSC/SOE agents, while taking such action as they could against the enemy in Latin America, were at the same time preparing an underground organization to carry on resistance after the Latin American countries had been invaded or had declared themselves allies of the Axis. In pursuit of this objective, BSC/SOE concentrated upon a number of definite operations.

For underground work in territory which may be occupied, the first prerequisite is thorough knowledge of the targets whose destruction would hamper the enemy: strategic communications, such as bridges, railway lines, air fields, wireless, telephone and telegraph stations; or sources of economic power such as electric plants, waterworks, mines and factories. Accordingly, the first job done by BSC/SOE agents in each Latin American area was the collection of information about targets to be attacked in case the enemy seized power. This work familiarized them with the strategic possibilities of their territory and developed the 'SO mentality' which their training in Canada (see Part VIII) had already implanted in them. For example, in Central America the following intelligence was produced and submitted to New York:

Costa Rica
 1. A comprehensive report on strategic areas and objectives throughout the country;

2. Individual reports on all the fifty-five air fields, with aerial photographs;
3. Reports on the chief petroleum storage installations, at Caldera, Puerto Limón and San José; with a list of all bulk oil stores;
4. A description of all power plants;
5. Maps of the Pacific and Atlantic (Northern) coastal railways, with notes on bridges and tunnels:
6. Photographs of the two ports of Golfito and Quepos, which have large docks capable of berthing heavy ships coming from the Pacific;
7. General, provincial and sectional maps of the republic, showing all targets.

Guatemala
1. Sketch maps showing all roads, railways, airports, emergency air fields and wireless stations;
2. Photographs of the airports of Chimaltenango, Guatemala City, Jutiapa, Puerto Barrios, Quetzaltenango, Quiche and Solola;
3. Report on the weak points in the IRCA railway from Guatemala City to San José and the Mexican frontier;
4. Map of Guatemala City.

Honduras
Blueprints of all the airports on the Caribbean coast, with notes on runways, approaches, lights, hangar facilities, radio contact, and so on.

General
1. Photographs of forty-seven air fields throughout Central America;
2. Reports on every new target which came into existence and changes in the strategic strength of each area.

It was necessary for agents to have good stores of explosives, light weapons and incendiary devices. The best supplied territory was Peru, for the chief agent there, being traffic manager of an important railway, not only had a large stock of dynamite and blasting gelignite under his personal supervision but knew every weak spot in the area. In Buenos Aires a Norwegian chemist was recruited to manufacture devices, and he was supplied with formulae for so doing. Incendiaries and explosives were conveyed by couriers from BSC to other areas such as Recife, where an attack on the fuel stocks of Lati was in prospect. Polish and Basque sea captains were particularly cooperative in this work. When the Foreign Office decided against the direct importation of such weapons into Latin America, dumps were set up in Trinidad and the Falkland Islands, from which they could be rushed to strategic areas in an emergency.

In order to organize underground resistance to invasions and revolutions inspired by the Axis, a shadow organization was needed in each territory. Its members had to be reliable, morally opposed to the doctrines of totalitarianism and well distributed in strategic points throughout their country. Again, the best prepared territory was Peru. The BSC/SOE chief representative there, as well as being manager of a railway, was a prominent member of the outlawed *Apra* Party, a personal friend of its leader, Haya de la Torre, and bound by strong links of creed and affections to the principal Apristas. The particular danger which was feared in Peru was a Japanese uprising (of which more is said in a later chapter). There were in the chief cities over 25,000 Japanese, whose leader had offered the revolutionary Sánchez Cerro a force of 11,000 men some time before the war. If supported by an aerial and naval attack on the then undefended Pacific coast, these Japanese could have paralysed, perhaps mastered the country. The Apristas claimed to have all preparations ready to counter-attack in such an event, and their strong discipline makes it probable that they would eventually have succeeded. In Argentina, the nucleus of such an organization was formed by the Basques under Aguirre's encouragement (see Part IV). They already had a society called *Acción Vasca*, from which trustworthy men were chosen. In all the other South American republics, similar organizations were set up.

To make these shadow organizations effective, it was essential to have secret wireless communications. BSC, therefore, planned a network of wireless transmitters throughout the subcontinent which could have relayed messages from a main station in unoccupied territory after an invasion, passing on directives and intelligence. A number of transmitters were despatched to Brazil, then the most threatened country, and courageous assistance was rendered BSC in this regard by a Polish sea captain called Lewandowski. Regrettably Lewandowski's ship was later stopped on the high seas by a German submarine and he was apprehended. Nothing has been heard of him since.

Arrangements were made to enlist trained wireless operators in various countries, and to send others to BSC's camp in Canada for training whence they returned to their field of operations fully prepared for activity should the necessity arise.

(b) After the Rio Conference

The second phase of BSC/SOE work in Latin America opened after Pearl Harbor and after the Rio Conference. The United States and the small Caribbean countries were now at war. Mexico and all the South American states except Argentina and Chile had broken off diplomatic relations with the Axis powers and were expelling their diplomatic missions. This was a great step forward which enabled BSC to develop plans along another line and indeed necessitated such reorientation.

But even then the danger of invasion could not be considered past. Indeed there were some grounds for believing it increased, for the Germans now had the active support of the Japanese, who, during the first four months of 1942, were spreading with terrifying speed and competence over the debris of three empires in the Far East. The Americans learned that Japanese ships were cruising off the vulnerable coast of western South America. A Nisei in Brazil asserted that all Japanese communities there were strategically disposed and militarily organized to take over the country, and reports of Japanese officers disguised as servants or tradesmen and of well-equipped Japanese 'scientific' expeditions in remote districts were unpleasantly reminiscent of reports from Malaya and the Philippines. They may have been mere canards, but, with the United States war potential still far from fully mobilized, they could not be ignored.

Throughout the first six months of 1942, WS's principal aim was to convince the Americans that Latin America must be protected and to show them how this could be done. He pointed out repeatedly how vitally important to the Allies were the strategic supplies of Latin America, and he stressed how vulnerable to invasion, to Axis-inspired revolution and to sabotage these supplies continued to be.

During one of the Prime Minister's visits to Washington, WS arranged for Mr Churchill and General Donovan to hear a report on the weakness and the importance of Latin America in global warfare. At a White House dinner shortly afterwards, Donovan brought up the subject, telling the President that the US Army and Navy were apparently not paying sufficient attention to it. Next day he saw General Marshall and told him the same thing. Throughout the succeeding months, the US Chiefs of

Staff were supplied by WS with reports and analyses which emphasized the Axis threat to Latin America. In addition, the Chiefs of Staff in London sent a telegram to the Joint Staff Mission in Washington saying that urgent steps must be taken, either with or without the help of the Americans, to 'end Axis machinations in South America' (see Part V). During General Marshall's visit to London, Sir Frank Nelson discussed the Latin American problem with him, while SOE headquarters took up the matter with the Joint Intelligence Committee. As a result of what he had learned, General Marshall decided that since the SOE organization in Latin America was already experienced and well equipped, it was of the utmost importance that it should be kept ready for use if required. At the same time, he determined to impress upon President Roosevelt once again the necessity for authorizing a US agency to set up a parallel organization, with which SOE could cooperate.

On General Marshall's return from London, he invited the SOE Division of BSC to submit to the US Chiefs of Staff a memorandum on what SOE could do in Latin America, the implication being that SOE would then be operating with the approval of the US Chiefs of Staff. The memorandum was prepared and delivered. It explained the possibilities of invasion, internal revolution and sabotage, as well as the operation of clandestine submarine bases and enemy radio stations. It recommended (1) that BSC/SOE should continue to collect and collate intelligence on enemy activity throughout Latin America, with special reference to activities which might threaten vital supplies; (2) that dumps of explosives and devices should be kept in readiness for any special operation called for by the Chiefs of Staff; and (3) that a secret network of wireless communications should be built up and maintained. This memorandum, together with the unremitting pressure exercised by WS, undoubtedly influenced the Chiefs of Staff.

At the time, it was hoped that General Donovan might be given the responsibility for building up an organization on the SOE level in Latin America, for this would have completed a grand design. SOE and the Donovan organization would together have covered the entire world, throughout most of which they were already collaborating successfully. But it never materialized. Donovan himself was opposed by many formidable rivals in the services and in the FBI, and so vigorous was their opposition and that of the State Department that Donovan's directive, when it was finally issued, specifically excluded him from the Western Hemisphere.

Nevertheless, the seeds which had been sown in the minds of the Chiefs of Staff and of the State Department had germinated and were beginning to take root. There was a conviction that something had to be done. The State Department embarked on a new and vigorous policy, exerting strong diplomatic pressure on South American republics to cut down Axis activities, to oust Axis agents and generally to put their houses in order. The denunciations of German espionage operating by means of clandestine wireless transmitters, which were presented to the Governments of Brazil, Chile and Argentina, were a direct expression of this policy (see Part VII). The Chiefs of Staff at the same time arranged to give military, naval and aerial protection to the most important and vulnerable areas which had all been specified in the early memoranda submitted to them by WS: for example, the Brazilian bulge opposite Dakar, the Galapagos islands, the oil refineries in Peru and the mining areas in Chile.

Gradually, United States intervention began to make itself felt in Latin America, and the republics which had once been wide open to invasion and revolution, now became a reservoir of power which could be used against the enemy. Lend-Lease munitions were supplied to them. Loans were lavished on them by the Export-Import Bank. US Intelligence officers, economic advisers and propagandists were borne south by aircraft in such steadily increasing numbers that the Brazilians nicknamed them 'parachute troops'. Thus the sub-continent was transformed from an objective of Axis attack into a base for supplying the Allies. Nevertheless it should not be forgotten that the direct threat to Latin America was not finally removed until the Allies invaded North Africa in November 1942, for, in fact, the Americans did not possess sufficient force to set up more than token defences.

Although the invasion threat disappeared in November 1942, BSC/SOE's work was not done. There was the possibility of sabotage of the sources of strategic South American supplies, and there was also the danger that Axis agents might inspire revolutions or undertake other subversive political activity.

To guard against the possibility of sabotage BSC set up the Industrial Security Officers' organization (see Part V). For countering subversive activity a new technique was developed. Before January 1942, the SOE organization had not been accepted as necessary by the Foreign Office and HM Ministers in South America. It was only after Pearl Harbor that the Foreign Office despatched a circular telegram to South American missions, explaining the history of SOE, stating that the foundations for its work should be established in Latin America, and defining its functions as:

1. Recruiting agents for Europe and the Far East;
2. Countering Axis activities;
3. Encouraging pro-Allied movements in a manner not open to HM Representatives.

Even then, there was still a certain reluctance to accept agents. In many quarters they were believed to be men who worked only by violent methods which would have embarrassed ministers and ambassadors. (There was an immortal telegram from Sir Esmond Ovey saying that he could not imagine himself sanctioning such operations until *after* the Germans had gained command of the Atlantic Ocean and cut off Britain's food supplies.) BSC/SOE agents were therefore instructed not to undertake any direct operations against the enemy.

But they soon devised other means of making the enemy's life a burden to him, means which were not only successful, but, so far from embarrassing the British Ministers to whom representatives were attached, pleased them and assisted their missions. When the BSC/SOE organization in Venezuela was curtailed, HM Minister said that although in the past he had been prejudiced against both SOE and SIS as a result of an unfortunate incident when he was stationed in Vienna, his experience of both organizations in Caracas had compelled him to change his mind. He added that, while he understood the necessity for reducing the SOE organization, he would be extremely sorry if the head of BSC/SOE Venezuela were not retained as an observer. HM diplomatic representatives in Ecuador, Colombia and Chile expressed themselves in similar fashion.

All but two countries in Latin America had now become belligerents or had broken relations with the Axis, but many of them were reluctant to do more than expel diplomatic missions. They had neither the legislative authority nor the administrative machinery to proceed further against the enemy, even if their native indolence and corruption had not weakened their will to do so. But that very indolence and corruption could be used by British and American agents to force the Germans, Italians and Japanese, who had once been so powerful, into the position of helpless, imprisoned and impoverished alien enemies. The technique devised might be called 'indirect operations', and while the Americans participated in much of this activity, BSC/SOE agents planned and executed the first moves. They used the police of the countries in which they were stationed; they exerted pressure on the Government through personal influence and through carefully prepared but apparently spontaneous demonstrations of public feeling. They instigated police raids. They arranged public denunciations of natives who hid their Axis sympathies under a cloak of patriotism. They drafted new anti-Axis laws and helped promote them. In one country the BSC/SOE organization assisted in producing a belated diplomatic rupture with the Axis, while in another it instigated a declaration of war on Germany. This work did not end until, in every country except Argentina, the Germans were eliminated or rendered powerless.

(c) After the Invasion of North Africa

The second phase lasted until 1943. By that time the whole pattern of the war had altered for the better. The North African invasion and the Pacific victories had beaten back the Axis from the approaches to South America. Mexico and Brazil had declared war, while Chile was about to expel the Axis representatives. It was, therefore, decided to dissolve the SOE organizations. Two BSC/SOE officers from New York toured all stations, paying off sub-agents and making the necessary arrangements. What was left of SOE in Peru was closed in January 1943; the organizations in Argentina, Brazil and Uruguay in February; Central America, Chile and Ecuador in March; Colombia in April; and Venezuela in May.

At the same time, it was felt that a sudden reversal in the fortunes of the Allies or a change in the troubled politics of South America was still not impossible. Moreover, the work that had already been done was so satisfactory that in some of the republics – in Chile, Colombia, Ecuador, Uruguay and Venezuela – the head BSC/SOE agent was retained as an 'observer'. In this more limited frame of reference, using not paid agents but the goodwill they had already acquired, and following the principle described above, these men were able to do continued damage to the enemy. Finally, after the successful invasion of Europe, the position was again reconsidered. The danger of a direct threat to South America had now vanished. Enemy influence had been virtually eliminated from all the South American countries with which BSC's SOE Division was concerned, and the problems of Argentina and Bolivia could be solved, if at all, only on the highest diplomatic level. Accordingly, the SOE stations in South America were finally closed on 30 September 1944.

The full story of the long SOE arm which BSC stretched down into South America can best be told country by country. The chapters which follow deal with them each in turn.

CHAPTER 2

Brazil and Argentina

(a) Brazil.
(i) The Lati Letter
(ii) Breaking the German Organization
(b) Argentina.

(a) Brazil
(i) The Lati Letter

Brazil, during the early part of the war, was the terminus for one of the most important Axis channels of communication with the American continent. Planes of the Italian transatlantic airline Lati were flying regularly between Europe and Brazil. They carried German and Italian diplomatic bags, couriers, agents, diamonds, platinum, mica, Bayer chemicals, propaganda films, books and all sorts and conditions of men and materials back and forth over the route. There was no thought in the minds of the Brazilian Government to hinder the airline's operations. One of President Vargas's sons-in-law was chief technical director of the line, and there were many other powerful Brazilians who had their own personal reasons for not wishing to see Lati's landing rights cancelled. Standard Oil, in spite of the protests of the US State Department, supplied it with fuel.

SOE/London ordered that something drastic should be done. Up in New York, in the offices of BSC, meetings were held and a plan was devised. In the summer of 1941 a telegram was sent to Brazil:

> We propose to try to convey to Brazilian Government a letter purporting to have been written by someone in authority in Lati head office in Italy to an Italian executive of Company in Brazil. Purpose of letter is to compromise company vis-a-vis Brazilian Government in hope that its concession in Brazil

LATI LINEE AEREE TRANSCONTINENTALI ITALIANE S.A.

Roma, 30 ottobre 1941 XX

Caro Coriente,

Io ricevuto la Vostra relazione che è giunta cinque giorni dopo essere stata spedita.

La relazione è stata portata subito a conoscenza degli interessati, i quali la considerano di grande importanza. Abbiamo condivisa con altri l'idea del Vostro punto di vista sulla situazione. Questo è un quadro completo della situazione che esiste laggiù e la Vostra è più dettagliata che quella i cui in mio complacimento. Il fatto desidero esprimerVi il mio complacimento. Informazioni più complete di quelle che abbiamo ottenuto da altri, mi ha riempito di soddisfazione.

Non vi è dubbio che il Cuscoccio sta cedendo alle lusinghe degli Americani e che soltanto un intervento violento da parte dei nostri amici venti può salvare il Paese. I nostri collaboratori di Berlino, in seguito alle conversazioni avute con il rappresentante a Lisbona, hanno deciso che tale intervento deve aver luogo al più presto. A Voi conoscete la situazione. Il giorno in cui si verificherà il cambiamento, i nostri collaboratori si preoccuperanno assai poco dei nostri interessi e la Lufthansa raccoglierà tutti i vantaggi. Per impedire che questo si verifichi dobbiamo procurarci al più presto altri amici influenti tra i venti. Faccio senza indugio. Lascio a Voi di decidere quali sarebbero le persone più adatte: forse Padilla o E.F. de Andrade

sarebbero più utili di C.M. il quale, per quanto attivo, conta poco.

I fondi di cui avrete bisogno saranno messi a Vostra disposizione. Non importa se i venti hanno bisogno di soma considerevoli: le avrete. L'importante è che i nostri servizi si avvantaggino di un cambiamento di regime. Informate.Vi di chi voglio nominare Ministro dell'Aeronautica e cercate di guadagnarvelo a qualunque.

3. dovrà essere tenuto al corrente di quanto avviene ma abbiamo convenuto che le trattative rimarranno completamente nelle mani della LATI la quale agirà nella sua capacità di ditta brasiliana che cerca di estendere e di migliorare i propri servizi.

Lo aspetto da Voi la massima discrezione. Come Voi dite nella relazione concernente la Standard Oil, l'Inglesi e gli Americani si intereserano di tutto e di tutti. Ed anche se è vero che — come giustamente affermate — i Brasiliani sono una nazione di cresciuta, non bisogna dimenticare che sono scimmie distrette a servire chiunque tiene le redini in mano.

Saluti fascisti,

[signature]

Gerente
Vicenzo Coriola
Linee Aeree Transcontinentali Italiane S.A.
(LATI Brasilia Divisão)

The 'Lati Letter', fabricated by Station M, which caused President Vargas to close the Italian airline

'There is no doubt that the fat little man is falling into the pocket of the American . . .'

will be cancelled. We would welcome your suggestions and also specimen letter from Head Office with signature of managing director or other important person. Also please give us full name of chief Italian executive in Rio office with whom Rome might normally be expected correspond.

Some weeks went by. Agents in Brazil worked delicately in and around the Lati organization in order to carry out New York's instructions without causing suspicion. On 6 September 1941, Brazil cabled New York:

Have obtained personal letter of August 17th from General Aurelio Liotta actual president Lati Rome . . . on paper exclusively used by president . . . Am sending letter first safe hand . . .

Three days later, on 9 September, New York cabled Rio:

We must know name and exact style of address of official in Lati organization in Rio to whom proposed letter should be addressed . . .

Rio's answer to this telegram said that the letter should be addressed to Commandante Vicenzo Coppola, the manager of Lati in Brazil. The original letter from General Liotta arrived in New York. It was at once sent up to Station M in Canada (see Part II) where BSC's scientific experts were instructed to simulate exactly the style of notepaper, the engraved letterhead and the form of type with which it was written. Fortunately, Station M had previously secured the very small amount of straw pulp that was available in North America. Straw pulp which is much used for production of papers in Europe was an essential requirement in this case, and after many hours of work Station M succeeded in producing a sheet of notepaper that was an exact duplication, physically and chemically, as well as in colour, of the one used by General Liotta writing from his office in Rome. The embossing was copied with microscopic accuracy. A typewriter was rebuilt to conform to the exact mechanical imperfections of the typewriter upon which the General's secretary had typed the letter and after it had served its purpose this was smashed into small pieces and dropped bit by bit into the Hudson River.

The letter – the final result of these efforts – would have been endorsed as an original by any technical experts who might have been called in to make a comparison. It was microphotogaphed and sent by safe hand to BSC's chief agent in Rio. A reproduction appears on the opposite page and the following is a translation of the text:

Dear Friend:

Thank you for your letter and for the report enclosed with it. These reached me within five days.

I discussed your report immediately with our friends. They regard it as being of the highest importance. They compared it in my presence with certain information that had already been received from the Prace del Prete. The two reports coincided almost exactly in their view of the present situation on your side of the ocean, except that yours was if anything more detailed. I congratulate you on this. It made me feel proud that on this occasion at least we should have known more than S. and his fellows.

There can be no doubt that the 'little fat man' is falling into the pocket of the Americans, and that only violent action on the part of the 'green gentlemen' can save the country. I understand that such action has been arranged for by our respected collaborators in Berlin following their recent conversations with the man in Lisbon. Our own friends however, do not put much faith in those said 'collaborators'; on the day when things begin to happen they will not trouble too much as to what *we* are going to derive from the new regime; it will be 'chacun pour soi', with all the plums for the Lufthansa. For that reason you must take immediate steps to make new friends among the 'green gentlemen'. Do this immediately. As to which new friends would be most useful and reliable, I leave that to your own judgment. Our friends seem to think that Padilha would be more useful than Q.R. who is very small fry, though active.

I am instructed to tell you that there will be funds available if required. I am told that, as far as the 'greens' are concerned, cash is a matter of the greatest interest. Do your best to make absolutely sure that all the requirements of our service are guaranteed under the new regime. Discover who they would propose to nominate as Minister for Air and make

the best dispositions possible. S. is to be informed as to what we are doing but it has been agreed that these matters shall be left entirely in the hands of Lati which will act in the purely commercial capacity of a registered Brazilian corporation which seeks a concession to extend and improve its business. All I ask is that you shall be very discreet. The English and the Americans have a finger in every pie, as your report regarding the Standard Oil affair indicates. The Brazilians may be, as you said, a 'nation of monkeys', but they are monkeys who will dance for anyone who can pull the string!
Salutations.
(signed) Aurelio Liotta

The 'little fat man' was an easily recognizable reference to President Vargas. All Brazilians would know that the 'green gentlemen' were the Integralists, an anti-Administration party which had already attempted a revolution against the President. As far as Vargas himself was concerned, the letter contained personal insult, abuse of his country, scorn of his foreign policy and a suggested encouragement of his political enemies, and it was reasonable to assume that this combination would cause him to react vigorously.
Meanwhile London cabled BSC, New York:

We are being continually pressed by authorities here, in particular Admiralty, for cessation of Lati. How is your plan proceeding? Can you arrange anything else in case present plan fails?

To which BSC replied:

Plan progressing and will be concluded within about three weeks. As you know, scheme aims at official termination of facilities which appears only feasible permanent cessation.
Destruction of craft or supplies would result temporary and comparatively unimportant stoppage.

The microfilm of the letter arrived in Rio. Then a robbery was arranged in Vicenzo Coppola's house, at which a bedside clock and other articles were stolen. Coppola called in the police and

BSC's agents thus achieved their first purpose, that of establishing the fact that the robbery had taken place.

Next, a Brazilian sub-agent approached an American Associated Press reporter, and told him, after pledging him to great secrecy, that he had taken part in the robbery at Coppola's house. Then he told him that he had found something that looked interesting and proceeded to show him the microphotograph of the letter which he said he had taken from Coppola's effects. The implication was that it had been sent to Coppola by General Liotta in microphotographic rather than in original form, because, owing to the nature of its contents, it was necessary to smuggle it into Brazil to ensure that it was not intercepted and read. The reporter rushed straight to the United States Embassy and showed the letter to the American Amabassador. The Ambassador, after consultation with the heads of his military mission, decided that the enlargements which had been made of the film were reproductions of a genuine letter, and straightway showed them to President Vargas personally.

He reacted in precisely the way that WS had hoped and surmised. He swore he would cancel Lati's landing rights in Brazil at once. On 20 November, BSC cabled London:

> Understand that Lati will only be allowed one repeat one more flight.

The letter itself was never published, probably because the references which it contained both to Vargas and to the Americans were too insulting. But the Americans decided to share the secret with their British colleagues. BSC's agent in Rio was shown by his US opposite a copy of the Lati letter, which, according to the American, had been 'pinched' by US Intelligence. BSC's agent expressed enormous interest and admiration, and congratulated his colleague upon his work.

Commandante Vicenzo Coppola had meanwhile drawn one million dollars from the bank the day before Lati was closed. He disappeared but was later arrested trying to cross the border into Argentina. He was sentenced to seven years' imprisonment and had his funds confiscated. Lati were forced to pay a fine of $85,000 for infringing Brazilian law. Their aircraft and landing fields and all their equipment were confiscated. Their crews and personnel were interned. In Brazil at any rate, their organization ceased to exist.

It was only a few weeks afterwards, in January 1942, that Brazil

Special Operations in Latin America

broke off relations with the Axis. In February 1942, BSC's agent in Rio reported that the US Embassy there had expressed the view that the Lati letter 'has been one of the main factors in persuading President Vargas to turn against the enemy'.

(ii) Breaking the German Organization

President Vargas broke off relations with the Axis in January 1942 following the Rio Conference. In August of that year, after the torpedoing of several Brazilian ships, the Government declared war on Germany. In Brazil, therefore, the difficult problem of pushing a pro-German government into a diplomatic break with the Axis did not arise. BSC agents were able to concern themselves with other matters.

The Government, both immediately before and after the declaration of war, conducted a reasonably energetic policy in regard to the suppression of enemy activities. Many Brazilians are corrupt, especially the Brazilian police, and at one time the latter were distinctly pro-German; but, nevertheless, they proved reasonably cooperative.

Before Pearl Harbor BSC/SOE agents had begun to gather information regarding the German espionage system and German sympathizers in the country. During 1941 and early 1942, messages such as these passed regularly through BSC's channels of communication:

From New York to Rio: 'Messrs. 'A' are to be appointed to act as 'B' at 'C'. The partners of this firm are 'D'. The firm is a branch of the 'E' firm at 'F' . . .'

"'A' is Carlos Fink & Company. 'B' is German secret service agent. 'C' is Recife. 'D' is Carlos Fink and Aloli Roessler. 'E' is Hamburg. 'F' is Augusto de Freitas & Company . . .'
From Rio to New York: 'Hellmuth von Muegge . . . who owns a ranch at Estado Do Rio, is chief of the Hitler Youth Movement . . .'
From New York to Rio: 'Koenig alias Kempter German agent is due to arrive Recife . . . probably from Rio. Please watch and report . . .'
From Rio to New York: 'Following are listed as Nazi agents in Brazil: Baron de Bianchi . . . Duca de Casalanza . . . Herbert von Heyer . . . Kurt Steffin . . . Huhn . . .'
From New York to Rio: 'One Vivian, calling himself H. Carlos, is travelling to Rio . . . will send reports . . . regularly via Lati . . . His address is Rio . . .'

From Rio to New York: 'Salomon Giovanni alias Sardos Jonos alias Jean Salomon alias Joao Saros . . . living in Rumanian Legation Rio . . . intelligent and dangerous agent . . .'
From New York to Rio: 'Karl Arnold and Alfredo Mueller, directors of enemy sabotage in South America . . . are keeping in touch with their organization through secret radio station in Carityba . . .'
From Rio to New York: 'Axis agents in Lisbon using signature 'Leo' and 'Leonardo' . . . communicating with following addresses in Brazil by means of microphotograph . . .'

There were many others of the same kind, and in each instance BSC/SOE agents made their investigations, penetrating the living quarters of the suspects, watching their habits and actions, listing their friends and contacts, and sometimes following a suspect thousands of miles across the country. The findings were frequently augmented by information supplied from other sources which was collected and forwarded by BSC in New York. The whole was documented and whenever the evidence was incriminating the Brazilian police were notified and were encouraged to take action.

There were rich and influential Germans in the strategic northern bulge of Brazil in the state of Pernambuco. This area was controlled by the chief BSC/SOE agent in Recife, and since the British community is not large in Recife, he was able to use with success an old established method to keep his activities under cover. He professed indifference to the war. He took no share in the patriotic projects of the British colony. He was derided by Englishmen and he was severely criticized for associating with a lot of doubtful Germans and Brazilians. It was a good cover, although it involved considerable personal sacrifice.

Much of his time was taken up with a family of important Swedish merchants called Lundgren. The family consisted of two brothers and a sister. The sister, in particular, was a fanatical Nazi who attended all local party meetings and lived next door to a notorious German agent called Sievert. Several sons of the family were in Germany 'for their education'. The firm employed many Germans, most of whom were open and enthusiastic Nazis.

In January 1942, just after Brazil had made her diplomatic break, BSC/SOE in Recife made a thorough investigation of the Lundgren firm. The resulting comprehensive report dealt especially with the Lundgren industrial colonies at Paulista and Rio Tinto. It contained complete lists of party members and dossiers on the chief suspects. It was substantiated by copies of letters, which local Nazis had written to Goebbels asking for more money and material and which had been intercepted by BSC/SOE agents. The report was handed to the Chief of Police in Recife. From him it went to the Governor, thence to the Army Staff of the district and thence to Rio. The Minister of Justice at once cabled the Governor of Pernambuco ordering a thorough investigation of the Lundgren colonies and the immediate arrest of all suspects.

The Pernambuco police had a fine opportunity to distinguish themselves and they took it. The arrests which they made included:

Karl Fink, head of the commission agency of Carlos Fink and Cia., Recife, who confessed to having sent intelligence back to Germany on Allied shipping.
Hans Heinrich Sievert, of Recife, who admitted being an agent of Herbert von Heyer, a notorious spy in Rio.
Martin Peter Friedrich Petzold, of Recife, who had in his possession a clandestine radio transmitter.
Edgar August Paul Schutt, an SS man employed by the Lundgrens.

These were only the leaders. BSC/SOE instigated the arrest of twenty others and the surveillance of as many more. In order to keep those still at large under observation, the police cancelled the driving licences and confiscated the cars and motorcycles of other suspects, not only Germans but Brazilians.

Unfortunately the *'Interventor'* of the state, whose name was Agamemnon Magalhaes, was in sympathy with totalitarian ideas and he adopted an obstructionist attitude. He shelved the new regulations of the Federal Government for controlling the movements of Axis nationals. He published in his own newspaper, *Folha da Manha*, an editorial recommending kindness and sympathy for the persecuted German minority. It was learned that his newspaper received financial support not only from Germany but also from the Lundgren family. During a search of the effects belonging to the German agent Schutt, a letter from Goebbels was discovered in which Goebbels wrote that the German Propaganda Ministry was relying on the Governor's newspaper and its management for full support. Foolishly, the Chief of Police lent this letter to the Governor, who, of course, destroyed it.

It was clear that the Germans and the Lundgrens would continue to be protected by Governor Magalhaes of Pernambuco so long as he remained in office. His official title of *'Interventor'* was well earned, the cynics sometimes said; for even though he might fail to perform some of his supervisory duties adequately, at least he became notorious for 'intervening' to effect the release of Axis suspects. But as soon as these suspects were released, BSC/SOE would produce new evidence and force their re-arrest. While they were in custody, BSC/SOE agents would continue to make things as unpleasant for them as possible, causing them to be called up for re-interrogation at all hours of the day and night. While they were out of gaol, BSC/SOE agents would watch them, would arrange for their telephones to be tapped and their correspondence to be intercepted and would embarrass them in every way possible.

Meanwhile the Federal Government was slowly responding to the pressure which BSC/SOE was exerting through influence in many quarters. In March 1942, the Lundgrens were ordered to remove all German, Japanese and Italian nationals from their coastal estates. Prosecutions were instituted against the Recife gang, some of whom, as previously mentioned, had already been arrested.

The agent Sievert, in whose house secret inks were subsequently found as well as a long report on the airbase, the port and projected naval base at Natal, was kept in gaol for some time, released, re-arrested, tried, acquitted, re-tried and sentenced to twenty years. Karl Fink was sentenced to seven years' imprisonment. Martin Petzold was tried in Rio, acquitted, re-tried and sentenced to twenty years. A key German agent named Christenson was tracked down and arrested in Rio. In repeated confessions he gave an almost complete exposé of the German espionage system in Brazil. His account, which was of the greatest importance, provided evidence which enabled the court to mete out many other severe sentences.

The German organization in Northern Brazil was almost broken. For the succeeding two or three months the remaining Germans lay low, and during that time there could have been very little intelligence going out of Brazil to Germany.

And then the sinking of five Brazilian passenger ships, one after the other, with considerable loss of life, was the cause of violent anti-German demonstrations throughout Brazil. BSC/SOE agents fanned the flames. In Recife every German and Italian shop or factory was completely wrecked. Sievert's firm, *Hermann Stoltz and Cia.*, was an empty shell when the people had finished with it. The Governor was obliged to organize a general round-up of Axis nationals. BSC/SOE agents came forward with their lists of suspects, of known propagandists and of those agents who – until then – they had been unable to persuade the police to arrest. By the middle of August 1942, ninety-five German and Italian nationals from these lists were in prison. The police were searching for a further sixty-nine. The Lundgren mills were commandeered by the Army, and thirty-three Germans working there were arrested. Thus in the short time between January and August 1942, the German organization in Northern Brazil was broken up and destroyed.

(b) Argentina

Argentina was the only South American republic which did not break relations with the Axis within a year of the Rio Conference. Because of this it would be natural to suppose that Argentina presented wide opportunities for SOE action. But this was not so. The action taken by BSC/SOE agents was confined chiefly to minor individual incidents connected with such matters as the combating of smuggling and the dissemination of propaganda. Action was not, as in Brazil, Chile and the other republics, connected with the broader issues of political manoeuvre and international intrigue.

There were two main reasons for this. First, until December 1942, the Foreign Office failed to associate itself with any clearly defined policy towards Argentina and her isolationist government. Secondly, the peculiar political structure of the country made positive action by agents an almost impossible task. The mass of the people were, surprisingly, rather pro-British and pro-Ally, mixing these sentiments with a strong tinge of hostility towards the United States. At the same time the leading army officers and many of the men in the ranks were pro-German. In the face of these two contradictory factions the Castillo Government remained obstinately isolationist.

In the early days, when Castillo and his Foreign Minister, Ruiz Guiñazú, were successfully resisting the attempt by the United States to induce all the South American republics to make a unanimous break with the Axis and were continuing to favour the representatives of Axis diplomacy and business who remained in Argentina, it was impossible to ascertain whether HMG wished for an attempt to be made either to overthrow Castillo or to induce him to alter his policy. The Americans, with some justification, continually complained about the equivocal British attitude to Argentine foreign policy. The chief BSC/SOE representative in Rio frequently reported that influential Argentinians had expressed the opinion that if HMG would make an announcement expressing frank disapproval of Argentine isolationism, there would be much more chance of expelling enemy interests from the country. Time and again BSC in New York reported to London and to HM Embassy in Washington on this point. Month after month went by, and with each month that passed the Germans entrenched themselves more strongly in the country and exerted more influence upon the Government. At last, in December 1942, the Foreign Office issued a strong statement condemning Argentina's policy.

The time, however, when useful action could have been taken, was gone. Argentina had by then moved so far away from the Allies that she was out of reach. BSC local representatives held long discussions with New York regarding the chances of forcing Castillo to change his policy; but there was little that could be done. Governed by an oligarchy, with a long history of electoral corruption, Argentina could have been diverted from isolationism only by large-scale bribery among the governing class or, alternatively, by a popular movement of overwhelming force. Bribery was considered. BSC had a good agent in constant contact with the nominal President, Ortiz. There was another in contact with General Justo, the man who might have succeeded Ortiz. But Ortiz, blind and diabetic, was busy eating himself to death; while Justo was out-manoeuvred and at last killed in an accident. The bribable politicians like Alberto Barcelo would have cost the earth, and it is very doubtful if they would have proved worth their hire.

The question of instigating a popular movement was debated at length, but the conclusion was reached that such a movement could not be successfully organized by foreigners. It could have been brought about only by the Radical and Socialist politicians, had they not been so corrupt, so old and so discredited that they commanded little popular support.

When the Foreign Office made its long-awaited announcement, agents did all that they could to see that it was read by the people throughout the country. Under the state of siege it was forbidden to broadcast any discussion of the declaration. The Foreign Minister at first forbade the press even to report that it had been made. Through the anti-Axis society, *Acción Argentina*, BSC agents arranged to have it printed in a leaflet called *Tricks of the Axis*, which was distributed to 100,000 persons throughout Argentina. Fifty thousand copies were passed out in strategic districts by hand. The other fifty thousand were posted. To prevent them from being seized and destroyed by the GPO, they were sent out in many different kinds of envelopes from many post offices all over the country, each envelope bearing full postage so that it did not appear to be a circular.

Argentina was a happy hunting-ground for numberless Axis agents, and the BSC/SOE representative made it his duty to keep track of as many of them as possible. But apart from compiling records and keeping New York and other stations informed of the movements of these agents, there was little that could be done. To denounce them to the Government would merely have been a waste of time. To take more drastic action would have given the Germans an opportunity of protesting loudly and perhaps of forcing the Government thereby to initiate restrictive measures against the British in the country.

When the Castillo Government was overthrown by the military revolution of June 1943, its successor, headed by Ramirez and Fárrell, was no easier to handle. It was only the threat of a complete economic blockade by the Allies that compelled Ramirez to sever relations with the Axis; only the US denunciation of Axis espionage in Argentina which compelled the Argentine authorities to break several of the spy-rings which they had hitherto tolerated. It was only the imminent surrender of the German army which compelled Argentina to declare war on Germany. She was obstinate to the last.

CHAPTER 3

Chile

(a) Encouraging a Break with the Axis
(b) The Politicians
(c) After the Break

(a) Encouraging a Break with the Axis

Chile stretches for over 2,500 miles along the west coast of South America, from the borders of Peru and Bolivia on the north down to Cape Horn on the south. To the east lies the Argentine, far greater, far stronger and far more wealthy, exercising continually a powerful influence upon her smaller neighbour.

Up to a point, therefore, Chile has to walk hand in hand with Argentina, and she was doing this when she refused to follow the other Latin American republics who broke relations with the Axis in January 1942. It was not until a year later that the breach occurred, and during the intervening period BSC/SOE agents played their part in bringing it about.

The closeness of Argentina was not the only reason for Chile's pro-Axis attitude. She knew well that her Pacific coastline could have been defended against a Japanese attack only by a first-class fleet and airforce, which she did not possess. Moreover, there was in the country a large, well-concentrated, industrious German colony. Chile's whole administrative machine, political and economic, her armed forces and her civil servants had for the past generation been infiltrated by Germans. Whether the Germans were naturalized or born in the country, they had at all times permeated through each stratum of the administration so that those working amongst them had to be prepared to encounter opposition, obstruction and difficulties at every step which they took. The Germans were concentrated mainly in the agricultural south. In Chile's internal life agriculture is important, and the foodstuffs which these German farmers produce have always been regarded as essential to the country. So in the face of Argentine pressure, an undefended Pacific coastline and a large number of Germans in the country, the Chilean Government was reluctant to abandon its position and was persuaded to do so in the end only as a result of several contributing factors including offers of military and economic assistance.

However, at the beginning of 1942, BSC/SOE agents, directed from New York, had already planned and were putting into effect their campaign. Their first move was to obtain incriminating evidence against Axis agents which they brought to the attention of the Chilean police. There was plenty of opportunity for this work but results were often disappointing. On one occasion when the police raided the homes and meeting places of the Nazis in the south of the country, the Chilean judge, Humberto Mewes Bruna, tried for many months to prove that Nazi activities constituted an offence equivalent to high treason. And although the impounded documents contained clear evidence to prove that the local NSDAP was controlled from abroad and was in fact an organ of the German Reich, there was nothing to show that its members had any plans for militant action against Chile.

After the Rio Conference, in January 1942, a considerable number of Germans and Japanese were arrested, but nearly all of them were soon set free upon giving certain minor undertakings. From BSC's point of view this was useless, and BSC agents therefore set about obtaining official contacts on several different levels. Four members of the secret police (*Investigaciones*) were placed on the payroll and given presents at frequent intervals. The chief BSC/SOE agent spent much time and trouble in winning the personal friendship of the Minister of the Interior, Raul Morales Beltrami, who occupied a position of great power which was almost similar to that of a Prime Minister. At the same time he began to build up close contacts with the leaders of the powerful left-wing parties so that soon BSC/SOE agents were in a position to obtain results by pressure and persuasion. They tried to persuade the politicians of the necessity for the enactment of strong anti-Nazi measures. As a result, in May 1942, the Chamber of Deputies voted to appoint a committee to enquire into Nazi activities. This, at any rate, was a step in the right direction.

The chief representative already had one or two friends upon the committee which was chosen, and he made it his business to enlarge his acquaintance. The committee was to receive a report from the secret police upon the work of the Nazis in Chile, and BSC/SOE agents, throughout the summer of 1942, assisted the

Chile

police in compiling this document. As well as the reports which they continued to obtain by direct investigation, agents were in touch with the Communist Party and from them obtained much useful information. All of it was passed on to the police, together with Censorship material which BSC in New York sent down for the purpose.

The final report which was submitted to the committee and to the Minister of the Interior in August 1942 was a formidable and comprehensive document. It combined all the information collected by the secret police and BSC/SOE, with additional details prepared by the FBI, of the German system of espionage in Chile. There is no doubt that its submission was the first important step towards convincing Chilean parliamentary and public opinion that a rupture of relations with the Axis was necessary. The seeds had been sown. It was important to keep them well watered and nourished, for the ground was still stony.

Accordingly BSC/SOE agents began to disseminate covert anti-Axis propaganda. In March 1942, when the Chilean ship *Tolten* was sunk off New York, they organized a demonstration that resulted in damage being done to a German-controlled theatre, which, with true German tact, was showing at the time the U-boat film *Submarines Westward*. They also made a successful raid upon the establishment of Takayasu Hombo, one of the principal Japanese agents in Chile, and did a great deal of material damage. Press outlets were constantly used for rumours and digests of information taken from European newspapers. One example amongst many was the May (1942) Vatican attack on German anti-religious activity, *The Cross and the Sword*. BSC/SOE arranged for this to be published throughout the country, while at the same time, and during subsequent months, a steady flow of useful articles appeared under Stockholm datelines or above the signatures of fictitious military experts.

A new anti-Axis society, Union for Victory (*La Unión para la Victoria*), was founded in September 1942, through the efforts of the chief BSC/SOE representative. Its ostensible purpose was to collect funds and to express in other ways sympathy for the Allies. Its real aim was the dissemination of propaganda in favour of a break with Germany, Italy and Japan. The Union for Victory was most useful – and so successful that the canny president Rios himself ultimately joined it as a member. For several months in the autumn of 1942, daily propaganda speeches were made, under the direction of BSC, over five Chilean wireless stations. BSC/SOE also assisted in arranging a festival for Aid to the

Democracies, which was attended by at least 100,000 people. A survey of Chilean opinion prepared by the US Censors a month later showed that this created a profound impression. A very large proportion of letters from Chile referred to it, expressing admiration or rage according to whether the writer was pro-Allied or pro-German. Subsequently, on 16 December 1942, BSC/SOE instigated an even more striking demonstration. As a protest against the crimes committed by Germany, all workers controlled by the great Chilean trades union federation C.T.Ch. stopped work for ten minutes. Rios, like every elected President of Chile, depended upon the support of organized labour, and this manifestation of its will produced a powerful effect on him. Popular opinion throughout the country began moving solidly towards a break with the Axis, and one part of BSC's job was accomplished.

(b) The Politicians

While endeavouring to sway public opinion and to discredit the Germans in the country, BSC/SOE agents sought for other ways and means of encouraging the Chilean Government to break with Germany. The cultivation of certain politicians by the chief BSC/SOE representative was perhaps as important a factor as any other in the campaign.

His plan was this: to bring together the several scattered left-wing parties so that there would be formed a strong 'united front' which would be influential enough to exert pressure upon President Rios. The pressure was to be exerted under the agent's covert guidance.

It was an ambitious plan, for Chile was suffering from the same disease of parliamentary degeneration which had brought about the downfall of France. There were in 1942 no less than five disunited left-wing parties, the Communists, Socialists, Socialist Workers, Democrats and Radicals. The BSC/SOE representative's task was to bring them together on the common ground of opposition to totalitarianism.

Throughout the year 1942 he made new friends in all the left-wing parties. He saw the leaders of the Radicals and the Socialists constantly. He argued with them and supported his arguments with documentary evidence. After a few months he began to make headway, and by June 1942, when the 8th National Convention of the Socialist Party took place, the question of a 'united front' was the question of the hour. The chief representative attended the meeting and he assisted in the framing of the four important resolutions which the convention passed. These called for:

(a) cessation of diplomatic relations with the Axis;
(b) reaffirmation of solidarity with all countries fighting against totalitarian aggression;
(c) immediate measures by the Government to destroy all centres of Nazi influence in Chile;
(d) unity of the left-wing parties in a national democratic front.

Meanwhile President Rios was watching, with some uneasiness, the growing unity of the left-wing parties. Whichever way he turned, he could not help hearing the loud voices of those who proclaimed their anti-Nazi resolutions.

BSC/SOE agents gained the confidence of the Communists by guaranteeing them their monthly cheques for newsprint for their newspapers and propaganda sheets. To bring the other parties into line, other appropriate means were used. On 24 June 1942, a *Frente National Democratico* or National Democratic Front of the five left-wing parties was precariously but effectively formed. The declared object was to summon the President to break relations with the Axis at once.

This pressure was too strong to be ignored. Just after Brazil's entry into the war, in August 1942, the Chilean Senate determined to review the whole problem in secret session. The Senators were very evenly divided on the question, with eighteen in favour of breaking relations, twenty against and seven undecided. The chief purpose of the debate, from the Allied point of view, was to discredit the Foreign Minister, Ernesto Barros Jarpa, who was then and thereafter the great upholder of neutrality and the main opponent of the Allies. Lest it be thought that he was merely an honest man attempting in a misguided way to do his best for his country, it should be noted that his cousin, the Chilean Ambassador to Berlin, was 100% pro-German. He himself had suspicious financial connections with German firms, and late in 1943 was known to have joined a movement for a totalitarian *putsch* on the Argentine model. What Barros himself wanted was a brief debate – he scheduled it to last for an hour and a half – and a vote of confidence on his policy. BSC/SOE and their newly united political friends out-manoeuvred him.

The principal speaker on the Allied side was Gregorio Amunategui, formerly president of the Liberal party. BSC/SOE agents provided him with many new and unanswerable arguments to use in his speech. There was a letter from a German officer, Otto von Zippelius, who had been instructor of the Chilean corps of *carabineros*. It was addressed to a member of the High Command in Berlin. It spoke reassuringly of the comparative immunity enjoyed by the NSDAP and other German organizations in Chile. There was a list of the details of the economic assistance given to Uruguay by the Allies. There were copies of articles published elsewhere in South America, criticizing Chile for refusing to break with the Axis. Finally, there was a telegram from the Foreign Office, emphatically denying that Great Britain approved of Chile's position. This last document was most important, because Barros Jarpa had several times categorically stated that Chile could rely on British support for her neutrality. Amunategui obtained additional material from Chilean sources – from BSC's friend Morales, who gave him a long report on German subversive activities in Chile, and from Benjamin Matte, the Minister of Finance, who gave him a memorandum on the economic advantages already gained by countries like Peru which had made the break.

BSC/SOE's chief representative procured for another speaker, the ex-Minister of Education, Rudecindo Ortéga, the text of a little-known speech made by Barros Jarpa just after the Pearl Harbor attack. Ortéga began by saying he was about to read a speech by a Chilean patriot. When he came to the peroration,

> If we stand heedlessly by in the face of this aggression, our grandchildren will be ashamed of the blood they bear in their veins!

there were cries of 'Whose speech is this?' Ortéga then pointed to Barros Jarpa and said, 'It is by our esteemed Minister of Foreign Affairs.' All through the speech Barros had been rudely interrupting the speaker, so that the effect which Ortéga obtained was extremely dramatic.

The debate spread over three sessions, lasting two days in all, instead of the hour and a half originally planned. The public were aroused, and at the end Barros Jarpa humbled himself so far as to ask that no vote should be taken. He had admitted defeat.

The wheel had turned a half circle and it was still turning. Chile was moving fast towards the breach with the Axis. In October 1942, President Rios decided to visit the United States. He was expected to announce the break just before his departure. But that same month the interrogation of a Nazi agent in Cuba, named Heinz Luning, exposed a number of German agents in Chile and implicated the German Bank. Sumner Welles delivered a speech accusing the Chilean Government of harbouring German spies and of causing the loss of Allied lives and ships. Immediately the wheel stopped turning, paused and began to spin the other way. Always ready to defend their dignity, the Chileans had decided that this admonition was an insult to their national honour tantamount to coercion by the United States. Rios postponed his visit indefinitely, and the Cabinet resigned *en bloc*.

But anti-Nazism had become too strongly implanted in the minds of the Government and of the people for that resentful attitude to last long. By December 1942, the situation was retrieved. Rios determined to send Raul Morales to Washington as his personal representative in negotiations with the Department of State. It may be wondered why he sent anyone at all and was not content merely to sever relations. The rather unsavoury reason is that Rios had determined to make the most of the situation. He would extract a *quid pro quo* from the richest nation in the world. The entire mission was to be kept secret. The connection between Morales and the BSC/SOE officers in Chile was by this time so close that Morales requested the chief agent to pass his confidential messages back from Washington to Santiago, through BSC channels, so that they should be hidden from the prying eyes of either the Chileans or the North Americans.

When Morales arrived in the US, a BSC representative from New York interviewed both him and his companion, the Socialist Oscar Schnake, several times. Thus WS was able to keep London and HM Embassy informed of every stage of the progress of the mission as well as passing advice and messages to the Chilean negotiators. The mission was successful and at long last, in January 1943, Chile announced a breach of diplomatic relations between herself and the Axis.

(c) After the Break

Now that Chile had severed diplomatic relations, BSC's agents made it their business to find out how this gesture could be made to result in material damage to the Axis. It was a problem similar to those which agents in other Latin American countries had faced, but among the wary, proud, evasive Chileans it was more difficult to solve than elsewhere. President Rios specifically confined the breach to the diplomatic sphere and he insisted at first that commercial relations should continue unaltered. With a certain gusto, he evaded the subsidiary obligations arising out of this pledge of Pan-American solidarity. Both he and the Foreign Minister made each new request received from the British or the Americans into a bargaining point with which to secure from the Allies agreements for the purchase of nitrate, for loans or for promises of continued economic assistance after the war.

In spite of this, much could be done locally, particularly in the sphere of economic warfare. The methods which the agents adopted in combating German economic activities, German banks, German companies and pro-German newspapers, were several, but the main one was, once again, the exercise of political pressure through undercover contacts. For example, both the American and British Embassies failed by exerting official pressure to persuade the Chilean Government to order the closing of the German news agency *PACH* and the German-inspired nationalist newspaper, *El Roto*. So in February 1943, the chief BSC/SOE representative approached his powerful friend Morales, and a week later both these Axis propaganda outlets were suppressed.

The chief representative was also instrumental in bringing together on a committee politicians representing every party – from the *Falange Nacional* on the right to the Communists on the left. The committee was formed under the auspices of the Free World Association (see Part II), which pledged itself to the full implementation of the Rio agreement and to the prosecution of economic war against the Axis. At the same time agents continued to arrange for the publication of articles in the large newspapers throughout the country, calling for a more earnest and realistic view of German economic penetration. NEW were requested to prepare a memorandum on the dangers which German finance meant to small nations, and, when this had been made available, it was widely distributed.

In April 1943, the General Economic Bill, which authorized the President to introduce the economic controls approved at the Washington Conference, was tabled. It was couched in the vaguest of terms, probably at President Rios's own request. As soon as it came up for approval, the chief representative persuaded Salvador Allende, the intelligent young Secretary of the Socialist Party, to press for the inclusion of a most important point, one dealing with the expropriation of Axis firms in Chile. Further, he influenced Benjamin Matte, the Minister of Finance and other key politicians to support the Bill in its amended form. After it was passed, he urged Matte to act upon it at once. Subsequently

Matte said to him: 'I have done what you asked. I have signed the decree liquidating the German banks.'

Thereafter BSC/SOE continued to wage vigorous war against the Axis economic interests. The *Banco Alemán Transatlántico*, the *Banco Germánico del Sur*, and the spearhead firms, Bayer, Schering, etc., were all due to be liquidated by the end of 1943 (see Part III). Most of the objects of Allied economic warfare were ultimately achieved and the back of German business in Chile was broken in spite of, rather than because of, the attitude of the President and his Government.

CHAPTER 4

Colombia

(a) The Law-Makers
(b) The Germans
(c) The Japanese and Others
(d) The Spanish Falange
(e) Acción Nacional
(f) Propaganda and Intelligence

(a) The Law-Makers

Colombia is a large, rich and populous country in the extreme north of the subcontinent. It borders on Panama, which was one of its provinces until the Americans in 1930 executed a successful operation and made Panama quasi-independent. Colombia is the only South American republic with ports on both the Atlantic and Pacific Oceans. Over half its export profits come from its excellent coffee, but it also has oil, gold and platinum, and many other valuable products which are still practically unexploited because of transport difficulties.

German influence has always been strong in Colombia. One of the three founders of the capital, Santa Fé de Bogotá, was a German called Nicolaus Federmann, agent of an Augsburg bank to which Charles V granted the right to conquer and settle part of the Caribbean coast. The first commercial airline in the world, *Scadta*, was founded in Colombia in 1919 by a group of young Germans. At the beginning of the war several of the largest commercial houses were owned by German families. They had been long and securely established as vital parts of the Colombian economic system. There were over four thousand Germans in the country, well distributed and organized with their usual efficiency. Italian influence was not marked. There was a colony of Japanese farmers. They looked childishly innocent of all subversive intentions, but after the start of Japanese aggression they had to be carefully watched. Finally, the Conservative party and the right wing generally, having been out of power since 1930, were embittered and aggressive, openly attacking the Liberal Government for sympathizing with the democracies, and serving as a megaphone for Axis propaganda of various types.

The chief targets for BSC/SOE in Colombia were, first, the Germans, and second, the friends and admirers of the Germans. The chief instrument used against them both was the National Police, particularly its secret branch, the Department of Investigations. For some time after the beginning of the war, this force was virtually powerless against the local Nazis, but BSC/SOE agents gave it a new lease of life. They encouraged and assisted and flattered it in such a way that very soon the National Police became a powerful and willing anti-Nazi instrument. The methods they used were as follows:

1. They suggested laws attacking enemy interests, helped to draw them up, and pushed them through the legislative machinery.
2. After each law was adopted, they discovered examples of its contravention by Axis nationals or entities.
3. They then produced, or alternatively persuaded the police to discover, evidence against the enemy personalities concerned so that their activities were curtailed.
4. With each such discovery, they pressed for the adoption of still more drastic measures against the Axis.

Their work culminated in Colombia's declaration of war on Germany in November 1943. It was satisfactorily concealed, for as HM Ministry of Information observed in a subsequent appreciation of Colombian politics:

The decision (to declare war) was an unexpected one, and there is little to show why it was taken at that particular time.

Liaison with the National Police was established early in 1941. The contact was the Director of Investigations, Arturo Vallejo Sánchez, with whom the head of BSC/SOE in Colombia built up a close personal and working relationship. When Pearl Harbor was attacked, the two of them were together for most of the following night, drafting a memorandum of security measures designed to put the local Nazis under control, and on 18 December it became a Presidential decree.

But enough had not yet been done. The most active Axis sympathizers were Colombian citizens of German birth, who, as things stood, were inviolate.

Accordingly, the chief representative in collaboration with his friend, Vallejo Sánchez, drafted a law penalizing 'fifth-column' activities as such, whether conducted by foreigners or by persons claiming Colombian citizenship. Specifically, it decreed sentences of six months to six years in a penal colony for any person conveying to the Axis powers intelligence on military affairs, international politics or economic and social conditions; for any persons convicted of sabotage (in the broadest interpretation of that word); and for anyone engaged in such subversive activities as belonging to anti-democratic political groups supported by foreign powers, spreading alarmist rumours, possessing clandestine radio stations and disseminating foreign propaganda 'contrary to the international orientation of the Government'.

In June 1942, the proposed law was submitted to the President for signature, but Eduardo Santos, who was just completing his Presidential term, was reluctant to approve a measure so radical and so likely to provoke subsequent criticism of his regime. He shelved it. At his retirement, Vallejo Sánchez was dismissed, and the chief BSC/SOE representative had to start all over again. Fortunately he had made many contacts in high places – the Secretary-General of the Foreign Ministry, the Director-General of the National Police, the new head of the secret police, and personal friends and confidential employees of the new President, Alfonso López. Utilizing these, he began to spread the idea that an anti-Fifth Column law was necessary and urgent.

Agents were assigned the task of mobilizing opinion in favour of the enactment of such a law. Through cut-outs, the press in Colombia was induced to print articles protesting against Axis-inspired subversive activities and revealing that the enemy was in fact plotting against the national security of the republic. Other articles were planted praising the National Police and demanding that they should be assisted in their work by more drastic and more flexible legislation. The chief representative himself engineered the arrest of various Colombian citizens of German birth who were found to be contravening existing laws and injuring the country's interests, and as each case 'broke', it was given wide publicity.

In the spring of 1943, an anti-Fifth Column bill was presented to Congress. But its enactment was delayed, for the Ministry of Finance requested an amendment which would give the Government more power over blocked accounts. By the time this was ready for submission, Congress had gone into recess for the summer. Ultimately the President and his advisers determined that the bill, as drawn, was too dangerous to submit to Congress. But all the work which had gone into it was not wasted. Most of its provisions were ultimately embodied in various decrees which the President signed piecemeal under special extraordinary powers which had been granted to him.

Meanwhile, the chief representative was conducting a parallel campaign. Its purpose was to procure the passage of a bill increasing the powers of the National Police. Local police forces in the provinces (or *Departmentos*) were slack, ignorant and sometimes afraid to take action against Axis sympathizers who were rich or well in favour with the Governor and the leading families. If the National Police themselves could be empowered to proceed against such persons on the ground that their activities endangered the entire nation, the local police could be bypassed. A bill to this effect was tabled.

Once again influential people were contacted. Arguments in favour of the bill were brought to the public's attention by inspired articles in the press, and the bill was, of course, enthusiastically supported by the heads of the National Police. Incidentally, it was not unwelcome to the President or to the Administration, because they realized that its passage would serve to increase their control over the provinces, where separatist movements were not infrequent. In spite of the violent opposition of the pro-Axis Conservative leader, Laureano Gómez, it was finally pushed through Congress, as Law No. 5 of 27 February 1943.

There was another law which required sponsoring, for as things stood Axis nationals would have been able to recover their frozen funds almost unimpaired at the end of the war. To provide against this contingency, the intelligence and planning section in New York proposed, in January 1943, that legislation should be devised which would require these frozen accounts to be expended on indemnifying Colombia for losses inflicted by the war. As a model, New York sent to Colombia a draft of a similar bill, H.R. 3672, introduced later in the US Congress.

H.R. 3672 was translated into Spanish and passed around among officials of the interested government department. It was publicized in the press and copies of it were distributed to the local insurance companies through Vallejo Sánchez.

Meanwhile Colombia was drawing closer to belligerency. Brazil declared war on Germany in August 1942. In April 1943, Bolivia followed suit, and invited her five northern neighbours to join her. BSC in New York, upon enquiring of HM Embassy in Washington, was advised that HMG's policy was 'to encourage declarations of war by all South American countries'. The word was passed to the south, where BSC agents had already prepared newspaper articles calling upon Colombia to declare war. These were now printed in the most influential Colombian newspapers – *El Tiempo*, *El Liberal*, *El Siglo*, and *La Razón*. HM Ambassador was apparently pleased with the strength and apparent unanimity of opinion in favour of war and he sent a despatch to the Foreign Office on the subject. When he showed the despatch to the chief representative, he was astonished to hear that the entire campaign was a BSC/SOE undertaking.

A few weeks later, the Colombian schooner *Resolute* was torpedoed off the coast, and its survivors machine-gunned by the attacking U-boat. The anti-German newspaper campaign gathered momentum, and was endorsed by many independent publicists. On 27 November 1943, Colombia declared war on Germany.

Now that Colombian property had actually been attacked and Colombian lives taken by the Germans, advocacy of the bill decreeing that Axis frozen assets should be used for indemnifying Colombia was an easier matter, and the bill was enacted on 29 December 1943. It laid down, *inter alia*, that:

> The Fiduciary Control to which the possessions of German citizens are subject ... will continue in force until such time as the indemnities and reparations arising out of damage caused by Germany or its nationals have been paid, as well as the expenses imposed on the National Treasury by the state of belligerence provoked by Germany.

But that was not the end. New York sent down to Colombia the draft of another American bill, together with instructions to the chief representative that he should arrange for the enactment of a similar measure in Colombia. It had to do with the subject of expropriating the assets of all German subjects or entities in Colombia, and it became law on 25 July 1944.

In result, the Germans lost assets valued at over seven million pounds sterling. The chief BSC/SOE representative pointed out that although it might appear that a considerable part of the amount expropriated would ultimately find its way back to the Germans, this was not so. Several million pounds, he said, would be utilized to maintain internees, to pay the fees and emoluments of administrative officials and, finally, to compensate the State for the material losses sustained in the sinking of Colombian ships and the murder of Colombian citizens; also for the economic losses involved by the diminution of Colombia's whole shipping potential, from the time when the sinkings occurred to the time when the ships could be replaced. He added: 'There are many other means of eating into the sum, and we feel sure, knowing the attitude of the officials mainly concerned, that very little of the total amount will ever find its way back to its original owners.' The Commercial Secretaries of the British and American Embassies were invited to prepare a list of the German interests whose expropriation would be most desirable. This list, duly submitted to the Colombian government, happily contained many old enemies such as Bayer and Schering (see Part III).

Decree No. 2643 of 30 December 1943 was the last of a series of laws inspired wholly or partially by BSC/SOE. This expanded and strengthened the powers already conferred on the National Police to control Axis nationals. It submitted them either to confinement in concentration camps, to limited residence in certain areas, or to regular surveillance. All German institutions of every kind were closed and their licences cancelled. Any foreigners, especially Germans, who could not be kept under proper surveillance were to be expelled from the country. Six were deported to the United States; over one hundred were interned.

Thus, after a campaign lasting just two years, the back of the German organization in Colombia was broken, probably for a long time, possibly for ever. The Germans were deprived of their businesses, their propaganda outlets, their *Volksdeutsch* institutions and their long-standing friendship with the Colombian nation which a German himself had helped to found.

(b) The Germans

In the two years, from 1942 until 1944, during which the legislative war was waged against Axis nationals in Colombia, direct action was instigated against individuals who were making trouble. BSC's chief SOE representative and his assistants were responsible for the arrest of many such persons. They included Germans, Japanese, members of the Spanish Falange and members of the Colombian Nationalist Party.

In May 1942, the chief representative obtained from the Colombian National Police a secret report on Germans and Nazi sympathizers holding official positions in the provinces of

Atlántico, Bolivar and Magdalena. This had been written for the President by his confidential agent, Eduardo de Heredia. Throughout the summer of 1942, reports were compiled by BSC/SOE agents, dealing with the key Germans in the principal towns of the country; and when these were pieced together a complete picture of the German organization emerged.

During the autumn of 1942 two Colombian destroyers left the port of Cartagena under sealed orders to refit and rearm at Baltimore. Immediately after they had sailed, the Berlin radio announced their destination and advised them to sail with lights on at night in order to avoid the risk of being torpedoed. Obviously there was a German information service in Cartagena which had wireless communication with Berlin.

De Heredia's report to the President had dealt in detail with the port of Cartagena. It had revealed that among many Axis sympathizers there was a suspect German named Wilhelm Dittmar or Dittmer, who had served as a bandmaster in the Colombian naval forces. He had been discharged from this post at the time of Pearl Harbor and, although ordered to leave Cartagena, he had remained in the city, spreading discreet and effective propaganda. It was ascertained further that he had induced the local authorities to declare him anti-Nazi and to unfreeze his funds.

In December 1943, after obtaining much concrete evidence against Dittmar, BSC/SOE agents suggested to the National Police that they should raid the house where he was living with his friend Erich Guter. The police found correspondence in the house proving that Dittmar had an organization under his control for gathering intelligence about the port. Guter was found to possess a wireless set as well as incriminating photographs and photostatic equipment. The raid and its resultant findings were given wide publicity in newspapers throughout the country in order that the heads of the National Police in other cities might be encouraged to emulate the action of their colleagues in Cartagena. Vallejo Sánchez, the head of the National Police, led this campaign by supplying articles to the big national newspapers *El Tiempo* and *El Espectador*. He was grateful for having been given the opportunity by BSC/SOE to lay his hands on Dittmar.

Rudolph Scheuplein of Medellín was another dangerous man. BSC/SOE agents learned that he had been giving directions to the new totalitarian party *Acna*. They investigated him and discovered that he was the local leader of the German *Arbeitsfront* and was in charge of its funds. He lived with one Karl Theodor Kurck. A full report was prepared, and this was handed to the National

Colombia

Police who were by now beginning to appreciate the assistance, particularly since BSC/SOE required no share in the eventual credit for success. They went to the house in which Scheuplein and Kurck lived, and there they found cash and securities worth some 16,500 pounds sterling. Since these funds should have been declared, they were seized and deposited in frozen accounts. The police also found numerous Nazi emblems, German flags, propaganda pamphlets and – more important – aerial photographs of strategic areas throughout the country. Amongst Kurck's private collection of material were 800 German propaganda pictures and three instruction booklets explaining their use.

Information from sources to which BSC had access in New York was often of value to the chief representative. For example when he reported that a certain Max Vogel was suspect and had been put under surveillance, New York sent him in return a copy of an intercepted letter showing that a notorious German agent in Mexico, George Nicolaus (see Part VII), was friendly with Vogel and had left some effects in his charge. This evidence was sufficiently conclusive to induce the police to search Vogel's house, and subsequently to arrest him. They ordered him to leave Colombia within forty-eight hours with the alternative of being sent to a penal colony in the jungle. Vogel chose to leave the country, and negotiations were conducted with a view to persuading the Colombians to hand him over to the British or Americans.

Eventually these negotiations were successful, but they cost the chief representative much effort and patience, for the Colombian authorities did not like the proposal, regarding it as irrational. The objections of two important officials were at last overcome only by the gift of a case of Scotch whisky to each of them. Scotch whisky in Colombia is a rare commodity. Vogel was flown to Trinidad, examined there by SIS and the FBI and finally interned in the US.

One of the more difficult tasks of BSC/SOE in Colombia was to arrange for the leading Germans in the territory to be repatriated, deported or interned. In October 1942, the Secretary General of the Foreign Ministry told the chief representative that if the latter would produce a list of the fifty most dangerous Nazis living in the country with a brief dossier on each, he (the Secretary-General) would set about securing their expulsion forthwith. The British Minister reported the offer to the Foreign Office, who replied: 'This seems an excellent proposal.' The Ministry of Economic Warfare took a different view. They said: 'Manpower is now one of the enemy's most acute problems', and the counter-espionage experts of SIS were understandably eager that known or suspected German agents should be allowed to remain in Colombia under surveillance.

It was the duty of WS carefully to weigh all the pros and cons of this question, to consult with MEW and with his SOE and SIS experts and to come to a decision. Finally a plan was produced with which everyone appeared to be satisfied, and instructions were sent to Colombia accordingly. Two lists were prepared, one naming forty-six Germans who would be given safe-conducts through to Spain subject to investigation and search at a British or American control point, and the other naming thrity-four who should be deported but would not be granted safe-conduct by the Allies. These lists were submitted to the President of Colombia and to the appropriate ministries. At the same time the inevitable and arduous task was begun of setting in motion the machinery which would influence government officials in favour of the plan. This was necessary, because in spite of the promise which the Secretary General had made, no time limit had been set. The campaign was still in progress when a far simpler solution was provided by Colombia's declaration of war.

Immediately thereafter, using the dossiers with which it had been provided, the Government deported six of the most dangerous Nazis to the USA for internment. Over 100 were placed in a concentration camp in Colombia, the creation of which had previously been recommended to the Foreign Ministry by BSC/SOE agents.

(c) The Japanese and Others

The Japanese in Colombia were not numerous, but it would have been unwise to neglect them, particularly in view of the suspicious activities of their leaders. There were many well-substantiated reports of Japanese 'geological expeditions' surveying the coast and the inland areas, where airfields could be improvised within striking distance of the Panama Canal and the Venezuelan oilfields. A month after Pearl Harbor, the Japanese Minister, Hisao Yanai, was caught in the act of photographing a large relief map of Colombia in the *Parque Nacional* in Bogotá. He was taken to the police station where his films were confiscated, and these, when developed, showed a remarkable concentration of interest on the Pacific coast. Yanai apologized with characteristic courtesy and he was allowed to go. The Japanese are unpredictable. It is difficult to imagine a parallel occidental case – to imagine Lord Halifax, for example, being caught redhanded photographing objects of military interest!

That same month after Pearl Harbor, the chief representative obtained proof that there was a radio transmitter in the Japanese Legation, which was being used for communicating with Japan. One of his informants heard signals on the special Japanese wave-length. Another produced confirmatory data on the Legation's monthly consumption of electric energy. When the diplomats were repatriated – in April 1942 – information was obtained through an employee of the Legation that one of the cases among their luggage contained the wireless transmitter. Its number was given, and the National Police were induced to open it during the railway journey to the coast. A fine Hallicrafter 'Skytraveller' set was found and removed. The case was refilled with stones of the same weight. Doubtless Hisao Yanai lost face when it was opened in Japan.

Then BSC in New York obtained an interesting map of the approaches to the Panama Canal which had on it Japanese markings (see Part VII). These appeared to indicate a possible aerial attack on the locks by aircraft taking off from some area on or close to the western coast of Colombia.

New York sent the information to the chief representative in that territory. He showed it to his contact in the National Police, who took him to the Minister of War, and then to the Chief of Staff. In result, the Japanese colony at Corinto was put under much closer control. All radio sets in the colony were confiscated. Articles were published in the local press renewing the warning against fifth-column activities by Japanese, and the appropriate precautions were taken at threatened areas along the coast.

(d) The Spanish Falange

The profoundly conservative, Catholic spirit of many of the people of Colombia was fertile ground upon which to sow the seeds of totalitarian ideals. Not only the Germans, but the Spaniards also, realized this. Even before Franco came to power in Spain, there was in Bogotá a small group of conservatives who showed their sympathy for the cause of the Spanish Falange. In February 1938, the Conservative newspaper, *El Siglo*, opened a subscription in aid of Franco's soldiers 'who are fighting for the liberty and integrity of the Mother Country'. The subscriptions amounted to $5870.78, which was spent upon food and cigarettes sent to the Nationalist Consul in Hamburg by the Hamburg America Line.

The movement grew as the mass of foreign priests and religious brotherhoods in the country began to take a more active part in it. By 1940, in certain districts where the Dominican monks travelled, virtually every peasant's hut was decorated with at least one photograph of Franco. By 1942, the Falangist movement was widespread, well organized, sufficiently provided with funds and working assiduously for an Axis victory.

In May 1942, BSC decided to open a campaign against the movement. Much material was despatched to the chief representative in Colombia: excerpts from Falangist correspondence intercepted by Censorship; the texts of indiscreet utterances by Franco, by Serrano Suñer and others. He used these, together with photographs and information obtained from the files of the National Police, as material for newspaper articles exposing the Falange as an organization sympathetic with and auxiliary to the Axis. The Spanish Minister protested, but because the articles were based upon fact and signed by Colombian citizens, his protests appeared ridiculous and produced no effect.

Meanwhile, individual Falangists were sought out by BSC/SOE agents, and investigated. The police were provided with details of their activities and persuaded to take action, so that one by one they were rendered ineffective. Toward the end of 1943, BSC/SOE reported to headquarters in New York, that the *Falange Española* in Colombia was completely dormant. Possibly it was dead.

(e) Acción Nacional

In Medellín, in the summer of 1942, a new party was born. It was called *Acción Nacional* or *Acna*. Its aims were familiar: to abolish all political parties; to create a corporate state; to oppose 'foreign imperialism'. Uniforms, drill, raised-arm salutes and 'strength through joy' clubs were organized on the Fascist pattern. No Germans openly belonged to *Acna*, but it had many members with pro-Axis records. Upon investigation it was learned that Scheuplein, who has already been mentioned, and a friend of his, one Hans Vieten, were financing the movement and supplying it with directives. Vieten's lawyer, Heriberto Royo Perez, was the founder of the party. In Bogotá, Juan Roca Lemus broadcast Axis news and commentaries over one of the radio stations and offered free pictures of Hitler and swastika pins to all his listeners. He was paid by Bayer. Vieten composed a handbill attacking the British and American blacklists, which *Acna* distributed. By these and other methods the party began to increase its activities.

With a trusted member of the Colombian secret police, the chief representative made a special trip to Medellín, the birthplace of the movement. Together they made a complete investigation of its totalitarian ideals, its ties with the Axis and its anti-democratic membership. The report was handed to a group of prominent Liberal members of Congress, who were impressed. They asked that the information should be published. President López, when shown the report, also approved of its publication. It was featured in newspapers during September 1942. In articles and editorials *Acna* was accused of being an outright fifth-column party. Many faint-hearted members wrote to the papers denying their membership. The publicity provoked a full-scale debate in Congress on subversive activity inspired by the Axis, and finally, on 10 October 1942, the organization was suppressed.

(f) Propaganda and Intelligence

In March 1943, the British Vice-Consul in Cartagena reported the arrival of several thousand copies of three books of Axis propaganda. One was called *Dictatorship in England* ('100 Families Rule the Empire') by G. Wirsing. Another was *I Talked with Bruno* by Benito Mussolini, and the third was *Gold, Guns, Democracies* by Pablo Zappa. They were all published by a blacklisted publishing house in Argentina, *Editorial La Mazorca*. They were consigned to Roberto Arrozola, who was a nationalist fanatic.

Cartagena had always been a nursery for Axis propaganda, so it seemed probable that this material would be freely distributed throughout Colombia unless immediate preventative action was taken. Accordingly, the chief representative obtained a police order for the confiscation of the whole consignment. He went down to Cartagena, brought all the books back to Bogotá and personally supervised their destruction.

BSC/SOE accomplishments in Colombia, as elsewhere in Latin America, were the result of indirect methods, and it is perhaps worth recording three main principles which were observed.

First, the Chief Representative made friends with men in key positions in the administration. Vallejo Sánchez had an unrivalled ability to find the pressure-point through which the maximum of effect could be produced with the minimum effort and publicity.

Others who could not be bought were won over by flattery or small favours. The occasion on which BSC procured several special radio valves for the head of the Colombian Air Force is a case in point.

Secondly, BSC/SOE worked with the police, but allowed them to take all the credit for achievements. Latin American officials are poorly paid. They can get advancement by being successful, so that when the Colombian police were offered the unpaid assistance of an organization which shunned publicity they were eager to accept.

Thirdly, operations were identified with the national interest. BSC/SOE's anti-German campaigns in Colombia succeeded because they were based, not on an appeal for sympathy with Britain's cause, but on an appeal to Colombians to safeguard their own security.

CHAPTER 5

Ecuador

(a) Expelling the Germans
(b) Proposed Declaration of War

(a) Expelling the Germans

In most South American countries cooperation between BSC/SOE and their US opposite numbers was satisfactory. In some it was very close. But in Ecuador it was virtually non-existent. US officials and agents took a strangely possessive attitude towards Ecuador, regarding it as their own exclusive sphere of influence. They did not want British help and they resented British interference.

Ecuador owns the Galapagos Islands. The Galapagos Islands constitute a strategic menace to the Panama Canal, and that was evidently the reason for the attitude of the Americans.

Nevertheless, the task of exposing and instigating the expulsion of German agents was chiefly performed by BSC/SOE agents. They drew up the first plan of action. They compiled the first list of the dangerous Axis nationals who deserved expulsion or internment. They furnished the FBI, upon their arrival, with basic information and with numerous contacts whom the Americans were soon employing as regular sub-agents. And BSC/SOE was on the point of inducing Ecuador to declare war on Germany when orders from the Foreign Office halted this operation.

The chief representative in Ecuador worked from Quito, for the most part, through the following three organizations:

1. The National Pro-Allied Committee, which was formed long before the United States entered the war. To it belonged representatives of all the foreign colonies in Ecuador. Since the immigrants were spread through practically every social stratum in the country, this Committee formed an excellent

informant service, commanding some 3,000 unpaid but reliable contacts. Its president was a stout-hearted old Frenchman, Pierre LaFargue, enthusiastically pro-British, bitterly anti-German and anti-Vichy, who gave up his business and worked all day and much of the night for the cause. When an Ecuadorean branch of the Inter-Continental Committee for Political Defence (created by the Rio Conference) was set up, LaFargue was invited to attend all its meetings. At these the BSC/SOE agent, through his friendship with LaFargue, was able to arrange for the latter to introduce many BSC/SOE proposals.
2. BSC/SOE's own network of agents, which at first, in preparation for a possible invasion, was spread throughout the country. Later agents were concentrated in Quito and Guayaquil, the two principal cities.
3. An organization of pro-Allied Ecuadoreans, led by the English-educated officer, Leonidas Plaza Lasso. Unfortunately, just as this organization was beginning to pull its full weight, Plaza and his brother were involved in an unsuccessful revolution against President Arroyo del Rio and were thrown into prison. If the revolution had succeeded BSC/SOE would have had one of their sub-agents as President of the republic!

Prior to Pearl Harbor and the Rio Conference, agents in Ecuador carried out a number of successful operations. In October 1941, sub-agents, directed by the chief representative in Quito, walked 30 kilometres across country and found near Riobamba a large radio transmitter belonging to *Sedta* Airlines which was transmitting messages to Germany. They knocked the German guard over the head, smashed the transmitter, then proceeded to the town of Riobamba itself and to the house of the Ecuadorean, Evangelisto Calero, where they knew that there was another transmitter. Taking advantage of the fact that it was Carnival time – there was a big party going on in the house – they entered stealthily and smashed the transmitter. The cost of the operation was insignificant. Sub-agents were paid no more than the equivalent of £4 each, which they considered a large reward.

At the beginning of 1942, BSC/SOE agents set about their main task of instigating the internment or deportation of Axis nationals. At that time there were some 5,000 Germans in the country, many of them violent Nazis and some of them active agents working in contact with outside sources. The job of investigating them was begun at once. Information was obtained from the National Pro-Allied Committee, from the immigration authorities, from police officials in certain cities and from many other sources. Thousands of names were sifted for the purpose of eliminating the harmless and leaving those who should be interned, deported or kept under surveillance. A photograph was stolen from the German Embassy, which showed forty Germans in Nazi uniform standing in front of the German Club. This provided proof that there had been an NSDAP organization in the country.

When the list was complete, the chief BSC/SOE representative handed it to the Government. For a few weeks he waited, but nothing happened. In March 1942, news was received that no Germans were to be expelled from the country. The list which BSC/SOE agents had prepared had been passed to the Germans by some high government official, and the Germans had paid a bribe to obtain their immunity.

The problem was therefore approached from another angle. The immigration authorities were persuaded to draw up a list of foreigners whose papers were not in order and who could be arrested for this offence without authorization from higher up. It was found that a number of the dangerous Nazis were vulnerable on this point, and as a result they were arrested together with two Falangist Spaniards. They were notified that they must either leave the country or be confined in a remote village under surveillance. One of the Germans was Paul Roehl, the Transocean agent for Ecuador. Roehl foolishly told the Minister of Justice that the Germans would soon take over the country and that the Minister and other Ecuadorean officials would then be made to face a firing-squad. The Falangist propagandist Valentín Fernandez Cuevas made the same error of judgment. He told the officials who arrested him: 'We shall be back in six months and, like the original Spanish conquerors, we shall crush you.' These men were interned and subsequently expelled from the country.

Meanwhile, the Americans were becoming more familiar with the territory and its problems, and they had begun to exercise increasing pressure on their own account. At this stage, however, BSC/SOE agents were still able to persuade them to cooperate, and when it was decided to make out another set of proposals for deportation, the FBI were responsible for one list and BSC/SOE for another. Together they included most of the dangerous men. But some bribery was necessary to secure action. BSC/SOE agreed with the chief of the secret police that he should be paid the equivalent of seven shillings and sixpence per head for every important German shipped out of the country, and half-price for unimportant Germans. The FBI paid 50% of these expenses. Although seven shillings and sixpence may seem a paltry sum, to the secret police it was considerable. The entire department was so poor that BSC/SOE found it necessary on several occasions to pay the expenses of arresting Germans and transporting them to the coast. Had they not done this, the arrests would never have been made.

The chief of secret police, spurred to action by thought of reward, was able in April and May of 1942 to arrange for 150 Germans and Japanese to be deported. These included 130 whose names had been submitted by BSC/SOE agents. The German organization was being broken up, and all that was required to complete the job was the expulsion of fifty more individuals. Agents accordingly intensified their investigations and by gathering information from official and unofficial sources were soon able to make up a complete dossier on each of the remaining Germans. The dossiers were submitted to the Ecuadorean police together with long memoranda prepared by the chief BSC/SOE agent, suggesting that the Germans had taken an active part against Ecuador in the disastrous Peruvian invasion. It was shown that employees of the German airline *Sedta* had made strategic photographs of the province of El Oro, and had passed these to the Peruvians; that two Germans deported in April 1942 had owned a ranch on the invasion route and had guided the Peruvian troops; and that one of these two was still in the country. He was Wolfgang Schmidt Hagius, nephew of von Papen and son of a colonel in the Kaiser's Army.

Meanwhile agents arranged an extensive newspaper campaign to arouse public feeling against the Germans and to encourage official action. Colonel Filemon Borja, who owned the pro-Allied newspaper *La Defensa*, was supplied with details of the German organization in Ecuador and with photographs stolen from the German Embassy. One of these showed the German Minister standing dutifully in line with a group of Nazis, listening to a speech by Walter Giese, the former *Landesgruppenleiter* for Ecuador. *La Defensa* brought out a special edition featuring the photographs, which were subsequently reproduced in all the important newspapers in the country, together with many articles and editorials on the subject. While the press campaign was in full swing, the famous Ecuadorean musician, Belisario Peña, returned to the country after spending three years in Germany, where he had regularly broadcast news and propaganda to South America for DNB. On the day he arrived, agents arranged for an open letter to him to be published in several newspapers. This gave details of his work for Germany and asked if he had returned to Ecuador to continue subversive activities for the Nazis. It proved an effective silencer.

But the Germans were not interned, and as time went on it became obvious that someone of considerable influence was working in their behalf. Eventually BSC/SOE discovered the source of the trouble.

Rafael Pino y Roca was the President's brother-in-law. He was an Ecuadorean citizen of good family, but ardently pro-German. He had been First Secretary and Chargé d'Affaires in Berlin for some years, had returned to become president of *Sedta*, and had managed, through his connection with the President, to delay the closure of that German airline for some time. Now he was using his influence with the President to save the Germans from internment and, through Nazi agents, was distributing anti-Allied propaganda.

It was agreed that efforts should be made to discredit Pino and to expose his pro-German activities. BSC/SOE, through their agents in the Post Office, obtained possession of a letter written by Ernst Panze, an important Nazi in Ecuador. In it he praised Pino y Roca for the assistance he had given to the German cause and suggested that Berlin should give him a subsidy of 1,500 sucres (about £30) a month, or, alternatively, capital up to 200,000 sucres (£3,800) to be invested in a business under German control. This was damaging information. Confirmation was obtained as a result of intercepting two letters which revealed that the chief of the secret police in Guayaquil, Manuel Carbo Paredes, was in the pay of the Germans. Owing to his senior position, he had always been informed of any new recommendation for internment or deportation. It was learned that he passed the news to the Germans, who, in turn, requested Pino y Roca to intervene with the President.

At this time, President Arroyo del Rio was about to visit Washington on one of those 'good neighbour' trips which were usually punctuated with banquets and oratory and culminated in loans from the Export-Import Bank. The intercepted letters were therefore passed to the US Embassy, which sent them to Washington by special courier so that they could be discussed with Arroyo during his visit. Copies were sent by HM Minister to the British Embassy in Washington. HM Minister pointed out how dangerous it was that an important police official in Guayaquil

– through which all British balsa supplies passed – should be in German pay.

It is not known whether or not the Americans mentioned the letters to Arroyo. It is quite possible that they did not, for inasmuch as the letters had been taken out of the President's own Post Office by his own officials for the account of a British agent, their source was extremely delicate. It is certain, however, that thenceforward the Ecuadorean Government began to exert more pressure on the remaining Germans. As a result of a BSC/SOE recommendation, which stressed the danger of sabotage, a number of the most dangerous Nazis were ordered to leave the coast and take up residence far in the interior of the country at points not touched by any railway.

In December 1942, a decree providing for the expropriation of their property was passed to the Finance Minister, who approved it. But when the President refused to sign it, the chief BSC/SOE representative decided to take action. He learned that the main reason which the President had given for rejecting the decree was that the liquidation of Axis firms would throw many Ecuadoreans out of work, lead to serious labour trouble, and increase anti-governmental feeling at the coming Workers' Congress. The representative therefore got in touch, through a cut-out, with the trade union leaders and induced them to propose a resolution at the Workers' Congress urging the Government to confiscate all property belonging to Axis nationals. The national economy, he said, would benefit, since firms which were then working with reduced staffs and a small turnover would recover and prosper as soon as they were taken over by friendly owners.

When the Workers' Congress met, the resolution was passed, and through press contacts, BSC/SOE agents gave it wide publicity. Thus the ground was cut from under the President's feet. The decree for expropriation came up for discussion at the next Cabinet meeting. On 11 June 1943, it became law. Pino y Roca, possibly because of BSC/SOE's exposure of his German contacts, was unable to exert sufficient influence to save his Axis friends. The total loss inflicted on the Germans amounted to about two million US dollars.

(b) Proposed Declaration of War

In April 1943, BSC received a directive from HM Embassy in Washington. Acting upon this directive, it instructed its chief representative in Ecuador to endeavour to induce the Ecuadoreans to declare war on Germany. Influential politicians were at once approached and an argument was used which could not but appeal to the Ecuadoreans. It was pointed out to them that, should Ecuador become one of the United Nations, she need have no further fear of another Peruvian invasion, because an attack on one of the United Nations would be regarded as an attack on them all, so that two other republics, Brazil and Bolivia, not to mention Great Britain and the United States, would be bound to come to her aid. The argument appealed strongly to the Minister of War, the Minister of the Interior, and General Astudillo, the Commander-in-Chief. The Ministry of War wrote officially to the Ministry of Foreign Affairs recommending a declaration of war. The Foreign Ministry called a meeting of its advisory council to consider the proposal, and a majority of the councillors were reported to be ready to support it.

At this stage, the US Chargé d'Affaires suddenly intervened. He assured the Foreign Ministry that there was absolutely no danger of a Peruvian attack, and the whole proposal was quashed. His action was surprising, particularly because he had previously been advised of BSC/SOE's plan and had approved of it, but apparently the US State Department had instructed its representatives not to encourage isolated declarations of war by South American republics. BSC/New York, upon referring the matter to London, was informed that the Foreign Office considered that the original directive from Washington must have been an error.

CHAPTER 6

Miscellaneous Operations

(a) Mexico, Cuba and the Central American Republics
(b) Venezuela
(c) Peru
(d) Uruguay
(e) Paraguay and Bolivia

When the SOE organization in Latin America was first formed, the danger to the whole sub-continent was so apparent that it was not possible to forecast accurately what the opportunities and necessity for action in individual countries would eventually prove to be. Consequently, the original coverage was complete, and it was only on the basis of first-hand experience that modifications were subsequently made.

(a) Mexico, Cuba and the Central American Republics

In Mexico, Cuba and the Central American republics the BSC/SOE representation was planned upon the assumption that the United States would remain neutral. Early in 1941 it appeared likely that the whole area from Mexico to Panama would be overrun by Axis agents, Axis diplomats, propagandists and businessmen. After Pearl Harbor, however, the Central American and Caribbean republics declared war; the Costa Ricans actually boasted of 'being in the war' before the United States, while Mexico broke off diplomatic relations and declared war five months later. All of them set about interning Germans and Japanese, closing down Axis propaganda media, and expropriating Axis properties, and meanwhile they were brought into the growing system of hemispheric defence set up by the United States. Admittedly, the restrictions on Axis nationals were often evaded, but as much pressure as could be borne was exerted by US representatives.

The original task of BSC/SOE agents was to make lists of all strategic targets, and after this had been fulfilled, the need for a Special Operations organization gradually disappeared. The representative in Cuba, who had been doing some useful covert propaganda, was withdrawn in the summer of 1942. In Mexico the chief representative confined his activities to propaganda campaigns, of which one deserves especial mention. A beautiful German actress named Hilde Krueger arrived in the United States from Norway in September 1939 and proceeded to Mexico in 1941. There she became the mistress of several influential men, including Miguel Alemán, the Minister of the Interior. She appeared to be a high-level propagandist rather than an espionage agent, and she used her influence to obtain privileges for Germans in Mexico. In February 1942, the BSC/SOE representative arranged a press campaign against her and other members of the Fifth Column, which occupied the headlines of *La Prensa*, the most influential paper in Mexico, for five days. As a result, she was arrested. Although she apparently fascinated the President's brother and other Ministers so greatly that she escaped imprisonment, she was discredited, and her operations could no longer be of use to her German friends.

(b) Venezuela

Venezuela, rich, backward and still dazed by a generation of tyranny under Gómez, presented few problems. Her oilfields represented one of the most important targets in the Western Hemisphere, but they were adequately defended by US forces. The populace was too ignorant and timid to be receptive to Axis propaganda nor would it have provided good material for a resistance movement. There was a strong and moderately pro-Allied government, with a first-class secret police. The most important aspect of German influence was German business, particularly drug companies, some of which had been founded more than a hundred years ago. The Economic Section of BSC, in conjunction with MEW, was responsible for ousting these.

As a result, there was not a great deal of work for BSC/SOE agents to do. The chief agent had a long acquaintance with the country and kept careful watch for signs of any uprising or disturbance which might constitute a danger to the Allied cause. He assured New York that Venezuela was comparatively safe except from seaborne or airborne attack. He kept in close touch with several 'free' organizations which supplied him with good information on suspect individuals and movements. The most useful of these was a group of Basque republicans, with whose help he arranged the penetration of the Spanish Embassy, which is described elsewhere (see Part IV).

A comprehensive rumour organization was run by agents in Venezuela. In particular, it was utilized for directing specific rumours to Spain for circulation there amongst German groups. Agents arranged for their Basque friends to include the rumours in letters addressed to defunct sports clubs and social organizations in various Spanish towns, where they were circulated by ex-members of these clubs who had been forewarned.

Although, as has been said, there was little German activity in the country, the Standard Oil Company, even after Pearl Harbor, continued to employ a number of Germans. BSC/SOE agents instituted a whispering campaign against them which failed. They then arranged, through their press contacts, for the publication of an editorial in a leading newspaper which suggested that the Government should investigate what was obviously a potentially dangerous situation. Simultaneously an even more vociferous attack was arranged through the left-wing press, and within a few days the Standard Oil Company was persuaded to dismiss its German employees.

(c) Peru

It has already been said that the BSC/SOE organization was better equipped in Peru to prepare for the possibility of an Axis invasion than in any other country of Latin America. And this was true. Yet, as events developed, what was originally the chief representative's main source of strength became a source of weakness.

Peru is one of the most troubled countries in the sub-continent, with an unstable economy, an exceptionally corrupt governing clique, and a working class which is partly represented by a savagely suppressed popular party, the *Alianza Popular Revolucionaria Americana* or *Apra*. Agents, in the early days, maintained close contact with the leader of *Apra*, Victor Raul Haya de la Torre, since his party would have been the only hope of organizing resistance to a Japanese invasion. A reasonable subsidy was paid to Haya in order that he might be able, despite governmental persecution, to keep his party in existence until the danger of an Axis attack had passed.

However it gradually became apparent that as a source of intelligence the *Apra* party was wildly unreliable. It was interested only in discrediting the Prado Government, and it tried to do this by inventing stories of dangers with which the Government would be unable to cope and circulating political canards with the avowed objective of breaking down the 'complacency of the democracies'. Consequently when the Japanese threat receded, there seemed no purpose in maintaining a separate BSC/SOE organization in Peru, and it was closed down.

To guard against a sudden renewal of the emergency, contact with *Apra* was maintained by the BSC/SOE representatives in neighbouring Chile who took onto their payroll Manuel Seoane, an Aprista exile high in the councils of the party. Unknown to him, all his correspondence with Haya de la Torre was copied.

(d) Uruguay

It was found that in Uruguay the people were already sympathetic with the Allied cause and anti-Axis movements were spontaneous. Accordingly, there was little scope for Special Operations. Two specific undertakings may be mentioned, however, as characteristic of the work which the BSC/SOE chief representative performed. The first was carried out in October 1941, when London cabled BSC:

> In order to arrange for interception of certain French vessels we need private code of *Compagnie de Navigation d'Orbigny* ... This company has agents in ... Montevideo ... Messrs. Williams, Calle Solis, Montevideo ... Please do utmost to secure copy ...

BSC/New York cabled its representative in Montevideo, who replied in a few days saying that, through an agent, he had obtained the required code. Its 150 pages were duly photostatted and sent to New York by courier.

The second operation was carried out in August 1942. There was in Uruguay a powerful broadcasting station, *Radio Continental*, which broadcast Axis propaganda to Uruguay, Argentina, Southern Brazil and other countries. It was blacklisted both by Great Britain and the USA, but nevertheless survived with the help of the German industrial union in Argentina.

In August 1942, a BSC/SOE agent completely destroyed it with especially prepared explosives. Because of war conditions, it was impossible to replace the equipment or reconstruct the building. Insurance was carried by a German company in Argentina which refused to pay the policy, because a story was fostered – and it was generally believed – that the owner had himself destroyed the building.

(e) Paraguay and Bolivia

Paraguay remained quiescent throughout the war and offered no scope for action. Bolivia required little attention after Pearl Harbor and the BSC/SOE representation there was withdrawn in June 1942. However, it happened before Pearl Harbor that Bolivia was the central point of one of the most important of all the special operations which BSC undertook in Latin America. That story is related in the next chapter.

CHAPTER 7

The Belmonte Letter

In May 1941, just five months before the discovery of the German map of South America, WS was given a message by J. Edgar Hoover. Hoover said that Major Elías Belmonte, who was Bolivia's violently pro-Nazi Military Attaché in Berlin, was believed to be planning a *coup d'état* to overthrow the pro-British Bolivian Government and to set up a pro-Axis dictatorship. Hoover added that President Roosevelt was most anxious that the evidence confirming this report should be obtained and passed to him with the utmost dispatch.

A BSC agent was rushed to La Paz to investigate, and a message from him to BSC in New York substantiated the information already received. It appeared that Major Belmonte in Berlin had been corresponding with the Bolivian Chief of Staff. The Bolivian Government itself had wind of the affair and was genuinely afraid that the projected *coup d'état* would-be attempted. On 18 May, more news came to BSC. There seemed to be reason for believing that the actual plans for the revolution were at that very moment on their way over to Bolivia by air in the German diplomatic bag addressed to the German Legation in La Paz. Diplomatic bags travelled on the Lati planes. The first point of call in the west for these aircraft was Recife, on the bulge of Brazil. BSC telegraphed its agent in Recife:

> Believed that incriminating documents of the highest importance are now on way from Berlin to La Paz by German diplomatic bag on Lati plane . . . These documents must repeat must be purloined at Recife . . . If you have reason think plane has already arrived and documents have gone out of your reach . . . cable urgently so as permit intervention elsewhere . . . Success of this operation is of utmost importance . . .

In Recife plans were made. One Lati plane arrived but it carried no passengers and no diplomatic bags. Then another and another, but there were no suspicious passengers nor were there any diplomatic bags aboard them.

For three weeks, agents in Latin America watched and searched for any clues which might assist in uncovering the German/Bolivian plans. Then suddenly, on 18 June, came a report from Rio de Janeiro. The report concerned one Fritz Fenthol whom BSC agents had been watching carefully ever since his arrival in Rio from Europe two months before (see Part III). He was suspected of being a German of great importance, and a girl secretary had already been planted on him in order to ascertain the object of his mission. Rio's report to New York stated that Fenthol had left for Buenos Aires by air, accompanied by a number of other Germans, and that he planned to proceed to Bolivia from Buenos Aires. Furthermore, the girl secretary had seen in his possession, the day before he left, an envelope addressed to the German Minister at La Paz. She had been unable to lay her hands on it.

This was important information. It was essential to obtain the envelope, for it might well contain the plans for the Bolivian revolution, Fenthol having possibly slipped into Brazil with them in April, just before BSC had received its first news of the plot and had begun to lay its plans for interception at Recife.

Fenthol arrived in Buenos Aires, where an agent, taking his time and judging his moment, successfully deprived him of the letter whilst he stood next to him in an over-crowded lift in the German Bank building. Fenthol was on his way up to the German Embassy, which was on the sixth floor of the building.

The letter was indeed from Major Belmonte in Berlin, and was addressed to Dr Ernst Wendler, German Minister at La Paz. It was taken at once by courier to New York where WS received it on 2 July. A photograph of it appears opposite and on the following page. Here is a translation:

> I am pleased to acknowledge receipt of your interesting letter in which you tell me of the actions which you and your personnel in the Legation and our Bolivian civil and military friends are taking in my country with so much success.
>
> Friends in the Wilhelmstrasse tell me that from information received from you, the moment is approaching to strike in order to liberate my poor country from a weak government and from completely capitalist tendencies. I go

CORREO AÉREO

**LEGACION DE BOLIVIA
EN
ALEMANIA**

BERLIN, 9 Junio de 1941

Al Excmo. Señor Doctor Ernst Wendler
Ministro de Alemania
La Paz

Estimado señor y amigo,

Tengo el agrado de acusar recibo de su interesante carta en la que me comunica de las gestiones que Ud. y su personal en la Legación, y nuestros amigos civiles y militares bolivianos llevan a cabo en mi país con tanto exito.

Me informan los amigos de Wilhelmstrasse que por informaciones recibidos de Ud. se acerca el momento de dar nuestro golpe para librar a mi pobre país de un gobierno debil y de inclinaciones completamente capitalistas. Yo voy más allá, y creo que el golpe debe fijarse para mediados de Julio pues considero el momento propicio. Y repito que el momento es propicio pues por sus informaciones al Ministerio de Relaciones en Berlin, veo con agrado que todos los Consules y amigos en toda la Republica de Bolivia, y especialmente en nuestros centros mas amigos, como Cochabamba, Santa Cruz y el Beni, han preparado el ambiente y han organizado nuestras fuerzas con habilidad y energía.

No cabe duda que tendremos que concentrar nuestras fuerzas en Cochabamba ya que siempre se ha prestado preferente atención a este punto. Sé por algunos amigos mios que se siguen reuniendo sin molestia alguna de las autoridades y que se siguen haciendo los ejercicios nocturnos. Más, veo que se han acumulado buenas cantidades de bicicletas lo que facilitara nuestros movimientos de noche ya que autos y camiones son demasiado bulliciosos. Por eso creo que durante las proximas semanas se debe obrar con muchisimo mas cuidado que anteriormente para despistar toda clase de sospecha. Deben evitarse las reuniones y las instrucciones se deben dar de persona en persona, en lugar de darlas en reuniones. Naturalmente que la entrega inicua de la LAB al imperialismo Yankee es un inconveniente ya que yo pensaba tomar control de esta organizacion inmediatamente a mi llegada a la frontera del Brazil, pero esto lo salvaré con los amigos aquí pues mi vuelo lo haré acompañado por otro avion que me seguirá todo el camino. Hemos recibido los planos detallados y mejorados de los lugares de aterrizaje mas convenientes. Este me hace ver, una vez más, que Ud. y su personal realizan un trabajo gigantesco para la realización de nuestro plan, todo en bien

First page of the Belmonte Letter, which
BSC purloined from a German agent.

CORREO AÉREO

LEGACION DE BOLIVIA
EN
ALEMANIA

BERLIN

No.
Asunto:

2.

Al Excmo. Doctor Ernst Wendler

de Bolivia. Tomo especial nota de lo que me escribe Ud. referente al elemento joven de ejercito. Efectivamente yo siempre he contado con ellos y seran ellos, sin duda, los que mejor me cooperarán en la magna obra que llevaremos a cabo en mi patria.

Como le digo mas arriba, es necesario que obremos con rapidez pues el momento es oportuno. Hay que deshacer el contrato del Wolfram con Estados Unidos y anular ó, en ultimo caso, modificar substancialmente, los contratos de Estaño con Inglaterra y Estados Unidos. La entrega de nuestras lineas aereas a los intereses de Wall Street es una traición a la patria. En cuanto a la Standard Oil que tanta actividad demuestra para una solución "honorable" para "restaurar el credito de Bolivia", esto es criminal. Desde mi corta estadía en el Ministerio de Gobierno vengo combatiendo esto. Que afan de entregar al pais a Estados Unidos so pretexto de ayuda financiera que nunca vendra. Me irrita! Estados Unidos seguirá su politica de antaño: conseguir grandes ventajas a cambio de pequeños emprestitos ni siquiera se nos permitirá manejarlos. Bolivia no necesita emprestitos americanos. Con el triunfo del Reich, Bolivia necesita trabajo y disciplina. Debemos copiar, aunque sea modestamente, el grandioso ejemplo de Alemania desde que asumió el poder el Nacional-Socialismo.

Ese famoso Tratado de Ostria
un verdadero crimen. Una vez
este sera una

Al Excmo. Doctor Ernst Wendler

fin, con un solo ideal y con un solo Jefe Supremo, salvaremos el porvenir de Sud America y comenzaremos, repito, una era de depuracion, orden y trabajo.

Hasta muy pronto, Señor Ministro.

Elías Belmonte P.

much further and believe that the coup should take place in the middle of July since I consider the moment to be propitious. I repeat that the moment is propitious since from your information given to the Foreign Office in Berlin I see with pleasure that all Consuls and friends in the whole Republic of Bolivia, and expecially in the centres which are most friendly to us such as Cochabamba and Santa Cruz, have prepared conditions and have organized our forces with skill and energy.

There can be no doubt that we shall have to concentrate our forces in Cochabamba since preference has always been given to this point. I know from some friends of mine that meetings are being held without being molested by the authorities and that there are nightly exercises. Further, I see that large quantities of bicycles have piled up which will facilitate our movements by night since motorcars and trucks are too noisy. For this reason I think that during the next weeks we should operate with greater care than formerly in order to avoid any kind of suspicion. We should avoid meetings and instructions should be given personally by word of mouth and passed from person to person instead of any meetings. Naturally the iniquitous cession of the LAB to Yankee imperialism is a nuisance, just when I had thought of taking control of this organization immediately on my arrival on the Brazilian frontier. However, I shall be able to put this matter right with my friends since during my flight I shall be accompanied by another aeroplane which will follow me all the way. We have received detailed maps showing the best and most convenient landing places. This shows me once more that you and your people are putting into force a gigantic piece of work for the realization of our plan, all for the good of Bolivia. I take special note of what you write me regarding the younger elements in the army. Actually I have always counted on them and it will be they, without doubt, who will give me the greatest cooperation in the important work which we are carrying out in my country. As I have said above, it is necessary that we should act rapidly since the moment is opportune.

We must undo the wolfram contract with the United States and cancel it, also substantially modify the tin contracts with England and the United States. The handing over of our airlines to the interests of Wall Street is treason to our country. As for Standard Oil which shows so much activity in bringing about an 'honourable' solution to 'restore the credit of Bolivia' – this is criminal. Since my short time in the government I have been fighting against this. Why hand over the country to the United States on the pretext of financial aid which will never come? This irritates me! The United States will follow their age-long policy: to obtain great advantages in exchange for small loans, and even these loans we are not allowed to administer. Bolivia does not need American loans. With the triumph of the Reich, Bolivia needs work and discipline. We must copy, though on a modest scale, the great example of Germany since National Socialism came into power.

This celebrated treaty Ostria has made with Brazil is a real pride. Once we are in control of the situation this will be one of the first things which we shall change. Already the government, with the support of my good friend Foianini, did all that was possible for this treaty not to be concluded. It is clear that the famous 'defeatist' Chancellor Ostria is completely influenced by capitalism and if he had his way we would already be an American colony.

I hope that the last word will be my flight from here in order to complete the work which will save Bolivia in the first place, and afterwards the whole South American continent, from North American influence. The other countries will quickly follow our example and then with one sole ideal and one sole supreme leader, we will save the future of South America and will begin an era of purification, order and work.

On 3 July WS cabled SOE in London:

On May 6th I was informed by the US authorities that certain documents were reported to be in transit from Bolivian Military Attaché, Berlin, to Bolivia . . . that President Roosevelt *most anxious* that these documents should be intercepted and passed to him with utmost dispatch . . . Immediate steps were taken . . . and as a result . . . document is today in my hands . . . US authorities are aware that some document was intercepted and are expressing anxiety that no time should be lost in passing it on to them if of interest . . . Summary of the letter is cabled separately . . . Cable most urgently approval hand over letter . . .

To which London replied:

The Belmonte Letter

> We agree US authorities should be given full details . . . Grateful if you would telegraph me full text of dispatch . . . most urgently required here by highest authorities . . .

And three days later London telegraphed again saying:

> We feel that Bolivian Government should be warned as soon as possible so that it may suppress coup if and when it takes place . . . We suggest you discuss matter frankly with US authorities and let them take action if they want . . . In any case absolutely essential warning should be conveyed through some channel with least possible delay . . .

WS handed the letter to J. Edgar Hoover, who was as gratified as he was surprised to receive it. He passed it at once to Secretary of State Cordell Hull, and Hull lost no time in informing the Bolivian Government of the whole matter.

The repercussions, felt throughout Bolivia, were spectacular:

1. On 19 July 1941, Wendler, the German Minister to Bolivia, was declared *persona non grata* and ordered out of the country. The Bolivian Chargé d'Affaires in Berlin was given seventy-two hours to leave Germany.
2. The manager of Bolivian Air Lloyd, the Transocean correspondent, and five other prominent Germans in Bolivia were arrested. The police searched the big commercial house of Sikinger, found a clandestine radio and lists of addresses for Axis propaganda and arrested the woman operator and several German accomplices.
3. The pro-Axis party, the *Movimiento Nacionalista Revolucionario*, or MNR, was temporarily broken up. Its leaders, Victor Paz Estenssoro, Armando Arce, Augusto Céspedes and Carlos Montenegro, all prominent in the 1943 revolution, were arrested. Four anti-Allied and anti-US newspapers connected with it were suspended. The US State Department sent photostat copies of the letter to Bolivia, where they were published in the local papers in order to justify the Government's action.
4. The Bolivian Ministry of the Interior announced the discovery of another 'non-Nazi and entirely military plot'. Thirty officers, including the chief of the Cochabamba military zone (on whom Belmonte relied, according to his letter) were arrested.

5. Extracts from the letter were published in the US press on 24 July and thereafter. It produced a profound effect upon the people, many of whom saw and understood for the first time that the Nazis really had plans for world domination.
6. The State Department assured Bolivia of full assistance from the US in case the expulsion of the German Minister should lead to any international incident.
7. Belmonte was struck off the Bolivian Army list. For some time he was broadcasting from Berlin to South America. In the summer of 1942 he arrived in Lisbon in an effort to get back to Bolivia, but was stopped by the joint action of British and US authorities, under impulse from BSC. Later, it was learned through secret channels that he had become a paid German agent and was in correspondence with his supporters in Bolivia. After the Bolivian revolution in December 1943, the new Government, including President Villarroel, almost certainly decided that Belmonte would be too dangerous a rival to bring home. His house in Berlin was incidentally destroyed during an air raid, and by last reports he was poor, though still proud. In August 1944, diplomatic correspondence intercepted by the Americans showed that his half-brother Ruben Sardon Pabón had asked Villarroel to permit him to return to Bolivia or to Spain.

Thus the discovery of the Belmonte Letter – three sheets of typed notepaper which changed hands in a crowded lift in a Buenos Aires building – probably averted a revolution, certainly expelled a Minister, caused the arrest of many dangerous men and at the same time considerably embarrassed the isolationist factions in the United States. Most important of all, it afforded President Roosevelt another sound argument with which to persuade the American people that they must make ready for war.

Conclusion

Such, briefly, was the story of BSC/SOE in Latin America. The story, as told, of the work done in each country, contains little detail; an effort has been made merely to draw a broad and general picture of the dangers which existed and the measures which were taken to offset them. The more spectacular operations took place, of course, before Pearl Harbor, and it may be said that they culminated in the Rio Conference of January 1942, for indirectly they all contributed to that end. Thereafter it was the task of the BSC/SOE organization to assist in exploiting and consolidating the advantages which resulted from the agreement reached at Rio.

The Intelligence and Planning Section in New York, under whose direction representatives worked, gathered together the information which came in from the field and supplemented it with intelligence from other sources. The section devised plans for each country and for Latin America as a whole, and advised upon the execution of concerted schemes. It built up comprehensive records which included background reports on the history, geography and military resources of each republic, biographies of practically every man of power in Latin America and analyses of the many political changes which took place in the various republics.

Thus BSC was enabled to make predictions with accuracy and regularity, and these it sent not only to SOE/London but, on occasion, to the Chiefs of Staff, to the Embassy in Washington and to the FBI in Washington. The FBI stated that in this way they received much information which was not available to them from their own sources. In fact, the BSC/SOE organization was responsible for approximately 90% of the high-grade British intelligence which came out of South America, although collection of intelligence was, of course, incidental to its main purpose.

Special Operations in Latin America

That this was so is undoubtedly due to the fact that no representative was appointed who did not already possess valuable contacts in the particular country to which he was assigned. The majority of representatives were, like the CSOs and the ISOs of BSC's Security Organization (see Part V), locally recruited and in private life had occupied responsible executive positions in British firms. All were chosen both on account of their natural aptitude for SOE work and because they were particularly fitted by previous experience to undertake it in Latin America. They were especially trained at the BSC school in Canada (see Part VIII), but although this was necessary no amount of training would have been substitute for the initial advantage which they possessed by reason of being already familiar with the political complexities and key personalities of the countries in which they would operate. It is, perhaps, a tribute to their quality that British connection with the activities described in the foregoing pages was not uncovered in a single instance.

PART VII

COUNTER-ESPIONAGE

CHAPTER 1

Purposes and Methods

(a) Early Collaboration with FBI
(b) Establishment of Counter-Espionage Section

(a) Early Collaboration with FBI

One of the best results of collaboration between WS and J. Edgar Hoover (see Part I) was in the field of counter-espionage. While the value of this did not become fully apparent until after the United States entered the war, BSC began early on to provide the FBI with material from its various sources – in particular correspondence intercepted and studied by Imperial Postal and Telegraph Censorship stations in Bermuda, Trinidad and Jamaica, without which the FBI would have been severely handicapped, for there was no postal censorship in the United States and, if the FBI wished to secure for themselves a letter addressed to a particular suspect, they had no other recourse than to purloin it from the post office.

For their successful prosecution of several espionage cases during 1940 and 1941 the FBI owed obligation to BSC. They reciprocated generously by making available to BSC details of their counter-espionage work carried out independently. Two typical instances will serve to illustrate this.

William G. Sebold was a naturalized American citizen of German birth. In 1939, he was in his native land and was approached by the German Intelligence Service with a request to act as an agent in the United States. He feigned agreement, and was fully trained in all aspects of espionage activity, including code and cypher work, radio transmission and microphotography. But he remained loyal to the country of his adoption, and kept the American Embassy fully informed of what was afoot. They instructed him to act as a double agent, and thus it happened that after his return to the United States, the FBI used him as a means to bring about the apprehension of numerous German agents. Under their direction he contacted the members of the German espionage ring with which he was associated, set up a radio station on Long Island and continued to send messages to Germany by wireless and other means until the FBI were satisfied that they had all the evidence necessary to bring the case to a successful conclusion.

In June and July of 1941 the arrests were made. At the trial which followed Sebold was the chief government witness, and the thirty-three accused included:

> Frederick Joubert Duquesne, who had a long record of espionage activity, particularly against Britain; he was one of the central figures.
> Axel Wheeler-Hill, a brother of a Bund leader from New York who had had a wireless transmitting set of his own.
> Herman Lang, an inspector of the Norden factory who had sold the Norden Bombsight to Germany;
> Conradin Otto Dold, Erwin Wilhelm Siegler and Franz Josef Stigler, German seamen on transatlantic ships, who had acted as couriers and had collected shipping news.

Nineteen of the accused pled guilty before or during the trial, and fourteen were found guilty. They were sentenced to long terms of imprisonment.

The case was obviously of major concern to BSC, and since many of those convicted had previously been known as good German-Americans, it did much to undermine the position of pro-German societies in the United States, which was one of BSC's principal objectives. The credit for it, however, belonged exclusively to the FBI who had conducted it without any outside assistance and had every reason to be proud of their achievement. But, despite the fact they were under no direct obligation to do so, they went out of their way to share knowledge they had gained with their British colleagues. They passed BSC a full transcript of the evidence and subsequently supplied written answers to questions based on this which were drawn up by SIS/London. In result much was learned both about enemy espionage in the United States and about American methods of countering it. The transcript revealed that all the convicted agents had been controlled by Hamburg, and for their communications had used not only short-wave radio and airmail letters but microphotographs, reduced to the size of small dots which could easily be concealed by couriers or in letters. Moreover, it contained evidence of all their transactions in the United States, even down to films of interviews between Sebold and his dupes, the numbers of the banknotes Sebold had paid out and copies of all the documents he had received from other agents.

The second instance concerns a case of a rather different kind and belongs to an even earlier period.

On 16 June 1940, one Herbert Hoehne arrived in San Francisco from Japan. He described himself as a Bayer commercial agent, but he was really a courier taking codes and confidential instructions to German Legations in South America. Two days later a certain Emil Wolff transited San Francisco on a Japanese ship. He had a similar mission.

The FBI arrested Hoehne in Los Angeles as he was leaving for Mexico and Wolff when he reached the Panama Canal Zone, both on the ground that they were acting as agents of a foreign government without registration.

The documents they were carrying, including German codes, were seized and copies were handed to WS by Hoover without the knowledge of the US Naval and Military Intelligence who were then strongly opposed to passing such information to the British. The Germans, of course, learned that the documents had been seized, but being aware of the attitude of the US services, did not believe that the documents would fall into British hands.

Wolf pled guilty and was sentenced to a prison term. Hoehne's trial was dropped, ostensibly so that the FBI should not be compelled to disclose the result of their inspection of his documents, but in reality to avoid making things difficult for the British, whose couriers were often necessarily employed on similar missions, though they were likewise not registered as agents of a foreign government.

Before Pearl Harbor, the FBI were already considering the possibility of assuming responsibility for counter-espionage in Latin America as well as the United States. British censors used to intercept letters from young men signing themselves 'Al' or 'Steve' to post-office-box addresses in New York, giving apparently innocent surveys of social conditions and of Nazi activities in Paraguay, Bolivia and other South American states. These were, in fact, FBI intelligence reports sent by mail to avoid the eyes of the State Department. From its own sources BSC was able to supply the FBI with much additional information, and in this way collaboration with them in counter-espionage work in Latin America was begun well before the Rio Conference, as a result of which they were enabled to conduct large-scale operations on their own account.

(b) Establishment of Counter-Espionage Section

Before Pearl Harbor, BSC regarded counter-espionage work as subsidiary to its function of combating those activities, notably subversive propaganda, in which the enemy engaged for the purpose of defeating Britain by neutralizing the United States and which the American authorities were powerless to suppress on their own initiative while the United States remained at peace. After Pearl Harbor, when the enemy could no longer attack British interests without automatically attacking American interests *de jure* as well as *de facto* and, conversely, was obliged largely to abandon indirect in favour of direct methods to undermine American strength, the position was reversed. Espionage now represented one of the gravest threats to the common security of Great Britain and the United States and BSC, relieved of the necessity of taking independent action against enemy agents, was able to accept the conduct of counter-espionage, in collaboration with American intelligence agencies, as one of its major responsibilities.

Towards the end of 1941, CSS decided that, since counter-espionage work entailed technical understanding of certain specialized and scientific methods, separate sections should be formed to undertake it in all SIS stations abroad. Such a section was established within BSC at the very time of Pearl Harbor, and this was fortunate, for it enabled immediate advantage to be taken of the greatly increased opportunity for engagement in counter-espionage without detriment to other activities of the SI Division, such as the penetration of the Vichy Embassy, which were then in progress (see Part IV).

There was, however, never any question of setting up a field organization in the United States, for apart from the fact that the employment of agents would have been a violation of the McKellar Act, it was obvious that far better results could be achieved by working on a policy level through established liaison channels than by any belated attempt to proceed unilaterally on an operational level. The FBI had already proved themselves willing to cooperate, and so far as the United States was concerned BSC's counter-espionage responsibilities were now as follows:

1. To continue, as before, to furnish the FBI with information

from its various sources. The quantity of this information increased considerably after Pearl Harbor and as a result of it BSC was enabled to initiate or largely assist seventeen of the twenty major espionage cases brought to the US courts during the war. A few of these cases are related in detail in Chapter 3.

2. To persuade the FBI to adopt methods of procedure which SIS regarded as essential practice. This was not an easy task and, as BSC's counter-espionage section learned by experience, had to be undertaken with great tact, for the FBI, justly proud of their past achievements, were naturally inclined to resent any interference in their affairs by a foreign agency. Yet it was very necessary. The FBI were devoted to traditional police methods, brought up to date by lavish expenditure on laboratory and other technical equipment. These methods, though admirably suited to crime detection, were sometimes found to be quite inappropriate to the efficient conduct of counter-espionage. For example, before they had been taught otherwise, the FBI would, after securing sufficient evidence to convict a particular agent, hand over the case to the public prosecutor instead of pursuing it further with the object of identifying more of the accused man's sources of information, channels of communication, paymaster, accomplices, methods of training and so forth. Or again, they would permit revelation in open court of secret sources which had to be protected if their usefulness was to continue.

3. To assist the FBI toward the active deception of the enemy through double agents, which in the British view, was the ultimate purpose of counter-espionage. The story of this work is related in Chapter 4.

BSC's counter-espionage section maintained close liaison with the RCMP in Canada, and was also concerned to ensure the maximum collaboration between the FBI and SIS in Latin America. SIS field stations throughout Latin America were under WS's administrative control between June 1942 and March 1943, and WS continued thereafter to direct the counter-espionage activities of stations in Central America. All SIS counter-espionage officers in Latin America sent copies of their reports and telegrams to BSC, and thus BSC was enabled to discuss problems of common interest with FBI headquarters and to plan future action conjointly.

Counter-Espionage

While the Western Hemisphere was the centre of BSC's activities, its responsibilities did not end there. OSS were authorized to conduct all American counter-espionage in the field outside the Western Hemisphere, and BSC had much initial concern with their plans for implementing this. The very close working relationship which developed between the counter-espionage divisions of SIS and OSS has been described elsewhere (see Part I), and it represented fulfilment of one of WS's chief purposes. London latterly became the centre of Anglo-American exchange of information and policy discussions relating to counter-espionage in Europe, but even so BSC's counter-espionage section continued to maintain day-to-day liaison with OSS headquarters. Likewise, it maintained liaison with the Army's G-2 and the Navy's ONI, who together controlled sources of information vital to the conduct of counter-espionage throughout the world and were the only US agencies with any knowledge of value concerning the Japanese Intelligence Service. Some months before the war ended a special unit was established in Washington under BSC's auspices to undertake a general study of the Japanese Intelligence Service in collaboration with G-2 and ONI. Its work is described in Chapter 5, which relates the story of BSC's concern with Far Eastern counter-espionage.

CHAPTER 2

Sources of Information

(a) Information from Censorship
(b) Clandestine Wireless Traffic

SIS had informants within many enemy organizations in occupied and neutral European countries. From these sources BSC sometimes learned that an agent was already operating in the Western Hemisphere or was being sent out to the Western Hemisphere, and thus was able to initiate investigation through its liaison channels – through the FBI or through its own representatives at Bermuda or Trinidad or through SIS stations in Latin America or through Canadian counter-espionage authorities.

But direct penetration of enemy organizations by SIS stations in Europe, though it proved of considerable assistance in a number of instances, did not represent BSC's chief source of information. The majority of espionage cases with which BSC was concerned flowed, as it were, from the very close watch which was kept on the enemy's means of communication. And the enemy's means of communication were, broadly speaking, of two main kinds – secret messages sent through the mail and clandestine wireless transmissions.

(a) Information from Censorship

Between enemy agents and censorship there was a continuing battle of wits. In addition to a variety of secret inks, some of which were known from the 1914–18 war, the Germans developed an entirely new method of concealing illicit messages which, though not impossible to detect, was certainly more ingenious and represented a greater potential menace to the effectiveness of censorship control than any means of avoidance hitherto employed. Hypermicrophotographs, each containing a page of typewriting shrunk down to the size of a single full stop, were concealed in letters which had otherwise all the appearance of innocence. The dots could be read under a 200-power microscope, with which several agents were supplied in portable form. To prepare them, however, an elaborate and non-portable apparatus was required.

British censors nicknamed the hypermicrophotographic method of communication 'Duff', because the dots were usually scattered sparsely through the letter like the currants in plumduff, although they were sometimes found under the stamp, or within the false back or on the flap of an envelope.

'Duff' could obviously not be detected by any cursory examination, and unless censorship had some original cause for suspicion it would inevitably slip by unnoticed. The same principle applied, though to a lesser extent, to secret inks and even plain language codes. Thus it was essential that censorship should be kept apprised by counter-espionage organizations of any information – for example addresses of known intermediaries – which would help it to determine the categories of correspondence to which especial attention should be paid.

BSC always maintained a very close liaison with Imperial Censorship through the latter's Assistant Director for the Western Hemisphere, with results which led to the apprehension or identification of many enemy agents whose activities might otherwise have remained uncovered.

From the counter-espionage point of view, Bermuda was undoubtedly the most productive of the various censorship stations in the Western Hemisphere, which was gratifying, for its very existence represented something of a gamble. Indeed the decision to establish it in the early days of the war was taken with grave misgivings, and afterwards there were several strong protests from Americans whose mail was delayed or censored by it.

However its success was overwhelming, and the FBI were given so much invaluable material from it that they never supported the protests with their authority. Bermuda's laboratory for developing secret inks was the admiration of the FBI and all American censors. Its specialists were the latter's instructors in a most difficult technique.

It was BSC's task not only to foster the productiveness of censorship sources but to utilize the information which flowed therefrom to the best advantage within its power. Not infrequently such information provided a lead to enemy activities in Latin America, and BSC was then able to maintain a certain measure of control over the investigations which it initiated through the relevant SIS station. In the United States, the procedure was usually of the following kind.

Censorship specialists at Trinidad or Bermuda – sometimes as a result of being specially alerted – would develop and read a secret message sent by mail from a German agent in the United States to an addressee in Europe. Pertinent details would be added from censorship records, and the whole passed to BSC.

After coordinating the information – and this would include making inquiries of headquarters and of the relevant SIS stations in Europe concerning the addressee – BSC would pass it on to the FBI, whose task it would then be to find the agent, put him under surveillance and to build up a sufficiently good case against him to bring him to trial.

The FBI's success in such instances was usually had by the application of two highly scientific methods. The first was the identification of handwriting and typewriting. Its laboratory would produce composite cards showing ten or fifteen characteristic letters of the alphabet in the hand of the agent. With these it would scan thousands and thousands of documents in which the agent's script might occur, looking for a reappearance of the same characteristics.

The second method was the careful analysis of personal information derived from the letters of agents (and in this work BSC often assisted). An agent who sends a message to Europe in secret ink must try to conceal it by writing it on the back of a perfectly innocent letter. It is more difficult than might be supposed to write a sensible, innocent letter of small talk, without giving away some pertinent detail of private life. In secret messages, the task is no easier, and even the smallest fact unwittingly revealed can be made the basis of a long investigation. For example, a letter in secret ink from a German in Colombia mentioned that his radio had been confiscated. Accordingly the FBI asked the Ministry of Communications whose radios had been confiscated, learned that only two Germans had suffered in this way, examined their handwriting, and thus found the culprit.

However, it seldom happened that the FBI could succeed with only one secret message as a basis for investigation. The more messages that were intercepted, the greater the chance, obviously, of finding a really pertinent clue. Thus it was often of very great importance that an illicit channel of communication should be kept open, despite its potential menace, by giving the enemy no cause to suspect that it had been detected. That meant, in effect, authorizing censorship to release, rather than to condemn, secret messages in such a way that they would reach the enemy without apparent sign that they had been tampered with *en route*. Such authorization, as will be shown by specific illustrations in a later chapter, was often obtained only with the greatest difficulty and sometimes not at all. To persuade the Americans – particularly the American Service agencies – that censorship was not merely a security measure designed to block the leakage of valuable information to the enemy but, imaginatively handled, was a powerful weapon of counter-espionage proved one of the most formidable obstacles which BSC had to surmount.

(b) Clandestine Wireless Traffic

In the autumn of 1940, systematic monitoring of the short-wave wireless traffic passing between Germany and enemy espionage groups in Latin America was started by the Royal Corps of Signals, the Federal Communications Commission, the FBI and the US Coast Guard Service (see Part IX). SIS also had a monitoring station in Rio which was at the time the headquarters of the German Intelligence Service in Latin America. The messages were decoded by the National Research Council in Canada, and by the FBI and US Naval Intelligence in Washington.

In the autumn of 1941, on WS's instructions, an officer of BSC began to analyse this traffic, and a few months later produced a comprehensive report on the structure, methods and purpose of German espionage in Latin America. His work was continued after Pearl Harbor as a routine function of the counter-espionage section, with results which led to the identification of many agents and rings.

The word 'led' is used advisedly, for even in encyphered wireless traffic agents were referred to only by their cover names, and, as in the case of a secret message sent by mail, interception did not in itself provide a means of identification but merely a basis for inquiry. If it was learned, for example, that one 'López' would sail on the *Cabo de Hornos*, then arrangements would be made for all passengers on that ship to be carefully interrogated. Or again, if it was learned that a secret message would be sent from Mexico on a certain date, censorship would be warned to examine all mail posted on that date for secret ink and microphotographs. In such instances, of course, the leads were clear enough; but frequently they were very obscure.

(It is, perhaps, worth noting here that one mistake often made by both German and British Intelligence services was to choose a cover name closely resembling the agent's real name. The different techniques of the two services reveal a characteristic difference in national temperaments. The Germans would pick a cover-name which was either an English or Spanish version of the agent's real name, or a German distortion of it. For example, a spy signing himself Fred Lewis was really Fritz Lehmitz. '*Casero*' means housekeeper, and was the name for von Schultz Hausmann. One Enrique Luni was Heinrich Luning – although he had procured a brand-new Honduran passport and could have chosen any Spanish name. The saboteur Alfred Langbein was named Kurzhals – Shortneck instead of Longleg. W. Banco in Mexico turned out to be Werner Barke.

On the other hand, the British would occasionally choose a name which contained a jocular allusion to the agent's personality or habits. Von Kotze, who had come from South Africa and was trying to get back, was called Springbok. A certain Popov was contacted by the password Scoot! A man who had jumped suddenly into wealth and fame by a spectacular public feat was nicknamed Upstart. An agent called Mosquera became Minaret. And a double agent was called Tricycle because his special pastime was going to bed with two girls at the same time.

Aliases of this kind, however amusing, are dangerous. A good alias has nothing whatever to do with the agent who bears it; it is part of a completely new personality. A bad alias is a hint to the enemy.)

Now although information derived from German clandestine wireless traffic was potentially of very great value, the British believed that it should be employed only with extreme caution. The Americans, on the other hand, were inclined at one time to handle it with reckless disregard for the possible consequences; and this gave rise, shortly after Pearl Harbor, to a serious divergence of policy between British and American Intelligence agencies – a divergence which BSC was called upon to mend.

The principle laid down by SIS was that clandestine wireless traffic should be regarded as a Top Secret source and jealously guarded against possible compromise: in other words that no action should be taken that might give the enemy reason to suspect that his messages were being read, thus prompting him to adopt new cyphers which might take years to break, for some of the cyphers he used in transmission to the Western Hemisphere he used also in areas of far greater tactical importance. Accordingly distribution was severely limited, and in the early stages decyphered versions of South American traffic were not even made available by headquarters to SIS representatives in Latin America.

On the American side, however, the procedure was quite different. Enemy communications were being monitored and decyphered, not by one US agency alone but by several, and the results were not kept particularly secret. Such instances as their circulation by the State Department to the American Ambassador in Uruguay, by the War Department to the US Military Attaché in Venezuela, who handed them to the British Consul; and by the Navy Department to all US naval observers in Brazil came to BSC's attention. Worst case of all, the Associated Press in Rio sent material to its New York Office (as a background article for the files), which was entirely based on a decyphered message and quoted one sentence from it verbatim.

A somewhat belated agreement was reached at the Western Hemisphere Intelligence Conference in April 1942 that such information should be released only with the approval of the Chiefs of Staff. It was belated, because a month before the Brazilian police had arrested dozens of Germans who were connected with various espionage groups in Brazil and were known to BSC through analysis of decyphered German clandestine W/T messages. It seemed obvious that the Brazilian police would never have taken such a step without very strong evidence. It was learned subsequently that the American Ambassador had in fact presented the Brazilian Government with a note requesting the arrest of the German agents and the closure of their stations – a request which he supported with a memorandum naming names and quoting intercepted messages. During the interrogation of at least one suspect the Brazilian police read out the contents of several intercepts in full.

Similar incidents occurred in Chile and Argentina, and it was not until the Service Intelligence departments became convinced of the vital necessity of safeguarding Top Secret sources that American policy regarding their use fell into line with the British view.

Meanwhile the arrests in Brazil accelerated BSC's work on the analysis of intercepts and also pointed to the desirability of pooling results with the Americans, since it was clearly ridiculous to countenance two parallel lines of independent research. Accordingly a meeting with interested FBI officers was arranged in June of 1942, and thereafter a very close liaison was maintained which proved extremely productive.

Sources of Information

As the war progressed and the volume of decyphered clandestine W/T traffic increased, it was realized that BSC should have access not only to messages passing to and from South America but to inter-European messages which could be regarded as pertinent to the work of United States counter-espionage generally.

The negotiations which ensued to make such information available to the appropriate American agencies were long and involved. However they were eventually concluded by stationing at SIS headquarters representatives from G-2, ONI, OSS and the FBI, who had the task of picking out messages of interest to their particular service. After despatch had been approved, the messages came by direct line to BSC, which then assumed responsibility for distribution.

Counter-espionage within the Western Hemisphere was thereby considerably facilitated, for the FBI obtained not only advance notice of the despatch of various agents to the United States but evidence of the reactions of the German High Command to information sent by their double agents and to arrests made in the United States. For example, the traffic revealed every step taken by one Jean Marie Gavaillez (a German agent who was eventually arrested on 25 May 1945). The FBI were pre-warned of his departure from Paris to Madrid, of his sailing on the *Magallanes* to New Orleans, and even of the times at which he would transit.

Again, while no one would have been likely to suspect from the state of the European war that the Germans at the beginning of 1945 would be taking active steps to send agents to the United States, it was learned from their clandestine W/T messages that in January they had four agents and, even more remarkable, in February nine agents under consideration for despatch.

CHAPTER 3

Some Illustrations of Espionage in the Western Hemisphere

(a) The 'Joe K.' Case
(b) Unmasking of a German Sabotage Organization
(c) The 'Fred Lewis' Case
(d) The 'Rogers' Case
(e) The Kobbe Case
(f) The Pozzi Case
(g) The Mexican 'Dot' Case

In the following pages a few of the major espionage cases with which BSC was concerned in the Western Hemisphere are related in detail; a few only, because more would impose a disproportionate demand on space.

The task of making a representative selection has not been easy. It has, however, been undertaken with a view to choosing those cases which illustrate most clearly the variety of methods employed and the importance of Anglo-American cooperation in counter-espionage work which BSC strove to make as close as possible.

(a) The 'Joe K.' Case

At about 9 o'clock on a rainy March evening two men paused at the corner of 45th Street and 7th Avenue in New York City. One of them stepped off the kerb without waiting for the traffic lights and was struck by a passing taxi. His friend disappeared into the crowd that gathered. A harassed policeman picked up the fallen man's despatch case and took it to the hospital, where the man later died. There are many such accidents in New York and this one did not appear to differ from the others. But because of careful work that had already been done by BSC and by the FBI, it proved

Some Illustrations of Espionage in the Western Hemisphere

very costly to the men who organized German intelligence on the *Tirpitzufer*. The espionage case that resulted came to be known to Allied Intelligence as the 'Joe K.' case.

The story begins in November 1940, when the Bermuda censors found a letter in the Clipper mail to Germany giving a list of shipping in New York harbour (mostly British and Allied), adding details of their arrival, departure, appearance and armaments, and including newspaper cuttings about shipping, aircraft and munition programmes in the United States. The writing on the cuttings appeared to be German, but the report was in tolerable, though Teutonic, English. It was signed 'Joe K'. The addressee was put on the watch-list; sorters were trained to look out for Joe K.'s handwriting on envelopes, and soon a fairly large number of letters to different addresses were found. They carried return addresses, in or near New York, which were evidently fictitious but which usually had a Christian name beginning with J. After a sufficient number had been collected, they were examined for secondary meaning. It became evident that Joe K. was a leading member of a large, probably German, espionage organization in the United States. It appeared that he was able to gather important information from contacts in nearly all strategic areas. A growing list of his addresses in Europe was kept under observation by Bermuda.

Another lead soon appeared. In March 1941, a letter to Portugal was intercepted at Bermuda, well written in perfect German. It contained elaborate details of aircraft supplied to Britain by the USA and of the United States Army training programmes. It was signed 'Konrad' and contained the following information:

> I have been in this beautiful country only a few months ... I made immediate efforts to find Joe, but up to now unfortunately without success. I do not quite know what my plans are yet; much depends on Joe.

Evidently Konrad was a trained military observer sent out to be part of Joe's organization. In subsequent letters Joe referred to meetings with 'Connie' – meaning Konrad.

Meanwhile, the Bermuda scientific examiners had been testing Joe's letters for secret writing, but without success until they tried iodine vapour. A secret message was then discovered; and all the previous letters were re-tested. Several of them, too, were found to contain secret messages, giving remarkably up-to-date information on aircraft production and shipping movements.

Konrad's letter was also tested, and was found to bear a message in secret ink saying that his address was c/o Joe and that he was posting duplicate reports via Portugal, China and Japan. He added, 'if further information on Puerto Rico is desired (see my report sent through Smith, China), please send Joe a telegram of good wishes'. BSC received all this information and passed it on to the FBI.

On 25 March, Bermuda intercepted a letter from Joe, containing messages in both open and secret writing which led to the solution of the case. In the letter Joe said that Phil (whom he also called Julio and Connie) had met with a fatal accident in New York, having been hit by a car, that he himself had called the ambulance without giving his name, that Phil's effects were at the Hotel Taft, and that the Spanish Consulate was paying the funeral expenses. He added many details, such as the number of the car and the exact time and place of the accident.

It so happened that, when the accident occurred in New York, the suspicions of the police were aroused by the nature of the documents found on the victim's person. The FBI were called in, and they reported, after scrutinizing the documents, that the dead man was probably a spy. At this stage BSC passed them the report from Bermuda about Joe's message, which provided confirmation. The victim had been carrying a Spanish passport issued in Shanghai under the name of Julio Lopez Lido, a postcard instructing the recipient to say 'I am Mr Konrad', many papers referring in open code to espionage activities, and letters from Dinnies Carl Wilhelm von der Osten. The last named lived in Denver, Colorado, and was already suspected of espionage. When interrogated, he admitted that the dead man was his brother, Captain Ulrich von der Osten, attached to German military intelligence. Thus Konrad, the trained military observer, known to Joe and his friends as Julio, Phil or Connie, was identified.

BSC and the Bermuda censors had meanwhile been working extremely hard on the case. It was observed that, in one of his messages, Joe scolded his correspondents in Europe for typing his letters, and told him that manuscript envelopes were not opened by censorship. Obviously then westbound letters from Europe to Joe were passing through unobserved. Accordingly, Bermuda decided to make a 100% examination of the first westbound Clipper mail at Bermuda after the winter interval.

They went through no less than 200,000 letters. They found, and sent to New York with great satisfaction, a letter from a businessman in Catalonia to Mrs Josephine Sturaro, 246 E. 51st

St, New York, which contained two private messages for 'Dear Joe'. The messages made reference to food parcels (which 'Joe K.' had in fact been sending) and, vaguely, to future business in the USA, whither the writer was bound. The censors concluded that he was *en route* to replace the deceased Capt. Ulrich von der Osten, alias Konrad, Julio, Phil or Connie, and accordingly the information was forwarded to the FBI. Future letters from the same man and to the same address were carefully picked out and similarly forwarded. It was only after three months that the FBI reported back on the writer's arrival. He was a *bona fide* businessman, a citizen of the USA; Mrs Sturaro was his sister; and Joe was his brother-in-law, a tobacco man from Kentucky. They were all above suspicion.

However, not long after, in mass testing of 15,000 westbound letters, Bermuda found a really valuable clue. It was a letter from Portugal to Mrs Pauline Noi at an address near New York, and it referred to Phil's accident. It was headed J/20, and was clearly the twentieth of a series of directives for Joe K. himself. It gave elaborate orders for improving his secret writing, coding and methods generally. (Joe later wrote an acknowledgment, which proved that although Bermuda had opened the letter, developed the secret ink and copied the message, he was not suspicious of British censorship.) The letter, with the name and address of the woman, was passed to the FBI.

In April 1941, SIS/London reported that in early March a German agent in Lisbon had telegraphed a code-message to 'Fouzie' in New York. They asked for identification of 'Fouzie'. The FBI were requested for help in identifying him, but replied that, since 10,000 cablegrams were filed every day in New York, identification was impossible. BSC then obtained the information from a contact in the cable company's office and passed the FBI the facts, which were that 'Fouzie' was the code name for Fred Ludwig, who lived in a suburb of New York. Two days later they replied 'Investigation has disclosed the Joe K. is identical with one Fred Ludwig.'

Meanwhile, the FBI had been investigating all the vague family references in the Joe K. letters. They might, of course, have been open code for the movements of his organization, but they might also refer to genuine persons and facts. For instance, he often mentioned his uncle Dave and his aunt Loney, on one occasion saying that they intended to sell their shop and subsequently that 'Mr H. sold his store'. Among the effects of the dead Konrad the FBI found a telephone number which they traced to a shop in a

New York suburb. They discovered that its owner had recently bought it from a couple named Dave and Loni Harris. Also in Konrad's belongings they found an address which proved to be that of Ludwig; and when they investigated him, they found that his aunt and uncle were in fact the Harris couple. Then they began to intercept his mail, and found that his handwriting was identical with that of Joe K. Thenceforward they had him under the closest surveillance. Bermuda protested several times against the clumsy opening of his mail, for it made some letters impossible to send on.

During the weekend of 28 June 1941, the FBI arrested several suspects in the Sebold Sawyer case (which has already been described) and some of them were actually with Joe at the time of their arrest. Joe accordingly began to make preparations for escape. Letters and postcards from him continued to flow through Bermuda, all showing that he knew he was being watched (he referred to his 'illness' or his 'competitors', for example) and was making his way towards a west-coast port. On 23 August 1941, Kurt Friedrich Ludwig, alias Joe K., was arrested in the western state of Washington. He was evidently *en route* for Seattle and Japan.

Other members of his ring, all known by cover-names from his correspondence, were arrested in August and September. They were either Germans or, like Ludwig himself, Americans of German origin. They were indicted for 'transmitting information relating to the national defence' along with 'certain representatives . . . of the German Reich'.

One particularly interesting agent was Paul Borchardt, a Jewish ex-officer of the German Army, who had worked for Haushofer and had lived in Britain for a year (not unsuspected) as a refugee. The FBI had got their first guidance to him from the German Consulate in New York. The consulate entrusted the destruction of its papers to the furnaceman in the building. A consular employee was always present while the pile of waste was being examined to determine that it contained no bombs, but he would leave as soon as the papers had been placed in the furnace. The furnaceman would immediately take the papers out again, having protected them from burning by throwing them into the fire in such a way that they choked off the draft. Upon reading some of them he had called up the FBI on his own initiative and thereafter regularly turned over his discoveries to them. One document was a decode of a restricted radio message received from Germany by the Consulate. It contained an order to seek out Borchardt (whose address was given) and to tell him to burn (or 'heat') a letter evidently received from his superiors in Germany.

Later, when Ludwig was in the country gaol, he tried to bribe a policeman. The policeman pretended to accept the bribe, and was told by Ludwig to send a cable to Borchardt in New York. BSC passed the FBI some pertinent information on Borchardt's previous career as a German agent. There was also a very striking piece of evidence: the report sent by Konrad to 'Mr Smith' of China, which Konrad had posted after leaving Hawaii, on a ship *en route* for the USA. The FBI had intercepted it because of the lead given them by Bermuda. It contained a report on the defences of Hawaii, with a map and photographs, and the observation that 'this will be of interest mostly to our yellow allies'. Introduced in evidence shortly after Pearl Harbor, it caused a great sensation.

All those who were implicated either pled guilty or were convicted. Ludwig and Borchardt received prison sentences of twenty years. The censorship expert, whose initial interest in the case had been chiefly responsible for opening it up, testified for the Bermuda censors and was thanked; but the part played by Bermuda censorship and BSC was deliberately understated for reasons of policy.

(b) Unmasking of a German Sabotage Organization

In March of 1942, the first clue to the existence of a German sabotage organization in Latin America was discovered through the interception of a message addressed to Abteilung 2 of the OKW. The message had been sent over the clandestine W/T station at Valparaiso and was signed 'Apfel'. It reported that 'Hirth' had been arrested and that he would have in any event to leave Peru, although efforts were being made to secure his release. It mentioned a 'Braun' and a 'Gersten', and also stated that 'Bohrer' was 'here' at present.

Who was 'Apfel' and where was he?

He appeared to be the head sabotage agent for all South America since he reported that his finances were sufficient to start work, though not in the northern republics. Peru was under his jurisdiction, and in one of his messages he asked whether his agents 'P' and 'J' in Buenaventura might leave the country at the next repatriation of Germans. The only Buenaventura of any consequence is in Colombia; and there were two dangerous Nazis there who could be identified with 'P' and 'J' – Oscar Poensgen and Bruno Johannsen.

'Hirth' was tentatively identified as Kurt Heuer, an active and dangerous Peruvian Nazi who had been deported from Peru about seventeen days after the message was sent. The FBI had apparently been opening his letters before that, for they stated that he had been receiving mail, through an intermediary, from Von Appen in Chile, and that the letters indicated that Von Appen was trying to get permission for him to enter Chile rather than be sent home.

In May 1942, Apfel received his final instructions – 'From the moment a country officially declares war begin work there immediately.' He was also instructed to sever at once all connections with the Valparaiso station which had been sending his messages.

Various suggestions about his real name were made. A genuine Apfel turned up in Peru, an ex-employee of the German Bank. There were many suspects in Chile, especially Carl Ludwig Jackel, the Nazi leader for the south, for it had been reliably reported that he was engaged in storing radio transmitters, explosives and other equipment in remote islands. But the successful lead was provided by SIS/Buenos Aires in November 1942, when it managed to recruit a good informant inside the German Bank.

This informant reported that one of the ringleaders of the intelligence service connected with the Bank was a certain Von Appen, whose name was 'often disguised as Apfel', that he had authority to draw funds without limit from the 'Winter Help' account held by the Bank, but that his whereabouts were unknown. Later the informant added that an ex-sea-captain by the name of W. Lange had visited the Bank, had withdrawn several long tubes from Von Appen's safe-deposit box and when asked by a bank official what they were had replied 'Dynamite'. Now SIS/Buenos Aires already knew of a Captain Wilhelm Lange who worked in Delfino's shipping agency. He was said to occupy an office at the very top of the building, from which vantage-point he could watch shipping passing through the harbour.

Further enquiries in the Bank elicited the fact that the safe-deposit was owned by one Alberto Julio Von Appen Oestmann, the Valparaiso representative of the Hamburg America shipping line. BSC meanwhile turned up more information on Von Appen, which revealed that he had had a five-year power of attorney granted him by the Hamburg America line, and that the name of his firm was the blacklisted Kosmos Shipping Agency.

In October 1942, after a protest from the Americans and a good deal of lobbying by SOE in Chile, the Chilean Government began to arrest and intern dangerous Germans. One of those arrested was Von Appen. During the course of his interrogation he stated that he was born in Hamburg in 1901, had been an officer on many Hamburg America ships, had joined the NSDAP in 1933 and had migrated to Chile in 1937, where he founded his Kosmos Shipping Agency. He denied, however, that he had any connection with Germany through private radio transmitters, and declared that he had neither heard the name of Apfel nor attempted to carry out sabotage activities.

As a dangerous alien, Von Appen was banished to a small town which he was forbidden to leave; and although, through Chilean laxity, he was still free to communicate with the outside world and to receive visitors, his teeth were now drawn.

In March of 1945, the Chilean ship *Lautoro* burst into flames off Valparaiso and became a total loss. Investigation showed that the cause was gross negligence on the part of the Chilean Navy. But a scapegoat was required. Von Appen was the obvious choice, and he was re-arrested. In the ensuing excitement the real cause of the damage to the *Lautoro* was entirely overlooked, and press reports implied that Von Appen had been responsible.

Under severe interrogation he supplied evidence of the existence of a widespread and well-knit organization in all South American Republics, with the exception of Ecuador. He revealed the identities of 'Hirth', 'P' and 'J', 'Braun', 'Gersten' and 'Bohrer'. BSC learned with satisfaction that it had been right in its deductions concerning 'Hirth' and 'P' and 'J'.

The fact that no sabotage was carried out was undoubtedly due in part to the efforts of the Industrial Security Section of the Security Division of BSC. For example, Von Appen admitted that the blowing up of the Cubatao Power Station (which supplies electricity to the cities of Sao Paulo and Santos) had been abandoned owing to the sharp watch kept by the officer on the job.

Von Appen stated that he had been recruited as long ago as 1939 and had received his sabotage training when he returned to Germany on a routine visit for his firm. It is not possible to judge how good that training had been; but one thing is certain. If he had not made use of an unauthorized channel for his communications, his organization might never have been uncovered.

(c) The 'Fred Lewis' Case

In February 1942, the Bermuda censors found German secret writing on a letter which had a New York address and was intended for a postbox in Spain, known to be used by an enemy agent. The message was signed Fred Lewis.

It contained accurate information which had to do with shipping leaving New York. It was followed by other messages all replete with intelligence material – some of it reliable, some of it incorrect – on the movement of troops, ships and material.

A report, together with copies of the letters, was passed to the FBI, but difficulties arose at once. BSC wished to have the letters released as soon as possible, in order that the writer might be given opportunity to reveal information which would assist in tracing him. The US Army and Navy on the other hand were unwilling that such potentially dangerous reports should go to Europe. Eventually a compromise was reached whereby only the messages containing inaccurate information were released.

As these letters continued to come in, the FBI set to work to find the writer, but the only Fred Lewis they could identify was a small Jewish lawyer, and there was no indication that he was connected with the case. The open letters themselves were signed by several different names, but the secret messages were invariably subscribed Fred Lewis, or F.L. They were all posted from New York.

The writer said little about himself. Once he asked for the name of the firm which was supposed to be 'realizing his button-patent', and on another occasion referred to a 'camouflaged royalty settlement from South America'.

In November 1942, BSC sent the FBI an analysis of the available facts about him. He was an air-raid warden; he had a garden; he was married, and he had had an illness during which he was nursed by his wife. He also referred to losing his house through foreclosure.

He had sent no letters since April, and from this fact there were three possible deductions to be drawn. Either he had given up in despair because (as he had often complained) he was without news from Germany; or he had found new intermediaries and cover-names; or he had been repatriated.

Equipped with these pertinent facts, the FBI tried to find him by checking on everyone who had taken out a button patent; by checking, too, on the handwriting of all recent repatriates, on persons whose homes had been foreclosed and on air-raid wardens. But their inquiries proved to no avail.

Meanwhile Bermuda was also working on the problem. Remembering that one of the letters mentioned receipt of a communication from Europe which had been tested by the censors for secret

```
                                    New York, N.Y., 18th of Febr.1942

                 S 4378.

Dear Joss:-

        It is almost a year, since I have seen you last,
and it now does not look as if we are going to meet again
for some time to come. Too bad that we had to get into this
war. I figured that it is probably would not take more than
a few months to lick the Germans, with the Russian apparent-
ly making a good job of it, but now that Japan has come
into this fracas, it seems that it will take a least an-
other year before we shall be able to lick the Germans as
well as the Japs. How I would love to roam again in Lisbon
and its beautiful surroundings, especially at this time of
the year, but that will simply have to wait now for the
duration of the war.
        Since writing you last, my health has constantly
improved, so much so that I do not have to stay indoors any
longer, but again can go out any time during the day, and
in all kinds of weather, and again attend to my business,
which I had been forced to neglect for quite some time.
Nothing more aggravating than being ill, but once you are
entirely over it, you look at the world again through rose
colored glasses, and Nature, even with its bare trees at
present, looks beautiful, a thing that cannot appeal to you
unless you have passed through a severe illness, after that
```

```
you feel like hugging the whole cockeyed world. But that does
not say that, in order for anyone to enjoy such feelings, I
should wish him to go through what I had to go through. But
it seems the good Lord sees to it that trees do not grow into
heaven, and whenever in His belief it is best to visit a ser-
ere illness on anyone, who, like me, has not been too good,
he does so in order to try to make us better human beings.
Whether, in my case, my really good intentions will materially
for any great duration, I cannot vouch for, but let's hope so.
        How is your family now getting along on foodstuffs?
Do you have any rationing at present or is everything still
plentyful? As it was at the time I saw you last? That is on
thing we do not have to worry about in this country. You can
get everything, even sugar, which up to now has not yet been
rationed, and if it actually should come to pass, we will still
get enough to go around, and as far as I hardly need say. It
would be a good lesson for many people, if rationing of sugar
would come, in order to stop some people needlessly overeating
same.
        I do hope that you and all of your family are en-
joying the best of health. When you see Alonso please give
his my kindest regards. And don't forget to write from time
to time.
                With all good wishes and best regards to you and
yours from my wife and myself,
                                Your friend
                                    Oliver.
        S 4378.
```

Reproduction of a letter written by 'Fred Lewis'. He intended this as an innocuous medium for the conveyance of secret writing. The first and last sentences of his opening paragraph provided a clue to his identity.

S.6278   10.II.42.

1. ZUM 10.II. ABFAHRT TRANSPORTER MIT 4000 MANN A.M.G.EBL.
2 GROSSE KRIEGSSCHIFFE, IN HOBOKEN 4 PRACHTER FLUGZ.
U. PANZER MOTORE. 16.II. BIM GEWERF 78.000 MANN, 1 PRACHTER
VISCHEN 19.II. 2. IST IM GEWERF 78.000 MANN, 1 PRACHTER
43000 T. LADET BUSCH TERMINAL BROOKLYN STAPELLAUF
NEL SCHWERE BOMBER U. SIEBEL DANGEICH. WILLINDLE
WOLL, FAIRCHILD U. KINDERTYP, POS-OST WESTBROOKLYN
BEOACHTE 7 FALLSCHIRMJAEGER, HABEN MUSTER SOVIE
DOOPS FREIHAFEN STAPELLAUF, VON ROMEO MATT MARIA
BERGDOERFER ZWISCHEN PIERS 15 WIE WIRD AUSGEBESSERT
ERACHWICK INSTANDSETZUNG FUER NEUER FLUGZEUG PANZER IM TRAM
4000 JAHRE INDET MILITARGERAETFABRIK TANKS U POWLER.
21 MIO MANNSCHAFTEN AM 19.II. 7M COMWOY STAHISEM
1 TRANSPORTER FLUGZ. FLUEZ. NIEDER VOELLIG ZAGESETZT.
IN GESCHICHTEN.— 24 U.S. DACCEIT MONTANAO. GOORG
INFERIALIEN ZT WOCHE NACH 1 BONA FÖR 9 JAGER
PARISER GASTATT. JEDOCH KRUEGER UEBER SPHERE
EROBERUNGEN IM SCHIFFBAU IKEN SPRENG TOMA
AM INDEUSK AM SCHIFFAHRT MES PAESHINGTOM HAT
6 AGENTE CAROLINA N AICEROPTER IST DEUTSCH HAT
I NEMT SM. ABER HUGE MAENEL WUSDIZULENERTEEN VAR
OBER MUELLER R.D. XMESSEWESNOTE SCHIFFAM
NACH SCHATZ HA MANUFACTURED VERTEIRENWÖRDVEN KONTE
KUPFERZWINDEN UMMED MEINE GUNVESTFAHR F.O. POGEBENS,
MESSING HAT LAGER LATOW, GISZOLICH AUSHLESEN
LICH HIGAEF, SCHROLLE LOTGLUCH AIR HONI MUCEL
...

S6278

IRTON LADEN 2 PRACHTER PANZER, FLUGZ.MOTORE
4-GESCHUETZE, IN HOBOKEN 4 PRACHTER FLUGZ
U. PANZER MOTORE ALLE ANGELAUFEN RUSSIA CONVOY
13 SCHIFFE ABFAHREN WILL NACH GR.BR. GROSSE LAGER
PROVIANTEL MUNITIONALLER WERKS U. N.Y. CITY
2 FALLSCHIRM JAEGER(TYPEN) VON IKESTAR, 112 164
DOUGLAS D4NY. MATT MARIA FAIRA HEIDESTADT
60% HITLER GEWEHRE, INPIE HEDEGVIK, DAS YS
NORFEN URSACHE MANGEN AN BES GEMOERT HERR
BELASTUNG, THIDRI PIER PERKAUFFE SOWIE FILIPAM
21 400 MANN LETZTE BRIEF WOCH BEIDE SEITEN
MIT GEWEHR U. MASSIN SCHRIFT, IN EINSEITIG
MARCH. SCHIFFT VERJAEGHTE. IN PIONIERE PRO
TEST TNOTEN STAK HENN ENTWICKELT GWP ISEDE
LICH HOCHMARISE EXSIVE VALET UEBERMUSSSUNG
...
HEIL HITLER!
.... ETWA

writing, it searched its records for all New York letters which had been so tested, and sent BSC the addresses they bore. The FBI then assembled a composite photograph of Lewis's handwriting (as seen both in the open letters and in the secret writing) and of his typing with the peculiarities of the machine emphasized. Bermuda checked all its condemned letters against this composite. The results were negative. But the method had been evolved nonetheless which would eventually solve the case.

In two of his letters Lewis mentioned that he had travelled in Portugal 'about a year ago'. This prompted the FBI to go over all the baggage declarations – some 50,000 in all – which had been made out by travellers entering the USA from Portugal between February and May 1941. It was a painstaking search, but it was rewarded. The Fred Lewis handwriting was found on a check made out by Ernst Fritz Detlev Heinrich Lehmitz, a naturalized American citizen of German origin.

Investigation of this man's background showed he had a house with a garden overlooking New York harbour, that the bank had foreclosed the mortgage on his property, that he was registered as an air-raid warden and that he had been ill. On 28 June 1943 – more than a year after the original evidence had come to light – the FBI arrested Lehmitz alias Fred Lewis.

He had gathered his information not only from watching the harbour, but from keeping a boarding house for merchant seamen and soldiers, and from working in a harbour restaurant frequented by munitions workers, shipyard workers, coastguards, sailors and seamen. The press said that 'the suspicious eyes of British censors at Bermuda' had spotted the secret writing and that the FBI had traced the postmarks to the house of Lehmitz. He was asked about a book on Brewster aircraft which he had mentioned in a letter, and gave the name of an Uruguayan-German engineer, Erwin Harry De Spretter, who had procured it for him. This man also was arrested.

Both the accused pled guilty, but were allowed to change their pleas since the possible penalty involved was death. After the case for the prosecution was presented they pled guilty again, and on 28 September 1943, each of them was sentenced to serve thirty years in the penitentiary.

(d) The 'Rogers' Case

While the Fred Lewis case was in progress, another series of letters in secret writing was passing through Bermuda. The first message intercepted was numbered 6. It was dated April 1942, and was addressed to the Swiss intermediary used by Fred Lewis.

The handwriting was skilful; the secret ink was ammonium vanadate, which had been used in the last war but not hitherto in this; and the letter gave details of aircraft output, shipbuilding and a new explosive. Since the typewriting in the cover letter was not identical with that in the Fred Lewis series, it was apparent that another well-informed agent, near the beginning of his career, was working on slightly different ground from Lewis.

The letters continued to pass through Bermuda at monthly intervals, until No. 14 arrived in March 1943. Who was the writer? Four of the first five letters intercepted were signed Rogers, or R.O. Gerson. They gave fictitious return addresses in the business district of New York.

Now on 29 November, a clandestine wireless station in Mexico had sent a message to Hamburg saying 'Rogers here again.' The next day Hamburg replied, 'We shall not write to Rogers further, but we demand his immediate return to his post.'

Accordingly, BSC suggested to the FBI that Rogers might be identified with a Count Albrecht Archibald Douglas who had escaped from an FBI roundup in 1941, passed through Mexico, and had been deported from Peru to Japan through FBI influence. This theory came to naught, however, when headquarters reported some months later that Douglas had reached Japan before Pearl Harbor, and for that reason could not be in the United States.

By November of 1942, the agent was clearly extremely worried. Letter No. 12 contained the sentences: 'Have been through hell on account of your mail. Your complete silence now imperative.' Evidently he had received communications from his employers in Europe and feared that their arrival would lead to his detection. It was suggested, therefore, that a fabricated letter should be sent through censorship to one of his postboxes with the object, of course, of eliciting the very kind of reply which he so evidently feared. The FBI agreed. Using No. 12 as a model (though without the entreaties, of course) they forged two letters together with secret messages under heading of a New York cover address.

They were sent to one of the Rogers intermediaries – Francisco Esteves. He was employed by the firm of *Zum Hingste* in Lisbon, which was known to be part of the German Intelligence network in Portugal, and he had been a German paymaster. Rather surprisingly, Esteves took the letters straight to the American Embassy in Lisbon, saying that he 'did not wish to give out information that would be detrimental to the USA'. He did not explain why he thought the information in the letters would be detrimental, although the covering messages were innocuous and the secret writing had not been developed.

SIS/Lisbon went into the matter and interviewed Esteves at length. He gave a good deal of information about *Zum Hingste* and his associates. One of them was a well-known German agent called Blum. Esteves knew that this man was a German agent, and declared that he was angry with Blum for using his name as an intermediary for intelligence reports without asking permission. He added that his motive in turning over the letters was to put himself in a good position with the Americans in case they won the war. The fabrication of these letters, however, produced no information about Rogers, and the practice was stopped.

The FBI then reverted to one of their favourite methods of identification. Having made a specimen of Rogers's handwriting and printing, they were prepared to go over every possible series of documents in which Rogers might have given his real name. But first information about his actual life had to be elicited, and this was done in various ways.

In letters numbers 11 and 12, the writer had said he would soon be in the US Army. Bermuda suggested that, since some of the Rogers letters were in block capitals, they might be compared with forms filled in by soldiers who had recently been conscripted. The FBI went over thousands of forms without success.

In October 1943, the FBI dug up an old wireless message from Germany to Mexico giving orders for the disposition of German agents. It contained the sentence, 'Rogers to report to here in future, and limit Dennis and Baxter remarks. Bremen.' It seemed that Dennis was the American Fascist, Lawrence Dennis, who used to publish a totalitarian propaganda sheet called *Weekly Foreign Letters*, and that Baxter was William Baxter who published an *International Economic Research Bulletin*. Both these publications would have been of interest to the German Intelligence organization. Rogers might have sent them over regularly, until Bremen told him to 'limit' them – that is discontinue them. The FBI, therefore, searched the subscription lists, and asked Bermuda for lists of private persons in the US who had posted such bulletins to Germany. Nothing was found.

The US cable censors suggested that a Hungarian called Roy Rogers, who entered the US in July 1941, might be the writer, since he had received a number of suspicious cables. A check was made on him, but his handwriting was found not to be identical with that of the Rogers messages.

Once again, eventual success was had only as a result of the most laborious procedure. Blum had requested his recruits to meet him in Italy in the first part of 1940. Mexican wireless traffic showed that Rogers had been in the US in March 1941. The FBI, therefore, examined all the baggage declaration forms filled out by travellers entering the US from Europe between December 1939 and March 1941. They discovered one, filled out in the handwriting of Rogers, which gave his real name.

He was Wilhelm Albrecht Von Pressentin, *genannt* Von Rautter, a comparatively noble German. Before arresting him, the FBI checked every other detail. First of all, they looked up his military record. He had been classified 1A on 30 September 1942, appealed, and had been reclassified. This corresponded to Rogers's remark that he would be in the army in two weeks, for the letter had evidently been written just after Von Rautter had been classified 1A. Then, his name appeared on the mailing list of both Lawrence Dennis and William Baxter. His rooms were searched, and he was found to possess a heavy lined paper of the type used to guide secret writing. Finally, it was learned that he had been paid $5,000 through the Bank of Mexico by one Simon. Simon was known to be an alias for Blum. The last step was to identify Von Rautter's handwriting with that of Rogers, which was satisfactorily done.

Von Rautter was arrested on 11 January 1944. He immediately burst into tears, told the whole story and pled guilty. His career was rather unusual.

His father and brother were Prussian Junkers, his mother English. His parents had been divorced because his mother, during the 1914–18 war, had assisted Allied prisoners interned on the family estate and had been denounced as a traitor by her husband. Von Rautter himself travelled a good deal. He was not a very stable character, but was apparently clever. When arrested, he was employed as financial adviser to a large stockbroking firm. He returned from the US to Germany in 1940 – according to his own account in order to look after his father's estate and to keep his stepmother from getting it all. While in East Prussia, Simon wrote to him from Hamburg suggesting that, if he were returning to the US, they might do some business.

Von Rautter said his first discussions with Simon had been strictly commercial, but meanwhile the Gestapo was apparently checking his record. When it was found satisfactory, he was invited to return to the USA and to send regular reports on matters of interest to the German Intelligence Service. There was an implied threat that his father and brother would suffer if he did not agree. He was trained in short-wave radio operation, the use of secret inks and codes.

As an agent, he was not very satisfactory. Before leaving, he was given a thirty-two-page list of American chemical companies, in each of which he was instructed to establish contact with an official; but he did not do so, nor did he set up a short-wave wireless transmitting station.

He was the Rogers who had been in Mexico in 1941 and the messages from Germany had been orders for him to return to the US and start work. Before opening the Rogers series of reports, he said, he had sent numerous letters to various European addresses, but he declared that all his information was obtained from newspapers and magazines. However, this may well have been no more than the usual German attempt to minimize guilt, for the thirteenth report in the Rogers series, written on 19 December 1942, contained the sentence, 'Burma attack planned.' The attack actually took place on the 22nd, and wherever he got this intelligence it was a little too good to have been derived solely from the newspapers.

He was indicted on 25 July 1944, the indictment being drawn up very discreetly so that no cover address, except Esteves, was mentioned. He pled guilty and was sentenced to twenty-nine years' imprisonment.

(e) The Kobbe Case

The Kobbe case provides an example of the three-way cooperation which existed between the FBI, BSC and the RCMP.

In August of 1942 a new Spanish consul was sent out to Vancouver. His name was Fernando Kobbe y Chinchilla.

There had seemed no good reason at the time for refusing his appointment, for, while the Department of External Affairs in Ottawa had been informed by London and Washington that he had once been pro-Axis, the available evidence suggested that he had since been converted. It was only after he had left Spain that new and more alarming facts concerning him began to emerge. It was learned from Top Secret sources that he intended to use his consular post as cover for espionage activities, having been recruited to work as a secret agent for the Japanese on the west coast of Canada. He himself boasted of possessing a code in which words were represented by Japanese names.

It was not possible to prevent Kobbe from taking up his appointment in Vancouver, but BSC, working through its liaison channels, made certain that his potential usefulness to the enemy would be countered. The FBI and the RCMP were informed of the facts.

The BSC representative at Trinidad was alerted and when Kobbe transited Trinidad *en route* to Canada, the diplomatic bag which he was carrying was opened without his knowledge and two cyphers found inside were photographed. After his arrival in Vancouver, his house was watched and his mail – both incoming and outgoing – was intercepted and examined by the RCMP, who had made all the necessary arrangements. It seemed certain that he had been rendered innocuous.

However, some months later – in March of 1943 – it was learned that he had sent his first secret intelligence report to Madrid and that this contained information on troopships sailing for the Aleutians. Since none of his letters and telegrams could have escaped the RCMP's net, his channel of communication was a mystery and it was thought possible that the report had in fact been invented by his immediate principal in Spain – one Alcazar de Velasco – to justify his recruitment and employment. Nevertheless, he could not be written off as harmless so long as there remained the merest possibility that he had an uncontrolled channel of communication at his disposal. Accordingly the task now was to secure evidence against him – irrefutable yet of a kind which could be used without compromising Top Secret sources.

In that, despite continuing efforts of one kind and another, no success was had until the following September.

It happened then that the FBI intercepted a large envelope, which was marked 'Diplomatic Mail' though it had been sent through the ordinary post. It was addressed from the Spanish Embassy in Washington to the Spanish Consulate in Montreal, and was found to include three letters for Kobbe in Vancouver. The envelope of one of these letters contained a message in secret writing as follows:

I have waited some time before getting into touch with you in case you are being watched.

Microphotographs of a complete new code, in which (as Kobbe had boasted on his way out) each word was represented by a

Japanese name, were also found, together with a formula for secret ink, a set of cover-addresses in Spain to which Kobbe could send his reports and $1030 in small bills. All of this equipment had been sent out to Kobbe by his immediate principal in Spain through the diplomatic bag.

The FBI had opened the envelope secretly. Without affixing censorship labels, they re-sealed it and put it back in the mail. When the envelope reached Canada it was also opened secretly by the RCMP, who noted its contents and passed it on. The two organizations were surprised to learn that the job had been done twice.

The only outstanding point was that the evidence against Kobbe could scarcely be used in a trial. In the first place, he had committed no crime. In the second place, the evidence would have disclosed that the FBI and RCMP clandestinely opened correspondence. As it turned out, however, the need for bringing him to trial did not arise. For the Canadians, satisfied that the envelope was not really privileged mail (it had been sent through ordinary postal channels and consuls in Canada have no diplomatic immunity in any case), authorized the use of its contents as the basis of an official protest to the Spanish Government against the behaviour of its representative. The matter was taken up on the highest level. HM Ambassador in Madrid formally protested to the Minister of Foreign Affairs, pointing out the inescapable conclusion that Kobbe was not the only Spanish consul engaged in nefarious proceedings of the kind exposed and that similar abuses were being perpetrated elsewhere.

In January 1944, Kobbe y Chinchilla was declared *persona non grata*, was escorted to the frontier of Canada by the RCMP, escorted to the port of New Orleans by the FBI and sent home to Spain. When last heard of, he was about to be tried by a tribunal of the Spanish Army.

(f) The Pozzi Case

In October 1942, the US censors at San Juan, Puerto Rico, were doing random testing of eastbound Clipper mail for secret writing. They found a letter in bad French from a man in Rio de Janeiro to someone in the Argentine Consulate at Marseilles, which, when tested, revealed an Italian message in secret ink. Much of it was indecipherable, but it was sent on to Bermuda, which produced a fuller and better decipherment and translation. The significant passage (as far as it was legible) read:

My dear Guido,
   At Trinidad the English subjected me to a severe interrogation, following denunciation . . . so-called intelligence service . . . funds they seized from me . . . Actually, during the voyage a law was issued concerning American profits in particular for effectiveness against espionage. In all the South American countries dollars can no longer be sold or bought except through the government bank in each separate country . . . commercial firms which have branches in the USA and are not included in the famous black lists: so as you can see, all of a sudden I found myself without money. Luckily Andrea B. Lópes helped me as much as he could . . . with the friend of the Mayroff firm . . . You will understand that I am now completely without funds, waiting for Lópes to bring me them as he promised, to obtain some for me in some way or other . . . the sum of 6400 taken from me at the home of the English Commercial Attaché at Rio. Now I beg of you to ask in Rome for arrangements to be made . . . to let me have funds, twenty thousand Argentine pesos are needed so that plans can be thought out for starting some business activity . . . to cloak my position and eliminate any suspicion . . . against the fifth column here . . . Italians are arrested simply because they speak Italian . . . The Americans . . . have already established three naval air bases at Pernambuco, Pará, and Porto Natal, with troops, airfields (ports of naval base type), anti-aircraft and coast artillery. As soon as I have these blessed funds I will visit the place so as to get more precise details for you by being right on the spot. I am working to get a watch over shipping movements in the ports of Rio and Santos. The Army is of no interest at the moment. I think I have found an excellent colleague, an old friend, owner of a firm which supplies . . . to the Army, the Navy, and the Air Force. He is an ex-Reserve officer, who on account of his gifts of intelligence . . . patriotism would be of . . . to me as a collaborator and also because through his business he has a free pass from the Brazilian government to enter all the Northern and Southern States. He is ready to work with me on condition that he is treated as if recalled to service. Let me know if you agree to this suggestion . . . and necessary details in my next letter . . . Buenos Aires get

orders and procure funds as I have not even been able to buy myself a radio to listen to the Monday broadcasts. My respectful greetings to our leaders and to you, dear Guido, a brotherly embrace.

FELICE
Vinceremo ('We shall conquer').

The secret ink was one of the common German espionage inks, but the writer was not well trained in its use, because the message was written in longhand. The cover letter was signed Willy Felix.

It was evidently the work of an Italian agent who had just been sent out to engage in espionage in South America. He had given away certain facts about himself which could be checked. Upon inquiry BSC learned that one Angelo Pozzi had been severely interrogated at Trinidad and had had his funds seized. He was the writer obviously enough.

What had happened in Trinidad was this. One of Pozzi's fellow passengers informed the authorities that he had seen Pozzi in August 1941 wearing the uniform of an Italian captain at the Argentine Consulate in Marseilles, and had been told that he was a member of the Armistice Commission.

On the basis of this evidence Pozzi was subjected to thorough search and interrogation. He was found to be hiding $2,000 in US currency, of which $1,400 was confiscated. He said he was an Italian by birth, had served as an officer cadet in the Italian army in 1917, had migrated to Brazil in 1923 and had become naturalized in 1929. He gave a reasonable account of his business activities in Brazil, and said he had gone to France and Monte Carlo for pleasure in April 1940. Admitting that he had met Italian officers in Marseilles, he said he had not worked in any official capacity for Italy. When confronted with the information against him, he persisted in denying that he had been in contact with the Armistice Commission, but explained rather lamely that he had been several times mistaken for another Italian in Marseilles who looked like him. Because no evidence was available to prove the denunciation or to disprove his Brazilian nationality, he was allowed to proceed to Rio. He said he was going to try to find his wife, an Austrian, from whom he had not heard for some time.

From the moment of his identification as a secret agent, he was, of course, placed under observation both by SIS and the FBI. During his stay in Rio he set out to cultivate the impression that he was pro-Allied and made an unsuccessful attempt to get in touch with British Intelligence. From Rio he went to Buenos Aires, where he made his purpose rather too obvious. He informed an SIS agent that he was very anti-Fascist and would like to work for the British, though he did not know how to make contact with the right people. He said he would be willing to go to Italy for sabotage work. He even provided this agent with a certain amount of information about Italian espionage.

It was known from clandestine wireless traffic that an agent had been sent to Argentina expressly to penetrate the British SIS, and there now seemed little doubt that Pozzi was that man.

Accordingly, SIS/Buenos Aires created a dummy intelligence organization, which he was encouraged to penetrate. There was some hope that he might be persuaded thereby to return to Europe, ostensibly as a British agent, via Trinidad, where he would be appropriately met. But this intent was frustrated by his inability or unwillingness to produce an Italian passport. In the end, SIS had to resort to trapping him into an admission of his guilt.

A meeting was arranged between Pozzi and an SIS agent at night, in a rather forbidding office in the suburbs of Buenos Aires. Another agent attended, disguised as an Argentine police official, with suitable manner and credentials. Pozzi was rather frightened when confronted with the 'police official', but at first resisted all attempts to break him down. However, when he was interrogated again and again about his post on the Italian Armistice Commission, and was told that his interrogators had definite proof that he had belonged to it, he finally confessed that he was an agent of Italian Military Intelligence.

At later interviews he amplified his statement which confirmed and, of course, greatly added to what was already known. He had been mobilized because he was in Italy when Mussolini declared war. Afterwards he was transferred to the Armistice Commission, for which he did a certain amount of intelligence work, though he had had no real experience or training. He was then recruited by Italian Military Intelligence, instructed in secret writing and codes, given the cover name of 'Felice' and the symbol 77, and told he would be head representative for Brazil.

He gave a long and interesting account of the structure of Italian Military Intelligence in so far as he had observed it, and of his codes and secret ink. He revealed the true identity of those among his associates to whom he had referred in his intercepted message. Andrea B. was an Italian agent in Rio or

Buenos Aires called Bonzo; Lopés was Bonassi, head of Italian SIS in Argentina; and Mayroff was a Neapolitan called Mayrhofer, who had a business in Buenos Aires and was on the blacklist. He stated that he had written three other letters like the Felice letter to three other postal addresses – and the fact that none of these was intercepted by censorship is an indication of the difficulties experienced in catching enemy agents.

Pozzi had apparently suffered from a common disease of his kind – lack of money – and had threatened to expose several of his colleagues unless he was better financed. He was now willing to cooperate with the British, and, as proof, signed a full confession which SIS held as a weapon over him.

For some time thereafter, he was interviewed at intervals and paid a regular salary. He gave a good deal of useful information on his contacts in South America, thus providing other leads. Bonzo, for example, was taken off a Spanish ship at Gibraltar and under interrogation gave a full story of the Italian espionage system in Buenos Aires as he had known it, confirming and amplifying Pozzi's story. More information of the same kind was secured by the FBI from interrogating other persons whose names Pozzi had supplied.

(g) The Mexican 'Dot' Case

On 1 December 1941, BSC informed Bermuda that certain correspondence which they were then intercepting from Mexico should be carefully tested for microdots – a method of secret communication (it has been described in a previous chapter) which, so far as was known to censorship, had not yet been used by enemy agents in the Western Hemisphere.

One month later, Bermuda detected microdots for the first time. The letter containing them was followed by twenty others of the same kind – eastbound and westbound between Mexico and Europe. Some of those originating from Mexico were sent by an agent with the cover name of 'Max', who was later to be identified as George Nicolaus.

The letters stopped suddenly after three months. But the reason for this soon became apparent.

The last letter was dated 19 February 1942, though it was not actually intercepted until the following April. Now on 28 February the Mexican police had arrested a number of German agents, including George Nicolaus and one Werner Barke. Both men were brought through the US *en route* to Germany, and

Barke was, in fact, repatriated. But shortly before the repatriation ship was due to sail, Nicolaus was searched by the FBI, and microfilms, containing information on US war production, were found concealed in the toes of his shoes.

The State Department, as it happened, refused to allow the FBI to prosecute him and instead ordered his internment at White Sulphur Springs, whither the German diplomats were destined to go. But the conclusion was nonetheless inescapable that he and his group had been behind the series of letters containing microdots.

A most promising field of investigation had seemingly come to an end; and indeed for a while the case was regarded as only of academic interest. But it was revived in November 1942, when Bermuda intercepted a letter from Mexico which contained thirty microdots. Clearly enough, German agents in Mexico, after a period of reorganization, were now active again. The dots were headed 'Y2983 for Guseck Berlin'.

Who was the mysterious Y2983? There was only one clue to his identity, and that was Max's account for November 1941, which included a payment of $200 to Y2983. He was, therefore, obviously known to George Nicolaus, and perhaps the latter could be persuaded to expose him.

At BSC's suggestion – a suggestion which was welcomed by the FBI – the State Department were requested through the Foreign Office to turn Nicolaus over for interrogation and trial. Regrettably, however, the State Department could do nothing, for though they were themselves anxious that Nicolaus's status should be changed to that of a prisoner charged with espionage, they were bound by their guarantee to the Mexican Government that he would be treated as an internee.

In the meanwhile, a second letter had been intercepted and this provided a new lead to the identification of Y2983; for it contained the message: 'Please advise my mother that my family and I are well. First name Clara, last address known to me Schaeferstrasse 22, Wannsee. Thanks!' But again the result was disappointing – at least for the time being. The address was that of a boarding house, and, though the 1939 German directory (the latest one available) gave the names of eight persons living there, these provided no useful clues in Mexico, despite the most thorough investigation.

Between November and the middle of February seven 'dot' letters were intercepted, but clearance could not be obtained from the Service authorities for the release of any of them. This was partly due to the fact that no one knew what the coded

Some Illustrations of Espionage in the Western Hemisphere

material contained. Accordingly BSC asked the FBI whether, in view of the obvious necessity of keeping the channel open, it would not be technically possible to clear certain letters for release by removing the offending messages. Shortly afterwards, the FBI replied that six letters had been cleared by this means, and BSC then requested Bermuda to release them at such intervals and in such a way as to arouse the least suspicion.

Y2983 was eventually unmasked through a lead unwittingly provided by his principals. In April 1943, Bermuda intercepted a letter containing instructions in microdots, which was addressed to a postbox in Mexico City. Investigation of the postbox by SIS/Mexico revealed that it had formerly been used by one Joachim Ruge. BSC passed this information to the FBI, who, on checking their records found that Ruge had written a letter in Honolulu in August 1940, while on his way to Mexico from Germany via Japan. The letter was addressed to Mrs Clara Ruge, Schaeferstrasse 22, Wannsee, Berlin, and began: 'My dear Mother . . .' The mystery of Y2983 was a mystery no longer.

Light was thrown on Ruge's organization by a letter which said in part:

> *Internal Report* – Franco has recently been released; efforts on behalf of Saunders are being continued; have not yet been able to achieve anything regarding Fernandez.

Actual identification of the organization was greatly faciliated when SIS and the FBI 'broke' simultaneously the coded messages which the letters contained. The code used was called the 'Max' Code.

In this connection, BSC recalled that there had been, in 1941, a number of cables sent from Volco, the cablegraphic address of Georg Nicolaus alias 'Max', to Brajob, Berlin. One Carlos Retelsdorf had transmitted them by clandestine wireless telegraphy to New York whence it was intended that they should be relayed to Germany. In fact, the relay station was operated by the FBI's double agent Sebold (see Chapter 1).

At BSC's suggestion the FBI searched their records to assemble all back messages which had passed through this channel and gave copies to BSC. Only a few of them had been decoded, but now the code had been broken further decodes could be made. One revealed instructions that in future the cover name 'Fernandez' was to be used instead of 'Frazer'. 'Frazer' had previously been identified as Edgar Hilgert, a known German agent who arrived in Mexico from Germany via Japan in November 1940, so that now 'Fernandez' was no longer an unknown agent.

It was apparent that many of the decoded messages received from the FBI had been badly translated, and as a result of retranslation and study by BSC further progress was made. A particular message had been translated as 'Glenn directs Franco undertaking impossible at present', whereas the correct reading was found to be 'Glenn now known as Franco. Undertaking impossible for the present.' Thus it happened that Franco was also identified, for 'Glenn' was known to be the alias of Carlos Retelsdorf.

Saunders was the last agent to be identified. SIS/Mexico provided the clue when it reported that Franz Wilhelm Buchanau, a suspect German agent, had been released from internment by the Mexican authorities, for this fitted in with Ruge's statements about Saunders.

Even after the most important *dramatis personae* in the case had been identified, work was continued on the old letters and messages in the hope that other agents – still operating – would be detected. Upon investigation of an old report from Mexico which contained a photostat of a receipt signed by Werner Barke, BSC suggested to the FBI that the signature looked remarkably like the 'W. Banco' which appeared on many of the Max letters. In due course, this deduction was confirmed by the FBI's laboratory.

No letters were intercepted after October of 1944, and the case was inactive when the European war ended. At that time it was still impossible, owing to political considerations, to round up the espionage ring or, as the vernacular has it, to 'break the case'. However enough had been learned of the organization, and sufficient preventative measures had been taken against its operations to make it useless to the enemy. In the latter task Ruge himself lent assistance in a somewhat humorous fashion. For that westbound letter which led to his unmasking told him of a new cover address in Barcelona for his communications, and he deciphered it incorrectly, with the result that all the letters he sent there were intercepted on their way back to Mexico, marked 'Return to sender, addressee unknown'.

The ways of most enemy espionage agents were, fortunately, not altogether infallible.

CHAPTER 4

Double Agents

    (a) The Problems and Advantages
    (b) The Double Agent 'Tricycle'
    (c) The Double Agent 'Springbok'
    (d) The Double Agent 'Lodge'
    (e) The Double Agent 'Pat J.'
    (f) The Double Agent 'Minaret'

(a) The Problems and Advantages

It has already been said that BSC had some success in assisting the FBI towards the active deception of the enemy through double agents.

While the use of double agents has been described as the ultimate purpose of counter-espionage, it is at the same time a risky and very intricate operation. A man or woman who is already permanently engaged in espionage on the enemy's behalf must be persuaded or coerced to retain his employment but to transfer his allegiance to the other side. The choice of the right moment to apply such persuasion or coercion is one of the most difficult decisions an intelligence officer can be called upon to make. His attempt may fail; and even if it appears to succeed, he has to face the possibility that the new double agent may return to his first masters and thus involve the officer in the appalling complications of the double double-cross.

If the operation is successfully accomplished, however, the results are usually profitable. The potential value of a double agent is inherent in his ability to do four things. First, he can give information about other agents and officers employed by the enemy, about their training, assignments and methods. Secondly, from the questionnaire with which he is supplied by his former masters he can explain what they want to know – and that is often an indication of the enemy's strategic plans.

Thirdly, if properly organized, he renders it unnecessary for the enemy to place new and possibly unknown agents in his operational area, and consequently makes an important contribution to security. Lastly, he can be used as a channel to pass strategic deceptive information to the enemy. It is to this end that double agents must be manoeuvred, for thus they play a valuable part in the cover plans for military operations of great magnitude.

The difficulties in exploiting them are many. Not the least lies in the personality and character of the man or woman concerned. Double agents, with the knowledge acquired from working with two intelligence services, are fully aware of their own value. While some may change sides for genuine ideological reasons or may accept initial employment by one side for the sole purpose of assisting the other, only too often they are motivated by a desire for money. In neutral countries, where it is not always easy to use coercion, their demands are often exorbitant. But even when they operate in the home country of a belligerent their wishes must be studied to some extent in order to obtain their cooperation and confidence, which are essential. One important double agent working from New York could give of his best only from a luxurious penthouse apartment, the bedroom charmingly furnished with the person of a famous and expensive French actress. Many of the FBI's troubles with double agents arose from their lack of understanding of the European mind and outlook, and their inability to place in charge of a double agent officers with a background likely to win his friendship and sympathy.

Another difficulty is that double agents are in constant danger of arrest by the local police who know nothing of their true purpose, of course. For example, SIS/Buenos Aires carefully recruited and built up a potentially valuable double agent inside the Spanish–German smuggling ring operating from the Argentine. But just before he could start real production he was arrested by the Argentines for smuggling, and disappeared.

Moreover, as already indicated, double agents may set out to penetrate the organization to which they have transferred their allegiance in order to report back to the enemy on its structure, methods and intent. Or they may even give him such information unwittingly. The double double-cross can arise, too, when the enemy discovers he has been betrayed and so in return deliberately feeds a double agent misleading information which will be accepted as accurate.

Finally, double agents cannot be used to deceive the enemy unless they are given, from time to time, true and useful intelligence material which they are permitted to transmit, for otherwise the enemy will realize that their information is of no value and will soon discard them. But the Armed Services were not unnaturally averse to releasing such information because of the danger inherent in so doing.

Conscious of these various pitfalls, the FBI were chary of using double agents in the early days of the war. They did, it is true, have one notable success in the Sebold/Sawyer case which has already been referred to in an earlier chapter. But their use of Sebold as a double agent was very limited, and he was not used as a channel for strategic deception. In those days they looked upon a double agent very much as a decoy whose usefulness was to uncover hitherto unknown agents. Hence, in the case of Sebold, the necessity of obtaining the release of valuable information from the Services did not arise, as he could be kept operating with comparatively low-grade material.

The question was not throughly examined before Pearl Harbor for, although both BSC and the FBI were interested in it, the US Services had not realized its importance, and were not prepared to give away any information. As has been related, it was difficult enough to get permission for the release of letters containing valuable intelligence sent by enemy agents in America, although it was imperative to do so in order to keep the channel of communication open and thus pave the way for the ultimate detection of the sender. In April 1942, BSC suggested to Hoover that the Chiefs of Staff should be invited to set up a joint inter-services committee which would be charged with the responsibility of facilitating the production of intelligence to be sent to Germany by double agents and of authorizing its release. BSC followed this suggestion with a paper on the care and 'feeding' of double agents, which was submitted to the Chiefs of Staff and accepted by them. Nevertheless, as had often happened in other instances, it was not acted upon consistently for many months. For example, an excellent double agent sent over by London was almost abandoned by the Germans because the FBI were unwilling or unable to get useful information to pass on to him.

Another difficulty, also purely American, arose from interdepartmental competition. The FBI occasionally employed double agents, and even G-2 made attempts to do so. Donovan's OSS employed more. Naturally each agency kept its operations secret from the other, with the result that the FBI would sometimes suspect and investigate an agent under the control of OSS.

In general, the theory and practice of double agents was one of the fields in which BSC/New York and SIS/London had to attempt to educate both the FBI and OSS, and it is open to doubt if they ever mastered the subject thoroughly. Nevertheless, as the war proceeded, an increasing number of double agents were put into operation in the Western Hemisphere and a number of them are worth consideration in some detail.

(b) The Double Agent 'Tricycle'

In 1937, a young Yugoslav student joined a club for 'free' political discussion in Freiburg, where he was finishing his education. The Yugoslav made two speeches to his fellow members, both strongly in favour of democratic government. But the apparent freedom of political thought was by no means as actual as he had supposed and after his second speech he was arrested by the German authorities and thrown into jail. He was released only after official representations had been made by the Yugoslavs to the German Government, and he was then expelled from the Reich. This incident was to serve Allied Intelligence well at a later date, for the young man developed an intense dislike for the Germans as a result of it. He later became known as the double agent 'Tricycle.'

In 1940, he was approached by the Germans in Belgrade and immediately got in touch with British Intelligence. As a result of careful handling, he was built up as a valuable source in the eyes of the Germans and during 1940 and part of 1941 he operated successfully between London and Lisbon. He was keenly anti-German, undoubtedly clever and loyal to his British employers. His tastes in clothes and entertainment were expensive – but then the Germans were paying largely for them. In fact, all he apparently wanted as a reward from the British was the post-war position of British honorary vice-consul.

After performing valuable service in Europe, he was sent by the Germans to the US in August 1941. The FBI were advised of his arrival and actually assisted in getting him his passage. However, they insisted on taking him over themselves. It was they who set up his wireless station, composed his messages and did his coding. BSC gave advice and supervision whenever possible, but was often deliberately bypassed by the FBI, since they were proud of their recent success with the Sebold/Sawyer case.

It did not work out. Tricycle disliked the comparatively unsophisticated Americans, and resented their inability to produce strategic information for him to pass on, while they in turn disliked his liberal manner of living. They kept making the impossible request that he should square up his financial affairs and reduce his expenses.

Eight letters were sent off by him in the autumn of 1941. One of these, in spite of BSC's warning, was not passed through Bermuda, but was sent to the Testing Department and fully developed. The others took much longer to arrive than might have been expected.

After some months the Germans sent him on to Rio. There he interviewed the Assistant Naval Attaché, Cmdr Bohny, and the German SIS chief, Alfredo Engels, who expressed complete confidence in him and instructed him to build a short-wave radio in New York for communication with Lisbon, Rio and Hamburg.

Throughout the first three months of 1942, the FBI passed out messages for him over his supposed radio, but gave BSC no copies of these, and no details concerning their success or failure. Tricycle was not even taken to see the radio station, with the result that he himself was in danger of being caught by a quick question from a German agent in the US or by a request to send a message on short notice. The Germans were complaining that his reports lacked meat and began to suspect – particularly after the arrest of Engels in Brazil – that Tricycle was working under control. After a protest by WS, Hoover appointed one of his senior and more experienced officers to take charge of the whole case, and set about obtaining a more regular supply of information from the Services.

However, despite his assurances, Hoover retained his original gang-busting ideals. When the Germans planned to send over some money for Tricycle, instead of allowing it to reach him without interference the FBI attempted to draw the courier into a trap, which would of course have notified the Germans that Tricycle was at least under the gravest suspicion. Throughout the middle of 1942, BSC, by making considerable efforts with the Joint Services Committee, elicited enough information to keep Tricycle at work. But in August 1942, the FBI finally decided to have no more to do with him, on the ground that he was a liar and was too expensive to justify his retention. In fact, it was a tacit admission of their incompetence in this particular instance.

(c) The Double Agent 'Springbok'

Perhaps the most interesting, if not the most successful, double agent employed by BSC was known as 'Springbok'. This man was a trained German agent whose wife was a well-connected Englishwoman. He himself was of noble descent and monarchical sympathies, his grandather having been Master of Ceremonies to Wilhelm I, and his monarchist father having been dismissed from a high governmental office at the accession of Hitler in 1933. In 1929, he went out to South Africa, where he built up a career as a fur buyer and miner. At the outbreak of war he lost his job and was nearly interned, but got out by proving to the South African Alien Investigation Department that he had for years had no contact with any German clubs or organizations. Then he tried without success to establish himself in Portuguese East Africa, was expelled, sailed for Europe rather than be interned, was captured by a French ship and was interned in Morocco until July 1940.

After the French Armistice, he was set free. The Germans gave him the option of entering the Army or doing intelligence work abroad. According to his statement, he chose the latter course because he no longer considered Germany his home and wished somehow to get in touch with his wife and children. In June 1941, he went to Brazil by Lati to join the espionage ring run by Alfredo Engels, as a collector of economic intelligence, particularly air information. After some months he was ordered to South Africa. He then approached the British, by the simple method of writing to the Consulate in Sao Paulo and asking for an appointment.

What he wanted was a chance to see his wife and children without being interned; some money, though not overmuch; and British citizenship after the war. In exchange, he gave a considerable amount of good new information and promised to work as a double agent in South Africa or elsewhere. The information he supplied comprised the following:

- a German letter-code, with the permanent key-word;
- the comb-cypher system used by German agents overseas;
- the formula for developing a German secret ink, with the key-word indicating that secret writing would be found in a letter;

– a formula for making secret ink out of phenolphthalein;
– a sketch of the structure of the German Intelligence organization in Brazil;
– a long report on the organization of German Intelligence HQ in Germany;
– names of prominent German agents in Brazil, including Alfredo Engels and Herbert Von Heyer (later convicted);
– detailed comments on the interrogations of German agents;
– the names of several prospective contacts and postboxes in South Africa – including Leibrandt, who he said had orders to assassinate General Smuts and destroy certain strategic bridges (Leibrandt was arrested in December 1941, convicted and executed);
– a report on a possible experimental ground for robot bombs.

Practically all of this was accurate, and some was new and valuable.

Although he was anxious to go to South Africa, headquarters preferred him to enter Canada, where he could be more reliably controlled. The South African authorities refused to allow him to return to the Dominion, where his wife was interned as a rabid Nazi. He was instructed to report to Germany that he could not get passage to South Africa, then to suggest North America, and finally to point out that information (for example on convoys) would be easier to obtain in Canada with less danger from the FBI. The Germans agreed.

Interviewed in Canada, Springbok produced still more information about the structure of the German Intelligence Service, personalities in it, and the German plans for sabotage in South Africa (illustrated by a map). The problem now was to get him into communication with Germany. A letter was prepared and sent down to Brazil in microphotographic form, saying that he had obtained a short-wave wireless transmitter and asking his opposite number in Sao Paulo, Werner Christoph Waltemath, to relay a message for him and open communication. He had already been directed to warn Waltemath by a letter in secret ink and two letters in open code, all facilitated through censorship by BSC. He asked Waltermath to tell Berlin he would soon be ready to communicate from Toronto through Brazil and had urgent information, although like all agents he needed money.

The RCMP were, of course, kept *au fait* with the plan as it progressed. In May 1942, BSC obtained from the British Chiefs of Staff in Washington a large quantity of excellent information for him, microphotographed it and sent it to his South American friends. But no regular W/T exchange was opened up between him and Waltemath.

In January 1943, another attempt was made to get into direct contact with the Germans, this time through a letter in secret ink to a postbox in Lisbon. The Germans were invited to reopen communication with Springbok under an alias in Toronto. In case the Germans moved him to the United States, the FBI were given the full story; and the help of OSS was enlisted to transmit the letter to Lisbon. But through bad staff work it was sent by sea bag on a slow ship and failed of delivery.

In March 1943, however, the Brazilian police were beginning to make wholesale arrests of German agents. The only link that Springbok had with Germany was Waltemath, and Waltemath lay very low in fear of being arrested. There were several attempts to establish communication between the two; but the task became even more difficult after Brazil entered the war in August, for then every German in Brazil was under strict control and wireless transmissions were monitored with increasing care.

The existence of Waltemath's set became known to the Sao Paulo police during their general clean-up, and they set about arresting him. And, while they were informed that Springbok himself (whom they knew to be connected with him) was under strict control, such is the vainglory of the Brazilians that they might have revealed the entire story to the newspapers, thus making Springbok forever useless. The FBI did what they could by arranging with the American press agencies to keep all mention of him out of correspondents' reports, but they could not control the Brazilian press. And in August 1943, the story appeared in Brazil, in Canada and in the United States. The RCMP covered up neatly. They announced to the press that Springbok had been arrested some time previously at the request of the British. As Springbok was living under a false name, he was able to remain safely in Toronto. Waltemath was sentenced to twenty-seven years' imprisonment for espionage in Brazil, and Springbok to the same term *in absentia*.

Springbok was now useless as a double agent. He was still employed (under a false name and nationality) by a Toronto firm, but frequent complaints were received by the firm and the RCMP about him, owing to his accent and Germanic appearance. BSC pressed headquarters to accept him for enlistment in the Pioneer

Corps, rather than for internment – in order to get him out of Canada. After all, there was a strong moral obligation to treat him well: he had never double-crossed the British in any way. But headquarters was reluctant to allow a German 'mercenary' to roam about Britain uncontrolled. After considerable persuasion, however, the authorities finally accepted him in February of 1945, and Springbok sailed from Halifax.

(d) The Double Agent 'Lodge'

A new problem in the employment of double agents in the Western Hemisphere arose in May 1944 with the despatch from Barcelona of a double agent known as Lodge, who had been selected to work in Montevideo under British control. Lodge was despatched from Spain by another double agent – one of the most important under British control. It was important that this operation should be successful in order that the reputation of the double agent in Spain should not suffer in the eyes of the Germans. The initial obstacles always encountered in moving a double agent and establishing him in a new area were successfully overcome, and Lodge arrived in Uruguay, where he was provided with a radio transmitter.

But now a greater difficulty arose. The operation had to be explained to the Americans. Lodge was instructed to establish radio communication between Montevideo and Hamburg. As his transmissions would certainly be monitored, it was essential to inform the American agencies concerned, and in particular the board known as Joint Security Control, which is responsible for the release of controlled strategic deception information to the enemy through American channels, and for release of all such material from the Western Hemisphere.

The matter was raised by BSC with General Bissell, as US Army member of the Joint Security Control. After considerable discussion, General Bissell finally agreed to the establishment of Lodge under British control, but added the ominous rider: 'This procedure is inconsistent with the existing arrangements between British and US authorities with respect to the establishment and use of double agents in South America for deception purposes.' The arrangement referred to by General Bissell had been drawn up in January 1943 by Colonel Bevan of the XX Committee and General Strong, then head of G-2. The Strong-Bevan agreement was unfortunately somewhat vague in terminology. It was interpreted by the Americans to prohibit the British from using double agents in South America. On the other hand, it was interpreted by BSC to mean only that deception material passed through double agents concerning the Western Hemisphere should first be approved by Joint Security Control (JSC) as the appropriate American authority. This difference in interpretation became the subject of protracted arguments between SIS and the Americans.

However, in the succeeding months, the Lodge operation continued successfully until finally, in November 1944, he established radio communication with Hamburg. At this point further difficulties arose. While the Americans jealously guarded their privilege of approving any information which might be sent by Lodge, they were not sufficiently energetic to provide such material themselves. For this reason, the SIS representative in Uruguay visited London and New York, and a plan was drawn up between him and BSC to provide Lodge with the necessary information to send to Hamburg. Part of the intelligence he sent out was to deal with events in Uruguay and would be supplied by the SIS representative in Montevideo; part, which would in fact be supplied by BSC, was to come from imaginary sources at his disposal who had access to information throughout the Western Hemisphere.

This scheme would have operated smoothly had not Lodge's employers in Hamburg insisted on receiving intelligence about Allied shipping movements out of the River Plate. BSC decided that the best way to satisfy the German requirements would be to release accurate information just too late to be of value. JSC was asked, therefore, to approve information of this kind and in every case to give a safe release date, taking into account speed and direction of the ship and the existing U-boat dispositions. JSC blandly approved the information in every case but refused to accept the responsibility of providing a safe date for its release. Nor could the US naval authorities be persuaded to indicate a safe date, although they presumably had in their possession all the relevant facts. In the face of this uncooperative attitude it was decided that, for the time being, Lodge should be forbidden to send any shipping information, and excuses were fabricated to satisfy the Germans that such intelligence was extremely difficult to obtain.

In spite of these and other difficulties, however, the Lodge operation continued until the end of the war in Europe with the use of material supplied by SIS in Montevideo and by BSC. Although no strategic deception of any great value was transmitted, the operation served its initial purpose of bolstering the reputation of the important double agent in Spain.

(e) The Double Agent 'Pat J.'

Fortunately not all the agents operating from the Western Hemisphere ran into the many difficulties encountered by Tricycle, Springbok and Lodge. A really successful operation was that carried out with the double agent known as 'Pat J.'

This man had been a German agent in the war of 1914–18. He was a Dutchman, who finally settled down in his own country as a dealer in radio and electrical equipment. Through his work he came into contact with Zeiss subsidiaries in Holland, and in 1940 he was recruited by the German Intelligence Service in The Hague. It was decided that he should be sent on an assignment to the United States after a period of training; and at the beginning of 1942 he arrived in Madrid on his way to America.

In Spain he underwent a change of heart and apparently decided that he would not work against the Allies of his own country. He had received permission from the Germans to visit the Netherlands Consulate on a passport matter, and seized this opportunity to tell the story of his recruitment to the Dutch authorities.

Headquarters was informed and requested BSC to ask if the FBI were prepared to accept Pat J. as a double agent to work in the United States. After consideration, the FBI decided in favour of the undertaking and Pat J. was assisted on his voyage over. The only trouble which arose was a bad attack of pneumonia on his arrival, but when he had recovered he was able to provide valuable information on the German Intelligence organizations in Holland and Paris.

That was in July 1942, and it was not until 1943 that, under supervision of the FBI, he was able to establish radio contact with his German masters. From then on the quality of his messages developed well, and he undoubtedly played a valuable part in the overall deception schemes.

Like so many German agents, he had the usual financial difficulties since payment through funds in neutral countries was by no means easy. The German tardiness in making payment to agents in the Western Hemisphere was a continual aggravation. Although the double agent was usually well taken care of financially by the British or Americans, he frequently had to pretend poverty in order to give verisimilitude to his supposed condition. On occasions this difficulty would create the ironic situation in which the Germans were making every effort to despatch funds urgently, while deception material was held up in order to maintain the pretence on the other side that sub-agents could not be paid and hence no information was forthcoming.

On one occasion, towards the end of 1943, the Germans advised Pat J. that funds would reach him shortly in the form of eight rare and valuable stamps. A German agent was despatched from Spain to Buenos Aires with funds to buy these stamps and send them to New York for Pat J. However, on arrival in Buenos Aires the agent apparently converted the funds to his own use and finally dropped dead of alcoholic excesses.

A few months later, a somewhat nervous New York Jew handed over $3,000 to an unknown man in a hotel bedroom in Manhattan. The Jew knew that the funds had reached him in contravention of the currency regulations, but he was under the impression that he was merely assisting a fellow refugee in distress. The final recipient of the money was Pat J., and it had been despatched by a Frenchman in Spain who had been working for the Germans for some years. This Frenchman was only a small pawn in the game, but it is worth noting here that during the war he had fleeced the German Intelligence Service by various means of 80 million francs. When last heard of, he was about to have the major part of his takings forcibly removed by the French authorities.

Further funds were sent to Pat J. at the end of 1944 by means of another German agent who flew from Lisbon carrying a diamond tie-pin and ring valued at about $6,000. Continued and ingenious methods of payment of a similar kind were ample proof of Pat J.'s success as a double agent, since they meant that the Germans clearly rated him highly. Pat J. was still transmitting when Germany capitulated, and it was planned that he should continue to do so in case of any possible revival of German clandestine activities.

(f) The Double Agent 'Minaret'

The case of 'Minaret' is another of the more successful operations carried out in the Western Hemisphere, though at one time it was jeopardized. Minaret, an Argentine national, arrived in Montevideo in July of 1941 from Spain and promptly reported to the US Embassy to tell his story. He had originally been recruited by the German Intelligence Service in Hamburg in 1939, and had carried out one or two minor missions on their behalf in Europe. He had no explanation as to why he had not told the truth earlier.

Nevertheless, it was decided that he could be profitably used as a double agent. It was originally planned that he should be controlled by the British and run from Uruguay, but after some negotiation he finally left for the United States to work under the control of the FBI. He established radio contact with Germany early in 1942. And then his troubles began.

In November of that year the FBI, who were experiencing their usual difficulties in obtaining deception material, allowed Minaret to send a most ill-advised message announcing in advance the replacement of Air Marshal Joubert as AOC in C, Coastal Command. Undoubtedly the FBI had picked up the news of this proposed change from their service contacts in Washington. Not only did they release this information without consulting BSC, but allowed Minaret to advise the Germans to broadcast the news to England.

The FBI were not at this time passing copies of Minaret's traffic to BSC, but they had reckoned without the fact that headquarters was monitoring and reading the messages. The only good that resulted from this piece of chicanery was that the FBI were forced in the future to provide copies of all such traffic to BSC, which in turn forwarded them to London.

Through study of the messages, headquarters inclined to the opinion that the Germans were aware that Minaret was controlled, and this opinion was strengthened when Minaret was supplied with a new cover address which was known to be badly 'blown'. It had been in possession of a spy whose arrest in Ireland in 1941 had been widely publicized. Nevertheless, the Germans had given ample proof of their gross carelessness in this respect, and their continued payment of large sums of money to Minaret, through a cut-out in Uruguay, tended to discount headquarters' fears. Minaret continued to transmit deception material on behalf of the Americans to the end of the European war.

One incident in Minaret's checkered career which occurred in January 1944 illustrates well the trouble which an unscrupulous double agent can cause. It also throws an interesting light on Minaret's character and motives. At the beginning of the year Minaret made a New Year's resolution – to take a holiday and to obtain more money. He calmly proceeded to blackmail the FBI, pointing out that unless his demands were met he would blow the whole operation to the Argentine Consul General in New York from where it would undoubtedly reach the Germans. His demands were exorbitant and could not be met. Nor was that all. He requested authority to take his mistress, who was interested in an operatic career, on a holiday to Buenos Aires with a view to studying the possibilities of the *Teatro Colón*.

The FBI turned to BSC for help. If they allowed Minaret to travel on a holiday with his mistress to the Argentine, would the British arrest him in Trinidad? They would guarantee to take him off British hands at the end of the war. Headquarters considered the case most sympathetically but regretfully decided that, in view of the fact that Minaret had voluntarily offered his services, no action could be legally taken against him.

Thrown back on their own resources, the FBI applied pressure to Minaret by threatening him with legal proceedings in the United States, should he take the action he contemplated. Minaret gave way, and although his relations with the FBI were apparently far from cordial, nevertheless the operation continued to the end of the European war.

It has not been possible to write in detail of all the double agents of varying importance who were operated from the Western Hemisphere – though there are many stories to tell of John Gold, Aspirin (named for the many headaches associated with him), Moonstone and Jar, Anthony and Bromo.

It is still difficult to assess the importance of the double agents in the Western Hemisphere in the overall deception picture, but Joint Security Control were satisfied that excellent deception had been carried out, particularly insofar as America's war potential was concerned. Tactical deception, clearly enough, could not have been carried out on any scale at such a distance. There is no doubt, however, that what was done to assist the Americans to establish double agents proved worthwhile, and it is gratifying to record that at the end of the war there were at least three controlled radio channels in daily contact with the enemy.

CHAPTER 5

Far Eastern Counter-Espionage

When BSC's counter-espionage section was formed, it was decided that it should not concern itself with Japanese espionage inasmuch as this work could not be undertaken satisfactorily by officers who, whilst fully qualified to deal with German or Italian espionage, had no Far Eastern experience.

Japanese espionage presents especial difficulties. Even Japanese names are a complicated subject which cannot be mastered by anyone not conversant with the language; for it is impossible in very many cases to identify a name except both by hearing it spoken and seeing it written. Often it is written in one way and pronounced in another. For example, the name for which the ideographs read 'small birds play' is pronounced '*Takahashi*' – 'Hawk's away'.

Japanese psychology cannot be properly understood by anyone who has not lived in the country. The roots of the Japanese espionage and security services, unlike those of Germany, can be traced back into antiquity; much relevant material is published in Japanese books, historical works or biographies, which have not been translated, but copies of which were available in 1942 only in North America. The study of the structure and functions of patriotic societies is an indispensable adjunct to the study of the intelligence services proper. And little was known about either of these subjects, although relevant material for the study of the secret activities of the most secretive of all nations was not lacking.

Accordingly, Far Eastern counter-espionage remained the responsibility of the head of the Far Eastern section, who previously had been engaged chiefly in Political Warfare (see Part II).

It was presumed that the Japanese would be unable to conduct much espionage in the United States, for their intelligence system before Pearl Harbor had been based exclusively on their Embassy and consulates, and there was no evidence that they had made arrangements in anticipation of the day when these would be denied to them. The presumption was proved correct. Indeed, it is a remarkable fact that, so far as is known, only one agent in the United States continued to convey intelligence to the Japanese after Pearl Harbor.

Velvalee Dickinson, who had acted as a Japanese agent before the war, when she had earned at least $60,000 as an employee of the Japanese Naval Intelligence Service, continued to work for her former masters without pay. She attempted to get intelligence through to Japan via an intermediary in the Argentine. She kept a dolls' shop in New York and her intelligence was transmitted in a plain-language code of Japanese manufacture. The first of her letters was intercepted at Bermuda where the censors rightly suspected that it contained plain-language code, for, while it made plentiful mention of dolls, it was apparently gibberish. Later, four other letters fell into the hands of the FBI who, by 22 January 1944, had obtained sufficient evidence to arrest her. She was subsequently convicted, but under interrogation and at her trial she was proved to be an obvious eccentric, far from representative of the usual agent. She made an hysterical scene in court and is reported to have become mentally deranged since her imprisonment.

There were, however, some indications that the Japanese planned, in the event of war with the United States, to transfer their centre of espionage in the Western Hemisphere to Mexico and eventually to Argentina. In the period preceding Pearl Harbor, an opportunity arose for BSC to investigate this possibility.

A special department of the Trinidad Censorship secretly opened a letter from the Argentine Embassy in Washington to the Foreign Ministry. It concerned two minor Japanese diplomats, who were being transferred from Washington to Buenos Aires, and it stated that the US Department of State suspected them of being members of the Japanese Intelligence Service. This information had never been passed to BSC by the State Department and the source was extremely delicate; but the opportunity could not be allowed to go unexploited.

The BSC representative in Trinidad asked New York for information. The reply stated that one member of the party, Hirasawa by name, was a dangerous agent belonging to an ultra-nationalist group. In 1939, he had organized the reshuffle in the Japanese Foreign Office which caused the resignation of Nomura and brought pro-Axis diplomats to the fore. In 1941, he was stationed in the Japanese Consulate at New York, where BSC's agents

Far Eastern Counter-Espionage

reported that he was empowered to send telegrams direct to Tokyo without reference to the Ambassador.

A representative of BSC flew to Barbados, where these and other Japanese had been removed from their ship, and the entire party was taken to Trinidad. Here they were interrogated, photographed, fingerprinted and searched. They were found to be carrying technical British and American publications of value in intelligence work, maps upon which locations of British and US naval bases in the Western Hemisphere were marked, lists of Hirasawa's contacts and about $40,000 in US notes, $15,000 of which were concealed in the lining of Mrs Hirasawa's handbag.

As diplomats, they were entitled to diplomatic privilege. But *were* they diplomats? A further despatch from the Argentine Foreign Ministry to the Embassy in Washington revealed that the Argentine Government had refused to accredit them, ostensibly because the personnel of all diplomatic missions in Buenos Aires was limited in number. Some days later, Japan evaded this restriction by raising its mission to the rank of Embassy, and the Argentine Government agreed to accept the party. But by now neither the British nor the Americans, whom BSC kept informed, had any intention of letting them go and, after much discussion, the Japanese sailed for Halifax under heavy guard.

In Halifax the party was further interrogated. A Japanese-Canadian employee of BSC, who had been recruited originally by the Far Eastern Section for Political Warfare work and who spoke and read Japanese fluently, was used to listen to their private conversations, whilst himself remaining unobserved. The FBI and the RCMP assisted at these interrogations and also in searching the forty-seven pieces of luggage carried by the Japanese.

Finally, after protests from the Japanese Government had duly been received, the party sailed for Japan minus their $40,000, their maps and their technical publications.

Thus corroborative evidence was obtained of the Japanese plan to transfer the centre of their intelligence work to Latin America, where it was the duty of SIS stations to make further investigations. In these they were handicapped by lack of expert staff. Indeed throughout the whole SIS organization in Latin America there was only one employee with knowledge of the Japanese language – a girl secretary in Santiago.

Meanwhile it was evident that Washington would be the centre for all Far Eastern counter-espionage intelligence and, as previously stated, the US Service intelligence departments possessed virtually the sum total of information available at the time concerning the structure of the Japanese espionage system as a whole. BSC had in mind, therefore, the possibility of setting up a unit of Far Eastern specialists to work jointly with the Americans. For this purpose, preliminary steps were taken to recruit the necessary staff. At the time, however, London did not favour such a plan, for they rejected virtually every suggestion to increase the staff of the Far Eastern section, without which the proposal could not be put into effect. Finally, in May 1943, London decided that BSC should cease to concern itself with Far Eastern work. The experts who had been assembled were all promptly recruited by American intelligence agencies.

WS, however, retained one officer to coordinate the reports from South American stations with FBI intelligence for, so long as Chile and Argentina maintained diplomatic relations with the Axis, the possibility of widespread Japanese espionage in Latin America could not be disregarded. Further, through the generosity, first of OSS and latterly of OWI, BSC had the advantage of the part-time services of the Japanese-Canadian mentioned above, who translated all documents in Japanese which SIS in Latin America obtained from their police contacts and other sources. On balance his work confirmed the conclusion reached eventually that Japanese espionage in Latin America was of little account. However, one example of it is perhaps worth recording. A diary, confiscated by the Chilean police from a suspected Japanese agent in Santiago, was found, after translation, to contain a formula for the use and development of secret writing. BSC forwarded the information both to Imperial and US Censorship, who were considerably interested in it, for it provided them with their only evidence that the Japanese had knowledge of a high-grade secret ink formula – one which they had received from their German colleagues.

It was not until March 1944 that SIS/London began to consider counter-espionage work against Japan as worthy of concentrated effort, and in that month the head of their counter-espionage division visited the United States to investigate at first-hand the possibilities of Anglo-American collaboration. His ultimate aim was to achieve some measure of integration in field work throughout the Far East on a similar basis to that already obtaining in Europe. But while this was not practicable for various reasons, he was informed that the Service agencies would not be averse to joint research with SIS in Washington.

After extensive deliberation, lasting several months, SIS decided to set up in Washington, under BSC's auspices, a section which would collaborate with G-2 and ONI on research primarily concerned with the structure of the Japanese intelligence services. However, while this idea was in itself still perfectly feasible, the choice of the officer to be in charge of the section was unfortunate, for, though he was a Japanese scholar (as it happened, the only one available to SIS), ONI unofficially informed BSC before his appointment had been confirmed that he was *persona non grata*. Nevertheless, after weighing all the evidence, CSS decided to send the officer to Washington, while at the same time giving the heads of G-2 and ONI written assurance that the officer was coming as his personal representative and had his full confidence.

Joint Anglo-American research regarding Japanese espionage began in November 1944, when as SIS Far Eastern unit was at last established in Washington. But during the next three months collaboration was no more than nominal. Both ONI and G-2 restricted their liaison to formal meetings held once a month, and they furnished little or no information of value. It soon became apparent to WS that the head of the unit was still far from liked by the Americans and was wholly unsuited to the task in hand. Accordingly, he recommended in strong terms to London that this officer should be recalled, and, when London intimated their intention of abandoning the whole project, pointed out that, in his view, the Americans were in principle still perfectly willing to collaborate with SIS.

In April 1945, CSS was persuaded to appoint a new head of the unit who was known to be acceptable both to ONI and G-2. Thereafter American collaboration was generously afforded. No objections were raised to the requisite increase in staff. *Inter alia*, G-2 agreed to supply copies of all Japanese Top Secret material which they had previously withheld; they allowed unrestricted access to their records; they supplied comprehensive reports on the various Japanese intelligence services, and asked the head of the unit to collaborate with them on equal terms in the interrogation of 140 Japanese diplomats captured by the American Seventh Army and brought to the United States. ONI were likewise cooperative.

Reviewing the problem in retrospect, it is, perhaps, regrettable that Anglo-American collaboration on Far Eastern counter-espionage intelligence, for which BSC had made plans immediately after Pearl Harbor, was not finally effected until five months before the capitulation of Japan.

PART VIII

ORGANIZATION FOR SECRET ACTIVITY OUTSIDE THE WESTERN HEMISPHERE

CHAPTER 1

Foreign Exiles and Minority Groups

(a) The Austrians
(b) Italians
(c) The Arabs

Reference has already been made to the work of organizing 'free' groups among the various foreign nationalities in the Western Hemisphere (see Part IV). This work was complementary – and in a sense preparatory – to BSC's entire recruiting programme.

Its main objective was to strengthen resistance movements in the occupied countries. Its subsidiary purposes were, first, to enlist the sympathies of resident minorities who had considerable influence in the lands of their adoption, and, because of this, were subjected, before Pearl Harbor, to ceaseless enemy propaganda; and secondly, to collect external intelligence (see Part IV).

'Free' groups were composed in the main of exiles and refugees from the Nazi tyranny, and they attracted members and support from the resident minorities in varying degrees. Some were formed spontaneously, while others, particularly of Axis nationality, BSC was under compunction to create. By no means all of them in the former category had any legitimate claim to be representative of the popular will within their own countries, and in several instances competing groups of the same nationality were mutually antagonistic. Furthermore there were several groups of an ultra-nationalist or quasi-Fascist complexion, whose existence was more harmful than beneficial.

BSC maintained contact with representatives of some twenty-one different nationalities, including Poles, Czechs, Hungarians, French, Austrians, Norwegians, Italians, Germans, Danes, Yugoslavs and Dutch. In working with them it was concerned:

1. To create 'free' or pro-British movements where none already existed.

2. To intervene in fratricidal disputes and to harness opposing democratic groups to a common purpose.
3. To assist those groups which were best qualified to influence opinion in their own countries. This assistance which was often considerable (for example, the Free French movement in the United States was initially dependent upon BSC for virtually all its resources) took the form of political guidance, financial subsidies, and the provision of facilities both for conducting propaganda and for collecting intelligence. As examples – BSC acted as adviser to a number of former statesmen, including Count Carlo Sforza, many of whom are now serving their own liberated countries as cabinet ministers or ambassadors; it enabled Subasic, subsequently Yugoslav Foreign Minister, to maintain contact with his countrymen at home; it kept the Czech and Polish secret services, among others, regularly supplied with intelligence of interest to them; and it controlled, through intermediaries, a number of foreign-language newspapers and periodicals in the United States – including the Hungarian *Szabadsag*, the *Slavonic Bulletin* and the *Nova Jugoslavia*.
4. To discredit – and if possible to suppress – the activities of groups or individuals who were politically undesirable. For example, the machinations of former Chancellor Bruening and Treviranus, of Otto Strasser and Carol of Roumania were carefully watched and appropriate counter-action was taken, either through press exposure or through United States and Canadian Government departments, whenever it was deemed advisable.

The work was essentially a Political Warfare undertaking, but, as may be judged, it also involved engagement in covert diplomacy and necessitated access to secret sources of information. To give a detailed account of it is not practical, for it would entail separate descriptions of nearly all the 'free' movements in the Western Hemisphere. However, a fair idea of the methods used, of the problems encountered and of the results achieved can be given by a brief survey of three widely separated foreign communities. The first of these, the Austrians, were a minority temporarily exiled from Europe, and had no roots in the United States. The second, the Italians, were a powerful resident minority, but with close European connections. The third, the Arabs, while relatively unimportant as a resident minority, were in a position to exert considerable influence in the Near East, which was, of course, an area of vital strategic importance.

(a) The Austrians

In its dealings with groups of Austrian emigres, of whatever political complexion, BSC laboured under an unfortunate initial handicap, for the majority of them claimed, without justification, to enjoy the official recognition of HM Government. It was thus all the harder to direct their activities to a single end. Of these groups three were important: the Legitimists, under the Hapsburg pretender, the Archduke Otto; the Socialists, under Julius Deutsch; and Austrian Action, under Count Ferdinand Czernin.

The Hapsburg group, which had the support of Hans Rott, a former member of the Schuschnigg Cabinet, and Rott's party, Free Austria, was adroitly kept in the public eye by the Archduke and his brothers, whose personal charm and social prestige won them many friends in both London and Washington. But the majority of the Austrian emigres were unsympathetic to the Legitimists. As the latter had not been represented in the Austrian Government at the time of the *Anschluss*, they could not claim to speak for the Austrian people. Further, Otto himself was unpopular with the exiled Czechs, Poles, Hungarians and Yugoslavs, who feared his imperial ambitions and even suspected him of being pro-Fascist. A born intriguer, he was incapable of holding himself aloof from politics and was perpetually meddling in the affairs of his fellow exiles.

To BSC the Legitimists were a lasting embarrassment. The Hapsburgs enjoyed an almost unrestricted freedom of movement and were opportunists by instinct. To counter their manoeuvres was difficult. But fortunately, through its liaison with the American press, BSC was generally able to arrange that the excursions of Otto to Canada, of Felix to Brazil, or of Robert to Portugal received a harassing publicity throughout the United States. For example, Walter Winchell (see Part II) was always eager to excoriate the Archduke, and his audience, as has already been said, was considerable.

The Socialists required less attention. Although well organized and bitterly opposed to the Nazi regime in Europe, they suffered from a lack of contact with current political feeling in Austria. Their leader, Deutsch, had left the country as far back as 1934, and some of his principal adherents even earlier. Nor were they popular with Austro-Americans. Thus, though BSC remained on friendly terms with them throughout, they were able to exercise little influence upon opinion either in the United States or in Austria itself.

Austrian Action, which proved the most useful of the Austrian groups, was controlled by Count Ferdinand Czernin, who though of a somewhat erratic temperament was nevertheless sincere, and a young publicist, Gregor Sebba, who had been arrested by the Nazis after the *Anschluss*. Upon his release he had travelled to the United States and had at once set about organizing his fellow refugees.

Using suitable cover, BSC financed Austrian Action extensively in its early days. Sebba wished it to be a militant group, but the absence of any official British support made this impossible. He had to confine himself, therefore, to more conventional forms of publicity – mass Austrian blood donations, the formation of a cultural section to arrange exhibitions of Austrian photography and the publication of a magazine, designed to present Austrian problems to the American people.

But, besides his public activities, Sebba laboured tirelessly with BSC to bring about a union of the divergent groups of Austrians in exile. In September 1941, he was successful in forming an Austrian Coordinating Committee, which represented a coalition of four previously independent bodies: Austrian Action, the Young Conservative Austrians, the Austro-American Centre and the Austrian Section of the American Committee on European Reconstruction. When, towards the end of 1941, Rott and some of his monarchist friends attempted to form a pro-Hapsburg government in exile, the new Coordinating Committee at once repudiated the unprecedented act in the press. Otto, in consequence, hastily disclaimed any part in the project.

Immediately after Pearl Harbor, Sebba succeeded in yet further uniting the Austrian emigres. A council was formed, consisting of three Legitimists, three anti-Legitimists and two neutrals. Only the Socialists remained unrepresented; and BSC concluded that its efforts of the two preceding years had not been wasted.

(b) Italians

There is a resident population of four and a half million Italians in the United States. Most of them are settled in the eastern industrial states – New Jersey, New York, Connecticut, Rhode Island and Massachusetts. In this area they form no less than twelve per cent of the total population and constitute a voting bloc which neither local politicians nor Washington can afford to ignore. At the same time the majority of them are poor, culturally backward and politically immature. In the communities of which they form a part they are generally regarded as socially inferior, and for this reason suffer from a sense of oppression. Mussolini, with his theories of racial superiority and national advancement, had an inevitable attraction for them, and when the European war broke out the weight of their influence was very definitely on the side of the Axis.

Nevertheless, there were refugees from Fascism in the United States, and there were elements of the resident minority who were basically pro-Allied. Among the more important Italian exiles and leaders of Italo-American groups with whom BSC maintained contact were Count Carlo Sforza; Augusto Bellanca, 'boss' of the large Italian bloc in the Amalgamated Clothing Workers of America; Luigi Antonini, who held a similar position in the International Ladies Garment Workers Union; and Don Sturzo, founder of the Christian Democratic Party in Italy, who, despite advanced age and ill health, was an active champion of the anti-Fascist cause. The task was to unite men of this calibre and others whom they represented in an organized movement. It was largely accomplished through the Mazzini Society, with which BSC had close connections.

The Mazzini Society was originally founded in June 1940, under the presidency of Professor Max Ascoli, who supplied it with most of its funds. It was, however, vitalized by Alberto Tarchiani, the former editor of the progressive Milan daily, *Corriere Della Sera*. Tarchiani, who worked as a BSC intermediary (his journey from Europe to the United States having been made possible by BSC), was fervently pro-British, and a man of very considerable energy and resource. Under his leadership, the Mazzini Society formed over fifty local branches in various parts of the country and a subsidiary youth organization. Moreover it won the support of the large and politically influential Italian-American Labour Council, and the support also of the *Federazione Colombiana* and of two Italo-American political parties.

The Society ran its own periodical, the *Mazzini News*, which was published monthly, had a mailing list of 30,000 leaders of Italian colonies and acted as a central news agency by supplying the Italian-language press with selected items. For the latter purpose BSC prepared many reports, including some which were based on information obtained from Imperial Censorship and from interrogations of travellers from Italy. The Society arranged regular Italian broadcasts, both domestic and short-wave. For these BSC supplied material from sources to which Italian-language newspapers did not have access: for example, material from intercepted letters which revealed rather strikingly the discontent both of Italian troops at the front and of their families at home. The Society distributed pamphlets and organized mass meetings, notably a Matteotti Memorial meeting which attracted vast crowds. Under its auspices Alberto Cianca, who had been brought out of North Africa by SOE and who subsequently emerged as one of Italy's leading political figures, went on a nationwide lecture tour which proved highly successful.

These activities – and more besides – were in the general cause of anti-Fascism. In addition, the Society undertook propaganda campaigns for specific purposes and one of these may be briefly described as illustration.

Generoso (Gene) Pope had considerable influence among Italo-Americans. He had entered the United States as a penniless immigrant, had made a fortune in the sand and gravel business and in time had become one of the 'bosses' of Tammany Hall. Thereafter, to increase his political power, he had bought the two Italian-language newspapers with the largest circulation in the country: *Il Progresso Italo-Americano* and *Il Corriere d'America*.

He had been an enthusiastic supporter of Mussolini from the outset, had paid an official visit to Fascist Italy, where he was feted, and had conducted a violent anti-British campaign at the time of the Abyssinian conflict. After the outbreak of the European war, he inevitably became one with the most militant isolationists, and early in 1941 launched an appeal for subscriptions to the Italian Red Cross which was to have culminated in a huge charity concert at Madison Square Garden.

At BSC's instigation, the Mazzini Society organized a counter-campaign. Its Italian news service distributed press releases which revealed Pope's Fascist background, were illustrated by photographs of Pope in the company of the Duce and pointed out the contrast between the anti-Allied reports in the Italian-language sections of his newspapers and the fulsome eulogies of President Roosevelt in the English-language sections.

This material was reproduced in such papers as the *New York Post* and *PM* and was circulated by other BSC-sponsored societies, including Fight for Freedom. Soon it attracted wide attention, and in result forced not only the cancellation of the projected concert but the premature closure of the whole subscription list. Moreover, Pope himself felt obliged to bow to the storm. In an interview with the *New York Post*, he affirmed that he was anti-Axis and he followed this up with similar statements in his own papers. His retraction assured the almost unanimous goodwill and support which were forthcoming from the Italian minority when the United States Government eventually declared war on the Axis.

Thus by the time of Pearl Harbor, the Mazzini Society had already fulfilled one of its main purposes. Thereafter, with BSC's support – and by the end of 1942 with the support of OSS also – it remained the focal point of the Italian anti-Fascist movement in the United States. Further, its influence extended to Latin America and was the medium whereby BSC was enabled to recruit agents in Central America for despatch into Italy (see Chapters 2 and 5).

(c) The Arabs

There were between 160,000 and 200,000 Arab-Americans in the USA. Of these 50,000 had been born in the Near East. While they were comparatively insignificant as a group within the USA, they nevertheless were important as a propaganda channel to the Arabic world, for the majority of them were in communication with their relatives in North Africa and Asia Minor.

After the fall of France, the Vichy French endeavoured to use their influence to mobilize Arab opinion in favour of the Axis. The most powerful Arab in the United States was Salloum Mokarzel, who was President of the Lebanese League of Progress – a society which was a coordinating centre of some sixty Syrian clubs in Canada, Brazil and Argentina as well as in the United States – and editor of the Arab newspaper *Al Hoda*. He was persuaded at the outset to support Vichy and Pétain.

BSC set about the task of converting him. Contact with him was made through Raoul Aglion, a prominent member of the Free French Movement (see Part II), who had long experience in the Near East. After lengthy negotiations, Mokarzel agreed in June 1941 to place the editorial policy of his paper under Aglion's control, and thenceforward BSC subsidized *Al Hoda* and supplied it with material. The paper's circulation was only 500 a day but it had many subscribers in French North Africa, and many of its readers in the United States forwarded their copies to friends and relatives at home.

As cover for his work, Aglion opened a Near East Information

Centre in New York, to which, at BSC's instigation, material comprising political news of interest to Arab-Americans, quotations from speeches of prominent Arab leaders and excerpts from the Egyptian press were cabled directly from SOE's Arab News Agency in Cairo. This material was passed to *Al Hoda* and was also used in Egyptian, Arabic, Turkish, Persian, French and Armenian programmes broadcast over the BSC controlled short-wave station WRUL (see Part II).

Further, BSC despatched packages of *Al Hoda* to SOE/Cairo for distribution, and extracts from the paper were cabled to the Arab News Agency in Cairo by the ostensibly independent *Britanova* (see Part II).

Al Hoda's new policy inevitably caused reaction from the Axis propaganda forces. A priest (said to have been sent by the Vichy Consulate) called on Mokarzel to remonstrate with him. He emphasized that Pétain was 'a faithful son of the church', and hinted that advertising and other favours would be forthcoming if Mokarzel would agree to discontinue his attacks. But Mokarzel remained firm, and immediately thereafter convened a meeting of the representatives of some forty Arab societies, at which resolutions were passed expressing support of 'the liberation of Syria and Lebanon from German domination'. The meeting was attended by a Reuters' representative and received wide publicity in the Arab press and radio.

The Vichy French then offered decorations to a number of prominent Syrians in the USA – but this move also proved ineffective. At Aglion's suggestion one of them wrote an open letter to the French Ambassador, Henry-Haye, saying that he could not accept a decoration from a Government which had constantly broken its promises and actively supported the enemies of his country. The letter was published in both American and Arab newspapers, and, in support of it, Aglion arranged for an Arab group in North Carolina to send Henry-Haye a telegram deploring the situation in Syria and Lebanon. 'When the German Army threatened your own country with an inferior force,' it ran, 'your Government surrendered with a superior force to save Paris and other cities in your country from destruction. Why not save from destruction another country which is not yours? Your General Dentz, knowing that the opposing forces are far superior, yet will cause destruction of a country for no other reason except collaboration with the Axis powers.'

At the beginning of July 1941, Mokarzel's organization followed a suggestion from BSC by inviting Jacques de Sièyes of the Free French Delegation to be the guest of honour at the Syro-Lebanese Convention in Detroit, while pointedly ignoring the French Consul who had presided over the gathering in previous years. Telegrams of support were sent to General de Gaulle and the British forces; anti-Vichy resolutions were passed; and the meeting, which represented, of course, a considerable slap in the face to Vichy, was publicized not only in America but throughout the Arab world.

In addition to the work which he undertook through *Al Hoda* and the Near East Information Centre, Aglion also formed, at BSC's instigation, the National Arab Committee for Democracy, which was nominally headed by the Lebanese scholar, Professor P.K. Hitti of Princeton, and another 'free' Arab Committee called *Groupe de Jeunesse Syrienne aux Etats-Unis*.

These societies, giving the impression of a strong pro-Allied movement among the Arabs in the Western Hemisphere, undoubtedly influenced public opinion in the Near East. They were the instruments used, for example, when SOE/London, at the time of the French invasion of Lebanon, requested BSC to arrange for cables supporting General de Gaulle to be sent from prominent Arabs in the United States to Lebanese leaders and to General Dentz, the French High Commissioner.

CHAPTER 2

Recruiting Secret Agents

(a) Recruiting Problems
(b) Methods Used
(c) Lessons Learned

Michael Budak (the name is an alias) was one of several hundred secret agents recruited by BSC and trained in a BSC school for operations in Europe. What is written of him in this and succeeding chapters applies in general terms to his fellows.

He was a Yugoslav Canadian, and was dropped one night by parachute into the country of his origin with instructions to join the Yugoslav forces of Marshal Tito. He did not know exactly what his chances were of fulfilling his mission, for he was not informed of the statistics. These revealed that there were three chances in a hundred that he would be incapacitated before he could begin operating, three in a hundred that he would be captured after arrival and in such case one in three that his captors would be the Gestapo. Thus when he landed safely on Yugoslav soil, he had a good chance of survival and of doing some very effective guerilla fighting against the Germans and their satellites.

(a) Recruiting Problems

One of the duties which WS undertook both for SIS and SOE was 'to recruit, train and despatch agents into enemy territory'. There were many unforeseen obstacles encountered in the way of fulfilling it.

To begin with, although the United States was the largest potential source of recruits in the Western Hemisphere, it could unfortunately never be exploited fully. So long as American neutrality lasted, the US Government did not wish recruits to be drawn from foreign or foreign-descended minorities, and could make their will effective through the Immigration authorities, the Department of Justice and the State Department, without whose permission it was virtually impossible for an agent to leave the country.

The case of a Bulgar named Alexander Stoyanoff provides illustration of the difficulty. This man was sent out by London to get false papers in America and return to Europe. The Immigration authorities, through their own enquiries, soon found out that his story was false, and BSC had to resort to a personal appeal on the highest level before Stoyanoff was cleared. Such pressure could be exercised in exceptional circumstances, and indeed, as will be shown later, several first-class agents were recruited in the United States directly by BSC. But to flout the will of the US Government as a matter of policy would obviously have been very unwise.

After the United States entered the war, BSC was obliged to give an undertaking to the FBI not to recruit any agents in its own behalf. As the result of an agreement with Donovan, a few agents recruited by OSS, at BSC's behest, were loaned to London. But this was an arrangement of which advantage could be taken only sparingly and very discreetly, for OSS had difficulty in securing a sufficient number of agents to fulfil their own needs. The manpower authorities were unwilling to allow any fit man of military age to leave the country, and a draft board release, without which an exit permit would not be granted, was extremely hard to obtain. In such circumstances great care had obviously to be taken not to abuse OSS's generosity and to guard against any disclosure that they were recruiting for the British.

Most of BSC's recruiting had, therefore, to be done outside the United States – in Canada and, to a lesser extent, in Latin America. The choice was rather limited, for it was found that with a few notable exceptions (to be described later) the members of foreign minority groups in the Western Hemisphere had insufficient interest in the land of their origin to be prepared to return to it, at the sacrifice of their existing comforts, on an arduous and dangerous mission; further, that many of them had forgotten their original language or could speak it only with an accent. Anti-Fascist intellectuals who had sought sanctuary in the Western Hemisphere were, in general, not of tough enough fibre to be suitable either for SOE or SIS work, while the majority of the roughnecks (particularly before the invasion of Russia) did not seem to care greatly who won the war.

Even when suitable candidates had been found and trained, BSC's difficulties were by no means over. Transport was always very limited and after Pearl Harbor was, for a time, practically unobtainable. Party after party were held up. Sometimes as much as three months would elapse before an agent reached the United States after recruitment in Latin America. Constant delays in sailing, changes in routine, and the multiplication of formalities to which attention had to be given represented, perhaps, the most irksome part of the job of recruitment. For nothing is more likely to discourage an agent and to damage his discretion than interruption in his plans for setting out upon his mission.

(b) Methods Used

The steps which led to Michael Budak's recruitment as a secret agent were quite straightforward. The first was taken after a meeting of the United Mine, Mill and Smelter Workers, of which Budak was a staunch member.

At that meeting he had spoken of 'the need for the Allies to open a second front in Europe', for like many left-wingers, including most of his friends, he was in sympathy with the Soviet Union on that score. One man whom he knew less well than some of the others, said, 'You guys talk a lot, but what are you really doing about the second front?'

Later Michael Budak talked to this man. He confessed that perhaps his own contribution to the war was not very impressive. But he wasn't certain where he would fit in best. The other mentioned casually that he had a friend who might be able to advise him, and that the three of them should have a chat.

Not long afterwards Michael Budak was introduced to a man who called himself 'Mr Crane'. His new acquaintance told him that he was a representative of the War Office, looking for personnel for special work in connection with the second front.

'What kind of work?' Budak asked.

The answer he received was not direct. 'It is the kind of thing that calls for courage and initiative,' Crane said.

At the end of the interview Budak realized that he had learned practically nothing about what kind of duties his interviewer had in mind, although the latter had managed to extract full details of Budak's past history, his character, experience, likes and dislikes, political affiliations or sympathies. If the recruiting officer had not taken a favourable view of Budak, the latter would have learned nothing more than that he had been introduced to a War Office representative who required men for some kind of special work.

However, the officer had been favourably impressed and had, therefore, taken Michael Budak one step farther along the way by telling him that he would be required to work in the country of his origin, whose language he spoke fluently (Yugoslavia, as it happened); that his activities there would be of a combatant nature; and that they would probably necessitate his functioning alone rather than as part of a unit. But there had been no mention of the type of training he would receive. He had not been told that his work would involve sabotage or that he would be likely to be dropped by parachute.

At the close of the interview Crane had impressed upon him that he must discuss the interview with no one, for his chances of selection would be jeopardized if any word of it leaked out.

There were two more interviews, and then Michael Budak learned that he had been tentatively accepted. He was given security instructions. He was told to cut down on his correspondence, to refrain from telling others about his past life and experiences, to withhold his real name as long as he had an alias to use, to remove all personal markings from his luggage and to put away all letters, photographs and other belongings which might betray his identity.

When these preliminaries were completed, Michael Budak became a student of the BSC Training School.

The procedure in his case was a fairly standardized method which BSC used, with variations, in recruiting nearly 300 men for work in enemy territories. In Canada, the principal recruiting ground, there was at first some thought of organizing small committees among the various foreign nationality groups with the object of founding organizations throughout the country with which BSC representatives could deal, and in fact extensive reports on key men of various nationalities were obtained from the RCMP. After further study, however, the plan seemed unwieldy and it was decided to work along different lines.

Successful recruiting operations among foreigners seemed to depend upon the ability of the recruiting officer to find a key contact man. The contrast between BSC's failure with Italians and its success with Yugoslavs illustrates this.

The Italians in Canada were in general unsuitable for work as secret agents. Those Italian-Canadians who were otherwise well qualified seemed to lack sufficient patriotic feeling for either the country of their birth or that of their adoption. Despite the fact that the RCMP cooperated fully, making files available and helping in every possible way, no key contact man could be found. It became necessary, therefore, to resort to direct approach, and a BSC representative interviewed 300 men throughout the principal centres between Montreal and the Rocky Mountains. The results

Organization for Secret Activity Outside the Western Hemisphere

were appalling. Only one recruit was found in the city of Montreal, and even he eventually proved unsatisfactory.

In 1942, a survey was made of the potential supply of Canadian recruits, with particular attention being paid to Yugoslavs. One important contact was developed in the course of this survey, and from that time onwards Yugoslav recruiting was a success. The key contact man would, from time to time, gather a group of candidates from various parts of Canada. When a suitable number had been found, a recruiting officer from the New York headquarters would visit Canada to interview the men in a small office acquired for the purpose. As soon as he had made the final selections, BSC, with the cooperation of various Canadian governmental departments, would secure passports, exit permits, releases from Selective Service and whatever else was necessary.

In the beginning, most recruits were civilians, and in the few instances when service personnel with the necessary background and training were found BSC secured their release by arrangement with the services. This general procedure was changed for a number of reasons. The principal one was that when the training school was established it was set up within the machinery of the Canadian Army. To make the recruiting procedure consistent with the training scheme, and also to take advantage of the improved security and discipline which were possible under military regulations, BSC made arrangements with the Canadian military authorities whereby recruits were enlisted into the Canadian Army.

This procedure worked out very well. It meant that men were put into uniform as soon as recruited. On completion of their training they went overseas on Canadian troopships. On arrival at a British port they would be discharged from the Canadian Army and absorbed by the War Office.

Later, the scheme was further simplified by arrangements which resulted in the services providing BSC with most of the raw material it required. Security reports of the services, and the opinions of commanding officers on the suitability of a potential recruit, obviously saved BSC a great deal of work.

Another special arrangement worked out with the Canadian authorities protected the agents recruited by BSC. It was agreed that men who served with BSC or its principals, whether or not they were at any time Canadian soldiers, should be entitled to receive the full benefits of a Canadian soldier under the Canadian War Services Gratuity Act. Similarly, the men recruited by BSC were given the right to the full benefit of Canadian Army pensions, regardless of whether or not they had ever served in the Canadian Army. The Canadian authorities could not have been more cooperative. They bore the whole of the costs and their goodwill was the mainstay of BSC's recruiting programme.

(c) Lessons Learned

Canada, then, was by far the most fruitful field of recruitment, and Yugoslav-Canadians the most successful recruits. Incidentally, the official recruiting officer in Canada for the Yugoslav Government-in-exile, Colonel Savich, did not cooperate with BSC. He was so indolent and so anti-Croatian that he found only one agent.

BSC learned that it was advantageous to search simultaneously for both SOE and SIS material, for by so doing elasticity could be lent to recruiting operations. The suitability of men for one or other type of work could be determined during their training period and the recruiting officer could thus be relieved of the burden of making the original decision himself.

SIS needed recruits of the kind hardest to find – men who had, in addition to such attributes as sound health, courage and resourcefulness, special facilities at their disposal for obtaining intelligence in a foreign country.

Although no success was had in finding Italian recruits in Canada, several Italians were recruited in Mexico on the instructions of BSC, and they did outstanding work as leaders of the underground in various large Italian cities.

Experience showed that the best agents were found amongst:

1. Emigrants (first generation citizens) from countries with a low standard of living such as Yugoslavia, Hungary or China.
2. Liberal-minded Canadians, young, ruthless and energetic.
3. Left-wing Yugoslavs, Spaniards and Italians; several Yugoslav Communists proved the most valuable material of all.
4. For high-level intelligence work, wealthy cosmopolitans of dual nationality, e.g. American and French.

In general result, BSC obtained far more recruits than London was able to accept. Fifty-six veterans of the Spanish war were produced in response to a request from SOE/London for 'individuals of any nationality for subversive work', but they were refused on political grounds. Lithuanian officers volunteered to return clandestinely to their country, but likewise were refused. By the beginning of 1943 BSC had developed an excellent organization in Canada for obtaining first-rate Balkan recruits, but SOE/Cairo had insufficient aircraft to transport the number suggested and asked for it to be cut down.

CHAPTER 3

Training

(a) Types of Instruction
(b) Classes of Students
(c) Helping the Americans

(a) Types of Instruction

Michael Budak's paramilitary course of training at the BSC school in Canada covered a wide variety of subjects. It was a distillation of all that was known about subversive methods, and because of the urgency for recruits at that particular time, a great deal of work was crammed into a short space of time – approximately one month in all.

The new recruit was taught the importance of accurate observation; and his own powers of observation were frequently put to practical test by moving or removing objects in his room. He was taught how to shadow a man and how to escape surveillance himself; how to creep up behind an armed sentry and kill him instantly without noise; and how to evade capture by blinding an assailant with a box of matches. In the 'unarmed combat' course he learned many holds whose use would enable him to break an adversary's arm or leg, or knock him unconscious or kill him outright.

He was given weapons training, too. He learned to handle a tommy-gun and to use several different types of revolvers and automatic pistols, firing them from a crouching position either in daylight or darkness. He was instructed in the use of a knife, which killed quickly and silently if driven upwards just below the ribs.

Much of his time was spent in mastering the arts of sabotage. He was taught the simplest way of putting a motor car out of commission without leaving trace of his interference. He learned how to attach explosives to a railway track or an oil tank in the way likely to cause the greatest damage; how to make simple types of grenades and explosive and incendiary devices using material that could easily be purchased.

Before the course was finished, he could make and write with secret inks, use different kinds of codes and cyphers for communication with agents, and interrogate a prisoner to best effect. He was trained in parachute jumping. He took part in night exercises in which one group of students would set out to sabotage a specified target, while others would be given the job of stopping them; and in exercises arranged with the RCAF, in which a raiding party would be dropped by parachute and would later carry out an attack supported by RCAF aircraft.

Practical tests were conducted, too, in the city of Toronto with the help of the Toronto City Police, who were undergoing counter-espionage and counter-sabotage training. A selected group of police in the counter-espionage squad, unaware that they were dealing with students, would be set on the trail of men whom they supposed were enemy agents. To pass this test Budak would have to evade the police.

(b) Classes of Students

The school trained more than 500 carefully selected students and conducted fifty-two courses. It was founded in December 1941, and the instructors and staff moved in on the day of Pearl Harbor.

Its scope grew beyond that originally planned for it, for it became a training centre – not only for agents recruited by BSC but for various British, Canadian and American officials engaged in secret or semi-secret work. Among those who attended its courses were:

- BSC personnel
- Industrial Security Officers
- many OSS officers
- US Naval Intelligence personnel
- US Military Intelligence personnel
- nearly a hundred members of the Office of War Information
- ten head FBI agents
- Canadian officials from the RCMP, Military Intelligence, the Department of External Affairs and the Wartime Information Board.

(c) Helping the Americans

Some account has already been given in a previous section

of the influence which the school had on the Office of War Information (see Part II). Its influence on OSS was greater, for BSC was chiefly instrumental in planning and developing the latter's training programme.

In February 1942, Donovan's organization had no training schools, although – to justify its existence – it needed them urgently. At the request of Colonel Robert Solborg, who was at that time head of the MO Division (the OSS equivalent of SO), two special courses for Donovan's men were arranged at the BSC school. Some of those who attended went straight into the field thereafter. Others became instructors and set up the first of Donovan's own training-schools.

After the OSS schools had been opened, the commanding officer of the BSC school was invited to inspect them, and made certain recommendations which were carried out and resulted in marked improvement. During a later reconstruction the entire OSS programme of training was once more revised, and then the BSC school was made over to them for finishing courses so that their output of students should not be interrupted. Meanwhile the O.C. of the BSC school was seconded to OSS as Advisory Director of Training. He ran weekend courses for their country section head officers, delivered key lectures in other courses and carried through a drastic reorganization of their programme.

Another SOE officer was seconded to OSS as early as April 1942, and he remained with them as instructor in close combat throughout the succeeding years. Still other officers of the BSC school, men with operational experience and a sound knowledge of field-work, assisted them from time to time.

OSS lacked not only experienced instructors, but books and equipment. BSC handed them its complete lecture book, which they used as the basis of their course, together with a wealth of material, published and unpublished, on pertinent subjects.

It also furnished them with supplies of special devices and explosives, such as incendiary pencils, fog-signals, lead delays, limpets, escape files, concealed compasses and models of ships and aircraft; thus they were able to go ahead with their programme unhampered by the necessity of waiting until such equipment could be produced in the United States.

When the training school was closed down in September of 1944, its entire stock was bequeathed to OSS, who received it gratefully, for they had nothing of comparable quality.

CHAPTER 4

Supplying the Underground

(a) Special Devices and Identity Papers
(b) Clothing from Enemy Countries
(c) Foreign Currency

(a) Special Devices and Identity Papers

The underground armies fighting the enemy in Europe and Asia required a wide variety of equipment, weapons and supplies to enable them to function efficiently. They could never get enough.

Besides recruiting and training many of the men, like Michael Budak, who became underground and guerrilla leaders, BSC obtained much that was required by them and by those with whom they worked. There were complete parachute outfits, including small spades which agents used to bury their parachutes after landing in enemy territory. There were special containers – released from an aircraft at the same time as an agent was dropped, containing wireless sets, weapons and other supplies he might need. And there were second-hand revolvers which were obtained without cost, for these were rounded up by the RCMP who assisted BSC most generously.

For sabotage operations there were any number of strange devices with strange names, the 'firefly', for example, limpets and the incendiary pencil.

A list of all the 'toys' (as SOE called them) which BSC obtained would make tedious reading. However, a rather unusual one was a gourd of curare poison, which produces instant death if injected into the blood stream. It was procured from up-country Venezuelan Indians and forwarded to London in April 1942. Some of the special devices which BSC supplied were invented by SOE, while others were developed through the collaboration of the SOE Division of BSC, OSS and the National Development and Research Council. Most of them were manufactured in the USA and Canada, and their total value was more than $6,000,000.

BSC also supplied essential identity papers for agents. It obtained passports of many countries both from Bermuda and through Latin American representatives, and it obtained original German documents from prisoners of war in Canada. Agents in enemy territory were apt to need new passports and documents at a moment's notice, so that the supply never exceeded the demand.

(b) Clothing from Enemy Countries

Agents needed genuine European clothing, for though SOE could manufacture a tolerable imitation, it was always *faute de mieux*. BSC was able to contribute to the supply in various ways.

Jamaica, Trinidad and Bermuda were asked to look out for suitable garments as well as articles such as knives, fountain-pens and suitcases which might be obtainable from European refugees on a 'new lamps for old' basis.

A friend of BSC in the Canadian Department of External Affairs acquired several suits of European origin from Canadian Immigration officers formerly posted in Europe. Clothes stored for prisoners of war and internees in Canada were sent over after protracted negotiations. And a Communist friend was persuaded to 'raid' for suitable garments a supply of clothing accumulated from a 'Bundles for Russia' drive he had helped to organize.

(c) Foreign Currency

The underground needed money. In a worldwide conflict – with the British, the Allies, the neutrals and the enemy all competing for supplies of money – many extraordinarily delicate stratagems for the purchase of foreign currency had to be devised and carried through in great secrecy. BSC was operating in the richest country in the world; several of its officers were skilled in financial matters; and the Latin American stations commanded another wide financial field. The friendly collaboration of Donovan provided safe assistance in procuring large quantities of currency, often at very short notice. And the New York bankers, Ladenburg, Thalmann & Co., with whom BSC maintained close and confidential relations, served on more than one occasion as discreet intermediaries.

At various times, from early 1941 to 1944, BSC bought for

London: German Reichsmarks, Italian lire, French francs, Polish zlotys, Dutch guilders, Norwegian kroner, Belgian belgas, Spanish pesetas, Netherlands East Indies guilders and Moroccan, Tunisian and Algerian francs. Furthermore, BSC kept London informed of sums of foreign money taken as prize at Bermuda, so that arrangements could be made for SOE or SIS to lay hands on them at the earliest possible opportunity.

An example of a more delicate transaction was one in which, after protracted discussions with the US Treasury and the Bankers' Trust Company, BSC joined with OSS to pay the dollar equivalent in New York for nearly two million Portuguese escudos. This money was required by agents of SOE and OSS, and it was made available to them through the Lisbon office of Bensaude & Co.

On another occasion, at the special request of the Bank of England, BSC procured 500,000 Argentine pesos. These were purchased in small parcels through intermediaries in Uruguay and Argentina, against payments from New York on an Uruguayan bank. The money was shipped over to Britain from New York.

Details of what was probably the most intricate of all these transactions may serve to illustrate the difficulties encountered. In this particular instance over eighteen million US dollars in large denominations were secretly transferred from New York to London for the use of SOE, SIS and Allied underground organizations in Europe before and during the invasion. It involved a long series of manoeuvres beginning in 1942 and ending two years later, which were known to no one outside BSC and SOE/London except Donovan himself and two of his officers. The difficulties apparent from the outset were:

1. The dollar notes could not simply be bought from the US Treasury by the British Treasury against a cheque, because such a cheque would necessarily pass through the entire American financial machine, with the result that both the despatch and the destination of the notes might easily become known to the enemy.
2. Since the notes were mostly to be used in occupied Europe, many of them would eventually fall into the hands of the Germans. Neither the US Treasury nor the Federal Reserve Bank could approve of this.
3. It was not thought desirable that even Donovan himself, who was being asked to cooperate in procuring the notes, should know for what they were intended, because the operations on which they were to be spent would suffer

rather than benefit from any American attempt to collaborate in them.

To circumvent these difficulties, it was arranged that one of Donovan's men should draw the notes in large denominations from the US Treasury. The first five million dollars were sent over in February–March 1943 and were exchanged for small notes – ones and twos and fives, collected in Britain – which, after being shipped back to the USA, were paid into the US Treasury by the same OSS officer who had drawn the large notes.

However, this method of exchange was at one time endangered by the fact that SOE/London, although they possessed the small notes, could scarcely ship them over as quickly as they received the large ones. One million dollars will go into one bag, in 50s and 100s; but one million in small notes occupies thirty or forty bags and takes more space than SOE/London could obtain for several weeks. At that time transport was extremely difficult; ships were taking four weeks to cross the Atlantic in convoy, and transport by air was very limited, particularly from England to America.

After the first three million had been drawn from the US Treasury, sent off to London and distributed to the Poles, for whom nearly half the total was earmarked, the US Treasury refused to permit any more drawings until a down payment was made. To the cold-eyed Treasury officials, an overdrawn account was an overdrawn account, even though the client was a US Government agency.

But meanwhile London was urgently asking for another two million. The deadline was mid-March, for that was the last lunar period during which there was sufficient darkness to allow planes to make the round trip from England to Poland. Partly by persuasion, partly by the ungrudging help of Donovan's men, and partly by the timely arrival in America of the first two million in small notes, the difficulty was overcome.

By 13 March 1943, the final consignment had arrived in London. Very little time was wasted there, and the shipment continued into Poland. It was landed in almost total darkness; the plane made the return journey safely; and the Polish underground was enabled to carry on for many more months without financial worries.

In July–August 1943, a further $5,250,000 was sent over to Britain, but on this occasion there were not sufficient dollar funds in Britain to make repayment in American currency. Somehow, a cheque or a series of cheques would have to pass to the

American Government from the British Treasury; and yet neither the American Treasury nor the Foreign Funds Control could be informed of the existence of the transaction or the reason for it.

Donovan's financial assistant solved the problem. He drew the notes from the Treasury on behalf of OSS, and handed them to SOE for shipment. The Treasury in Britain repaid them by sending a cheque to the Ministry of Supply, which instructed the New York Supply Mission to draw equivalent cheques in favour of Donovan's financial assistant himself; and he then passed the payment back to OSS. Large payments for unspecified purposes by the Ministry of Supply or its mission in New York were common enough for these transactions to pass unnoticed.

Finally, in May-September 1944, a further $8,000,000 was transferred in exactly the same way. This time Donovan's financial assistant asked to be informed roughly where the money would be spent, by whom, and under whose authority; he also asked whether it would be circulated or hoarded and whether any large sums would fall into enemy hands. He was given this information on the understanding that he would keep it to himself, and thus the transfers were carried out without hindrance.

CHAPTER 5

Agents at Work

    (a) In French Territories
    (b) Spain and Portugal
    (c) Italy
    (d) The Balkans
    (e) Red Tape and Failures
    (f) Facilitating Agents Recruited Elsewhere

Graduates of the BSC training school operated in Europe, Africa, Australia, India and the Pacific area. A few case histories may serve to illustrate the different types of agents who were turned out – their failures, difficulties and successes.

(a) In French Territories

In addition to several French-Canadian trainees who entered France to work with the resistance groups, there were a few highly specialized agents who visited occupied France for BSC and returned with valuable information. One of these was a Franco-American manufacturer who made two such trips. He and his brother controlled an important French industrial concern. He had served in both the French and United States armies in the last war, had lived for twenty years in Paris but had retained his American passport. On his way out of France in 1941, he called at the British Consulate in Lisbon where he handed in some information on the economic situation in France, with particular reference to the automobile industry, which he knew well. In August 1941, his brother also arrived from France with a useful report on factories working for the Germans.

    The brother who had left France first was subsequently introduced to a BSC officer by a contact to whom he had brought personal messages from Paris. He said he was willing to return to France using his own business as cover, and to bring back information on the business he knew. He entered France in August 1941 and returned in October, with a long report on the monthly schedules of the chief automobile manufacturers, tyre production, motor and aircraft factories, textile, chemical and other industries, and on general political trends.

In November 1941, he went to France again, stayed until January 1942, and brought back a still more useful report, for it was of wider scope. He also supplied BSC with the name of a friend in Lyons who was prepared, if contacted by SIS, to collect information from acquaintances in the rubber, steel and electrical construction trades.

In due course he undertook to return once more. This time, since the US had entered the war, he would travel under the auspies of Donovan's COI; but it was agreed that he should also report to SIS, from whom he got a list of fifty-two separate questions to answer. Applications for his visa were entered with the French Embassy; and since the Embassy had already been penetrated by BSC (see Part IV), it was possible to watch the progress of the various formalities, and to ascertain that he was not suspected, at least by the Vichy authorities.

Meanwhile he was trained both at the BSC school in Canada and at the OSS school in Washington. When his visa came through, it was valid for only fourteen days. He became nervous, because, when he remembered the ease with which he had made his previous trips, it seemed to him that his visa had taken a very long time to obtain. Both Donovan and BSC decided, therefore, that he should not return to Europe; and since Vichy shortly afterwards broke off relations with the USA, a good agent was thus saved.

In the spring of 1941, both SIS and SOE asked BSC to find American agents capable of entering North Africa to investigate and, if possible, counter German infiltration into that strategic territory. Many possible recruits were interviewed, but those who had suitable cover, and at the same time the right character for the job, were few.

The first man who was sent proved indiscreet after he reached Europe. The next was more successful. He was a middle-aged American lawyer, long the Paris partner of one of the wealthiest New York law firms. He was recruited by BSC because of his intimate knowledge of the French character and his good relations with influential French personages. He visited Vichy France, Spain, Switzerland and North Africa from July 1941 to February 1942, returning with reports on the attitude of Pétain,

German policy in France, and notes on half a dozen personal interviews with Pétain and Weygand. Some material he was able to provide was helpful in making psychological preparations for the North African campaign.

(b) Spain and Portugal

Agents for Spain were always easily obtained; but because of the Foreign Office ban on subversive activities against Franco, only intelligence and propaganda agents could be used.

In May 1941, SOE/London conceived the plan of sending to Spain a number of pro-British Americans or South Americans, who, by conversational propaganda, would dispel the Spanish belief that Germany was the only important power and that all other nations were either weak or too remote for concern. Buenos Aires was asked for recruits. They produced an Argentine and an Uruguayan. Both were employed by the Bank of London & South America, but London obtained their release by application to the head office of the bank.

They were directed to emphasize the following propaganda themes:

1. Allied victory is certain, with Lend-Lease and American resources.
2. If Spain joins the Axis, she will cut herself off from Argentina and the Spanish-American world.
3. Argentina dislikes the imperialist intentions of the Falange.
4. South American Catholics are disturbed by Axis domination over religious instruction.
5. Serrano Suñer is an Axis hireling.

They sailed for Spain in July 1941. There had been the usual delay in securing visas and passages for them, but the time was put to good use by elaborating on their directives, preparing lists of influential Spaniards whom they were to see and getting them excellent letters of introduction. They remained in Spain for four months and apparently did good work.

With the cooperation of José Bensaude, the shipowner, an agent was recruited and despatched into the Azores when a German invasion of Portugal and the islands was thought to be impending. He was engaged in October 1941 and retained until January 1943, by which time the danger had disappeared. An interesting but incidental result of his work with SIS was that the Ministry of

Economic Warfare took steps to increase the allotment of rations to the Azores, for he had reported that German propagandists fostered anti-British feeling by blaming the blockade for shortages of food, tyres and raw materials.

(c) Italy

BSC recruited its first agent for Italy in August 1940 from amongst a batch of Peruvian cadet airmen who had arrived in New York after a year's training in Italy. Arrangements were made for their interrogation and they gave some useful information on the general situation in Italy and on the Italian air force in particular. A few of them appeared likely recruits, and one was engaged. His cover was good. He had left a wife in Italy and could easily return to get her, while the Italian Ambassador in Lima, being a friend of his family, would give him his visa.

After visiting Peru, he left for Italy with instructions to investigate the output of Italian aircraft factories, the exact losses of the Italian air force, and the extent to which the Germans dominated it. He was expected to pass this information to SIS/Madrid on his way back to Peru. But he never returned.

In September 1941, he asked SIS for his fare home, which was sent. By February 1942, it was evident that he had been arrested. Foolishly, he had told a friend of his about his mission. The friend was an Italian airman, one Vittorio Morando, who not only denounced him but made a serious attempt to penetrate SIS/Madrid by offering his services and giving the agent's name as a reference.

Perhaps on the basis of BSC's experience with Italians it would be fair to say that approximately 50% of Italian recruits were useless and 50% satisfactory.

The Italian recruits obtained in Mexico in 1942 (mentioned above) were good examples of the latter category. Despite travel bottlenecks and other difficulties they all reached their destinations. One man had to go from British Honduras to Jamaica in a small fishing boat, while others travelled via the USA, after special arrangements had been made with the help of OSS to smuggle them through the country, for they had been unable to obtain transit visas.

An outstanding Italian agent was the revolutionary, Emilio Lussu, alias Dupont, alias Grienspan, whose work BSC assisted. In June of 1941, through its Italian contacts, BSC discovered that Lussu was in Lisbon. He was organizing a committee to help anti-Fascist Italian refugees in French internment camps. He sent over several good men who worked for BSC among the Italian colonies in America.

BSC encouraged the Mazzini Society (see Part VIII) to send him $6,000, passed correspondence for him through the bag and asked London to contact him. London were enthusiastic about him and liked particularly his plan to start an anti-Mussolini revolution in Sardinia. In the spring of 1942, he was brought out of Lisbon. He procured a visa under a false name, with the assistance of OSS, reached the United States and contacted several other friends, all of whom were then active in Italian anti-Fascist work. He obtained names of people who would assist him in pursuing his revolutionary plan, discussed the Italian problem with BSC officers and was shipped out of Halifax again in April.

By November 1942, he was in the south of France. He was working, as always, independently of SOE, but was in touch with the organization. He was in Rome a year before the Allies entered, and he prepared the *coup* by which Sardinia came over to the Allied side. Returning to Rome, he was an active underground member of the *Partito d'Azione* in Rome at the time of the city's liberation.

One of the most valuable agents was an Italian, who, after working for BSC for some while, was transferred to SOE in Europe and rose to become a Lieutenant Colonel in the British Army. He was indeed the first of BSC's recruits, for he was enlisted by WS when both were travelling in the same ship *en route* to America from England in June of 1940.

His record was outstanding. He was second in command of the mission which went to Sicily when the first troops landed there, and he was instrumental in recruiting Sicilians for work behind the Allied lines. He performed similar missions at Salerno and Anzio. In December 1944, he was parachuted into the hinterland behind Milan with the object of making contact with and encouraging the members of the Committee of Liberation. Subsequently he became head of the SOE mission in the Milan area.

The Committee of Liberation had the highest respect for him and took their orders from him without question. The capture of Milan, for which he deserves much of the credit, was a model operation. He led the liberation forces into Milan and personally took over the Milan radio station. He was the first Allied officer to speak over the Milan radio and was later granted the freedom of the city. He has been awarded the DSO and MC.

(d) The Balkans

For propaganda and subversive work in Europe directed from the Middle East, BSC recruited and despatched many agents. Late in December 1941, SOE told BSC that a number of wireless operators were needed at once for the Balkans. Fourteen good candidates were soon found – three Greeks, two Montenegrins and the others Croats and Dalmatians. However, they were all American citizens, so that they were liable to be claimed either by the American Army or by Donovan. Although Donovan was anything but ready to use them, the State Department were making it increasingly difficult to get agents out of the country.

It took four months to complete the necessary formalities, and these included a demand from London that the recruits should all be inoculated for yellow fever and typhoid – a demand which was eventually satisfied by the use of serum smuggled into the United States from Canada. But when they were at last ready to leave, SOE/Cairo informed BSC that the means did not exist for infiltrating them into Europe from the Middle East. Only the Greeks and the Montenegrins embarked.

By dint of much contrivance the others were kept together in a single team, and were finally despatched to England and the Middle East in June 1942. They proved highly successful. They were the first men to be dropped into Yugoslavia, with instructions to make contact with the partisans, and it was on their advice that British liaison officers were sent to join Marshal Tito.

(e) Red Tape and Failures

There were some recruits who failed to live up to expectations. For this there were various reasons in various individual cases. But possibly the most common contributing factor was red tape, which so ensnared the machinery of recruiting, training and infiltration that the agent became impatient, frightened, bitter, difficult to handle and temporarily unsuited for discharging his responsibilities.

An illustration of red tape and its effect is provided by the story of Karl Hans Sailer, an Austrian Social Democrat who was living in the United States as a refugee. London requested BSC to contact Sailer and obtain his agreement to proceed to the Middle East as quickly as possible. No hint was given as to what he was needed for. On 6 January 1942, he said he would be willing to go if his family were supported in America.

There followed a series of difficulties which took nearly six months to overcome. First, Sailer had no passport. He had entered America under a 'merchant's visa', issued by the US Consul in Marseilles. However, by a confidential arrangement with the Consul-General in New York, BSC was able to supply him with a British passport.

The next difficulty was to secure an exit permit for him. Through the intervention of OSS, he was granted one, although it was not easily obtained even so. He wanted a re-entry permit too, but no such permits were issued for aliens of his status. All he got was a verbal guarantee that he would be allowed to return provided Donovan could satisfy the State Department that 'nothing had occurred during his absence to alter his desirability'. These difficulties surmounted, it was found that there was no transport available to him because of the sudden increase in American priority travel.

At last, in May 1942, BSC succeeded in securing Sailer passage on a troopship. But he rejected it, at first insisting on travelling by air or by sea via Lisbon (which would have been extremely insecure from his point of view), and then refusing to leave at all.

However, he was persuaded after some weeks to modify his last decision; and as a result of protracted negotiations, an air priority was obtained for him, and he left in October 1942.

When his mission was completed, the State Department were asked to sanction a re-entry permit for him, and upon being assured (again with Donovan's help) that Sailer had no Communistic tendencies, they agreed. But the American Consul in Jerusalem refused to issue the permit on the ground that SOE in the Middle East had 'furnished misleading information' about Sailer's position. The Consul had apparently mistakenly supposed that the Americans knew nothing of what Sailer was doing. It took another six months before this final difficulty was cleared up. Sailer eventually arrived back in the United States ten months after the completion of his mission!

Recruiting for Germany was, on the whole, unsuccessful, partly because suitable recruits were hard to find and infiltration was difficult to arrange. In July 1941, Bermuda detained Richard Blacha, a German-Polish hybrid from Silesia who had stowed away on the *Excalibur* at Lisbon. He said he had deserted from the German Army before the attack on France and was anxious to work against the Nazi regime. BSC arranged to interrogate him in Canada.

London suspected him of being an *agent provocateur*, and,

although the result of his interrogation in Canada was not entirely to his discredit, he was sent back to London under guard. Subsequently, BSC had access to a grim note from the Polish SIS which asserted that, after Blacha's alleged desertion, he had several times visited his brother, who was a German officer.

The Bulgar, Alexander Stoyanoff (alias Vilmar) – to whom reference has already been made – proved very unsatisfactory. He arrived from London in July 1941, with instructions to obtain German and Bulgarian visas and re-enter Europe. His ultimate purpose was to murder Adolf Hitler.

It was largely due to his indiscretions that he got into trouble with the American authorities, and his behaviour was no more commendable after BSC had seen him safely out of the country. At Bermuda he had to be put under restraint, for he became quite hysterical and it seemed evident that he was a drug fiend. Upon arrival in Lisbon, he became fearful of proceeding to Germany and returned to London, where he threatened to commit suicide. For a while SOE debated the advisability of arranging his internment, but in the end decided against it. Instead they sent him over to Canada where he passed into obscurity.

Sven Hammerum, a naturalized US citizen of Norwegian origin, was another failure. In the autumn of 1940 he travelled from Oslo to the USA on a US vessel, with the intention of returning to Norway on a Norwegian vessel. He claimed to be on friendly terms with German officers and to possess a good knowledge of targets, concentration areas and key points in Norway.

After some discussion, BSC decided to send him to Denmark and Norway via Portugal, France and Germany. SIS/London were so advised and were asked for:

1. Addresses in Sweden with which Hammerum could communicate;
2. Particulars of secret inks he could use.

After two weeks, London provided an address in Sweden, but BSC was alarmed to learn that its Norwegian agent was expected to write from inside occupied territory to a man in a neutral country who possessed the obviously Anglo-Saxon name of 'C. Montagu Evans, Esq.'

It was pointed out to London that the address was unsuitable. Two more weeks passed, and London reported that Stockholm could not understand the objection to an English name. An explanation of the objection was telegraphed immediately and

London came back with the statement that 'This matter has become too complicated to be dealt with by telegraph.'

BSC had originally telegraphed explicitly:

> Sending Hammerum to Denmark and Norway via Portugal, France and Germany. He can communicate to addresses in Sweden . . . Can you provide these?

However it now seemed obvious that London mistakenly supposed that Hammerum himself was to go to Sweden, and thus saw no danger in the suggestion that he should communicate with an Englishman.

A month passed before the misunderstanding was cleared up, and then something happened which caused further delay. When Hammerum applied for a visa in the German Consulate at New Orleans, the Consul asked him to 'undertake a task for Germany for which he would be highly rewarded'. In brief, the Consul's proposal was that he should travel to England as a seaman on a Danish or Norwegian ship, that on arrival he should sign off or go sick or find some other excuse to leave the vessel and that he should then make his way to London, where he would be contacted and receive further instructions.

This proposal altered the circumstances of the case, for an opportunity to penetrate the enemy's organization in the United Kingdom could obviously not be ignored. Accordingly it was agreed that Hammerum should undertake the mission for the Germans, and, after appropriate briefing, he sailed.

When he reached England he had neither money nor his seamen's papers. He said that he had left the latter with the BSC officer with whom he had been in touch in New York. His stay in London was disappointing. He did not make contact with the German agent, and, despite his desire to fulfil the original mission planned for him, London decided to ship him back to America.

On 2 March 1941, more than five months after he had been recruited, Hammerum returned to the USA. He complained to BSC that he had not been met in London, that he had been manhandled, placed under arrest and then passed from one unhelpful person to another; further that his efforts to secure the arrest of several dangerous characters had been unappreciated.

It is difficult to apportion the blame for his failure. It can safely be said, however, that the long delay to which he was subjected contributed to it. Men became agents at the risk of their lives and of the welfare of their families. Inevitably they were impatient with delays which often appeared to them the result of needless red tape and inefficiency.

(f) Facilitating Agents Recruited Elsewhere

In common with other stations in large central cities, BSC was concerned with facilitating the passage, payment and communications of agents recruited in places outside the sphere of its jurisdiction, chiefly in London. What remains on record of this work does not adequately represent the time and effort it involved. It was, however, continuous and often resulted in considerable difficulties. A case in point, one of many, follows.

SOE/London, in the course of organizing attacks on targets in France, came into contact with an underground association of Spanish Republicans – evidently Communists – who were willing to cooperate in exchange for supplies. To avoid offending Spain, London determined that orders to the organization should be transmitted through New York.

Chief of this underground organization was Geoffrey Marshall, who had commanded a British destroyer at Jutland, and after the war had joined the Communist Party. He entered the United States in 1930, where he organized Communist groups in California, was arrested in 1932 and was deported in the following year. He then went to Moscow, turned up in Spain at the beginning of the civil war, was given command of the destroyer *Alcalá Galiano*, and escaped after the victory of France. For a while he worked for SIS in southern France, but was dismissed in October 1940. He returned to London, and there he continued to control his Communist association.

London attached great importance to the maintenance of this liaison, particularly because some of Marshall's men were being sent into Germany and Belgium as conscripts. BSC was, therefore, instructed to pass messages from London to two of Marshall's lieutenants who would be sent to New York. They, in turn, would relay them – evidently by seamen on Spanish vessels – to the Peninsula and southern France.

The two lieutenants arrived late in October 1941. They were Joseph Alexander Steven and Julie Angela Marshall. The girl was Geoffrey Marshall's daughter and, although she and Steven travelled on separate British passports, they were evidently living together as man and wife. They had no contact with BSC except for passing messages and receiving money, were not allowed access to BSC's records and were dissuaded from sending communications in their private code.

Agents at Work

Their work was valuable, however. At the beginning of 1942, SOE/London resolved to renew the subsidy to their organization in Europe. But because of the McKellar Act they could not be permitted to stay in the United States. To register them as agents of the British Government was out of the question. Yet had they remained without being registered, the FBI might have learned of their relationship with the British – which would doubtless have led to serious embarrassment, particularly in view of their Communist connections.

After some trouble, Uruguayan visas were obtained for them. But upon their arrival in Uruguay it was found impossible for them to stay – still less (as had been hoped) for them to acquire Uruguayan citizenship.

From excellent sources the BSC representative in Montevideo learned that they were Communists, and since the Uruguayan Government was very anti-Communist, he felt justified in insisting that they should be removed to avoid compromising his own work, for he had been instrumental in securing their visas. He agreed, however, that 'they were first-class people, capable of carrying out their mission with efficiency and success'.

Steven refused to go to Argentina, because he feared he would be recognized there. He and his companion were sent back to England. They were uncompromised, and they bequeathed BSC a list of no less than 500 names of members of their organization, or sympathizers, in the New York area.

CONCLUSION

Such, then, in outline only, is the story of BSC's part in the recruitment and training of agents. The difficulties were many, and if too much emphasis has been placed on them the excuse must be that this book is intended to serve not only as a record of the past but as a guide to the future.

The value of the work performed by agents in enemy territory can hardly be overestimated. As SHAEF stated in a report dated 13 July 1945, 'Without the organization, communications, material, training and leadership which SOE supplied (with the assistance of OSS from November '43 onwards on the formation of SFHQ) "resistance" would have been of no military value.' As it happened, in no previous war were 'resistance forces', in General Eisenhower's words, 'so closely harnessed to the main military effort'. To quote but one instance from the SHAEF report above mentioned, the programme of railway sabotage in France and Belgium 'reduced the stock of serviceable locomotives to a point where there was an actual deficiency in the number required by the enemy at the time of and following the Normandy landing. Sabotage in France alone between September 1943, and September 1944, accounted for almost as many as the total disabled by air action during the same period.'

BSC contributed its share to the number of qualified and fully trained men needed by SOE in the task of organizing resistance movements, both militarily and politically, throughout occupied Europe. But, more important perhaps, BSC was able to provide the Americans with the basis, which otherwise would have been lacking, of their recruiting and training programme. At the time of writing, something of the exploits and achievements of OSS is being made known to the American public. A recent editorial in the *New York Herald Tribune* states

... OSS – that Sphinx-like service which maintained so

Conclusion

complete a secrecy throughout the war that the telephone operators at its Washington office would not even admit its existence – has recently been feeding (a steady stream of publicity) into the newspapers and magazines, conveying some idea of its accomplishments. As first set up, its primary function was simply the expert collation and analysis of information supplied by the various older intelligence agencies. From this, however, it advanced to the more desperate business of getting information through its own operatives, and thence to acting in almost any secret enterprise which its own ingenuity suggested or into which its services were invited. It did almost everything from spreading calculated 'black propaganda' in Germany to dropping rescue teams in the Manchurian prisoner-of-war camps, from running a supply line across the Aegean to Greek patriot guerrillas to bolstering Siam in her peculiar 'underground' alliance with the Allies. Thirty-one of its own officers were captured and executed in the course of such missions. Thirty-three more are listed as missing, while hundreds of civilian colleagues in enemy-held countries probably gave their lives in its service.

The tribute is well deserved. It does not, however, disclose – quite properly, of course – that OSS's emergence from a passive to an active role would hardly have been possible without BSC's cooperation, that many of the OSS 'operatives' were recruited through BSC and that all were trained according to methods which BSC learned and evolved before Pearl Harbor.

PART IX

COMMUNICATIONS NETWORK

CHAPTER 1

Developing Speed and Security

(a) Growth of Communications Division
(b) Development of *Telekrypton*
(c) *Telekrypton* Lines in North America
(d) Transatlantic Lines
(e) *Rockex I*
(f) *Rockex II*

(a) Growth of Communications Division

It was not until late in 1941 that BSC found itself faced with any serious problem in communications. Up to that time, by agreement with the FBI, SIS telegrams exchanged between New York and London passed, via Washington, over an FBI wireless channel which linked FBI headquarters with HMG Communications Centre, Whaddon, Buckinghamshire, the transmitting and receiving station for all SIS wireless traffic. It was necessary only that some form of landline should exist between Washington and New York, where a code room of six was sufficient to handle the daily correspondence and to manipulate, with some wariness, the teleprinter which connected them with the outside world. Such SOE telegrams as were exchanged with London (and these were few) passed along the same route, in SIS cyphers. Traffic between BSC and points other than London was carried by Western Union cables.

In October 1941, the head of HMG Communications Centre (more briefly known as XW) paid a visit to the United States, largely to settle two matters which were causing anxiety. First, England was desperately short of the special wireless equipment needed for secret communications, and the USA was the only potential source of supply. Secondly, London were concerned with the possibility of Nazi *coups d'état* in South America. These, if successful, would gravely impair the usefulness of both SIS and

SOE work in that region unless something were done promptly to instal a secret communications network, which could keep agents in touch with suitable points in British territory in the event of their having to go underground. A local problem had also arisen at New York. Since the establishment of a branch office of BSC in Washington, some completely secure means of inter-communication had become necessary, as neither telephone nor teleprinter was proof against line-tapping. This was a matter that required the study of an expert communications engineer.

In result, WS and XW agreed to appoint an officer who would be charged with the duties: (a) of advising upon the immediate communication problem of BSC, (b) of acting, under the general supervision of WS, as the agent of SIS and SOE in the Western Hemisphere for the purchase of secret wireless equipment and the procurement of the results of any research in this field which might prove useful, and (c) of giving technical advice regarding the installation of any South American communications network which SIS and SOE might jointly approve. An expert with the required combination of talents was found in Canada, and his appointment was endorsed by SOE/London. It was decided that he should also be responsible for liaison between the Radio Security Service, London, and such US or Canadian agencies as wished to exchange with RSS intelligence bearing upon enemy clandestine wireless activity.

The first task of the new Communications Officer was to delegate certain of his duties. In January 1942, an RSS Section came into being; in March, a Purchasing Section. Communications proper formed yet another section, with which the old BSC Code Room was incorporated. In the following June, what became known as the Traffic Exchange Section made its appearance. Twelve months later a small engineering laboratory was added for the development of special cyphering devices. These, together with an Accounts Section and Mail-room, gave the Communications Division, as it was by now called, the shape it was to have throughout.

The work of the Division as a whole must be judged from the performance of its component sections, which will have to be told separately. Independent as these sections may appear to have been, it was only because each was responsible to a single head who, through WS, was constantly in touch with the general activity of SIS, SOE and Security Services in the Western Hemisphere that the Division became a satisfactory clearing-house for vast quantities of both friendly and enemy intelligence as well as secret equipment of all kinds.

(b) Development of *Telekrypton*

In a paper published in 1926, an American engineer, G.S. Vernam, pointed out that it would not be difficult to convert a standard teleprinter into a cyphering machine. His theory was that the five-unit electrical impulses produced by a teleprinter, when directly connected with a wire, could be mixed at the moment of transmission with a second series of impulses to give a third and meaningless series. This last would appear upon the receiving teleprinter as a mere jumble of characters unless the second series of impulses were removed before the message was printed. It was, in effect, the principle that A plus B equals C and that C minus B produces A once more – the familiar principle of the one-time recyphering table. Vernam had shown how this could be applied by transmitting the impulses produced from a piece of five-unit teleprinter tape, perforated at random, simultaneously with an *en clair* message. At the opposite end of the wire the jumbled impulses were filtered through an identical piece of perforated tape and reappeared as *en clair* characters upon the receiving teleprinter.

The idea was sound, and the Western Union Telegraph Company had gone so far as to manufacture a limited amount of the equipment necessary for Vernam's cyphering process. However, it had no commercial success, and in December 1941, two *Telekrypton* cyphering machines (such was the trade name) were still lying in the Western Union warehouse.

In many respects the Western Union *Telekrypton* was well suited to BSC's need for secure local communication between Washington and New York. It had, however, two weaknesses. The code tape, which consisted of a string of random teleprinter characters, was joined at the ends to form a loop. This loop ran through the transmitter continuously as a message was being sent, and, although the *mélange* which passed down the wire was impressive, it would not have given much difficulty to a cryptographer. Secondly, the machines were far too complex for their purpose and would obviously be difficult to keep in running order.

Despite this, *Telekrypton* looked promising, and to the evident surprise of Western Union BSC bought the two machines. First they had to be remodelled and unnecessary working parts eliminated. Then the loop of code tape required improvement. It was clear that what was needed was not a loop, but a limitless quantity of tape, perforated at random and in duplicate, and cut into convenient lengths. One set of these could then be used for encyphering, and its twin at the far end of the wire for decyphering. Individual lengths could be destroyed after a single use and the level of security would be the same as that of one-time tables.

The difficulty was to find a means of tape-perforation which would ensure a completely haphazard series of five-unit teleprinter characters. At first, manufacture by hand was attempted, the operator scanning a novel and copying odd letters as she went. This was slow, however, and it did not follow that the tape would be completely without pattern. Hand-punching was, therefore, replaced by a mechanical device, somewhat like a cornucopia filled with glass and steel beads. The beads made random contact with a tape-perforator as they dropped through the bottom of the container, and tape was produced accordingly. This process in turn proved unsatisfactory, as the beads had an irritating habit of getting stuck or crushed on their journey. Ultimately a less spectacular, but thoroughly efficient, tape-puncher was developed. This was operated electronically and gave completely random results. With its installation BSC had a means of communication by landline which was both rapid and secure.

(c) *Telekrypton* Lines in North America

Although this electronic tape-puncher was not completed until the beginning of 1943, the *Telekrypton* cyphering equipment, supplied with hand-punched code tapes, came into operation on a line between BSC/New York and BSC/Washington in January 1942. After a few days, during which it was studied with suspicion by both its operators and the office at large, *Telekrypton* was accepted as part of the general furniture of life. It proved to be so successful that in February, at a meeting with representatives of the Canadian Military and Naval Intelligence and of the Department of External Affairs held in New York to discuss the improvement of communications between Ottawa, BSC and the United Kingdom, it was decided to install a line fitted with *Telekrypton* between BSC and Ottawa. The line came into operation in May 1942. By the following July, BSC was also connected by *Telekrypton* with its new transatlantic wireless transmitter at Oshawa, Canada, which is described below.

In the course of the next two years other lines were thrown out from BSC to connect it with the Signals Security Agency of the US War Department, Arlington, Va. (January 1943), with the BSC Security Office in downtown New York (February 1943), with the offices of the Combined Chiefs of Staff, Washington (November 1943), and with the Communications Annexe of the US Navy Department, Washington (February 1944). In each case *Telekrypton* was used, save with the Signals Security Agency. For administrative reasons it was found simpler that SSA should provide BSC with its own standard cyphering machine, a device similar to the BSC version of *Telekrypton*, except that it used multiple loops of coding tape instead of unique lengths. These loops, which had to be changed constantly during transmission to maintain security, caused considerable inconvenience and by mutual agreement the SSA equipment was eventually discarded in favour of the British Typex which was sure, though slow.

From the above it can be seen that between Pearl Harbor and the beginning of 1944 the Communications Division became the centre of a system of teleprinter lines which kept BSC in immediate touch with its vital centres of liaison in the US and Canada. It remains to describe how trunk communications with the United Kingdom were extended and improved.

(d) Transatlantic Lines

As was mentioned earlier, SIS and SOE telegrams exchanged with London were at the outset handled by the FBI. This arrangement continued in force for some six months after the establishment of the Communications Division. By July 1942, however, BSC had a wireless transmitter of its own (known as Hydra) at Oshawa, Canada, and both SIS and SOE traffic was accordingly diverted along this route. Hydra came into being at an opportune moment, for shortly before the FBI had suggested – a little disingenuously perhaps – that the transmission of BSC correspondence by their Washington wireless channel would be greatly simplified if telegrams were sent *en clair* to FBI headquarters and encyphered there instead of at New York. BSC replied that the need for simplification was fully understood and that in future any telegrams sent to the FBI for relay would be *en clair*. It so happened that it was never found necessary to send any.

While Hydra continued after July 1942 to be the regular channel of communication with HM Government Communications Centre on all SIS and SOE matters, the growth of a Traffic Exchange Section as an agency for the British Government Code and Cypher School (GCCS) within the Communications Division called for substantially more extensive transatlantic communications than Hydra could provide, and thus increasingly greater use had to be made of the public cables. These, however, were becoming more choked month by month with the avalanche of government traffic passing ceaselessly over the Atlantic in both directions. Accordingly, as some insurance against a possible interruption of cable communications, it was decided that BSC must try to obtain a private cable for its own use.

This was not easy, and it was only after several months of negotiation (backed by the US War Communications Board) with Western Union that the lease was obtained (May 1943), not of a complete cable but of what is known as a Varioplex sub-channel. This consists of the fourth part of a multiplex channel, which is itself only a portion of what the public talks of as a 'cable'. By an automatic process at the cable-head, the co-tenants of a given multiplex are able to send traffic simultaneously, one character from each message being transmitted in rotation. But the time of transit of a message is thereby proportionately lengthened. A complete 'cable' is capable of some 50,000 groups or words during the twenty-four hours. A Varioplex, if used continuously and simultaneously by all its customers, can pass not more than 6,000 or 7,000 for each of them. Nevertheless, this direct link proved of great use in clearing urgent telegrams to GCCS, as inter-communication was practically instantaneous; and by taking advantage of the human frailty and fitful traffic lines of its bedfellows BSC was able, on occasion, to transmit up to 17,000 groups daily.

The channel ran directly from the BSC teleprinter room to the teleprinter room at GCCS. During the preliminary tests the usual operators' chat was exchanged. It came as something of a shock to the New York operator, who breezily started off with 'HIYA, THERE, UK,' to be answered within seconds by a prim 'VERY WELL THANK YOU, AND YOU?' The Communications Division was getting its first evidence of the fact that national differences of idiom and temperament are more nakedly revealed on international lines of communication than anywhere else. Tones and inflections do not exist, only cold print. The mistranslation into English of the words *'le gouvernement français demande une explication'* in a French diplomatic note once led to a temporary coldness between the Quai d'Orsai and the Foreign Office. On a teleprinter it is easier still to take as an insult what was meant as a courtesy. Tempers rise quickly, and the blame for mistakes is automatically laid to one's opposite number.

No acrimony developed between BSC and London. BSC was a British agency under British control and accustomed to British ways. But it was not so simple to maintain harmony on the direct lines connecting London with the US Naval Communications Annexe in Washington, for example, and much unnecessary friction arose from the innocent efforts of each side to persuade the other to adopt its own procedure and nomenclature, its own methods of filing, and so on. It is likely that friction of this sort will soon become magnified out of proportion to its original cause, and that its effects will not be confined to the communications room in which it starts. It is unwise to deal with allies directly in communications matters, even if they speak the same language. An intermediary under one's own control should be used.

The Western Union Varioplex afforded temporary relief to the Division, which by the summer of 1943 was faced with the problem of clearing upwards of 50,000 groups of miscellaneous traffic daily by cable. But its difficulties were not over. Towards the end of the year the director of US Naval Communications, a man of salty character and vocabulary, complained that the heavy traffic passing over the BSC Varioplex to and from London prevented the full use of the parallel Varioplex rented by his own Department between GCCS and Washington. BSC accordingly limited its Varioplex traffic to some 3,000 groups daily. Since much of what BSC had been transmitting and receiving was naval material, handled on the US Navy's behalf, the result was a greatly increased load on the Navy's own Varioplex. This, as the Naval Communications director had apparently failed to foresee, meant a corresponding rise in the Navy's cable bills. The unhappy Communications Division therefore found the bulk of the traffic switched back to it without warning, but with the proviso that the BSC Varioplex was to be used as sparingly as ever.

As the director of Naval Communications was not the least influential of the members of the War Communications Board, the Division bowed to the storm and cast about for other means of transmitting urgent material in bulk across the Atlantic. This, fortunately, it found. For over a year previously it had been passing an increasing amount of traffic to the Commercial Cable Company, a subsidiary of International Telephones and Telegraphs. Commercial Cables were a small firm in comparison with Western Union and were at the beginning of the war in a relatively poor way of business. A steady government file was extremely welcome to them, and therefore they had always given BSC traffic priority in despatch. This had led BSC to make more and more use of Commercial Cables, and by the end of 1943 its file of traffic, which had swollen considerably since the previous summer, occupied two-thirds of the company's total cable capacity.

Consequently it was not difficult to come to an informal understanding with Commercial Cables whereby in return for a still larger daily file a complete cable should be earmarked for the exclusive use of GCCS and BSC and the cable-heads in London and New York should be connected directly with the communication rooms of the two. Traffic could thus flow without interruption of any kind from the one room to the other, only a few minutes being lost in transit.

The new direct cable had all the advantages and none of the drawbacks of the Varioplex, and from February 1944 onwards, it remained, together with the Varioplex itself and Hydra, the route by which urgent material passed to and fro between New York and London. Not even the three together, however, were enough to carry the average day's load in its entirety. By the second half of 1944 this had risen to something like 175,000 groups. The balance was absorbed by the remaining channels of Commercial Cables (at times the Company's entire resources were engaged by BSC), by Western Union and by the Radio Corporation of America.

(e) *Rockex I*

It is necessary to say a little more at this point of that enfant terrible, *Telekrypton*. In an earlier section a rough description was given of the way in which *Telekrypton* behaves when – in communications parlance – it is *working to line*. This was the aspect of it which had interested Vernam and Western Union. Neither was concerned to ask whether the device could be used like other coding machines to encypher a piece of plain English and itself print the encypherment instead of transmitting it to a distant point in the form of electrical impulses. Could it be *Telekrypton* would become an all-purpose machine, independent of landlines and capable of producing encyphered texts which could be sent anywhere indifferently by any means of communication available.

In time of peace there is little stimulus to invent equipment for which there is no general demand. Governments are almost the only customers for cyphering machines; commercial firms prefer codebooks. But governments are by habit content with what they have, unless some major crisis forces them to pay closer attention to security and speed. And then, the conversion of *Telekrypton* into an all-purpose machine was not likely to be a simple matter. Suppose the words SMITH HAS ARRIVED were encyphered on the standard *Telekrypton* principle. As they are typed on the teleprinter, so the perforations equivalent to each letter or space appear one by one *en clair* on a piece of five-unit tape. This tape passes through a transmitter, which converts the perforations into impulses. But the haphazardly perforated code tape is fed through the transmitter at the same time, and the impulses produced represent, therefore, a fusion of the two tapes, character by character. Now if the spaces between words are included, SMITH HAS ARRIVED consists of seventeen characters. Seventeen characters will accordingly be produced when the message is encyphered. But what is a character to a teleprinter is not one to the human eye, and the encyphered jumble will look something like:

OF7; M?
/6D Z

Ostensibly this hotch-potch consists of only twelve characters, even if the spaces are included. Moreover, something has gone wrong in the middle, as the last five characters have been dropped a line.

The explanation is that a teleprinter keyboard, unlike that of a typewriter, consists in lower case of the twenty-six letters of the alphabet only. Figures, punctuation marks and the other garnishings found on a typewriter are all confined to the upper case. To pass from the lower case to the upper, a key labelled *Figs.* is provided. But if this is pressed, its effect is not that of a shift key on a typewriter. It produces merely a particular perforation in the five-unit tape. This perforation, like the house that Jack built, generates an impulse which travels down the wire and warns the receiving teleprinter which in turn prints the succeeding impulses, not as letters, but in upper case. It will continue to do so until a second impulse comes down the line, caused by the pressing of the *Ltrs.* key. Upon receipt of this, it will switch back to letters.

Now although SMITH HAS ARRIVED consists of letters only, it does not follow that when each character is fused with a character upon type the result will be a letter. In the encypherment given above, the 'S' and 'M' happened to coincide with characters upon the tape which produced 'O' and 'F'. But when 'I' passed through the transmitter, it was unfortunate enough to meet with an 'X'. The result was the peculiar impulse signalling a figure shift, and although 'I' itself disappeared into thin air, it left its mark on 'T', its successor, which instead of being encyphered as a letter, became the figure 7. OF7 consists, therefore, of four characters, not three.

In the same way the A of ARRIVED met with an E on the code tape. Fused together, A and E produced the impulse signalling that the teleprinter carriage should rotate one space and continue on a fresh line, an impulse known as a 'line feed'. Thus the apparent absence of any encyphered equivalent of A is accounted for by what looks like a piece of slipshod typing.

Obviously no communications system, public or private, could undertake to transmit texts encyphered in this three-dimensional fashion. Yet, unless all the irregularities remained exactly in their original form, the message would be indecypherable on receipt. The only solution of the difficulty would be so to modify the *Telekrypton* encyphering process that, while retaining its security, the machine would produce a text consisting wholly of letters, wholly of figures, or of a mixture of both. These could then be blocked in groups of five, and there would be no risk of corruption in transit.

By the autumn of 1942 it was apparent that BSC would have to attempt some such rebuilding of *Telekrypton*. Since the beginning of the year the volume of telegrams passing between New York and London had increased steadily and the existing hand code room was hard put to keep abreast of them. In particular, many of those exchanged with the Radio Security Service were tabular in form and, except by the most desperate expedients, could not be reproduced in anything like their original shape by code books and one-time tables. If these telegrams could be encyphered mechanically in a form acceptable to Hydra or a commercial cable company, the saving in time and labour would be very great. A teleprinter fitted with *Telekrypton* is speedy (it will encypher and decypher at the rate of sixty-five words per minute), and it is also constructed to throw material into page form. Provided, therefore, that there were some means of eliminating from the encyphered copy produced by *Telekrypton* the oddities described above, the problem of quick and secure communications between New York and London would be solved for good.

After some weeks of experimentation an answer to the problem was found. The abnormal characters produced by the figure and letter shifts, line feed, space bar and so on were given numerical equivalents. By making certain mechanical changes, a teleprinter was so reconstructed that when the fusion of an *en clair* character with code tape character produced a letter shift, the impulse which resulted caused, not a letter to shift, but the figure 3 to appear in the encyphered text. Similarly, a figure shift became the figure 4, and a line feed the figure 5. Furthermore, these impulses did not travel down a wire to a distant receiver, but were converted immediately into their equivalents in print. As an *en clair* message was typed and the code tape fed into the transmitter, so the encyphered text issued from the side of the machine, printed on paper slip and blocked into groups of five mixed figures and letters. SMITH HAS ARRIVED now appeared as WFZH5 IV43R BTVPP YY. The seventeen characters are still present in the encyphered version, but are masked less disconcertingly. Line feeds and the like have become the figures 5, 4 and 3.

A message of this kind could be transmitted without difficulty by either wireless or cable. On receipt it would be copied as it stood on a similarly constructed teleprinter, an identical code tape being run through the machine during the process. This machine, owing to its special construction, would treat the figure 5, when it occurred, as a line feed, deduct from it the coincident character on the code tape, and print the resulting *en clair* character – in this case the letter H.

It was found necessary to use six such figures in all (from 2 to 7 inclusive) as the equivalents of symbols significant only to a teleprinter. These six figures, together with the twenty-six letters of the alphabet in endless combinations, composed the text of all messages encyphered by the new version of *Telekrypton*, later named *Rockex I* in memory of its place of birth: Rockefeller Centre, New York. By January 1943, BSC had supplied London with a machine of its own, and thenceforward *Rockex I* was used to the limit of its capacity.

Rockex I remained the standard means of encyphering and decyphering almost all SIS telegrams passing between London and New York throughout 1943 and 1944, and it also proved invaluable for the transmission, via BSC, of an uninterrupted flow of Top Secret intelligence between GCCS and the Combined Chiefs of Staff, Washington. In the course of time, however, the machine showed certain minor weaknesses. The chief of these was the mixed character of the cypher text which it produced. Figure-letter texts are disliked by cable companies, as they are awkward to transmit. Accordingly a higher rate is charged for them. They are also less easy to transmit by wireless than plain letters. The Communications Division, therefore, with the encouragement of GCCS, set itself the problem of modifying *Telekrypton* yet again in such a way that while the principle of the unique code tape was retained the machine would encypher in letters only, block these in groups of five and automatically print messages of any length in pages of fifty such groups each.

(f) *Rockex II*

In March 1944, *Rockex II* made its appearance. Its principle was basically that of the original *Telekrypton*, as encypherment took place by means of the fusion of an *en clair* with a haphazardly perforated tape. *Rockex II*, however, was so built that upon the meeting in the transmitter of an *en clair* with a code tape character, only those capable of producing one of the twenty-six letters of the alphabet were allowed to have offspring. Thus, on the old *Telekrypton*, *en clair* S meeting X on the code tape would be encyphered as O. The same was true of *Rockex I*. The same also of *Rockex II*. On the old *Telekrypton*, however, an *en clair* I meeting an X on the code tape was encyphered as a line feed. On *Rockex I* it was encyphered as the figure 5. On the eugenic *Rockex II* the meeting would take place, but the code tape X would merely bow to the *en clair* I (which remained frustrated in the transmitter) and itself pass on to be printed as X on the encyphered page. *En clair* I would wait for the next character on the code tape, which it would marry forthwith if it proved capable of producing a letter as offspring. Otherwise it would again wait.

The effect of this new device was that SMITH HAS ARRIVED tended to have more than seventeen characters, when encyphered. It appeared as something like MLEYZ MUHOQ VBESN MLKFT. Here three code tape characters have failed to marry with their opposites and have survived in their original form. Which letters are *en clair*, however, and which are encyphered matters nothing. The original text is itself invariably encyphered, sooner or later, and the besprinkling of the final text with a number of dummy letters is, as any cryptographer knows, a measure of increased security.

In order that messages encyphered by *Rockex II* might be printed automatically in groups of five letters each, in lines of ten groups and in pages of fifty groups, the five-unit code tape which had been used for *Telekrypton* and *Rockex I* was discarded in favour of a six-unit tape. The sixth perforation warned the machine when to start a new group, line or page, leaving the other

Developing Speed and Security

five free for the business of coalescing with their opposites on the *en clair* tape which remained five-unit as before. The introduction of a more elaborate code tape called for changes in the electronic tape-puncher, which had been designed to meet the much simpler needs of *Telekrypton* and *Rockex I*.

The construction of the new tape-puncher required a good deal of ingenuity and patience. Something like four hundred blueprints had to be drawn before the parts could be machined, and even when the unit was at last assembled exhaustive tests were necessary to ensure that it had no hidden weakness. This delayed the debut of *Rockex II* until the spring of 1944. But the delay proved well worthwhile. *Rockex II*, when finally completed, was undoubtedly one of the most efficient machines of its kind in existence. It was fast, completely secure, and capable of working directly to line or of printing an encyphered text in neat pages of fifty groups. In decyphering it reproduced an *en clair* message in precisely its original format, and even if during transit certain letters of the encyphered text had been incorrectly transmitted by a wireless or cable operator, *Rockex II* would still decypher the message without trouble, omitting from it only those characters which were corrupt.

By the summer of 1944 a model of *Rockex II*, together with the new tape-punching equipment, had been shipped to England and there successfully demonstrated. It was decided that *Rockex II* should be adopted officially by the British Government as one of its standard cyphering devices, and plans for its production in England on a large scale were drawn up by the Cypher Policy Board.

CHAPTER 2

Hydra and the South American Scheme

(a) First South American Scheme
(b) Start of Hydra
(c) Other South American Proposals
(d) Hydra's Reorientation and Growth

One summer's day in 1943 an American general stated with emphasis to two British officials visiting the Pentagon Building in Washington that, if he could have his way, he would transfer all army communications between Washington and GCCS from the submarine cables to wireless channels. Cables, he said, might be tapped by U-boats, and copies of the cypher traffic thus intercepted passed to Berlin. The general had forgotten that wireless signals can be intercepted without even the inconvenience of a descent to the depths of the Atlantic.

The British visitors were startled, expressed polite agreement, and remained unconvinced, as did the general's subordinate officers. But while the flow of traffic by cable between the United States and England continued undiminished, the general had almost stumbled upon an important truth. Cable communication can always be interrupted by accident or sabotage. Wireless communication, despite jamming and periodic blackouts, is nothing like so vulnerable. In particular, it is the one quick means of keeping in touch with a number of distant points, either separately or simultaneously, when they happen to be out of the reach of cables or landlines.

(a) First South American Scheme

In 1941, as has been said already, there was grave danger that the widely flung network of agents, both SIS and SOE, in Latin

America might be cut off overnight from the usual commercial channels of communication with London. In the original plan to prepare for this emergency, Canada was selected as the best site for a main transmitting and receiving centre. This station would be capable of maintaining contact with London on the one hand and with a subordinate trunk station, possibly placed in Jamaica, on the other. Jamaica, in turn, would be in daily touch with at least two out-stations further south. (Santiago, Chile, and Montevideo were considered as possibilities.) These out-stations would act as clearing centres for the traffic of agents scattered throughout the lower half of South America and equipped with disguised, short-range transmitters. Agents in the northern areas and in Central America would be in direct touch with Jamaica.

In its draft form this scheme was endorsed by both SIS and SOE, London. The cost of operation was to be shared equally by both, and only at the fringe of the network, between out-stations and agents, was any distinction to be made in the handling of the two types of traffic. It remained for the Communications Division of BSC, after making a technical survey, to recommend final sites for the trunk and out-stations and in consultation with the SIS and SOE officers at New York to recruit and train the operating staffs for both these and the tentacles in the field.

(b) Start of Hydra

When it was first drawn up the plan was a good one. The political situation in many Latin American republics was explosive, and the United States had no emergency communications system in this part of the world which could have been used in the event of a crisis. The Communications Division accordingly went ahead with its preparations. The first matter to settle was a site for the Canadian trunk station. This, fortunately, did not take long. For some months previously SOE had maintained a training camp for its agents at Oshawa, Ontario. The camp was isolated, and several acres of level ground were available for the erection of antennae and transmitting and receiving houses. The camp was also an ideal spot for the training of operators. With SOE approval, therefore, it was arranged that a transmitting station should be built at Oshawa and operators trained at the existing SOE school.

Next, a suitable transmitter had to be obtained. This was a more difficult matter than might be supposed. Transmitters of any power had already vanished from the market in the United States, as the American armed forces had a prior right of purchase on all that could be manufactured and were unlikely to listen to any British appeal for help. However, by March 1942, a second-hand one-kilowatt transmitter had been bought from a Toronto amateur, and a week or so later the Philadelphia broadcast station, WCAU, was persuaded to sell BSC a ten-kilowatt transmitter for which it had no further use.

These two prizes were shipped to Oshawa, overhauled and housed in the new buildings. The Canadian Government assigned BSC special operating frequencies without too close a scrutiny into the use to be made of them, while operators were recruited as fast as possible from the body of Canadian amateurs still available and were put through comprehensive training courses. By July 1942, Hydra made its first tests with England and was ready for continuous operation.

(c) Other South American Proposals

The march of events in the Western Hemisphere during the six months following Pearl Harbor put a somewhat different complexion on the South American scheme. In the first place, the United States Government was now closely interested in the defence of Latin America. Secondly, heart-searchings had begun among the Latin Americans themselves, particularly in Brazil which had previously harboured flourishing German and Japanese colonies. South America, with the exception of Argentina, was swinging pronouncedly towards open friendliness with the Allies or towards a far more meticulous neutrality than hitherto. A much closer watch was being kept on the activities of foreign residents, particularly on suspicious wireless transmissions, and Brazil took the lead in enlisting American help to build up a wireless monitoring system of its own. Encouraged by the initial success of its good neighbour policy, the US State Department was at the same time coming more and more to regard Latin America, from the Mexican border to Tierra del Fuego, as its own sphere of influence, in which independent British interference, especially if it were subterranean, would be unwelcome.

All this made it inevitable that both London and BSC should hesitate before putting into effect a scheme which could no longer be justified on the ground of immediate emergency and which, if carried out as originally planned, would undoubtedly antagonize the Latin American Governments and Washington alike. Although in May 1942 the Communications Division did ship to Santiago a 250-watt transmitter from a consignment

Hydra and the South American Scheme

intended for England, this was done upon special instructions from London and with the understanding that the transmitter would be used by SIS/Santiago for purely local purposes, and not as part of the South American scheme proper.

There was still, it is true, a case of sorts for proceeding with the Jamaica station. This might be used as an all-purpose link with Hydra and later, if circumstances changed, be turned into a relay point for the traffic of agents. In fact, the US Army Signal Corps put forward a specious argument for its establishment. In the summer of 1942 enemy submarines were active in the Caribbean. Allied losses were considerable, and while Caribbean waters were covered by naval patrols as far as possible, the Caribbean is a large sea. It was said that the submarines (although no evidence was forthcoming to support the statement) were in constant touch with German agents ashore by means of ultra high-frequency wireless, and thus it was argued that if the agents were apprehended it would be simple to discover where the submarines obtained stores and fuel.

The Signal Corps lost no time in producing a plan of campaign. Half a dozen wireless transmitting stations were to be built at selected points along the coast of the Caribbean, from Yucatan to Trinidad. These would relay to some central point, such as Jamaica, all suspicious signals intercepted by subsidiary listening posts established at intervals along the coast. It was suggested that BSC should furnish the Jamaica station and a quota of operators. The Signal Corps would undertake to do the rest.

On paper the scheme looked plausible. But ultra high-frequency transmissions have only a visual range, and it did not take long to see that if coverage was to be complete, listening posts would have to be set up at something like twenty-five-mile intervals along a thousand miles of largely uninhabited coastline. Each would need special receiving equipment which was unobtainable. Each would need a transmitter which was likewise unobtainable. And each would have to be manned by at least four specially trained operators.

BSC therefore declined the invitation to participate and refused also to be tempted by a revised plan whereby the listening posts were to be replaced by locally hired natives of proven integrity and great patience, who would report any suspicious happenings to the six main relay stations for transmission to a central intelligence office.

The proposal to erect a station in Jamaica was finally abandoned in October 1942, because of the universal shortage of wireless equipment of all kinds, and because of the still improving political temper of Latin America.

(d) Hydra's Reorientation and Growth

Though the South American scheme was dropped Hydra remained, and continued to play a useful and increasingly important part in the BSC communications system.

Of the two transmitters installed at Oshawa in March 1942, the smaller was at first held in reserve and the larger used until late in 1943 for SIS and, to some extent, SOE traffic between New York and London. It was operated manually, and, given reasonable atmospheric conditions, had no difficulty in handling the 3,000 or 4,000 groups exchanged daily. If conditions were bad, BSC was warned and telegrams were diverted to the cable.

However, by December 1943, the Communications Division had undertaken considerable commitments for GCCS and the US War and Navy Departments. Consequently, a greatly increased load of traffic had to be passed over the Atlantic. Much of this load was carried by the cables, but it was clear that Hydra could offer an equally rapid and much cheaper route if full use were made of both transmitters and if high-speed, automatic operation were substituted for manual. Extra staff were therefore engaged, SIS traffic switched from the large to the small transmitter which was well able to handle it and the large transmitter itself converted to automatic operation.

By February 1944, Hydra was carrying the new load well. On an average, 10,000 groups were transmitted daily and 7,000 received. As atmospheric conditions improved during the spring and summer, the volume rose to 30,000 transmitted and 9,000 received. This made yet a further increase in operating staff necessary, and an awkward housing problem might have resulted save for the fortunate coincidence that SOE was already thinking of dissolving its training school, which had by now served its purpose. The Communications Division, therefore, applied in July for permission to take over the buildings and land in their entirety. This was granted, and in the following October SOE formally vacated the property.

With the approach of winter, atmospheric conditions naturally deteriorated, and there was a corresponding decrease in the quantity of traffic passed. But this was offset in part by the introduction early in 1945 of a mechanical device, known as a 'convertor', which enabled Hydra greatly to enlarge its output during its limited hours of operation.

This convertor, designed and built in the BSC laboratory after the completion of *Rockex II*, automatically transformed five-unit teleprinter tape into two-unit morse tape. A high-speed morse transmitter, such as Hydra, is fed with perforated tape, each perforation representing a dot or a dash. Normally this is produced by hand upon a machine known as a *Kleinschmidt*, which looks rather like a typewriter. The process is not fast, and the transmitter is invariably hungry for more tape than even a small battery of *Kleinschmidts* can supply. The convertor helped greatly towards the solution of this difficulty. Traffic reaching Oshawa from New York by landline was not henceforward received in printed form and copied on a *Kleinschmidt* by hand. Instead, it was taken on five-unit teleprinter tape and passed directly into the convertor whence it emerged at high speed as morse tape and was fed continuously into the wireless transmitter.

Thanks to this mechanical improvement, Hydra became a channel along which a substantial volume of traffic could flow steadily throughout the year.

CHAPTER 3

Illicit Wireless Intelligence

(a) Monitoring Enemy Transmissions
(b) Problems of Multilateral Liaison
(c) The Menace of US Inter-Departmental Strife
(d) Listening Posts in Latin America

(a) Monitoring Enemy Transmissions

RSS came to be what it was largely by accident. In 1939, a small group of signals officers was seconded to work with MI5 and the Special Branch of Scotland Yard on the problem of detecting and scotching enemy agents in Great Britain who might attempt to communicate with Germany by wireless. In principle this was a wise precaution. In practice RSS earned no glory. Despite its best efforts at detection, such agents as obtained a footing in the country were either so clumsily trained or so obviously continental in appearance that they found themselves upon the gallows before they had had time even to erect an antenna. Even cases of Fifth Column activity, which were sedulously reported by patriotic citizens, turned to dust and ashes. Allegations that a next-door neighbour was engaged in secret wireless transmissions were investigated with care. But the matter was invariably explained by a faulty water-tap, a rattling window-blind, or, most embarrassing of all, by the perfectly legitimate use at midnight of a piece of harmless earthenware by a man of advancing years.

During 1940, in the course of its search for unauthorized wireless signals in Great Britain, RSS stumbled upon certain transmissions between points on the Continent, particularly in the newly occupied areas of France, which seemed to fall into no previously known category. As a matter of interest a number of these messages were intercepted and sent to the Government Code and Cypher School for examination. There it was found that although some were in cyphers of a comparatively high grade, others could be broken without difficulty. These when read showed that RSS had by accident come upon a quite elaborate communications system operated by the German Abwehr.

From then on RSS devoted more and more attention to the study of German secret communications within Europe. As time passed, wireless networks of a bewildering complexity were gradually mapped and the traffic passing over them was systematically intercepted. The last drop of information was distilled, not merely from the contents of the messages themselves, when these were readable, but from the incautious chat exchanged by German operators, from direction-finding (D/F) bearings and from a close analysis of the form and procedure favoured by different transmitting centres.

These clandestine networks, which in the palmy days of the Reich stretched from the North Cape to Lourenço Marques and from Buenos Aires to Sebastopol, carried a strange *pot-pourri* of intelligence – operational, meteorological, political, economic and nondescript. The Abwehr was only one of many agencies which found clandestine wireless communication useful. With them were the German Military and Naval Intelligence, the Gestapo and the *Sicherheitsdienst*.

It was natural that even while the United States was still officially neutral its government departments charged with the security of the Western Hemisphere should be interested in activity of this kind. Canada had likewise intercepted certain of these signals and wanted to learn more of their nature. On the other hand, RSS itself was anxious to obtain from the Americans and Canadians all available information regarding illicit wireless services operated from Canada, the United States and Latin America.

As early as 1941 BSC had tried to meet the need for some kind of liaison in this unfamiliar field. But the work required a special knowledge of both wireless operation and German foibles. It was decided by WS and XW that it should become the responsibility of the new Communications Division. An RSS officer was attached to the section in January 1942 to promote the full exchange of illicit wireless intelligence between Great Britain, the United States and Canada.

(b) Problems of Multilateral Liaison

At that time, as afterwards, the interception and study in the United States of enemy clandestine wireless transmissions were in the hands of three agencies: the FBI, the Federal Communications Commission (FCC) and the Coast Guard. This last, as soon as the United States declared war, came under the control of the Navy Department, and thenceforward represented both the armed services in all matters touching German, though not Japanese, illicit wireless activity.

Such a variety of bureaux did not simplify the exchange of RSS intelligence, particularly as each agency regarded itself as independent of the others. The reason for this lay in the different character and duties of the three.

It was once remarked of a well-known Oxford scholar that, while he had no enemies, he was hated by all his friends. Something of the same kind would express the feelings towards the FBI of its fellow US agencies. The pre-war reputation of the FBI rested largely on its efficient incarceration of gangsters. This had been shrewdly publicized, since continued publicity is the surest way in the United States of becoming a national institution, and, as war drew on, the press was not allowed to forget that the FBI was being equally successful in tracking down undesirable aliens and spies. The periodic fanfares acclaiming its coups naturally caused resentment among the Services, who were showing the same energy but were forbidden to make public mention of their work. The FCC was similarly displeased, since it received little credit for the substantial help which it often afforded the FBI.

Nevertheless, the FBI did much that was unquestionably of great value, and by early 1942 it had firmly entrenched itself as the agency responsible for the security of the United States, and had authority also to operate in Latin America. In consequence, it was allowed by Presidential decree to maintain a cryptographic branch as part of its Technical Research Laboratory. This office was small and not particularly effective. Little exchange of cryptographic intelligence took place with the US Services and none with the United Kingdom, which by agreement worked only with the War and Navy Departments. Furthermore, the supply of encyphered intercepts available to the FBI from its own sources was meagre. It possessed no major wireless receiving stations which could systematically cover enemy transmissions and was therefore dependent upon the FCC for most of the material which it studied. At the same time, BSC as a whole had worked so closely with the FBI before Pearl Harbor that the Communications Section naturally began by regarding it as its prime source of clandestine wireless intelligence within the United States.

The Federal Communications Commission was a child of the

Roosevelt Administration and therefore shared the criticism which was directed at the New Deal. As a civilian body, it was disliked by the Services, which treated its help as a mere *pis aller* until their own wireless interception networks were completed. As a potential competitor in the detection of enemy agents using wireless, the FBI looked upon the FCC with some jealousy and tried to obtain a *de facto* control over its activities. In truth the Radio Intelligence Section of the FCC approximated more closely to RSS itself than any other agency in the United States. Its primary duty was to run to earth unlicensed broadcasting stations or amateur operators, who were forbidden to make transmissions during time of war. In this it acted much as did RSS in relation to MI5, although it was watching for purely civil as well as for criminal offenders. Like RSS also, it inevitably came across many unidentified transmissions between points outside the United States, and it set itself to classify them. Most of these signals were intra-European and could be heard only spasmodically even by an interception system as widely flung as that of the FCC. But FCC direction finding was so good that the source of many such transmissions was determined accurately.

Technically excellent as the FCC was, liaison with its Radio Intelligence Section was a matter for caution. The FCC was a civilian department engaged in semi-public work. Its security was poor. It was also too curious. To intercept the transmissions of an agent and by D/F to find out the house from which he is making his signals is one thing. To decypher the messages which he is sending is another. The FCC was well equipped for the first task. It had no business with the second. Nevertheless, in the early part of 1942, it formed an unofficial cryptographic section and had some success with low-grade enemy cyphers. The section was hurriedly disbanded upon the protests of the FBI and Service Departments, but the inquisitiveness which had brought it into being remained and had always to be guarded against when information was exchanged between RSS and the FCC.

In the days of Prohibition one of the first duties of the US Coast Guard had been the suppressing of rum-runners, who drove a brisk trade between the West Indies and points north. After more primitive methods of communication had failed, rum-runners found that low-powered wireless transmitters were handy when a rendezvous had to be arranged or cancelled at short notice. Simple codes and cyphers were used, and the whole system had the air of a German Abwehr network in miniature.

To counter this the Coast Guard had set up wireless receiving stations along the Atlantic shore of the United States, kept a continuous watch for suspicious signals and maintained a small cryptographic office for studying intercepted messages. Hence, on the outbreak of war, the Coast Guard was already experienced in the tricks of the illicit wireless operator and was designated by the Army and Navy to search for surreptitious enemy transmissions in case these should affect the security of the Services or prove of operational importance.

The cryptographic section of the Coast Guard was therefore expanded. Liaison was established with GCCS, and its existing receiving stations were provided with more operators and better equipment. Like RSS, the Coast Guard engaged in the interception and 'discrimination' of German illicit signals. In addition, it decyphered these whenever possible, but here its duty ended. All decoded intelligence was passed to the Office of Naval Intelligence, and it was for ONI to decide what action, if any, should be taken. Nor did the Coast Guard attempt to search for possible Japanese illicit transmissions. These, it was felt, were better left to the Army and Navy, whose operators were accustomed to the Japanese morse code and whose cryptographic sections had the necessary Japanese linguists.

Clearly, the RSS Section of BSC was likely to find liaison with the Coast Guard profitable. Although its interception system was far smaller than that of the FCC, it was efficient and the FCC traffic files were available to fill gaps. On the other hand, the Coast Guard's cryptographic section was incomparably better than that of the FBI, and it had the further advantage of being in constant touch with those of the War and Navy Departments and with GCCS.

Such were the three recognized, but obstinately quarrelsome, agencies in the United States which waited to try the diplomatic powers of BSC. In Canada matters were simpler. There the official responsibility for detecting unauthorized wireless transmission lay with the Department of Transport, a smaller brother of the FCC. Since 1939, the Department of Transport had lent its receiving stations in central and eastern Canada to the Canadian Navy for operational work, while its West Coast station was fully engaged in the interception of Japanese diplomatic traffic on behalf of the Ottawa Cryptographic Unit and GCCS, described below. This left it with nothing save a number of itinerant inspectors, whose duty it was to sift any written or verbal reports of illicit transmissions that might come to hand and report their findings to the Royal Canadian Mounted Police for action.

The need for some kind of search for suspicious signals originating in Canada was met by the Canadian MI-2, the branch of the office of the Director of Military Intelligence responsible for intercepting and sifting the operational wireless traffic of the enemy. MI-2, whose operational interception was done on the west coast, had also a station at Ottawa. As early as 1941 it was found possible to assign certain of the receivers at this station to RSS work and, although no clandestine activity within Canada came to light, much that was of interest both to the DMI and to RSS itself was picked up, particularly from the German services then active between Hamburg and South America. The material intercepted was passed to the Canadian cryptographic bureau, known as the Examination Unit of the National Research Council, and also to RSS. At the beginning of 1942, however, Canada was still largely in the dark regarding German illicit wireless networks in general, and Canadian interception was not linked with that of agencies in the United States.

Accordingly, BSC arranged that in future any intelligence exchanged between RSS and the FBI, FCC and US Coast Guard should also be made available to Ottawa, with New York acting as a clearing-house. In return, Canada accepted the suggestion that BSC should act as her liaison with the United States on all RSS matters and agreed to integrate interception at Ottawa with that of other centres, so that duplicated effort might be avoided. On this basis BSC acted as Canada's intermediary for the next three years. Relations remained cordial throughout and Canada made a valued contribution to the endless task of keeping abreast of German illicit wireless activity.

(c) The Menace of US Inter-Departmental Strife

It has been said that the Communications Division began by considering the FBI its first, though not its only, source of RSS intelligence. There was good reason for this. The FBI had long worked with BSC on SIS, counter-espionage and security matters and had itself expressed a wish to extend this collaboration to the study of the secret wireless communications of German agents.

Before Pearl Harbor BSC was an undercover agency, winked at by the Department of State. Apart from its liaison with the office of the Coordinator of Information (later OSS), it maintained contact only with the FBI, which protected it from official curiosity and guaranteed its good behaviour. After Pearl Harbor when the question of RSS liaison arose, the status of BSC was very different. It was now a mission which, though engaged in highly secret work, had legitimate grounds for exchanging a variety of intelligence directly with US Government departments whose duties were divergent from those of the FBI. The circulation of RSS intelligence was a test case. RSS had much to offer, the FBI little of its own to give. RSS was interested in discovering, intercepting, and identifying every illicit transmission made. It studied the decypherments of what it intercepted only to obtain further knowledge of the enemy's communications system. The first object of the FBI, on the other hand, was to read what the enemy was saying and take action upon it, and for that purpose it maintained a cryptographic section. For its supply of encyphered material it depended almost wholly upon others, and it consequently had an imperfect grasp of the problems peculiar to RSS. Nevertheless, the FBI took the stand that it should act as an intermediary between BSC and other US agencies in these matters.

For the time being BSC was content to accept this position as far as the FCC was concerned. By patient prodding a limited quantity of intelligence was obtained chiefly in regard to the transmitters then active in South America. But this was slow in coming and usually 'cold' before it reached RSS. The Coast Guard exchanged no information with the FBI, and if BSC had not been prepared to approach it directly, a promising vein of intelligence might have remained untapped.

The approach was made through the British Joint Staff Mission so as to give emphasis to the connection of RSS with the Services. As a result, a satisfactory liaison was set up, and for some months relations between BSC and the Coast Guard grew steadily closer and more informal. It was understood by both sides that no information received from the Coast Guard was to be divulged to the FBI. Nor was BSC prepared to pass to the Coast Guard anything it might learn from the FBI. To do so would at once have entangled the office as a whole in US domestic squabbles.

Such a policy had its embarrassments. BSC might know from FBI reports that an enemy agent in Rio was about to begin transmission to Germany one midnight on a frequency of 11,000 kilocycles, using the call XYZ. The Coast Guard, ignorant of this, might pick up XYZ, not on 11,000 k/c, but on 12,000, and wonder what it was. The FBI, meanwhile, listening on 11,000 would hear nothing. Only BSC would know that the agent must have changed his plans at the last minute. BSC similarly watched in silence, while the Coast Guard avidly studied material which had been transmitted to Germany from New York, unaware that it had been concocted by the FBI next door for its New York double agent to send to Hamburg.

For some time the FBI took no official notice of the liaison between BSC and the Coast Guard. In June 1942, however, the Research Laboratory complained on the ground that it contravened the *entente* between the FBI and BSC, whereby the former was to act as the link between BSC and all US Government agencies, save OSS. BSC replied that the *entente* had ceased to have meaning since Pearl Harbor, but that it was perfectly willing to let the FBI obtain RSS intelligence on its behalf from the Coast Guard if it could do so.

The FBI replied that it both could and would. The Communications Division of BSC accordingly informed the Coast Guard that direct liaison would cease forthwith, and for the next six weeks waited in patience for the FBI to procure the promised intelligence. None was forthcoming. BSC, therefore, feeling that concessions enough had been made, told the FBI that as contact with the Coast Guard and FCC had become purely nominal, it must with regret propose to London that the exchange of RSS intelligence with the United States be dropped altogether.

The threat was effective. Two or three days later the FBI suggested that the needs of BSC might be met by some sort of round-table meeting held at frequent intervals and attended not only by the Coast Guard, FBI and FCC, but by ONI and G-2. BSC accepted the proposal with the request that the Signals Security Agency of the War Department (SSA) be invited as well, since SSA, while not directly concerned with the illicit wireless activity of agents, was interested in German 'secret diplomatic' wireless traffic, which had recently become an additional RSS commitment.

The meetings began at the end of August 1942. ONI and G-2 found themselves on strange territory and therefore soon ceased to attend. But the remaining representatives continued to meet weekly throughout the next twelve months. The atmosphere, which at first was frigid, became more tolerable as time passed, but nothing could remove the antipathy of the Services to the FBI. Their more valuable items of intelligence were imparted, hurriedly and *sotto voce*, either before the meetings began or after they had been adjourned. So empty of content, in fact, did the meetings themselves finally become that in August 1943 the Coast Guard and SSA jointly suggested to the other members that the meetings were superfluous, giving as their reason the excellence of day-to-day communication between their respective offices and BSC. The FCC agreed with alacrity, and the FBI found itself unable to protest. Separate liaison was therefore resumed and from that time onwards BSC had immediate access to the records of the Coast Guard, FCC and SSA alike. Liaison with the FBI continued at the same time. But it was arid and conducted only by correspondence.

(d) Listening Posts in Latin America

It was not uncommon to receive at New York, even before the creation of an RSS Section, reports from SIS and SOE centres in Latin America describing enemy illicit wireless activity in circumstantial and often picturesque terms. A Peruvian monastery, an Argentinian hen-house, a lonely Costa Rican shack were all, it was alleged, the repositories of transmitters flashing intelligence to Germany. The case of the Lady from Rio Hacha, contained in the following memorandum from Barranquilla, dated 14 August 1942, is typical of the less melodramatic.

> I am informed that in a house at the corner of Carrera 7 de Agosto and San Roque, occupied by a lady from Rio Hacha, whose name I have been unable to obtain, there is a radio transmitter, and my informant tells me that various people have reported to him that they have heard sounds of morse code being transmitted. I am also told that almost daily four or five Germans meet at this house and spend some time there pouring (sic) over large scale maps which are in the house.

Little could be done upon receipt of a report of this nature. Morse, tuned in by accident on a receiving set, can sound very like a transmission. A transmitter requires a special antenna, which to a trained observer will reveal a great deal about the transmitter itself. An agent transmitting regularly has to make quite elaborate tests before he can be sure that his control is likely to hear him, and if these tests are satisfactory he will adhere closely to an arranged time-table, for otherwise regular communication would be impossible.

Few if any of the SIS and SOE posts in Latin America were equipped to investigate technically the many stories reaching them of enemy illicit transmission. It was therefore no discredit to them that much dross reached New York, but little gold. On the other hand, BSC could be of small help unless technical information was supplied. Without it, the only possible procedure was either to give instructions that a suspected house be searched unobtrusively for further evidence of transmissions or to sift all British and US records of illicit signals, together with the D/F bearings taken upon them, in the hope of finding something which would confirm a given SIS or SOE report.

The first of these courses was most undesirable. If an agent is engaged in secret wireless communication, whether local or distant, it is always more profitable to intercept his signals and learn from them something of his associates than to put him on his guard by loitering about his place of work. This left the alternative of trying to match recorded suspect transmissions with alleged illicit operators. But D/F bearings, unless taken locally, are so inaccurate and the statements reaching BSC from Latin America were so vague that here, too, little could be accomplished.

As far as traffic between Latin America and Germany or Japan was concerned, this dilemma was not serious. Monitoring stations in Great Britain or the United States were sure of intercepting most of the messages passed by any transatlantic or transpacific service that might become active. But they could not intercept local transmissions of low power within Central or South America and that some such transmissions were going on seemed possible.

The only way to settle the question and to discover also the true worth of SIS and SOE accounts of enemy illicit wireless communication was to set up listening posts at strategic points in Latin America itself, manned by operators who could not only recognize a disguised transmitting antenna but also listen systematically for suspicious signals audible in their neighbourhood. This BSC decided to do, and in the summer of 1942 it set about arranging Embassy or business cover for the new monitors and shipping equipment to selected places. Fortunately there was no difficulty in recruiting the monitors themselves, as the abandonment of the South American scheme (previously described) had left the Communications Section with a surplus of trained men.

The first posts were set up in October 1942, and by the following spring there were small stations at Barranquilla, Caracas (soon transferred to Trinidad), Montevideo, Santiago, Lima and Quito. These, together with a station which had previously existed at Sao Paulo, thanks to the energy of SIS/Rio, effectively covered South America. Central America was watched by monitors at Panama City, San José and later Belize. In March 1944, a further station was installed at Buenos Aires. While they were all instructed to assist local SIS or SOE officers to the best of their ability, their interception was controlled by the RSS Section of BSC with which they were in touch daily by cable. Thus they wasted little time in investigating signals already known to be operational, authorized, or harmless.

A study of the reports of these listening posts over a period of three or four months gave the RSS Section a much closer idea of the areas of Latin America in which illicit wireless transmissions could be expected. At the beginning of 1942 six known stations had been active. One of these was at Santiago, Chile, the other five in Brazil. All were German, and all were in regular contact with Brussels, Hamburg, or Berlin. No evidence of similar Japanese links had been found, although there were many reports suggesting that Japanese fishing boats off the coasts of Lower California and Mexico might be transmitting shipping intelligence to agents ashore. By October 1942, however, when the first of the BSC monitors was installed, German espionage in South America had received a grave wound. Mass arrests of agents had been made in Brazil (August 1942), and with FCC help the Brazilian Government had set up a D/F network of its own. The five original clandestine stations were silent. Only Santiago survived. It thus seemed likely that now, if ever, efforts would be made to resume communication with Germany from the Argentine, from Uruguay, from the northern and north-western republics or from Central America.

Nothing was reported, though listening posts were shifted patiently from place to place, careful records were made of atmospheric conditions in both populous and remote districts and local rumours were immediately followed up. It was soon shown that in Central America, Colombia, Venezuela, Ecuador and Peru human credulity had outdistanced nature. So limited were the hours during which signals could have been either transmitted or received with any accuracy that regular clandestine communication by wireless, had it been attempted, would certainly have been intercepted. BSC therefore felt with some confidence that it need not be worried overmuch by tales of enemy stations north of Chile and Brazil. As a precaution it retained listening posts in Central and upper South America until the spring of 1944. But it had become clear long before that that Germany looked not to the north but to the Argentine for its daily intelligence bulletins, while the Japanese were not interested in the possibilities of illicit wireless at all.

Illicit Wireless Intelligence

It was largely due to the BSC monitoring stations at Sao Paulo and Montevideo that in January 1943 the first attempt to re-establish clandestine wireless communication between Germany and South America was detected. The new service, which was soon proved to work between Berlin and Buenos Aires, was better disguised than its predecessors in Brazil. Operators' chat was reduced to a minimum, frequencies were changed even during a single transmission and authorized commercial call-signs were used. After a short while, a large German naval wireless station at Bordeaux was made a relay point for outward-bound traffic, which was given the appearance of normal operational signals. Thanks to the efforts of the US Coast Guard and GCCS, the material was readable almost from the start, and the BSC posts, which alone could consistently hear the messages exchanged, were able to fill the frequent gaps in the RSS and Coast Guard files.

The Buenos Aires–Berlin service remained active until September 1944, when the Argentine Government arrested all but one of the agents who operated the Buenos Aires transmitters. Throughout this time it was covered continuously by the BSC stations, and even after its abrupt suspension the same watch was maintained, for there was evidence in transmissions from Prague and Berlin early in 1945 that the enemy had not given up hope of establishing communications with the Argentine once more.

The successful interception of the Buenos Aires–Berlin traffic in itself repaid BSC for the pains it had taken to see that each post was currently supplied with all the technical intelligence necessary to it. But the South American monitors were also in a position to cover intra-European links which, from time to time, might not be audible in Great Britain, the United States or Canada. They proved, in fact, most profitable auxiliaries in a campaign which required endless patience and alertness and which no one agency could hope to conduct from British or American soil alone.

CHAPTER 4

Complexities of Traffic Exchange

    (a) Traffic Analysis
    (b) Conference on Exchanging Traffic
    (c) BSC as the Focal Point
    (d) Three Main User Agencies
    (e) Differences Over Diplomatic Traffic
    (f) Operational Traffic
    (g) BSC's Load Increased
    (h) Solving US Navy's Problems

While the work done by BSC on behalf of the Radio Security Service had that piquant flavour which the public likes to associate with all 'back room' activity, its virtues and limitations will perhaps become clearer if the parallel, though more general, duties of the Traffic Exchange Section of the Communications Division are set side by side with it. To arrange that intercepted wireless traffic should reach the hands of those who could make the best use of it in the shortest possible time was the Traffic Exchange Section's responsibility. This responsibility was not without its own special problems.

To a limited extent, RSS was able to help with the complex task of keeping a watch for every operational wireless signal made by the enemy, since clandestine wireless networks frequently carried traffic of an operational nature. But the problem of intercepting and analysing the ceaseless flow of military, naval and air-force traffic, both German and Japanese, passing between general headquarters, subordinate commands and an infinity of units in the field, at sea, or in the air, rested with the Signals Intelligence branches of the three services. These, in turn, worked in the closest possible partnership with GCCS.

(a) Traffic Analysis

To decypher signals is not the only way of discovering what the enemy has in mind. A great deal of collateral intelligence can

Complexities of Traffic Exchange

be extracted from the external features of a message, from its address, its place and time of origin and the route by which it was sent. A naval example will serve to illustrate the value of such 'traffic analysis'. In May 1941, the German battleship *Bismarck* slipped from her home port and cruised to the north of Scotland, looking for convoys of merchantmen. Except when sighted, she kept wireless silence. British naval forces lost touch with her in the North Atlantic, and for twenty-four hours it looked as though she had escaped pursuit. Traffic analysis showed, however, that whereas Wilhelmshafen alone had hitherto been in communication with her, German wireless stations in Occupied France, as far south as Bordeaux, were suddenly being used as relay points. Her movements could be roughly plotted by following transmissions from the French coast. The Home Fleet was warned, and a Catalina sighted her in the area predicted. She fled, was intercepted, and was sent to the bottom on 27 May. This was but one occasion of many when what the enemy was saying mattered less than to whom and how he was saying it.

As with cryptography, traffic analysis had its difficulties. Just as the enemy made the cryptographer's task harder by striving to perfect a cypher which was at once unbreakable and suited to operational conditions, so he was well aware that the mere fact that he was transmitting from one point to another was itself of significance to the other side. Hence encyphered call-signs, coded addresses, the elaborate relay of traffic which might more easily have been transmitted direct, dummy messages, wireless silence and innumerable other lubricities, all of which had to be taken into account before the true value of intelligence derived from traffic analysis could be estimated.

Something should be said here of yet another type of wireless traffic, which is in a sense complementary to the operational transmissions described above. This is known as 'Diplomatic' or 'Government' traffic. Diplomatic traffic is the endless flow of messages passing along commercial channels of communication between governments and their representatives in foreign capitals. Some of this traffic is *en clair*. Most is encyphered. It differs from both operational and clandestine signals in two respects. First, since it is transmitted only by the wireless or cable services available to the general public, interception of it is a relatively straightforward matter. Secondly, intelligence of value may be derived from the correspondence of friendly powers no less than from that of the enemy. Coverage must therefore be worldwide.

While the USA was still neutral, Great Britain depended for

its supply of diplomatic wireless intercepts upon a number of fixed monitoring stations within the Empire. Traffic was taken at Mauritius, at Abbottabad in the Punjab, at Point Grey on the west coast of Canada and at a number of points in the British Isles. Coverage was adequate, though not without gaps. In particular, transmissions between Berlin and Tokyo gave trouble, as did certain commercial wireless links in Latin America.

With Pearl Harbor, however, matters changed overnight. Cryptographic liaison with the United States, which had previously been restricted and *sub rosa*, could now become open and complete, in regard to both operational and diplomatic codes and cyphers. Moreover, US wireless interception could now be aligned with that of Great Britain to furnish both countries with a maximum range of coverage. What kind of working agreement was reached will be shown in later paragraphs. The first major step was taken in April 1942, when a British joint service mission, headed by an Admiralty representative, arrived in Washington to discuss with the US Service Departments a pooling of ideas in the field of wireless intelligence and the regular exchange of intercepted traffic.

This Washington conference was attended by a naval and military delegation from Canada and by two members of the Communications Division of BSC. The Communications Division was interested in the discussions partly because they were to include the subject of illicit wireless intelligence and partly because at this stage of the war the better acquainted BSC could become with the progress made in the interception and classification of Japanese wireless signals in general, the better able it would be to identify at their first appearance the transmissions of Japanese agents, which were expected daily.

(b) Conference on Exchanging Traffic

On both counts, BSC found the conference of benefit. It found also that as the meetings progressed and the problems of wireless interception, traffic analysis, radio finger-printing and the like were examined in turn, one requirement took on an ever increasing importance. While it was agreed by all that the smooth exchange between the United States, Great Britain and Canada of wireless intelligence, intercepted enemy traffic and miscellaneous technical information was most desirable, no means of carrying out such an exchange under a unified control existed.

The representatives from Great Britain hoped to remedy this by persuading the US Services to set up something equivalent to the British 'Y' Committee, an inter-service body which had been responsible to the Chiefs of Staff since the outbreak of war in Europe for integrating wireless interception and for supervising the production of wireless intelligence. Indeed, after a forceful presentation of the case by the head of the British delegation, the conference proposed as its twenty-sixth recommendation that: 'a permanent committee, with representation from interested services of the United States Government and the British Empire and a chairman of high rank and considerable influence, be established in Washington for the purpose of coordinating the activities of our respective Communication Intelligence organizations.'

Despite the thunder of these polysyllables, BSC had its misgivings. Amity between the US War and Navy Departments was not at that time remarkable, particularly in those branches concerned with communications and signals intelligence. The Office of Naval Communications regarded itself, with some justice, as a professional agency of long experience, able to perform its duties without outside help. The Army Signal Corps, on the other hand, faced with a programme of vast and rapid expansion, was both conscious of its own temporary shortcomings and resentful of the professed self-sufficiency of the Navy. It therefore seemed improbable that the proposed inter-allied 'Y' Committee would meet with the approval of the US Chiefs of Staff. In view of the fact that certain civilian offices, such as the FCC and FBI, were likely to press for representation on it, it seemed improbable that it would ever come into existence.

Pondering this, and emboldened by their possession of a landline between New York and Washington, by their new line to Ottawa, their code room of six, and their faith in Hydra, the BSC representatives suggested to the conference that until the international 'Y' Committee should be set up in the United States, Great Britain and Canada might be willing to accept the limited hospitality which the BSC communication system could offer to their more urgent traffic. New York, they pointed out, was a convenient relay point, and the Communications Division was already accustomed to the three-way exchange of clandestine wireless intelligence.

The suggestion was courteously received. A short discussion followed, and in consequence it was proposed as the thirty-fifth recommendation of the conference: 'a limited amount of the traffic to be forwarded to London by radio from the United States be handled by the British Security Coordination transmitter at Toronto.'

(c) BSC as the Focal Point

Legend has it that in the remote past certain men who were cast from cliffs into the sea because of their misdeeds found themselves suspended between earth and ocean, the one being unwilling to receive them and the other to take them back. The position in which the Communications Division found itself during the six months following the Washington 'Y' conference was equally disconcerting. BSC had been known previously to the British 'Y' Committee and GCCS only as an office engaged in SIS and SOE work in the Western Hemisphere. There was, therefore, some reluctance to believe that it was able to, or indeed should, undertake duties of a broader kind. This hesitation was all the more natural in view of the known differences between the US Service Departments on the one hand and agencies such as the FBI and OSS, with which BSC had long worked closely. At the same time, the US Army and Navy were uncertain whether even a temporary use should be made of a mission which they felt had not the official support of the British Signals Intelligence authorities. Yet a start had still to be made somewhere with the exchange of certain types of wireless intelligence and intercepted enemy traffic by faster means than the diplomatic bag.

Time passed, and it became clearer daily that no international or even American 'Y' Committee would come into being. It was doubtful also whether London would be prepared to ratify more than a portion of the recommendations of the Washington conference, which it was felt had in some respects exceeded its intended terms of reference.

The need for immediate action itself brought about a makeshift solution. In June 1942, the branch of GCCS concerned with diplomatic intercepts found that it urgently needed certain Japanese government traffic from the US files. Such traffic was intercepted by the US Army, and had therefore to be obtained from SSA (or as it was then styled, SIS), the Army cryptographic bureau. For want of a better alternative, BSC was asked to serve as a relay point and, by the use of certain simple security devices, to prepare the material for cabling as it was received from SSA. BSC readily consented, since while SSA was willing enough to furnish any traffic asked for, it was not in a position to cable it.

At the same time, BSC was being called upon to help Canada

Complexities of Traffic Exchange

Although the United States had failed to set up a 'Y' Committee as a result of the Washington conference, Canada had done so promptly. Modelled on its predecessor in Great Britain, the Canadian committee consisted of representatives from Naval, Military and Air Intelligence, the Department of External Affairs and the Department of Transport. The Communications Division of BSC, which had worked closely with Canada on RSS matters for the previous six months, was also urged to send an officer as technical consultant to the meetings of the Committee as regularly as possible.

In extending this invitation to BSC, the Canadian 'Y' Committee had more in mind than the strengthening of its existing RSS liaison. At that time (June 1942), when a Japanese invasion of the Canadian west coast still seemed possible, Canadian MI-2 possessed one monitoring station at Victoria, BC, which was engaged in the interception of Japanese military operational signals, while a second was on the point of completion at Grande Prairie, Alberta. But MI-2 was new to the task of operational interception; the Ottawa cryptographic section had neither the staff nor the equipment necessary for the study of Japanese operational cyphers and its knowledge of traffic analysis was rudimentary. It was thus inevitable that Canada, regardless of any hesitancy in London, should feel collaboration with the United States to be a matter of urgency. It was no less inevitable that the Canadian 'Y' Committee should look to BSC as a tried friend for assistance in making this collaboration effective.

So it happened that by July 1942 BSC found itself acting as a relay point for Japanese military traffic intercepted in Canada and needed in Washington, and becoming, because of its first-hand knowledge of persons and policies in both places, the accepted interpreter to each of the views of the other.

At the same time, it was suggested to the British 'Y' Committee by the head of the recent mission to Washington that the BSC Communications Officer be appointed technical representative of the Committee in the Western Hemisphere, with the duty of procuring from the United States or Canada any scientific information bearing on wireless interception and communications which the Committee might need. The proposal had the support of XW who was equally interested in keeping abreast of this type of intelligence, and it was formally approved.

Recognition of the BSC Communications Division by the 'Y' Committee went no further at this time. For its general liaison with the American and Canadian 'Y' Services, the Committee proposed to send to Washington an officer who would be independent of BSC, and for the rapid exchange of operational and diplomatic intercepts, together with miscellaneous wireless intelligence, a special 'Y' transmitter was to be purchased and installed at Toronto. This last was to be under RAF control.

News of these intentions was received at both Ottawa and BSC with some uneasiness. Ottawa felt that its existing communications with Washington via New York were entirely satisfactory and that the superimposition of a new exchange centre for 'Y' traffic and intelligence would lead only to confusion. It pointed out also to the British 'Y' Committee that wireless transmitters were at the moment almost unobtainable, that Hydra was already in operation and that the need of the Committee for a wireless relay station in Canada could be fully met if, with the consent of XW, the surplus capacity of Hydra were used for 'Y' purposes. On its side, BSC urged strongly that the establishment of a separate British 'Y' office in Washington be considered afresh, since both XW and 'Y' liaison would inevitably suffer if US Government Departments, long divided among themselves, were asked to have dealings with two parallel British missions instead of one.

After some discussion in London these arguments prevailed. It was decided to postpone the appointment of a Washington 'Y' liaison officer, and XW consented to share Hydra with the 'Y' Committee, provided that SIS communications did not thereby suffer. Finally, in the autumn of 1942, the 'Y' Board, which directed the 'Y' Committee on matters of broad policy, ruled that BSC should become the recognized centre in the Western Hemisphere for the three-way exchange between the United States, Canada and Great Britain of 'Y' traffic, as the need for such an exchange might from time to time arise.

(d) Three Main User Agencies

With the knowledge that it had the support of the 'Y' Board, BSC was at length able to set about promoting officially as effective an interchange as possible of 'Y' intelligence and intercepted material. How its communications system was gradually enlarged and modified in order to accommodate large masses of operational traffic will be described later. Its first and more immediately important task was to find a means of improving the general coverage of the commercial wireless channels carrying diplomatic traffic and to bring about a ready exchange of diplomatic intercepts upon request, while at the same time allowing no one country cause to think that it was giving more than it received. The difficulties that faced BSC in this regard will become clearer if something more is said of the three agencies, British, American and Canadian, which studied material of this kind.

The British agency concerned was, of course, GCCS. Since the early days of the war in Europe, GCCS had been split physically into two halves. Its 'civil side', which was concerned with diplomatic and commercial codes and cyphers, had its offices in London. Its 'service' side, which worked on operational codes and cyphers, was at some distance from London. The division had been made for administrative reasons at a time when no regular exchange of intercepts with agencies abroad had been contemplated.

The London Section was a cryptographic office only. It remained dependent for its intake of code and cypher traffic upon the large communications centre which formed part of the country Section and which alone was in touch with all 'Y' monitoring stations. It was not itself equipped for transmission or relay. In these circumstances it was natural, though unfortunate, that the London Section should regard as something of an inconvenience requests from the United States or Canada for files of traffic of which it possessed only a single copy and which it could not prepare for despatch by cable or diplomatic bag without considerable difficulty and delay. The temptation to disregard such requests was increased by the feeling that agencies in the Western Hemisphere were newcomers, seeking to rival an established professional, and were perhaps being more hasty than judicious in their demands upon London.

Unlike GCCS, the Signals Security Agency of the US War Department, which was responsible for the study of diplomatic, commercial and military operational codes and cyphers, was a geographical unit. It suffered, however, in its early days from a dichotomy of a different kind. Cryptography and the interception of material for cryptographic study were regarded as two unrelated pursuits. Hence, those sections at SSA which were engaged in cryptography had little or no means of directly influencing interception, while the branch which controlled interception had no means of knowing whether it was using its resources to the best effect, for it lacked expert cryptographic guidance. This was particularly noticeable in the diplomatic field, where the types of material filling the air varied greatly in character and importance. It was not, indeed, until late in 1943, after several of its higher officers had seen at first hand the close partnership between cryptography and interception that existed in the country Section of GCCS, that SSA was remodelled along similar lines. Before that time differences of view between the two branches had to be accepted as inevitable.

The Ottawa Cryptographic Unit was the Canadian member of the Anglo-American-Canadian trio. Canada took no direct interest in cryptography until after the outbreak of war in Europe. Even at the time of Pearl Harbor, the small 'Examination Unit' which had been set up under the control of the Department of External Affairs was engaged only in the study of French Government traffic passing between Ottawa and Vichy by cable, and of such clandestine enemy wireless signals as were intercepted by the new MI-2 station on the outskirts of Ottawa, which had been operating for a short while.

Early in 1942, at Canada's invitation, a GCCS officer was lent to the Unit, and under his guidance extra staff was recruited in the course of the next year, and regular cryptographic liaison was instituted between Ottawa and both GCCS and SSA. The Examination Unit did not venture into the operational field, and its work on diplomatic material remained restricted to Vichy French and Japanese. For its supply of intercepts it depended on the Department of Transport station at Point Grey, near Vancouver, upon the Canadian Cable Censor and – to a lesser extent – upon the MI-2 station at Ottawa.

(e) Differences Over Diplomatic Traffic

From the differences between these agencies in experience, structure and policy, BSC soon concluded that it would be idle to expect any basic readjustment of interception, whereby well-defined and separate tasks would be assigned to each country and the resulting traffic files exchanged upon request, although it was upon this principle that operational interception was conducted with marked success. But operational interception was concerned with the activities of a common enemy. Diplomatic interception was directed, more often than not, at those of common friends. Hence the reluctance of any one country to entrust to another work which it might have reason for doing more thoroughly itself.

The tendency to build up self-dependent monitoring systems for the interception of diplomatic traffic, regardless of any overlapping which might occur, was naturally strongest in Great Britain and the United States. Canada was still too young as a world power and too new to work of this kind to be sure of her own needs. Yet she, too, for want of any definite understanding with the United States, was content to look to her own resources for material needed by the Examination Unit without enquiring whether the same material was not already available at SSA, whose stations were geographically so close to hers.

In the circumstances, it appeared to BSC that two things could be done to improve matters. First, Canada might be persuaded so to alter her interception programme as to complement, rather than duplicate, that of SSA. In addition, the principle might be established that even if SSA and GCCS followed independent policies in interception the traffic files of each should be available to the other without restriction. In that event, Canada would likewise offer her intercepted diplomatic traffic to both GCCS and SSA and in return would request from them whatever she wished.

Accordingly, it was suggested to SSA and the Canadian 'Y' Committee that a meeting be called to review the interception and exchange of diplomatic traffic. Both welcomed the proposal, and the meeting took place in Washington in January 1943. Two members of the Communications Division attended on behalf of GCCS.

Attracted possibly by the venue, the Canadian delegation was a remarkably large one, few members of the 'Y' Committee being absent. This, in turn, led to a formidable increase in the number of SSA representatives, so that what BSC had hoped would be a small and workmanlike gathering ended as a conference of considerable formality. Some progress was made. It was agreed unanimously that in future a committee consisting of one representative from SSA, one from Ottawa and one from BSC should meet from time to time to report on the interception and circulation of diplomatic traffic. This committee would have in its hands schedules of the coverage maintained by each country, so that excessive duplication could be detected. It was agreed that these schedules should become the basis of formal requests for intercepted traffic. The requests were to be revised monthly.

The conference adjourned, feeling that it had accomplished all that was expected of it. But when the committee of three held its first meeting, it found that certain difficulties were unresolved. In the first place, Canada still hesitated to make more than minor adjustments in her coverage on the ground that there was always a residue of messages which she could intercept and which SSA could not. In fact, almost all of these 'unique' intercepts could have been supplied by Great Britain. But since the London Section of GCCS continued stoutly to find reasons for withholding from Canada copies of its current traffic, Canada clung to her former policy.

Secondly, SSA showed itself to be sharply divided from GCCS over the form that a request for intercepted diplomatic traffic should take. As has been said, the provision of traffic for its cryptographers to study was the duty of the branch that controlled interception. This 'Traffic Centre' was less interested in obtaining messages of cypher type A, B, or C than in making sure that no diplomatic message sent by a known transmitter was missed, regardless of its cryptographic character. Which kinds of message were important and which unimportant was a matter for the cryptographers to decide after the complete file had been handed to them. Hence in drawing up its request for diplomatic traffic intercepted by GCCS, SSA merely listed those transmitters that were either wholly or partly inaudible to its own stations and asked for the miscellaneous traffic that it had missed.

The request, when it was forwarded by BSC, received a frosty welcome from the London Section of GCCS. The Section maintained that it was concerned with cryptography, not with the sorting of traffic by transmitters, and that the cryptographic branch of SSA, not its Traffic Centre, which understood nothing of the cryptographers' true needs, should be the agency empowered to request intercepted material. Nor was the Section equipped for the despatch of large quantities of material by cable.

SSA remained unmoved. It pointed out to BSC that it was not for London to define the duties of its various branches. SSA might otherwise justifiably criticize the isolation of an important part of GCCS from its Communications Centre. Further, it drew attention to the special 'Exchange Section' which it had itself newly set up for the sole purpose of sorting and despatching to London, via BSC, any type of material that GCCS might request, regardless of the form which the request might take.

This unhappy deadlock continued for the greater part of the year 1943. The working committee appointed by the January conference met at intervals and did what it could to improve interception, particularly in Canada. But the exchange of intercepted diplomatic traffic between the United States and Great Britain remained as one-sided as ever, and BSC was left with the thankless task of attempting at intervals to justify the views of London to SSA and of SSA to London.

Complexities of Traffic Exchange

Finally, in the autumn of 1943, representatives of the Communications Division visited London in an effort to set matters right by personal discussions, since feeling at SSA had become strong enough to endanger SSA's good relations with GCCS as a whole. The mission was fortunately successful. By the beginning of 1944, the responsibility for sorting and despatching diplomatic traffic to the United States had been transferred from the London Section of GCCS to a new 'Exchange Party', similar to the Exchange Section of SSA and situated in the main GCCS Communications Centre.

GCCS, London, continued to correspond directly with the cryptographic branch of SSA on all technical matters, while the SSA Traffic Centre was in constant touch, through BSC, with an office which even the most bizarre requests could not disturb. In consequence, tranquillity was soon restored.

Canada likewise enjoyed the benefit of the change. Since it was now possible for her to obtain currently from GCCS what diplomatic traffic she wished, her Examination Unit came to depend less and less upon the intercepts of Canadian stations, and during the year 1944 both sets and operators were released for assignments which no longer duplicated the work of others.

(f) Operational Traffic

Although, in quantity, diplomatic messages formed but a fraction of the wireless transmissions for which a daily watch was kept, it has been thought worthwhile to describe in some detail the steps by which an accord was at length reached between Great Britain, the United States and Canada on their interception and disposal. The question of their disposal, in particular, served to throw into sharp relief the divergent views and methods of the agencies that studied such texts, and the slowness with which a satisfactory answer to the question was found illustrates the problems that faced BSC in its role of mediator, endeavouring on the one hand to win the confidence of the United States and Canada, and on the other to serve the interests of Great Britain.

Paradoxically, the exchange of operational traffic, to which most of the communications system of BSC was devoted, caused the Communications Division far fewer embarrassments. The reason for this was simple enough. Upon America's entry into the war, it was agreed that Great Britain should have the direction of all 'Y' and cryptographic work relating to the war in Europe, while the United States would assume control in the war against Japan.

On the whole, the pact was faithfully observed. Hence in the operational field interception and cryptography were controlled by two benevolent despots, whose spheres of authority did not overlap, a welcome contrast to the individualism that flourished so sturdily elsewhere. BSC thus found its duty virtually limited to the relaying of intercepted material and cryptographic intelligence to one or other of the centres designated to work upon it, and the difficulties encountered by the Communications Division were physical rather than political. Such disagreements on matters of principle as occurred from time to time were settled by international conference.

Since German operational transmissions, with few exceptions, were inaudible in the Western Hemisphere, the Division was engaged almost entirely with the relay of Japanese traffic, both military and naval, the interception and study of which was by agreement under the general supervision of the US War and Navy Departments. Military (and military air) traffic was the responsibility of SSA, naval (and naval air) traffic that of OP-20-G, a branch of the Office of Naval Communications and the naval equivalent of SSA.

The year 1942 was largely a preparatory period during which the US Army was engaged in building monitoring stations, training operators in the Japanese morse code, experimenting with traffic analysis and assembling and educating a body of cryptographers to work upon Japanese operational cyphers. Great Britain was expanding her own nucleus of Japanese cryptographers as rapidly as possible. At the same time, she was establishing at New Delhi what became known as the Wireless Experimental Centre (WEC), the successor to a smaller monitoring and cryptographic section that had existed at Singapore in the days of peace. In Brisbane a similar agency was taking shape, the Central Bureau (CBB), staffed jointly by the Australian and United States Services. Canada, as has been said already, was interested only in the interception and traffic analysis. But she too was occupied during much of 1942 with the building of stations, the recruiting of operators and the training of a 'Discrimination Unit' at Ottawa.

Thus it was not until 1943, when the widely scattered agencies responsible for the interception and study of Japanese military wireless messages had had time to equip themselves for their work, that any assignment of cryptographic tasks or any fine adjustment of coverage could be attempted. Before that time, although intercepted traffic and a limited amount of wireless and cryptographic intelligence was exchanged, it was not in accordance with any single and consistent policy. BSC, insofar as it appeared on the scene, acted merely as a forwarding agent. Miscellaneous military intercepts received by wire or by safe-hand from Ottawa were passed by safe-hand to GCCS and SSA. Similar traffic from SSA was passed to GCCS and Ottawa.

(g) BSC's Load Increased

In the spring of 1943 representatives of SSA, WEC and CBB met at GCCS to review the situation. As a result, it was agreed that henceforward the interception of Japanese military traffic should be generally supervised by SSA, although SSA undertook to allow for the special demands which local theatre commanders might make from time to time upon such centres as WEC and CBB. It was further agreed that definite cryptographic commitments should be undertaken by each centre, and that each should be currently informed of the progress of the rest. Traffic would be supplied to the various centres in accordance with their commitments.

A second meeting followed at Washington in June 1943, in order that Canada, who had not been represented at the previous meeting, might have an opportunity of stating her position. In general, she acquiesced readily in the decisions already taken. She pointed out that her Discrimination Unit, which was producing valuable intelligence by means of traffic analysis, was handicapped by a shortage of material for study. She would like, therefore, to obtain from SSA as many of its current intercepts as possible, regardless of their cypher type, to supplement her own supply. With some hesitation, caused by the fear that Ottawa might duplicate what was already being done in Washington, SSA agreed to provide as much traffic as the existing lines of communication would carry.

The result of these two conferences was a steady increase in the load placed upon the BSC landlines. As interception was now governed by an agreed plan and fresh monitoring units kept making their appearance, the volume of traffic intercepted became ever larger, and although only messages encyphered in a limited number of cryptographic systems were passed by BSC to GCCS and WEC, additional lines between both SSA and New York and Ottawa and New York were needed to carry them. So large indeed was the file despatched daily by SSA, in order to meet the needs of GCCS and WEC alone, that BSC had to ask Ottawa to forgo its claim to the entire intake of SSA and to rest content instead with copies of whatever material reached New York for relay to Great Britain and India. To this Ottawa generously consented.

Despite the growth in volume of the military intercepts that reached BSC daily, the Communications Division had not as yet to face the problem of finding room for them on its transatlantic cable or wireless channels. It was sufficient to forward the daily file by diplomatic bag. But by the beginning of 1944, enough progress had been made in the study of Japanese military cyphers to require the speedier delivery of messages intercepted in the Western Hemisphere. GCCS therefore requested BSC to transmit as many of these as possible by Hydra.

At that time the relay by wireless of intercepted enemy cypher traffic was notoriously irksome. Since wireless communication has no privacy, such traffic must be re-encyphered to prevent its identification by enemy listening posts. *Rockex II* was still on the drawing boards of the BSC laboratory, and the only device available for such a re-encypherment was the standard British Typex machine, which was manually operated. BSC had experimented with the use of Typex during the previous autumn, when a few Japanese meteorological messages had been relayed to GCCS. But now a permanent body of operators was recruited and trained, and the exacting task of re-encypherment on a large scale begun.

The use of Hydra for the relay of Japanese military traffic during 1944 varied with the progress of the cryptographers and also with the needs of the US Navy (OP-20-G), which itself had claims upon the services of BSC. Thus in May 1944, as the result of a further international conference which met in Washington, the Communications Division ceased transmitting the complete text of military intercepts to GCCS by Hydra. Instead, a summary of those elements of each message which were of cryptographic interest was prepared at New York from material supplied by SSA and MI-2 and encyphered in Typex. GCCS received this daily from Hydra and relayed a copy to New Delhi.

In the following October, the summary was in turn superseded by a file of naval traffic, which required the full attention of the BSC Typex Section. Military intercepts received from Washington or Ottawa had, in consequence, to be forwarded by a channel other than Hydra. After negotiation with GCCS, it was decided (November 1944) that the complete file should be fed automatically, without editing or re-encypherment, on to the cable that linked BSC directly with GCCS. Provided that the traffic was restricted to the direct cable, there would be no loss of security. At the same time, Hydra, which would otherwise have been idle, was used for the relay of the encyphered correspondence exchanged between SSA, GCCS and WEC, which had hitherto been transmitted by cable.

Finally in the spring of 1945, when sufficient *Rockex II* equipment had become available for the automatic re-encypherment of enemy intercepts, Hydra reverted to its former role, transmitting to Great Britain upwards of 70,000 groups of Japanese military traffic daily. Early in 1945, WEC made good an old undertaking by passing to Hydra, via GCCS, a quantity of its own intercepts for the use of SSA. To BSC these were not particularly welcome, since SSA had long complained that the manuscript copies of India's traffic, which had hitherto reached Washington only by diplomatic bag, were generally both illegible and obsolete when received.

Such, in broad outline, was the part played by BSC in effecting an exchange between widely distant points of the materials from which were reconstructed the movements and designs of the Japanese military forces. Prominence has been given to the relay of intercepted enemy cypher traffic, because it was here that BSC found the problems of distribution hardest. But it should be borne in mind that, together with the mass of enemy intercepts that passed continuously into and out of New York, there came also an uninterrupted flow of telegrams containing cryptographic 'chat', reports of progress, intelligence derived from traffic analysis and the miscellaneous comments and queries which each Signals Intelligence Centre daily circulated among the rest. All of these BSC had to despatch to their destination with a minimum of delay. Since channels of communication were already congested, the responsibility was not a light one.

(h) Solving US Navy's Problems

While the physical problems posed by the relay of naval operational intercepts and cryptographic intelligence were largely similar in character, there was a sufficient difference in temper and policy between SSA and OP-20-G (or OPG, as it came to be called) to relieve the Communications Division of any fear of monotony in its dealings with Washington. Of Canada nothing need be said. The naval monitoring stations in eastern Canada were under the direct control of the Admiralty, to which reports on enemy submarine movements in the Atlantic were cabled from Ottawa. The single station on the west coast, at Gordon Head, Vancouver Island, was directed by Washington, and it was from Washington that its Japanese naval intercepts reached BSC. On the naval side, therefore, the Communications Division was required to work with OPG alone.

In one sense this simplified matters. There was no massive exchange of naval traffic between Washington and Ottawa. Nor had BSC to undertake the intricate task of despatching selected naval material in three directions simultaneously. But on the other hand, Canadian Naval Signals could never be invoked as an ally of weight in disputes with Washington, and the absence of an effective British counterpoise in the Western Hemisphere tended to give the authority of OPG something of an autocratic colour, which was lacking in the control exercised by SSA.

There were other reasons for the determination with which the US Office of Naval Communications assumed direction of the general interception and study of Japanese naval wireless messages. Until the collapse of Germany the Royal Navy had been preoccupied with the duty of clearing European waters of the enemy. The conduct of the war at sea against Japan had fallen almost wholly to the United States. There existed no British naval forces in the Pacific or adjacent waters commensurate with the ground forces in India and South-East Asia. Hence, whereas a Signals Intelligence Centre such as WEC, which served the Indian High Command, was a constant reminder to SSA that collaboration in military 'Y' and cryptographic work must always be a matter of give and take, OPG hardly felt such a brake in its dealings with the British naval 'Y' and cryptographic unit at Colombo. If, however, circumstances gave OPG a more commanding position in the Japanese field than SSA ever acquired, the Director of Naval Communications could justly anticipate British criticism by pointing out that when German naval cyphers were proving troublesome, OPG had placed cryptographers and equipment unstintingly at the service of GCCS without any attempt to question the use made of them.

Although BSC had been appointed a clearing-house for intercepted wireless traffic before the end of 1942, it was not until May 1943 that the Communications Division found itself undertaking the relay of naval as well as of military material. In view of the quantity of traffic that BSC was later to handle on behalf of OPG, the diffidence with which OPG made its first request for assistance is, in retrospect, a little surprising. Possibly it sprang from the reluctance of every navy to put trust in landsmen. However

Complexities of Traffic Exchange

that may be, two of the junior officers of OPG visited the BSC branch office in Washington and enquired, with something of a conspiratorial air, whether BSC could provide them with copies of wireless messages exchanged between French, Spanish and Italian naval attachés and their respective governments, and intercepted in Great Britain. GCCS, they thought, might be willing to forward these messages by cable, but the OPG Communications Centre was not at the moment in a position to accept them. Nor were those in higher authority at OPG prepared to take any action in the matter.

BSC promised to obtain the messages from GCCS, to remove the disguise which would be added to them before their transmission by cable, and to relay them by landline to its Washington office. Thence they would be delivered by messenger to OPG. The offer was accepted gratefully, and within a few days the file began to reach Washington.

It soon became apparent that the messages were taking longer to travel from BSC, Washington, to OPG, via the main US Navy mail-room, than they were to cross the Atlantic. BSC therefore suggested to OPG that a supplementary landline be installed between its Washington office and the Naval Communications Annexe, which housed OPG. BSC was prepared to provide the necessary equipment and to bear the cost of the line.

The offer seemed to the Communications Division to be a tempting one, since OPG would receive traffic intercepted in Great Britain rapidly, and in edited form, without having to meet cable or line charges and without inconvenience to its communications staff. But there was hesitation in accepting it. Individual officers stated that, while they were personally in favour of a line connecting BSC with OPG, others (who remained anonymous) were less certain of its value, and the Commandant himself oscillated so violently between the two parties that BSC began to feel that it was fighting with shadows. As a last resort, it pointed out to OPG that the Western Union Telegraph Company was not prepared to reserve a line indefinitely and that unless a decision in the matter were soon reached its offer would have to be withdrawn. A meeting of all interested officers followed at OPG. The tenuous opposition at length vanished, and the installation of the line was unanimously approved. By July 1943, traffic had started to pass over it.

Once the lotus had been tasted, OPG rapidly forgot its earlier misgivings. In the following October a substantial portion of the operational messages intercepted at Colombo was urgently required in Washington. There was, at the time, no means of transmitting these either by cable or by wireless across the Pacific. GCCS, however, was receiving by wireless copies re-encyphered in Typex. For lack of trained Typex staff, OPG was not able to accept from GCCS these re-encyphered copies as they stood. It, therefore, turned to BSC for help. BSC was equally unprepared to handle a large file of traffic in Typex. It arranged, however, with GCCS that the second encypherment should be removed at the GCCS Traffic Centre. The messages would then be given the same simple disguise as was used in the relay by cable of diplomatic traffic. They would be cabled to BSC where this disguise would in turn be removed. BSC would then forward them by land-line to OPG, edited in the fashion standard with the US Navy. Together with the Colombo file, GCCS also proposed to cable to New York a quantity of related operational traffic, intercepted at the naval 'Y' station, Flowerdown, England.

For the following twelve months intercepts from Colombo and Flowerdown continued to reach BSC by cable from GCCS. There they were edited and relayed. But the flow of traffic, if uninterrupted, was sluggish, in spite of its quick passage through the BSC Traffic Room and the installation (February 1944) of direct landlines between New York and the Naval Communications Annexe. Complaints came ever more loudly from OPG that, whereas operational traffic intercepted by US stations which had been passed by OPG to BSC for relay to GCCS since November 1943 was never more than twenty-four hours old upon its arrival in New York, material from Colombo was frequently delayed for 130 hours, and material from Flowerdown for at least thirty-six.

Service between Flowerdown and Washington was improved by adjustments in the GCCS Traffic Centre, and eventually Flowerdown's intercepts reached OPG in six hours, a creditable achievement in communication. Colombo offered a harder problem. Here the reason for delays was partly inability of the Colombo Typex staff to keep abreast of its commitments, and partly a bottleneck in the GCCS Typex Room, where material from Colombo awaiting decypherment had to take its turn with a mass of other incoming traffic.

These difficulties were not finally overcome until October 1944. By then, the Colombo cypher staff had been reinforced and BSC was itself in a position to decypher a large Typex file daily. The GCCS Typex Room, therefore, ceased to intervene in the relay to New York of intercepts from Colombo. As much of the file as possible was forwarded, as it stood, via Hydra. The remainder reached BSC by commercial wireless channels. After removing the second encypherment, BSC relayed the messages to OPG. The time that elapsed between their interception at Colombo and their receipt in Washington dropped from 130 hours to 24; and from then on all was well. Even after the opening, in May 1945, of a transpacific wireless channel, which connected OPG with Colombo through Pearl Harbor and Guam, BSC continued to supply OPG with the bulk of the operational intercepts that it required from 'Y' stations under British control.

With the US Navy, as with the Army, it must not be forgotten that intercepted enemy cypher traffic formed only part of the load that had to be carried by the lines of communication linking each cryptographic centre with the rest. If OPG was rather more magisterial than SSA in its assignment of tasks and its control of interception, the interchange of decoded intelligence, progress reports and the like was no less lively between the Communications Annexe, GCCS, Colombo, Pearl Harbor and Melbourne than it was between Arlington Hall, GCCS, New Delhi and Brisbane. From early in 1944, both OPG and GCCS made continuous use of the Communications Division for the relay of traffic of this kind, much of which could not be carried by the wireless and cable channels directly connecting the two.

CHAPTER 5

Purchasing Secret Equipment

(a) The Trials of *Aspidistra*
(b) Exceptional Priority Position
(c) Relying on Friends
(d) Final Favoured Position

The Communications Division of BSC became an agency for the purchase of secret equipment on behalf of XW. The mere buying of goods is a sober affair but the catholic needs of those whom the Purchasing Section represented and the ceaseless competition it faced from rival and more influential customers in the American market tested its ingenuity to the full. No one can procure from harassed manufacturers at one moment a consignment of bows and arrows, and at another a thousand special wireless valves without acquiring something of a flair for the unorthodox.

Until the end of 1941 the needs of XW for wireless equipment of all kinds, whether in the form of finished transmitters and receivers or of their components, were met partly by the British wireless industry and partly by American firms, who were discreetly approached by a former business associate resident in the United States. His purchases were shipped to Great Britain by the officer commanding the Third Battle Squadron, Halifax. As time passed, a second undercover purchasing agent was enlisted, and to supplement the efforts of the two an understanding was reached with the Radio Corporation of America, whereby orders placed with its London office would be passed to its factories in the United States but would be paid for in sterling.

At the time of his visit to America, it became apparent to XW that some kind of local control over his purchasing agents was desirable if full advantage was to be taken of the American market. Further, he required a representative who would see to it that RCA factories in the United States carried out their contracts as expeditiously as possible. Accordingly, with the concurrence of WS, it was arranged that the BSC Communications Officer should also be responsible for the supervision of XW purchases in the Western Hemisphere. He was asked at the same time to undertake a similar duty for SOE, since SOE orders for wireless equipment, although not on the same scale as those of XW, were being met only after considerable delays.

(a) The Trials of *Aspidistra*

As has been mentioned, it became necessary in March 1942 to delegate the more routine duties connected with the purchase of goods for XW and SOE to a Purchasing Section. But the Communications Officer himself remained far from idle. As far back as the spring of 1941, XW had undertaken to obtain, install and operate a high-powered broadcasting transmitter on behalf of the Political Warfare Executive. At that time such a transmitter could be bought only in the United States. In June 1941, therefore, an engineer from HM Government Communications Centre was sent to America to negotiate a suitable purchase. As it happened, the National Broadcasting Company was about to receive from its parent, the Radio Corporation of America, a transmitter designed for its New York station WJZ. This transmitter, which was capable of generating more than 700 kilowatts, was the largest ever built. Some conception of its size can be formed if it is remembered that a 50 kilowatt transmitter is normally regarded as adequate for broadcasting. The plum was a tempting one. Negotiations were opened with NBC and RCA for its purchase, and it was finally agreed that RCA, after making certain technical modifications, should sell it to the British Government for $1,300,000. Power was to be supplied to the transmitter, known thenceforward as *Aspidistra*, by a sixteen-cylinder Diesel engine, whose only peer was a Diesel engine in Jerusalem which furnished the whole of Palestine with electricity.

RCA agreed to deliver *Aspidistra* by 30 November 1941, so that it could be installed fifty feet beneath the earth in south-east England, undergo tests and be ready for continuous operation by 30 April 1942. But unforeseen technical difficulties arose and at the time of the appointment of the BSC Communications Officer, *Aspidistra* was still at the RCA factory in Philadelphia.

BSC pressed RCA to increase its efforts. But the entry of the United States into the war brought an immediate shortage of materials and skilled labour, and it was clear, even in February 1942, that the completion of the work would still require some weeks. To make matters worse, the United States Government, which was well aware of the value of such a transmitter, approached BSC with the suggestion that *Aspidistra* might be more usefully employed if it were set up under American control in China. BSC countered this by pointing out that the large modulation transformer, which weighed fifteen tons, could not be transported over the Burma Road. The force of this argument was admitted, but to forestall attack from a fresh quarter, BSC quickly rented a warehouse near the RCA factory, which it filled with as much of the transmitter as was completed. RCA were thus able to reply with a shrug to further enquiries that since a considerable part of the equipment was already in the hands of the British Government it was impossible to re-negotiate its sale.

By July 1942, almost all the component parts of the transmitter had reached Great Britain safely. But even then the Purchasing Section congratulated itself too soon. Three antenna-towers, each 350 feet high, without which *Aspidistra* was impotent, had been designed and built in the United States. Such was their size that they had to be carried across the Atlantic on three separate vessels. All three were sunk. BSC had therefore to start again and arrange for the building of three fresh towers, this time under far more difficult conditions than before.

The new towers were at length delivered, and this time reached Great Britain safely. But BSC was not yet rid of *Aspidistra*. The transmitter required valves of a special type, and by a government order the entire output of such valves was allocated to the US Navy. Appeals to the Navy Department and to the civilian agencies that controlled production and priorities were unavailing. Only the President could instruct that an exception be made in favour of BSC. XW was informed of the impasse. He, in turn, saw to it that the attention of the Prime Minister was called to the matter. A cable followed from Downing Street to the White House, setting the facts before the President. Within two days BSC received a message from the White House that its needs would be met, and on 23 November 1942 *Aspidistra* at last resounded over Europe.

If the purchase and shipment of *Aspidistra* caused the Purchasing Section considerable anxiety, the reward was ample. Not only was the transmitter used for twenty-one hours daily throughout the invasion of North Africa, but it played a vital role, under the direction of the Air Ministry, in protecting RAF squadrons during the saturation bombing of German industrial and communications centres which began in 1943. Enemy broadcasting stations were being openly used to direct the Luftwaffe to the RAF targets for the night. *Aspidistra* accordingly started to broadcast on the same frequencies, and such was its power that the enemy's signals were extinguished. Later, a series of prearranged tunes was broadcast from the same stations, each signifying a given district in Germany, and from these tunes the Luftwaffe took its instructions. After some study their meaning became apparent to the Air Ministry. Thereafter, if a German station broadcast a tune which directed the Luftwaffe to Hamburg, *Aspidistra* drowned its efforts with another, which ordered it even more insistently to Munich.

(b) Exceptional Priority Position

Quite apart from the problems presented to BSC by *Aspidistra*, the entry of the United States into the war brought about a control of production and distribution that made the purchase of even the most commonplace goods a far more intricate matter than it had been previously. Two Government agencies, in particular, were likely to cause the Purchasing Section embarrassment unless an understanding could be reached with them whereby orders from London would be given clearance without any enquiry into the purpose for which the equipment in question was needed. These two agencies were the War Production Board and the Board of Economic Warfare. The War Production Board was empowered to mobilize the industrial resources of the United States for war and to determine in what order of priority claims for raw materials, goods and services should be met. BSC was likely to receive but cold comfort from the Board unless it could in some way convince its members of the urgency of its needs without at the same time compromising its security.

Here the Purchasing Section was fortunate. With the assistance of XW, who appealed to the British Supply Council in North America, it obtained an introduction to the Council's Chief Priority Officer. He, on learning the delicate nature of the case, generously offered to use his influence with his American counterpart, the Chief Priority Officer of the War Production Board. A meeting with the latter followed, and it was arranged that permission for all purchases, the purpose of which might not be divulged, should in future be obtained by a direct application on the part of BSC to the Chief Priority Officer of the Board. The only limiting conditions were that BSC should first obtain the concurrence of OSS before making an application, and that the total value of goods purchased in any one year should not exceed $500,000.

Since both XW and BSC worked in the closest partnership with OSS, the arrangement was eminently satisfactory. The secret nature of the agencies which it represented had proved in the end not a fatal disadvantage but an asset to the Purchasing Section. Its direct access to the source of all priorities gave it a freedom denied even to the British Supply Mission upon whose far more cumbrous machinery it would otherwise have had to rely.

The Chief Priority Officer of the British Supply Council in North America was equally helpful to BSC in its dealings with the Board of Economic Warfare. This agency, which controlled the export from the United States of all raw materials and finished products, even to Allied countries, might have caused BSC serious inconvenience. It was arranged after negotiation with the Board that a 'blanket' export licence should be granted for all purchases made by BSC on behalf of the British Government. The concession, obtained in the summer of 1942, held good until early in the following year, when the Board of Economic Warfare was abolished and its functions taken over, so far as BSC was concerned, by the Office of Lend-Lease Administration.

Even though a further restriction of exports followed, and the BSC blanket licence was withdrawn, the Purchasing Section suffered only from an increase of clerical work. It was necessary now to obtain a separate export licence for every crate of goods shipped from the United States, and each application for a licence had to be accompanied by a detailed description of the contents of a given crate, together with an invoice from the supplier supporting this description. Provided these requirements were complied with, BSC obtained its licences without trouble. If it seemed that security might be jeopardized by disclosing the nature of any piece of equipment, it was despatched to Great Britain in that cavernous receptacle, the diplomatic bag.

Thus, before the end of 1942, the Purchasing Section of BSC had established itself securely as a substantial customer in the American market, despite widespread and constant competition. It was the sole channel through which XW orders reached American manufacturers, since its special relationship with the War Production Board enabled it to procure equipment far more rapidly than any other mission or individual. It had also purchased wireless sets and their components, from time to time, on behalf of SOE.

Its success with SOE orders proved a mixed blessing. Until the beginning of 1943, these had been confined to the relatively small quantity of wireless equipment which SOE bought in the

United States for cash. The rest of its wireless equipment needs had been ordered under Lend-Lease through the British Supply Mission, Washington. The rubber boats, explosives and other 'toys' required for special operations had also been procured through Lend-Lease, with the help of OSS. Because of heavy demands upon the market, there had been frequent delays in the delivery of goods ordered through the Supply Mission. These delays contrasted unfavourably with the promptness with which BSC, using less conservative methods, was able to execute its cash purchases for SOE. SOE therefore suggested to BSC that it should, in addition to buying wireless equipment for cash, use its influence to expedite orders placed through the Supply Mission.

With some misgivings, the Purchasing Section promised to do what it could, and an SOE officer was seconded to it to give assistance. Before long it became plain that any attempt on the part of BSC to interfere in what the Supply Mission regarded as its own business would cause resentment. It might also prejudice the standing of BSC with the War Production Board, since BSC had not hitherto requested special consideration for Lend-Lease orders. After a short time, therefore, the Purchasing Section regretfully excused itself from a duty that was daily growing more embarrassing. SOE/London concurred. As an alternative solution to its difficulties, it obtained the consent of the Treasury to raising the limit set upon each of its cash purchases in the United States from $1,000 to $5,000. This increase, it was hoped, would make it possible to obtain all urgently required items through BSC, instead of through the Supply Mission. The plan suited the Purchasing Section well, and it confined its work for SOE to the buying of wireless equipment and other goods which were needed quickly for cash.

(c) Relying on Friends

By the spring of 1943, the new status accorded the Communications Division as a whole by the 'Y' Board had attracted the attention of yet other agencies to the Purchasing Section, which soon found itself buying for the 'Y' Committee, GCCS and the Director of Naval Intelligence, as well as for XW and SOE. This popularity, while flattering to the Section, also caused it some concern since it coincided with fresh rumbles from those sleeping volcanoes, the War Production Board and the Office of Lend-Lease Administration.

By this time, the US War and Navy Departments were ordering

yearly some $87,000,000 worth of wireless equipment alone. Many types of raw material and finished components were being reserved by the War Production Board for the exclusive use of the US Services. In the early months of the year, for example, upwards of two hundred such limitation orders had been issued within this single corner of the American market. It thus came as no surprise when, in June 1943, BSC was asked to present for review by the War Production Board and the Office of Lend-Lease Administration a detailed estimate of the purchases it proposed to make during the next twelve months. The document had to show not only the quantity and nature of the items required but the tonnage of raw materials that would be needed for their manufacture and their value in dollars.

The Purchasing Section patiently complied, and was rewarded with the announcement that it would be permitted by the United States Government to buy up to $750,000 worth of wireless equipment during the year 1943–4. But satisfactory as it was to know that so considerable a quantity of goods could be exported once they had been obtained, there still remained those ancient rivals, the US Army and Navy, whose priorities with manufacturers were always as good as and sometimes better than those commanded by BSC.

From that time onwards the Purchasing Section had to live by its wits. The War Production Board was still its good friend. But the Board could be of no help when the complete output of a factory had been allocated to one or other of the US Services or when a piece of equipment of an improved type was being produced secretly under Army or Navy control. Information regarding such 'classified' equipment could be obtained without too much difficulty from the Intelligence Branch of the Army Service Forces or from the Office of Naval Intelligence, with both of which the Purchasing Section was in constant touch. But to obtain permission to purchase even a small quantity of it was another matter. Here BSC was obliged to appeal to the generosity of either the Army Signal Corps or the Office of Naval Communications, stressing the fact that the equipment it needed would, when in British hands, be used directly to the advantage of the United States.

Sometimes such an appeal was successful; often it failed. But in making it, the greatest care had to be taken to see that it was not misconstrued as 'another piece of British double-dealing'. With equipment of all kinds as scarce as it was, this could happen only too easily. Once, for example, after BSC had obtained a consignment of teleprinters through the Office of Naval Communications for cryptographic work at GCCS, the rumour started in Army Signals, which had had its eye on the same teleprinters, that on their arrival in England they were handed over to Reuters. Such fantasies were hard to rebut, but fortunately BSC suffered little damage from them.

Besides the help it received, on occasion, from the US Services in obtaining restricted items of equipment, BSC was able to meet a limited number of XW requirements through OSS. Under an agreement made between XW and OSS at the time of the establishment of an OSS office in London, it was laid down that the reserves of either could be drawn upon by the other for urgently needed items, whether the operation for which they were to be used was a joint one or not. In 1943, OSS was still heavily indebted to XW. It was not difficult, therefore, to arrange that certain types of US Army and Navy equipment held in OSS stocks should be made available to XW if they were otherwise unprocurable. These restricted items, however, while precious in themselves, formed only a fraction of the goods ordered through BSC. By alert anticipation of other customers in the open market the Purchasing Section carried out the bulk of its commitments.

(d) Final Favoured Position

By the summer of 1944, when the part to be played by Great Britain in the war against Japan had been defined at the Quebec Conference, it became clear that the existing limit of $750,000 set upon the purchases made by BSC had become wholly inadequate. XW operations in the Far East were alone likely to require equipment costing far more than that sum. At almost the same time the Board of Economic Warfare was separated from the Office of Lend-Lease Administration and set up independently, under direct Presidential control, with the title of Foreign Economic Administration. In addition to performing the duties of the old BEW, the FEA was given the power, formerly held by the War Production Board, to assign priorities in the American market to foreign purchasing missions.

One of the first acts of the new office was to take out of the hands of the British Supply Mission the task of estimating the yearly needs of those agencies which the Mission had previously represented. It was anticipated, therefore, that it would show considerable curiosity regarding the agencies represented by BSC, when the Purchasing Section presented a greatly increased estimate for the year 1944–5. The situation was not a comfortable one.

But help came once more from the War Production Board. Its Chief Priority Officer, who had long been familiar with BSC, put its case to the Foreign Economic Administration. Officials of the War and Navy Departments supported him. Consequently, when BSC offered its new estimate for approval, no embarrassing questions were asked, and permission was granted for the purchase of equipment during the next twelve months to the value of $1,500,000. Further, the Purchasing Section was absolved from making in future separate and detailed application for the priority ratings and export licences that it might require. Instead, it received a combined priority rating and export licence, which permitted the purchase and shipment of goods to the value of $1,500,000 without further formality. No other foreign agency had ever been granted such a privilege. The Section was able to work in peace.

Conclusion

Such was the Communications Division. Its duties were many, and its history varied. It was not always successful in its undertakings. Telegrams (invariably from CSS to WS) were from time to time delayed. Others (inevitably from WS to CSS) were incorrectly transmitted. The Traffic Centre was known to despatch to SSA a file of traffic intended for OPG. The Purchasing Section shipped to Liverpool a telephone system ordered by a station in South America and, on recovering it, shipped to South America a crate of automobile parts instead. But, when set against the volume of traffic which the Division handled and of goods which it bought and shipped, such mistakes may seem small and may perhaps be forgiven. If it is borne in mind that the Communications Division, like the rest of BSC, was an experiment on the part of a country which is congenitally conservative in amalgamating functions which have previously been regarded as alien to one another, its achievements may be considered illuminating. As has been remarked before, there is strength in unity. Or, as *Rockex II* mightly darkly have put it, RTWKF WTREJ ZPDHU.

Index

A
Abetz, Otto 190
Abwehr 35, 467
Acción Argentina 299
Acción Nacional, Colombia (*Acna*) 316, 320-1
Acción Vasca 281
Acna 316, 320-1
Admiralty Delegation 266
AEB American Corporation 159
Afifi, Sheikh Youssef 103
AFL *see* American Federation of Labor
Africa
  BSC Security Division liaison 272
  see also French North Africa
agents
  BSC recruitment xxviii, 85, 416-22
  BSC role xxxii
  choice of cover name 356-7, 438-9
  dual-nationality 421
  ideal 421
  loan by Americans to British 417
  OSS, recruitment 40-2, 43-4
  US restrictions after Pearl Harbor xxxiii
  see also counter-espionage; intelligence
Aglion, Raoul 63, 413, 414, 415
Aguirre, José 216, 217
Air Commission 266
Al Hoda 62, 413, 414
Alba Pharmaceutical Company 145
Albanian broadcasts, WRUL 61
Albert, Heinrich 56
Alberto, Joao 181
Alcalá Galiano, SS 440
Alcazar de Velasco, Angel 376
Alcoa 253
Aldecoa, Mauricio Abaroa 181
Aldrey, Juan Guillermo 177
Alemán, Miguel 331
aliases, choice of 356-7, 438-9

Alien Property Custodian, US 153
Allen, Robert S. 128-9
Allende, Salvador 308
allied personnel, checking 264-5
aluminium 253
Alvarez del Vayo, Julio 71
Amalgamated Clothing Workers of America 82, 411
America First Committee 68, 70, 71-5, 245-6
  CIO and 81, 83
  congressional franking case and 77, 78-9
  Far Eastern Committee 73
  Irish alliance 85
American Astrologers' Convention 104
American Committee on European Reconstruction 410
American Communist Party 82
American Council on Public Affairs 86
American Defenders of Freedom 70
American Federation of Labor 70, 80, 81
American Friends of Irish Neutrality 85
American Institute of Public Opinion *see* Gallup Poll
American Irish Defence Association 85-6
American Labor Committee to Aid British Labor 70, 80-1
American Legion 71, 74, 86
American Neutrality Act x
American people
  American infiltration of British missions 267-8
  'Americanism' 66-7, 68
  anti-British elements 239-40
  attitudes post-Pearl Harbor 223-4
  attitudes to British xxvi
  foreign exiles 407-15
  German-speaking 239
  interventionism, BSC fostering of 55

509

Index

Irish-Americans as BSC recruits 85
isolationism 55, 68, 81-3, 86, 223-4
Italian-speaking 239
Japanese residents, use in BSC campaign 93-4
minority groups 407-15
national characteristics 103-4
pro-British groups 67-71
pro-British propaganda xxx-xxxiii
working class organization 81
see also USA
American-Irish Historical Society 85
'Americanism' 66-7, 68
Amunategui, Gregorio 305-6
Ancient Order of Hibernians 85
'Andrea B.' 378, 380-1
Angell, Sir Norman 71
'Anna' 32-3, 105
'Anthony' 398
anti-trust laws (US)
German firms in USA and 136, 140
Standard Oil and 150
antimony, Latin American sources 256, 257, *259*
Antofagasta railway 257
Antonioni, Luigi 411
'Apfel' *see* Von Appen Oestmann
Apra (Alianza Popular Revolucionaria Americana, Peru) 281, 332-3
Arab News Agency 93
Arab-Americans 413-15
Arabic world, propaganda to 413, 414
Aranha, Oswaldo 155
Arce, Armando 341
Argentina
arrest of Germans following decyphering operations 358
BSC/SOE operations 245, 280, 281, 298-300
factory security 260
German wireless intelligence from 476-7
Japanese espionage and 400, 401
in planned German redistribution of South America 276, *277*, 278
platinum smuggling through 180
proposed collaboration with Axis powers 153
rumour spreading 113-14
as source of raw materials 256, *259*
support for Fenthol 155
support for Nazis 125-6

Armenian broadcasts 61, 414
Army Staff Mission, British 266
Army, US
Airforce A2 38
Opinion Research Division 226
Psychological Warfare Department 118
Signal Corps 463, 481, 504
see also Military Intelligence; Signals Security Agency (US War Dept)
Arnold, Karl 295
Arnold, Thurman W. 150
Arpels, Louis 193
Arpon Gandara, Angel 176-80
Arroyo del Rio, Carlos 324, 327-8
Arruzola, Roberto 321
Artucío, Hugo Fernandez 71
Ascoli, Professor Max 411
Asensio, General José 216
Aspidistra 499-501
'Aspirin' 398
Associated Press (AP) 97, 113, 293, 358
Astor, Vincent 17, 192
astrological predictions, propaganda use 102-4
Astudillo, General Ricardo 329
Attorney General, US, congressional franking case and 80
Augusto de Freitas & Co. 294
Australia, Fifth Column in Japan and 93
Australian Broadcasting Commission 97
Australian Commonwealth Security Service 271, 272
Austria, OSS agents in 43
Austrian Action 62, 410
Austrian Coordinating Committee 410
Austrians in USA, BSC contacts 407, 409-10
Axis
invasion threat xxxi, xxxv
Mexican blockade attempt 1940 5-6
propaganda in USA 66-87, 223, 224-5
in South America 113-14, 153, 255, 256, *258*, 282-4, 321-2
Tricks of the Axis (leaflet) 299
Aznar family 166-7
Azores, BSC agent in 433-4

B

Backer, George 20
Bage, SS 167, 182
Balkans
allied airmen rescue by OSS 43

510

Index

BSC agents 436
  recruits 422
  see also Greece; Yugoslavia
balsa wood, Latin American sources 256, 259, 327-8
Baltimore Sun 20, 55-6, 199
Banco Alemán Transatlántico 309
Banco Germánico del Sur 309
'Banco, W' 357, 384
Bank of England 428
Bank of London & South America 433
Bank of Mexico 374
Bankers' Trust Company 428
banks, German
  in Chile 307, 308-9
  Peru 366
Barcelo, Alberto 299
Barfleur (converted cruiser) 210
Barke, Werner 357, 381-4
Barnes, Joseph 115, 225
Barros Jarpa, Ernesto 305, 306
Barton, Bruce 72
Basque freighters 166-7
Basques 216-17, 231-2, 281, 332
bauxite 250, 253-4, 256, 259
Baxter, William 373, 374
Bayer drug company 145, 309, 320-1, 349
BBC (British Broadcasting Corporation) 64
Béarn (aircraft carrier) 208
Beaverbrook, Lord 11, 21
Behn, Sosthenes 157
Behrisch, Arno xvii
Bell, Walter x
Bellanca, Augusto 411
Belmonte letter 335-42
Belmonte, Major Elias 335, 342
Beltram, Diego 161
Beltrami *see* Morales Beltrami, Raul
Benceny 167-8
Benoit, Charles 204, 205-6
Bensaude & Co. 428
Bensaude, José 433
Berle, Adolf A. Jr 47, 48-9, 137, 150-1
Bermuda Censorship 79, 80, 151, 152, 347, 354
  interception of coded letters 400
  in 'Joe K' case 361, 362
  in Mexican 'dot' case 381-4
  WS' responsibility for ix, xxviii
Bernstein, Henri 189, 197

Bertrand-Vigne, Colonel Georges 190, 193, 199
Bevan, Colonel John H. 393
BEW *see* Board of Economic Warfare
Bianchi, Baron de 294
Biddle, Francis 129
'the Big X' *see* Sage, Lieut Colonel 'Jerry'
Biggs, Ernest xvii
Bilbo, Theodore G. 67
Bismarck, sinking of 479
Bissell, General Clayton 393
Blacha, Richard 437
blackmail
  by press 123
  of FBI by 'Minaret' 397-8
Blum ('Simon') 373, 374-5
Board of Economic Warfare, US 501, 502, 505
Bohny, Cmdr 389
'Bohrer' 365, 367
Bolivia
  BSC/SOE operations 334, 335-42
  in planned German redistribution of South America 276, *277*, 278
  proposed collaboration with Axis powers 153
  SOE organization terminated 286
  as source of raw materials 256, *259*
Bolivian Air Lloyd 341
bombsight, US, details to British 11
Bonassi (head of Italian SIS in Argentina) 381
Bonzales, Dr Cesar 177
Bonzo (Italian agent) 380-1
Borchardt, Paul 364-5
Borja, Colonel Filemon 326
Borkin, Joseph 140-1, 143-4
The Bormann Brotherhood (Stevenson) xviii
Bowes-Lyon, Hon. David 54, 120
Bowles, Chester 72
Boyer, Charles 189
Braden, Spruille 132
'Braun' 365, 367
Brazil
  arrest of Germans following decyphering operations 358
  BSC Special Operations in 275
  BSC/SOE activity 288-98
  character of people 294
  diamond smuggling 174-5
  German intelligence organization 391
  Germans in 294-8

Index

monitoring system 264
in planned German redistribution of South America 276, *277*, 278
platinum smuggling through 180
ports covered by BSC Consular Security Officers 245
Rio SIS station x
shipping fleet 167
SOE organization terminated 286
as source of raw materials 256, *259*
Bren gun plans 191, 199
Brewster aircraft 371
bribery, Ecuador 325-6
Britain
  agents, BSC involvement 440-1
  Anglo-American joint intelligence committee xxv-xxvi, 47
  Donovan's support for 8-9
  election of 1945 222
  government approval for liberation plan for Martinique 210
  imperial policy 121
  invasion threat, BSC Security Division and 269-71
  representation in USA 66-7
  shipping, anti-sabotage precautions 246-7
  US attitude to xxvi
  US public opinion toward 223-4
Britanova 59, 93, 414
British Broadcasting Corporation 64
British Guiana *see* Guiana, British
British missions, in USA, security 265-8, 270
British and Overseas Features 59
British Overseas Press Service 59
British Purchasing Commission x, xxvi, 191, 193, 241, 242, 266
  Credit and Investigation Section 240, 241
  involvement in WS's organization xxx
  Shipping Security Section 240, 241
British Security Coordination
  choice of representatives 344
  cities with direct representation xxix
  commenting system 229
  Communications Division *see* Communications Division
  Counter-Espionage section 350-2
  creation xxx-xxxi
  CSOs *see* Consular Security Officers
  external intelligence 231-5

failure and delay of operations 436-40
functions, summary xxxv-xxxvi
Intelligence and Planning Section 343
intelligence role xxxi
ISOs *see* Industrial Security Officers
post-Pearl Harbor xxxiii-xxxiv
pre-Pearl Harbor xxxi-xxxiii
purpose 240-1
PWE *see* Political Warfare Executive
RSS section *see* Radio Security Service
rumour factory 109-14
Security Division 241-2, 249, 264-8, 269-72
SO mission *see* SO mission
three-way cooperation with FBI and RCMP 375-7
three-way exchange USA/Canada/GB 482-4
training school xi, xxxii, 4, 121-2, 261-2, 344, 423-5, 461
Washington office set up 26
British Security Manual 266
British Supply Mission 502, 505
British-American Ambulance Corps 189
broadcasting *see* radio broadcasts
'Bromo' 398
Brousse, Charles xix(n.11), 107, 194, 195, 196, 198, 204, 206
Bruce, David xvi, 40
Bruening, Heinrich 408
Brunschwig, Captain Roger 189
BSC *see* British Security Coordination
Buchalter, Louis (Lepke) 124
Buchanau, Franz Wilhelm ('Saunders') 384
'Budak, Michael' 416, 418-21, 423-5
Bulgaria 14
Bullitt, William 201
Buna (synthetic rubber) 148-9
Burma, OSS operations 37-8
butterfly trays mystery 173-4
Butyl (synthetic rubber) 148-9
Buxton, Ned 39
Byrnes, James F. 132

C

cable communications
  disadvantages 460
  establishment of transatlantic cable 453-4
Cabo de Buena Esperanza, SS 166, 168, 181

Index

Cabo de Hornos, SS 162, 166, 169, 178, 356
Cabral de Queroz, Joaquim 181
Cadet, Mme 196, 198
Calero, Evangelisto 324
cameras, acquired by OSS/BSC cooperation 32
Campbell, Sir Ronald Ian 131, 132, 267
Canada
  assistance to WS xxvii
  BSC training camp xi, xxxii, 121-2, 261-2, 344, 423-5, 461
  cooperation with BSC 104-9
  Department of External Affairs 228, 271
  diplomatic traffic 486-9
  Discrimination Unit 490, 491
  Examination Unit 471, 486, 489
  Hydra scheme 460-2, 484
  liaison with xxviii
  MI-2 branch 471, 483, 486
  National Research Council, decoding of radio messages 356, 471, 486
  Oshawa transatlantic wireless transmitter 451-4, 464, 465
  Ottawa Cryptographic Unit 486
  recruitment of BSC agents 417, 419-21
  responsibility for enemy illicit transmissions 470-1
  Schering holding company 141-2, 143
  Vichy-controlled islands 212-13
  Washington conference on exchanging traffic 480-2
Canadian Army, 'Military Research Centre No.2' xi
Canadian Aviation Bureau 264
Canadian Broadcasting Corporation 104
Canadian Club of New York 171
Canaris, Admiral 35, 36
Cantril, Hadley 222-3, 226
Caracas, representative despatched xxviii
Carbo Parades, Manuel 327
Caribbean coast, proposed wireless transmitting stations 463
'Carlos, H.' 294
Caroe, Sir Olaf 132
Carol of Roumania 408
Carraredo 181
Cartagena (port) 316, 321
cartel agreements, German companies and US subsidiaries 136, 140, 152-3
Carter, Boake 224

Cartoux, Maurice 191, 192
Carvalho, Silvestre de 181-2
Casablanca, SS 42
The Case for American-Irish Unity (pamphlet) 86
'Casero' 357
Castillo, Ramon 298, 299, 300
Catholics
  in America First Committee 71
  Irish, BSC and 86
CBB *see* Central Bureau of Brisbane
CBS *see* Columbia Broadcasting System
CD (Head of SOE), Donovan and 24, 28, 33
Celler, Emanuel 126
censorship
  USA 347
  see also Imperial Censorship
Central America, BSC/SOE operations 330-1
Central Bureau of Brisbane 490, 491
Central Europe, OSS in 42
Cepsa (oil refinery) 147, 150
Céspedes, Augusto 341
Chamberlain, John, article on OSS 34-46
Chandler, Albert B. 132, 267
Chase National Bank 156
Chautemps, Camille 201-3
Chepha 139, 141, 142
Chesters, Charles 40
Chicago Daily News 12
Chicago Tribune 71
Chichibu, Prince 95
Chief Industrial Security Officers 228, 261
Chile
  arrest of Germans following decyphering operations 358
  BSC Special Operations in 275, 301-9
  German interests 301, 303-7, 308-9
  in planned German redistribution of South America 276, *277*, 278
  ports covered by BSC Consular Security Officers 245
  proposed collaboration with Axis powers 153
  SOE organization terminated 286
  as source of raw materials 256, *259*
China, OSS operations 37-8
chincona bark, Latin American sources 256, *259*
Chinese, in USA, as agents 421

513

Index

Chinese broadcasts in Japan 96
choice of staff *see* recruitment
Christenson 297
chromium, Latin American sources 256, *259*
Churchill, Winston xii, xvi, 10, 13-14, 41, 282
Cianca, Alberto 412
CIO *see* Congress of Industrial Organizations
ciphers *see* codes and cyphers
CISO *see* Chief Industrial Security Officer
Civilian Defence and Information Bureau 71
Clauzel, Ghislain 208
clothing, European, supply 427
Coast Guard, US
   BSC and 472, 473
   cryptographic section 470
   decoding of German wireless transmissions 477
   enemy clandestine wireless transmissions and 467-71
   liaison with CSOs 249
   monitoring of broadcasts 356
   relations with fellow US agencies 469-70, 472, 473-4
   responsibility for security 269, 270-1
cocaine, smuggling to Germany 182-3
codes and cyphers
   BSC training 424
   Compagnie de Navigation d'Orbigny 333
   concealed messages 353-6
   course of action over 357
   Cypher Policy Board 459
   decoding of radio messages 356, 471, 477, 486
   development 448
   French, acquisition by BSC 187, 194, 196, 198, 204-8
   from V. Dickinson 400
   German, acquired by 'Springbok' 390-1
   Italian xvi, 194, 214-16
   Japanese characters to represent words 376-7
   Rockex I 457-8
   Rockex II 458-9
   SIS 447
   Spanish 216-17, 376-7
   supplied by 'Springbok' 390
   Telekrypton cyphering machine 449-51, 454-6

Venezuela, Spanish Embassy 217
COI *see* Coordinator of Information
Coit, Richard x
Colombia
   BSC/SOE operations 310-22
   German influence 310-11, 314-18
   platinum in 180
   ports covered by BSC Consular Security Officers 245
   SOE organization terminated 286
   as source of raw materials 256, *259*
   Vichy French organizations 208
Colonial Office 228, 254
Columbia Broadcasting System (CBS) 64, 225-6
columnists (newspapers), BSC's contacts 56
Commandante Pessoa, SS 172
Commercial Cable Company 453, 454
Committee to Defend America by Aiding the Allies 71, 72, 85, 92, 94-5, 96
Communications Centre, Whaddon 447
Communications Division (BSC) xxxv, 28, 447-59
Communications Officer, appointment 448
   as focal point 482-4
   Hydra scheme 461-2, 464-5
   operational traffic 490
   as purchasing agent 498-506
   Purchasing Section 448, 502, 506
   relationship with FBI 471-2
   responsibility for detection of illicit wireless services 467
   RSS *see* Radio Security Service
   TES *see* Traffic Exchange Section
   Washington conference on exchanging traffic and 480-2
   work with OPG (OP-20-G) 493-7
   see also radio; wireless
communists
   in Chile 304-5, 308
   in USA 49-50, 81-2, 244, 245, 440
   see also Soviet Union
Compagnie de Navigation d'Orbigny 333
Confederación de Trabajadores de Chile (C.T.Ch.) 304
conference on exchanging traffic 480-2
Congress of Industrial Organizations 81-2
Congress, US
   congressional franking case 75-80
   distribution of German propaganda 76

Index

'Connie' *see* von der Osten
Consular Security Officers 168, 228, 243-52, 271-2
  ports covered 244
  posts created xxx
contraband
  examples of 170-4
  see also smuggling
'convertor' for Hydra 464-5
convoy duty, US for British merchant shipping 12-13, 15
convoying, America First campaign against 72
Coon, Carleton 34
Coordinator of Empire Requirements 266
Coordinator of Information (COI) 63-4
  abolition 28-9
  American Irish Defence Association and 86-7
  British Security Coordination 24-8, 55, 100, 115-18
  BSC and 24-8, 55, 100, 115-18
  FBI and 27, 29
  involvement in Station KGEI 97-8
  work with BSC 24-8, 55, 100, 225
copper, Latin American sources 256, 259
Coppola, Commandante Vincenzo 290, 292
Il Corriere d'America 412
Corriere Della Sera 411
Costa Rica 330
  BSC/SOE intelligence 279-80
Cot, Pierre 189
Coughlin, Father Charles E. 71, 226
Council for Democracy 70
counter-espionage 347-403
  after Pearl Harbor xxxiii
  British/US cooperation 358-9
  British/US divergence of policy 357-8
  Far Eastern 399-403
  OSS 30
  smuggling and 183-4
  sources of information 353-9
  see also agents; intelligence
counter-propaganda
  against America First Committee 73-4
  against US anti-British feeling 69
  see also propaganda
cover names, choice 356-7
'Crane, Mr' 418
crew control 168
La Critica 113

Croatia, BSC agents 436
The Cross and the Sword 303
cryptography 468-70, 486
  see also codes and cyphers; wireless intelligence
CSOs *see* Consular Security Officers
CSS (Head of SIS) xvii
  counter-espionage organization 350
  delay in response to WS 49-50
  directive on counter-espionage 184
  Donovan and 9-12, 24
  Japanese negotiations and 218
  SIS Far Eastern unit and 403
  Standard Oil information and 147
  warning on Axis 69
  Willkie and 18
C.T.Ch. (Confederación de Trabajadores de Chile), 304
Cuba
  BSC/SOE in 331
  BSC/SOE operations 330-1
  Havana, representative despatched xxviii
  opium smuggling 172
  as source of raw materials 256, 259
Cubatao Power Station 367
Cuiaba, SS 182
Cunningham, Admiral Sir John H.D. 14
Curie, Eve 189
Curran, Father Edward Lodge 71
'Cynthia' (BSC woman agent) xiii, xv, 193-6, 198, 204-8, 214-16
cyphers *see* codes and cyphers
Czech broadcasts, WRUL 61
Czech Embassy, press attache 110
Czech language bureau, ONA 59
Czech 'traitor', BSC operation against 104-5
Czechs in USA 407, 408, 409
Czernin, Count Ferdinand 409, 410

D

Dahl, Roald xi
Daily News see New York Daily News
Dalai Lama, OSS and 36-7
Dalmatia, BSC agents 436
Dan, Baron 95
Danes, in USA, BSC contacts 407
Daughters of the American Revolution 86
Davis, Elmer 29, 119, 121
de Carvalho, Silvestre 181-2
de Casalanza, Duca 294

Index

de Chambrun, José 190, 199
de Chambrun, René 189-90, 199
de Freitas, Augusto & Co. 294
de Gaulle, General Charles Joseph xv, 189, 204, 210-11, 212-13, 415
de Heredia, Eduardo 316
de la Grandville, Comte xix(n.11), 206
De La Sota family 166-7
de Sièyes, Count Jacques 189, 210, 414-15
De Spretter, Erwin Harry 371
de Wohl, Louis 62, 102-4
de Zuylen, Baroness 206
La Defensa (Ecuador newspaper) 326
delays caused by red tape 436-40
Delfino's shipping agency 366
Deltram, Diego 161
Dennett, Prescott 78
Dennis, Lawrence 373, 374
Dentz, General Henri F. 414
deserters, BSC Security Division and 268
destroyers *see* shipping
Deutsch, Julius 409
Deutscher Handels- u.Wirtschaftdienst 160
devices *see* equipment
Dewey, Thomas E. 18, 220, 221, 222
diamond smuggling 152, 174-80, 251
Dickinson, Velvalee 400
Dictatorship in England (Wirsing) 321
Dilling, Elizabeth 80
diplomatic traffic 479
  BSC and 486-9
  USA/Canada/GB differences over 486-9
Director of Naval Intelligence, liaison with BSC Security Division 271
Dittmar, Wilhelm (Dittmer) 316
DNB (news agency) 68, 69
DNI *see* Director of Naval Intelligence
dock workers *see* seamen
Dolan, Lieut. Brooke 36
Dold, Conradin Otto 348
Dolivet, Louis 71
dollar transfer from US to London 428-30
Dollfuss, Engelbert 153
Donovan, William Joseph xxvii, 8-15, 21, 24-33
  American Irish Defence Association and 86-7
  Axis threat to Latin America and 282-3
  broadcast propaganda and 63-4
  broadcast to US nation 15
  character and history 39-40
  congressional franking case and 79
  as coordinator of information 24-8
  Far East propaganda and 99-101
  FBI liaison with BSC and 46-7
  foreign currency supply 427
  Hoover and 47-8
  OSS, future plans for 45-6
  OSS and 28-9
  OSS failures 38
  proposed Latin American action 283
  publicizing of Japanese atrocities and 118
  Roosevelt and 13, 14, 16-17, 48, 69
  SOE report on Axis in Latin America and 255
  thanked by Truman 32-3
  visit to Balkans 14
  visits to Britain 9-10, 13-14
  see also Office of Strategic Services (OSS)
Dorra, Dr Clement 63
double agents 385-98
  methods of payment to Pat J. 395-6
  problems 385-8
double double-cross 385, 386
Douglas, Count Albrech Archibald 372
Drew-Brook, Tommy xiv
Dreyfus, Armand 141
drug companies *see* pharmaceutical companies
Dubinsky, David 70
'Duff' (hypermicrophotographic communication) 354
Duffy, Father 86
Dulles, Allen 40, 42-3
Dumont, Georges 171-2
Duperial ammonia factory 263
DuPont 157
'Dupont' 434-5
Duquesne, Frederick Joubert 348
Dutch, in USA, BSC contacts 407
Dutch Guiana *see* Guiana, Dutch
Dutch West Indies, oil, importance to Britain 253

E

economic warfare *see* Board of Economic Warfare; Ministry of Economic Warfare
Ecuador
  BSC/SOE operations 323-9
  platinum in 180

Index

police bribery 325-6
ports covered by BSC Consular Security Officers 245
proposed declaration of war 328-9
SOE organization terminated 286
as source of raw materials 256, *259*
Eddy, Colonel 'Bill' 34-5
Eden, Anthony 120, 220
Editorial La Mazorca (publishing house) 321
Egypt, astrological predictions 103
Egyptian broadcasts 61, 414
Egyptian consulate, New York 63
Eifler, Colonel Carl 37
Eire government 86
Eisenhower, General Dwight D. 442
Elliott addressing machine 77
Ellis, Colonel C.H. ('Dick') Ellis x, xiii-xiv, xviii
Emile Bertin, SS 208, 210
Engels, Alfredo 389, 390, 391
Enigma machine xvi
L'Epoque 189
equipment
  BSC provision for COI 28
  for European underground organizations 426-30
  procurement by OSS/BSC cooperation 32
  procurement through Donovan 9, 11, 14, 19, 31, 32
  purchasing secret 498-506
  for underground armies 426-7
El Espectador 316
essential oils, smuggling of 171-2
Esteves, Francisco 372, 373, 375
Europe
  operational traffic 489
  Political Warfare 54, 55-65
European secret services, BSC and 408
Excalibur, SS 171, 437
explosives, for BSC/SOE operations 280-1, 283
Export-Import Bank 284

F

fabrication 104
  Lati letter 288-94
  letter to trap 'Rogers' 372
  see also forgery
factories
  Latin America, security 260

security 243
USA 241-3
failures, BSC operations 436-40
Falange Española 315, 319-20, 325, 433
Falange Nacional (Chile) 308
Falkland Islands, weapons dumps 281
Far East
  BSC influence over American propaganda 99-101
  counter-espionage 399-403
  Political Warfare 88-101, 116
Farbenindustrie, I.G. 110, 135, 143-6, 148-50, 154, 157, 183
Farish, Major Lynn 43
Fárrell, Edelmiro J. 300
Faymonville, Colonel 38
FBI *see* Federal Bureau of Investigation
FCC *see* Federal Communications Commission
FEA *see* Foreign Economics Administration
Federal Bureau of Investigation (FBI)
  blackmail by double agent 397-8
  bribery of Ecuador police and 325-6
  COI and 27, 29
  cryptography 356, 468
  double agents, management of 386, 387-9, 392, 397
  enemy clandestine wireless transmissions and 467-71
  German firms in USA and 136
  Hoover and 3-7
  identification of correspondents 355
  industrial security, Latin America 260-1, 263
  Japanese ships, control 166
  liaison with BSC x, 7, 47-50, 229, 250-1, 343, 347-52, 447
  liaison with BSC Communications Division 471-2
  liaison with BSC Security Division 242
  liaison with SIS x, xxv, 4
  monitoring 356
  OSS and 47-8
  relations with fellow US agencies 468, 473-4
  RSS and 472-3
  security responsibility 269
  SIS and 359
  SOE report on Axis in Latin America and 255

517

Index

three-way cooperation with BSC and RCMP 375-7
training 424
'Tricycle' and 388-9
wireless channel 447
see also Hoover, J. Edgar
Federal Communications Commission
BSC and 472-3
cryptographic section 469
enemy clandestine wireless transmissions and 467-71
monitoring of broadcasts 356
Radio Intelligence Section 469
relations with fellow US agencies 468-9, 472, 473-4
Federal Grand Jury 79
Federazione Colombiana 411
Federmann, Nicolaus 310
'Felice' 378-9, 380
'Felix, Willy' 379
Fenthol, Fritz 154-5, 336
'Fernandez' 383-4
Fernandez Cuevas, Valentin 325
Fernandez, Dr Pablo Emilio 177-8
Fifth Columnism
Colombia 312
Japan 88-9, 96-7
Latin America 312
propaganda, BSC/COI investigation 115-16
USA 12, 57, 223, 224-5, 226
Fight for Freedom: Labor News 84
Fight for Freedom Committee 74, 80-1, 83-4, 85, 412
Fink, Carlos/Karl 294, 296, 297
Finnish broadcasts, WRUL 61
Fischer, Maurice 174
Fish, Hamilton 73, 74, 78-80
Fleming, Ian xviii, xx(n.18)
Flynn, Edward J. 86
Foianini, Dionisio 340
Folha de Manha 296
Ford, Henry 71
foreign currency, for agents, supply 427-30
Foreign Economic Administration, US, radium smuggling and 173
Foreign Economics Administration (US) 505
foreign exiles, USA 407-15
Foreign Office
agreement on neutral ships 166

Argentina, policy towards 298-9
British policy in India and 131
BSC information 228
Chile, policy towards 306
Colombia and BSC 314, 317
Ecuador and 323, 329
industrial security in S America and 257, 262
invasion of St Pierre and Miquelon and 212
Japanese attack and 218
Japanese propaganda and 88-9
W. Phillips, recall 267
SOE functions defined by 284-5
weapons dumps decision 281
foreign-language communication
broadcasting 60-1
newspapers 58-9
Forgan, Russell 40
forgery, BSC organization 104-9
Forinvent 139, 141, 142
'Fouzie' 363
France
Bordeaux, German naval wireless station 477
BSC French broadcasts 61, 414
French in USA, BSC contacts 407
OSS agents in 42
see also French; Vichy French
'France Forever' 189
Franck, Louis x
'Franco' 384
Franco, Generalissimo Francisco 166, 227
franking, congressional franking case 75-80
Fraser, Ingram xiv
'Frazer' 383
Free French
broadcasts, WRUL 62-3
BSC involvement 231, 408
occupation of Vichy-controlled islands 212-13
US Delegation 189, 210, 415
'free' movements, BSC role in xxxii-xxxiii, 231
Free World Association 61, 62, 70-1, 308
Freedom for Ireland organizations 86
Freedom (news-sheet) 193
Freeman-Mitford, Unity 234
French see also France; Henry-Haye; Vichy French

Index

French Committee of National Liberation 180
French Guiana *see* Guiana
French North Africa, as OSS base 42
French territories, BSC agents in 431-3
The Friends of Democracy 224
'The Friends of Fritsch' 155
frigoríficos 262, 263
Fritzsche Brothers 171
Fuhrmann, Arnulf 276

G

G-2 *see* Military Intelligence, US (G-2)
Gaelic American 85
Galapagos Islands 255, 323
The Galilean 226
Gallup, Dr George 221, 222, 226-7
Gallup Poll 221, 222-3
   to assess US public opinion toward GB 223-4, 226
game of 'Vik' 107-9
Garreau-Dombasle, Maurice 189
Gavaillez, Jean Marie 359
GCCS *see* Government Code and Cypher School (GCCS)
General Aniline and Film Corporation 144, 157
General Electric Company 96, 157, 160
German Bank
   Chile 307
   Peru 366
German Library of Information 76
German Railroad Bureau 76
Germans in Central America 33-1
   Mexico, ships 5
Germans in South America 276, *277*, 278
   Argentina 276, *277*, 278, 358, 476-7
   Brazil 294-8, 358, 391
   Chile 301, 303-7, 308-9, 358
   Colombia 310-11, 314-18
   Ecuador 323-8
   Peru 365, 366
   submarine campaign 250
   Venezuela 331-2
Germans in USA xxvi, 239
   America First Committee 72-3
   BSC contacts 407
   businesses 133-55
   WRUL broadcasts to 61
Germany
   BSC agents 437-9
   codes and cyphers 390-1

dollar holdings 158-9
double agents 385-98
economic agents 153-5
foreign exchange control 158
German-American indebtedness 156-60
Military and Naval Intelligence, communications networks 391, 467
OSS work in 42-3
planned redistribution of South America 276, *277*, 278
propaganda 67-8, 75-80, 89-91, 92
smuggling operations 152, 164-80, 166-7, 173, 174-80
Swedish business connections 135, 158, 159-60
Swiss business connections 135, 136
Switzerland, German agents in 42-3
threat to USA 18-19
Vatican attack 303
wireless communication with Latin America 474-7
see also Fifth Columnism
'Gerson, R.O.' 372
'Gersten' 365, 367
Gestapo
   communications networks 467
   OSS penetration 43
   Vichy, in USA xv, 189-93, 201
Giese, Walter 326
Gill, Harry xvii
Giovanni, Salomon (Sardos Jonos; Jean Salomon; Joae Saros) 295
Giraud, General Henri 202
'Glenn' 384
Goering, Hermann 234
Gogai (Japan) 116
Gold, Guns, Democracies (Zappa) 321
Gold, John 398
Golddiskontbank 156-7, 158
Gómez, Juan Vicente 181
Gómez, Laureano 313, 331
Goodrich Rubber Company 149
gossip column
   Pearson and Allen 129
   see also rumours
Gottlieb, Ernst 159
Government Code and Cypher School (GCCS) 451-2, 454, 457-8, 464, 466, 482, 485, 486-9, 491, 492-7
   liaison with US Coast Guard 471, 477
'government traffic' 479

Index

Government, US
　belief in coordinated Foreign Intelligence Service 32
　British support 8-9
　departments, BSC Security Division, involvement in 271
　Far East policy, BSC and 99-101
　German firms and 136
　interdepartmental rivalry 481
　investment in Britain's defence 14-15
　principle of direct aid to Britain 12
　reports of Cabinet meetings 129
　responsibility for security 269
　WS's contacts 16-17
Gowen, Albert Younglove 18-19
Graf Spee internees 125, 126
Graf Spee sinking, pro-British feeling in USA and 68
Grandville, Comte de la xix(n.11), 206
Greece, BSC agents 436
Greek broadcasts, WRUL 61
Greek National Herald 59
'green gentlemen' 291, 292
Green, William 70, 80
'Grienspan' 434-5
Groupe de Jeunesse Syrienne aux Etats-Unis 415
'Guard' telegrams 267-8
Guatemala
　BSC/SOE intelligence 279-80
　representative despatched xxviii
Guiana
　British, bauxite production and shipping 253-5, 259
　Dutch 254, 256, 259
　in planned German redistribution of South America 276, 277, 278
Gulf Oil 260
Gustav, King of Sweden xvii
Guter, Erich 316

H

Haiti, representative despatched xxviii
Halifax, The Earl of 68, 131, 267
Hamburg America shipping line 366
Hammer, Ernst 138, 143
Hammerum, Sven 438-9
handwriting, identification 355, 369, 371
Hannegan, Robert E. 130
Hansen-Sturm, Gunther 73
Hapsburgs in USA 409, 410
harassing suspects 168-9

Harriman, W. Averell 21
Harris, Dave and Loni 363-4
Haushofer, Karl 364
Hausmann, von Schultz ('Casero') 357
Havas (pro-Nazi French News service) 193
Hawaii, defence details 365
Haya de la Torre, Victor Raul 281, 332, 333
Hayashi, Dr Kiroku 95
Hearst, William Randolph, newspapers 20, 21-2, 96, 224
Heiyo Maru, SS 94-6
Henry-Haye, Gaston xiv-xv, 104, 188-90, 192, 195, 196, 197, 199, 200, 201, 206, 414
Heredia, Eduardo de 316
Hermann Stoltz and Cia 297
Heuer, Kurt ('Hirth') 365, 366
Highet, Gilbert x-xi
Hilgert, Edgar ('Fernandez', 'Frazer') 383-4
Hill, George 77-80
Hill, Tom xi, xii
Hillman, Sidney 82, 83
Hiranuma, Baron 95
Hirasawa (Japanese agent) 400-1
'Hirth' 365, 366, 367
Hitler, Adolf
　belief in astrology 102-3
　planned murder 438
　plans for South America 276-8
　Wiedemann information about 235
Hitler – Wanted for Murder 84
Hitler Youth Movement 294
Hitti, Professor P.K. 415
Hoare, Sir Samuel 61
Hochschild, Mauricio 155
Hoehne, Herbert 349
Hohenberg *see* Von Clemm
Hohenzollerns 79
Holdsworth, Gerald xvii
Holt, Rush 76, 80
Hombo, Takayusu 303
Home Guard, procurement of rifles 11
'Home on the Range' 130
Honduras, BSC/SOE intelligence 279-80
Hoover, J. Edgar xvii-xviii, 3-7
　Belmonte letter and 335, 341
　collaboration with BSC 3-7
　creation of BSC and xxx
　Donovan and 47-8

520

Index

industrial protection in Latin America 260
Pearson and 129
relationship with BSC 3-4, 47-50
US neutrality and 5-6
Winchell and 124
WS and xxv, 49
see also Federal Bureau of Investigation
Hopkins, Harry L. 38, 128, 130
Houdry, Eugene J. 189, 210, 211
Houston, USS 117
Howard, Roy 20-1
H.R. 3672 (US bill) 313
Hughes, John 40
Huhn (agent) 294
Hull, Cordell (US Secretary of State) 8, 13, 98, 118, 128, 129, 130, 131, 195, 198, 199, 341
Hungarians, in USA 407, 408, 409, 421
Hungary, oil fields 232
Hyde, Harford Montgomery xii-xiii, xiv
Hydra wireless transmitter 451-2, 460-5, 484, 492-3
hypermicrophotographs 353-4
see also microphotographs

I

I Talked with Bruno (Mussolini) 321
Ickes, Harold 128, 129, 219(n)
identity papers, for agents, BSC supply 427
I.G. Farben 110, 135, 143-6, 148-50, 154, 157, 183
Igazmondo 62
Ikeda, Seihin 95
IMICO (International Mortgage Investment Corporation) 151-2
immigration authorities, US, responsibility for security 269
Imperial Censorship 228, 347
help to BSC 105, 353-6
liaison with xxviii, 4
procedure over illicit communications 355-6
see also Bermuda Censorship; Trinidad Censorship
India
US criticism of British policy 131-2
Wireless Experimental Centre (WEC), New Delhi 490, 491, 492, 493
India League of America 267
Indo-China

dissemination of information on German Fifth Column in Japan 93
Japanese/French secret agreement 98
Industrial Intelligence Centre, London ix
industrial security, Latin America, BSC and 260-1, 367
Industrial Security Officers 261-3, 284, 424
Industrial Security Plan xxxiv, 260
informants, smuggling 169
Ingersoll, Ralph 20
inks *see* secret inks
Inouye, Viscount Tadashiro 95
Inspection Board of the United Kingdom and Canada 241, 243
insulin, smuggling 172
Integralists 292
intelligence
Anglo-American cooperation xxv-xxvi, 47, 401-3
BSC role xxxi
Donovan as COI *see* Coordinator of Information
external, BSC 231-5
Germany, communications networks 391, 467
Italian Military, S America 380-1
Japanese 400-3
need for Foreign Intelligence Service, US 32
South America, BSC xxxi, xxxii, xxxiv, 227-30, 279-80
US xxxiv, 32-3, 35-6, 219-27
see also agents; counter-espionage; Military Intelligence; Naval Intelligence; Office of Naval Intelligence; Secret Intelligence Service
Intelligence and Planning Section, BSC 343
Inter-Continental Committee for Polical Defence 324
Interessen Gemeinschaft Farbenindustrie Aktiengesellschaft see I.G. Farben
International Business Machines 60
International Economic Research Bulletin 373
International General Electric Company 96, 157, 160
International Ladies' Garment Workers Union 70, 411

Index

International Mortgage Investment Corporation (IMICO) 151-2
International News Service 20, 140
International Telephone and Telegraph Corporation 157, 453
interrogation of seamen 169, 270-1
interventionism, US 55
'Interventor' 296-7
'Intrepid' xviii
Iraqui broadcasts, WRUL 61
Irish-Americans
 in America First Committee 71
 BSC campaign 84-7
Ishida, Mr 95
Islands for War Debts Committee 78
isolationism, USA 55, 68, 81-3, 86, 223-4
ISOs *see* Industrial Security Officers
Istanbul, Britanova transmissions 93
I.T.& T. 157, 453
Italian Armistice Commission 380
Italian language bureau, ONA 59
Italian Military Intelligence, S America 380-1
Italian-American Labour Council 411
Italians in Canada, as agents 419-20
Italians in Mexico, as agents 421
Italians in South America 258
Italians in USA xxvi, 407, 408, 410-13, 421
 WRUL broadcasts to 61
Italy
 BSC agents in 434-6
 codes and cyphers xvi, 194, 214-16
 Committee of Liberation 435
 insulin supplies 172
 see also Lati

J

'J' (Johannsen, Bruno) 365, 367
'J'accuse' 203
Jackel, Carl Ludwig 366
Jamaica, proposed transmitter 463-4
Jamaica Censorship ix, xxviii, 347
Japan
 atrocities, publicizing 118
 BSC contacts 90-1
 BSC PWE against 54, 58, 88-101
 BSC as relay point for communications 483
 BSC rumour factory and 110
 BSC/COI cooperation 116
 counter-espionage 399-403

German merchants selling Japanese merchandise in S America 153
 German propaganda in 89-91, 92
 heavy industry, BSC report 232
 Hydra use for military traffic 492
 operational traffic 489, 490
 OSS operations against 36, 37-8
 secret agreement with France over Indo-China 98
 shipping lines 165
 US embassy, BSC penetration 217-18
 wireless communication with Latin America 474-7
Japan News Week 91
Japan Plan 118
Japanese
 in Colombia 318-19
 in Peru 281
 in South America 258, 282
Japanese character 399
Japanese illicit transmissions, monitoring 470
Japanese intelligence, Anglo-American cooperation 401-3
'Jar' 398
'Jerry Dagger' *see* Sage, Lieut Colonel 'Jerry'
Jewish Telegraph Agency 58
'Joe K' case (*see also* Ludwig, Fred) 360-5
Johannsen, Bruno ('J') 365
Johansson, Elsa xvii
Johnson, Calvin 267
Joint Security Control 393, 394, 398
Joint Staff Committee, US, proposal 387
Joint Staff Mission, British 266
'Jonos, Sardos' 295
Jordan, Mrs Jessie x
Joubert, Air Marshal 397
JSC *see* Joint Security Control
'Julio' *see* von der Osten, Ulrich
Justo, General Agustin P. 299

K

Kabayama, Count Aisuke 95
Kachins, in war against Japan 37
Kadono, Chokuro 95
Kaneko, Count Kentaro 95
Kansas City Star 59
Karlow, Peter 41-2
Kasai, Juiji 94-6

Index

kayaks, acquired by OSS/BSC cooperation 32
Kent, Sherman 38
Kérillis, Henri 189
KGEI Station 96-8, 100
King, Admiral Ernest J. 219(n)
Kleinschmidt (machine) 465
Knox, Frank (US Secretary of the Navy) 8, 9, 10, 12, 13
Kobbe y Chinchilla, Fernando 375-7
Koch, Eustace 234
Koenig ('Kempter') 294
Konoye (Prime Minister of Japan) 95
'Konrad' *see* von der Osten, Ulrich
Kosmos Shipping Agency 366
Krueger, Hilde 331
KSFO Station 96
Kurck, Karl Theodor 316-17
Kurusu, Saburo 98, 217-18
'Kurzhals' 357
KWID Station 100

L

Labor Union advertisements 84
labour organizations, USA 80-4
  British connections 81
Ladenburg, Thalmann & Co. (bankers) 427
Lady from Rio Hacha 474
LaFargue, Pierre 324
LaGuardia, Fiorello H. 81, 86, 221
Lais, Admiral Alberto xiv, xv-xvi, 214-16
Lal, Chaman 132
Lança, Dr Teutonio 182
landline, Washington-New York 447
landing craft, acquired by OSS/BSC cooperation 32
Lang, Herman 348
Langbein, Alfred 357
Lange, Captain Wilhelm 366
Langer, Senator 128
Lati Airline (Linee Aeree Transcontinentali Italiane, S.A.) 150, 151, 166, 280-1, 335-6, 390
Lati letter 288-94
Latin America
  American intelligence activities xxxiv
  Anglo-American liaison 250
  anti-German propaganda article 92
  Axis naval attack rumours 113-14
  BSC intelligence 227-30
  BSC rumour material in 110
  CSOs in 250
  establishment of SOE organization xxxi
  I.G. Farben contacts 145-6
  industrial security 255
  intelligence role of BSC xxxi, xxxii, xxxiv
  raw materials 256
  recruitment of agents 417
  SIS stations, liaison with xxviii, 4
  vital industries 253-7
  wireless traffic with Germany and Japan 474-7
  see also South America
Lautoro, SS 367
Laval, José *see* de Chambrun, José
Laval, Pierre 190, 195, 201, 202, 205
Lazareff, Paul 193
Lazareff, Pierre 189
League of Human Rights, Freedom and Democracy 70
Leahy, Admiral William D. 131
Lebanese League of Progress 413
Legitimists (Austrian emigres) 409
Lehman, Herbert H. 81
Lehmitz, Ernst Fritz Detlev Heinrich ('Fred Lewis') 357, 367-71, 372
Leibrandt (German agent) 391
Lemmon, Walter 20, 60, 62
Lend-Lease 31, 99, 242, 284
  America First campaign against 72
  see also Office of Lend-Lease Administration
'Leo' 295
'Leonardo' 295
letter-writing campaign 106-9
letters
  fabrication to indict enemy agent 104-5
  interception, US Censorship/CSO cooperation 252
  microphotographs in 348-9, 353-4, 381-4
  opening and resealing 4
  rumours transmitted in 110
Lewandowski, Captain 281
'Lewis, Fred' *see* Lehmitz, Ernst Fritz Detlev ('Fred Lewis')
Lewis, John L. 40, 81-3, 245
L'Herminier, Commander 42
El Liberal (Colombia) 314
Life magazine 19, 33, 34-46
lighter flints, smuggling 172-3
Lindbergh, Colonel 9, 19,

Index

70, 71, 72, 73, 74-5, 84, 104
line-tapping 448
Lins de Barros, Joao Alberto *see* Alberto, Joao
Liotta, General Aurelio 200-2
Lippman, Walter 20
listening posts 463
  Latin America 474-7
Lithuanians, as agents 421
Lloyd Brasileiro shipping line 167, 172-3
'Lodge' (double agent) 393-5
London Agreement 29-30
López, Alfonso (President of Colombia) 312, 321
'López' (Bonassi) 378, 381
Lothian, Marquess of xxv, xxvii, 48, 88-9
Luce, Henry 19
Ludwig, Kurt Friedrich/Fred ('Fouzie', 'Joe K') 363-4, 365
Lundgren firm 295-8
'Luni, Enrique' 357
Luning, Heinrich (or Heinz) 307, 357
Lusso, Emilio ('Dupont', 'Grienspan') 434-5

M

McCloy, John J. 131
McConaugh, James 44
McCormick, Colonel Robert 71
MacDermot, Francis (Eire) 86
McGlynn, Michael 85
MacInnes, Helen xi, xii
McIntyre, Marvin 130
McKellar Bill/Act (1942) xxxiii, 47-8, 350, 441
Maclean's Magazine xvi
MacLeish, Archibald 225, 226
Magalhaes, Agamemnon 296-7
Magallanes, SS 359
Magyar Amerikai Oljipari Resveny Tarsasag (MAORT) 150, 154
Malaya, rubber industry 148, 150
Malaya Broadcasting Corporation 97, 99-100
Maloney, William Power 80
Manzanillo 94-5
MAORT (Magyar Amerikai Oljipari Resveny Tarsasag) 150, 154
map division
  countries with BSC direct representation xxix

OSS 41
  map of South America, German redistribution plan *277*
Marinho de Lima, José 182
Maritain, Jacques 189
Marshall, Geoffrey 440
Marshall, General George C. 282-3
Marshall, Julie Angela 440-1
Martinique 208-12
Mason, Edward 38
Massin, Pierre Ernest 171
Matapan, Battle of xv, xvi
Mathis, Emil 191
Matsimaga, Toshio 117-18
Matsuaira, Tsuneo 95
Matte Larrain, Benjamin 306, 308-9
Maurois, André 190, 197, 202-3(n), 203-4
'Max' 381
'Max' Code 383
Mayalde, Conde 166
Mayrhofer ('Mayroff') 381
Mazzini News 411
Mazzini Society 411-13, 435
Mediterranean Fleet, Donovan and 13
Mella Alfageme, José Alfaro 169-70
Mello Franco, Afranio 113
Menzies, Colonel Sir Stewart ix, xiv
Merchant Navy
  deserters 268
  US convoys 12-13
merchant shipping, British, US convoys for 12-13
mercury, Latin American sources 256, *259*
MEW *see* Ministry of Economic Warfare
Mewes Bruna, Humberto 302
Mexican 'Dot' case 381-4
Mexico
  BSC/SOE operations 330-1
  I.G. Farben in 146
  Italian agents from 434
  Italians as agents 421
  Schering trading company 139
  SOE organization terminated 286
  as source of raw materials 256, *259*
  Vichy French organizations 208
Mexico City
  Axis blockade plans of 1940 5
  representative despatched xxviii
Meyer, Eugene 131
MI5 ix, x
mica, Latin American sources 256, *259*

524

Index

microphotographs 348-9, 353-4
  Mexican 'Dot' case 381-4
Middle East, American supplies to 14
Milch, Erhard 70
Military Intelligence, Canadian
  Director 471
  liaison with BSC Security Division 271
Military Intelligence, US (G-2) 4-5, 38, 48, 229, 251, 260, 263, 269, 352, 359, 387, 403, 473
  suspicion of British 349
  training 424
'Military Research Centre No.2' xi
'Minaret' (double agent) 357, 396-8
Ministry of Economic Warfare (MEW) (UK) 144, 147, 160, 166, 173, 184, 228, 318, 331
Ministry of Information 59, 113, 311
Ministry of Supply Mission 265
Ministry of War Transport 271
Minoga, Mauricy 175
minority groups, USA 407-15
Miquelon, occupation 212-13
Mitchell, Hamish x
Mitsubishi 153
Miyoshi, Shigemichi 95
MNR (*Movimiento Nacionalista Revolucionario*) 341
Mokarzel, Salloum 413
Molotov, Vyacheslav 234
money *see* foreign currency
Monte Albertia, SS 183
Monte Amboto, SS 167
Monte Gurugu, SS 167, 168, 169-70
Monte Naranco, SS 181
Montenegro, BSC agents 436
Montenegro, Carlos 341
'Moonstone' 398
Morales Beltrami, Raul 302, 306, 307, 308
Morando, Vittorio 434
Morgenthau, Henry Jr 128, 129, 199
Moroccan broadcasts, WRUL 61
Morton, Sir Desmond ix
Mosquera ('Minaret') 357
Movimiento Nacionalista Revolucionario (MNR) 341
Moyne, Lord 121
Mueller, Alfredo 295
Mufarrij, Fuad 63
Mukai, Mr 95
Murphy, Robert 35

Murray, Major Henry 44
Murray, Philip 82, 83
Musa, Jean Louis 163, 190-3, 199, 200, 201, 204
Muselier, Emile 211
Mussolini, Benito 39-40, 321, 411, 435

N

La Nación (Buenos Aires) 59
Nagai, Matsuzo 95
Nagashima, Yoshiharu 95
Natal (S America) 255
National Arab Committee for Democracy 415
National Broadcasting Company 64, 499
national differences
  'Americanism' 66-7, 68
  Anglo-American linguistic problems 452-3
National Maritime Union of America 244
National Secret Service 230
National Service Act, US, BSC support 126
National Union of Seamen (British, in America) 248
Naval Communications Annexe, US 451, 453
naval cyphers *see* codes and cyphers
Naval Intelligence, British 13
Naval Intelligence, US
  decoding of radio messages 356
  director, liaison with BSC Security Division 271
  industrial protection in S America 260
  suspicion of British 349
  training 424
  see also Office of Naval Intelligence (ONI)
Naviera Aznar 166-7
Navy Department, US, control of US Coast Guard 468
Nazis
  pro-Nazi propaganda, dissemination 75-80
  ridicule campaign 107-9
  Station M abusive pamphlet campaign 109
  in USA 68, 239-40
NBC *see* National Broadcasting Company
Near East
  broadcasts to 62, 63
  Information Centre 413-14

Index

Nelson, Sir Frank 283
neutrality, US x, xxv, xxvi, 5-6
  Hoover and 3-4, 5
  infringement, Mexican example 5-6
New Spain, as part of planned German redistribution of South America 276, 277, 278
New York Committee to Defend America *see* Committee to Defend America by Aiding the Allies
New York Daily Mirror 112, 199
New York Daily News 58, 224
New York Herald Tribune 92, 98, 199, 200, 201, 202, 225, 442-3
  article on Westrick 57
  BSC contacts with 20, 55-6, 58
  Donovan and 12
New York Post 20, 55, 92, 112, 412, 413
New York Times 20, 55, 58
New Yorksky Dennik 59
New Zealand, BSC liaison 271, 272
news agencies
  BSC use of 58-9
  see also DNB; Transocean
newspapers
  BSC use of 55-6, 58-9, 61, 123-32
  see also press
Nicolaus, George ('Max') 317, 381-3
Nicolson, Harold 203(n)
NID 18 271
Nigeria, astrology, astrological predictions 103
Nippon Yusen Kaisha 165
Noi, Mrs Pauline 363
Nomura, Chagashi 400
Non-Sectarian Anti-Nazi League to Champion Human Rights 69-70
Norden Bombsight 348
Normandie, SS 250
North Africa *see* French North Africa
Norwegians, in USA, BSC contacts 407
Nova Jugoslavia 408
NSDAP organization 68, 302, 325, 367
  Ecuador 325
nurses, drafting 126
Nyassa, SS 163
Nye, Gerald P. 74, 75, 76

O

observation, BSC training 423
O'Dwyer, William 221

Office of Facts and Figures (US) 118, 226
Office of Lend-Lease Administration 502, 504, 505
  see also Lend-Lease
Office of Naval Communications 481, 504-5
Office of Naval Intelligence (ONI) 4-5, 38, 229, 269, 270, 352, 359, 403, 470, 473
  Ships Observers' Scheme and 164-5
  see also Naval Intelligence, US
Office of Public Opinion Research, Princeton University 222-3
Office of Strategic Services (OSS) xxxiii, 28-33, 34-46, 119, 229, 231
  abolition 32
  Chamberlain article 34-46
  cooperation with BSC 29-3, 61-2, 231, 424-5, 442-3
  counter-espionage 352
  double agents 387-8
  equipment purchasing 503, 505
  failures 38-9
  foreign currency deals with BSC/OSS 428-30
  future plans 44-6
  Japanese agents and 402
  Life article on 34-46
  loan of agents to British 417
  map division 41
  recruitment 40-2, 43-4
  rescue operations, allied airmen 43-5
  SIS and 29, 359
  SOE and 29-30
  training 43-5, 424-5
  see also Coordinator of Information; Donovan
Office of War Information, USA (OWI) 28-9, 119, 120
  BSC training school, use of 121-2, 424
  Japanese agents and 402
  Survey Division 226
Ogilvy, David xiv
Ogura, Masatsune 95
oil companies
  S America 260
  see also Standard Oil
oil supply, BSC reports 232
Okuma, Marquis Nobutsune 95
OKW 365
ONA *see* Overseas News Agency (ONA)

Index

ONI *see* Office of Naval Intelligence
operational traffic, exchange 489-91
OPG (OP-20-G) 493-7
opium smuggling 172
Order of the Purple Heart 78
Ortéga, Rudecindo 306
Ortiz, Roberto 299
Osaka Yusen Kaisha 165
OSS *see* Office of Strategic Services (OSS)
Ostria Gutierrez, Alberto 30
Ott, Eugen 97
Otto, Archduke *see* Von Hapsburg, Archduke Otto
Oumansky, Constantine 82
Overseas News Agency (ONA) 58-9, 93, 112, 113
Ovey, Sir Esmond 285
OWI *see* Office of War Information, USA (OWI)
Oxelösund xvii

P

'P' (Poensgen, Oscar) 365, 367
PACH (German news agency in Chile) 308
Paget, Sir James ix, x
Pan American Airways 181, 264
Panair 181
Panama
  in planned German redistribution of South America 276, *277*, 278
  ports covered by BSC Consular Security Officers 245
  representative despatched xxviii
  Schering trading company 139
Panama Canal 323
  Japanese interest 318, 319
Panuco, SS 248
Panze, Ernest 327
Paraguay
  BSC/SOE operations 334
  in planned German redistribution of South America 276, *277*, 278
Partito d'Azione 435
Passport Control Office
  change to BSC xxx
  growth under WS xxviii(note)
  nature of post of officer xxvii
  role ix
passports, BSC supply 427
'Pat J.' (double agent) 395-6
Patch, General 42

Patterson, Paul 20
Paul, Prince of Yugoslavia 14
payment of double agents, unusual methods 395-6
Paz Estenssoro, Victor 341
Pearson, Andrew Russel (Drew) 123-4, 127-32, 267
Peenemünde 43
Pelley, William Dudley 68, 226
Peña, Belisario 326-7
'Pepino' 108
Pepper, John x, xiii, xiv
perfumes, essential oils for, smuggling 171-2
Perkins, Mrs Frances 132
Pershing, General John Joseph 11-12, 18, 19
Persian broadcasts 61, 414
personnel
  security 264-8
  vetting 264-5
Pertinax (journalist) 189
Peru
  BSC/SOE operations 280, 281, 332-3
  German sabotage operation 365
  in planned German redistribution of South America 276, *277*, 278
  ports covered by BSC Consular Security Officers 245
  proposed collaboration with Axis powers 153
  SOE organization terminated 286
  as source of raw materials 256, *259*
  Spanish Legation smuggling activity in 182-3
  threat to Ecuador 329
Pétain, Marshall Phillipe 104, 188, 201, 202, 414
petroleum, Latin American sources 256, *259*
Petzold, Martin Peter Friedrich 296, 297
pharmaceutical companies, BSC investigation 145-6, 331
'Phil' *see* von der Osten, Ulrich
Philadelphia Enquirer 59
Philby, Kim xviii
Phillips, William (Pres. Roosevelt's special envoy) 131, 267
Pino y Roca, Rafael 327, 329
Pioneer Import Corporation 151-3
A Plan for Pre-determining the Results of Plebiscites . . . 227

Index

platinum smuggling 161-2, 180-3, 251
Playfair, Giles xi
Plaza Lasso, Leonidas 124
PM newspaper 20, 412
Poensgen, Oscar ('P') 365
Poles in South America 281
Poles in USA 407, 408, 409
   Polish broadcasts, WRUL 61
Polish language bureau, ONA 59
political pressure organizations, BSC's contacts 56
Political Warfare Executive ix, xxx, xxxi, xxxiv-xxxv, 16-23, 53-4, 119-20
   against European enemy 55-64
   against Japan 88-101
   Far Eastern Section 90, 99-101, 116
   foreign exiles and minority groups 408
   letter-writing campaign 106-9
   relations between UK and US and 11-12
   transmitter, BSC Communications Division purchase 499-501
   US high-level contacts 16-18, 22
   see also propaganda
polls
   US, accuracy 220-2
   see also Gallup poll; public opinion poll
Pope, Generoso (Gene) 412
Popov 357
ports *see* shipping
Portugal
   BSC agents in 433-4
   control of ships 166
Portuguese broadcasts, WRUL 61
postal censorship 347
Pozzi, Angelo 377-81
Prace del Prete 291
La Prenza (newspaper, Mexico) 331
President Lincoln (US liner) *see Cabo de Buena*
President Wilson (US liner) *see Cabo de Hornos*
presidential elections 220-1
Presidential elections, US, prediction of results 220
press
   America First, material to counter 74
   campaign, in Colombia 314, 316
   foreign-language, BSC contacts 408, 412
   as propaganda channel 55-6, 123-32
   PWE contacts 19-23

   use by BSC in rumour campaigns 110
   Vichy French BSC campaign 198-204
   see also newspapers; propaganda
press campaign
   against Standard Oil in Venezuela 332
   Ecuador 326
   Mexico 331
Proclaimed List (US) 140
Il Progresso Italo-Americano 412
propaganda, anti-British
   America First Committee 72
   Axis in South America 151, 321-2
   Axis in USA 66-87, 223, 224-5
   Fifth Column 115-16
   German 67-8, 75-80, 89-91, 92
   in USA xxvi
propaganda, pro-British xxx-xxxiii, 61-2, 84, 223-4
   Arabic world 413-15
   astrological predictions 102-4
   Chile 303-4
   Donovan and 63-4, 99-101
   in Far East 99-101
   I.G. Farben, campaign against 144-5
   Latin America, article 92
   over German financial dealings 160
   Spain 433-4
   Standard Oil, campaign against 150
   US xxx-xxxiii
   see also counter-propaganda; Political Warfare Executive; press; radio; rumours
prophecies, astrological, in propaganda campaign 102-4
Provost-Marshall General's Office, US security and 269
psychiatrists, for OSS recruitment 44
Psychological Warfare Board, SHAEF 227
Psychological Warfare Department, US Army 118
public opinion polls
   of CIO delegates 83-4
   in election campaigns 220-2
   potential 226
Publicity 226
Pulitzer Prize, suggested for *New York Herald Tribune* 57
PWE *see* Political Warfare Executive

Q

Quadir, Major Altaf 132

Index

Quebec Conference 505
Queen Elizabeth (ship) 249
Queen Mary (ship) 249
The Quiet Canadian (Hyde) xii, xiii
quinine (chinchona bark), Latin American sources 256, *259*

R

radio broadcasts
  Donovan's organization 26-7
  Japan 96-8
  PWE 19-23
  stations 96-8, 100, 112
  use by BSC in rumour campaigns 110, 111
  used by isolationists 224
  see also Communications Division (BSC); wireless communication; WRUL
radio commentators
  BSC's contacts 56
  see also Pearson; Winchell
Radio Continental (Uruguay) 333-4
Radio Corporation of America 454, 498, 499
Radio Security Service (RSS) 448, 466-7
  Canadian services and 470-1
  FCC and 469
radio valves, acquired by OSS/BSC cooperation 32
radium smuggling 173
railways
  Antofagasta railway 257
  sabotage, France and Belgium 442
Ramirez, President Pedro Pablo 125-6, 300
La Razón 314
RCMP *see* Royal Canadian Mounted Police
Ream, Louis 40
recruitment of agents
  BSC xxviii, 85, 416-22
  OSS 40-2, 43-4
  see also training
Red Star 113
red tape, delays caused by 436-40
Redman, H.V. 89
Reichsbank 156, 159
Reid, Helen Ogden 20
Research and Analysis Branch (OSS) 30, 31

resistance movements, BSC support for 407
Resolute 314
Retelsdorf, Carlos ('Glenn', 'Franco') 383-4
Reuters 414, 505
Rhine-Westphalia Electric Power Corporation 158
Ribbentrop, Joachim von 56, 151, 152
Ribiero Lópes, Antonio 193
Richards, Atherton 40
Rickman, Alexander xvii
ridicule campaign 107-9
Rieber, Thorkild 56, 57
Rieth, Kurt Heinrich 153-5
rifles for Home Guard, procurement 11
Ring of Freedom 70
Rio Conference
  Anglo-American joint committee following 47
  rumour campaign before 113
Rios, Juan Antonio 303-4, 306, 307-8
Robert, Admiral George 103-4, 208, 211-12
Robertson Guantes, Guillermo 168-9
Robertson, Norman xii
robot bombs 391
Roca Lemus, Juan 320-1
Rockex I 457-8
Rockex II 458-9, 493, 507
Roehl, Paul 325
Roessler, Aloli 294
'Rogers' case 371-5
Rogers, Roy 373-4
Romains, Jules 189, 197
Romney, Alfred (alias Rosenfeld) 159
Roosevelt, Eleanor, cow named after 128
Roosevelt, Franklin Delano
  in 1944 Presidential election 220-1
  America First opposition to 72, 73
  Belmonte letter and 335
  BSC and 16, 126-7
  CIO support 84
  Donovan and 6, 13, 14, 16-17, 24-6, 48, 69
  on FBI/SIS liaison xxv-xxvi
  information from Japanese embassy 218
  Pearson and 129-30
  planned redistribution of South America by Germany and 278
  reaction to BSC Fifth Column report 224-5

Index

support for ALCABL 81
Vichy French in US and 198
Winchell and 124
Roosevelt, James 95-6, 218
Rosenfeld, Alfred *see* Romney, Alfred (alias Rosenfeld)
Rosenman, Samuel I. 223
Rostow, Walt 38
Rothermere, Lord 234
El Roto (newspaper) 308
Rott, Hans 409, 410
Roumania
  Carol of Roumania 408
  oil fields 232
Roumanian broadcasts, WRUL 61
Roussy de Sales, Raoul 189
Royal Air Force
  Coastal command 11
  fuel oil supply 253
  pamphlet drop 116
Royal Canadian Air Force 424
Royal Canadian Mounted Police 104, 228
  BSC comments to 229
  illicit transmissions and 470
  liaison with BSC 271, 351, 419
  SOE report on Axis in Latin America and 255
  Springbok and 391-2
  three-way cooperation with FBI and BSC 375-7
  training 424
Royal Corps of Signals 356
Royal Dutch Shell Oil Company 260
Royal Navy
  fuel oil supply 253
  in Latin America 250
  transfer of US destroyers to 9, 10-11
  US destroyeers 6
Royo Peres, Heriberto 320
RSS *see* Radio Security Service
rubber
  Latin American sources 256, *259*
  shortage, USA 148
Ruge, Joachim (Y2983) 382, 383
Ruiz Guiñazú, Enrique 155, 298
rumours
  I.G. Farben 144-5
  Japanese communications 93
  rules 111
  rumour factory, BSC 109-14
  Venezuela 332
  see also propaganda

Rumrich, Gunther x
Russia *see* Soviet Union

S

sabotage
  anti-sabotage training 261
  attempts on Station WRUL 62-3
  BSC training 423-4
  by Americans of German and Italian extraction xxvi
  clause in BPS contract 242
  equipment supplies 426-7
  German operation 365-7
  of S American raw materials 256-7
  shipping, anti-sabotage precautions 246-7, 249-50
  threat of, measures xxx
Sage, Lieut Colonel 'Jerry' 44
Sailer, Karl Hans 436-7
St Cergue, SS 248
St Pierre (Newfoundland)
  occupation 212-13
  Vichy France projected wireless station 191-2
St Thomas (Virgin Islands), port 254
'Salomon, Jean' 295
San Francisco Chronicle 59
San José, representative despatched xxviii
Sànchez Cerro, Luis M. 281
Sandstede, Gottfried 278
Sangroniz de Castro, José Antonio 176-80, 183
Santiago
  enemy transmitters 476
  SIS transmitter 462-3
Santos, Eduardo 312
Sardinia, plan for anti-Mussolini revolution 435
Sardon Pabón, Ruben 342
'Saros, Joao' 294
'Saunders' (Buchanau, Franz Wilhelm) 384
Savich, Colonel 421
Scadta (airline) 310
Scandinavian Seamen's Club 244
Schering A.G. 135, 136-43, 309
  export manager as BSC agent 144
Schering/Bloomfield 136-43
Scheuplein, Rudolph 316-17, 320
Schiaparelli, Else 204
Schiaparelli Parfum Inc. 171
Schmidt Hagius, Wolfgang 326

Index

Schnake, Oscar 307
Schutt, Edgar August Paul 296
'Scoot' 357
Scripps-Howard newspapers 20
seamen
  BSC anti-sabotage measures 248-9
  vetting 264
  see also shipping
Sears-Roebuck 72
Sebba, Gregor 410
Sebold, William G. 347-8, 349, 364, 383, 387
Sebold/Sawyer case 364, 387
secret agents *see* agents
secret communications network, need for 448
secret inks 353, 354, 372, 424
  supplied by 'Springbok' 390-1
  used in fabrication of letters, Station M 106
Secret Intelligence Service (SIS) ix, x
  BSC and xxx, xxxiv, 54, 228, 229, 229-30
  BSC report xii
  dummy intelligence organization, Argentina 380
  enemy illicit wireless communications and 474-5
  ISO information to 262-3
  in Japan 89
  Japanese agents and 401, 402-3
  JSC and 394
  liaison with Hoover's FBI 4, 6
  monitoring of broadcasts 356
  OSS and 29
  recruits 421
Secretary of the Navy, US *see* Knox, Frank
Secretary of State, US *see* Hull, Cordell
Secretary of War, US *see* Stimson, Henry
Section D xvii
security, British and American divergence of policy 357-8
sedition case, 1942 80, 226
Sedta airlines 324, 326, 327
Seguin, Paul 193
Senegalese broadcasts, WRUL 61
Seoane, Manuel 333
Sequel to the Apocalypse (booklet) 145, 150
Serbo-Croat broadcasts, WRUL 61
Serpa Pinto, SS 174, 181
Serrano Suñer, Ramon 433

Service Departments (US) 5
Services Intelligence departments, US, opinion of COI 27
SFE *see* Survey of Foreign Experts (SFE)
Sforza, Count Carlo 408, 411
SHAEF 442
  Psychological Warfare Board 227
Shell Oil *see* Royal Dutch Shell
Sherman Anti-Trust Act 140
Sherwood, Robert xii, 17, 64, 115, 119, 120, 225
shipowners, liaison with BSC 165
shipping
  abuse of ships' stores 252
  acquired through BSC/OSS cooperation 31-2
  American-controlled, alien seamen 270
  anti-sabotage precautions *246-7*, 249-50
  BSC inspection 243-52
  destroyers, transfer from US to Royal Navy 9, 10-11
  labour trouble 244, 245, 248
  smuggling, controlled by Germany 166-9
  see also seamen
Ships Observers' scheme 161-6, 168
Shirer, William L. 20, 112
Shoriki, Matsutaro 95
Sicherheitsdienst, communications networks 467
Sicily, recruitment of agents 435
Siegler, Erwin Wilhelm 348
Siemens & Halske 157
Siemens-Schuckert B.A. 169
Sievert, Hans Heinrich 296, 297
El Siglo (Colombia) 314, 319-20
Signals Security Agency (US War Dept) 451, 473, 482, 485, 486-9, 491, 493
Sikinger (Bolivia) 341
'Silver Shirts' 68
Simon, André 203(n)
'Simon' (Blum) 374
Simovic, General 14
Singapore
  SO news service 97
  SO section 91, 98
  USA transmitters 99
Siqueira Campos (ship) 167
SIS *see* Secret Intelligence Service (SIS)
sisal, Latin American sources 256, *259*
Slavonic Bulletin 408

Index

Slovak broadcasts, WRUL 61
'Smith of China' 362, 365
smuggling
  cooperation between CSOs and other BSC agents 251-2
  methods 161-2
  prevention of 161-84
  see also contraband
Smuts, Field Marshal Jan Christiaan 391
SO.1 *see* Political Warfare Executive
SO mission (British Security Coordination) in Latin America 275-344
  after Pearl Harbor 282-7
  before Pearl Harbor 276-82
Social Justice 226
Society of Patriotic Japanese Residing Abroad 93
SOE *see* Special Operations Executive (SOE)
Soejima, Count 95
Solbert, Colonel 118
Solborg, Colonel Robert 425
Somerville, Admiral xvi
Sousa 181
South Africa
  BSC liaison 271
  German intelligence 391
South America
  Axis strength 255, *258*, 260
  BSC/SOE intelligence 279-81
  CSO activities 249, 250-1
  enemy plans 16
  enemy smuggling activities 166-70
  German submarine campaign, 1942 250
  Hydra scheme 460-2
  map *277*
  ports covered by BSC Consular Security Officers 245
  see also Latin America
Soviet Union
  US communists and 82
  see also communists
Spain
  BSC agents in 433-4
  codes and cyphers 216-17, 376-7
  control of ships 166
  diplomatic cyphers 216-17
  Falange Española 315, 319-20, 325, 433
  smuggling activities 166-7, 168-9, 176-80

Spanish
  as agents 421
  in Colombia 319-20
Spanish broadcasts, WRUL 61
Spanish language bureau, ONA 59
special operation, equipment 503
Special Operations Executive (SOE) ix, x, 53-4
  anti-British groups targetted 69, 228
  BSC PWE and 119
  BSC radio propaganda and 61
  BSC report xii
  closure of stations 286
  illicit wireless transmissions in Latin America and 474-6
  ISO scheme, involvement in 261-2, 263
  OSS and 29-30, 31-3
  report on Axis in Latin America 255, 260
  in South America (BSC/SOE) 284-6
  WS appointed CD's representative in Western Hemisphere xxx, xxxiv
spies *see* agents
Spinks, Dr C.N. 91-2, 93, 97
Spretter, Erwin Harry de 371
'Springbok' (double agent) xiii, 357, 390-3
SSA *see* Signals Security Agency (US War Dept)
staff recruitment *see* recruitment
stamps, smuggling 173
Standard Oil 145, 147-51, 154, 155, 260, 288, 332, 339-40
stars *see* astrological predictions
State Department, US, Donovan and 27
Station M 104-9
Steffin, Kurt 294
Stephenson, William ix-x, xvi-xvii, xviii, xxvii-xxviii
  Axis threat to South America and 282-3
  building of US secret organization xxvii
  communication problems of BSC and 448
  Donovan and 9, 11-12
  Germans in Colombia and 318
  Hoover and 3-7, 47-50
  methods to counter US isolationism 20
  prediction of result of US Presidential elections 220
  report on BSC x-xii
  Winchell and 125
Sterling Products 145, 146

Index

Stettinius, Edward R. Jr 128, 132
Steuben Society 77
Steven, Joseph Alexander 440-1
Stevenson, William xviii
Stigler, Franz Josef 348
Stimson, Henry (US Secretary of War) 8, 9, 13, 118, 132
Stoltz, Hermann and Cia 297
Stork Club 124
Stoyanoff, Alexander (alias Vilmar) 417, 438
Stragnell, Gregory 138, 143
Strasser, Otto 408
Strong, General George 48, 393
Strong-Bevan agreement 393-4
Stuart, Father James 37
Sturaro, Mrs Josephine 362-3
Sturzo, Don Luigi 411
sub-chasers for blockade running 31-2
Subasic, Ivan 408
submarines, use of wireless 463
subversive propaganda *see* Political Warfare Executive; propaganda
Sulzberger, A.H. 20
Suñer *see* Serrano Suñer, Ramon
Supply Council 266
Survey of Foreign Experts (SFE) 30-1
Suzuki, T. 88
Sweden
  banks, dealings in German financial matters 158, 159-60
  holding companies for German-owned businesses 135
  Swedish firm in Brazil 295-6
Swedish broadcasts, WRUL 61
Swiss Bank Corporation 138, 139, 141, 142
Switzerland
  banks, dealings in Reichsmarks 158
  German agents in 42-3
  holding companies for German-owned businesses 135, 136
  shipping in South America 167
Syrians, in USA 62-3, 413, 414
Syro-Lebanese convention 414
Szabadsag 408

T

Tabouis, Genevieve 189
Takaishi, Singoro 95
Takashima, Seiichi 95
Takekoshi, Yosaburo 95
Tammany Hall 412
Tanaka, Captain 95
Tanaka, Tokichi 95
Tarchiani, Alberto 411
Tass 112
Tatkries 234
Taylor, Edmond 115, 225-6
Teagle, Walter 154
Telekrypton 449-51, 454-5, 458
Texas Oil company 56, 57
'Their Aims – Our Aims' (pamphlet) 70
Thomas, R.J. 82
Thompson, Dorothy 70
Thorkelson, Jacob 76
Thorpe, Elizabeth xiii, xv, 193-6, 198, 204-8, 214-16
El Tiempo (Colombia) 314, 316
tin, Latin American sources 256, *259*
Tinkham, George Holden 76
Tito, Marshall 416, 436
Tocopilla 255
Tokugawa, Prince Iyemasa 95
Tokugawa, Marquis 95
Tolstoy, Lieut. Colonel Ilya 36-7
Tolten, SS 303
Torch operation 32, 38
Toronto, BSC training in 424
Torrente López, Felipe 178
Townsend, Ralph 80
Toyoda (Foreign Minister, Japan) 95
'toys', supplies 426-7
Traffic Exchange Section Communications Division, BSC 448, 451-2, 478-97
traffic analysis 478-80
training
  BSC school xi, xxvii, xxxii, 121-2, 261-2, 344, 423-5, 461
  OSS 43-5
transatlantic communications 451-4
Transfer Trust Company 159
transmitters 99, 281-2, 451-2, 460-5, 476, 484, 492-3, 499-501
Transocean News Agency 68, 69, 341
Treasury, British 22, 266, 428-30
Treasury, US, foreign currency deal with BSC/OSS 428-30
Treviranus, Gottfried Reinhold 408
Tricks of the Axis (leaflet) 299
'Tricycle' (double agent) xix(n.11), 357, 388-93
Trinidad, weapons dumps 281

Index

Trinidad Censorship 347, 376, 379
  as base for rumour-spreading 110-11
  Japanese intelligence material 400-1
  as source of raw materials 256
  WS' responsibility for ix, xxviii
Truman, Harry S., on OSS 32-3, 132, 150
tungsten, Latin American sources 256, 259
Turkish broadcasts 61, 414
typewriting, identification 355
Typex machine 451, 492, 496

U

Uchida, Nobuyo 95
Ukrainian Daily News 59
Ulokoigbe (Nigerian priest) 108
underground, occupied countries, BSC and xxxii
underground armies, supplying 426-30
Underwood-Elliott-Fisher 154
Union for Victory (Chile) (*la Union para la Victoria*) 303
unions, combatting isolationism 81-3, 86
United Automobile Workers 82
United Irish Societies 86
United Mine Workers 40, 81-2
United Nations war relief fund 81
United Press (UP) 97, 113
Uruguay 306
  BSC/SOE operations 333-4, 441
  double agents based in 393, 396-7
  Fuhrmann plot 276
  Montevideo SIS station x
  in planned German redistribution of South America 276, *277*, 278
  ports covered by BSC Consular Security Officers 245
  rumour-spreading 110
  SOE organization terminated 286
USA
  Anglo-American joint intelligence committee 47
  British missions in, security 265-8
  BSC, benefits from xxxii
  diplomatic traffic 486-9
  economy, dependence on S America 148
  German-American indebtedness 156-60
  multilateral liaison with BSC 467-71
  need for intelligence service 32-3
  threat from Germany 18-19

see also American people; individual government departments and agencies

V

V-weapon developmental program 43
Valero Alcaraz, Carlos 161
Vallejo Sánchez, Arturo 311, 312, 313, 316, 321-2
vanadium, Latin American sources 256, 259
Vanderbilt, Bill 40
Vargas, Gerulio 288, 292, 293
Varioplex sub-channel 452
Vatican
  attack on German anti-religious activity 303
  French broadcasting station 62
Vauzanges, Jacques 210, 211
Venezuela
  BSC/SOE operations 331-2
  diamond smuggling 175-80
  oil, importance to Britain 253
  oil fields 150
  ports covered by BSC Consular Security Officers 245
  rumour-spreading 110
  SOE organization terminated 286
  as source of raw materials 256, *259*
  Spanish embassy, cypher books 217
Vernam, G.A. 449, 454
Veterans of Foreign Wars 71, 86
vetting of personnel 264
Vichy French
  agents in USA 189-93, 198-204
  in Arabic countries 413
  Canadian islands 212-13
  codes and cyphers 187, 194, 196, 198, 204-8
  Gestapo xv, 189-93, 201
  government, gold reserve 208
  Latin American organizations 208
  naval cyphers 194, 196, 198, 204-8, *209*
  secret agreement with Japan over Indo-China 98
  ships fuelled by Standard Oil 149-50
  see also France; French
Viereck, George Sylvester 79-80, 224
Vieten, Hans 320, 321
'Vik' (game to ridicule Nazis) 107-9
Villarroel, Gualberto 342

Index

'Vilmar' *see* Stoyanoff, Alexander
Virgin Islands 254
'Vivian' (agent) 294
Vogel, Max 317
Von Appen Oestmann, Alberto Julio ('Apfel') 365, 366-7
Von Beck 234
Von Clemm, Karl 152
Von Clemm von Hohenberg, Werner Conrad 151-2
von der Osten, Dinies Carl Wilhelm 362
von der Osten, Captain Ulrich ('Connie', 'Konrad', 'Julio', 'Phil') 362
Von Faupel, Wilhelm 112
Von Gienanth, Ulrich 73
Von Hapsburg, Archduke Otto 409, 410
Von Hapsburg, Felix 409
Von Hapsburg, Robert 409
Von Heyer, Herbert 294, 296, 391
Von Hohenberg *see* Von Clemm
Von Kotze ('Springbok') (agent) 357, 390-3
Von Levetzow, Werner 109
Von Muegge, Hellmuth 294
Von Rautter, Wilhelm Albrecht (Von Ressentin) ('Rogers') 374-5
Von Ribbentrop, Joachim 56, 151, 152
von Thermann, Baron Edmund 278
Von Wagenheim, Baroness 56
Von Wimmersberg 160
Von Zippelius, Otto 306

W

WABC Station 112
Walewick, Jacques 178
Wallace, Henry A. 220
Wallenberg, Marcus 159
Waltemath, Werner Christoph 391, 392
War Department, US, liaison with Security Division of BSC 242-3
War Production Board 501-3, 504, 506
War Trade Department of Brit embassy 27
Washington conference on exchanging traffic 480-2
Washington Merry-Go-Round (Pearson and Allen) 129
Washington Post 131, 199
Washington Times Herald 58-9
Wavell, Field Marshal the Rt Hon. Viscount 14
weapons

dumps, South America 281
training, BSC school 423
for underground armies 426-7
WEC *see* Wireless Experimental Centre
Weekly Foreign Letters 373
Welles, Sumner 128, 198, 307
Weltzien, Julius 138, 143
Wendler, Dr Ernst 336, 338, 341
Western Hemisphere Intelligence Conference xi, 358
Western Hemisphere Weekly Intelligence Bulletin 228-9
Western Union Telegraph Company 191-2, 212, 447, 449, 452, 453, 454, 495
Westrick, Doctor Gerhard 56-8
Weygand, General Maxime 36
Wheeler, Burton K. 9, 76, 77, 80, 84, 86-7
Wheeler-Hill, Axel 348
whispering campaigns *see* rumours
White, William Allen 72
Wiedemann, Captain Fritz 232-5
Willkie, Wendell L. 17-18, 220
Winchell, Walter 20, 106-7, 123-7, 409
Winter, William 96-8
Winthrop Chemical Company 145
wireless communication
 BSC, in S. America 281, 283
 BSC Communications Division 447-59
 clandestine traffic 356-9
 France, OSS 42-3
 from Ecuador 324
 German with South America 474-7
 transatlantic 451-4
 US agencies and 471-2
 see also Communications Division (BSC); radio broadcasts
wireless equipment
 British shortage 447-8
 BSC transmitters in S America 281-2
 purchase 498-504
Wireless Experimental Centre (WEC), New Delhi 490, 491, 492, 493
wireless intelligence
 FCC Radio Intelligence Section 469
 German 476-7
 illicit 466-77
 see also codes and cyphers
wireless transmitters 99, 281-2, 451-2, 460-5, 476, 484, 492-3, 499-501
Wirsing, Gerhard. 79, 321
Wiseman, Sir William ix, 233, 234-5

Index

Wohl, Louis de 62, 102-4
Wolff, Emil 349
wolfram, Bolivia 339
Woll, Matthew 70, 80
woman agent ('Cynthia'), reason for success 194
Wood, Robert E. 72
Wooten 233
Wren, Walter ('Freckles') x
WRUL Station 20, 59-65, 64, 113, 414

X

X-Ray (publication) 226
XW (head of HMG Communications Centre) 447-8, 483-4, 498, 501, 505

Y

Y2983 382, 383
'Y' Committees 481-4, 487, 503

Yanai, Hisao 318-19
Ybarra, Conde de 166
Ybarra Line 166, 176
Yonai, Admiral 95
Yoneyama, Umekichi 95
Yugoslav Bulletin 62
Yugoslavia 14
  BSC agents 436
  BSC rumour factory and 110
Yugoslavs
  in Canada, as agents 420, 421
  in USA 407, 408, 409, 421
Yuki, Mr 217

Z

Zappa, Pablo 321
Zeiss 395
Zum Hingste (firm) 372, 373
Zuylen, Baroness de 206

Also available from St Ermin's Press . . .

ST ERMIN'S
PRESS

I SPY

The Secret Life of a British Agent

Geoffrey Elliott

Who was Major Kavan Elliott, womaniser, rogue, wartime saboteur and peacetime spy?

Behind the cover of an apparently respectable business career, Elliott's nomadic life entangled him in a complex web of deception, glamorous women, Communist double agents and interrogation at the hands of the Gestapo and the Hungarian secret police. Was the hero who dropped blind into Serbia in 1942 on a mission for Special Operations Executive – and spent much of the war in a Nazi prison camp – a courageous dare-devil or a philandering scoundrel?

This is the extraordinary, authentic story of the quest undertaken by Kavan Elliott's son for the truth about his remarkable father. Geoffrey Elliott's meticulous research led him across Europe, tracing the men who captured his father as a British spy in Yugoslavia, imprisoned him in Germany, and expelled him from Hungary in 1949. During the search he discovered that Kavan's personal life was almost as complex and colourful as his clandestine activities: a tale of two families, a bevy of beautiful mistresses, and a business life which ricocheted from Croydon to the Caribbean, and ended in a faked robbery on a sub-post office in Berkshire.

From the torture chambers of Budapest to the classified archives of the British Secret Intelligence Service, *I Spy* reveals an astonishing legacy of espionage, betrayal, romance and double-dealing.

Hardback; 304pp; 8pp b/w photographs
£18.99

COUNTERFEIT SPIES

Genuine or Bogus? An Astonishing Investigation
into Secret Agents of the Second World War

Nigel West

Of the many hundreds of accounts of wartime adventures by secret agents behind enemy lines, which are authentic and which are the fantasies of hoaxers and Walter Mittys? Did either Elizabeth Denham or Josephine Butler really undertake dozens of missions into occupied territory? Was the plastic surgeon George Borodin actually employed by British Intelligence to alter the appearance of vulnerable spies? How many young volunteers were recruited by Churchill to supply him with an independent source of information? Did a black OSS agent organise an undercover resistance network in Nazi-controlled Paris? Was the ill-fated Allied attack on Dieppe deliberately betrayed to enhance the reputation of a double agent? Have dozens of authors and their publishers been duped into peddling fiction dressed up as fact?

This compelling investigation of clandestine operations of the Second World War reveals a catalogue of bogus claims, doctored photographs, faked documents and manufactured archival records. The spurious tales of more than two dozen authors are placed under the expert's microscope, compared to the recently declassified files of hitherto secret organisations, and exposed as exaggeration, embellishment or outright fraud.

Hardback; 320pp; 8pp b/w photographs
£18.99

St Ermin's Press books are available from:
Little, Brown and Company (UK),
P.O. Box 11,
Falmouth,
Cornwall TR10 9EN.

Fax No: 01326 317444
Telephone No: 01326 372400
E-mail: books@barni.avel.co.uk

Payments can be made as follows: cheque, postal order (payable to Little, Brown and Company) or by credit cards, Visa/Access. Do not send cash or currency. UK customers and B.F.P.O. please allow £1.00 for postage and packing for the first book, plus 50p for the second book, plus 30p for each additional book up to a maximum charge of £3.00 (7 books plus).

Overseas customers including Ireland, please allow £2.00 for the first book plus £1.00 for the second book, plus 50p for each additional book.

NAME (Block Letters) ....

....

ADDRESS...

....

....

☐ I enclose my remittance for ....

☐ I wish to pay by Access/Visa Card

Number ☐☐☐☐☐☐☐☐☐☐☐☐☐☐☐

Card Expiry Date ☐☐☐☐